Crusades
Volume 5, 2006

# *Crusades*

Edited by
Benjamin Z. Kedar and Jonathan S.C. Riley-Smith
with Jonathan Phillips

*Crusades* is published annually for the Society for the Study of the Crusades and the Latin East by Ashgate. A statement of the aims of the Society and details of membership can be found following the Bulletin at the end of the volume.

Manuscripts should be sent to either of the Editors in accordance with the guidelines for submission of papers on p. 253.

*Subscriptions: Crusades* (ISSN 1476–5276) is published annually.

Subscriptions are available on an annual basis and are fixed, until after volume 3 (2004), at £65, and £20 for members of the Society. Prices include postage by surface mail. Enquiries concerning members' subscriptions should be addressed to the Treasurer, Professor James D. Ryan (see p. 252). All orders and enquiries should be addressed to: Subscription Department, Ashgate Publishing Ltd, Gower House, Croft Road, Aldershot, Hants GU11 3HR, U.K.; tel.: +44 (0)1252 331551; fax: +44 (0) 1252 344405; email: journals@ashgatepublishing.com

Requests for Permissions and Copying: requests should be addressed to the Publishers: Permissions Department, Ashgate Publishing Ltd, Gower House, Croft Road, Aldershot, Hants GU11 3HR, U.K.; tel.: +44 (0)1252 331551; fax: +44 (0)1252 344405; email: journals@ashgatepublishing.com. The journal is also registered in the U.S.A. with the Copyright Clearance Center, 222 Rosewood Drive, Danvers MA 01923, U.S.A.; tel.: +1 (978) 750 8400; fax: +1 (978) 750 4470; email: rreader@copyright.com and in the U.K. with the Copyright Licensing Agency, 90 Tottenham Court Road, London, W1P 9HE; tel.: +44 (0)207 436 5931; fax: +44 (0)207 631 5500.

# Crusades

# Volume 5, 2006

*Published by* ASHGATE *for the*
*Society for the Study of the Crusades*
*and the Latin East*

Published by
Ashgate Publishing Limited
Wey Court East
Union Road
Farnham
Surrey, GU9 7PT
England

Ashgate Publishing Company
110 Cherry Street
Suite 3-1
Burlington
VT 05401-3818
USA

Ashgate website: http://www.ashgate.com

Typeset by N²productions

Transferred to Digital Printing in 2012
ISBN 978-0-7546-5656-2

MIX
Paper from
responsible sources
FSC
www.fsc.org
FSC® C004959

Printed and bound in Great Britain
by Printondemand-worldwide.com

# CONTENTS

## ARCHAEOLOGY, TOPOGRAPHY

## REVIEWS

# Abbreviations

| | |
|---|---|
| *AOL* | *Archives de l'Orient latin* |
| *Autour* | *Autour de la Première Croisade. Actes du colloque de la Society for the Study of the Crusades and the Latin East: Clermont-Ferrand, 22–25 juin 1995*, ed. Michel Balard. Paris, 1996 |
| *Cart Hosp* | *Cartulaire général de l'ordre des Hospitaliers de Saint-Jean de Jérusalem, 1100–1310*, ed. Joseph Delaville Le Roulx. 4 vols. Paris, 1884–1906 |
| *Cart St Sép* | *Le Cartulaire du chapitre du Saint-Sépulcre de Jérusalem*, ed. Geneviève Bresc-Bautier, Documents relatifs à l'histoire des croisades 15. Paris, 1984 |
| *Cart Tem* | *Cartulaire général de l'ordre du Temple 1119?–1150. Recueil des chartes et des bulles relatives à l'ordre du Temple*, ed. Guigue A. M. J. A., (marquis) d'Albon. Paris, 1913 |
| CCCM | Corpus Christianorum. Continuatio Mediaevalis |
| *Chartes Josaphat* | *Chartes de la Terre Sainte provenant de l'abbaye de Notre-Dame de Josaphat*, ed. Henri F. Delaborde, Bibliothèque des Écoles françaises d'Athènes et de Rome 19. Paris, 1880 |
| *Clermont* | *From Clermont to Jerusalem: The Crusades and Crusader Societies 1095–1500. Selected Proceedings of the International Medieval Congress, University of Leeds, 10–13 July 1995*, ed. Alan V. Murray. International Medieval Research 3. Turnhout, 1998 |
| *Crusade Sources* | *The Crusades and their Sources: Essays Presented to Bernard Hamilton*, ed. John France and William G. Zajac. Aldershot, 1998 |
| Setton, *Crusades* | *A History of the Crusades*, general editor Kenneth M. Setton, 2nd edn., 6 vols. Madison, 1969–89 |
| *CS* | *Crusade and Settlement: Papers read at the First Conference of the Society for the Study of the Crusades and the Latin East and Presented to R.C. Smail*, ed. Peter W. Edbury. Cardiff, 1985 |
| CSEL | Corpus Scriptorum Ecclesiasticorum Latinorum |
| *EC, 1* | *The Experience of Crusading 1: Western Approaches*, ed. Marcus G. Bull and Norman J. Housley. Cambridge, 2003 |
| *EC, 2* | *The Experience of Crusading 2: Defining the Crusader Kingdom*, ed. Peter W. Edbury and Jonathan P. Phillips. Cambridge, 2003 |
| FC | Fulcher of Chartres, *Historia Hierosolymitana (1095–1127)*, ed. Heinrich Hagenmeyer. Heidelberg, 1913 |

| | |
|---|---|
| *GF* | *Gesta Francorum et aliorum Hierosolimitanorum*, ed. and trans. Rosalind M. T. Hill and Roger Mynors. London, 1962 |
| GN | Guibert of Nogent, *Dei gesta per Francos*, ed. Robert B. C. Huygens CCCM 127A. Turnhout, 1996 |
| *Horns* | *The Horns of Hattin*, ed. Benjamin Z. Kedar. Jerusalem and London, 1992 |
| *Kreuzfahrerstaaten* | *Die Kreuzfahrerstaaten als multikulturelle Gesellschaft. Einwanderer und Minderheiten im 12. und 13. Jahrhundert*, ed. Hans Eberhard Mayer with Elisabeth Müller-Luckner. Schriften des Historischen Kollegs, Kolloquien 37. Munich, 1997 |
| Mansi. *Concilia* | Giovanni D. Mansi, *Sacrorum conciliorum nova et amplissima collectio* |
| MGH | Monumenta Germaniae Historica |
| *MO, 1* | *The Military Orders: Fighting for the Faith and Caring for the Sick*, ed. Malcolm Barber. Aldershot, 1994 |
| *MO, 2* | *The Military Orders*, vol. 2: *Welfare and Warfare*, ed. Helen Nicholson. Aldershot, 1998 |
| *MO, 3* | *The Military Orders*, vol. 3: *Their History and Heritage*, ed. William G. Zajac. Aldershot, 2006 |
| *Montjoie* | *Montjoie: Studies in Crusade History in Honour of Hans Eberhard Mayer*, ed. Benjamin Z. Kedar, Jonathan Riley-Smith and Rudolf Hiestand. Aldershot, 1997 |
| *Outremer* | *Outremer. Studies in the History of the Crusading Kingdom of Jerusalem Presented to Joshua Prawer*, ed. Benjamin Z. Kedar, Hans E. Mayer and Raymond C. Smail. Jerusalem, 1982 |
| PG | Patrologia Graeca |
| PL | Patrologia Latina |
| PPTS | Palestine Pilgrims' Text Society Library |
| *RHC* | *Recueil des Historiens des Croisades* |
| *Darm* | *Documents arméniens* |
| *Lois* | *Les assises de Jérusalem* |
| *Oc* | *Historiens occidentaux* |
| *Or* | *Historiens orientaux* |
| RHGF | *Recueil des Historiens des Gaules et de la France* |
| RIS | Rerum Italicarum Scriptores |
| NS | New Series |
| *ROL* | *Revue de l'Orient latin* |
| RRH | Reinhold Röhricht, comp., *Regesta regni hierosolymitani*. Innsbruck, 1893 |
| RRH Add | Reinhold Röhricht, comp., *Additamentum*. Innsbruck, 1904 |
| RS | Rolls Series |

SRG      Scriptores Rerum Germanicarum

WT      William of Tyre, *Chronicon*, ed. Robert B. C. Huygens, with Hans E. Mayer and Gerhard Rösch, CCCM 63–63A. Turnhout, 1986

# Two Types of Vision on the First Crusade: Stephen of Valence and Peter Bartholomew

*John France*

Swansea University

Visions and visionaries always posed problems for the church. They were part of the very fabric of Christianity, but the visionary claimed direct contact with the God and, therefore circumvented and, implicitly, threatened the authority of the official hierarchy of the church. Holy men were always a potential threat. St. Simeon the Stylite (c. 396–459) held court for nearly forty years perched on a high column near Antioch in Syria, producing a rash of emulators whose indiscipline and excess had to be curbed by imperial legislation. They were sometimes linked to the *Circumcelliones* who terrorized North Africa.[1] The sense of righteousness which monasticism bred might easily lead to disorder and heresy. The monks from the Egyptian desert were all too ready to participate in the sack of the Serapeum, the greatest library of the ancient world, in 391. For this reason the church was deeply concerned to control monastic turbulence by strong discipline embodied in such rules as that of Pachomius and "The Master."[2] In the church of the Roman Empire the bishop was the key officer, the guarantor of order amongst the faithful, whose truly Roman political spirit passed into medieval practice. It is no wonder that Pope Gregory I the Great (590–604) so strongly approved of the *Rule* of St. Benedict, for it firmly subordinated the potential turbulence of ascetic holy men to the power of the abbot and the local bishop; it domesticated monasticism and made it a buttress, not a challenge to the established social and religious order.[3] Gregory of Tours was only too happy to record the ignominious death of a self-proclaimed Messiah. St. Boniface and the Frankish church were much troubled by Aldebert, a "charismatic holy man" in the eighth century.[4]

All too obviously, in the view of the official hierarchy, visionaries and wonder-workers offered only traps for the unwary. In the words of a modern authority: "The word of a visionary cannot be taken as certain proof that a vision was supernatural in origin" because such manifestations might be the result of "diabolical intervention"

---

[1] Peter Brown, *The World of Late Antiquity* (London, 1971), pp. 104, 98, 103.

[2] Philip Rousseau, *Pachomius: the Making of a Community in Fourth-century Egypt* (Berkeley, 1999); David Knowles, *Pachomius to Ignatius* (Oxford, 1966).

[3] St. Benedict is known only from the inclusion of a *Life* in the *Dialogues* of Pope Gregory I, written c. 593–94, some 45 years after the saint's death. A fine edition is, Gregory the Great, *Dialogus*, ed. Adalbert de Vogüé, Sources chrétiennes 251 (Paris, 1978).

[4] Norman Cohn, *The Pursuit of the Millennium* (London, 1957), pp. 39–43; Peter Brown, *The Rise of Western Christendom* (Oxford, 1996), pp. 422–23.

or "the pathological state of the individual."[5] But how to distinguish between good and evil manifestations? The Church claimed to be the sole arbiter, and it is a symptom of its growing confidence that from the tenth century the process of canonization was increasingly systematized and controlled through the papacy.[6] It is hardly surprising that the problem of visions should be manifested on the First Crusade because it arose in an acute, and then recent, form from a great crisis in the affairs of the western church in which radical ideas about the role of monasticism and the church had been bruited.

The great reform of the Church, which culminated in the "Investiture Contest," sprang from a demand for new and better standards of clerical behaviour within the church. There is a vigorous debate about how far the monastic reformers of the late tenth and early eleventh centuries, especially at Cluny, were concerned to change the Church as a whole. Some have argued that they were revolutionaries who saw themselves as "superior to bishops" and wanted "a society guided towards the good by truly pure men." Others have taken the view that Cluny was primarily interested in purifying monasticism and its observance.[7] But whatever view is taken of this controversy, Cluny's condemnation of clerical corruption, and especially simony, had a very powerful impact on contemporaries. It was an institutionalized reproach to what many regarded as the corruption of the contemporary secular church, made the more powerful by the way in which monks enlisted visions and the supernatural in their support.[8] In the ferment of ideas in the early eleventh century, heresy emerged. Leutard, the simple peasant who about 1000 dreamt that a swarm of bees entered his body "through nature's secret orifices" attacked the role of the clergy and a tradition of heresy established itself in his diocese of Châlons-sur-Marne.[9]

But heresy was a relatively rare phenomenon. Far more important was the eremetic movement of the eleventh century which became highly influential. This was an age of spiritual renewal, out of which arose the great Orders of Citeaux

---

[5] Jorden Aumann, "Visions," in *The New Catholic Encyclopaedia of America 14* (Washington DC, 1967), 716–17.

[6] The first papal bull of canonization which we have is that of St. Ulric, bishop of Augsburg (923–73), on which see Eric W. Kemp, *Canonization and Authority in the Western Church* (Oxford, 1948), pp. 57–58.

[7] Georges Duby, *The Three Orders: Feudal Society Imagined*, trans. Arthur Goldhammer (Chicago, 1980), p. 140. By contrast, Gerd Tellenbach, *Church, State and Christian Society at the Time of the Investiture Contest*, trans. Ralph F. Bennett (Oxford, 1940), pp. 42–47, 76–85, 93–95, 186–92, sees Cluny as largely self-absorbed: in this he follows the majestic study of Ernst Sackur, *Die Cluniacenser in ihrer kirchlichen und allgemeingeschichtlichen Wirksamkeit bis zur Mitte des elften Jahrhunderts*, 2 vols (Halle, 1892–94). There is a good survey of this controversy in H. E. John Cowdrey, *The Cluniacs and the Gregorian Reform* (Oxford, 1970), pp. xii–xxvii, whose own conclusion is that Cluny was becoming more and more concerned with the wider importance of its ideas from the time of St. Odilo (994–1048). See also, John France, "Glaber as a Reformer," *Studia Monastica* 34 (1992), 41–49.

[8] Thomas Head, *Hagiography and the Cult of Saints. The Diocese of Orléans 800–1200* (Cambridge, 1990), pp. 135–201.

[9] Rodulfus Glaber, *Histories*, ed. and trans. John France (Oxford, 1989), pp. 88–91.

and Chartreuse.[10] It was also an age of radical experimentation and dissatisfaction with the established order, and many of those involved were sharply critical of churchmen, the church and its institutions, and spread their ideas by preaching. A notable example was Robert of Arbrissel (c. 1055–1117) who fled to the forest of Craon where there was a virtual colony of hermits including Bernard of Tiron and Vitalis of Savigny.[11] Robert is remembered as the founder of the abbey of Fontevraud but he rose to fame as a dynamic wandering popular preacher and was criticized by Bishop Marbode of Rennes for his savage anticlericalism:

> In the sermons in which you are in the habit of teaching the vulgar crowds and unlearned men, not only, as is fitting, do you rebuke the vices of those who are present, but you also list, denounce, and attack, as is not fitting, the crimes of absent ecclesiastics … but perhaps it suits you that when, in the opinion of the common people the Church's order is grown vile, you alone and your like are held in esteem.[12]

It was long thought that Urban II (1088–99) commissioned Robert to be a recruit for the crusade after he gave a sermon before him at the Council of Angers in early February 1096, but it seems more likely that the pope persuaded Robert to join the Augustinian house of La Roë as a means of curbing his excesses, and it was not until 1098 that Robert resumed his wandering life.[13] There was always something subversive about Robert, who appointed an abbess, Petronilla, to rule his double house of Fontevraud, and this is possibly why he was never canonized despite the great prestige which later accrued to this foundation.[14]

Men like Robert saw their role as the purification of this world. Another was Peter the Hermit who was a great popular preacher with a vast following amongst the poor in Northern France and who, though never officially licensed by the pope, recruited and organized what is usually called "The People's Crusade" which

---

[10] Henrietta Leyser, *Hermits and the New Monasticism* (London, 1984) provides a good short introduction to this dynamic movement. See also Laura Raison and René Niderst, "Le mouvement érémitique dans l'ouest de la France à la fin du XIe siècle et au début du XIIe siècle," *Annales de Bretagne* 55 (1948), 1–46.

[11] It is an indication of Robert's impact that there are two contemporary lives: Baldric of Dol, *Vita Roberti de Arbrisello* PL 162:1048–57 and Andrew of Fontevraud, *Vita Altera B. Roberti de Arbrisello* PL 162:1057–78. An excellent modern study is that of Jacques Dalarun, *Robert d'Arbrissel, fondateur de Fontevraud* (Paris, 1986).

[12] Translated and quoted in John M. Porter, "Preacher of the First Crusade? Robert of Arbrissel after the Council of Clermont," in *From Clermont to Jerusalem. The Crusades and Crusader Societies 1095–1500*, ed. Alan V. Murray (Turnhout, 1998), p. 49.

[13] Porter, "Preacher of the First Crusade?," pp. 48–51.

[14] Attempts to canonize Robert have all failed, though he used to be revered as a *beatus* at Fontevraud and still does in his birthplace at Arbrissel. The Bollandists list him as a *beatus* in the *Acta Sanctorum*, Feb.III, 593 and he is similarly designated in the entry by Jacques M. Bienvenu, "Roberto d'Arbrissel, beato," in *Dizionario degli Istituti di Perfezione, VII* (Rome, 1983), pp. 1065–68; this work has a papal imprimatur. I must thank Professor Bernard Hamilton for his help in elucidating Robert's status.

preceded the official crusade and came to grief in Asia Minor in 1096. He used to be regarded as the originator of the crusade, and recently an effort has been made to suggest that as such he played an independent role, but this has not been generally accepted.[15] It is important to recognize that the title "People's Crusade" is a gross misnomer. The expeditions to which we give that title were, in reality, no different in their social composition from many of the other contingents on the crusade. Numerous small forces lacked a great "Prince", but subsequently attached themselves to one. The forces which Peter inspired arrived early at Constantinople and became associated with other groups, notably the Italians, to whom they were complete strangers. There is no evidence that Folkmar and his Saxons, whose expedition was broken up by the Hungarians in June 1096, had ever even met Peter. These disparate elements caused trouble at Constantinople and were shipped across to Asia Minor. They provoked the Turks of Nicaea and were heavily defeated. This is hardly surprising in view of their disparate nature and lack of a single leader. As a result, later chroniclers found it convenient to belittle and disparage them as social inferiors. However, they seem to have had knights and substantial men, including counts, in their ranks.[16] Anna Comnena characterizes Peter and his followers as poor men, but her purpose was to create a picture of spiritual simplicity in contrast to the greed and ambition of Bohemond.[17]

We know remarkably little about Peter the Hermit. Albert of Aachen wrote shortly after the crusade and records that, while on pilgrimage, he had been scandalized by Islamic control of the Holy Sepulchre and had a vision of Christ telling him to preach its liberation. The Greek princess Anna Comnena later recalled a rather similar story. However, she wrote some forty years after the event and probably drew on recollections of Peter's early arrival in Constantinople. Moreover, she would have wanted to suppress the fact that Alexius I Comnenus (1081–1118) had asked the papacy for help in 1095, thereby helping to provoke the great

---

[15] Heinrich Hagenmeyer, *Le vrai et le faux sur Pierre l'Hermite* (Paris, 1883) established that Urban II, not Peter, was the true originator of the crusade, but Ernest O. Blake and Colin Morris, "A Hermit goes to war: Peter the Hermit and the origins of the First Crusade," *Studies in Church History* 22 (1985), pp. 79–107 have attempted to revive the idea of Peter as the originator of the crusade, and they are followed in this by Jean Flori, "Faut-il réhabiliter Pierre l'Ermite? Une réévaluation des sources de la première croisade," *Cahiers de civilisation médiévale* 38 (1995), 35–54, and in his book *Pierre l'Ermite et la Première Croisade* (Paris, 1999), who thinks that the French sources suppressed mention of Peter's role because a crusade originating in such circles was socially and religiously unacceptable. However, Flori apparently did not know the article by Marion D. Coupe, "Peter the Hermit – A Reassessment," *Nottingham Medieval Studies* 31 (1987), 37–46, who suggests that the tradition of Peter as originator of the crusade grew up in Germany where the arrival of his forces may have been the first inkling of the crusade.

[16] John France, *Victory in the East. A Military History of the First Crusade* (Cambridge, 1994), pp. 88–95.

[17] Anna Comnena, *Alexiad*, trans. Edward R. W. Sewter (Harmondsworth, 1969), p. 309. On Anna, see John France, "Anna Comnena, the Alexiad and the First Crusade," *Reading Medieval Studies* 10 (1983), 20–32.

expedition.[18] Albert suggests that Peter was a preacher before his adventures in the Holy Land, and this is substantiated, at greater length, by Guibert of Nogent. Guibert did not go on the crusade himself, and used the work of an anonymous South Italian eyewitness, the *Gesta Francorum*, as his main source for the crusade, but drastically rewrote it, using other material to fill in gaps. He provides no account of Peter's preaching of the crusade, but does describe his life as a wandering preacher whose rhetoric earned him lavish gifts which he gave to the poor, even to prostitutes. Clearly these gifts indicate that Peter's appeal was much wider than merely to the poor. Guibert shares Marbod of Rennes's contempt for the poor, and Albert of Aachen speaks of detestable people who went on the crusade led by a pig and a goat. But such aristocratic characterization of these expeditions should not be accepted at face value, and it is notable that Albert paints quite a flattering portrait of Peter.[19]

Such charismatic visionaries as Robert of Arbrissel and Peter the Hermit had a very wide appeal which continued over a long period of time. In the early twelfth century a popular preacher, Tanchelm, held Antwerp in thrall. This would not have been possible without support from substantial people. He had many successors elsewhere, some of them heretics, notably Peter Waldo whose Waldensian followers would persist through to the Reformation. Waldo was devoted to the ideal of apostolic simplicity, an idea supported also by St. Francis. But Francis was committed to obedience to the papacy and was acclaimed by Innocent III (1198–1216). To a degree, their contrasting fates show the deep ambivalence of the official church to the charismatic.[20] What these preachers had in common was that they were on the periphery of power. They disliked the riches of the institutional Church and tended to emphasize the virtues of poverty which they opposed to the

---

[18] Albert of Aachen, *RHC Oc.* 4. Book 1 chaps. 1–22. A new edition and translation of Albert's work by Dr. Susan B. Edgington is due to appear in Oxford Medieval Texts in 2006. Because of this, references to Albert are by book and chapter. I am grateful to Dr. Edgington for the use of her text. Anna never mentions Pope Urban, with whom Alexius had had extensive contacts, or his appeal for help to the Council of Piacenza in 1095; *Alexiad*, p. 309, and France, "Anna Comnena, the Alexiad and the First Crusade," 20–32.

[19] Guibert of Nogent, *Dei Gesta per Francos* ed. Robert B. C. Huygens, CCCM 127A (Turnhout, 1996); trans. Robert Levine, *The Deeds of God through the Franks* (Woodbridge, 1997), Book II. Guibert was one of many early copyists of the anonymous *Gesta Francorum et aliorum Hierosolimitanorum*, ed. Rosalind Hill (Edinburgh, 1962), on which see John France, "The Use of the Anonymous *Gesta Francorum* in the Early Twelfth-Century Sources for the First Crusade," in *Clermont*, pp. 29–42 and "The Anonymous *Gesta Francorum*, the *Historia Francorum qui ceperunt Iherusalem* of Raymond of Aguilers and the *Historia de Hierosolymitano Itinere* of Peter Tudebode; an analysis of the textual relationship between primary sources for the First Crusade," in *Crusade Sources*, pp. 39–70. There is a recent study of Guibert by Jay Rubenstein, *Guibert of Nogent. Portrait of a Medieval Mind* (New York, 2002), who remarks on his contempt for Peter, especially p. 97.

[20] Cohn, *Pursuit of the Millennium* provides useful information about such preachers, though his interpretation is now rather dated. Malcolm Lambert, *Medieval Heresy. Popular Religious Movements from the Gregorian Reform to the Reformation*, 2nd edn (Oxford, 1992); John Moorman, *St Francis of Assisi* (London, 1963). For studies of other northern French preachers see Charles Dereine, "Les prédicateurs 'apostoliques' dans les diocèses de Thérouanne, Tournai et Cambrai-Arras durant les années 1075–1125," *Analecta Praemonstratensia* 57 (1983), 171–89.

corruption of wealth. This is not to say that they were social revolutionaries or that they had a developed doctrine of apostolic poverty. But the notion of gaining virtue by giving to the poor was deeply ingrained in Christianity and provided them with an appeal to all classes. Moreover, pilgrimage, so popular in this age, emphasized equality before God, and, in a religious sense at least, was enthusiastically accepted across the social spectrum. Urban II offered all, rich and poor, an equal opportunity for salvation, and the conditions of the crusade imposed suffering upon all.[21]

Of course, it was not equal suffering, for it is clear that the wealthiest amongst the crusaders fared better than the poorest. The lot of those in between must have corresponded to one extreme or another according to circumstances. At times of particular stress almost everybody must have felt terrified and impoverished. Moreover, the participants in the First Crusade existed in a state of heightened spirituality. They were, we may guess, an atypically pious group, almost all of whom must have been moved, to a greater or lesser extent, to join the crusade to serve God and to expunge their sins. The eyewitness sources preach the message that success could only come by God's favour and failure was the consequence of His displeasure. These circumstances made the crusaders susceptible to religious appeal. Further, in some respects, the crusade was a microcosm of western European society. It was controlled by an alliance between the Church, represented by the papal legate, Adhémar of Le Puy, and the princes. We can see this official structure working to maintain and control the spirit of the crusaders. Adhémar preached regularly to the army and urged the rich to support the poor. In moments of crisis he went further. By December 1097 the crusaders had been besieging Antioch for three months. They had exhausted the food supplies in the immediate area, and the foraging expedition sent into Syria at the end of December fought off an enemy relief force on 31 December, but failed to acquire much food. As a result, the army was starving in the bitter winter.[22] In these circumstances Adhémar prescribed a period of religious celebrations including a three-day fast, together with masses and celebrations, and the expulsion of women from the camp.[23]

But there are indications from an early stage that this leadership could be seen as exclusive: the anonymous author of the *Gesta Francorum* felt betrayed by the agreement made with Alexius Comnenus.[24] This introduced the risk that, as in Europe, ecclesiastical critics could also arise and influence events. In June 1098 the First Crusade found itself at the nadir of its fortunes. They had besieged Antioch in October 1097, but it was a formidable city and its ruler was able to call on many allies. After a winter of starvation during which two major Muslim relief forces were

---

[21] A very vivid picture of the sufferings of the crusaders is drawn in Jonathan Riley-Smith, *The First Crusade and the Idea of Crusading* (London, 1986), pp. 58–90.

[22] For the severity of this crisis, see France, *Victory*, pp. 236–44.

[23] *GF*, p. 74; Raymond of Aguilers, *Liber*, ed. John H. and Laurita L. Hill (Paris, 1969), p. 54; Albert of Aachen, Book 3, chaps. 57–58.

[24] *GF*, p. 12.

beaten off the spring brought some relief as allied ships landed food at the nearby port of St. Simeon, and the blockade of the city was considerably tightened. In May 1098 one of the leaders of the crusade, the southern Italian Norman, Bohemond, made contact with a traitor – probably a renegade Armenian – who betrayed his towers to the crusaders in a secret assault on the night of 2/3 June 1098. They failed, however, to gain possession of the citadel which was situated on Antioch's curtain-wall. On 5 June a huge relief force led by Kerbogah, atabeg of Mosul, acting on the authority of the caliph of Baghdad, besieged Antioch where food supplies were sadly depleted after a long siege and the excesses of the crusader sack. The crusaders were now besieged by an enormous Muslim army outside the city. The citadel passed to Kerbogah's control and because it stands on the circuit of the walls his troops threatened to descend through it into the city. So the Christian army found itself engaged in a life-and-death struggle in the most adverse of military circumstances. In these conditions crusader morale plummeted as deserters, called "rope-dancers" because they fled the city by sliding down ropes, fled to the coast. On 12 June Bohemond set fire to an area of the city to smoke out shirkers, and all the chroniclers report high prices and starvation: "All things were very dear ... . So terrible was the famine that men boiled and ate the leaves of figs, vines, thistles and all kinds of trees. Others stewed the dried skins of horses, camels ... we endured this misery, hunger and fear for six and twenty days."[25]

In this moment of supreme crisis enter two visionaries, the priest Stephen of Valence and Peter Bartholomew. Although the fact of their visions is well known, their different natures have not been remarked upon.[26] Our knowledge of these men is limited but instructive: Stephen was unequivocally a priest, while Peter was a poor man from Arles, yet he showed a knowledge of letters when examined. This suggests a parallel with Peter the Hermit, who we know had some education. The best source for the doings of these men and other visionaries is the chronicler Raymond of Aguilers. He was a canon of the cathedral of St. Mary of Le Puy, and he tells us that he was raised to the priesthood at Antioch and served as chaplain to Raymond count of Toulouse, the leader of the biggest army on the crusade, that of the Provençals. In view of the charges that have been made against Raymond's veracity, it is worth noting that he is sometimes very frank about unwelcome matters. He admits that Adhémar was at first very sceptical of Peter's revelations, and later reports that Peter Bartholomew, having pretended to be illiterate, was forced to admit not only that he was literate, but that he had real knowledge of the liturgy.[27]

---

[25] *GF*, pp. 62–63.

[26] Colin Morris, "Policy and Visions: the case of the Holy Lance at Antioch," in *War and Government in the Middle Ages: Essays in Honour of J.O. Prestwich*, ed. John Gillingham and James C. Holt (Woodbridge, 1984), pp. 33–45, has drawn attention to the political nature of these visions.

[27] Raymond of Aguilers, pp. 88, 108, 72, 76, and see below, pp. 18–19.

Raymond and the anonymous author of the *Gesta* give much the same account of Stephen's vision. On the night of 10 June Stephen was cowering in a church, terrified that the Turks would break out from the citadel, when Christ appeared asking who was the commander of the army – and when Stephen replied that it was Adhémar, he was told to communicate the divine will to him. This respect for hierarchy is the hallmark of a vision whose message was essentially that, if the army repented of its sins, God would show aid within five days; the revelation ended with a vision of the Virgin entreating Christ to aid His people – a familiar iconographic theme. Adhémar accepted this vision for it was inspiring, yet at the same time disciplined and respectful of authority. He used the interest it engendered to demand that the leaders take an oath not to desert.[28] The differences between the two accounts are minor in substance, except that the *Gesta* says that Stephen's vision came first while Raymond asserts that it was after that of Peter Bartholomew. Since we know that Raymond used the former in writing his own account, either he changed the order to reduce the significance of Stephen's vision and magnify that of Peter Bartholomew, or he was correcting an error by the anonymous writer.[29]

Peter Bartholomew, by contrast, revealed not one but a series of visions. In the fifth and latest at Antioch on 10 June [5] St. Andrew had appeared to him after he had joined in an unsuccessful sally against the forces of Kerbogah, and simply bid him reveal what he had been told on four previous occasions.[30] On 30 December 1097 [1] St. Andrew and a companion, who was in fact Christ, appeared and took Peter to the Church of St. Peter in Antioch and showed him the "Lance of the Lord," instructing that he should tell the leaders and return to dig it up when the city was captured.[31] But before the lance was revealed, the first element in the vision struck a jarring note. Peter was told to convoke a meeting of Adhémar, the count of Toulouse, and Peter Raymond of Hautpoul, and to transmit to them divine displeasure that the legate had not sufficiently preached God's word to the people or blessed them with the cross. This is a much less respectful visionary; and another theme is notable – all the three named leaders are Provençals, and this exclusivism will recur later. Peter, however, felt he was too humble and said nothing. Then on 10 February [2], near Edessa, where he had gone in search of food, St. Andrew reprimanded him for his failure to reveal the divine message. In reply Peter pleaded that he was too humble a person to convey such a message. In response he was told that he had been chosen because he was humble and poor – the explicit message is that God's choice, not status or wealth, is all important. Here "holy poverty," so

---

[28] Raymond of Aguilers, pp. 72–74; *GF*, pp. 57–59.

[29] *GF*, pp. 57–60; Raymond of Aguilers, pp. 72–74.

[30] Peter had a large number of visions and they will be numbered here in the text in square brackets, as [1]. For the failure of this sally, see France, *Victory*, p. 275.

[31] John xix.33–34 does not name the soldier who wielded the spear thrust into the side of Christ on the cross, apparently to ensure he was dead. It is likely, as Morris, "Policy and Visions," p. 35, says, that the western name Longinus is based on the Greek word for a lance.

dynamic in Christian history, appears and it so dominates Raymond of Aguilers' work that historians have treated the lance as the symbol of the poor. Once again, Peter feared to reveal his visions. On 20 March, Palm Sunday [3], at St. Simeon's port, where perhaps he had gone in search of food, Peter was again told to reveal the divine message, along with some rather obscure instructions on how the count should behave at Jerusalem. He replied that he was afraid to go back to Antioch because there were many of the enemy between St. Simeon and Antioch, but was assured that they would not hurt him. Apparently his lord, William Peter, overheard part of this vision.[32] However, Peter claimed that when he returned to Antioch, he could not assemble the Provençal leaders as instructed. Then in May [4], at the port of Mamistra, on his way to Cyprus to find food, he was ordered to reveal all and his ship was miraculously prevented from sailing. It was only after the fifth vision that he made his revelation which Adhémar dismissed as fraudulent; Raymond of Toulouse, however, was enthusiastic and placed the visionary in the care of his chaplain Raymond, none other than the chronicler, who now becomes not merely a recorder but also an actor, in the drama of events. Then, five days after the vision of Stephen which could thus be interpreted as foretelling (and confirming) the event, on 14 June, an almost entirely Provençal party dug in the church of St. Peter at Antioch and found the lance. Amongst them was Raymond of Aguilers, who tells us that he kissed the relic when only its very tip was exposed.[33]

It is obvious that this is a very different kind of vision from that of the priest Stephen. It is not respectful of the hierarchy of power, directly criticizing the papal legate and opposing his authority by a divine commission. Moreover, while Stephen dealt in revelations, Peter offered a tangible token of God's favour, the "Lance of the Lord." We should not forget how far popular devotion revolved around relics as material signposts to salvation.[34] On the night following, 16 June, Peter had another vision [6], and this time he seems to have had no hesitation in revealing what has been rightly characterized as a highly political revelation.[35] Andrew again appeared with a companion and proclaimed that the lance had been given to the count of Toulouse alone, upon whom was thus conferred the leadership of the army, "but only as long as he shall remain steadfast in the love of God." The implication was, of course, that Peter, as God's emissary, would be the judge of Raymond's steadfastness. Moreover, in this vision St. Andrew revealed his companion to be none other than Christ himself. This hardly comes as a surprise to the reader, for in

---

[32] Identified as William Peyre of Cunhlat by Jonathan S. C. Riley-Smith, *The First Crusaders, 1095–1131* (Cambridge, 1997), pp. 86–7, 216, 226.

[33] Raymond of Aguilers, pp. 68–72, 75.

[34] Peter Brown, *The Cult of the Saints: its Rise and Function in Latin Christianity* (London, 1981); Nicole Herrmann-Mascard, *Les reliques des Saints. Formation coutumière d'un droit* (Paris, 1975); Daniel F. Callahan, "The Peace of God and the Cult of Saints in Aquitaine in the Tenth and Eleventh Centuries," *Historical Reflections* 14 (1987), 445–66; Patrick J. Geary, *Furta Sacra: Thefts of Relics in the Central Middle Ages* (Princeton, 1978).

[35] Raymond of Aguilers, pp. 75–76; Morris, "Policy and Visions," pp. 33–45, 41.

the very first vision he had been described as "fairer than the children of men," a phrase from the Psalms commonly applied to Christ.[36] Through Andrew, Christ gave various instructions for the commemoration of the finding of the lance, and these prompted the bishop of Orange and Raymond of Aguilers to question Peter about his acquaintance with church liturgy. At first Peter denied any such knowledge, but he ultimately admitted to knowing something of it, though he claimed to have forgotten much. In this vision, Peter emerges as a powerful religious figure, somewhat in the mould of Robert of Arbrissel, who appears to envisage himself and the count as the Moses and Aaron of the crusader army. His divine warrant is presented very carefully by Raymond of Aguilers, with the mysterious figure named as Christ precisely to validate the pretensions of this new prophet. In the dire emergency at Antioch the leaders of the crusade, even Adhémar, had little alternative but to tolerate Peter because his proclamations might help morale in the army.

Many of the contemporary sources say that the discovery of the lance had a dramatic effect on the army's mettle. The author of the *Gesta Francorum* was by no means a devotee of the count of Toulouse, but writes of "boundless rejoicing" on its discovery and adds "From that hour we decided on a plan of attack." Albert of Aachen was similarly enthusiastic. Anselm of Ribemont was a distinguished and pious lord of the second rank who wrote a letter home to the West in July 1098 in which he proclaimed "when this precious gem was found, all our spirits revived." Most importantly, a letter from all the princes to Pope Urban on 11 September 1098 said much the same.[37] However, although the lance was found on 14 June, it was not until 28 June that they actually sallied out to attack the encircling Turks; which hardly suggests a sudden and irresistible upsurge in morale. Moreover, shortly before the battle, the leaders sent an embassy to Kerbogah, led by Peter the Hermit, and there are grounds for thinking that they were prepared to abandon the city in return for their lives.[38] There were certainly more revelations, and this strengthens the notion that there was no sudden upsurge in spirits. Raymond of Aguilers speaks vaguely of more visions and Albert of Aachen describes one granted to a Lombard priest. Shortly before the battle St. Andrew again appeared to Peter [7] commanding that the crusaders should repent of their sins and employ as their battle cry, not *Deus Vult* used hitherto, but *Deus Adiuua*.[39] Why, then, are the sources so unanimous in their view of the inspiring effect of the lance?

The reason seems to be that it was carried into battle on 28 June when the crusaders destroyed the army of Kerbogah in an extraordinary victory. It was

---

[36] Vulgate Ps. 44.3, translation used here is AVR Ps. 45.2; Raymond of Aguilers, p. 16, n. 2.

[37] *GF*, p. 65; Albert of Aachen Book 4, chap. 43; Heinrich Hagenmeyer, *Die Kreuzzugsbriefe aus den Jahren 1088–1100* (Innsbruck, 1902), pp. 159, 162.

[38] Morris, "Policy and Visions," p. 41; Thomas S. Asbridge, *The First Crusade. A New History* (London, 2004), pp. 229–32.

[39] Albert of Aachen, Book 4, chap. 20; Raymond of Aguilers, pp. 77–78. This is conventionally dated 21 June, but the context suggests a date far closer to the battle against Kerbogah on 28 June.

actually borne at the head of the Provençal forces by Raymond of Aguilers.[40] Thus the lance became a great token of victory, a tangible manifestation of God's favour to the crusader army. The material nature of the lance as a token of victory must be insisted upon. At Jerusalem the crusaders discovered the "True Cross," and down to Hattin in 1187 it was carried into battle against the Muslims. There is room to doubt whether the lance inspired the crusaders to victory, but in retrospect it was the most obvious manifestation of divine favour which was the only explanation that the crusaders could conceive for their astonishing victory. Moreover, the military crisis which ended on 28 June 1098 was succeeded by a political crisis when the army effectively fragmented as a result of serious disagreements over policy amongst the leaders. The lance thus became a symbol of the unity which had prevailed before a time of troubles. In this turbulent period Peter Bartholomew, as the bearer of the lance and, in effect, God's prophet, was able to play a significant, though sometimes ambivalent, role.

When the crusader armies passed through Constantinople all the leaders had promised to return former Byzantine territories to the Emperor Alexius Comnenus. The precise territorial range of this promise is not known to us, although it certainly included Antioch and its surroundings, and it is certainly not clear what the emperor offered in return. However, the army benefited enormously from the alliance, particularly because they were able to draw upon Cyprus as a logistical base during the long and bitter siege of Antioch (October 1097–June 1098). In May 1098 news reached the crusader leaders at Antioch of the approach of a huge relief army under Kerbogah. At the same time Firuz, who commanded three towers of the Antioch defences, approached Bohemond and offered to betray the city to him. Bohemond demanded rule over the city once it has been secured. But the leaders so valued the Byzantine alliance that even in this emergency they would only make a conditional promise to Bohemond: that he should have the city if Alexius did not come to take control.[41] In early July 1098, after their victory over Kerbogah, the leaders conferred and sent a high-level delegation led by Hugh of Vermandois, brother of the king of France, and Baldwin of Hainaut to notify Alexius. Moreover, they delayed the resumption of the journey to Jerusalem for an extraordinarily long time, until 1 November. This would have allowed Alexius to receive the news at Constantinople, to raise an army and to march to Antioch. In the meantime the intention was that the army, tired after its ordeal, should rest and so avoid marching in the heat of summer.

The army quickly became embroiled in bitter quarrels. Bohemond was not prepared to wait upon the emperor's response. The count of Toulouse had been ill at the time of the battle against Kerbogah and so had been entrusted with guarding against the citadel. When the garrison saw that Kerbogah had been defeated they offered to surrender, but some southern Italians present insisted that it should be to

---

[40] Raymond of Aguilers, pp. 81–82.
[41] On the benefits of the Byzantine alliance see France, *Victory*, pp. 195–96; *GF*, pp. 44–47, 72.

Bohemond, not the count of Toulouse. Barely had Hugh of Vermandois and Baldwin of Hainaut departed when, on 14 July, Bohemond made a treaty with the Genoese and granted them a quarter within the city on condition that they support him against his enemies, although they stipulated that they would remain neutral if he fought the count of Toulouse.[42] By November, when the army gathered again, all our sources make it clear that the main dispute was between Bohemond, who demanded Antioch, and Count Raymond, who wanted to adhere to the Byzantine alliance, and this appears to have emerged as early as 14 July.

In the course of the summer of 1098 the army learned about events at Philomelium in late June 1098 during Kerbogah's siege of Antioch. At the time of Antioch's fall to the crusaders, Stephen of Blois, a major leader of the northern French forces who had in the spring been chosen as leader of the crusade, was ill at Alexandretta.[43] When he understood how dangerous the situation of the army had become, he fled and reached the Emperor Alexius at Philomelium. Anna Comnena would have us believe that her father was marching to the aid of the crusaders at Antioch, but it seems more likely that he was following up the crusader victories in Asia Minor and subduing key places to his authority.[44] However this may be, Stephen's news persuaded Alexius to abandon his campaign and retreat to Constantinople. The *Gesta Francorum* presents this in a highly dramatic narrative as a Greek betrayal. By contrast, Raymond of Aguilers simply condemns Stephen without mentioning the emperor. Albert of Aachen is fairly neutral, but states that Alexius fled.[45] We do not know when news of Philomelium reached the crusaders at Antioch, but it must surely have been after the sending of Hugh of Vermandois and Baldwin of Hainaut to Constantinople. Undoubtedly news of this "betrayal" must have strengthened the claims of Bohemond, although the count of Toulouse remained devoted to the Byzantine alliance. The best evidence we have of its impact is a letter sent by all the leaders to Pope Urban on 11 September 1098. In this letter they begged the pope to come to complete the work of the crusade and, in particular, to drive out of Antioch all the heretics, including the Greeks. This letter may well have been powerfully influenced by Bohemond who added a *post scriptum* of his own which is virulently hostile to Byzantium. Since Adhémar is known to have pursued a policy of friendship to the Greek Church and to have restored John the Oxite as Greek patriarch of Antioch on the fall of the city, the condemnation of the Greeks as heretics can only indicate a remarkable change in crusader thinking.[46]

---

[42]  Hagenmeyer, *Kreuzzugsbriefe*, pp. 155–56.

[43]  France, *Victory*, pp. 269–70.

[44]  *Alexiad*, pp. 349–50.

[45]  *GF*, pp. 63–65; Raymond of Aguilers, p. 77; Albert of Aachen, Book 4, chaps. 37, 40.

[46]  Hagenmeyer, *Kreuzzugsbriefe*, pp. 161–65, and for the letters indicating Adhémar's cooperation with the Greek patriarch of Jerusalem, then exiled in Cyprus, pp. 132, 142–44. Hagenmeyer drew attention to the problems posed by this letter, not least because it was sent by the princes as a group, but in the middle Bohemond speaks for himself, as well as adding a *post scriptum* in which Alexius is savagely denounced. However, Hagenmeyer recognized that there is no evidence of a text without these dubious

One of the reasons for writing this letter was undoubtedly to tell the pope of the death of Adhémar on 1 August. This occurred at a time when the leaders of the army had dispersed: Raymond of Toulouse was perhaps at his base of Ruj in the Orontes valley, while Bohemond was securing Cilicia; Baldwin of Boulogne had seized Edessa, and it seems that his brother, Godfrey of Bouillon, accompanied by Robert of Flanders, was supporting him by campaigning in the Afrin valley.[47] Into this vacuum of leadership stepped Peter Bartholomew who revealed a vision [8] which he had on the night of 3/4 August.[48] There had appeared to him Christ, St. Andrew and Bishop Adhémar who spoke first, testifying to his sin in doubting the lance, for which he had been punished by the fires of hell. Then St. Andrew spoke in a series of instructions directed to the count of Toulouse, reaffirming that the lance was God's gift to him, and demanding that he dispose of the city of Antioch to a just ruler and at all costs not to the Byzantines as had been done so unjustly with Nicaea. The count was ordered to see to the election of a Latin Patriarch for Antioch, to become reconciled with Bohemond and to lead the army onwards to Jerusalem. Finally, all the rich were enjoined to support the poor. In this, Peter was voicing the exasperation of the rump of the army in Antioch at the turn of events. They hated the Byzantines because of Alexius's desertion, and cared little about Antioch. That in the situation at Antioch the vision could be read as favouring Bohemond's possession of the city is, therefore, hardly surprising. The mass of the army resented the quarrels of the senior notables which had left them leaderless and uncertain. They wanted to press on to Jerusalem, which was the goal for which they had come. In effect this was a manifesto for the crusade. The visionary, Peter Bartholomew, appears here giving orders, directing, acting as a governor and spiritual leader whose secular arm is Raymond of Toulouse. While Raymond of Aguilers emphasized the poor, the visionary spoke in terms which would have been understood by all and would have appealed to a wide social range within the army.

With this vision Peter Bartholomew established himself as a new force in the army, and he was influential precisely because the aspirations to which he gave vent were shared throughout the ranks, and, indeed, by the leaders themselves. But the leaders hesitated because they could see that without a settlement over Antioch it was possible that either Bohemond or the count would not press on to Jerusalem. This dispute further involved the whole question of the Byzantine alliance which was caught up in the fate of Antioch. In addition there was the question of the leadership. Bohemond had been by far the most able military leader, but the count commanded the largest force in the entire crusade and enjoyed the sanction of

---

passages. Thus we have to see the denunciation of the Greeks as heretics as evidence of a change in attitude to the Byzantines amongst the leaders, almost certainly in the light of knowledge of Philomelium. Bohemond expelled John the Oxite from Antioch in 1100, and replaced him with a Latin, Bernard of Valence, on which see Thomas S. Asbridge, *The Creation of the Principality of Antioch 1098–1130* (Woodbridge, 2000), pp. 195–98.

[47]  France, *Victory*, pp. 308–10.

[48]  Raymond of Aguilers, pp. 84–88.

God expressed through the gift of the lance. Neither would defer to the other. On 11 September the leaders had been reduced to appealing to Urban to come and take over the command. They must have known this was impossible, but it was a way of delaying, of plastering over the cracks in the crusader leadership. Further, the hierarchy may have begun to worry about their ability to capture Jerusalem. Baldwin of Boulogne had managed to seize Edessa by playing upon the Armenian factions within the city. The crusaders had seized Antioch but at the cost of tremendous casualties. They could not have known for certain how effectively they had broken the power of the Seljuk Turks and the Abbasid Caliphate. But they would have been aware by this time that Jerusalem had fallen in July 1098 to the Fatimids, and that any attempt to seize it by force would be a risky business in the face of their power. Moreover, the crusaders, at the suggestion of Alexius, had sent an embassy to Egypt in June 1097, and in February/March 1098 they seem to have concluded some kind of understanding with Fatimid emissaries and dispatched another embassy to Cairo. It was, therefore, possible that Jerusalem might fall to them by negotiation.[49] These were compelling reasons for hesitation. But while the leaders could live well in conquered northern Syria, the bulk of the army needed to ravage to subsist, and anyway they were deeply conscious of the task before them – Jerusalem.

In September, Count Raymond agreed to support Duke Godfrey in an expedition to the city of Azaz, whose ruler, Omar, had sought crusader help against the efforts of his overlord, Ridwan of Aleppo, to curb his independence.[50] Such alliances with Muslims may have seemed rather puzzling to the broad mass of crusaders. Godfrey did well from this, but Count Raymond profited little and undertook a great raid into hostile territory. Raymond of Aguilers says that he did this to relieve the famine and tedium of the poor at Antioch. Peter Bartholomew then had another vision [9] at Ruj, in a tent he shared with Bishop Isoard of Apt (1095–1102), a chaplain called Simon and Raymond himself. Simon heard something of the vision – a saintly figure demanding that the bishop, who subsequently shared his experience with Raymond of Aguilers, should reaffirm his belief in the lance.[51] Peter Bartholomew reported a vision of Christ and St. Andrew, together with an unnamed figure, but it was St. Andrew who spoke. His message was really very simple: the count should dismiss his evil advisers and press on to Jerusalem. The bluntness of the criticism is remarkable and it put the count on the defensive. In fact, Raymond went on to capture Albara where, on 25 September, he made Peter of Narbonne the first Latin bishop in the East, returning to have him consecrated by the Greek patriarch of Antioch.

On 1 November the leaders gathered at Antioch and the bickering over the fate of the city reached its climax. Bohemond demanded recognition of his control of

---

[49]   On Crusader–Fatimid relations see France, *Victory*, pp. 325–26.

[50]   This affair is nicely elucidated by Asbridge, *First Crusade*, pp. 243–44.

[51]   Raymond of Aguilers, pp. 89–91.

Antioch, but the count of Toulouse, who controlled a substantial section of the city, stood by the oath to Alexius and the Byzantine alliance. The other leaders, Godfrey of Bouillon, Robert Curthose duke of Normandy and Robert count of Flanders, probably sympathized with Bohemond, but they did not wish to be perceived to have broken their oaths, and, more importantly, feared that, if they supported either protagonist, the other would refuse to continue. This was much more than a mere quarrel over personalities. However, according to Raymond of Aguilers, the mass of the army did not understand such matters, condemned both parties cynically and considered electing a worthy knight to lead them to Jerusalem. This revival of the spirit of the "People's Crusade" should not be dismissed, because Albert of Aachen later tells us that much the same pressures forced Duke Godfrey and Robert of Flanders to leave Antioch. The upshot of all the quarrels, Raymond says, was that Bohemond and Raymond came to a "discordant peace" (*discordem pacem*) under which, as the account in the *Gesta* makes clear, each protagonist retained his position in the city.[52]

The army then left Antioch and besieged Marra, which was close to Count Raymond's city of Albara, from 28 November to 11 December. The city resisted strongly and terrible hardships were experienced because this area of Syria had been devastated by earlier raiding. It is unlikely that the attack on Marra was anything more than a stop-gap activity to occupy the army, because many of the leaders were not present.[53] In yet another vision [10], at Marra on the night of 30 November/1 December, St. Andrew appeared to Peter Bartholomew, but this time with St. Peter, in the guise of poor men – a device that emphasized the sanctity of poverty. St. Peter denounced the immorality of many in the army and the oppression of the poor; but he gave his assurance that Marra would be captured. The change in tone and content is very evident. Peter had this vision in the chapel of Count Raymond and there is none of the blunt criticism which had marked his previous vision. Although the army went on to capture Marra, quarrels again broke out when Bohemond tried to use his quarter of the city as a bargaining counter for the count to relinquish his part of Antioch – the *discordem pacem* had broken down. Popular exasperation fanned by the visionary now exploded. About Christmas 1098 Count Raymond was faced with a blunt demand, led by the bishop of Albara and some nobles, for the crusade to move on. Although Peter Bartholomew was not present on this occasion, the protestors made reference to the lance, and this indicates the appeal of the relic and the widespread sympathy which Peter's manifesto had aroused, though for the moment the visionary's activity was curbed. Count Raymond's difficulty was that his army, although the biggest on the crusade and swollen by the presence of virtually all the poor, was not big enough to attack

---

[52] For the Council see *GF*, pp. 75–76; Raymond of Aguilers, pp. 92–94; Albert of Aachen, Book 5, chap. 28.

[53] We can be certain that Bohemond and Raymond were at Marra, and perhaps also Robert of Flanders. See France, *Victory in the East*, pp. 311–13.

Jerusalem alone, and the other leaders might well resent any effort he made to assume leadership. Moreover, any movement away from Antioch might leave his forces in the city at the mercy of Bohemond. On 4 January 1099 he offered the other leaders large money-fiefs to serve him until Jerusalem was captured – Robert of Normandy accepted and so did Bohemond's nephew Tancred. The latter's emergence at this point is interesting; originally he had commanded a small element of Bohemond's force and even now had few troops, perhaps 40 knights, but such were the losses in the army that this was by now a powerful independent force. In Marra the people were breaking down the walls in frustration but on 13 January the march finally began.[54]

It is unlikely that Raymond of Toulouse intended to take his army to Jerusalem. Bohemond was now clearly intending to stay at Antioch where there were also the substantial forces under the command of Robert of Flanders and Godfrey of Bouillon who appear to have taken the southern Italian's part in the quarrel. It was probably for this reason that, on 14 February, after a prosperous march south aided by the tribute of several Muslim cities, the count began the siege of Arqa, a dependency of nearby Tripoli. Here the army could be supplied by sea from Christian Laodicea, Cyprus and Antioch. To press on further south would be to incur the hostility of the Fatimids and perhaps jeopardize the chances of a peaceful liberation of Jerusalem. The siege, however, went badly. In Antioch popular feeling forced Robert of Flanders and Godfrey to march south, although they only went as far as Jabala, still holding aloof from Count Raymond. A false rumour of an enemy attack led them to join Raymond at Arqa. Tancred stirred up animosity between the northern French and the Provençals and broke away from Count Raymond amidst much bad feeling which was only modified by lavish gifts to the newcomers. At the same time desire to press on to Jerusalem became stronger and stronger. In early April 1099 an imperial embassy arrived and asked the leaders to postpone the march to Jerusalem until June so that Alexius could join them. Public opinion exploded against Count Raymond, who was ready to agree and wished to conquer Arqa, and Godfrey made himself popular by urging the army on to Jerusalem.[55]

It was when the quarrels over the siege of Arqa were reaching their height that Peter Bartholomew met his nemesis, fundamentally because of the contradiction between his position as spokesman of the mass of the army and his championship of the Provençals. Peter had owed his strength to his ability to speak the mind of the army as a whole, but there had always been in his visions a strong note of Provençal patriotism. His ability to express himself freely seems to have been curbed by his assimilation into the household of the count of Toulouse, and he had played no direct role in the "rebellion" at Marra, though others had taken up his theme. Peter's close association with the chaplains and household of Count Raymond was likely, in a

---

[54] Raymond of Aguilers, pp. 95–102; France, *Victory*, pp. 314–16; Asbridge, *First Crusade*, pp. 269–76.

[55] Albert of Aachen, Book 5, chaps. 35, 36; Raymond of Aguilers, pp. 111–12, 125–26.

period of acute political rivalry, to politicize the relationship and thereby bring into question the authenticity of the lance with which Count Raymond's prestige was so closely associated. Quite apart from Adhémar's scepticism, it is evident that others, notably the bishop of Orange, had had their doubts. Now the leading sceptic was Arnulf of Choques, chaplain of Robert of Normandy and later patriarch of Jerusalem.

Opposition was brought to a head by Peter Bartholomew's vision [11] on 5 April 1099 at Arqa. This is narrated in the chronicle of Raymond of Aguilers who appears to have transcribed a legal document, prepared for the subsequent trial of the lance, which included several supporting visions by other people.[56] In this vision Christ appeared on the cross, supported on either side by Saints Peter and Paul. Christ spoke of his five wounds, comparing them to five ranks within the crusader army. Of these, the first were like Christ himself, the second like his apostles, the third like those who mourned his death, the fourth like the crucifiers and the fifth like Judas. Since there were five armies present at Arqa – those of Count Raymond, Robert of Normandy, Robert of Flanders, Godfrey of Bouillon and Tancred – little effort was needed to see the point, especially as Christ was made to suggest that the various groups could easily be identified by preparing an assault on Arqa. The visionary's association with Count Raymond and this overt endorsement of the unpopular siege of Arqa had divorced him from much of his popular support and opened the way for his enemies. Arnulf of Choques brought up the question of Adhémar's doubts. A whole series of supportive visions were then adduced by those whom Raymond of Aguilers called the "good clergy": the priest Ebrardus, Peter Desiderius, Stephen of Valence, the bishop of Apt and Raymond of Aguilers himself all recounted stories supporting the lance and especially Adhémar's post-mortem approval. The most interesting among them was that of the priest Ebrardus who had been at Tripoli seeking food just before Antioch fell and was addressed by a Syrian Christian who claimed to have had a vision of St. Mark saying that the lance would be found in the city and the Christian army would be victorious. Raymond himself told how a priest, Bertrand, had seen Adhémar and his dead standard-bearer Heraclius, both of whom urged all to believe in the lance. Stephen of Valence repeated his earlier vision and the bishop of Apt his story of overhearing part of one of Peter's visions. Peter Desiderius had seen a vision of Adhémar singed in hell for his doubt of the lance. At first Arnulf was ready to accept this, but he reaffirmed his doubts, and Peter Bartholomew resolved to undergo trial by fire.

On 8 April 1099 Peter Bartholomew undertook the trial. Its outcome was ambiguous because Peter survived the ordeal. Raymond of Aguilers says he was injured by the enthusiasm of the mob as he emerged and died of these injuries on 20 April. He reproached Raymond of Aguilers for having, through doubt, wished him to undergo the test. He could be certain of this, he said, because it was revealed

---

[56] Raymond of Aguilers, pp. 112–20.

to him in a vision [12] of Adhémar and the Virgin. Peter then gave instructions for the housing of the lance near his home town of Arles.[57] Not only is the outcome of the trial in doubt, so is its consequence, for the count of Toulouse carried the lance into battle at Ascalon after the capture of Jerusalem, while later writers would refer to it as a token of victory and it has a place in the famous crusading hymn *Ierusalem laetare*.[58] Ralph of Caen described it as an invention by the count of Toulouse, but he was writing a life of Tancred, is unremittingly hostile to all things Provençal and wrote with much hindsight some twenty years after the event.[59]

Far more important for us is to recognize why it was that there was a trial at all. Peter's Provençal leanings had undermined the basis of his popular support; these two themes in his visions had ultimately come to be opposed to one another, and it was this which gave Arnulf and his backers their chance. Before then, Peter had been articulating the desires of thousands of his fellow crusaders of all ranks. So Peter belongs to that great tradition of charismatic visionaries who were ultimately unable to retain their support. But what of Raymond of Aguilers? Historians have been quick to note his role in events – he has been dismissed as credulous and his work as unworthy of belief, a mere pawn, *ein gewissen und skrupelloser Priester* entrapped in a *Schwindel*, a *Lügengespinst* perpetrated by his master the count of Toulouse who used the lance to give himself political prestige in the quarrel with Bohemond and the contest for leadership.[60] Others have not been so charitable and seen Raymond as involved in self-justification, simply defending all that the Provençals and their leader had done in the East.[61] More recently, it has been suggested that the invention of the lance was the result of a conspiracy of clerics who were not under the control of the count of Toulouse and who sought to manipulate the crusade for their own naive objective of pressing on to Jerusalem.[62] Conspiracy theories are attractive but it is very hard to explain the emergence of Peter in these terms, for his first series of visions emerged in entirely understandable circumstances and had little of the political resonances which later appeared. The explanation of the role of Raymond of Aguilers is much more complex. He came from Le Puy, in the very heart of the pilgrim movement, a city at the crossroads of two great routes to Compostella – from Cluny to the east and from Paris to the north. The shrine of St. Mary of Le Puy was already important in its own right and the pilgrim trade was generating great wealth there.[63] Close to the city there was also the famous shrine of St. Michael on the Aguilhe, with which Raymond of Aguilers

---

[57]  Ibid., pp. 121–24.

[58]  Morris, "Policy and Visions," p. 43.

[59]  Ralph of Caen, *Gesta Tancredi RHC Oc.* 3, especially 675–78, 681–84.

[60]  Klemens Klein, *Raymond von Aguilers: Quellenstudie zur Geschichte des ersten Kreuzzuges* (Berlin, 1892), pp. 63, 82.

[61]  Paulin Paris, *La Chanson d'Antioche*, 2 vols (Paris, 1848), 1:21.

[62]  John H. and Laurita L. Hill, *Raymond IV de Saint-Gilles, 1041 (ou 1042)–1105* (Toulouse, 1959), pp. 89–90, 92.

[63]  Louis Bréhier, *Adémar de Monteil. Un evêque à la première croisade* (Le Puy, 1923), p. 4.

may have been associated.[64] To the south lay the important holy places of St. Faith of Conques and St. Peter of Moissac and not far away was St. Julien of Brioude. Rosalind Hill once remarked that: "It is impossible to understand Raymond of Aguilers without seeing the wonder-working shrines of Provence."[65] For Raymond, brought up in this world of miraculous shrines and the fervour of the pilgrim movement, the immanence of God, a common and powerful contemporary notion, must have seemed especially vivid. One of the canons of Saint Julien-Brioude, Robert, had founded the abbey of La Chaise Dieu in 1046 in an early manifestation of the eremetic movement, and during Raymond's lifetime it was enjoying its "century of saints."[66] Raymond of Aguilers was a reformer – he admired Adhémar, whose installation as bishop of Le Puy had been accompanied by a bitter military and political conflict with the old order which was terminated only by the direct intervention of Gregory VII (1073–85).[67]

In Raymond of Aguilers, therefore, there met the very spirit of eleventh-century piety and pilgrim fervour, and a familiarity with the prophetic tradition which was enjoying a brief revival in the eremetic movement. Raymond articulated the revelations of the visionary, and there can be no doubt that he did this with care and skill. We should not be hypnotized by the notion that the lance was the token of the poor. Rich, poor and middling, clergy and laity, were all susceptible to the new religious spirit and the desire to go on to Jerusalem, the goal for which they had come. There was a real community of interest across all classes – at Christmas 1098 we have noted that it was poor, knights and nobles who together pressured the count into marching south.[68] Holy poverty was a powerful idea with a wide appeal amongst Christian people which is not confined to the poor themselves; it is a powerful theme in the visions and personified in the visionary himself. The major leaders of the crusade and their advisers were concerned with politics, with great responsibilities and rivalries – the fate of the Byzantine alliance, the question of command, the resources of the army for its great task – but they were not immune to the basic driving force of the crusade. Raymond of Toulouse's restless activity in the summer of 1098, as well as the influence of the visionary, gave him great prestige and in the end he was forced to still his doubts and lead the march to Jerusalem. But he was not alone. In February 1099 Godfrey of Bouillon and Robert of Normandy,

---

[64]    There is no certainty about the term "Aguilers" but it is possible that it is a latinization of Aguilhe, the great finger of rock which stands close to Le Puy and bears an important shrine of St Michael. A mark of its medieval popularity are the scrapes cut into the rock face of the vertiginous path leading up to the little chapel to house pilgrims overnight. G. J. d'Ademar-Laubaume, *Adémar de Monteil, Légat du Pape sur la première croisade* (Le Puy, 1910), p. 8 notes a charter of Adhémar witnessed by Raymond d'Aguilhes, "Chancelier de l'evêque du Puy," but this person cannot certainly be identified with our chronicler.

[65]    In a private letter to the present writer.

[66]    Leyser, *Hermits* (see above, n. 10), p. 33.

[67]    Ademar-Laubaume, *Adémar de Monteil*, p. 13.

[68]    On the community of interest of all groups see William Porges, "The clergy, the poor and the non-combatants on the First Crusade," *Speculum* 21 (1946), 1–23.

facing the same kind of pressure from their followers, were also forced to swallow their misgivings and march towards Jerusalem.

Raymond of Aguilers, his colleagues and the count of Toulouse were caught up in the complex network of beliefs, interests and forces which underlay the crusade. This is the primary importance of the chronicle of Raymond of Aguilers – that he was an eyewitness close to major events and controversies. When Peter Bartholomew revealed the lance it was not an entirely exotic event (as it would be for us) – God was revealing His support for God's people on God's errand. Raymond of Aguilers is the chronicler of an expedition which he saw as the continuation of the divine revelation; he articulates and explains what he sees, because he believed it and lived it. That there was a degree of political opportunism in the actions of the count of Toulouse is undoubted, but there was no conspiracy. The prophetic spirit, as we may call it, of Peter Bartholomew, was revealed at a crisis of authority in the history of the crusade and became a real force in events. Peter was not a calculating politician – the themes in his visions change according to circumstances and they are sometimes contradictory. In the end his association with Count Raymond and his Provençal patriotism exposed him to attack, and that was his undoing. But the spirit which he represented lived on. In the pages of Raymond of Aguilers he is replaced by a new visionary, Peter Desiderius, whom we have noted as one of those supporting the lance at the time of the trial. In late April he had a vision of St. Andrew commanding the count to desist from the siege of Arqa – which he reluctantly did – and press on to Jerusalem. Raymond used this vision to recall Desiderius' earlier visions at Antioch which revealed holy relics, perhaps by way of establishing his *bona fides*. At Jerusalem, Desiderius suggested that the army, recollecting Joshua at Jericho, should march, as barefoot pilgrims, around the city as part of the preparations for the final assault, which it duly did.[69] But Desiderius was far more like Stephen of Valence, a disciplined cleric – his was not the visionary role of Peter Bartholomew which represented so faithfully the spirit of contemporary piety, and therefore of the crusade, which transfixed Raymond of Aguilers the chronicler, and dominates his account of events.

---

[69]   Raymond of Aguilers, pp. 131–34.

# Vengeance and the Crusades

*Susanna Throop*

University of New Hampshire at Manchester

In 1935 Carl Erdmann's *Die Entstehung des Kreuzzugsgedankens* was published, sparking a re-examination of the developments of 1095 and 1096, and, eventually, of the motivations and justifications lying behind subsequent military expeditions as well.[1] But, despite this scholarly activity, the idea of crusading as vengeance has never been fully and comprehensively explored.[2]

There is nonetheless a view commonly held by historians regarding the idea of vengeance and the expedition known as the First Crusade. According to the accepted viewpoint articulated by Jonathan Riley-Smith, the relationship between vengeance and crusading at the time of the First Crusade was located predominantly in the minds of the laity. The desire for vengeance manifested itself at the beginning of the First Crusade in the attacks perpetrated by the crusaders on European Jews, but subsequently this desire dissipated; by the end of the crusade, all that remained were "residual feelings."[3] According to this model, the idea of crusading as vengeance faded into oblivion in the later part of the twelfth century, confined to anomalous medieval writers who were behind the times ideologically; as Erdmann himself concluded, the idea of vengeful crusading in the twelfth century was surely nothing more than "an obvious improvisation suggestive of how immature the idea of crusade still was."[4]

In fact, the textual evidence points to entirely different conclusions. This article demonstrates that the popularity of the idea of crusading as vengeance was not limited to the laity, and, instead of fading away after 1099, the ideology grew more widespread as the twelfth century progressed. The primary aim here is to present the evidence alongside preliminary analysis, reserving further, more detailed interpretation for future publications.

There are several methodological issues facing research such as this, some of which must be discussed here. Faced with the questions of which terms in Latin and Old French should be examined, and whether it is appropriate to group them together and at the same time exclude other terms, the field of research has been limited as much as possible by focusing on the Latin root-words *vindicta* and *ultio*,

---

[1]  Carl Erdmann, *Die Entstehung des Kreuzzugsgedankens*; *The Origin of the Idea of Crusade*, trans. Marshall W. Baldwin and Walter Goffart (Princeton, 1977).

[2]  For brief treatments of the subject see: Paul Rousset, *Les origines et les caractères de la première croisade* (Neuchâtel, 1945); Jonathan S. C. Riley-Smith, *The First Crusade and the Idea of Crusading* (London, 1986); Jean Flori, *Croisade and chevalerie* (Brussels, 1998).

[3]  Riley-Smith, *The First Crusade and the Idea of Crusading*, p. 55.

[4]  Erdmann, *Origin of the Idea of Crusade*, p. 113.

and the Old French *venjance*. For the purpose of discussion these terms have been translated into the modern English *vengeance*. There is reason to believe that *vindicta*, *ultio*, and *venjance* were understood as roughly equivalent terms in the Middle Ages: Hebrew words such as *nâqam* in the Old Testament were translated into either *vindicta* or *ultio* in the Latin Vulgate, and *vindicta* was translated into the Old French *venjance*, as in the case of the Latin poem *Vindicta Salvatoris* and its Old French version, *La Venjance de Nostre Seigneur*. It is also reasonable to translate the medieval terms into the modern English word *vengeance* for similar reasons, although the choice of the specific term *vengeance* is primarily based on linguistic similarity, and by no means implies that the medieval and modern words all signify precisely the same concept.

For the sake of clarity this research is restricted to the medieval terms *vindicta*, *ultio*, and *venjance*, despite the abundance of similar nouns like *retributio* in the sources. Medieval writers gave *retributio* both positive (reward) and negative (punishment) connotations, making it semantically distinct from, though undoubtedly related to, *vindicta* and *ultio*.[5] This present analysis has not labelled events in the sources as "vengeful" or "acts of vengeance," relying instead on the commentary of medieval contemporaries. When the word *vengeance* is used here to translate or discuss a medieval text, it is because *vindicta*, *ultio*, or *venjance* was used by the medieval author. Moreover, a distinction is drawn between the concept of a crusade in its entirety as one act of vengeance, and the frequent descriptions of individual battles or skirmishes as acts of vengeance for previous raids or ambushes. It is the former alone that has been considered evidence for the idea of crusading as vengeance.

Histories and chronicles have formed the backbone of this research. This is because of both their value, and the fact that any new interpretation intended to address a common assumption must by its nature look at the material that is commonly examined. This study has also utilized letters and literature in order to illustrate contemporary crusading culture in western Europe. Because the goal is cultural illustration rather than the establishment of points of fact regarding actual crusading events, the sources have been separated by date of composition, rather than by the date of the events described within the texts. In a few cases the date of composition has been difficult to establish, and those texts are discussed in the appropriate subsection below.

---

[5] For example Gratian, *Decretum* C.23 q.3 c.1, in *Corpus iuris canonici*, ed. E. Friedberg, 2 vols (Leipzig, 1879–81), 1:896 (*Quot sunt differentiae retributionis*).

**1095–1137**

For the period from 1095 to 1137 this paper will examine three different kinds of sources: letters, eyewitness accounts of the First Crusade, and narrative accounts written by non-participants. Only two letters of the First Crusade, out of the twenty-three compiled by Hagenmeyer, contained a reference to crusading as vengeance. The first was the letter from the lay leaders of the expedition to Urban II, written in September 1098 from Antioch, in which the leaders claimed "we the *Hierosolymitani* of Jesus Christ have avenged the injury of the highest God."[6] Subsequently, in 1100 Paschal II wrote concerning the First Crusade to the consuls in Pisa "when the Christian people gathered an army in the name of God ... they most strenuously avenged the earthly Jerusalem from the tyranny and yoke of the barbarians."[7] While the letter from the lay leaders of the First Crusade simply stated that they had avenged an unspecified injury done to God, the letter from Paschal II made it clear that it was the seizure of Jerusalem by the Muslims that had been avenged. These two letters show the presence of the idea of crusading as vengeance on the cusp between the eleventh and twelfth centuries, but this evidence is mitigated by the fact that the vast majority of the letters made no connection between the First Crusade and vengeance.

Another source that argues for the presence of the idea of crusading as vengeance at the end of the eleventh century is the so-called "encyclical of Sergius IV." This document has been the object of fierce scrutiny and debate for more than a century now; some historians have argued for its authenticity, whilst others have argued for a dating in the late eleventh or early twelfth century.[8] One scholar has even concluded that the "encyclical" must date from the late twelfth century, due to its apparent ideological link with the papal propaganda of Innocent III.[9] In all likelihood, Schaller's argument relied overmuch on incorporating the "encyclical" within an earlier tradition of pious pilgrimage and underplaying links between the "encyclical" and the ideology of Urban II.[10] To date, Gieszytor's arguments have been the most in-depth and convincing, drawing upon a wealth of material and textual evidence to conclude that the "encyclical" most likely dates from the late eleventh or early twelfth century. His argument for dating it to Urban II's visit to

---

[6]  Heinrich Hagenmeyer, ed., *Epistulæ et chartæ ad historiam primi belli sacri spectantes* (Innsbruck, 1901), p. 164. All translations in this article are my own.

[7]  Hagenmeyer, *Epistulæ*, p. 180.

[8]  The former most recently Hans-Martin Schaller, "Zur Kreuzzugsenzyklika Papst Sergius IV," in Hubert Mordek, ed., *Papsttum, Kirche und Recht im Mittelalter: Festschrift für Horst Fuhrmann zum 65. Geburtsag* (Tübingen, 1991), pp. 135–54. Argued previously by Carl Erdmann and Paul Kehr. The latter most recently Aleksander Gieysztor, "The genesis of the crusades: the encyclical of Sergius IV (1009–1012)," *Medievalia et humanistica* 5 (1948), 3–23, and 6 (1948), 3–34. Argued previously by Julius von Pflugk-Harttung and Paul Riant.

[9]  Ursula Schwerin, *Die Aufrufe der Päpste zur Befreiung des Heiligen Landes von den Anfängen bis zum Ausgang Innocenz III* (Berlin, 1937), p. 301.

[10]  Schaller, "Zur Kreuzzugsenzklika Papst Sergius IV," pp. 148–49.

the Abbey of Moissac in 1095 is much less convincing, but that does not alter the validity of his argument for the more general dating of the document to the late eleventh century.

The "encyclical," which was never widely distributed, called upon Christians in western Europe to take back Jerusalem in the wake of the destruction of the Holy Sepulchre by the Caliph al-Hakim in 1009. The text described the proposed expedition as an act of vengeance: "we are going into the area of Syria, so that we might avenge the Redeemer and his tomb."[11] Furthermore, the "encyclical" presented the destruction of Jerusalem in 70 C.E. by Titus and Vespasian as an early analogue of the proposed expedition: "just as it was in the days of Titus and Vespasian, who avenged the death of the Son of God."[12] These examples from the "encyclical" suggest that vengeance was owed for the death of Christ. Clearly, the "encyclical of Sergius IV," taken together with the two First Crusade letters already discussed, demonstrates that the idea of crusading as vengeance was in existence in the late eleventh century, albeit to a limited degree. The "encyclical" also signals the existence of the legend of the destruction of Jerusalem that would become the text known as *La Venjance de Nostre Seigneur* by the end of the twelfth century.[13]

The remaining sources for the period were written slightly later than the letters, in the early twelfth century. Among these sources, the eyewitness accounts were written by people who, as far as can be determined, actually participated in the events they described. It seems reasonable to think that the eyewitnesses were more likely to reflect accurately the atmosphere on the First Crusade than those who were never there. The atmosphere on the 1096 expedition itself is an important issue that must be addressed if possible, since the accepted view posits that the desire for vengeance evaporated shortly after the taking of Jerusalem in 1099.

Five Latin eyewitness accounts are under discussion: the *Gesta Francorum*, Fulcher of Chartres' *Historia Iherosolymitana*, Peter Tudebode's *Historia de Hierosolymitano Itinere*, Ekkehard of Aura's *Hierosolymita*, and the *Liber* of Raymond of Aguilers.[14] In the first four texts, there were almost no references to vengeance of any kind, and absolutely no reference to the idea of crusading as vengeance.[15]

---

[11]  Ibid., p. 151.

[12]  Ibid.

[13]  For an excellent overview of the evolution of this legend from the account of Josephus to the dramatizations of the later Middle Ages, see Stephen K. Wright, *The Vengeance of Our Lord: medieval dramatizations of the destruction of Jerusalem* (Toronto, 1989), pp. 1–29.

[14]  *Gesta Francorum et aliorum Hierosolimitanorum*, ed. Rosalind Hill (Oxford 1962); Fulcher of Chartres, *Historia Iherosolymitana*, ed. Heinrich Hagenmeyer (Heidelberg, 1913); Peter Tudebode, *Historia de Hierosolymitano Itinere*, ed. John H. Hill and Laurita L. Hill, Documents relatifs à l'histoire des croisades 12 (Paris, 1977); Ekkehard of Aura, *Hierosolymitana*, *RHC Oc* 5 (Paris 1895); Raymond of Aguilers, *Liber*, ed. John H. Hill and Laurita L. Hill, Documents relatifs à l'histoire des croisades 9 (Paris, 1969).

[15]  The *Gesta Francorum* did depict those killed at Nicæa as martyrs who ascended to heaven saying "Lord, avenge our blood, which was shed for you" (*GF*, p. 17). However, it is not clear from the text that

In the fifth account, that of Raymond of Aguilers, the idea of crusading as vengeance surfaced twice. According to the text, the English went on the First Crusade "having heard the name of the Lord of vengeance on those who unworthily occupied the land of Jesus Christ's birth and of his apostles."[16] The taking of Jerusalem was summarily described: "the sons of apostles avenged the city and the fatherland for God and the fathers."[17] Like Paschal II in his letter of 1100, Raymond suggested that vengeance was owed for the Islamic occupation of Jerusalem.

The account of Raymond of Aguilers confirms that the idea of crusading as vengeance was in existence at the time of the First Crusade. In fact, the idea of holy war as vengeance for God dates back well before 1095, making it likely that the understanding of the First Crusade as vengeance may have been an adaptation of a previous trend, and not an entirely new ideology specific to the crusades.[18] But the main point is that, despite the existence of the idea of crusading as vengeance, understanding of the ideology at the time of the First Crusade does not seem to have been as widespread as previous historians have thought. Not only did the majority of letters and eyewitness accounts omit the idea, but even the one eyewitness account that did discuss crusading as vengeance also contained passages that seem to suggest vengeance was an inappropriate activity for crusaders: Raymond of Aguilers ostentatiously noted two occasions when the crusaders showed restraint, rather than otherwise, claiming that their minds were fixed on the journey ahead of them rather than on the desire for vengeance.[19] The letters and eyewitness accounts simply do not reveal the inflamed lust for vengeance that supposedly pervaded the crusading armies at the end of the eleventh century.

It could be argued that the evidence appears this way because the idea of crusading as vengeance circulated among the lower ranks of the crusaders, and thus found little outlet in written texts, especially those written by members of the Church. However, what evidence is available suggests otherwise. As shown above, the lay leaders of the crusade, who were hardly humble rabble, as well as Pope Paschal II, gave credence to the idea of crusading as vengeance. Raymond of Aguilers likewise referred to crusading as vengeance, while at the same time other members of the Church such as Ekkehard of Aura and Fulcher of Chartres ignored it. The evidence in this case simply does not allow for the ideological separation of the laity and the professed religious, or of those of low and high rank.

The eyewitness accounts of the First Crusade did not emphasize crusading as vengeance, but six narratives written by non-participants did: these are the accounts

---

in calling for God to avenge them, the dead Christians were requesting a crusade *per se*; it was not unusual to call for God to avenge injury and wrongdoing.

[16] Raymond of Aguilers, *Liber*, p. 134.

[17] Ibid., p. 151.

[18] Flori, *Croisade and chevalerie*, p. 189.

[19] Raymond of Aguilers, *Liber*, p. 38.

of Albert of Aachen, Baldric of Bourgueil, Guibert of Nogent, Orderic Vitalis, Ralph of Caen, and Robert of Rheims.[20]

In Albert of Aachen's account, when Peter the Hermit first witnessed the Islamic occupation of the Holy Sepulchre in Jerusalem "he called on God himself to be the avenger of the injuries he had seen" and then proceeded to Rome to urge the First Crusade.[21] Orderic Vitalis wrote that "with the permission of divine judgment the detestable Saracens crossed the borders of the Christians, invaded the holy places, killed the Christian inhabitants, and polluted the holy things with their filth, but after a long time they rightly suffered deserved vengeance at the hands of the northern peoples."[22] According to Robert of Rheims, Urban II at Clermont asked his audience "therefore to whom will this work of vengeance, this work of recovery, fall, if not to us?"[23] In response to Urban's appeal, according to Orderic Vitalis, all Christendom prepared for the expedition to the East: "valuable estates were sold for little and arms were taken up with which divine vengeance would be exercised."[24] In general, these writers called for Christians to enact divine vengeance both for the Islamic occupation of Jerusalem and the purported sufferings of Christians at the hands of the Muslims.

Robert of Rheims commemorated the fall of Antioch with a little verse inserted in the narrative:

> Divine vengeance thus wished to avenge itself
> on the dog-like people, and thus it was pleased.[25]

In this passage, the crusaders were acting out the will of God by taking vengeance on the Muslims for an unspecified injury. Similarly, Orderic Vitalis recounted that Baldwin I rallied his men at Jaffa, saying "let us arm ourselves manfully to take vengeance for God."[26] Although the injury was unspecified, to contemporaries it clearly demanded vengeance.

Yet another slightly different tone appeared in a sermon preached before the walls of Jerusalem were scaled, according to Baldric of Bourgueil: "I say to fathers and sons and brothers and nephews: for if some outsider struck one of your own, would you not avenge your blood? How much more ought you to avenge your God, your father, your brother, whom you see blamed, outlawed, crucified; whom you

---

[20] Albert of Aachen, *Liber Christianae expeditionis*, *RHC Oc* 4 (Paris, 1879); Baldric of Bourgueil, *Historia Jerosolimitana*, *RHC Oc* 4 (Paris, 1879); Guibert of Nogent, *Dei Gesta per Francos*, ed. Robert B. C. Huygens, CCCM 127A (Turnhout, 1996); Orderic Vitalis, *Historia Æcclesiastica*, ed. Marjorie Chibnall, 6 vols. (Oxford, 1969–80); Ralph of Caen, *Gesta Tancredi in expeditione Hierosolymitana*, *RHC Oc* 3 (Paris, 1866); Robert of Rheims, *Historia Iherosolimitana*, *RHC Oc* 3 (Paris, 1866).

[21] Albert of Aachen, *Liber*, p. 272.

[22] Orderic Vitalis, *Historia*, vol. 5 p. 4.

[23] Robert of Rheims, *Historia*, p. 728; internal reference to Psalm 67.22.

[24] Orderic Vitalis, *Historia*, vol. 5 p. 16.

[25] Robert of Rheims, *Historia*, p. 805.

[26] Orderic Vitalis, *Historia*, vol. 5 p. 348.

hear clamoring and desolate and begging for aid."[27] In this example of rhetoric, the crusaders were to avenge Christ himself, their father and brother, who (it was suggested) was suffering the Passion at that very moment in time and crying out for assistance. Crusaders were urged to view their relationship with God in terms of family, and thereby to follow the customs of vengeance they were familiar with.[28] Moreover, at the same time, the passage plays upon the powerful image of the suffering Christ calling for help.

The application of biblical texts to the First Crusade led to yet another "injury" committed by the Muslims. Guibert of Nogent applied Zechariah 12.6 to the First Crusade, explaining that "therefore *they devoured all the people to the right and to the left in a circle* [means that] while over here the elect, whom the right hand signifies, are incorporated into the piety of Christianity, over there the reprobate, who are known to pertain to the left, are devastated with deserved vengeance of slaughter."[29] For Guibert, vengeance was deserved by the Muslims not for one specific action but rather because they were "reprobate."

It is in the twelfth-century histories of the First Crusade written by non-participants, both monastic and otherwise, that the idea of crusade as vengeance was most visible. That said, these writers did not confine themselves to one theme. Much of the rhetoric concerning martyrdom and the imitation of Christ thrived in these accounts. The important point is that these writers emphasized vengeance more than the Latin eyewitnesses did. Indeed, however limited their treatment of vengeance, it was greater than that of the eyewitness accounts, making it extremely unlikely that the idea of crusading as vengeance peaked before 1100 and then slowly faded away.

Although there were only a small number of examples of the idea of crusading as vengeance from this period, nevertheless it is notable that writers played upon a wide variety of subcategories of the idea of crusading as vengeance: vengeance for an unspecified injury to God and Christianity, vengeance for the Islamic occupation of the Holy Land and treatment of the Christians living there, and vengeance for the sufferings and/or death of Christ. Moreover, in the writing of Guibert of Nogent, there was a hint that the Muslims deserved vengeance simply because of who, or what, they were.

---

[27] Baldric of Bourgueil, *Historia*, p. 101; internal reference to Isaiah 63.3.

[28] For more on the medieval understanding of family, see David Herlihy, "Family," *American Historical Review* 96 (1991), 1–16. For more on the medieval relationship between vengeance and social ties, see Daniel L. Smail, 'Hatred as a Social Institution in Late-medieval Society,' *Speculum* 76:1 (2001), 90–126 and Paul R. Hyams, *Rancor and Reconciliation in Medieval England* (Ithaca, NY, 2003).

[29] GN, p. 304.

**1138–1175**

The mid-twelfth century sources, those dating roughly from 1138–75, revealed an interesting pattern of evidence. First, in some texts the vocabulary of vengeance was applied to crusading. Second, the moral value of vengeance in general was presented in a more universal and unambiguously positive fashion. But third, and crucially, the ideology did *not* appear in a number of key crusading texts from the period.

Peter the Venerable stressed that the First Crusaders had taken vengeance for the Islamic occupation. In a letter to Louis VII of France in 1146, Peter directly compared the First Crusade to Old Testament wars when "by the command of God they exterminated the profane people with warlike strength, and avenged the land for God and themselves."[30]

The Byzantine emperor Manuel I, writing to Eugenius III in 1146 about the Second Crusade, stated that he knew that the Franks were coming "in order to avenge the holy churches, and because Edessa [was] held by the impious enemies of God." Manuel I emphasized both the general need to take vengeance for injuries done to the Church in the East and also the more specific need to take vengeance for the fall of Edessa.

The anonymous author of the *Gesta Stephani* wrote regarding the Second Crusade that:

> Therefore when the disgraceful news of such an intolerable expulsion had been made known to the pious ears of the mother Church, the kingdoms were agitated, the powers of the world were shaken, the whole world joined together manfully to avenge the shame of this universal injury. And especially the strong youths of all England, all marked with the strength of a manly heart and a constant mind, came together for this most particular [act of] vengeance.[31]

Just before this passage, the injuries that demanded vengeance were explicitly listed: the Muslims were "hostile to [the Christian] religion," they had seized Christian cities (including Jerusalem), killed some Christians and taken others hostage, and "what is a crime to say, they sought to abolish the temple, destroy the holy places, and delete the name of Christ."[32]

But other writers of historical accounts were much less clear about why vengeance was required in the East. For example, Bernard of Clairvaux, although he also utilized the vocabulary of vengeance, was less specific when he wrote to "the universal faithful" about the Second Crusade in March 1147, reminding them

---

[30] Peter the Venerable, *The Letters of Peter the Venerable*, ed. Giles Constable, 2 vols. (Cambridge, MA, 1967), 1:327.

[31] *Gesta Stephani Regis Anglorum*, ed. Kenneth R. Potter (Oxford, 1976), p. 192.

[32] Ibid., p. 192.

that during the First Crusade "God elevated the spirit of kings and princes to take vengeance on the nations and eradicate the enemies of the Christian name from the land."[33] From Bernard's perspective, the First Crusaders had taken vengeance by eliminating non-Christians from the Holy Land. An annalist claimed that the Second Crusade was "to avenge the injury done to the Christian religion on the pagans."[34]

When it came to describing the arm of the Second Crusade that attacked Lisbon, the generality was marked. There was a sermon by Peter, bishop of Oporto, described in the *De expugnatione Lyxbonensi* in which crusading was referred to as "divine vengeance," "vengeance for the blood of [the Church's] sons," "vengeance taken upon the nations," and "deeds of vengeance."[35] By the end of the narrative, the author stated that the taking of Lisbon was "divine justice ... vengeance upon the evildoers."[36] Aside from one apparent reference to Christian deaths, no specific injury was singled out; rather, the vocabulary of vengeance hinged upon the perception of the Muslims as "evildoers."

The Old French crusading song *Chevalier, mult estes guariz*, composed between December 1145 and June 1147, remarked that the Christian knights "went to serve [God] in his need ... in order to provide God with vengeance."[37] By interpreting the need for vengeance in terms of men fulfilling their lord's need to take vengeance, in effect the song eliminated the need for more specific justification: if the lord needed vengeance, vengeance must be sought. This kind of attitude may have underlined other unspecific references to vengeance, though it is impossible to say that with any certainty unless the textual evidence itself confirms it.

Similarly, the Occitan troubadour Marcabru wrote circa 1146–47 that "since the son of God summons you to avenge him on the lineage of Pharaoh, you indeed ought to be joyful."[38] In another poem Marcabru was somewhat more specific, writing that vengeance was owed for injuries done to God throughout the world: "the Lord who knows all that is, and all that will be, and that was, has promised us crowns and the name of emperor ... as long as we take vengeance for the wrongs they do to God, both here and there towards Damascus."[39] Wrong had been done, and vengeance was owed.

In the texts outlined above, crusading was described as an act of vengeance. In addition, it was discussed with less ambiguity. Many of the crusading texts written in the early twelfth century explicitly referred to occasions when the crusaders did

---

[33] Bernard of Clairvaux, '*Epistolae*', ed. Jean Leclercq and Henri M. Rochais, *S. Bernardi Opera*, 8 vols. (Rome, 1955–77), 8:432.

[34] *Gesta Abbatum Lobbiensium*, MGH Scriptores 21 (Hanover, 1869).

[35] *De expugnatione Lyxbonensi*, ed. and trans. C. W. David (New York, 1936), pp. 76, 78 and 80.

[36] Ibid., p. 182.

[37] *Les chansons de croisade*, ed. Joseph Bédier (Paris, 1909), p. 10.

[38] *Marcabru: A critical edition*, ed. Simon Gaunt, Ruth Harvey, and Linda Paterson (Cambridge, 2000), p. 310.

[39] Ibid., p. 438.

*not* seek out vengeance. Raymond of Aguilers noted that when the crusaders were attacked at Scutari and Durazzo, they deliberately did not retaliate.[40]

There were no references to such self-conscious passivity or acts of non-violent mercy in the texts examined for the period 1138–75. In Odo of Deuil's *De profectione Ludovici VII in orientem*, he repeatedly described the crusaders taking vengeance upon those attacking them (namely, Greeks and Muslims). Unlike Raymond of Aguilers' First Crusaders, the French leaders of the Second Crusade were depicted leaving Adalia "mourning that they were not able to avenge their injuries."[41] They had however been able to take further action during a previous ambush: "all [the crusaders] unanimously ran against them, and those whom they could, they killed, in consequence of their own who had died, and avenging their own injuries."[42] The crusading texts from the mid-twelfth century do not endorse the righteous affirmation of pacific behaviour.

Of course, most of the time the vocabulary of vengeance was presented as an understood social commonplace, with little commentary of any sort offered by the authors. But when vengeance *qua* vengeance was commented on in the mid-twelfth century, it was discussed as a good thing. As Bernard of Clairvaux wrote to the Knights Templar, "a Christian glories in the death of a pagan, since Christ is glorified; in the death of a Christian, the generosity of the King is revealed, since the knight is led forth, about to be rewarded. Moreover a just man rejoices over [the former], since he sees vengeance [done]."[43]

That said, there were a number of key sources for crusading during the period from 1138 to 1175 that did not include the idea of crusading as vengeance. Eugenius III, Hadrian IV, Alexander III, and Suger of St. Denis did not refer to the ideology in their letters, even in the well-known papal bull *Quantum praedecessores*.[44]

Some narrative accounts avoided the ideology as well. Caffaro of Genoa did not utilize the idea of crusading as vengeance at all, even steering clear of language that accompanied the vocabulary of vengeance in other sources.[45] Henry of Huntingdon omitted the specific vocabulary of vengeance in his account of the First and Second Crusades.[46] Instead, he described the taking of the Holy Sepulchre in Jerusalem in 1099 thus: "therefore assaulting the city and climbing its walls with ladders, the sons of God took the city, and killed many rebels (*rebellantes*) in the temple of the Lord,

---

[40] Raymond of Aguilers, *Liber*, p. 38.

[41] Odo of Deuil, *De profectione Ludovici VII in orientem*, ed. and trans. Virginia G. Berry (New York, 1948), p. 110.

[42] Ibid., p. 126.

[43] Bernard of Clairvaux, *Liber ad milites templi de laude novae militiae*, ed. Jean Leclercq and Henri M. Rochais, *S. Bernardi Opera*, 3:217.

[44] Eugenius III, *Epistolae*, RHGF 15 (Paris, 1878); Eugenius III, *Opera*, PL 180 (Paris, 1855); Alexander III, *Epistolae*, PL 200 (Paris, 1858); Hadrian IV, *Epistolae*, PL 188 (Paris, 1855).

[45] Caffaro of Genoa, *De liberatione civitatum Orientis*, ed. Luigi T. Belgrano, *Annali Genovesi di Caffaro e de'suoi continuatori* 1 (Rome, 1901).

[46] Henry of Huntingdon, *Historia Anglorum*, ed. Thomas Arnold, RS 74 (London, 1879), pp. 225–30 and 279.

and cleansed the holy city of the unclean peoples."[47] Henry noted that the capture of Edessa led to the Second Crusade, but did not use the vocabulary of vengeance; the Christians simply went "to fight the pagans who had taken the city of Edessa."[48] Vincent of Prague was likewise matter-of-fact about the Second Crusade and did not use the vocabulary of vengeance: "no small [number] of Christians were moved to defend Jerusalem against the king of Babylon."[49]

The *Annales Herbipolenses* described the beginning of the Second Crusade in 1147 with vitriolic language aimed at those who promoted the crusade rather than at its target: "for some pseudo-prophets, sons of Belial, witnesses [*testes*] to the Antichrist, who seduced Christians with inane words, compelled all kinds of men with vain sayings to go against the Saracens to liberate Jerusalem."[50] The fierce disapproval in the text may have been the result of the notorious failure of the Second Crusade, and certainly many writers of historical accounts of the Second Crusade focused on its disastrous outcome rather than the motives that drove people to take part. Otto of Freising also talked of vengeance taken on the Christians rather than through their actions.[51] Perhaps the absence of the ideology was because of this focus on outcome (thus failure) rather than on motivation and justification.

But even when these writers did devote a line or two to the reasons for the crusading, they did not use the vocabulary of vengeance. For example, Helmold of Bosau recorded that Bernard of Clairvaux "exhorted princes and certain people of the faithful to march to Jerusalem to seize the barbarous nations of the east and subject them to Christian laws."[52] Odo of Deuil depicted the bishop of Langres exciting people at Bourges at Christmas 1145, "warning all of the depopulation and oppression of the Christians and the insolence of the pagans, that with their king they would fight with Christian reverence for the King of all."[53] Otto of Freising described the First Crusaders without the vocabulary of vengeance: "confident in the strength of the cross, with Godfrey as their leader, a journey to fight against the enemies of the cross in the East was announced."[54] These writers hit upon familiar themes: the centrality of Jerusalem, the need to conquer Islamic territory, the ill-treatment of Christians by the Muslims, the desire to fight against the enemies of the cross. But these themes were not discussed with the vocabulary of vengeance.

---

[47] Ibid., p. 229.

[48] Ibid., p. 279.

[49] Vincent of Prague, *Annales*, MGH Scriptores 17 (Hanover, 1861), p. 662.

[50] *Annales Herbipolenses*, MGH Scriptores 16 (Hanover, 1859), p. 3.

[51] Otto of Freising, *De gestis Friderici seu rectius Cronica*, ed. Franz-Josef Schmale (Darmstadt, 1965), p. 220.

[52] Helmold of Bosau, *Chronica Slavorum*, ed. Heinz Stoob (Berlin, 1963), p. 216.

[53] Odo of Deuil, *De profectione Ludovici VII in orientem*, p. 6.

[54] Otto of Freising, *Chronica sive Historia de Duabus Civitatibus*, ed. Walther Lammers (Darmstadt, 1961), p. 502.

## Sources dating from approximately 1176–1203

The examination of fifteen narrative crusading accounts composed between 1176 and 1204 (ten in Latin and five in Old French), and of the poetry and the papal letters for the period, has revealed that no fewer than fourteen texts referred to a crusade as an act of vengeance, and eight of the fifteen did so repeatedly. The extremely high proportion of texts referring to the ideology in the last third of the century demonstrates that the idea of crusading as an act of vengeance was presented even more frequently in later twelfth-century crusading texts than in texts from either the early or mid-twelfth century. Furthermore, the concept served as a primary source of rhetoric for some writers, such as Innocent III.

Many passages focused on the need to avenge the Islamic occupation and Christian deaths in the East. William of Tyre wrote that the preaching of the Second Crusade involved the cry for vengeance for the injuries done to eastern Christians:

> There were those who disseminated their words near and far among the people and the nations and solicited provinces idle and dissolute from a long peace to avenge such injuries. Lord Eugenius III ... directed the powerful men in deed and sermon to diverse parts of the West, who announced the intolerable hardships of their Eastern brothers to the princes and the people and that they ought to rouse themselves to go to avenge the injuries of fraternal blood.[55]

Similarly, the account of Ambroise described the response to the Third Crusade thus:

> Neither the old nor the young
> wished to hide his heart;
> they showed the weight on them,
> and their need to take vengeance
> for the shame done
> against God who had not deserved
> that his land had been destroyed,
> where his people were so harried
> that they did not know what to do.[56]

For Ambroise, as for so many, the injuries deserving of vengeance were the Islamic occupation and the treatment of Christians in the East, injuries which had shamed God and obligated the Christians in the West to act. The *Gesta Regis Henrici Secundi* recorded a letter from Henry II to Aimeric the patriarch of Antioch in 1188, in which Henry wrote "now however the Lord ... has thus excited the sleepy

---

[55] WT 16.18, pp. 739–40.

[56] Ambroise, *Estoire de la guerre sainte*, ed. Marianne Ailes and Malcolm Barber, *The History of the Holy War: Ambroise's Estoire de la Guerre Sainte*, 2 vols. (Woodbridge, 2003), 1:2. See also 1:112.

Christians to His service, so that everyone who is of the Lord, girds himself with his sword, and judges a man blessed and faithful who leaves his father and mother and all things in order to avenge the injuries of the Holy Land for Christ."[57] The *Itinerarium peregrinorum* remarked that Joscius, archbishop of Tyre, was partly responsible for getting news from the East to the West: "announcing that the inheritance of Christ was occupied by the gentiles to all the faithful, some he moved to tears, while others he inflamed to vengeance."[58] In *Plorans ploravit Ecclesia*, written in 1198, Innocent III hoped that God "would arm sons to avenge the paternal injuries, and brothers to avenge the fraternal wounds."[59] In his 1198 letter *Si ad actus*, Innocent III promised the count of Forcalquier indulgence for his sins "if he would personally take vengeance for the injury of the Crucified One, seizing the journey as befits such a prince, and praiseworthily persisting in the defence of the eastern land."[60]

Other passages focused directly on the injuries done to Christ, God and the cross. The *Itinerarium peregrinorum* described the crusaders as "avengers of the injury of the cross."[61] Peter of Blois, in his *De Hierosolymitana peregrinatione*, called for vengeance for Christ's blood: "the blood of Naboth clamored, the blood of Abel clamored from the earth for vengeance, and found an avenger. The blood of Christ clamors for aid, and does not find any to help."[62] The comparison drawn between Christ, Abel, and Naboth suggests that Peter of Blois was not writing about the metaphysical blood of Christ, but rather the actual blood of Christ spilt at the crucifixion. The *Gesta Henrici Secundi* described attacks against southern French heretics as an act of vengeance for Christ's injuries in three separate passages, noting "behold … it was clear to the Christian princes, that they should avenge the injuries of Christ."[63] The 1187 lament of Berter of Orleans, calling for vengeance for oppressed Christianity, was cited in the *Gesta Henrici Secundi* and the (other) chronicle of Roger of Howden:

> Against which the prophet wrote,
> that from Zion the Law would march away,
> did the Law perish there?
>> Shall it not have an avenger?
>> Where Christ drank
>> The chalice of the Passion.

---

[57] *Gesta regis Henrici Secundi*, ed. William Stubbs, RS 49 (London, 1867), p. 39; see also Roger of Howden, *Chronica*, ed. William Stubbs, RS 51 (London, 1868), p. 343.

[58] *Itinerarium peregrinorum et gesta regis Ricardi*, ed. William Stubbs, RS 38 (London, 1864), p. 32.

[59] Innocent III, *Plorans ploravit Ecclesia*, ed. Othmar Hageneder and Anton Haidacher, *Die Register Innocenz' III* 1 (Graz, 1964), p. 431.

[60] Innocent III, *Si ad actus*, ed. Othmar Hageneder and Anton Haidacher, *Die Register Innocenz' III* 1 (Graz, 1964), p. 611.

[61] *Itinerarium peregrinorum*, p. 59.

[62] Peter of Blois, *De Hierosolymitana peregrinatione*, PL 207, col. 1063.

[63] *Gesta regis Henrici Secundi*, p. 220; see also pp. 199 and 228.

The hater of the cross oppresses the cross
from which oppressed faith mourns,
who does not rage in vengeance?
    As much as he values his faith,
    he will save the cross,
    he whom the cross redeemed.[64]

According to Roger of Howden, in October 1191 Richard I of England wrote to
Garnier of Rochefort, abbot of Clairvaux, that "the friends of the cross of Christ ...
flew forward to avenge the injuries of the Holy Cross."[65] Similarly, he reported that
in 1191 Pope Celestine III wrote that Richard "armed himself to avenge the injury of
the Redeemer."[66] In 1201, again according to Roger of Howden, the Master of the
Hospital in Jerusalem wrote "if we were to have the good aid of the Christians, with
the favourable grace of heaven, we would think to rightly avenge the injuries of
Christ and the Christians."[67] Richard of Devizes ironically noted of Richard I that
"the devotion of that man was such, so suddenly, so swiftly and so hastily he ran, nay
flew, to avenge the injuries of Christ."[68] The *Itinerarium peregrinorum* noted that
Richard count of Poitou took the cross "in order to avenge the injury of the cross."[69]
Gerald of Wales noted that Peter, bishop of St. David's, also took the cross to avenge
an unspecified injury done to God: "I will go to avenge the injury of the highest
father."[70] Celestine III wrote to the archbishop of Canterbury in 1195, "[the people
of God] girded on themselves the material sword to attack the persecutors of the
faith, so that they might avenge the injury of the cross with swift vengeance."[71] In
his letter *Quanta sit circa*, Innocent III expanded on Matthew 16.24, writing "he
who wishes to come after me, let him deny himself, and take up his cross, and follow
me, having taken on the sign of the cross to avenge the injury of Jesus Christ."[72] In
the 1198 letter *Post miserabile*, he wrote "the apostolic seat cries out, as though a
trumpet lifting up its voice, desiring to excite the Christian people to the warlike
battle of Christ and to avenge the injury of the Crucified One" and "but now our
princes ... while one seeks to avenge his own injuries on another, there are none so
moved by the injury of the Crucified One."[73] In *Justus et misericors*, written in 1201,
he noted that "we rejoice in the Lord, because He, Who gave cause for penitence,

---

[64] Ibid., p. 27; see also Roger of Howden, *Chronica*, pp. 330–31.

[65] Roger of Howden, *Chronica*, p. 130.

[66] Ibid., p. 151.

[67] Ibid., p. 187.

[68] Richard of Devizes, *Cronicon de tempore regis Richardi Primi*, ed. and trans. John T. Appleby
(London, 1963), p. 4.

[69] *Itinerarium peregrinorum*, p. 32.

[70] Gerald of Wales, *Itinerarium Kambriæ*, ed. James F. Dimock, RS 21.6 (London, 1868), pp. 14–15.

[71] Celestine III, *Misericors et miserator*, PL 206, col. 1108.

[72] Innocent III, *Quanta sit circa*, ed. Othmar Hageneder and Anton Haidacher, *Die Register
Innocenz' III* 1 (Graz, 1964), p. 22.

[73] Innocent III, *Post miserabile*, ed. Othmar Hageneder and Anton Haidacher, *Die Register Innocenz'
III* 1 (Graz, 1964), pp. 499 and 500.

has bestowed the state of penitence within many, and mercifully has inspired them, that, taking up the sign of the cross, they wish to avenge the injury of Jesus Christ."[74] In 1203 Innocent further wrote "we beget this letter with tears ... advocating the word of the Lord, and exhorting Christian friends by name to avenge the injury of Jesus Christ."[75]

Other passages gave less specific reasons for vengeance. Rigord attributed the following speech to Philip Augustus of France after he took the cross in 1190: "we however, with the counsel of God, will take vengeance."[76] Gervase of Canterbury recorded that, in a 1177 letter to the Cistercian chapter, the count of Toulouse wrote: "I ... will gird on my sword, and I confess that I am constituted in this thing the avenger of the anger of God and the minister of God."[77] Roger of Howden recorded another song sung on the journey to Jerusalem in 1190:

> Therefore the God of the Hebrews lifted up
> the Christian princes, and their strength,
> to avenge the blood of the saints,
> to aid the sons of those dead.[78]

As well as the papal letters, vernacular literature from the late twelfth century also highlighted both specific injuries, such as the Islamic occupation, and more general injuries done to Christ and the cross.[79] The Islamic occupation of the Holy Land was a crucial factor for vengeance. After the fall of Jerusalem, the *Chanson de Jérusalem* noted that:

> They had fought a great tourney to avenge God,
> they had taken and conquered a very rich land[80]

---

[74] Innocent III, *Justus ad misericors*, RS 51.4, ed. William Stubbs (London, 1871), p. 165; also in *Die Register Innocenz' III* 4.

[75] Innocent III, *Cum in manu*, ed. Othmar Hageneder and Anton Haidacher, *Die Register Innocenz' III* 6 (Graz, 1997), pp. 163–64.

[76] Rigord, *Gesta Philippi Augusti*, ed. Henri-François Delaborde, in *Oeuvres de Rigord et de Guillaume le Breton* 1 (Paris, 1882), p. 102.

[77] Gervase of Canterbury, *Chronica*, ed. William Stubbs, RS 73.1 (London, 1879), p. 270; internal reference to Romans 13:4.

[78] Roger of Howden, *Chronica*, pp. 37–38.

[79] Like the "encyclical of Sergius IV," the Old French epics known collectively as the *Crusade Cycle* have been debated for many years, as scholars have tried to pinpoint dates of origin for various poems and parts of poems. To date, Robert Cook has offered the most logical and straightforward approach to the first three poems of the *Crusade Cycle*. (Robert F.Cook, *"Chanson d'Antioche," chanson de geste: le cycle de la croisade est-il epique?* (Amsterdam, 1980)). Following Cook, I argue that speculation on earlier origins of the poems is simply that: speculation. The earliest extant texts of these works date from the very late twelfth and early thirteenth centuries, and as such those texts are creatures of that era, despite the correct assumption that related oral compositions surely predated the written epics. For a different viewpoint, arguing against Cook, see Susan B. Edgington, "The First Crusade: Reviewing the Evidence," in *The First Crusade: Origins and Impact*, ed. Jonathan Phillips (Manchester, 1997), pp. 55–77.

[80] *La Chanson de Jérusalem*, ed. Nigel R. Thorp, The Old French Crusade Cycle 6 (Tuscaloosa, 1992), p. 146.

and in the text Bishop Arnulf commented:

> We came into Syria to take vengeance
> on those who held and governed it vilely.[81]

Also in the *Chanson d'Antioche*, the crusaders were depicted as those who went "to avenge the condition [of the Holy Sepulchre]," to "take vengeance on the lineage of the Antichrist," and to "avenge God on his enemies."[82]

More often, the first poems of the Old French Crusade Cycle called for vengeance for injuries done to God, specifically the crucifixion itself. The *Chanson de Jérusalem* described the First Crusaders as "those who had come to avenge God," "to avenge the Lord," "who crossed the sea to avenge ... Lord Jesus," and those who asked God to "allow us to take vengeance on all [his] enemies."[83] Even more specifically, *Jérusalem* claimed that the crusaders "had passed over the sea to avenge his [Christ's] body."[84] The *Chanson d'Antioche* described the crusaders as

> The noble barons who love God and hold him dear,
> [who] went overseas to avenge his body.[85]

The same poem also directly linked the crucifixion, the prophecy of the destruction of Jerusalem, the subsequent defeat of the Jewish rebels by Titus and Vespasian in 70 C.E., and the First Crusade, just as the "encyclical of Sergius IV" had previously done. In laisse 8, the *Chanson d'Antioche* narrated the dialogue between Jesus and the two robbers during the crucifixion. In the poem, the robber on the right said to Jesus:

> Now it would be well if it happened that you are avenged
> on these slavish Jews by whom you have been wounded.[86]

Whereupon Jesus prophesied vengeance and the destruction of Jerusalem:

> Friend ... the people are not yet born
> who will come to avenge me with sharp lances,
> and will come to kill the faithless pagans
> who have always refused my commandments.[87]

---

[81]  Ibid., p. 149.

[82]  *La Chanson d'Antioche*, ed. Suzanne Duparc-Quioc, Documents relatifs à l'histoire des croisades 11 (Paris, 1977), pp. 22, 23 and 36; *La Chanson d'Antioche*, ed. Jan A. Nelson, The Old French Crusade Cycle 4 (Tuscaloosa, 2003), pp. 50, 51 and 58–59.

[83]  *La Chanson de Jérusalem*, pp. 39, 58, 65 and 125.

[84]  Ibid., p. 90.

[85]  *La Chanson d'Antioche*, ed. Duparc-Quioc, p. 20; *La Chanson d'Antioche*, ed. Nelson, p. 49.

[86]  *La Chanson d'Antioche*, ed. Duparc-Quioc, p. 26; *La Chanson d'Antioche*, ed. Nelson, p. 53.

[87]  *La Chanson d'Antioche*, ed. Duparc-Quioc, p. 26; *La Chanson d'Antioche*, ed. Nelson, p. 53.

Finally, the robber on the left mocked the credulous robber on the right, who retorted:

> Over the sea a new people will come
> to take vengeance for the death of their father ...
> the Franks will have all the land through deliverance.[88]

The narrator then described the destruction of Jerusalem by Titus and Vespasian, which was labelled vengeance.[89] These passages from the *Chanson d'Antioche* drew a parallel between the Jews, responsible (in the poem) for the crucifixion of Christ, and the Muslims; both groups were subject to the vengeance of the Christians for the injuries they had purportedly done to God.

The *Chanson d'Antioche* continued to assert that the First Crusade itself was vengeance for the crucifixion. The crusaders were "they who came to avenge God on the servile slaves who wounded him and his holy name"[90] and "to avenge the wound that God suffered on the cross to save his kingdom."[91] When the crusaders despaired inside the besieged Antioch, Adhémar, bishop of Le Puy, reminded them:

> You have all well heard the commandments from God,
> and we have the [holy] lance, that we know truly,
> by which he [Christ] suffered for us death and torment,
> when the criminal Jews cruelly killed him.
> We are all his sons, and we will take vengeance.[92]

In the poem Christ himself validated this categorization of the crusade as vengeance for the crucifixion, speaking to Anselm of Ribemont in a vision. Anselm later passed the message on to Godfrey of Bouillon:

> The time has come that God named ...
> and his sons will avenge him for his redeeming death.[93]

Although writers in the late twelfth century did still sometimes explicitly call for vengeance for the Islamic occupation of the Holy Land and Christian deaths, much more frequently vengeance was owed for "the injuries of Christ" or "the injury of the cross," phrases that could have been, and most likely were, interpreted in a variety of ways. For example, Innocent III repeatedly called for vengeance for the injuries of Christ, the "Crucified One," leaving it open to interpretation whether

---

[88] *La Chanson d'Antioche*, ed. Duparc-Quioc, p. 27; *La Chanson d'Antioche*, ed. Nelson, p. 54.

[89] *La Chanson d'Antioche*, ed. Duparc-Quioc, pp. 29 and 223; *La Chanson d'Antioche*, ed. Nelson, pp. 54–55.

[90] *La Chanson d'Antioche*, ed. Duparc-Quioc, p. 53.

[91] Ibid., p. 68.

[92] Ibid., p. 363; *La Chanson d'Antioche*, ed. Nelson, p. 289.

[93] *La Chanson d'Antioche*, ed. Duparc-Quioc, p. 481; *La Chanson d'Antioche*, ed. Nelson, p. 387 (Appendix 8).

he meant the injuries done to the metaphysical body of Christ, that is the Church and Christians, or the physical injuries done to the human body of Christ during the crucifixion. Occasionally texts, like the *Chanson d'Antioche*, narrowed down the interpretive options by making it clear that the First Crusade was vengeance for the crucifixion of Christ.

## Conclusion

Evidence for the broad idea of crusading as vengeance can be subdivided in a number of ways. Often the texts emphasized the need to avenge the Islamic occupation of the Holy Land and the deaths of Christians in the East. But sometimes, apparently with more frequency as the century wore on, vengeance was simply owed for unspecified injuries done to God, Christ, the "Crucified One," or the cross. These vaguer exhortations to take vengeance were sometimes presented side by side with more specific motivations, such as vengeance for the Islamic occupation of the Holy Land, and both the vague and the specific calls for vengeance appeared both in texts written by the highest Church authorities (namely Innocent III) and in vernacular works such as the Old French Crusade Cycle.

By the end of the twelfth century the concept of crusading as vengeance was widespread. Epic poetry, general chronicles, papal bulls, and crusading narratives all referred to the idea at length. However, it is less immediately evident why the idea of crusading as vengeance waxed and waned as it did in the twelfth century. The cultural factors that may have affected the ideology, such as developments in theology and canon law, anti-Jewish attitudes, devotion to the crucifixion, and customary vengeance practices, will need to be evaluated alongside specific historical factors such as the failure of the Second Crusade and the impact of papal personalities in order to shed light on the development of the ideology. And how did the ideology of crusading as vengeance fare in the thirteenth century? These questions will be addressed in future publications by this author and, hopefully, others.

At the moment it seems reasonable to conclude that, rather than fading away after the taking of Jerusalem in 1099, the idea of crusading as vengeance grew in significance as the twelfth century progressed; and undoubtedly it was propagated as ardently by educated members of the Church such as Bernard of Clairvaux and Innocent III as it was by the redactors of vernacular literature.

# The Military Orders as Monastic Orders

*Tom Licence*

Magdalene College, Cambridge

In spiritual affairs and temporal, the twelfth century was an age when one's interests were advanced by associating with the influential. Those who renounced the world for religion were believed to amass influence in heaven. By conferring gifts upon them the laity hoped to share that influence, and the statement that such gifts were made for the good of their souls became formulaic in their charters.[1] Sometimes donors explained their motives or why a particular monastic establishment had been chosen for preferential treatment. Having considered bonds of kinship or fealty and the obligations of practicality, these donors were free to invest in one of three broad categories of (living) religious. The first comprised saintly individuals, whose solitary contemplation fostered an intimate knowledge of matters divine and detached insights into the affairs of men. The second comprised enclosed communities, perhaps young and zealous, perhaps moderate and well-established, but either way hopeful arks of salvation sailing away from worldly sin on voyages of inner purification. The third comprised charitable communities which risked polluting that purity to effect tangible good deeds in the world. Our task is not to determine the extent to which contemporaries assessed these three alternatives and weighed their options accordingly, but to locate the Temple and Hospital within this spiritual diagram. This is necessary because some of monasticism's greatest historians have completely ignored them, even though they belong in the third category with the canons regular.[2] Although Colin Morris, Hugh Lawrence, Janet Burton and the archaeologists Patrick Greene and Roberta Gilchrist have at least acknowledged that these orders should feature in the history of Western monasticism, surrounding debates remain unresponsive to their reintegration. Too many discussions of active spirituality for example still revolve around the

---

[1] The formula "pro salute anime X" was universal. Whether "salute" should be translated as "health," "safety" or even "salvation" is less clear. It also became a legal formula to ensure that a gift was given in free alms. Joan Wardrop wrote: "the number of charters containing requests for [specific additional spiritual] benefits in itself testifies to their reality in the eyes of those who asked for them" – J. Wardrop, *Fountains Abbey and its Benefactors 1132–1300* (Kalamazoo, 1987), p. 243.

[2] Neither George G. Coulton in his four tomes on *Five Centuries of Religion* (Cambridge, 1923–50), nor David Knowles in his four relevant volumes on monasticism and the religious orders, found any room for either Temple or Hospital. *The Heads of Religious Houses* (Cambridge, 1972) also omits them entirely, although *Religious Houses of England and Wales* (London, 1940) includes them. Richard W. Southern's *Western Society and the Church in the Middle Ages* (Harmondsworth, 1970) follows this approach to monastic history, discussing monks and canons but ignoring the military orders. In light of this neglect it seems strange that Dugdale, Tanner, Fosbroke and the Victoria County Histories had all addressed the military orders.

canons regular and later the friars. Add the military orders and active spirituality is augmented enormously. How then should this affect our understanding of the trends within contemporary monastic benefaction? In short, it forces us to consider the possibility that charity, commonly associated more with the thirteenth century, was successfully competing with enclosed religion early in the twelfth.

Although some religious carefully distinguished between the different orders within the Church, there is no evidence that benefactors were particularly interested in such technicalities. Both knights and bishops described entry into canonical or military orders as ways of "leaving the world" because in spirit they were, even without the strict seperation enjoined upon monks and anchorites.[3] Donors to all orders also spoke of altruistic motives, but donations to the Temple and Hospital, as we will see, were attracted by the blend of asceticism and charity, rather than that of asceticism and withdrawal which sold the enclosed orders. Part of this appeal lay in channelling one's investments to the Holy Land where the imagined presence of their ultimate recipients, Christ and his saints, loomed large. Consequently Western preceptories were modelled on the alien cells of Benedictine priories, designed to fund foreign mother-houses.[4] Grant formulae often acknowledged this structure, proffering gifts directly upon the two orders. Where individual houses or brethren were named, gifts were placed "in their hands".[5] Donors who embellished basic charter protocol with their own commentary moreover sometimes praised the orders' deeds in the East.[6] The importance of the East in prompting initial benefactions is also confirmed by its appearance in foundation charters. Robert of Ros founded Temple Ribston (1217x24) "to sustain the Holy Land"; some Richerenches donors observed in 1141 that their preceptory had been built "to sustain the Templars," presumably overseas.[7] Even though explicit references to succouring the Holy Land are rare (Templar Sandford managed only two in nearly five hundred charters), it is fair to assume that this motive was normally implicit.[8] Indeed it can be argued that donors only specified a use for their gifts when they did

---

[3] For examples see *The Early Charters of the Augustinian Canons of Waltham Abbey, Essex 1062–1230*, ed. Rosalind Ransford (Woodbridge, 1989), p. xxvii and no. 507, and *Cart Tem*, nos. 20, 61.

[4] Roberta Gilchrist, *Contemplation and Action: The Other Monasticism* (London and New York, 1995), pp. 103–104. There is no historical substance to the old myth that Templar houses were known as preceptories and Hospitaller ones as commanderies, and the two labels remain interchangeable.

[5] For gifts entrusted to Raymond of Puy and Hugh of Payns, see *Cart Hosp*, no. 210, and *Cart Tem*, nos. 30, 59.

[6] For a few examples see *Cart Hosp*, nos. 124 and 551 and *Cart Tem*, nos. 16, 32, 46.

[7] Ed. R. V. Taylor, "Ribston and the Knights Templars," *Yorkshire Archaeological and Topographical Journal* 7 (1882), 429–52, p. 432 and *Cart Tem*, no. 230. The first Sandford grant (no. 1 in the cartulary) also mentioned succouring the Holy Land.

[8] John Walker, "Crusaders and Patrons: the influence of the Crusades on the Patronage of the Order of St Lazarus in England," in *MO, 1*, 327–32, p. 332. Concern for the East may be attributed to Templar patrons just as a belief in the worthiness of enclosure is attributed to patrons of monastic houses. The claim that their benefactions fluctuated with the preaching of the crusades, however, has yet to be substantiated.

not wish them to be channelled abroad. One gift at Templar Reims for example was split into four. Only the first quarter was to be sent to the Holy Land, the second being allocated to the poor, while the third and the fourth were to provide pittances for brothers who attended the anniversary masses of the donor and of his kinsmen respectively.[9] Where they do occur, references to the East might mirror the concerns expressed in crusade appeals or alms-raising circulars to which donors were responding. The Ribston grant (coinciding with the Fifth Crusade) and a raft of Polish charters from 1232 are likely examples of this impassioned interchange.[10]

Patrons of the military orders often claimed that love was their inspiration (the phrase *intuitu caritatis* is common in their charters) and occasionally stepped beyond charter protocol to explain this in personal terms. Constance, countess of St. Gilles praised the Hospital's "innumerable kindnesses, performed day and night in the service of humanity". William the Fat, grand admiral of Sicily, justified granting the Hospitallers two *casales* in Mazzara and a house in Palermo on the grounds that their pious activities had impressed him.[11] Templar charity was similarly infectious. Helen Nicholson, having traced twenty epics, romances and love songs of the thirteenth century in which the Templars appear, has shown that only half of those appearances are military in nature and the rest charitable.[12] Louis VII thanked the brethren for ceaselessly protecting poor and rich pilgrims alike, drawing upon the common image of Templars fighting continually in the Holy Land, which paralleled that of monks praying continually in monasteries.[13] Perhaps this was the "flame of true charity" which burned bright in the Temple according to Innocent II. Thierry, count of Flanders, meanwhile imagined the sacrifice of those "far away who would willingly die to protect him" and gratefully showered them with gifts.[14] Bishops Elbert of Châlons-sur-Marne and Joscelin of Soissons could expound Templar charity at length. The widow Lauretta erroneously interpreted warfare against God's enemies as a gospel duty and commended the Templars accordingly.[15] Passionate

---

[9] "Obituarium Templi Remensis" in *Mélanges Historiques. Choix de Documents*, vol. 7 (Paris, 1882), 303–32, p. 326. Robert of Staynburn granted half a toft specifically to the chapel of St. Andrew at Temple Ribston because he wanted the income to sustain the lamp before Mary's altar. See ed. R.V. Taylor, "The Ribston Templars," *Yorkshire Archaeological and Topographical Journal* 9 (1886), 72–98, p. 79.

[10] See ed. Winfried Irgang, *Urkunden und Regesten zur Geschichte des Templerordens im Bereich des Bistums Cammin und der Kirchenprovinz Gnesen* (Vienna, 1987), nos. 6, 7 and 8.

[11] *Cart Hosp*, 551 (1178x9): "humanitatis obsequio"; *Cart Hosp*, 2, no. 1178 (1203).

[12] Helen Nicholson, "Knights and Lovers in the Military Orders in the Romantic Literature of the Thirteenth Century" in *MO, 1*, 340–45, p. 340. Charitable activities depicted included supporting and lodging poor knights, burying the dead and providing a place of penance, retirement or refuge.

[13] *Cart Tem*, no. 561 (1149–50) and for an example of this common image see no. 231 (1141): "iugiter militantibus". The ideal of ceaseless sacrifice appeared early in the Templar rule, ed. D. Schnürer, *Die Ursprüngliche Templerregel* (Freiburg, 1903) – hereafter Schnürer, no. 2, and its reflection in the charters shows that it was employed to win patrons.

[14] *Cart Tem*, no. 16 (1128): "illis tantum remotis qui in seruicio meo cum armis obierint".

[15] Ibid., nos. 46 (1132), 59 (1133–34) and 62 (1133–34): Lauretta described the Templars as "cotidie aduersus impiissimos istos, secundum euangelium, uiriliter bellantibus".

collective responses were not unusual. The Puysubran donors, although "sinners and unworthy," were moved by "the martyrdom, injuries, tribulations and famines which befell Christ's poor in Jerusalem".[16] The fate of distant poor also troubled Queen Matilda, wife of Philip Augustus, who arranged that alms should be sent overseas after her death and put to whatever use necessary to serve them.[17] One cleric who visited the Jerusalem Hospital introduced his report with a laudatory discourse on its Christian charity.[18] Both orders were characterised as charitable and both found sponsors, male and female, clerical and lay, in popes, kings, barons, bishops and of course the humble poor themselves who responded to this. The likely explanation is that illness, injury and the dangers of pilgrimage and battle affected all. Such was the human condition, and it would have taken either a barren imagination or a hard heart not to find at least the ideological vocations of the Temple and Hospital instinctively appealing.

Blending with donors' altruism was concern for their own salvation. Megan McLaughlin, exploring the era 750–1100, argues that intercession was believed to incorporate its object into a religious community, as a dweller in its prayers and sharer in its devotions.[19] This idea, if it lingered, may have offered spiritual comfort while traditional penitential theology fell apart from the late eleventh century onwards. As monks began asserting that no amount of penance could make adequate satisfaction for sin, they forced a dilemma upon the laity whom they nevertheless continued to reprimand. The formulation of indulgence doctrine eventually provided a solution, but it took a century, and the intervening period of comparative penitential uncertainty gave rise to a host of notional calculations based upon reciprocity. Gifts to God were seen as shrewd investments since he promised to repay many times over, while the worthier the recipients, the greater their influence as advocates before the heavenly tribunal. Estimations of spiritual recompense were left to the discretion of confessors or even lay donors themselves. Henry Lacy, for example, hoped that his gifts to the Temple would not only help him to heaven but also his mother, father and all his friends, alive and dead.[20] Adalbert, count of Périgord, a donor of humbler expectations, gave the Hospital part of Malefage forest as a metaphorical "cup of cold water". The biblical reference was carefully selected. Christ had said, "If anyone favours one of my disciples with even a cup of cold water he will be rewarded" and Adalbert meant to hold him to his word.[21] Thierry, count

---

[16] *Cart Hosp*, no. 6: "nos peccatores, quamuis indigni, cogitantes de passionibus et de iniuriis et de doloribus et de peniuriis quas sustinent pauperes Xpisti in ciuitate Ierosolima ..."

[17] *Cart Hosp*, vol. 2, no. 1167 (1203).

[18] Benjamin Z. Kedar, "A Twelfth-Century Description of the Jerusalem Hospital" in *MO, 2*, 1–26.

[19] Megan McLaughlin, *Consorting with Saints: Prayer for the Dead in Early Medieval France* (Ithaca and London, 1994), pp. 102–32.

[20] *Records of the Templars in England in the Twelfth Century: The Inquest of 1185*, ed. Beatrice A. Lees (London, 1935), no. 262: "ut perhennis uita nobis omnibus donetur".

[21] *Cart Hosp*, no. 40 (1116): "concedo et irreuocabiliter dono calicem aque frigide remuneranti Deo, atque Ierosolimitano ... Hospicio," cf. Matt. 10.42 (author's paraphrase).

of Flanders, and his wife Sibyl gave because the Lord had promised to multiply such gifts back upon the giver.[22] Maurice Latroche and Henry his son responded to preaching, for Archbishop Manasses of Orleans, who confirmed their gifts to the Temple, wrote that they had been moved by the claims of holy writ. Whatever these claims, they were no doubt similar to those harnessed by all religious establishments to authenticate their promises of spiritual rewards. Donors also commonly expressed fears about sudden death, but in grants to the Temple such comments may be significant for Bernard had presented the Templars as fearless in the face of death and ready to embrace it. The Cistercians won admirers (and critics) through a staunch hope in their own salvation and it is possible that the early Templars appealed to donors who shuddered at the grave by courting the same spiritual authority.

Why though did donors find comfort in religious communities? Joan Wardrop has rightly followed Susan Wood in identifying "the sense of belonging to the house and sharing in its benefits" as the motive underlying most monastic benefaction.[23] Harder to discern are the reasons patrons sought the benefits of one house over another. Family tradition, proximity and the competing pastoral services on offer, such as prayer, votive masses or prime spots for burial, could steer potential donors, but donors would also align themselves with a house or order because they esteemed its spiritual vocation. Cistercians had their zeal and impressive asceticism, friars their poverty and urban pastoral appeal, and the Temple and Hospital alleviated burdens of human suffering. As an idea, sharing in the benefits of a religious community was universal, but when applied to any one of these it became highly subjective, beauty being in the eye of the beholder. The Temple and Hospital, however, possessed spiritual resources that other orders were unable to tap. First, both associated themselves with the merits of crusading. Around the year 1120 Raymond of Puy wrote to prelates in the West promising not only the Hospital's prayers and benefits to its benefactors but also surety of God's mercy, glory and heavenly crowns "as if they themselves were fighting in Jerusalem".[24] This was a bold offer given that fighting in Jerusalem, at least in a crusade context, constituted a fully satisfactory penance. Innocent II invested the Temple with comparable divine influence by insisting that family and friends should share in the brethren's own substantial indulgence.[25] If Henry Lacy viewed this as fully satisfactory, then

---

[22] *Cart Tem*, no. 98 (1134x47): "attendens per religiosas personas quod legitur: 'Si quid Deo datur, si subtili consideratione pensatur, non est donum sed mutuum, quia, fructu multiplicato, ad dantem reuertitur' …"

[23] Wardrop, *Fountains*, p. 235, quoting Susan Wood, *English Monasteries and Their Patrons in the Thirteenth Century* (Oxford, 1955), p. 122.

[24] *Cart Hosp*, no. 46 (1119x24): "quasi ipsi militent in Hierosolimis."

[25] *Papsturkunden für Templer und Johanniter*, ed. Rudolf Hiestand, Vorarbeiten zum Oriens Pontificius 1 (Göttingen, 1972) – hereafter Hiestand – no. 3 ("Omne Datum Optimum," 1139): "tam remissionis peccatorum … etiam familias et seruientes uestros uolumus esse participes."

his belief (although such beliefs were widespread) that a sizeable donation to the Temple might secure eternal life for himself and kindred becomes comprehensible. Although the terms of the satisfaction were unclear, penitential theology was still malleable and Raymond's alms-raising letter shows that the Hospital's campaigners were capable of promulgating such promises and probably of competing with enclosed religious, some of whom still contended that enclosure was necessary to salvation.

Second, the Hospital through its legends claimed to have been piling up good deeds since biblical times: a mountain of merits which enclosed orders, at best tracing their origins to Augustine or Benedict, struggled to provide.[26] With the emergence of those legends the Hospital began to carve out shares from that mountain for grateful benefactors. While the Hospital's earliest patrons therefore only expected to become sharers in its future activities, or to benefit "in life and death," later ones began to apprehend the extent of the spiritual wealth on offer.[27] By 1151 Alfred and Sibyl Bendaville were able to hope that Christ would make them, along with their parents, ancestors, friends, offspring (William, Roger and Gilbert) and lord, sharers "in all the worthy things done in Jerusalem from the days of the apostles until the end of time".[28] Indeed the number of applicants named for this privilege, although not unusual, may suggest that the Bendavilles believed they were drawing upon a spiritual treasury as substantial as its description implied. Other grants to the Hospital were equally explicit or simply referred to sharing in past and future deeds.[29] The extended time-scale in these charters can only be explained by the exploitation of the legends (circulating in Europe by 1143) as an incentive to benefaction. This practice is also evident in two forged thirteenth-century Hospitaller alms-raising letters. Here benefactors were offered shares in the prayers of the order's 4,000 houses and in the merits of its 4,000 brethren who fought the infidel, before being treated to an inspirational account of the Hospital's legendary good deeds.[30] Temple patrons, on the other hand, never expressed the belief that they were shareholders in an ancient institution and this is perhaps the strongest evidence that the Templars had no circulating foundation legends of their

---

[26] The treasury of merits doctrine, which assisted in the explanation of indulgences, was only formulated by c. 1230 but was evolving during the twelfth century.

[27] For example, *Cart Hosp*, no. 22 (? 1112): "in cunctis beneficiis qui in iamdicto loco fiant factis usque in diem iudicii;" and no. 54 (1121–22): "suscipiunt nos … in parte orationum et beneficiorum sanctissimi Hospitalis de Iherusalem in uita et in morte."

[28] *The Cartulary of the Knights of St John of Jerusalem in England, Secunda Camera, Essex* , ed. Michael Gervers (Oxford, 1982), no. 111: "quatinus nos et illos participes faciat Ihesus Christus Dominus noster de omnibus bonis que facta sunt in Ierusalem a diebus apostolorum uel facienda sunt usque in finem seculi."

[29] For example, *A Cartulary of Buckland Priory in the County of Somerset*, ed. Frederic W. Weaver, Somerset Record Society 25 (London, 1909), p. 166; and Gervers, *Cartulary*, no. 171 (c. 1185); "ut mereamus participari de bonis que fiunt uel fient in sancta domo hospitalis."

[30] Karl Borchardt, "Two Forged Thirteenth-Century Alms Raising Letters used by the Hospitallers in Franconia," in *MO, 1*, 52–57, p. 54. The origins of these numbers are unknown.

own. In contrast, a Cistercian house like Fountains could claim neither a share in the merits of crusading nor a spiritual treasury dating back to the apostles. It could offer the "prayers, benefits and masses of the abbey," a stake in all the good deeds ever done in the reformed order of Saint Benedict, but that was all – and the order had only been founded at the turn of the century.[31]

To encourage generosity to the Temple and Hospital, senior religious made benefaction a penitential exercise and attached prayers and benefits of their own. In the late 1120s William, archbishop of Aux, freed anyone who granted a penny each month to the Temple from forty days of penance. Innocent II in 1131 remitted one-seventh for Hospital donors, Celestine II in 1144 remitted the same for annual donors to the Temple, Hadrian IV offered an indulgence for Templar benefactors' petty sins and Lucius III remitted a sixth of their penance.[32] Heraclius, patriarch of Jerusalem, dedicated the Templars' new church near the Thames while visiting England in 1185 to plead for a new crusade. Over "the little door" was inscribed a promise of sixty days' indulgence for all who would honour the anniversary of its dedication each year with a visit.[33] Its predecessor, the Old Temple of St. Mary at Holborn, claimed a twenty-day indulgence from Theobald, archbishop of Canterbury, who also offered the prayers and benefits of his church to any annual alms-giving pilgrim. Becket renewed the promise, describing the visiting and venerating of holy places as a work of piety and charity acceptable to God. Although Archbishop Roger of York only offered a ten-day indulgence for the same exercise (1169x81), it too was accompanied by the prayers and benefits of St. Mary's, York.[34] Honorius III offered a fifteen-day indulgence in 1217 to all pilgrims who attended the anniversary of the dedication of the Paris Temple church, and Gregory IX doubled this modest indulgence in 1230.[35] Such grants were routine responses either to lay pressure or requests from the brethren themselves, but once again they reveal that, in spiritual terms, the Temple and Hospital boasted similar credentials to other religious communities in the eyes of both religious and lay.

Although some consciences were appeased by benefaction, others demanded a greater commitment. Taking the habit was one option, entering into confraternity another and serving for a set period with the Templars a third. Taking the habit of Temple or Hospital required vows of poverty, chastity and obedience, acceptance of the order's rule and customs, and a determination on the part of the postulant to relinquish worldly things for divine. All professed brethren (knights, sergeants and

---

[31] Wardrop, *Fountains*, p. 260: "particem facimus omnium bonorum que fiunt et fient in ordino nostro usque in sempiternum."

[32] *Cart Tem*, no. 6 (1126x30); *Cart Hosp*, no. 91; Hiestand, nos. 8, 27 and 176.

[33] *Records*, ed. Lees, p. lvii. Workmen destroyed the inscription in 1695.

[34] Ibid., nos. 6, 7 and 8: "inter precipua pietatis et caritatis opera unum est quod Deo acceptum esse credimus loca uidelicet sancta uisitare et uisitando uenerari."

[35] Henri de Curzon, *La Maison du Temple de Paris: Histoire et Description* (Paris, 1888), p. 67. For indulgences attached the Temple in the Corona de Aragón, see Alan Forey, *The Templars in the Corona de Aragón* (London, 1973), p. 169.

brother-chaplains) were bound by these strictures. Laymen could either volunteer to fight for a set period with the Templars or have this duty enjoined upon them as penance, as it was upon Becket's murderers. Count Fulk V of Anjou volunteered such service before becoming king of Jerusalem, and Alexander III, in 1166, provided a plenary indulgence for all who would pledge their swords to the Temple for two years.[36] The terms of confraternity are more debatable. Not only are they clouded by charters, which use *frater* and *confrater* interchangeably, but the concept lacked close ecclesiastical definition and interpretations of it varied between religious houses and developed over time.[37] Where detectable, confraternity in the Temple and Hospital normally involved the gift of one's body for burial, a promise either to join the order concerned should the confrère ever choose to enter religion or upon death, and a token benefaction. Sometimes confraternity was by subscription. In return a share was granted in prayers and benefits and possibly access to pastoral care, influential friends and mundane favours. By comparison the Cistercians were reluctant to grant special privileges to lay benefactors, successive general chapters prohibiting their burial until 1217, and Augustinian Waltham appears to have viewed confraternity as a rare privilege.[38]

Did these pious investors see one particular saving quality in "the poor knights of Christ" and "the poor brethren of the Hospital"? A clue may lie in their common appellation. Bernard praised the Templars' ascetic poverty. Innocent II saw Christ's decision in that of the Hospitallers: "when possessed of all riches he became a pauper for us".[39] Before the two orders amassed property and privileges recruits were moved by this example. Raymond Berenger III, count of Barcelona and Provence, took the Templar habit in 1130. "Merciful God," he wrote, "possessed of all riches became a pauper for me ... and I have done likewise for him."[40] Luke 14.13, which appeared in the Hospital's legends and later inspired St. Francis, also compelled potential postulants to enter the Temple. Someone at least had persuaded Nicholas of Bourbouton that unless he renounced all he possessed he could not become Christ's disciple, and Nicholas responded by joining the Templars.[41] Acalaide also wanted to shed her riches like Jesus, believing this would lead her to true contrition and salvation, while Raymond of Luzençon became "a pauper for

---

[36] *La Règle du Temple*, ed. Henri de Curzon, Société de l'Histoire de France (Paris, 1886) – hereafter Curzon – pp. 65–67; Hiestand, no. 53.

[37] For confraternity in the Temple see Elisabeth Magnou, "Oblature, classe chevaleresque et servage dans les maisons méridionales du Temple au XIIe siècle," *Annales du Midi* 73 (1961), 377–97.

[38] Wardrop, *Fountains*, pp. 240–42. Fountains broke this rule. For confraternity at Waltham, see Ransford, *Waltham*, pp. 98–103.

[39] *Cart Hosp*, no. 122 (1137): "cum omnium diues esset, pro nobis est pauper effectus."

[40] *Cart Tem*, no. 32 (1130): "Hec quippe omnie facio, ut misericors Deus qui, cum diues esset in omnibus, pro me pauper factus est, peccata et offensiones meas clementer dimittat, et me, pro ipse pauperum factum, in diuitias glorie sue intromittere dignetur."

[41] Ibid., no. 371 (1145): "Nunc autem ueritati que dicit: nisi quis renunciauit omnibus que possidet, non potest meus esse discipulus;" cf. Lk. 14.33

God".[42] To become poor in order to serve the poor was a twofold emulation of Christ, and the appearance of this ideal in benefactors' charters shows that the young Temple and Hospital won recruits with it. Enclosed orders boasted poverty as part of their ascetic withdrawal but won recruits through zealous reform or strict solitude, while the appeal of the canons regular – who fulfilled a variety of needs – lay in their affordability rather than any austerity. Only the friars would define poverty as their cause to provide an orthodox alternative to austere heretics and to emulate Christ. A hundred years earlier, the ideal of charitable poverty characterised many small religious hostelries in the West but defined the Temple and Hospital as institutions.[43] Both Templars and Hospitallers were also amenable to entry *ad succurendum*, a service Cistercians were disinclined to provide.[44] In 1144, Templars arrived at the deathbed of Geoffrey Mandeville, earl of Essex, and dressed him in their habit. Afterwards they were obliged to hang this excommunicate's body in a lead water pipe from a tree in their orchard at Old Temple until Geoffrey was procured a papal absolution in 1163.[45]

Confraternity or 'fraternity' – well attested in Templar and Hospitaller charters – could be both pastoral and practical.[46] By 1112 a Hospitaller confraternity was operating at Cervera in Catalonia, where members were expected to remain faithful to the Hospital and its brethren, bear their fellowship honourably and confer gifts upon the order. William of Ceriza signed up, as did Berenger Bernard and his wife Ermesende, expecting the Hospitallers in turn to remember them in all their masses, alms and benefits.[47] Another land grant secured Peter Bernard the last rites of a Templar confrère and the privilege of burial at Mas-Deu. Should he relinquish his possessions, he wrote, the knights would consent to feed and clothe him as one of their own.[48] Elsewhere spiritual association was procured by subscription. Every

---

[42] Ibid., no. 68 (1133): she became a *paupercula*; no. 207 (1141).

[43] Although the Temple and Hospital, unlike the friars, were not doctrinally opposed to the acquisition of property, it was needed to fund their activities overseas and does not appear to have undermined their early appeal to poverty.

[44] Cistercians believed that the saving power they attached to their habit deserved greater commitment.

[45] *The Book of the Foundation of Walden Monastery*, ed. Diana Greenaway and Leslie Watkiss (Oxford, 1999), pp. 18–19. A variant account occurs in *Chronicon Abbatiae Rameseiensis*, ed. William D. Macray, RS 83. Geoffrey confronted the Templars with a dilemma. Their own brethren were exempt from excommunication but association with excommunicated knights was forbidden (although an unfortunate mistranslation in the French rule transformed this prohibition into a command – see Curzon nos. 12 and 13). Assuming the brethren were following correct procedures, an agreement on Geoffrey's *ad succurendum* entry, which the Templars were subsequently obliged to honour, must have been made prior to his excommunication.

[46] See Forey, *Corona*, pp. 42–48 and 53–54.

[47] *Cart Hosp*, no. 21; no. 22 (Jan 1111 for? 1112): "in ipsa fraternitate, in sacrificiis et elemosiniis, et in cunctis beneficiis."

[48] *Cart Tem*, no. 299 (1143). A distinction between Templar knights (*cauallaria*) and confrères (*confratres*) is evident in this charter.

year, upon the feast day of Saint Remigius, Geoffrey of Tournai parted with two shillings for his fraternity with the Hospital.[49] At Cardington (Shropshire) in 1185 the Templars owned the parish church where the vicar Arnulf paid three marks a year for the benefice and an extra shilling for his confraternity. Within the parish ten of the Templars' tenants belonged to the same confraternity, including two widows, a priest and the priest's wife, who each annually contributed between a penny and sixpence for membership.[50] Such lists are rare, although another survives from Novillas, and they raise certain questions.[51] Did this annual subscription, apparently graduated in accordance with wealth, procure any pastoral or practical benefits more quantifiable than spiritual association? At some houses, as we have seen, rich donors expected the privileges of confraternity in return for a single impressive grant, while others were able to obtain specific favours from the brethren. Templar Novillas, for example, proved amenable to unusual requests. Gerald the priest granted it land in the mid-twelfth century on two conditions: first, that should some illness leave him hard up the brethren would pay him ten shillings; secondly, that should he wish to go on a pilgrimage they would provide him with a mount. In 1217 Peter Sanchez got them to take care of his son until the age of ten, while Temple Holborn in 1144 was ready to receive, if not to bury, the excommunicated Geoffrey.

Although intercession was primarily the vocation of enclosed orders, lay patrons could place great trust in the prayers of Templars and Hospitallers. Roger I of Sicily, agreeing that "the constant prayer of the righteous avails much," took the Hospitallers under his protection at Palermo in October 1137. "On our behalf," he wrote, they "disturb the kingdom of heaven with constant intercession, and with constant prayers never refrain from hammering upon the door of paradise that it may be opened to receive us."[52] During the last quarter of the twelfth century specific prayer requests began to proliferate in monastic cartularies. As the expectations of pious laity grew and indulgence doctrines and Purgatory took shape, vague hopes of spiritual association were supplanted by demands for prayers and liturgical activities specially tailored to the needs of donors' souls. The increasing importance attached to detailing terms and conditions within the written contract might have played a part in this. Unlike the Cistercians and Carthusians, the Temple and Hospital appeared as eager as many Benedictine houses to shoulder this growing pastoral burden. Roger Moulins' statutes of 1182 stipulated that five Hospitaller clerks should read the Psalter every night on behalf of the order's benefactors, while Templar statutes decreed that confrères, consoeurs and benefactors, alive and dead,

---

[49] *Cart Hosp*, no. 156, section 4 (1144x51).

[50] *Records*, ed. Lees, p. cvii.

[51] For the list of confrères and consoeurs at Templar Novillas and their payments see Forey, *Corona*, p. 376.

[52] *Cart Hosp*, no. 124: "Scriptum namque est 'Multum ualeat deprecatione iusti assidua'" (a modification of Jas 5.16); the Hospitallers "pro nobis orationibus assiduis interpellant regem celorum et, ut nobis ianua paradisi aperiatur, pulsare assiduis precibus non desistat."

should be included in the prayers which closed each chapter.[53] The Templars went a step further and added sixty paternosters, dedicated to brethren and benefactors, to their daily liturgical routine. Thirty assisted the dead through Purgatory, thirty sought pardon and deliverance for the living, and the Templars were instructed to make these new paternosters a priority "above all" – including attendance at the daily offices and the saying of the paternosters already prescribed as a substitute for those unable to attend. In fact, only a thoroughly debilitating malady justified their omission.[54] With such a duty required by their statutes the Templars, apart from fighting in the East, could claim real dedication to the well-being of members' and patrons' souls.

The Temple and Hospital also responded to multiplying demands for masses, the beneficial recreation of Christ's sacrifice attracting growing interest among sponsors and spectators alike. "Votive" masses were those volunteered on behalf of a particular saint during one's life, while masses for the dead could be requested either for a short period or at regular intervals (annually, biannually and so on) after death. "Chantry" masses, multiplying by the thirteenth century, required constant access to an altar and the services of a priest, and were meant to be sung in perpetuity, as long as funds lasted. Throughout his life the priest Herbert Ventelay benefited from a votive mass of the Holy Spirit which the Templars at Reims had agreed to celebrate on his behalf. After his death the mass for the dead was offered for his soul "in perpetuity". Parishioners at Shoreham in Sussex could request votive masses in the local Templar chapel and travellers could offer oblations there.[55] Private chapels like that of William fitz Nigel sometimes boasted Hospitaller chaplains for daily mass, in this case supplied by Garnier of Nablus and the Clerkenwell chapter; many Templar and Hospitaller churches and chapels served both brethren and local parishioners.[56] At Perton (Somerset) the Hospital maintained one such benefice at a thriving parish church. In the 1220s it could depend upon four marks from oblations at Easter, twenty shillings on Lady Day, two marks at Christmas, half a mark at the Purification of the blessed Virgin, four marks for burials, one mark for purifications and three marks for confessions in Lent and offerings at the cross. St. Bartholomew's, inherited by the Templars at

---

[53] Anne-Marie Legras and Jean L. Lemaitre, "La pratique liturgique des Templiers et des Hospitaliers de Saint-Jean de Jérusalem," in *L'écrit dans la société médiévale: divers aspects de sa pratique du XIe au XVe siècle*, ed. Caroline Bourlet and Annie Dufour (Paris, 1991), 77–138, p. 87, cf. *Cart Hosp*, nos. 627 and 504 where the rules of the Jerusalem Hospital (1177x81) required a priest to celebrate for the souls of the dead daily. Curzon, no. 541.

[54] Curzon, no. 286: "surtout." These two different sets of paternosters – the new ones intended for the spiritual well-being of benefactors and members, and the earlier ones prescribed as a substitute for the offices – should not be confused.

[55] "Obituarium," p. 325; ed. William H. Blaauw, "Sadelescombe and Shipley: The Preceptories of the Knights Templars in Sussex," *Sussex Archaeological Collections* 9 (1857), p. 236: "missas uotiuas."

[56] *Cart Hosp*, no. 869 (1189). In some instances the chapels were divided into two storeys – see Gilchrist, *Action and Contemplation*, p. 90.

Le Puy-en-Velay and served by a brother-chaplain, provided parishioners with burials and obits in return for donations.[57] Pastorally active among parishioners, the incumbents also cared for their own brethren. In 1187 the conscientious Clerkenwell chapter only granted the benefice of a Hospitaller chapel to the vicar Randolph after he agreed to celebrate regular Sunday masses for any Hospitallers who happened to be staying there.[58] When inventories were made of the Templars' chapels during the trial, all were stocked with at least the basic equipment required for divine office if not lavishly ornamented like the Templar church at Saint-Eulalie. Sometimes liturgical paraphernalia had been bequeathed by devoted brother-chaplains like Doard, who left Temple Reims his chalice, missal, breviary and altar cloths.[59]

Endowments for priests and chapels dedicated to perpetual masses proved popular. In an early example from c. 1186, Garnier of Nablus and chapter agreed to provide a dwelling at Fryerning for the chaplain Henry of Maldon so that he might celebrate mass for the soul of the late Margaret of Mountfichet in a private chapel assigned to that purpose.[60] Over the next generation such arrangements multiplied. In 1216 King Richard's widow Berengaria established a Hospitaller chantry for her husband's soul. Mary, widow of Peter Monzòn, endowed a lamp before her namesake's altar in the Church of the Holy Redeemer at Novillas in 1221 and specifically requested a Templar chaplain to sing mass there.[61] Three Hospitaller priests celebrated mass in their church at Corbeil every day from June 1225 for the souls of the late King Phillip, his queen and others, while at Le Puy-en-Velay Guy Malemouche made provisions for his soul. His will of March 1227 opted for a chantry at his parish church of St. Marcellus, burial with the Templars at Le Puy-en-Velay (along with an appropriate donation) and a hundred shillings each for the Franciscans and Dominicans to further their good works.[62] Templar Sandford, founded to help the Holy Land c. 1240, also housed a chantry for its founder, and Henry III paid eight pounds a year for three permanent chaplains at New Temple. The first celebrated mass for king and queen, the second for all Christian people and the third for the faithful departed. Henry and Eleanor apparently also granted their bodies for burial there, a remarkable favour – although they ended up at

---

[57] Weaver, *Buckland Priory*, no. 14; ed. Augustin Chassaing, *Cartulaire des Templiers du Puy-en-Velay* (Paris, 1882), p. vii.

[58] Weaver, *Buckland Priory*, no. 350.

[59] "Obituarium," p. 328.

[60] For Anglo-Norman chantries see David Crouch, "The Culture of Death in the Anglo-Norman World," in *Anglo-Norman Political Culture and the Twelfth-Century Renaissance*, ed. C. Warren Hollister (Woodbridge, 1997), 157–80, p. 177. See also Kathleen L. Wood-Legh, *Perpetual Chantries in Britain* (Cambridge, 1965), pp. 4–8. The arrangement described – an early chantry – must at least date before 1190 and although the words "in perpetuity" are not used, the home and garden provided for Henry speak for themselves.

[61] *Cart Hosp*, 2, no. 1451 (Le Mans, 1216); Forey, *Corona*, p. 384: "set ex nostris fratribus debet esse capellanus."

[62] *Cart Hosp*, 2, no. 1817, and see also no. 1836 (June 1225); Chassaing, *Cartulaire*, no. xxv.

Westminster.[63] To choose burial with a religious house was to express trust in its sanctity and allegiance to its cause. Helen Nicholson's assembled romance tales reveal that burial with the Temple likewise appealed to chivalrous imaginations; unsurprisingly, the Paris Temple's rotunda and nave were paved with tombs.[64] Eight marble knights still clutch their swords or pray heavenwards at New Temple, London.

In its heyday the Paris Temple church was a hive of devotional activity where several local religious confraternities, such as the Croisés, came to celebrate their obits. Preaching talent was sought from other orders so that brethren, parishioners and pilgrims alike could enjoy the sermons of friars and regular canons on grand feast days. So many visitors and worshippers thronged the rotunda that an additional choir-nave was constructed in 1217 to accommodate them.[65] In smaller communities religious life could revolve around Templar or Hospitaller chaplains. Brother Adam, who from 1241 served the Templar chapel of St. Peter at Cockham (Sussex), presided over parochial processions. One assembled at a cross outside St. Peter's on Palm Sunday, those at Easter and Pentecost circled the font with chrism and oil, while a fourth on the vigil of St. Mark circumnavigated the village corn. To ensure masses were provided, the Templar master Robert of Sandford granted Adam four acres and five shillings and four pence a year, along with two loads of wheat and two of barley.[66] The Hospitallers received the church of St. Nazaire from Archbishop Bérenger of Narbonne in 1160 on the condition that when its incumbent died they should select a new vicar from among their own brethren, "born and ordained in our province," whose cure of souls would be supervised by the archbishop.[67] Parishioners at these churches endowed lamps, offered oblations and probably commissioned some of the gilt reliquaries, ornamental crucifixes, embroidered vestments and handsome chalices recorded in the Templar inventories. Sometimes bonds formed with fellow religious. Around the year 1180 the canons of Oseney and the Sandford Templars agreed to remember each other in their prayers while the then provincial master, Richard of Hastings (d. 1185), witnessed charters at Waltham. Crispin, one of his nephews, was a canon at the abbey and Mathew, Crispin's brother, was miraculously cured of a foot infection there. Richard himself gave the canons three relics and the Templar Brother Roger, almoner to Henry II from 1177, donated a relic and witnessed several Waltham charters.[68] In the 1140s the abbot and brethren of Augustinian St. Vaas committed themselves in brotherly love to assisting the Templars "enlarge the body of our Lord Jesus Christ". Life, they

---

[63] "The Sandford Cartulary", ed. Agnes M. Leys, *Oxfordshire Record Society* 19 (1937), no. 1; Dugdale, *Monasticon Anglicanum*, 6, II, p. 818.

[64] Curzon, *La Maison du Temple*, p. 100.

[65] Ibid., pp. 67, 72 and 86. The Croisés appeared before 1225.

[66] Blaauw, "Sadelescombe," pp. 259–60.

[67] *Cart Hosp*, no. 295.

[68] Ransford, *Waltham*, pp. 165–66 and 183.

wrote, was assailed by death, memory by forgetfulness and truth by falsehood, and they chose to make their stand against these three impediments with others who had renounced the world.[69]

To trace the development of a major religious order's devotional identity in many countries over nearly two hundred years is to identify themes and emphases. This process is admittedly imperfect. When attempting to explain what military orders meant to their members and friends as religious institutions we are obliged to interpret medieval thought-patterns through the partial reflections they have left in a scattering of sources neither preserved nor assembled for this purpose. Our surest indication of a concept's importance in an order's spirituality – whether the adoption of poverty, the practice of charity or the emulation of Christ – must therefore be the frequency and diversity of its appearances. To dismiss such concepts as gestures, or to deny any distinction between Templar devotion to Christ and devotion to Christ throughout Christendom, is to deconstruct the very religious identities that won these orders recruits and benefactions and inspired their unique vocations.[70] At the same time we must acknowledge that these identities themselves were fluid. In reality Templars in East and West genuflected before a host of different saints and adopted various provincial liturgies. Some nurtured chivalrous dreams of fighting in Jerusalem, others a spiritual longing to emulate the suffering Saviour and more, perhaps, a perturbation of fleshly temptations only pacified by the comforting purity of the Virgin. Many might simply have been content to farm Templar estates and say their paternosters with little regard for inner religion. Whatever the blend, the order's heart, both structurally and spiritually, was in the Holy Land. From here sprang a profound devotion to Christ and here lay the backdrop of a balanced religious vocation, alternating between action and contemplation as battle continually raged and subsided.[71] Great sacrifices were involved, not only the risk of physical death, and death to the world through the adoption of monastic vows, but the willingness to leave loved ones behind for a distant unknown land with no guarantee of being reunited. At the time of the Temple's foundation both monasticism and crusade were flourishing but the early Templars arrested pious imaginations by radically combining the two. To this formula they added poverty and charity, as befitted both the zealous spirit of the age

---

[69] *Cart Temp*, no. 226 (1141–47): "Quoniam uita morte, memoria obliuione, ueritas impugnatur falsitate, nos contra hec tria impedimenta … cum fratribus nostris, militibus Templi … specialem societatem omnium spiritualium bonorum habemus … ut in augmentum corporis domini nostri Iesu Christi fraterno quoque auxilio magis magisque proficiamus."

[70] Tom Licence, "The Templars and the Hospitallers, Christ and the Saints", in *Crusades* 4 (2005), 39–57.

[71] Tom Licence, "The Spiritual Appeal of the Military Orders," unpublished M.Phil. thesis (Cambridge, 2003), pp. 7–10.

and the biblical crusader landscape where each day the dust, sweat and blood spoke of Christ's present humanity.

Neither bound to perform priestly duties like many regular canons nor restricted by enclosure like most monks the lay brothers of the Temple and Hospital were free to pursue innovative charitable functions, namely warfare and care of the sick. With memberships and vocations independent of the normative characteristics of monastic religion, two orders arose that were at first structurally unique and which opened exciting avenues of devotional expression. Rivalling new and old orders alike in the West, they acquired benefactors and associates from across the social spectrum who believed that Templar and Hospitaller prayers, masses and spiritual merits were efficacious in safeguarding their souls. In numerous parishes Templar and Hospitaller brother-chaplains ministered to the laity while their orders accommodated increasing demands for burial, prayer and masses, promising both quantifiable and associative benefits in return. Historians of Western monasticism have, to put it bluntly, ignored all this, which is why their otherwise scholarly surveys must be supplemented with further research on Templar and Hospitaller religion. More might be done towards reconstructing the presentation of these orders at personal, regional and institutional levels by collating the scriptures selected and sentiments articulated in benefactors' charters and comparing them with those associated with other orders. Such research would also help refute the persistent conviction – still circulating despite plentiful evidence to the contrary – that charters only contain protocol that reveals little about benefactors' motives and beliefs.

# La Vision des Ordres Religieux-Militaires par les Chrétiens Orientaux (Arméniens et Syriaques) au Moyen Age (du début du XIIe siècle au début du XIVe siècle)

*Marie-Anna Chevalier*

Université Paul Valéry – Montpellier III

La précocité de la présence des ordres militaires, particulièrement des deux premiers d'entre eux – le Temple et l'Hôpital de Saint-Jean de Jérusalem – dans la principauté d'Antioche, la principauté arménienne de Cilicie et le comté d'Edesse a favorisé les contacts entre leurs membres et les chrétiens orientaux. L'Arménie cilicienne, voisine des Etats latins d'Orient, était, dans une certaine mesure dans la sphère d'influence de ces Etats. Elle adopta certaines de leurs pratiques, mit en place une organisation féodale, se dota d'une chancellerie latine, et fit siens certains titres francs donnés aux officiers – tels que ceux de maréchal ou de connétable. La plupart de ces transformations semblent avoir été effectuées pendant le règne de Lewon Ier.[1] Les *Assises d'Antioche*, traduites en arménien par le connétable Sembat avant 1266,[2] étaient également utilisées dans le royaume. Malgré ces modifications majeures, la cour arménienne conserva son identité et ses caractères propres. L'ordre teutonique, parrainé par les empereurs germaniques, fut particulièrement bien accepté en Arménie, Lewon Ier ayant reçu une couronne royale de l'empereur par l'intermédiaire de l'archevêque Conrad de Mayence.[3] Les autres ordres militaires n'entrent pas dans le cadre de notre étude, bien que leur histoire, particulièrement celle de Saint-Lazare, soit loin d'être dénuée d'intérêt. Nous possédons un large éventail de sources chrétiennes orientales, dont les auteurs, pour quelques uns d'entre eux, ont témoigné un certain intérêt à l'égard ces congrégations. Nous disposons de chroniques et de chronographies, d'histoires, de tables chronologiques, de colophons,[4] d'ouvrages liturgiques, d'écrits sur l'Eglise

---

[1] Victor Langlois, *Le Trésor des Chartes d'Arménie ou Cartulaire de la chancellerie royale des Roupéniens* (Venise, 1863), pp. 19, 30–31, 40–52, et Claude Mutafian, *Le royaume arménien de Cilicie, XIIe–XIVe siècle* (Paris, 1993, 2001), p. 45. Lewon (1150–1219), de la dynastie des Řoubêniens, fut prince d'Arménie cilicienne de 1187 à 1198, et devint le premier roi de ce pays en janvier 1198. Il régna jusqu'à sa mort, en 1219.

[2] *Assises d'Antioche*, éd. du texte et trad. par Léonce Alichan (Venise-Saint-Lazare, 1876). Sembat (1206/8–1275) était l'un des frères du roi d'Arménie Hétʿoum Ier, il exerça la fonction de connétable du royaume.

[3] Conrad de Mayence était à la fois chancelier impérial et légat du pape. Lewon fit appel à ce personnage pour obtenir une couronne après la mort de l'empereur Henri VI.

[4] Les colophons sont des annotations que les copistes, les relieurs et les divers personnages qui ont eu les manuscrits entre les mains, ont fait dans la marge ou à la fin d'un ouvrage original. Apparus dès le Ve

arménienne, d'élégies, mais aussi de sources "latinisantes", tels que les documents diplomatiques et autres écrits émanant de la cour royale arménienne, sur le thème que nous allons aborder. Les chartes octroyées aux ordres militaires nous permettent de percevoir un autre type de regard porté sur les frères par les souverains arméniens, ce point de vue pouvant diverger de celui que certains d'entre eux ont adopté dans leurs chroniques – lorsqu'ils en ont rédigé –; cette forme de représentation retient d'autant plus notre attention qu'elle est conditionnée à des intérêts politiques et, soumise directement au regard, cette fois, des principaux intéressés. A l'exception de trois chroniqueurs syriaques – Michel le Syrien,[5] l'Anonyme syriaque[6] et Bar Hebraeus –,[7] tous les autres auteurs chrétiens orientaux auxquels nous allons nous référer sont Arméniens. Ils prennent en considération des événements qui ont trait aux ordres religieux-militaires dans les Etats latins d'Orient, fondés au lendemain de la première croisade, et dans l'Etat arménien de Cilicie, situé à la frontière septentrionale de la principauté d'Antioche. L'origine géographique de ces auteurs varie en fonction de leur confession: les Arméniens qui évoquent ces ordres sont, en majorité, issus de l'Arménie cilicienne et, les chroniqueurs syriaques, ici de confession jacobite, viennent, pour la plupart, du comté d'Edesse. Ces écrivains avaient une certaine connaissance des ordres religieux-militaires, plus ou moins précise selon les auteurs, puisque dès les années 1130, on trouve des membres de ces congrégations dans le comté d'Edesse et dans la principauté d'Antioche.[8]

---

siècle, les colophons arméniens connaissent leur apogée aux XIIIe–XVe siècles. Voir Gérard Dédéyan, "Les colophons de manuscrits arméniens comme source pour l'histoire des croisades," dans *Crusade Sources*, pp. 89–110.

[5] Michel le Syrien fut le patriarche jacobite d'Antioche de 1166 à 1199. Parmi ses œuvres figure une histoire universelle qui va jusqu'à l'année 1195 (*Chronique de Michel le Syrien, patriarche jacobite d'Antioche (1166–1199)*, éd. et trad. par Jean B. Chabot, 4 vols. (Paris, 1899–1910)).

[6] On doit plusieurs livres à l'"Anonyme syriaque", dont le *Livre des événements ecclésiastiques* et la *Chronique civile*, ce dernier ouvrage (débutant avec les événements du VIIIe siècle) fut achevé après 1237, mais ne nous est parvenu que jusqu'en 1234. Cependant, cette chronique semble avoir été l'œuvre de deux auteurs, le premier d'entre eux étant un ecclésiastique d'Edesse qui aurait séjourné au couvent de Barsaumâ. Cf. Monique Amouroux-Mourad, *Le comté d'Edesse (1098–1150)*, (Paris, 1988), pp. 3–4.

[7] Grégoire Aboû'l-Farâdj, dit Bar Hebraeus, né à Malatya, vécut ensuite dans les Etats latins et en Cilicie, puis il partit pour la Mésopotamie et l'Azerbaïdjan, où il fut élevé à la dignité de maphrien (grand métropolite (jacobite) de la partie orientale du patriarcat d'Antioche), en 1264. On lui doit une chronique ecclésiastique et une chronographie (*The chronography of Gregory Abû'l Faradj, the son of Aaron, the Hebrew physician commonly known as Bar Hebraeus, being the first part of his political history of the world*, trad. par E. A. Wallis Budge, 2 vols. (London, 1932)). Il mourut en 1286.

[8] Pour les premières donations en faveur des ordres militaires dans le comté d'Edesse, voir Amouroux-Mourad, *Comté d'Edesse*, p. 141; pour les débuts de ces ordres en Cilicie, voir Jonathan S. C. Riley-Smith, "The Templars and the Teutonic Knights in Cilician Armenia," dans *The Cilician Kingdom of Armenia*, éd. Thomas S. R. Boase (Edinbourg et Londres, 1978), pp. 92–117, et Marie-Anna Chevalier, "Quelques aspects de la présence des Templiers en Cilicie," dans *Relations historiques et culturelles franco-arméniennes*, Septième conférence scientifique internationale à Erévan les 20 et 22 septembre 2000 (Erevan, 2001), pp. 88–102.

La représentation des ordres militaires[9] par les auteurs chrétiens orientaux nous renvoie à plusieurs problèmes: comment les écrivains arméniens et syriaques désignaient-ils ces ordres? Les désignaient-ils toujours expressément? Sur quels aspects de ces institutions ont-ils mis l'accent? Quelles particularités intrinsèques à ces ordres religieux au caractère atypique ont le plus marqué les auteurs? Quelle est l'image globale qu'ils en renvoient? Leur point de vue évolue-t-il avec le temps? Est-il fluctuant selon la fonction, le milieu, et le degré d'implication du narrateur?

## Des modes de désignation variables

Les ordres militaires sont désignés de diverses manières, selon les auteurs envisagés leur origine ethnico-religieuse, et leur degré de connaissance de ces ordres.

### La non-désignation des ordres religieux-militaires

Certains écrivains arméniens ne se soucient pas de les mentionner, dans des circonstances où leur présence est, par ailleurs, avérée. C'est le cas du catholicos Grigor IV Tegha[10] qui, dans son *Élégie sur la prise de Jérusalem [par Saladin]*,[11] évoque la prise de la forteresse de Baghrâs par le sultan ayyoûbide Saladin, événement qui eut lieu en septembre 1188. Le catholicos ne prit pas soin de signaler la présence des templiers, alors détenteurs de ce château, ni, *a fortiori*, d'évoquer le sort qui leur fut réservé:

> Ils [les troupes de Saladin] allèrent camper dans une vaste plaine,
> Auprès d'un lac qui s'étend en ces lieux,
> Et investirent la place forte
> Que l'on nomme Sara (Baghrâs).[12]

Parfois, les auteurs ou les copistes des colophons, font également abstraction des ordres militaires, alors qu'ils font mention d'événements qui les touchent directement. Lorsque le roi d'Arménie, Lewon Ier, mourut, en 1219, il transmit son royaume à sa fille cadette, Zapêl (Isabelle), en laissant pour consigne au régent du royaume, Adam de Gaston, et au bailli, Kostandin de Papérôn, de lui faire épouser

---

[9] Pour ce qui concerne la représentation des ordres militaires dans la société médiévale, consulter l'ouvrage d'Helen Nicholson, *Templars, Hospitallers and Teutonic Knights. Images of the Military Orders, 1128–1291* (Leicester, 1995).

[10] Le catholicos est le chef de l'Eglise arménienne. Grigor IV Tegha (1133–89) exerça cette fonction de 1172 à 1189.

[11] *RHC Darm*, 1:272–307.

[12] *RHC Darm*, 1:303. Baghrâs, appelée également Gaston dans les sources latines et franques, était une forteresse située au sud de l'Amanus et orientée vers la plaine de Cilicie. Elle défendait le sud-est des Pyles syriennes et se trouvait à moins de 30 kilomètres au nord d'Antioche.

quelqu'un de son rang.[13] Par conséquent, en 1223, la reine se maria avec Philippe, fils du prince d'Antioche Bohémond IV. Cependant, le nouveau roi, accusé par les seigneurs arméniens d'être pro-latin et de détourner des richesses appartenant à la couronne arménienne en direction de la principauté d'Antioche, fut emprisonné et mourut en 1225.[14] Le bailli Kostandin voulut alors faire épouser à Zapêl son fils, Hét'oum. Celle-ci partit se réfugier auprès des Hospitaliers, auxquels son père, le roi Lewon, avait donné la ville de Séleucie en 1210.[15] C'est à propos de cet épisode précis que le copiste d'un missel, Hovhannês, nous dit:

> Le père Sarkis est venu chez nous et nous a apporté la mauvaise nouvelle que la reine, épouse du roi Lewon, est venue de Chypre à Séleucie, pour voir sa fille, qui était la reine [épouse] du roi Het'oum. Et ils emmenèrent la reine [Zapêl] à Séleucie, et là-bas elle a vu sa mère, et a trompé le père du roi, le baron Kostandin, et est entrée à Séleucie, elle s'est insurgée avec sa mère, et elles chassèrent le baron de la forteresse en l'insultant. Cela s'est passé ainsi et nous sommes dans la crainte et la peur: mais Dieu connaît le futur.[16]

Soit par méconnaissance du fait que la forteresse appartenait à l'ordre de l'Hôpital, soit pour ne pas jeter l'opprobre sur cet ordre prestigieux, en l'associant à l'attitude de la reine qu'il désavoue, Hovhannês ne signale ni la présence des frères de l'ordre, ni leur implication dans cette affaire.

D'autres auteurs, mentionnent, quant à eux, les ordres militaires dans leurs chroniques, mais sans le faire de façon systématique. Il advient parfois qu'ils omettent de les évoquer, alors que leur rôle ou leur présence est indéniable.

Michel le Syrien qui, par ailleurs, est très attentif aux faits concernant les ordres religieux-militaires, néglige de les mentionner à diverses reprises: par exemple, lorsque, pendant l'expédition de Manuel Comnène en Cilicie, en 1158, les principaux dirigeants latins, vinrent à la rencontre du basileus, afin de le réconcilier avec le prince arménien T'oros, les templiers étaient présents, mais le patriarche n'y fait pas allusion; il n'en parle pas non plus quand il s'intéresse, dans son récit, à l'expédition commune aux Grecs, Latins et Arméniens menée contre Alep;[17] et,

---

[13] Kirakos de Gandzak, *Histoire d'Arménie*, éd. Mélik-Ohandjanian (Erevan, 1961) (en moyen arménien), pp. 187–90; Kirakos de Gandzak, "Histoire d'Arménie," dans *Deux historiens arméniens*, trad. par Marie-Félicité Brosset, (St. Petersburg, 1870), pp. 92–93; *La Chronique attribuée au Connétable Smbat*, introduction, trad. et notes par Gérard Dédéyan (Paris, 1980), pp. 93–94. Voir aussi Mutafian, *Le royaume arménien de Cilicie*, pp. 50–52.

[14] Kirakos, éd. Mélik-Ohandjanian, pp. 187–90; Kirakos, trad. Brosset, p. 93; *Chronique du royaume de la Petite Arménie par le connétable Sempad*, *RHC Darm*, 1:647–48; Dédéyan, *Chronique Smbat*, pp. 95–96; Mutafian, *Le royaume arménien de Cilicie*, pp. 52–54.

[15] *Cart Hosp*, pp. 115–16, n° 1344. Séleucie est une ville à l'ouest de la Cilicie, sur la rive droite de l'embouchure du Kalykadnos.

[16] *Colophons de manuscrits arméniens (XIIIe s.)*, éd. A. S. Matevossyan (Erevan, 1984) (en moyen arménien), 2: 166, n° 122.

[17] "En l'an 1470, Manuel, empereur des Grecs, envahit la Cilicie. [...] Les rois de Jérusalem et d'Antioche, avec le patriarche des Francs, vinrent le trouver et se mirent d'accord avec lui. Ils le

lorsqu'il signale la venue d'un voleur à Baghrâs au début des années 1160, il ne précise pas davantage que les détenteurs de la forteresse étaient les templiers.[18]

Un autre auteur syriaque, plus tardif, Bar Hebraeus, mentionne également cette dernière anecdote, toujours sans indiquer quels sont les propriétaires de Baghrâs, ce qui est logique dans la mesure où, pour ce qui concerne les événements du XIIe siècle, il s'inspire, entre autres, du récit de Michel le Syrien;[19] ici, on retrouve, mot pour mot, le même passage. L'auteur ne fait pas non plus mention des templiers lorsqu'il est question, pour les musulmans, de vider de son contenu la forteresse de Baghrâs, après sa conquête par Saladin ou, lors de son investissement par les Arméniens.[20]

Malgré ces quelques omissions, les deux auteurs syriaques susmentionnés sont, de manière générale, relativement au fait des actions auxquelles les ordres militaires ont participé.

## La désignation générique de "Francs"

Après le stade de non-désignation des ordres religieux-militaires, le premier pas vers une désignation est leur identification aux "Francs." En effet, cette dénomination, relativement imprécise, et bien qu'elle soit révélatrice de l'origine géographique de leur recrutement, assimile les membres des ordres aux autres Francs, qu'ils soient croisés de fraîche date ou anciennement établis en Terre sainte, sans égard pour la particularité de leur institution. Le récit du départ de Zapêl pour Séleucie par l'historien Kirakos de Gandzak[21] est significatif à cet égard:

La reine ne consentit pas à être la femme de l'enfant,[22] elle se révolta et alla à Séleucie chez les Francs qui [sont] là-bas, parce que sa mère était de la nation franque de l'île de Chypre. Et Kostandin prit toute son armée et assiégea la ville jusqu'à ce qu'ils lui remettent la reine à contrecœur. Et il l'emmena et la donna en mariage à son fils.[23]

Cet extrait met en avant le fait que les Francs aient accueilli Zapêl, soulignant ainsi une forme de solidarité entre gens d'une même nation, puisque la mère de

---

réconcilièrent avec Thoros, qu'ils lui amenèrent [...]. Tous les chrétiens grecs, francs et arméniens s'allièrent pour s'emparer d'Alep, de Damas et de toute la Syrie," Michel le Syrien, 3.316.

[18] "En cette année, les Francs voulurent s'emparer d'un brigand franc qui était à Bagras. Il s'enfuit et alla trouver Nour ed-Dîn," ibid., p. 318.

[19] "And in [that] year there was a certain Frank who was a robber in Baghrâs, and because the Franks wanted to seize him, he fled and went to Nûr ad-Dîn," Bar Hebraeus, p. 287.

[20] Ibid., pp. 336–37.

[21] Kirakos de Gandzak (1203–72) fut l'auteur d'une histoire de l'Arménie de 301 à 1265. Pendant quelques temps prisonnier des Mongols, il parvint à s'enfuir. Son histoire est riche de renseignements concernant les conquêtes de ce peuple.

[22] Il s'agit de Hét'oum, le fils de Kostandin.

[23] Kirakos, éd. Mélik-Ohandjanian, p. 189. On retrouve ce passage dans: Kirakos, trad. Brosset, p. 429.

Zapêl, la reine Sybille, était la fille du roi de Chypre Aimery Ier.[24] Donc, soit dans le but de montrer une certaine forme de cohésion chez les Francs, soit par méconnaissance des hospitaliers de Saint-Jean de Jérusalem, – cette dernière hypothèse étant cependant de loin la plus plausible puisque, à aucun autre moment de son récit, Kirakos ne mentionne les ordres militaires, même en tant que "Francs" –, l'auteur réduit les ordres à la nation dont ils sont issus, ne tenant aucun compte de leurs fonctions ou de leur mission.

*Les chevaliers des ordres militaires en tant que "frères"*

Un autre terme est utilisé pour désigner ces religieux combattants, assez courant celui-ci, particulièrement sous la plume des clercs syriaques, et, dans une moindre mesure, chez quelques auteurs arméniens: il s'agit de celui de "frères." Ce nom est conservé par les chrétiens orientaux – qu'ils soient Syriaques ou Arméniens – tel que le prononçaient alors les Latins, et transposé dans leurs langues respectives en transcription phonétique. Afin de mieux rendre compte de cela, Jean-Baptiste Chabot, dans son édition de la chronique de Michel le Syrien, traduit ce mot en transcrivant "Phrêr"[25] (tout en n'excluant pas le terme de "frères");[26] il désigne même une fois les templiers comme des "frères Phrêr,"[27] témoignant, par cette redondance, du fait que Michel le Syrien utilisait le nom "Phrêr" comme un nom propre et celui de "frère" comme un nom commun (employé à propos de n'importe quel type de moine), les "frères Phrêr" étaient alors des moines particuliers puisqu'ils appartenaient à la catégorie des "Phrêr," à savoir des ordres militaires. E. A. Wallis Budge, malgré sa traduction en anglais de la chronographie d'Aboû`l Faradj, conserve le mot français de "frères"[28] (ou, du moins, le met parfois entre parenthèses à côté des mots anglais "*Brothers*" ou "*Brethren*"), et même, dans un cas précis, il transcrit: "Maistir of the Frîrê,"[29] c'est-à-dire le maître des frères, se rapprochant ainsi davantage de la prononciation syriaque. Albert Abouna, quant à lui, dans sa traduction en français de la chronique de l'Anonyme syriaque, encadre le mot frères de guillemets pour souligner cette particularité.[30]

Chez les auteurs arméniens, Grigor Yérêts[31] mentionne aussi les "frères" – sans

---

[24] Cyril Toumanoff, *Les dynasties de la Caucasie chrétienne de l'Antiquité jusqu'au XIXe siècle. Tables généalogiques et chronologiques* (Rome, 1990), p. 428.

[25] Michel le Syrien, pp. 201–203, 207–208, 235, 286–87, 314.

[26] Ibid., 3.201–203, 314, 324–25.

[27] "Les Francs voulaient qu'on donnât les places fortes que les Arméniens avaient enlevées aux Grecs à ces frères *Phrêr*," ibid., p. 314.

[28] Bar Hebraeus, pp. 283, 308–309, 370, 381, 389–90.

[29] Ibid., p. 288.

[30] *Anonymi auctoris chronicon ad A.C. 1234 pertinens II*, trad. par Albert Abouna, introduction, notes et index par Jean-Maurice Fiey, *CSCO, SS* 154 (Louvain, 1974), p. 141.

[31] Grigor Yérêts fut prêtre (d'ailleurs *"yérêts"* signifie, entre autres, "prêtre," en arménien), il prolongea la chronique de Mattʿeos d'Oufha (connu en Occident sous le nom de Matthieu d'Edesse) jusqu'en 1162.

plus d'indication sur leur appartenance à tel ou tel ordre militaire – en transcription phonétique arménienne du mot français, ce qui est bien rendu et expliqué dans la traduction qu'a faite Édouard Dulaurier de sa chronique,[32] tandis que dans la traduction, beaucoup plus récente de Ara Dostourian, ce dernier traduit (ou plutôt interprète) directement par templiers[33] le mot arménien de "frerk‛" (il s'agit du mot "frer" avec la marque du pluriel en arménien). Un colophon évoque aussi: "les combattants, qui sont appelés 'frerk‛' ",[34] lors de leur mise en captivité par Saladin, après le désastre de Hattîn, en juillet 1187. Le connétable Sembat, dans la chronique qui lui est improprement attribuée,[35] désigne les membres des ordres religieux-militaires de deux manières, et fait ainsi la transition entre deux types d'auteurs, puisque, soit il les mentionne comme "frères"[36] ou "frères aux vêtements marqués de la croix"[37] (bien que, dans l'esprit de l'auteur, cette formule s'applique plutôt aux templiers),[38] soit comme templiers[39] ou comme hospitaliers[40] désignés en tant que tels (cependant, il n'évoque à aucun moment les chevaliers teutoniques).

Au sujet de cette dénomination de "frères," deux hypothèses sont envisageables: d'une part, il s'agit peut-être, de la part des chrétiens orientaux, d'une volonté de conserver le terme français, bien que celui-ci ait un sens assez large, afin de respecter et de présenter au mieux l'entité des ordres religieux-militaires; n'ayant pas d'équivalent dans leur langue, cette dénomination leur permettait de mettre en relief la singularité des membres de ces ordres par rapport à ceux d'autres congrégations. L'autre hypothèse, qui n'est pas contradictoire avec la précédente, serait que les auteurs en question ne possédaient pas une connaissance très précise des ordres religieux-militaires et, par conséquent ne désignaient pas leurs membres en fonction du nom de l'ordre auxquels ils appartenaient, mais simplement, par l'hyperonyme de "frères." Ce qui conforte cette théorie est l'amalgame commis par Michel le Syrien entre templiers et hospitaliers lors de son récit de l'"Histoire des 'Phrêr' francs," où il présente les templiers comme des fondateurs d'hôpitaux,[41]

---

[32] *Chronique de Grégoire le Prêtre* (Grigor Yérêts), *RHC Darm*, 1:171–72, 184, 188, 189, 194; *Chronique de Matthieu d'Édesse (962–1136) avec la continuation de Grégoire le Prêtre jusqu'en 1162*, trad., annotée et éd. par Édouard Dulaurier, Bibliothèque historique arménienne (Paris, 1858), pp. 337–39, 350–51, 354–57 et 361.

[33] *Armenia and the Crusades, 10th to 12th centuries, The Chronicle of Matthew of Edessa*, introduction, commentaire et trad. par Ara E. Dostourian (Lanham, NY, 1993), pp. 262–64, 270–71, 273–77.

[34] *Colophons de manuscrits arméniens (V–XIIe s.)*, éd. A.S. Matevossyan (Erevan, 1988) (en moyen arménien), 1:272–73, n° 280.

[35] Cette chronique serait plutôt l'œuvre d'un de ses frères, le chancelier Vasil († 1275), archevêque de Sis et chancelier. Sur l'auteur potentiel de la chronique, voir l'introduction de Dédéyan, *Chronique Smbat*, p. 26.

[36] Dédéyan, *Chronique Smbat*, pp. 45, 62–63.

[37] Ibid., pp. 59, 116–17.

[38] Cf. les remarques de G. Dédéyan à ce propos, ibid., p. 62, note 63.

[39] Dédéyan, *Chronique Smbat*, p. 96.

[40] *Sempad, RHC Darm*, 1:645, 648; Dédéyan, *Chronique Smbat*, p. 89.

[41] Michel le Syrien, 3.203, pour la citation, voir infra.

fonction propre à l'ordre de l'Hôpital de Saint-Jean de Jérusalem (et, plus tard, à celle de l'ordre de Sainte-Marie des Teutoniques), mais en aucun cas à celui du Temple, qui avait pourtant, comme tous les autres ordres religieux, des activités caritatives non négligeables. Malgré tout, d'autres auteurs, comme le connétable Sembat, sont au fait des événements qui touchent aux ordres militaires, et ceci, en identifiant quelquefois les templiers et les hospitaliers. On pourrait penser que ce manque de précision est caractéristique des auteurs syriaques, du fait de leur absence de contact avec les membres de ces ordres. Mais cela semble peu probable étant donné l'implantation précoce de ces derniers dans le comté d'Edesse.[42]

*Une désignation correspondant au nom de l'ordre*

Le troisième mode de dénomination des frères des ordres religieux-militaires est leur désignation par le nom de l'ordre dont ils font partie. Ce type de dénomination est adopté par des auteurs ayant une connaissance relativement poussée de ces ordres. Les personnages de la famille et de l'entourage royal, qu'il s'agisse du roi lui-même, d'officiers royaux ou de prélats, les côtoyant de façon régulière, étaient prédisposés à écrire à leur propos. En effet, les templiers, les hospitaliers et les chevaliers teutoniques étaient présents à la cour du souverain arménien. On les retrouve aussi aux côtés du roi lors des cérémonies et des grands événements religieux. Ce fut le cas par exemple, lors du couronnement de Raymond-Roubên, pendant l'Epiphanie de l'année 1212. Le grand maître de l'Hôpital de Sainte-Marie des Teutoniques, Hermann de Salza, et le seigneur de Séleucie, un hospitalier de Saint-Jean de Jérusalem, ainsi que d'autres membres de ces congrégations, étaient présents auprès de Lewon Ier.[43] Parmi les chrétiens orientaux, seuls les Arméniens désignent les ordres militaires par leur nom (à l'exception d'une mention dans la chronique de l'Anonyme syriaque)[44] et, parmi ces Arméniens eux-mêmes, ce sont les plus hauts placés qui sont les plus précis. On peut le voir à travers les différentes chartes – rédigées en latin – promulguées par la chancellerie royale arménienne:[45] par exemple, Lewon Ier fait une donation à la "maison de l'Hôpital," le 15 avril 1210; il évoque les "maître et couvent de la sainte maison de l'Hôpital" et se

---

[42] Amouroux-Mourad, *Comté d'Edesse*, p. 141. L'auteur mentionne des donations en faveur des hospitaliers, dans ce comté, dès le début des années 1130.

[43] "Wilbrandi de Oldenborg, Peregrinatio, iterum edita," dans *Peregrinatores medii aevi quatuor, Burchardus de Monte Sion, Ricoldus de Monte Crucis, Odoricus de Foro Julii et Wilbrandus de Oldenborg*, éd. Johann C. M. Laurent (Leipzig, 1864), pp. 177–78, et Wilbrand d'Oldenbourg "Itinerarium Terrae Sanctae," dans *Itinera hierosolymitana Crucesignatorum (Saec. XII–XIII)*, éd. et trad. Sabino De Sandoli, 4 vols. (Jérusalem, 1978–84), 3:222–23.

[44] "Plus de cent cinquante nobles parmi les frères des Templiers et des Hospitaliers furent pris et envoyés en prison à Damas," dans l'Anonyme syriaque, p. 148.

[45] En Arménie cilicienne, le chancelier du royaume était souvent l'archevêque de Sis. Cependant, il était assisté dans sa tâche par un chancelier latin et par des scribes. Cf. Langlois, *Trésor des Chartes d'Arménie*, p. 19. On peut se demander dans quelle mesure le chancelier latin a eu une influence sur la manière de représenter les ordres religieux-militaires dans les chartes qui leur étaient adressées.

recommande, ainsi que son petit-neveu Raymond-Ṙoubên, et leurs terres, à "frère Garin de Montaigu" et au couvent de l'ordre;[46] les autres chartes émises par ce roi en faveur de l'Hôpital, sont, en substance, aussi précises. Pour ce qui concerne les teutoniques, Lewon Ier évoque, en avril 1212, les "frères [...] de la Sainte maison de l'Hôpital des Teutoniques."[47] Le roi d'Arménie, en conflit ouvert avec les templiers pour la possession de la forteresse de Baghrâs, désigne précisément l'ordre et ses membres. Il mentionne "le maître et le couvent du Temple" dans une charte de 1199,[48] "le maître du Temple" et les "templiers," dans une autre lettre adressée au pape Innocent III, datée du 1er octobre 1201.[49] Il en est de même dans les autres actes émis par sa chancellerie. Hétʿoum Ier[50] et son épouse, la reine Zapêl, le 22 janvier 1236, font don "à la maison de l'Hôpital des Allemands par la main du saint et du religieux maître frère Hermann et du frère commandeur cher à Dieu Littoldi" de la cité d'Harouniye et de ses dépendances, cette maison étant également appelée, dans le même acte: "l'armée des frères de l'Hôpital des Allemands."[51] Raymond-Ṙoubên, héritier présomptif de la couronne d'Arménie et prince d'Antioche, fait une donation à la "maison de l'Hôpital des malades de Jérusalem," et cite avec précision les membres de cet ordre qui confirment ce privilège, ainsi que leur rang,[52] il continue à désigner l'ordre de l'Hôpital de la même manière dans ses autres actes, à quelques nuances près, telles que: "la maison de l'Hôpital des pauvres de Jérusalem;"[53] en mars 1219, il octroie aussi une charte de franchise "au maître et aux frères de l'Hôpital de Sainte-Marie des Teutoniques."[54] Le grand seigneur Kostandin de Sarvandikʿar, ayant pourtant un contentieux avec l'ordre, nomme respectueusement: "le très grand maître des hospitaliers allemands, le frère Jean,"[55] le 15 juin 1271, lors du règlement du litige, dans une charte rédigée, quant à elle, en

---

[46] *Cart Hosp*, pp. 115–16, n° 1344.

[47] Langlois, *Trésor des Chartes d'Arménie*, pp. 117–20; Ernst Strehlke, *Tabulae Ordinis Theutonici ex tabulari regii berolinensis codice potissimum*, éd. préface et ajouts de Hans E. Mayer (dans la 2ème éd.), (1ère éd., Berlin, 1869; 2ème éd., Jérusalem, 1975), pp. 37–39, n° 46, et Kurt Forstreuter, *Der deutsche Orden am Mittelmeer*, Quellen und Studien zur Geschichte des Deutschen Ordens, Bd. 2 (Bonn, 1967), p. 234 (le chapitre 8 concerne l'Arménie, pp. 59–67 et, en appendice, pp. 234–37, on trouve une édition partielle des chartes, qui corrige la publication de Strehlke).

[48] Innocent III, *Epistolae*, *PL*, 214: col. 810–12, n° 252; *Acta Innocentii PP. III (1198–1216) e registris vaticanis aliisque eruit*, éd. Teodosiï T. Haluscynskyj (Vatican City, 1944).

[49] Innocent III, *PL*, 214: col. 1003–1006, n° 43; *Acta Innocentii PP. III, id.*, p. 559, n° 7.

[50] Hétʿoum Ier (1215–70) fut le premier roi arménien de la dynastie hétʿoumienne; Lewon Ier étant mort sans descendance masculine, Hétʿoum épousa, dans les circonstances que nous avons déjà eu l'occasion d'évoquer, la fille de ce roi, Zapêl. Il régna de 1226 à 1269.

[51] Langlois, *Trésor des Chartes d'Arménie*, pp. 141–43; Strehlke, *Tabulae Ordinis Theutonici*, pp. 65–66, n° 83; et, Forstreuter, *Der Deutsche Orden*, pp. 235–36.

[52] Frère Garin de Montaigu, maréchal de la maison de l'Hôpital, frère Goubert, commandeur de la maison de l'Hôpital d'Antioche, frère Girent Dedoluc, et frère Bernard, *Cart Hosp*, pp. 70–71, n° 126.

[53] Ibid., p. 175, n° 1441.

[54] Strehlke, *Tabulae Ordinis Theutonici*, pp. 41–42, n° 51.

[55] Léonce Alichan, *Sissouan ou l'Arméno-Cilicie, description géographique et historique* (Venise-S. Lazare, 1899), p. 239, et dans *Les Gestes des Chiprois*, *RHC Darm*, 2:840, note d.

arménien. Et, le catholicos Hovhannês, dans une lettre adressée au pape Innocent III, aborde la querelle qui oppose Lewon aux "templiers."[56]

Dans sa *Table chronologique*, le roi d'Arménie Hét'oum II[57] mentionne nommément les templiers – en tant que propriétaires de Château-Pèlerin –[58] et, les chevaliers teutoniques comme "*Alaman Frerk*" (frères allemands), à propos de leur entreprise de restauration de la forteresse de Montfort.[59]

Deux personnages célèbres de la famille royale arménienne des Hét'oumiens se sont également intéressés aux frères des congrégations militaro-religieuses. Il s'agit de l'auteur de la chronique que l'on attribue au connétable Sembat, frère du roi Hét'oum Ier, qui évoque les "chevaliers du Temple,"[60] "le maître de l'Hôpital,"[61] mais qui nous dit aussi, au sujet des chefs militaires de la campagne en Egypte et de leurs troupes, lors de la cinquième croisade: "en compagnie de leurs maîtres, les maisons des Frères, le Temple et l'Hôpital, avec tous leurs moines."[62] Le second personnage, Haython l'Historien ou Hét'oum de Korykos,[63] dans sa *Flor des estoires des parties d'Orient*, signale la mobilisation, aux côtés du prince de Tyr, à l'appel de Ghâzân, des "maistres [du Temple] e de l'Hospital e leur covent."[64] Le même auteur, dans sa *Chronique*, indique les faits marquants de la vie des ordres militaires et, par conséquent, les mentionne fréquemment. Son récit est précis, puisque les noms des grands maîtres et de certains dignitaires sont cités. On trouve par exemple mention de la mort du "maître des hospitaliers frère Garin de Montaigu"

---

[56] Innocent III, *PL*, 215: col. 692–94, n° 120.

[57] Hét'oum II (1266–1307) était le fils du roi Lewon II. Il régna de façon discontinue sur l'Arménie cilicienne de 1288 à 1293, de 1295 à 1296, de 1299 à 1301, tiraillé entre sa vocation religieuse et ses responsabilités politiques. Il fut le régent du jeune roi Lewon III de 1301 à 1307.

[58] *Table chronologique*, *RHC Darm*, 1:484.

[59] Ibid., p. 485. Château-Pèlerin et Montfort étaient tous deux situés dans le royaume de Jérusalem; Château-Pèlerin était établi sur le littoral palestinien, entre les villes de Haïfa et de Césarée, et Montfort se trouvait au nord-est de la vie d'Acre.

[60] Dédéyan, *Chronique Smbat*, p. 96.

[61] Ibid., p. 89.

[62] Ibid., p. 90. Le roi de Hongrie André II et le duc d'Autriche Léopold VI dirigèrent la 5ème croisade prêchée en 1216 par le pape Honorius III. Malgré la défection du roi de Hongrie en 1217, une expédition fut lancée à l'initiative de Jean de Brienne en direction de l'Egypte. Le grand maître du Temple, Guillaume de Chartres, et celui de l'Hôpital, Garin de Montaigu, participèrent à cette campagne dont le départ eut lieu en mai 1218.

[63] Hét'oum de Korykos (1240/5–1314), appelé aussi Haython, à la fois historien, bailli et connétable, était le fils du prince Ochin, lui-même frère du roi Hét'oum Ier. Sur ce personnage, voir Claude Mutafian, "Héthoum de Korykos, historien arménien, un prince cosmopolite à l'aube du XIVe siècle," dans *Cahiers de recherches médiévales* 1 (Orleans, 1996), 174–83.

[64] Haython, *La flor des estoires des parties d'Orient*, *RHC Darm*, 2:196–99 (version française) (2:320–21, pour la version latine). Traduit par: "maîtres du Temple et de l'Hôpital avec les frères," dans "La Fleur des histoires de la terre d'Orient," trad., présenté et annoté par Christiane Deluz, dans *Croisades et pèlerinages, récits, chroniques et voyages en Terre sainte, XIIe–XVIe siècle*, éd. Danielle Regnier-Bohler (Paris, 1997), pp. 851–52. Sur les expéditions conjointes (ou en projet) aux Francs, Arméniens et Mongols au début du XIVe siècle sous le commandement de Ghâzân, le khan mongol de Perse, contre les Mamloûks, voir Alain Demurger, *Jacques de Molay* (Paris, 2002), pp. 139–57.

en 1227,[65] ou encore de celle du "maître du Temple, frère Armand de Périgord" en 1244,[66] et de bien d'autres encore. Dans un colophon, Hét'oum revient sur la prise d'Acre, événement qui eut lieu en 1291, par al-Ashraf Khalîl: cette ville "qui était la maison de la principauté du Temple et de l'Hôpital et des autres princes renommés."[67]

D'autres auteurs ayant rédigé des colophons mentionnent expressément les ordres militaires et ceci, toujours à propos de la chute d'Acre. C'est le cas de Gêworg de Lambroun: "la ville très célèbre et bien bâtie, Acre, que tenait la nation des frères, la maison du Temple, et de l'Hôpital"[68] et de Hovhannês de Yerzenk:[69] "En 740 (8 janvier 1291–7 janvier 1292), le fils d'Alfi, qui avait pour nom Malik Ashraf, sot et brutal, prit la ville d'Acre très renommée et très peuplée; celle-ci était détenue par la nation des frères, la maison du Temple et de l'Hôpital."[70]

Quelques hommes d'Eglise désignent également les ordres religieux-militaires par leur nom: Mekhit'ar de Dashir[71] nous fait part de la présence du grand maître du Temple et du commandeur de l'Hôpital, entre autres, lors de son entretien avec le légat du pape.[72] Stép'annos Orbélian,[73] l'évêque arménien de Siounik', nous dit que Acre servait "de résidence et de capitale aux trois rois francs, les templiers, les hospitaliers et les Allemands."[74] Et, le continuateur de Samouêl d'Ani signale, quant à lui, que les "frères du Temple" étaient prêts à livrer Frédéric II au sultan égyptien.[75]

Ces différents modes de désignation – du plus vague au plus précis et au plus explicite – des ordres militaires sont déjà un témoin de la représentation dont ils font l'objet de la part des chrétiens orientaux et de la façon dont ces derniers appréhendent leur mode de vie, leur rôle dans l'Orient latin, leur évolution. Toutes

---

[65] *Chronique d'Hét'oum l'Historien (XIIIe s.)*, dans *Chroniques Mineures*, 2 vols. (Erevan, 1956) (en moyen arménien), 2:64.

[66] Ibid., p. 66.

[67] Matevossyan, *Colophons (XIIIe siècle)*, pp. 718–20, n° 579.

[68] Ibid., pp. 701–703, n° 570.

[69] Né aux alentours de 1250 et mort vers 1330, Hovhannês de Yerzenk dirigea l'école fondée par le catholicos Hakob Ier, il composa plusieurs ouvrages parmi lesquels: *Recueil des commentaires sur la grammaire, Discours sur les mouvements célestes, Deux panégyriques, Commentaire de l'Evangile de Matthieu.*

[70] Matevossyan, *Colophons (XIIIe siècle)*, pp. 706–13, n° 574. La chute de la ville d'Acre, alors capitale du royaume de Jérusalem, en 1291, sous les coups du sultan mamloûk al-Ashraf Khalîl, fils d'al-Mansoûr Kalâwoûn, marqua la fin des Etats créés par les croisés au Proche-Orient. La plupart des Latins se replièrent sur l'île de Chypre.

[71] Mekhit'ar de Dashir a vécu au XIIIe siècle. Docteur en théologie (*vardapet*), il fut envoyé en mission à Acre par le catholicos Kostandin Ier.

[72] *Relation de la conférence tenue entre le docteur Mekhitar de Dashir, envoyé du catholicos Constantin Ier, et le légat du pape, à Saint-Jean d'Acre, en 1262, RHC Darm*, 1:695–96.

[73] Stép'annos Orbélian (1260?–1304), fut prêtre au couvent de Noravank. Il occupa la fonction de métropolitain de Siounie, et reçut le titre de *protofrontès* (premier suffragant du patriarche, le plus élevé en grade de tous les évêques).

[74] Stép'annos Orbélian, *Histoire de la Siounie*, trad. par Marie-Félicité Brosset, 2 vols. (St. Petersburg, 1864–66), pp. 245–46.

[75] Samuel d'Ani, "Tables chronologiques," dans *Collection d'historiens arméniens*, éd. Marie-Félicité Brosset, (St. Petersburg, 1876), 2:470–71.

les dimensions inhérentes à la mission des ordres religieux-militaires et aux fonctions induites par celle-ci sont également envisagées, au moins partiellement, dans les écrits des chrétiens orientaux.

## Une vision pluridimensionnelle des ordres militaires

### La dimension religieuse et spirituelle des frères

Les frères intéressent plus vivement les chrétiens orientaux pour leurs faits d'armes que pour leur mode de vie monacal et leur dimension spirituelle. Cependant cet aspect religieux des ordres militaires est perceptible à travers les termes utilisés pour qualifier ces ordres ou les membres qui les composent. Les documents les plus riches à cet égard sont les actes provenant de la chancellerie royale arménienne, où les souverains accolent des épithètes révélateurs de leur respect et parfois même d'une forme de vénération envers certaines de ces congrégations. Etant donné le différend qui opposa Lewon Ier aux templiers, on comprend aisément que ce sont plutôt les hospitaliers et les teutoniques qui sont l'objet d'une telle considération; Lewon Ier parle de "sainte maison de l'Hôpital,"[76] et Raymond-Řoubên, de "sacro-sainte maison."[77] De cette façon, la vie spirituelle des hospitaliers de Saint-Jean de Jérusalem est magnifiée dans ces chartes et l'ordre acquiert un caractère sacré. L'aspect religieux des teutoniques est encore plus flagrant dans la charte de donation de Lewon Ier datée d'avril 1212, dont voici un extrait:

> Je donne et concède aux frères vénérables et religieux de la Sainte maison de l'Hôpital des teutoniques se comportant en lieu et place des Maccabées pour la défense de la maison d'Israël, desquels je suis *confrater* et desquels je souhaite être associé à leurs bienfaits et à leurs prières […].[78]

Ici, Lewon va bien au-delà des simples épithètes pour témoigner de la pratique religieuse des chevaliers teutoniques, il évoque à la fois leur vie de prières et leurs activités caritatives. De plus, il établit un parallèle entre leur action militaire motivée par la foi dans le royaume d'Arménie et celle des Maccabées, famille de l'Ancien Testament, qui a combattu contre Antiochus IV Epiphane, en Judée.[79] Dans le même

---

[76]  *Cart Hosp*, pp. 115–16, n° 1344; pp. 164–65, n° 1426; pp. 165–66, n° 1427.

[77]  Ibid., pp. 70–71, n° 1262; pp. 122–23, n° 1355.

[78]  Langlois, *Trésor des Chartes d'Arménie*, pp. 117–120; Strehlke, *Tabulae Ordinis Theutonici*, pp. 37–39, n° 46; et, Forstreuter, *Der deutsche Orden*, p. 234.

[79]  *Idem*. La référence aux Maccabées était fréquente dans les chroniques franques de l'époque des croisades, et les chevaliers des ordres militaires étaient souvent comparés à ces héros de l'Ancien Testament, voir Alain Demurger, *Chevaliers du Christ. Les ordres religieux-militaires au Moyen Age, XIe–XVIe siècle* (Paris, 2002), pp. 188–89. Les Maccabées étaient également cités régulièrement dans l'historiographie arménienne médiévale.

document, et de façon plus classique, il est fait mention de la "sainte maison de l'Hôpital des teutoniques", comme précédemment pour les hospitaliers.

Comme dans la charte précédente, émise par Lewon Ier, ses successeurs, Hét'oum et Zapêl, dans une donation à l'Ordre de Sainte-Marie des Teutoniques, utilisent des procédés laudatifs du même registre:

> Parce que nous avons vu la sainte et religieuse maison de l'Hôpital des Allemands comblée et remplie de toute bonté dans tout et pour tout marquée de la croix, se battant contre les ennemis de la croix du Christ et par cela vainquant leurs ennemis dans les combats, distinguée et renforcée dans le service des malades, pourvoyant toujours par des dons aux [besoins des] pauvres. […] Comme les frères de la sainte maison des Allemands accomplissent toute la loi écrite et chrétienne et ils ont souhaité pour cette vie transitoire et ils ont mérité le royaume de Dieu immortel et éternel, comme il est écrit: "Là où je suis, là mon ministre sera;"[80] et de nouveau "Là où deux ou trois se trouvent réunis en mon nom, je suis au milieu d'eux."[81] A cause de cette sainte maison, demeure de Dieu, nous proclamons et nous voulons être des leurs dans tous leurs bienfaits.[82]

Le couple royal souligne dans ce passage les trois aspects principaux caractérisant l'ordre de Sainte-Marie des Teutoniques: la spiritualité (avec les termes de "sainte", "religieuse" et "marquée de la croix"), mais, au-delà même de cette spiritualité, c'est surtout la place et le rôle des teutoniques dans l'accomplissement des desseins divins qui sont mis en exergue dans la dernière partie de l'extrait; leur dimension et leur valeur militaires sont signalées avec un certain enthousiasme et, leur hospitalité, qui va de pair avec leur charité ("service des malades", "dons aux pauvres"), est également évoquée. Ainsi, aux yeux des rois arméniens, la spiritualité des chevaliers de l'ordre est le principe qui les guide dans toutes leurs actions. Cette dimension spirituelle transcende donc l'ordre et rayonne sur toutes ses activités (la pratique religieuse, les activités guerrières et l'attention portée aux plus démunis) en les dotant d'un caractère sacré.

Les auteurs de certaines chroniques font percevoir cet aspect des membres des ordres militaires à travers les adjectifs, les appositions ou les groupes nominaux qu'ils leur associent. Grigor Yérêts nous en offre une exemple en comparant les templiers à des "envoyés du ciel," et en les désignant comme "milice qui aime le Christ," lorsqu'ils apportèrent leur aide à Stép'anê, frère du prince arménien T'oros II.[83]

---

[80]  Jn 12.26.

[81]  Mt 18.20.

[82]  Langlois, *Trésor des Chartes d'Arménie*, pp. 141–43; Strehlke, *Tabulae Ordinis*, pp. 65–66, n° 83; et, Forstreuter, *Der deutsche Orden*, pp. 235–36.

[83]  Grigor Yérêts, pp. 171–72, Dulaurier, *Matthieu d'Édesse*, pp. 337–39, et Dostourian, *Matthew of Edessa*, pp. 262–64. L'auteur qualifie à nouveau les templiers de "milice du Christ," dans Grigor Yérêts, p. 188; voir aussi Dulaurier, *Matthieu d'Édesse*, pp. 354–57, et Dostourian, *Matthew of Edessa*, pp. 273–77.

Et lorsque l'auteur de la chronique attribuée au connétable Sembat nous parle des "Frères aux vêtements marqués de la croix,"[84] il entend non seulement décrire le manteau orné de la croix dont sont vêtus les chevaliers du Temple, mais cette façon de les désigner évoque aussi tout ce que ce symbole recouvre.

Certains auteurs présentent avec davantage de précisions le mode de vie monacal des ordres militaires. Les trois vœux de pauvreté, chasteté et obéissance sont exposés. Michel le Syrien met essentiellement l'accent sur la pauvreté individuelle des frères: "ne possédant absolument rien en propre, mais mettant en commun toutes leurs possessions."[85] Le patriarche jacobite mentionne la sentence pour celui qui n'aurait pas respecté ce vœu: "Si on reconnaît que quelqu'un a caché quelque chose à la communauté, ou si on trouve qu'il possédait en mourant quelque chose qu'il n'avait pas donné à la communauté, ils ne le jugent pas de digne de sépulture."[86]

La chasteté de ces chevaliers est également évoquée dans la chronique de Michel le Syrien: "Pour eux, ils s'imposèrent la règle de vivre monastiquement, ne prenant pas de femme,"[87] ainsi que dans un colophon du XIIIe siècle, rédigé par un copiste nommé Housik: "Près de la forteresse gardée par Dieu, Baghrâs, à la frontière de la ville d'Antioche, […] dans laquelle les pères agréables à Dieu et les combattants qui vivent dans le célibat sont installés."[88] Il s'agit des prêtres et des chevaliers de l'ordre du Temple installés à Baghrâs.

L'obéissance apparaît en filigrane dans les écrits du patriarche jacobite: "Il n'est permis à personne […] de s'absenter sans la permission du supérieur; […] ni, quand on reçoit l'ordre d'aller quelque part pour y mourir, de dire: 'Je n'irai pas'."[89]

---

[84] Dédéyan, *Chronique*, pp. 59, 116–17.

[85] Michel le Syrien, 3.202. Il dit également: "quiconque devenait frère avec eux, donnait à la communauté tout ce qu'il possédait," "Leur usage est celui-ci. Il n'est permis à personne de posséder en propre, soit maison, soit argent, soit biens quelconques," "Et cependant ils étaient tous pauvres et détachés de tout," pp. 201–203. La règle des templiers est ferme sur ce point: "nous demandons fermement que rien ne soit gardé et qu'aucun frère ne possède rien, ni victuaille, ni linge, ni laine, ni autre chose, hormis son sac," *Règle et statuts de l'Ordre du Temple*, éd. Laurent Dailliez (1ère éd., Paris, 1972; 2ème éd. augmentée par Jean-Pierre Lombard, Paris, 1996), p. 111, art. 44.

[86] Michel le Syrien, 3.202.

[87] Ibid. On peut lire dans la règle du Temple: "Que la fleur de chasteté apparaisse en tout temps entre vous," Dailliez, *Règle*, p. 114, art. 53, et "Nous croyons qu'il est une chose périlleuse à toute religion de regarder les femmes en face. Et pour cela qu'aucun d'entre vous ne présume pouvoir embrasser une femme, une veuve, une pucelle ni sa mère, ni sa sœur, ni sa tante, ni aucune autre femme. Ainsi donc, la chevalerie de Jésus-Christ doit fuir de toute manière d'embrasser les femmes par quoi les hommes ont continué maintes fois à tomber; qu'ils puissent conserver et demeurer perpétuellement devant Dieu avec pure conscience et une vie sûre," p. 118, art. 68; ou encore pp. 106–107, art. 27: "La chasteté est la sûreté du courage et la santé du corps, car si un frère ne promet pas la chasteté, il ne peut venir au repos éternel, ni voir Dieu, etc."

[88] Matevossyan, *Colophons (XIIIe siècle)*, pp. 158–59, n° 114.

[89] Michel le Syrien, 3.202. Le patriarche ajoute: "A la fin de l'année, sur celui qui accepte et promet de porter le joug, ils récitent des prières et le revêtent de leur habit." A propos du vœu d'obéissance, il est dit dans la règle du Temple: "Il est une chose convenable à tous les frères qui sont profès, […] qu'ils aient une ferme obéissance à leur maître. Car aucune chose n'est plus chère à Jésus-Christ que l'obéissance," Dailliez, *Règle*, p. 109, art. 35.

La vie quotidienne des ordres militaires fait aussi l'objet d'une attention particulière chez Michel le Syrien. Les prières[90] ont une place importante parmi les activités des frères, mais le patriarche ne s'y appesantit pas.[91] On voit, avec beaucoup plus d'éloquence, dans le colophon du copiste Housik, l'importance des offices pour les templiers (de Baghrâs): "Ils glorifient sans relâche la très sainte Trinité, qui est bénie pour l'éternité, avec des psaumes et des bénédictions, jour et nuit, avec des chants religieux et des voix douces."[92]

Michel le Syrien s'intéresse également à la façon dont les templiers s'organisent au sein de leur ordre (il évoque les modalités d'entrée dans la congrégation, la répartition des tâches entre les frères, la hiérarchie entre les membres),[93] à leurs usages en matière de nourriture [94] et d'habillement,[95] correspondant à leur mode de vie monacal.

La charité envers les pauvres est l'une des fonctions propre à tous les ordres religieux, qu'ils soient militaires ou pas, et templiers, hospitaliers et teutoniques ne font pas exception dans ce domaine. Raymond-Řoubên ne s'y trompe pas lorsqu'il parle de "maison des pauvres de l'Hôpital de Jérusalem"[96] à propos des hospitaliers; Hét'oum et Zapêl non plus lorsque, dans la charte qu'ils accordent à l'Ordre de Sainte-Marie des Teutoniques, ils nous disent que ces derniers: "pourvoient toujours par des dons aux [besoins des] pauvres."[97] Michel le Syrien est assez disert sur ce sujet, et énonce cela de façon parfois un peu générale: "Ils sont familiers et

---

[90]   Dans la Règle primitive de l'ordre, il est établi que les Templiers doivent: "toujours, avec un pur désir, entendre les matines et l'office divin en entier, selon les observances canoniales et les us des maîtres réguliers de la Sainte Cité de Jérusalem" (c'est-à-dire des chanoines du Saint-Sépulcre), la particularité de leur mission et ses incidences possibles sont prises en compte puisque, il est précisé ensuite: "Mais si, pour les besoins de la maison et pour ceux de la chrétienté d'Orient, chose qui adviendra souvent, un frère est envoyé hors de la maison et qu'il ne puisse rendre le service à Dieu, il doit dire pour matines treize *pater noster*; pour chacune des heures, sept, et pour les vêpres, neuf. Mais nous préférons qu'il dise l'office dans son ensemble," dans Dailliez, *Règle*, pp. 101–102, art. 9 et 10.

[91]   "Ils récitent des prières," Michel le Syrien, 3.202.

[92]   Matevossyan, *Colophons (XIIIe siècle)*, pp. 158–59, n° 114.

[93]   Michel le Syrien, 3.202.

[94]   "Leur nourriture est ainsi (réglée): le dimanche, le mardi et le jeudi, ils mangent de la viande, et les autres jours, des œufs, du lait et du fromage. Les prêtres seuls qui officient dans leurs églises boivent du vin chaque jour, avec le pain, ainsi que les soldats, c'est-à-dire les cavaliers pendant leurs exercices, et les piétons dans les combats," ibid., p. 202. D'après la règle du Temple, les frères peuvent manger de la viande trois fois par semaine, ce qui correspond aux dires de Michel le Syrien; les autres jours, ils se nourrissent de légumes ou de soupe, Dailliez, *Règle*, p. 104, art. 17, 19 et 20 (ce dernier article a pour objet les périodes de jeûne). Les habitudes alimentaires des membres des ordres militaires sont aussi établies en fonction de leurs activités guerrières.

[95]   "Leur vêtement est un habit blanc très simple, et en dehors de lui, ils n'en peuvent revêtir d'autre. Quand ils dorment, ils n'ont pas la permission de quitter leur habit ni de déceindre leurs reins," Michel le Syrien, 3.202. La règle établit les couleurs des robes des frères, le manteau blanc pour les chevaliers, des robes noires pour les écuyers et les sergents. Sur la tenue vestimentaire des templiers, voir Dailliez, *Règle*, pp. 106–108, art. 27, 28, 29 et 30.

[96]   *Cart Hosp*, pp. 122–23, n° 1355.

[97]   Langlois, *Trésor des Chartes d'Arménie*, pp. 141–43; Strehlke, *Tabulae Ordinis Theutonici*, pp. 65–66, n° 83; et, Forstreuter, *Der deutsche Orden*, pp. 235–36.

charitables pour tous ceux qui adorent la Croix."[98] Mais il sait aussi être plus précis sur ce thème.[99] Il évoque également une distribution de nourriture par les templiers lors d'une famine à Jérusalem, et l'esprit de sacrifice de ces chevaliers du Christ qui voulurent continuer à donner la même quantité de froment aux pauvres malgré l'amenuisement inquiétant de leurs réserves. Michel le Syrien, dans son enthousiasme, fait mention d'un miracle divin qui permit aux frères de retrouver leurs celliers à nouveaux pleins, après avoir pris leur généreuse décision.[100]

L'ordre de l'Hôpital et celui des teutoniques sont également caractérisés par les soins qu'ils prodiguent aux malades et leurs activités hospitalières,[101] ce qui n'est pas le cas de la milice du Temple. Les souverains arméniens y sont sensibles: Raymond-Roubên désigne l'ordre de l'Hôpital de Saint-Jean de Jérusalem sous le nom de: "maison de l'Hôpital des malades de Jérusalem"[102] et, pour Hétʿoum Ier et son épouse Zapêl, la maison de l'Hôpital des Allemands s'est "distinguée et renforcée dans le service des malades."[103] Michel le Syrien expose tout le processus d'accompagnement aux malades par les frères, quelle que soit l'issue pour leurs protégés: "Ils fondèrent dans tous leurs pays, et surtout à Jérusalem, des hôpitaux, de sorte que tout étranger qui tombe malade y trouve sa place; ils le servent et prennent soin de lui jusqu'à ce qu'il soit guéri, et alors ils lui donnent un viatique et le renvoient en paix, ou bien, s'il meurt, il prennent soin de sa sépulture."[104]

Michel le Syrien va au-delà d'un simple embellissement des faits dans sa perception des ordres religieux-militaires, puisque, quelquefois, il associe des phénomènes surnaturels ou encore naturels mais exceptionnels, liés aux astres, à la

---

[98] Michel le Syrien, 3.203.

[99] "Sur tout ce qui rentre des récoltes de froment, de vin, etc., ils distribuent aux pauvres un dixième; toutes les fois qu'on cuit le pain dans une de leurs maisons, on en réserve un sur dix pour les pauvres. Les jours où on dresse la table et où les frères mangent le pain, tout ce qui reste est donné aux pauvres. Deux fois par semaine, ils distribuent spécialement aux pauvres du pain et du vin," ibid., pp. 202–203. Le patriarche s'intéresse aux dons à l'égard des plus démunis dans certaines conditions spécifiques: "Quand quelqu'un meurt, ils font célébrer pour lui quarante messes; ils nourrissent les pauvres, pour lui, pendant quarante jours et quarante personnes chaque jour," ibid., p. 202. Ici, les propos de Michel le Syrien sont conformes à ce que l'on peut lire dans la règle du Temple: "Nous prions aussi et commandons par notre autorité pastorale, qu'un pauvre soit nourri de viande et de vin jusqu'au quarantième jour en souvenir du frère mort, comme s'il était encore vivant," Dailliez, *Règle*, p. 102, art. 11. Sur la charité, voir aussi les articles 21 p. 105, et 71 p. 118.

[100] "A cette époque, il y eut une grande famine à Jérusalem. Or ces *phrer* […] donnaient et distribuaient aux pauvres, selon leur coutume, sans diminution […]. Le Seigneur, […] les visita. Dès que les économes entrèrent, ils trouvèrent tous les celliers surabondamment pleins et regorgeant de froment, d'orge, de vin et de légumes," Michel le Syrien, 3.207–208.

[101] A propos des activités hospitalières des frères de l'ordre de Saint-Jean de Jérusalem, voir Susan B. Edgington, "Medical care in the Hospital of St John in Jerusalem," dans *MO, 2*, pp. 27–33; et, sur celles des teutoniques, Klaus Militzer, "The role of hospitals in the Teutonic Order," dans *MO, 2*, pp. 51–59, et Bernard Demel, "Welfare and Warfare in the Teutonic Order: a survey," dans *MO, 2*, pp. 61–73.

[102] *Cart Hosp*, pp. 70–71, n° 1262.

[103] Langlois, *Trésor des Chartes d'Arménie*, pp. 141–43; Strehlke, *Tabulae Ordinis Theutonici*, pp. 65–66, n° 83; et, Forstreuter, *Der deutsche Orden*, pp. 235–36.

[104] Michel le Syrien, 3.203.

mention de la milice du Temple. On en a déjà eu un aperçu lorsqu'il a été question de l'approvisionnement miraculeux des celliers de l'ordre dans la Ville sainte. Le patriarche signale également la mort de "quarante cavaliers 'Phrer' [...] avec quatre cents autres chrétiens, et le diacre Bar Qorya." lors d'une éclipse du soleil, reliant les deux événements.[105]

L'ultime aspect de cette dimension religieuse et spirituelle des membres des ordres militaires, perceptible dans les écrits des chrétiens orientaux, est la foi poussée à son paroxysme, jusqu'à sa dernière limite, celle du martyre. Dans la chronique du Pseudo-Sembat, on assiste au sacrifice ultime des templiers et des hospitaliers pour l'amour de Dieu. Après le désastre de Hattîn, en 1187, Saladin proposa aux membres des ordres militaires d'apostasier et de se convertir à l'islam en échange de "présents" et d'"honneurs" mais, les frères, en dépit de cette offre avantageuse, firent le choix de mourir à la suite de la poignante exhortation attribuée par l'auteur au maître du Temple.[106] Le martyre des frères est expressément mentionné par certains chroniqueurs, tel Grigor Yérêts évoquant le siège d'Ascalon par les chrétiens, en 1153: "Dans ce siège, la valeureuse nation des Franks éprouva bien des fatigues, partagées par son brave et saint roi, pendant une année entière. Un grand nombre d'entre eux et de Frères obtinrent la couronne du martyre."[107] Pour Michel le Syrien, les templiers "considèrent comme des martyrs ceux qui meurent dans les combats."[108] Il existe donc dans l'esprit des auteurs des sources chrétiennes orientales deux types de frères martyrs: ceux qui sont morts pour avoir refusé d'abjurer leur foi (chez le Pseudo-Sembat), et ceux qui ont perdu la vie pour leur cause, à savoir le combat en faveur du retour de la Terre sainte aux mains des chrétiens et, contre ceux qu'ils considéraient comme des infidèles, c'est-à-dire les musulmans (dans Grigor Yérêts et Michel le Syrien). Cette dernière caractéristique de la dimension religieuse et spirituelle des ordres militaires est celle qui nous permet de faire le lien avec la représentation du caractère martial de ces chevaliers du Christ.

---

[105] Ibid., pp. 235–36.

[106] "O frères, voici qu'ils sont venus les jours du salut de nos âmes, qui nous permettront de gagner le Paradis; je vous en conjure, demeurez unanimes et inébranlables dans l'amour du Christ; nous mêlerons aujourd'hui notre sang à son sang salvifique; ne craignons pas ceux qui tuent les corps et ne nous laissons pas abuser par les attraits d'une vie passagère," dans Dédéyan, *Chronique Smbat*, pp. 62–63. Cependant, ce discours ne semble pas avoir été prononcé par Gérard de Ridefort, seul templier à être sorti indemne de cet épisode, mais par un chevalier de l'ordre appelé Nicolas (d'après l'*Itinerarium Peregrinorum et gesta regis Ricardi*, cité par Sirarpie der Nersessian, *The Armenian Chronicle*, p. 753, note 40, et *Etudes*, p. 362, note 40, et par Gerard Dédéyan, *Chronique Smbat*, p. 62, note 64).

[107] Grigor Yérêts, p. 184, Dulaurier, *Matthieu d'Édesse*, pp. 350–51, et Dostourian, *Matthew of Edessa*, pp. 270–71.

[108] Michel le Syrien, 3.202.

*La vocation militaire des frères*

Il semble évident, pour les chrétiens orientaux, que les membres des ordres religieux-militaires ne sont pas des soldats ordinaires, les termes de "milice invincible" et de "milice du Christ" qui leur sont attribués par Grigor Yérêts[109] témoignent d'une forme de représentation de la mission divine dont ils sont investis.

La mission originelle des frères était revêtue d'un caractère militaire certain; c'est ce qui ressort d'ailleurs des écrits du patriarche jacobite:

> Au commencement du règne de Baudouin II, un homme franc [...] avait fait vœu [...] de se faire moine, après avoir aidé le roi à la guerre pendant trois ans, lui et les trente cavaliers qui l'accompagnaient [...]. Quand le roi et ses grands virent qu'ils s'étaient illustrés à la guerre, et avaient été utiles à la ville par leur service de ces trois années, ils conseillèrent à cet homme de servir dans la milice, avec ceux qui s'étaient attachés à lui, au lieu de se faire moine, pour travailler à sauver son âme seule, et de garder ces lieux contre les voleurs.[110]

En effet, le but initial de la fondation de l'ordre était la protection des pèlerins et la défense des lieux saints.[111] Ce n'est que plus tard que les templiers participèrent à des combats aux côtés des souverains latins et même arméniens.

Le regard que portent les Arméniens et les Syriaques sur la dimension guerrière des frères est perceptible à travers le récit des combats auxquels ces derniers participent, qu'il s'agisse de campagnes militaires ou de la défense de territoires ou de forteresses. Hétʿoum l'Historien, dans sa *Flor des estoires des parties d'Orient*, expose la manière dont les troupes chrétiennes, comprenant les templiers et les hospitaliers, se sont assemblées à l'appel du Khan mongol Ghâzân, en vue de combattre conjointement les Mamloûks;[112] le même auteur fait mention, dans sa chronique, de nombreuses batailles où les membres des ordres militaires se sont illustrés et où ils ont souvent trouvé la mort,[113] par exemple lors de la prise de Tripoli par le sultan Kalâwoûn en avril 1289.[114] Plusieurs copistes et historiens relatent dans les colophons la vaine défense d'Acre par les ordres militaires, en 1291.[115] Le Pseudo-Sembat, quant à lui, mentionne la participation des frères à plusieurs

---

[109] Grigor Yérêts, pp. 171–72, 188, 189; Dulaurier, *Matthieu d'Édesse*, pp. 337–39, 354–57, et dans Dostourian, *Matthew of Edessa*, pp. 262–64 (traduit par "aimés du Christ"), 273 ("forces invincibles").

[110] Michel le Syrien, 3.201.

[111] Sur la fondation de l'ordre du Temple, voir Alain Demurger, *Les Templiers. Une chevalerie chrétienne au Moyen Age* (Paris, 2005), pp. 27–31; Alain Demurger, *Vie et mort de l'ordre du Temple* (Paris, 2ème éd., 1989), pp. 15–52; Demurger, *Chevaliers du Christ*, pp. 36–40; et Malcolm Barber, *The New Knighthood. A History of the Order of the Temple* (Cambridge, 1994), pp. 1–37.

[112] Haython, *Flor*, pp. 196–99 (pp. 320–21, pour la version latine), et Haython, trad. Deluz, pp. 851–52.

[113] Haython, *Chronique*, pp. 60, 65, 66, 67, 68, 74, 75–76, 77.

[114] Ibid., p. 79.

[115] Matevossyan, *Colophons (XIIIe siècle)*, pp. 701–703, n° 570; pp. 706–13, n° 574; pp. 718–20, n° 579.

combats, en particulier, à Hattîn, comme nous avons déjà eu l'occasion de le voir.[116] Cependant, ces sources se contentent d'une simple évocation de la participation des ordres militaires sur le champ de bataille ou lors d'un siège. Elles ne s'appesantissent pas sur leurs techniques de combat, les moyens ou les stratégies mis en œuvre, mais évoquent seulement l'issue des rencontres, et présentent les frères dans la victoire comme dans la défaite, en témoignant du sort qui leur est réservé en cas de revers.

Templiers, hospitaliers et teutoniques sont représentés parfois comme des prisonniers à la suite d'une défaite. Dans un colophon arménien du XIIe siècle, le copiste écrit, à propos de Saladin: "Il captura le roi et les combattants, qui sont appelés 'frères'."[117] Toujours au sujet de la bataille de Hattîn, l'Anonyme syriaque nous dit de façon plus circonstanciée: "Plus de cent cinquante nobles parmi les frères des templiers et des hospitaliers furent pris et envoyés en prison à Damas, sauf le vieux prince Renaud auquel ils coupèrent la tête en présence de Salāh al-Dīn, avec beaucoup de chefs qui furent tués devant sa tente."[118]

La mort des frères des ordres religieux-militaires est fréquemment mentionnée dans les sources chrétiennes orientales, que ce soit lors de grandes batailles, comme à Harim, en 1163,[119] ou à Hattîn, en 1187;[120] pendant des sièges, par exemple lors de la prise d'Ascalon par les chrétiens, le 19 août 1153,[121] ou à l'occasion de combats plus circonscrits. Cette mort revêt souvent un caractère particulier, atypique, puisqu'elle s'apparente, comme on l'a vu plus haut, au martyre.

La perte de villes et de forteresses détenues par les frères est également envisagée par les chrétiens orientaux, par exemple, celles de Baghrâs en 1268, par les templiers,[122] ou encore celle du Krak des Chevaliers par les hospitaliers et celle de Montfort par les teutoniques, en 1271,[123] le cas le plus flagrant et l'un des plus récurrents dans les divers récits étant celui de la perte de la ville d'Acre.[124]

Malgré l'estime ressentie par certains chroniqueurs à l'égard des frères, la vaillance et la valeur militaire des chevaliers du Christ sont parfois remises en cause;

---

[116] Dédéyan, *Chronique Smbat*, pp. 62–63.

[117] Matevossyan, *Colophons (Ve–XIIe siècle)*, pp. 272–73, n° 280.

[118] L'Anonyme syriaque, pp. 148–49.

[119] "Nour ed-Din mit le siège contre Harim. Alors cinq princes se réunirent: le prince d'Antioche, le comte de Tripoli, Thoros de Cilicie, le grec Doucas de Tarse, et le Maître des Frères, avec environ treize mille cavaliers et piétons. Ils se rencontrèrent avec Nour ed-Dîn et les Francs furent honteusement taillés en pièces. [...] Tous les Frères furent tués. [...] Nour ed-Din s'empara de Harim et du couvent grec de Siméon," Michel le Syrien, 3.324–25. On retrouve le même passage, presque mot pour mot, dans Bar Hebraeus, p. 288.

[120] Dédéyan, *Chronique Smbat*, pp. 62–63.

[121] Grigor Yérêts, p. 184; Dulaurier, *Matthieu d'Édesse*, pp. 350–51; et, Dostourian, *Matthew of Edessa*, pp. 270–71.

[122] Mentionnée par Hétʿoum l'Historien dans Haython, *Chronique*, p. 74.

[123] Ibid., p. 75.

[124] Orbelian, pp. 245–46; Matevossyan, *Colophons (XIIIe siècle)*, pp. 701–703, n° 570; pp. 706–13, n° 574; pp. 718–20, n° 579.

c'est ce que l'on constate dans un colophon écrit par Hovhannês de Yerzenk, également au sujet de la chute d'Acre:

En 740 (8 janvier 1291–7 janvier 1292), le fils d'Alfi, qui avait pour nom Malik Ashraf,[125] sot et brutal, prit la ville d'Acre très renommée et très peuplée; celle-ci était détenue par la nation des frères, la maison du Temple et de l'Hôpital, la nation courageuse s'est montrée faible et lâche devant les impies. La ville fut assiégée et prise, et [les habitants] furent passés au fil de l'épée ou emmenés en captivité.[126]

Un autre type de perception du rôle militaire des ordres est à prendre en considération. C'est la façon dont, à travers les différentes chartes émanant de la chancellerie royale arménienne, chacun des ordres est perçu par les souverains. Par conséquent, cette représentation varie en fonction de l'état des relations entre le souverain en question et l'ordre mentionné dans la charte. A titre d'exemple, Lewon Ier se plaint de façon quasi permanente du comportement hostile des templiers envers lui, hostilité allant parfois jusqu'au conflit ouvert,[127] l'ordre du Temple soutenant les intérêts du comte de Tripoli aux dépens de ceux du petit-neveu du roi d'Arménie, Raymond-Ṙoubên. *A contrario*, Lewon se félicite de l'attitude réservée des hospitaliers dans ce même conflit.[128] Ce roi et, plus tard, Hétʿoum Ier évoquent avec reconnaissance le soutien militaire apporté par les maisons des Hôpitaux de Saint-Jean de Jérusalem et de Sainte-Marie des Teutoniques à leur royaume.[129]

La hiérarchie des ordres militaires intéresse quelques auteurs chrétiens orientaux. Michel le Syrien tente de reconstituer, d'une façon générale, la structure interne des ordres, en évoquant les fonctions des uns des autres:

Les prêtres seuls qui officient dans leurs églises boivent du vin chaque jour, avec le pain, ainsi que les soldats, c'est-à-dire les cavaliers pendant leurs exercices, et les piétons dans les combats. Les ouvriers travaillent chacun à son métier, et de même les ouvriers des champs; dans toute ville ou village où ils ont une maison, il y a un chef et un économe, et, sur leur ordre, tous ceux qui s'y trouvent travaillent chacun à son ouvrage. Le supérieur de tous est à Jérusalem: il commande à tous, et il n'est jamais permis à aucun d'eux de faire quelque chose de personnel.[130]

En effet, parmi les membres des ordres militaires, on trouvait des frères clercs, des prêtres ou des frères chapelains, qui assuraient le culte, et des frères laïcs, chevaliers et sergents, qui combattaient. Il y avait également du personnel pour

---

[125] Il s'agit du sultan mamloûk Al-Ashraf Khalîl.

[126] Matevossyan, *Colophons (XIIIe siècle)*, pp. 706–13, n° 574.

[127] Lettre de Lewon Ier au pape Innocent III, cf. Innocent III, *PL*, 215: col. 687–92, n° 119.

[128] Ibid.

[129] *Cart Hosp*, pp. 115–16, n° 1344, et pp. 118–19, n° 1349; et dans Langlois, *Trésor des Chartes d'Arménie*, pp. 117–20, 141–43; Strehlke, *Tabulae Ordinis Theutonici*, pp. 37–39, n° 46, pp. 65–66, n° 83; et, Forstreuter, *Der deutsche Orden*, pp. 234, 235–36.

[130] Michel le Syrien, 3.202.

s'occuper de l'agriculture et de l'artisanat nécessaires à la vie des congrégations. Hétʿoum l'Historien, quant à lui, possède une bonne connaissance des dirigeants des ordres puisqu'il identifie et nomme, dans sa chronique, les différents maîtres des trois plus grands ordres militaires, au gré des événements qu'ils traversent, et parfois même des dignitaires, tels que le maréchal du Temple.[131]

*Une dimension politique*

A la vocation militaire de ces ordres, s'ajoutent de façon sous-jacente des activités politiques. Elles sont perceptibles à plusieurs niveaux: d'une part la possession de forteresses – on a vu les cas de Baghrâs et de Séleucie – et de villes – par exemple Acre –, souvent situées à des positions clefs, donne aux congrégations et à leurs dirigeants un rôle décisionnel non négligeable lors de rassemblements de chefs chrétiens, qu'il s'agisse de princes latins (et/ou arméniens) implantés au Proche-Orient ou de croisés fraîchement débarqués, en vue d'offensives éventuelles contre les musulmans. De plus, les frères jouent également, aux yeux des chrétiens orientaux, et particulièrement des Arméniens, un rôle diplomatique non négligeable. Ainsi un chevalier teutonique, à l'instigation de son ordre, entreprend de défendre les intérêts de Lewon Ier auprès du pape Innocent III.[132] Par un prêt au roi d'Arménie, les frères de l'Hôpital contribuent, quant à eux, au financement du mariage de sa fille Rita avec le roi de Jérusalem, Jean de Brienne.[133] Et, les templiers, pourtant anciens adversaires de Lewon Ier, parviennent à déjouer un complot ourdi contre le roi, en dénonçant une conspiration.[134] Les Arméniens constatent, à travers leurs écrits, l'omniprésence des ordres militaires dans la vie des Etats latins d'Orient et dans celle du royaume arménien de Cilicie, sur les plans tant militaire que politique.

*La perception de la richesse des ordres religieux-militaires*

La dimension économique des ordres militaires apparaît dans les sources chrétiennes orientales à travers la représentation des biens, qu'ils soient meubles ou immeubles, des frères.

---

[131] Haython, *Chronique*, p. 60.

[132] Lettre d'Innocent III à Lewon Ier, cf. Innocent III, *PL*, 216: col. 54–56, n° 45.

[133] *Cart Hosp*, pp. 165–66, n° 1427.

[134] Raymond-Ŕoubên fut responsable de ce complot, en 1217: "Then Liôn, the king of the Armenians, the brother of Rûfîn the Armenian, because he, Rûfîn the Frank, was the son of his brother's daughter, was enraged and he came to Antioch; and he made the people of Antioch swear oaths of fealty to him. Then this stupid man seeing that he was reigning became puffed up with pride and he wished to seize Liôn, who had made him king, so that he might reign over Cilicia also. Then when the Brethren (Frères) knew of the plot they informed Liôn concerning him, and he escaped without injury," dans Bar Hebraeus, p. 370.

C'est, comme souvent, Michel le Syrien, qui nous offre une vue globale de la richesse de ces ordres. Il mentionne d'abord les premières donations qui leur ont été faites: "Le roi leur donna la Maison de Salomon pour leur habitation, et des villages pour leur subsistance. De même, le patriarche leur donna quelques-uns des villages de l'Eglise;"[135] puis, le patriarche dévoile un de leurs modes d'expansion, l'accueil de nouveaux membres: "Quiconque devenait frère avec eux, donnait à la communauté tout ce qu'il possédait: soit villages, soit villes, soit toute autre chose. Ils se multiplièrent, se développèrent et se trouvèrent à posséder des pays, non seulement dans la contrée de Palestine, mais surtout dans les contrées éloignées d'Italie et de Rome."[136] Pour finir, il s'émerveille devant l'étendue des richesses de ces congrégations: "Ils possédèrent des forteresses et bâtirent eux-mêmes des places-fortes dans tous les pays de la domination des chrétiens. Leur richesse se multiplia en or et en choses de toute sorte, en armures de toute espèce, en troupeaux de moutons, de bœufs, de cochons, de chameaux, de chevaux, au delà de celle de tous les rois."[137] Dans les faits, les ordres militaires disposaient certes de nombreux casaux, villages, villes et châteaux, avec les terrains attenants, mais c'est une extrapolation que de dire qu'ils détenaient des pays entiers, bien que le sens du mot "pays" soit alors plus proche de celui de "régions."[138]

Dans un second temps, et de façon plus concrète, dans les actes de donations des souverains arméniens, les différents types de territoires possédés par les ordres militaires sont décrits. On le voit, par exemple, dans la charte octroyée par Lewon Ier, en avril 1212, aux chevaliers teutoniques:

> Je donne et concède dorénavant et à perpétuité des tenures de terres et de casaux extrêmement bonnes et très vastes […]; en premier, le célèbre château nommé Amouda et les casaux nommés plus bas qui lui sont rattachés avec leurs appartenances et leurs confronts […].[139]

Dans cette même charte, Lewon accorde des franchises aux frères, permettant à ceux-ci d'acheter et de vendre tout ce qui est nécessaire à leur entretien.

---

[135]  Michel le Syrien, 3.201.

[136]  Ibid., pp. 201–202.

[137]  Ibid., p. 203.

[138]  Sur le patrimoine et les activités financières des ordres militaires en général, voir Alan J. Forey, *The Military Orders from the Twelfth to the early Fourteenth Centuries* (London, 1992), pp. 58–77, 98–132; Demurger, *Chevaliers du Christ*, pp. 160–66; pour ce qui concerne plus spécifiquement les Hospitaliers, voir Jonathan S. C. Riley-Smith, *The Knights of St. John in Jerusalem and Cyprus, 1050–1310* (Edinburgh, 1967), pp. 421–69, et Michel Balard, "I possedimenti degli Ospedalieri nella Terrasanta (secoli XII–XIII)," dans *Cavalieri di San Giovanni e Territorio*, éd. Josepha Costa-Restagno (Bordighera, 1999), pp. 473–505; pour les templiers, voir Barber, *New Knighthood*, pp. 229–79; Demurger, *Templiers*, pp. 273–329; et pour les teutoniques, Kristian Toomaspoeg, *Histoire des Chevaliers teutoniques* (Paris, 2001), pp. 77–95.

[139]  Langlois, *Trésor des Chartes d'Arménie*, pp. 117–20; Strehlke, *Tabulae Ordinis Theutonici*, pp. 37–39, n° 46; et, Forstreuter, *Der deutsche Orden*, p. 234.

Dans un troisième temps, ce sont les chroniques qui se font l'écho des biens des congrégations militaro-religieuses, évoquant la possession de telle ou telle forteresse par telle ou telle maison.[140]

La représentation que se font les chrétiens orientaux des ressources des ordres militaires donne une idée de la puissance territoriale et de la richesse de ces derniers. Cependant, cette vision reste assez superficielle, puisque aucun renseignement n'est apporté sur le mode d'exploitation de leurs domaines, les différentes taxes qu'ils en retirent, ou sur la participation ou, du moins, la contribution des frères à d'autres activités économiques. Malgré tout, une de leurs activités financières, le prêt, est signalée dans une charte de Lewon Ier, daté du 23 avril 1214. Le roi atteste avoir reçu 20,000 besants sarrasins du grand maître de l'Hôpital, Garin de Montaigu, pour l'aider à financer le mariage de sa fille Rita avec Jean de Brienne. Cette somme ayant été prélevée sur les aumônes de l'ordre, Lewon engage le territoire de Čker et tous les casaux qui s'y trouvent pour le recouvrement de cette dette.[141]

La perception des ordres militaires par les Arméniens et les Syriaques dans toutes les dimensions constitutives de leur entité et de leur identité, démontre un intérêt particulier des chrétiens orientaux envers ces moines à la mission si atypique. De cette mission sont induites leur force militaire, mais aussi leur mainmise sur des territoires parfois étendus et sur des forteresses d'une importance stratégique, ce qui implique à la fois le rôle politique incontournable des ordres mais aussi une richesse incontestable. Cependant, c'est la dimension spirituelle des frères, et leur combat dénué de tout intérêt personnel et de toute attente de satisfaction matérielle, livré seulement au nom du Christ, qui frappe le plus les écrivains orientaux. Malgré tout, tous les auteurs des sources dont il est ici question ne sont pas figés sur cette image, loin de là. Ils portent chacun un regard différent, et parfois même un jugement, sur ces ordres et sur leurs actes.

## D'un jugement sévère et sans concession au panégyrique

### Les reproches faits aux ordres militaires

De manière générale, les chrétiens orientaux ont une image relativement favorable des ordres militaires. Cependant, dans certains cas, ils émettent un jugement sans indulgence face à ce qu'ils estiment le plus souvent être un relâchement de leurs valeurs, qu'elles soient spirituelles ou militaires. D'autres auteurs conservent une

---

[140] Par exemple, dans Haython, *Chronique*, l'auteur signale la construction du château de Montfort par les teutoniques (p. 64), la possession de Baghrâs et de la Roche Roussel par les templiers (p. 74), ou encore celle du Krak des chevaliers par les hospitaliers (p. 75). Dans Bar Hebraeus, p. 381, l'auteur nous dit que Séleucie est aux mains des frères (hospitaliers) et, dans la *Table chronologique* du roi Hét'oum II, dans *RHC Darm*, 1:484, 485, il est fait mention des templiers à Château Pèlerin et, à nouveau des frères allemands à Montfort.

[141] *Cart Hosp*, pp. 165–66, n° 1427.

certaine distance à leur égard, évoquant les faits qui les concernent d'une façon relativement abrupte, sans s'apitoyer sur leur sort ni louer leur courage, mais sans les vilipender non plus.

Divers types de reproches sont faits aux ordres religieux-militaires: le premier et non le moindre est la dégradation de leurs institutions et l'altération de leur mission originelle; il est formulé par Nersês de Lambroun,[142] dans ses *Réflexions sur les Institutions de l'Eglise*:

> Ils trouvèrent des corporations religieuses régies par des lois différentes, corporations qui associent les institutions monastiques, en vivant dans le monde, à l'habit militaire, et qui se proposent pour but de faire une guerre implacable aux ennemis du voisinage. L'origine de cet ordre est louable, si Satan toutefois ne mêle pas finalement son ivraie avec la bonne semence, suivant une parole que les gens frondeurs peuvent nous appliquer, et nous leur rétorquer, ainsi que nous ne l'ignorons pas. Mais, dans la suite, les institutions de cet ordre ne furent plus ce qu'elles avaient été dans le principe.[143]

C'est donc la manière dont les ordres ont évolué qui est stigmatisée par l'archevêque de Tarse. Au-delà de ces propos, il faut également souligner le fait que, dans l'Eglise arménienne, il n'était pas admis que les clercs puissent combattre ou même porter des armes (sauf dans des situations où ils couraient un réel danger). La *Lettre encyclique* de Nersês Chenorhali[144] est éloquente à cet égard: "Les armes de notre stratégie ne sont pas matérielles, ainsi que le précise l'Apôtre, mais spirituelles et divines. [...] Nous vous supplions donc de renoncer dorénavant à ces habitudes non canoniques et de ne pas porter d'armes."[145]

L'Eglise arménienne et ses représentants les plus illustres avaient donc, on peut le penser, un *a priori* défavorable envers les ordres militaires puisque, se référant aux préceptes de l'Evangile, en citant Paul, dans l'Epître aux Romains (13, 12), Nersês Chenorhali conseille aux prêtres "de revêtir les armes de la lumière," et non celles des ténèbres.[146] Cela excluait toute compatibilité entre vie religieuse et métier des armes. Mais, si Nersês de Lambroun paraît accepter, dans ses propos, la

---

[142] Nersês de Lambroun (1153–98) fut supérieur du couvent de Skewr̃a, et archevêque de Tarse. Il produisit de nombreuses œuvres, parmi lesquelles l'*Explication de la Divine Liturgie* (1177), le *Discours synodal* (1178), la *Lettre adressée au roi Léon* (vers 1195) ou encore *Discours*. Sur la vie de Nersês de Lambroun, voir aussi N. Bogharian, *Les écrivains arméniens* (Jérusalem, 1971) (en arménien), pp. 253–59, et L. Zekiyan, "Nersês de Lambroun," dans *Dictionnaire de spiritualité*, 11: col. 122–34.

[143] *Réflexions sur les Institutions de l'Eglise et Explication du mystère de la messe*, RHC Darm, 1:571.

[144] Nersês Chenorhali (1102–73), fut catholicos de 1166 à 1173. Parmi ses ouvrages, nous pouvons évoquer son *Encyclique*, les *Epîtres sur la question de l'Union avec les Grecs*, *Au sujet de la conversion des Fils du soleil* et *Elégie sur la prise d'Edesse*.

[145] Nous remercions M. Mariam Vanerian pour nous avoir aimablement communiqué sa traduction de la *Lettre encyclique*, dont nous avons reproduit un extrait ici. Voir aussi Nersês Chenorhali, *Lettre encyclique* (Erevan, 1995) (en arménien ancien), pp. 118–41.

[146] Nersês Chenorhali, *Lettre encyclique*, pp. 118–41.

combinaison guerre/monachisme, ses critiques envers l'ordre du Temple semblent relativement précoces.[147]

Sur le plan militaire, les frères sont parfois jugés sans complaisance également, surtout lorsqu'ils se trouvent dans l'incapacité de défendre efficacement un territoire ou une ville qui leur a été confié: on a vu l'exemple de Hovhannês de Yerzenk, qui traite les templiers et les hospitaliers de lâches, à la suite de la prise d'Acre[148] par le sultan mamloûk al-Ashraf Khalîl.

Le manque de loyauté des templiers est également pointé du doigt par le continuateur de Samouêl d'Ani:

> Le monarque allemand vient dans l'île de Chypre, avec une armée nombreuse, et se rend en pèlerinage à Jérusalem. Les frères du Temple écrivent à Kamel, sultan d'Egypte, qu'ils lui livreront l'empereur, auquel le sultan fait remettre leur lettre, pour le convaincre de la trahison de ses nationaux, et lui livre de bonne amitié Jérusalem. La paix s'étant établie entre eux, l'empereur vint et menaça les frères de son courroux.[149]

Même si l'existence d'une telle lettre n'est pas attestée, on trouve l'écho de cette trahison et la mention de ce document dans la chronique de Matthieu Paris,[150] cela fut repris par Ernst Kantorowicz.[151] Par ailleurs, le chroniqueur Sibt ibn al-Djawzi évoque la menace de l'assassinat de l'empereur par les templiers.[152]

---

[147] Cependant, dès leur origine, les ordres religieux-militaires ont fait l'objet de diverses critiques, en Orient comme en Occident. On les accusait d'être envieux, cupides, orgueilleux, déloyaux, violents, etc. Voir Nicholson, *Templars, Hospitallers and Teutonic Knights*, p. 129. Dans la seconde moitié du XIIe siècle, Gautier Map, à l'autre extrémité de la chrétienté, en Angleterre, dans ses *Contes pour les gens de cour* (trad. Alan K. Bate (Turnhout, 1993), pp. 100–101), émettait le même constat que Nersès de Lambroun sur la déformation de l'objectif initial des templiers, tout en critiquant également leur enrichissement. Il rejoignait les religieux arméniens sur le fait de condamner l'utilisation des armes par des moines, et s'appuyait sur l'exemple donné par le Christ et les apôtres qui avaient préféré la parole au glaive. Nous remercions le professeur Jonathan Riley-Smith pour les précieux conseils qu'il nous a prodigués et qui a attiré notre attention sur le parallèle qui existe entre ces deux témoignages – concordants malgré la distance qui séparait leurs auteurs –, ce qui en dit long sur la désaffection que connaissait déjà le Temple dans certains milieux culturels, et ceci, à travers toute la chrétienté, moins d'un siècle après sa fondation. Le concept de l'usage de la force par des hommes d'église, et particulièrement des moines, était encore loin d'être accepté par tous.

[148] Matevossyan, *Colophons (XIIIe siècle)*, pp. 706–13, n° 574. Cf. supra.

[149] Samouêl d'Ani, p. 471.

[150] *Matthaei Parisiensis, monachi sancti Albani, Chronica majora*, éd. Henry R. Luard, 7 vols., RS 57 (London, 1872–83), 3:177–79.

[151] Ernst Kantorowicz, *L'empereur Frédéric II* (Paris, rééd. de 2000), p. 177.

[152] *Chroniques arabes des croisades*, textes recueillis et présentés par Francesco Gabrieli (Paris, 2ème éd., 1996), p. 302. L'ordre du Temple ne pouvait être favorable à Frédéric II de Hohenstaufen, en raison de l'excommunication qui avait été prononcée contre l'empereur germanique en 1227 par le pape Grégoire IX. Cependant, malgré l'interdiction papale, l'empereur avait déclenché la sixième croisade en prenant la mer le 28 juin 1228, s'aliénant de ce fait le soutien des ordres militaires, à l'exception de celui des chevaliers teutoniques. L'animosité des templiers à l'encontre de l'empereur eut pour conséquence la volonté de ce dernier d'assaillir leur maison à Acre, il fut cependant obligé de se retirer sans avoir eu le temps de concrétiser son projet, à cause de l'invasion de son royaume de Sicile par Jean de Brienne. Si les

Celui qui porte le regard le plus implacable sur les templiers, tout en se positionnant lui-même en victime, est le roi Lewon Ier dans ses lettres au pape Innocent III. Il se plaint de la mauvaise volonté de l'ordre à son égard, de son refus de combattre à ses côtés pour défendre les frontières du royaume puis, plus grave, de ses actions militaires contre ses intérêts et, comble de l'inacceptable, contre des chrétiens![153] Le souverain arménien, étant personnellement impliqué, nous offre donc une représentation particulièrement négative de l'ordre du Temple puisque, ne pouvant être à la fois juge et partie, il ne devait être que partial. De plus, Lewon Ier, en refusant de rétrocéder aux frères leur ancienne forteresse de Baghrâs, qu'il avait lui-même reprise après la conquête de Saladin, ne pouvait pas s'attendre à une attitude conciliante de leur part.

*Un point de vue neutre*

Une autre catégorie d'écrivains est beaucoup moins passionnée et tente d'exposer les faits relatifs aux frères combattants d'une façon relativement neutre, sans user d'adjectifs péjoratifs ou mélioratifs pour les qualifier. L'information en elle-même les intéresse davantage que l'interprétation qu'ils peuvent en tirer. La *Chronique* d'Hét'oum l'Historien est représentative à cet égard. Sans faire de reproche ni de louange aux membres des ordres religieux-militaires, Hét'oum s'intéresse à tous les événements importants qui jalonnent leur histoire, que ce soit la date de leur fondation, la mort de leurs grands maîtres et de certains de leurs principaux dignitaires, la construction et la perte de leurs forteresses, les campagnes auxquelles ils participent, leurs combats défensifs, l'issue de ces conflits, les donations et les ventes à leur profit, leurs actions diplomatiques et quelques anecdotes les concernant.[154] Dans sa *Table chronologique*, Hét'oum II adopte la même démarche pour évoquer les templiers et les chevaliers teutoniques,[155] approche également reprise dans certains colophons de manuscrits.[156] Et, parmi les chroniqueurs syriaques, l'auteur anonyme mentionne les frères lors d'un combat contre Saladin, et l'emprisonnement de ceux-ci après le désastre de Hattîn, sans exprimer une quelconque opinion sur leur manière de combattre ou sur leur sort.[157]

---

hospitaliers ont fini par adopter une attitude plus conciliante envers Frédéric II, ce ne fut pas le cas des templiers qui se joignirent aux barons de Terre sainte contre lui. Voir Jean Richard, *Histoire des croisades* (Paris, 1996), pp. 321 et 323.

[153]   Cf. Innocent III, *PL*, 214: col. 810–12, n° 252, et col. 1003–1006, n° 43; 215: col. 687–92, n° 119.

[154]   Haython, *Chronique*, pp. 60, 65, 66, 67, 68, 74, 75–76, 77 et 79. Hét'oum de Korykos adopte également un ton neutre pour évoquer les ordres du Temple et de l'Hôpital dans Haython, *Flor, RHC Darm*, 2:196–99 (2:320–21, pour la version latine), et Haython, trad. Deluz, pp. 851–52.

[155]   Dans *RHC Darm*, 1:484 et 485.

[156]   Matevossyan, *Colophons (XIIIe siècle)*, pp. 701–703, n° 570; pp. 718–20, n° 579.

[157]   L'Anonyme syriaque, pp. 141–42, 148–49.

*Un regard favorable et bienveillant envers les ordres militaires*

On constate, à travers les sources mentionnant les membres des ordres militaires, une gradation dans le respect éprouvé par leur auteurs et même parfois, dans leur admiration. Lorsque Lewon Ier ou Raymond-Ṙoubên accordent des chartes de donations ou de franchises aux hospitaliers, ils désignent l'ordre comme "sainte" ou "sacro-sainte maison", et le grand maître est toujours précédé de l'épithète "vénérable."[158]

La perception des templiers, qu'il appelle les "Frères aux vêtements marqués de la Croix," par le Pseudo-Sembat, est élogieuse, en particulier pour décrire leur courage face à Saladin devant le choix qui s'offrait à eux après le désastre de Hattîn.[159] Cependant, bien que le chroniqueur mentionne la plupart des faits essentiels concernant les templiers et les hospitaliers en Arménie cilicienne, il n'évoque pas la querelle d'Antioche dont ils furent, avec le comte de Tripoli, Raymond-Ṙoubên et le roi Lewon Ier, les protagonistes, peut-être dans un souci de préserver l'image des frères qui aurait pu être entachée par la mention de leur implication dans ce conflit.

Dans sa *Chronographie*, Bar Hebraeus considère, dès l'année 1156, pendant laquelle Renaud de Châtillon lança une offensive contre le prince arménien Tʿoros II,[160] que les templiers "œuvrent dans l'intérêt de tous les chrétiens."[161] Les frères du Temple continuent à bénéficier d'une image favorable lorsque, en 1217, ils dénoncent à Lewon Ier le complot fomenté par Raymond-Ṙoubên pour s'emparer de sa personne et régner à sa place.[162] L'auteur rapporte aussi le fait que les hospitaliers, chez lesquels Zapêl était partie se réfugier à la suite du décès prématuré de son époux, "protégèrent honorablement" la reine,[163] et qu'ils firent dire à Kostandin qui la leur réclamait: "Nos maisons et nos bastions sont les villages de refuge des chrétiens, et nous ne pouvons livrer une femme, une reine, qui a cherché refuge auprès de nous."[164] Le grand métropolite fait donc partie des chrétiens orientaux qui ont conscience de la mission et du but que se sont fixés les ordres militaires et dévoile certaines des qualités et valeurs qui en découlent, telles que leur loyauté et l'asile qu'ils offrent aux chrétiens.

Certaines sources chrétiennes orientales vont plus loin dans l'estime portée aux ordres militaires et font parfois de véritables dithyrambes.

---

[158] *Cart Hosp*, pp. 70–71, n° 1262; p. 71, n° 1263; pp. 115–16, n° 1344; pp. 122–23, n° 1355; pp. 164–65, n° 1426; pp. 165–66, n° 1427; p. 175, n° 1441; p. 176, n° 1442.

[159] Dédéyan, *Chronique Smbat*, pp. 59–63.

[160] Offensive lancée à l'instigation de l'empereur byzantin Manuel Comnène. Le véritable objectif du prince d'Antioche était cependant de remettre aux frères les forteresses de l'Amanus, jadis prises aux Francs par les Grecs.

[161] Bar Hebraeus, p. 283.

[162] Ibid., p. 370.

[163] Ibid., p. 381.

[164] Ibid., pp. 389–90.

*Une vision laudative*

On distingue une vision extrêmement élogieuse des ordres militaires dans quelques chroniques du XIIe siècle et dans certaines chartes de la première moitié du XIIIe siècle. Pour Grigor Yérêts, les templiers sont des "envoyés du ciel,"[165] la "milice qui aime le Christ,"[166] et une "milice invincible."[167] Ils obtiennent "la couronne du martyre" en combattant les musulmans.[168] De surcroît, le chroniqueur arménien met en exergue le soutien des chevaliers du Temple aux Arméniens, un soutien à la fois militaire, contre le sultan saldjoûkide mandaté par Manuel Comnène,[169] et diplomatique – les templiers plaidant la cause du prince T῾oros II devant ce même empereur.[170]

Michel le Syrien est celui qui détaille le plus le mode de vie des ordres militaires; de ce fait, il ne tarit pas d'éloges sur la discipline que les frères s'imposent à eux mêmes, ni sur leur utilité tant au combat qu'auprès des pauvres et des malades qu'ils secourent avec une constance sans faille.[171] Le patriarche se fait également l'écho de leur droiture et de leur intégrité lorsqu'il évoque l'occupation et le pillage du couvent de Barsaumâ, qui eut lieu le 18 juin 1148, par le comte Josselin.[172] Il nous fait part de la réaction des templiers devant cet événement: "Quelques Francs qui l'accompagnaient étaient du nombre des Phrêr, c'est-à-dire 'frères'; en voyant cela ils lui dirent: 'Nous sommes venus avec toi pour faire la guerre aux Turcs et secourir les Chrétiens, et non pas pour piller les églises et les monastères', et ils l'abandonnèrent et s'en allèrent sans avoir mangé du pain ou bu de l'eau."[173]

On peut classer le colophon du copiste Housik dans cette catégorie de sources laudatives envers les ordres militaires, puisque son auteur voue une véritable admiration aux templiers, desquels il loue le zèle, tout en évoquant leur chasteté et leur dimension militaire.[174]

---

[165] Grigor Yérêts, pp. 171–72, Dulaurier, *Matthieu d'Édesse*, p. 338, et Dostourian, *Matthew of Edessa*, p. 263.

[166] Grigor Yérêts, pp. 171–72, trad. par "milice chérie du Christ" dans Dulaurier, *Matthieu d'Édesse*, pp. 338, 354, trad. par "aimés du Christ" dans Dostourian, *Matthew of Edessa*, p. 263 et par "soldats du Christ," p. 273.

[167] Grigor Yérêts, p. 189, Dulaurier, *Matthieu d'Édesse*, p. 355, et Dostourian, *Matthew of Edessa*, p. 273.

[168] Grigor Yérêts, p. 184, Dulaurier, *Matthieu d'Édesse*, pp. 350–51, et Dostourian, *Matthew of Edessa*, p. 270.

[169] Grigor Yérêts, p. 189, Dulaurier, *Matthieu d'Édesse*, p. 338, et Dostourian, *Matthew of Edessa*, p. 263.

[170] Grigor Yérêts, p. 188, Dulaurier, *Matthieu d'Édesse*, p. 354, et Dostourian, *Matthew of Edessa*, p. 273.

[171] Michel le Syrien, 3.201–203, 207–208, 235, 314, 324.

[172] Pour plus de détails sur les circonstances de cet événement, voir l'Anonyme syriaque, pp. 113–15, et Gérard Dédéyan, *Les Arméniens entre Grecs, Musulmans et Croisés. Etude sur les pouvoirs arméniens dans le Proche-Orient méditerranéen (1068–1150)* (Lisbon, 2003), pp. 1238–39.

[173] Michel le Syrien, 3.287.

[174] Matevossyan, *Colophons (XIIIe siècle)*, pp. 158–59, n° 114. Voir *supra*, les citations d'extraits du colophon.

La vision laudative des ordres passe souvent par l'évocation de leur foi, de leur générosité et de leurs qualités militaires, ainsi, les documents diplomatiques qui encensent le plus les frères sont les deux chartes de donations émises par la chancellerie des souverains arméniens, en faveur de l'ordre de Sainte-Marie des Teutoniques, que nous avons eu l'occasion de présenter à propos de la description de la dimension spirituelle des ordres. Dans la première, datée d'avril 1212, Lewon Ier assimile les teutoniques aux Macchabées, et mentionne leurs "bienfaits" et leurs "prières." Sa bienveillance envers l'ordre est renforcée lorqu'il ordonne que ses hommes "ne puissent exiger par la force, de ces mêmes frères, quelque service ou taxe (*tributum*) ou redevance (en nature) (*angariam*) ou quelque levée d'impôt de quelque manière que ce soit, mais au contraire qu'ils soient tenus de les aimer, de les honorer et de les vénérer pour tout et en toute chose, comme il sied aux hommes pieux."[175] La seconde charte, accordée par Hétʻoum Ier et Zapêl, le 22 janvier 1236, évoque la charité des frères et leur vaillance au combat. Ils sont d'autant plus favorables à cet ordre qu'ils en sont *confratres* et que les chevaliers teutoniques ont proclamé qu'ils les protégeraient ainsi que leur royaume.[176]

L'appréciation des actions et de la valeur des ordres militaires varie considérablement en fonction de la dignité des auteurs, de leur proximité d'avec ces congrégations, de contentieux potentiels ou, au contraire, d'une reconnaissance pour services rendus ou à rendre.

Alors que nous aurions pu penser à une similitude de point de vue des auteurs chrétiens orientaux sur les ordres religieux-militaires, en raison d'une proximité géographique et de certaines affinités culturelles, la réalité se révèle être toute autre. En effet, les sociétés arméniennes et syriaques sont différentes et cela se ressent à travers la tonalité des chroniques; celles écrites par les Syriaques mettent l'accent sur les aspects économiques et religieux des événements, tandis que celles rédigées par des Arméniens (vivant dans une société de type féodal) sont plus axées sur les faits militaires. Toute la palette des modes de désignation, des types de jugements, des perceptions du rôle des ordres s'offre à nous. Cependant, nous pouvons tenter de dégager certaines grandes tendances. De façon générale, les auteurs syriaques sont favorables aux ordres militaires, dont ils connaissent le mode de vie (surtout Michel le Syrien) mais, pour le reste, ils sont peu précis, surtout lorsqu'il s'agit de distinguer les templiers des hospitaliers, qu'ils préfèrent tous appeler "frères." La plupart des auteurs arméniens issus du haut clergé, qu'ils soient catholicos, évêques ou encore responsables d'écoles monastiques, ont un regard plus dur envers les ordres religieux-militaires, considérant que ceux-ci ne respectent plus la mission

---

[175] Langlois, *Trésor des Chartes d'Arménie*, pp. 117–20; Strehlke, *Tabulae Ordinis Theutonici*, pp. 37–39, n° 46; et, Forstreuter, *Der deutsche Orden*, p. 234.

[176] Langlois, *Trésor des Chartes d'Arménie*, pp. 141–43; Strehlke, *Tabulae Ordinis Theutonici*, pp. 65–66, n° 83; et, Forstreuter, *Der deutsche Orden*, pp. 235–36.

qu'ils s'étaient fixés, et cela, dès la fin du XIIe siècle; de plus, il n'était pas concevable pour cette élite de l'Eglise arménienne de concilier vie monacale et activités guerrières. Les clercs arméniens qui, eux, exerçaient des fonctions plus modestes, ne taisent pas leur admiration pour les templiers, qu'ils voient comme des modèles de vertu et d'abnégation. Quant aux souverains arméniens et à leur entourage familial, leur représentation des ordres militaires diverge selon que nous considérons les actes à valeur juridique, souvent très élogieux (sauf envers les templiers), ou les récits à contenu historique, beaucoup plus détachés et neutres. Cependant, on perçoit clairement que c'est cette dernière catégorie d'auteurs qui connaît le mieux les ordres militaires, leurs grands maîtres, leurs principaux dignitaires et la plupart des événements qui les touchent.

La majorité des mentions relatives aux templiers, hospitaliers et teutoniques dans les sources arméniennes concernent des faits militaires, qu'il s'agisse de combats, de chevaliers faits prisonniers ou tués, etc. Il n'est pas étonnant de constater que ce soit cette caractéristique des ordres religieux-militaires que l'on rencontre le plus fréquemment dans les sources puisque l'objet même des chroniques et des histoires est de narrer ce type d'événements. Cependant, la double identité des membres de ces ordres est souvent mise en valeur, par l'adjonction de mots tels qu'"envoyés du Ciel" ou "milice du Christ"; de plus, certains auteurs prennent l'initiative de parler de la vie monacale des frères de façon plus développée. La représentation des ordres militaires fluctue davantage en fonction des écrivains qu'avec le temps, puisque l'on trouve des critiques acerbes comme des propos louangeurs à leur sujet au XIIe et au XIIIe siècle.

Bien qu'il y ait une singularité de chaque perception, et qu'aucun auteur ne puisse se défaire du prisme déformateur de sa pensée et de son milieu – son témoignage étant l'articulation entre l'acte qu'il pose et la société qu'il reflète –, une tendance générale transparaît dans les écrits des auteurs chrétiens orientaux, celle d'une représentation des ordres religieux-militaires comme des combattants désintéressés de tout bien matériel, présents sur tous les fronts et sacrifiant leur vie sur l'autel de leur foi.

# Conrad III and the Second Crusade: Retreat from Dorylaion?[1]

*Jason T. Roche*

University of St. Andrews

Since the seminal work of Bernhard Kugler in the latter half of the nineteenth century, it is conventionally held that, during the progress of King Conrad III of Germany towards Ikonion[2] (modern Konya), Anatolia, during the Second Crusade (1147–48), the crusaders were defeated in battle by Turkish forces at Dorylaion (modern Eskişehir) and accordingly, forced to turn around and retreat to Nikaia (modern Iznik).[3] The locating of the defeat and subsequent retreat from Dorylaion rests solely on Kugler's interpretations of just two Greek texts: John Kinnamos and Niketas Choniates, and their very brief references to the crusade in Asia Minor.[4] At various times in their career both historians were imperial secretaries attached to the court and the emperor's person. Choniates' political and rhetorical gifts in particular were recognised and he rose to important posts within the central and provisional administration. Yet their histories do not extensively utilize imperial documents; indeed, they are largely dependent upon various forms of eyewitness accounts such as first-hand narratives of specific events that may, or may not, have been officially issued for public consumption, living testimony and verse encomia.[5] However, despite the use of first-hand material, it has been contended elsewhere that Kinnamos' and Choniates' testimonies concerning the crusade, written perhaps some 35 and 55 years later respectively, betray a number of weaknesses when compared to contemporary and near contemporary sources. The texts' inherent limitations are born out of, amongst other things, lack of supporting evidence, personal ambition, necessary dependence upon distorted oral testimony

---

[1] The writer would like to thank Professor Jonathan Phillips for his useful comments on the initial draft of this paper.

[2] Contemporary Greek place names are used throughout.

[3] Bernhard Kugler, *Studien zur Geschichte des Zweiten Kreuzzugs* (Stuttgart, 1866) and the modifications and additions to this found in his *Analekten zur Geschichte des Zweiten Kreuzzuges* (Tübingen, 1878) and *Neue Analekten* (Tübingen, 1883).

[4] Kugler, *Studien*, pp. 152–53; Nicetae Choniatae, *Historia*, ed. I. Bekker, Corpus Scriptorum Historiae Byzantinae (Bonn, 1835), p. 89; Niketas Choniates, *O City of Byzantium, Annals of Niketas Choniates*, trans. Harry J. Magoulias (Detroit, 1984), p. 39; Ioannes Cinnamus, *Rerum ab Ioanne et Alexio Comnenis Gestarum*, ed. A Meineke, Corpus Scriptorum Historiae Byzantinae (Bonn, 1836), p. 81; John Kinnamos, *Deeds of John and Manuel Comnenus*, trans. Charles Brand (New York, 1976), p. 68.

[5] Niketas Choniates, *O City of Byzantium*, pp. xvi–xvii; John Kinnamos, *Deeds*, pp. 5–6; Paul Magdalino, *The Empire of Manuel I Komnenos, 1143–1180* (Cambridge, 1993), pp. 4–26 and 413–88.

and, perhaps most significantly, Byzantine rhetorical conventions, in particular the stereotypical notion of the Latin "barbarian" crusader.[6]

For such reasons, we should not confer unwarranted and, as will become apparent, misconstrued significance on the geographical information contained in the Greek sources. It is thus necessary to readdress the conventional dependence on Kinnamos and Choniates for the history of Conrad's crusade and it is the intention of this paper to question the traditional notion that Conrad turned back at Dorylaion. This aim is facilitated by analysis of the topographical evidence contained within a plethora of contemporary and near contemporary sources. The depicted image of the location the crusade ultimately reached contrasts sharply with what is known of Dorylaion in the twelfth century.

The twelfth century was not a period that witnessed the prolific production in Anatolia or, indeed, the traditional Muslim heartlands to the east, of contemporary Persian, Arabic or Turkic sources that were concerned with events on the western marches of the Turkish world.[7]

Conversely, there are literally dozens of contemporary and near contemporary Latin texts and a smaller number of Syriac sources that refer to the passage of Conrad III through Anatolia.[8] There are many of questionable authority; the briefer *annales* merely recount the outstanding events making it frequently impossible to identify the degrees of separation between the author and his sources of information. Often it is clear that an author had some form of access to another account, whether this is evident in the source content or literary style; such sources of information are not addressed below.

However, there is a significant minority of detailed *annales* and chronicles that are not only contemporaneous to the events they relate, but are derived from eye-witness testimony. There are other important contemporary and near contemporary texts for which we cannot identify original sources of information. Nonetheless, they provide considerable and unique plausible and corroborative testimony, or are far removed geographically from further sources; in both instances, this suggests

---

[6]   Jason T. Roche, "Niketas Choniates as a source for the Second Crusade in Anatolia," in forthcoming denkschrift in honour of Professor Isin Demirkent (2007); "Conrad III and the Second Crusade: Anatolia Reconsidered," unpublished Ph.D. thesis, University of St. Andrews.

[7]   Of the extant contemporaneous sources only the Arabic text of Ibn al-Qalanisi refers to the crusade in Anatolia. However, his useful testimony offers little topographical evidence and is not utilised herein. Ibn al-Qalanisi, *The Damascus Chronicle of the Crusades, Extracted and Translated from the Chronicle of Ibn al-Qalanisi*, trans. Hamilton A. R. Gibb, University of London Historical Series 5 (London, 1932), pp. 279–82.

[8]   On the western Latin texts addressed below see: Giles Constable, "The Second Crusade as Seen by Contemporaries," *Traditio* 9 (1953), 213–79. For a detailed analysis see: Wilhelm Wattenbach and Franz-Josef Schmale, *Deutschlands Geschichtsquellen im Mittelalter vom Tode Kaiser Heinrichs V. bis zum Ende des Interregnum* (Darmstadt, 1976); Kugler also analysed a number of the important Latin texts: Kugler, *Studien*, pp. 1–36.

that the authors had access to first-hand material.[9] This important minority of valuable source evidence is not free from occasional overt subjectivity and textual inaccuracies. Notwithstanding, when it is gleaned for tangible data relating to Conrad's crusade in Anatolia, it is possible to identify common significant threads evident through the offered sources. The recurring image of the barren landscape the crusaders ultimately reached seriously questions Kugler's reading and, hence, the subsequent historiography that Conrad turned back at Dorylaion.

The name Dorylaion is of course familiar to crusade historians as the plain on which the armies of the First Crusade defeated a Turkish force under the command of the Seljuk Turk, Kılıc Arslan in 1097.[10] It is well known that Dorylaion's location on the north-western edge of the Anatolian plateau did, and still does, represent the limit of comparatively fertile, cultivated and populated country that is characteristic of the coastal plains and river valleys of Asia Minor. It is equally well known that a route from the plain of Dorylaion south-east towards Ikonion soon passes through the steppe-like terrain of the plateau. This is a predominately scorched and waterless landscape during the month of October,[11] that is, the month Conrad advanced towards Ikonion.[12] Nevertheless, for comparative purposes with the contemporary and near contemporary topographical evidence, it is necessary to reconstruct an image of Dorylaion in the twelfth century before illustrating what contemporary learned Byzantines knew about the region.

The major Roman, Byzantine and modern road from Nikaia to Dorylaion, via Lefke (near modern Osmaneli), and modern Bilecik and Bozüyük follows natural routes of communication by rivers. This facilitates the perennial availability of fuel

---

[9] Constable confers a high degree of authority to such texts and likewise treats them as independent sources. Constable, "The Second Crusade," 213–79.

[10] For an analysis of this famous battle see: John France, *Victory in the East* (Cambridge, 1994), pp. 169–85. France rejects Anna Komnene's evidence that the First Crusade marched east from Nikaia to Lefke and her statement that the battle took place "on the plain of Dorylaion" because, as he rightly argues, the crusaders could not have reached Dorylaion in two days from Lefke. Accordingly, he revises the established route and relocates the site of the battle to a locality he suggests the crusaders could have reached given the time frame. However, France does not explain why Anna mentions Lefke and Dorylaion. It may be that Anna, writing some half-century after the event, incorrectly presumed that the famous battle of 1097 took place at Dorylaion because the plain was synonymous with the Turkish presence in north-west Anatolia. Also, her mention of the army marching to Lefke is likely to be correct or at least reflects customary military practice. There is no doubt that the road via Lefke was the only Byzantine military route to Dorylaion from Nikaia, reflecting serious logistical and topographical considerations; conversely, it appears that the route suggested by France was never used by armies during the Byzantine age, which accordingly, places his hypothesis in doubt. The writer proposes to readdress this in the future. Anna Komnene, *The Alexiad of Anna Comnena*, trans. Edward R. A. Sewter (Harmondsworth, 1969), p. 341. For references to the Byzantine military route between Nikaia and Dorylaion, see n.13 below.

[11] Admiralty (Naval Staff, Intelligence Division), C.B. 847C (2): *A Handbook of Asia Minor 3, Part 2 The Central Plateau West of the Kyzyl Irmak* (London, 1919), p. 54. For a very useful survey of Turkey's medieval topography see: Michael Hendy, *Studies in the Byzantine Monetary Economy, c.300–1450* (Cambridge, 1985), Section 1.

[12] Wilhelm Bernhardi, *Konrad III*, 1 (Leipzig, 1883), pp. 629–30.

and pasture, and indeed it is mostly lush and fertile along its whole length.[13] It is certain that this was the route the crusade embarked upon and subsequent allegations in the sources suggesting the army was purposely guided away from this road due to "typical" Greek perfidy have long been recognised as dubious.[14]

By the time of the Second Crusade, Dorylaion, situated between the rivers Bathys (modern Sarisu) and Tembros (modern Porsuk) was little more than rubble having been virtually razed to the ground by the Turks soon after the Battle of Mantzikert (1071).[15] However, the relatively lengthy entry for Dorylaion in Belke and Mersich's *Tabula Imperii Byzantini* indicates that on account of Dorylaion's position in the communications infrastructure of north-west Anatolia, its favourable location between the two rivers, the wide plain surrounding the city (that provided outstanding pasture for the imperial stables) and its famous thermal springs, the city was a place of great import.[16] Moreover, it should be noted, that Dorylaion was the second *aplekton* in the Byzantine mustering system, which naturally, would need to be located in such a verdant area in order to provide an army with adequate water and provisions.[17]

Given the presence of the two rivers and abundant pasture, it is not surprising that Türkmen tribes inhabited the environs of the former city. Indeed, during the twelfth century, it appears that the heaviest concentration of Türkmens in the north-west was by the Bathys and Tembros rivers in the Dorylaion plain.[18] It is

---

[13] For the route between Nikaia and Dorylaion see: William M. Calder and George E. Bean, *A Classical Map of Asia Minor* (London, 1958); Klaus Belke and Norbert Mersich, *Phrygien und Pisidien*, Tabula Imperii Byzantini 7 (Vienna, 1990), pp. 141–43; David French, *Roman Roads and Milestones of Asia Minor, fasc.1 The Pilgrims' Road*, British Archaeological Reports International Series 105 (Oxford, 1981), p. 105, map 3; Jacques Lefort, "Les communications entre Constantinople et la Bithynie," in *Constantinople and its Hinterland*, ed. Cyril Mango and Gilbert Dagron (Aldershot, 1995), pp. 207–20; Christophe Giros, "Les fortifications médiévales," in *La Bithynie au Moyen Âge*, ed. Bernard Geyer and Jacques Lefort (Paris, 2003), pp. 209–24; Jacques Lefort, "Les grandes routes médiévales," in *La Bithynie*, pp. 462–72. By reference to the above sources, analysis of the contemporary geopolitical situation and Byzantine military practice, in addition to the examination of the various potential routes' topographies and the topographical and geographical detail contained within contemporary texts, the writer has established that this was the only military route from Nikaia to Dorylaion used during our period and accordingly, the route Conrad was led upon. See map opposite.

[14] For example see: Kugler, *Studien*, pp. 152–53; Bernhardi, *Konrad III*, p. 631.

[15] Belke and Mersich, *Phrygien und Pisidien*, pp. 238–42; Andrew Stone, "Dorylaion revisited: Manuel I Komnenos and the refortification of Dorylaion and Soublaion in 1175," *Revue des Études Byzantines* 61 (2003), 183–99.

[16] Belke and Mersich, *Phrygien und Pisidien*, pp. 238–42.

[17] George Huxley, "A list of *Aplekta*," *Greek, Roman and Byzantine Studies* 16 (1975), 87–93.

[18] Speros Vryonis, Jr., *The Decline of Medieval Hellenism in Asia Minor and the Process of Islamization from the Eleventh through the Fifteenth Century* (Berkeley, 1971), p. 188. John Kinnamos and Niketas Choniates make several references to the Türkmens of the plain. Ioannes Cinnamus, *Rerum*, pp. 190–91 and 295–96; John Kinnamos, *Deeds*, pp. 145 and 220–22; Nicetae Choniatae, *Historia*, pp. 227–28 and 657–58; Niketas Choniates, *O City of Byzantium*, pp. 99–100 and 273. Also see: Bar Hebraeus, *Political History of the World*, part 1, trans. E. A. Wallis Budge (Oxford, 1932), p. 306; Michael the Syrian, *Chronicle*, ed. and trans. Jean-Baptiste Chabot as *Chronique de Michel le Syrien*,

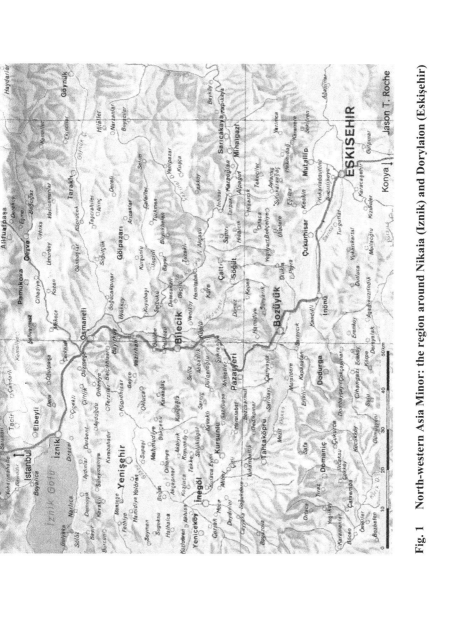

**Fig. 1**  North-western Asia Minor: the region around Nikaia (Iznik) and Dorylaion (Eskişehir)

Jason T. Roche

clear that the verdant strips of land by the rivers and the road here were ideal for a pastoral nomadic existence. An oration[19] by Euthymios Malakes relates that, during Dorylaion's reconstruction in 1175, "the Romans lived luxuriously on the Persian produce and luxuriated in the good things of the barbarians and drove their herds and flocks." It appears that the Türkmens were supplementing their pastoral nomadic existence with some agriculture in the plain. As Andrew Stone has pointed out, this detail of the Byzantine army being able to forage for its subsistence whilst Dorylaion was being rebuilt, supplements Choniates' account that frequently mentions foraging expeditions.[20] Choniates also relates that the Türkmens endeavoured to stop the Byzantines foraging and ultimately the reconstruction of Dorylaion as they "knew that they would be in danger should they be forced to abandon the fertile plains of Dorylaion on which herds of goats and cattle grazed, romping in verdant meadows."[21]

It is possible that the Byzantines were able to gather necessities from Greek-speaking inhabitants of the plain. A second oration by Euthymios Malakes delivered on Epiphany 1176, suggests that Byzantine villagers were paying tribute to the Turks the previous year.[22] It is worth quoting Kinnamos at length here as he clearly illustrates why Byzantine inhabitants may have resided in the plain despite the Türkmen presence:

> This Dorylaion was once as great a city as any in Asia and worthy of much note. A gentle breeze blows over the land, and plains extend around it, extremely smooth and exhibiting an extraordinary beauty, so rich and fertile that they yield abundant grass and produce splendid grain. A river, fair to see and sweet to taste, sends its course through the midst. Such a multitude of fish swims in it that, while fished in abundance by the people there, there is no lack.[23]

It is clear that what is meant in these twelfth-century Greek sources as the plain of Dorylaion, namely, the region around the rivers Bathys and Tembros where the ruined city and road were situated, was a perennially verdant and inhabitable region in the twelfth century.[24] It was certainly attractive to Türkmen tribes who appear

---

*patriarche jacobite d'Antioche (1166–1199)*, 3 vols. (1905; repr. Brussels, 1963), 3:369. For further references to the Türkmens of Dorylaion see: Stone, "Dorylaion Revisited," 183–99.

[19]  On contemporary Byzantine verse encomia see: Magdalino, *Manuel I Komnenos*, pp. 20–21 and Ch. 6.

[20]  Quoted in: Stone, "Dorylaion Revisited," 183–99; Nicetae Choniatae, *Historia*, pp. 227–28; Niketas Choniates, *O City of Byzantium*, pp. 99–100.

[21]  Nicetae Choniatae, *Historia*, pp. 227–28; Niketas Choniates, *O City of Byzantium*, pp. 99–100.

[22]  Stone, "Dorylaion Revisited," 183–99.

[23]  Ioannes Cinnamus, *Rerum*, p. 294; John Kinnamos, *Deeds*, pp. 220–22.

[24]  Just as British Naval Intelligence reports confirm that it was fertile in the early twentieth century before the introduction of modern agricultural techniques. Admiralty (Naval Staff, Intelligence Division), C.B. 847A: *A Handbook of Asia Minor 1, General* (London, 1919), pp. 91–93 and 227; Admiralty (Naval Staff, Intelligence Division), C.B. 847B: *A Handbook of Asia Minor 2, Western Asia Minor* (London, 1919), pp. 112–13.

to have practised some agriculture in the "rich and fertile" meadows that yielded "abundant grass" and produced "splendid grain" and that may have contained Greek-speaking villages despite the Türkmen presence. Incidentally, this all infers that this region had not suffered for some time from devastating border warfare and the scorched-earth policies that appear to have been occasionally employed by both Turks and Byzantines in some frontier regions.[25]

What we know of the topography of the major route from Nikaia to Dorylaion and of Dorylaion itself, which is one of a predominately lush and fertile country, is in stark contrast to the grim image presented in the contemporary sources of the terrain the crusaders were ultimately guided into and were confronted with in October 1147 before the decision was made to retreat. It is to these Latin sources that we must now turn; it should be noted that the writer has applied the most neutral translation to the pertinent words and phrases so as not to bias the furnished evidence.[26]

The Würzburg annalist, who had met survivors of the crusade, has the Byzantine emperor Manuel I Komnenos counselling King Conrad III in Constantinople in the following manner: "The road you must take to the land of the Saracens is very remote, difficult beyond measure because of the emptiness and dangers and it is more burdensome to lead a numerous army into waterless places."[27] The Latin *solitudine* is translated as "emptiness" here, but it is worth noting that Elizabeth Hallam abridges the sentence to read, "it is even more difficult and burdensome to lead such a huge army through the dry wilderness ..."[28] and of course, *solitudine* can be translated as "wilderness" as well as "desert". Manuel's counsel continues: "I consider it to be better to withdraw from your animosity for the time being, choosing to reconsider an inexpedient proposal rather than, by proceeding inadvisably, fail en route by hunger, thirst and grave famine or with limbs becoming exhausted on account of the great hardship, to sustain the raids and attacks of the gravest enemy, and God forbid, suffer the extreme penalty of death."[29] In fact, it is not certain that Conrad had an audience with Manuel at this juncture and whatever the case may be, and as we shall see, what the Würzburg annalist is essentially relating here is what he knows to have actually occurred.

---

[25] Vryonis, *The Decline of Medieval Hellenism*, pp. 147–48. Dorylaion had probably not been the site of border warfare since it was lost to the Byzantines sometime after Mantzikert (1071).

[26] The writer is indebted to Peter Maxwell-Stewart for his initial assistance with the Latin texts.

[27] "Ceterum via qua ad terram Saracenorum ire debetis, remotissima est, solitudine et periculis ultra modum difficilis, et eo difficilior, quanto in locis arentibus ducenda multitudo exercitus est gravior." *Annales Herbipolenses*, MGH SS 16:4. Also see: Constable, "The Second Crusade," 213–79, esp. 243–44 and 268–69; Wattenbach, *Deutschlands Geschichtsquellen*, pp. 148–51; Kugler, *Studien*, pp. 31–34.

[28] Elizabeth Hallam, *Chronicles of the Crusades* (London, 1989), p. 136.

[29] "melius esse considero, ut animositate vestra interim cedatis, eligentes ab inutili proposito potius animum retrahere, quam inconsultius procedendo fame siti et inedia gravi in via deficere, vel etiam fatiscentibus membris ob magnitudiem laboris, gravissimorum hostium incursus et impetum, extremum vite supplitium passuri quod absit, sustinere." *Annales Herbipolenses*, MGH SS 16:4.

The Syriac fragment attributed to the Jerusalemite Mar Simon, an eyewitness to some events in the Levant, states that the crusaders were treacherously sent on their way from Constantinople "by roads that led to barren and uninhabited regions."[30] The Würzburg annalist records that after leaving Nikaia[31] the army "made its way towards Iconium" and "So it entered a very extensive emptiness. They found nothing which seemed suitable to be used as food."[32] Gerhoh of Reichersberg, who includes material in his treatise *De investigatione Antichristi* derived from eyewitness reports, affirms that "While the army was walking towards Iconium, it was overwhelmed by effort, hunger and thirst in the wilderness."[33] The Latin term *in deserto* is here most neutrally translated as "wilderness" although we do not know precisely what Gerhoh and his contemporaries had in mind when they used such terms. We should note, however, that he refers to a lack of water *in deserto* and perhaps then, the *desertum* Gerhoh perceived was the "extensive emptiness" and the "barren and uninhabited regions," which the Würzburg annalist and the aforementioned Syriac source state the crusaders were ultimately guided into. Indeed, a later anonymous Syriac chronicle composed before 1240 declares that "The emperor caused them to go by a bad road and sent with them guides to lead them to a desert where neither water nor any needful thing was to be found ... they found no house nor villages where they could buy, not even water, they wandered in a dry desert and knew not where to go."[34] The anonymous *Notae Pisanae*, an addendum to Bernard Maragone's contemporary *Annales Pisani*, states that the army entered "the territory of the Turks which consisted entirely of wastelands and [the army] was unable to find provisions."[35] In the plural, the Latin *deserta* is best translated here as "wastelands" although it could be translated as "unfrequented places". Helmold of Bosau's *Chronica Slavorum*, based predominantly on oral testimony and written circa 1167–68,[36] Gerhoh of

---

[30]  William R. Taylor, "A New Syriac Fragment Dealing with Incidents in the Second Crusade," *Annual of the American Schools of Oriental Research* 11 (1931), 120–30.

[31]  15 October 1147. Bernhardi, *Konrad III*, p. 629.

[32]  "Iconium tendebat. Ingressi igitur solitudinem longissimam, cum nichil eorum que usui ciborum apta viderentur invenirent." *Annales Herbipolenses*, MGH SS 16:5.

[33]  "Exercitus namque versus Iconium gradiens labore, fame ac siti in deserto confectus." Gerhoh of Reichersberg, *De investigatione Antichristi Liber 1*, MGH Libelli de Lite Imperatorum et Pontificum Saeculis XI et XII Conscripti 3, p. 375. In some aspects, Gerhoh appears to have relied on the *Annales Herbipolenses*. *Annales Herbipolenses*, MGH SS 16:5–8. However, there is sufficient additional testimony to suggest that he also conversed with eyewitnesses. See: Constable, "The Second Crusade," 213–79, esp. 268; Kugler, *Studien*, pp. 34–36.

[34]  Arthur S. Tritton, "The First and Second Crusades from an Anonymous Syriac Chronicle," *The Journal of the Royal Asiatic Society of Great Britain and Ireland* (1933), 69–102 and 273–306, esp. 298.

[35]  "la terra del Turchi, qui habebat tota deserta, ke nulla victualia habere potuit." *Notae Pisanae*, MGH SS 19:266. Also see: Constable, "The Second Crusade," 213–79, esp. 228, 233, 265 and 273.

[36]  "transducti in desertum maximum." Helmold of Bosau, *Chronica Slavorum*, ed. Johann M. Lappenberg and Bernhard Schmeidler, MGH SS.r.G (Hanover, 1909), p. 117. Also see: Constable, "The Second Crusade," 213–79, esp. 223, 237 and 273; Wattenbach, *Deutschlands Geschichtsquellen*, pp. 427–37.

Reichersberg,[37] The very valuable and detailed Pöhlder annals (*Annales Palidenses*),[38] which is derived from eyewitness reports, and the chronicle of *Casus Monasterii Petrishusensis*, composed in 1156, all independently describe the terrain the crusaders ultimately advanced into as a "wilderness" (again translating *desertum* as "wilderness" here).[39]

Both Helmold of Bosau and Michael the Syrian (whose chronicle finished in 1195 and was based predominately on oral testimony and contemporary works) stressed that many of the crusaders perished in this terrain because they were unable to find food or water.[40] The Würzburg annalist verified that the crusaders "entered the wilderness next to Iconium. Nor was it enough that for so many days up until that point they had found nothing that was pleasing to eat; still more, they lacked water, which they had found so far to support life."[41] The *Historia Pontificalis* of John of Salisbury, who was known to many of the surviving crusaders, and the *Chronicon* of William of Tyre, who wrote some thirty years later and who may have likewise spoken to survivors of the passage through Anatolia, both describe this environment as "uninhabited land" (the Latin terms *desertis locis* and *loca deserta* respectively are translated here as "uninhabited land").[42] However, it should be noted, that the English translations of Helmold of Bosau and John of Salisbury render *desertum* and *desertis locis* respectively as "desert."[43] Conceivably, the translators are aware

---

[37] "iter per desertum quoddam versus Iconium ingressus est; ingressus est per desertum." Gerhoh of Reichersberg, *De investigatione*, p. 375.

[38] "arripuit iter deserti." *Annales Palidenses*, MGH SS 16:48–51 and 82–83. Much of the lengthy account of Conrad's crusade in Anatolia presented in the *Annales Palidenses* seems to be reproduced in the *Annales Magdeburgenses*, which, nonetheless, offers additional important crusade testimony. *Annales Magdeburgenses*, MGH SS 16:105–107 and 188–90. The *Annales Magdeburgenses* in turn appears to be part replicated in the *Annales Casinenses*, *Pegavienses* and *Sancti Pauli Virdunensis*. *Annales Casinenses*, MGH SS 19:310; *Annales Pegavienses*, MGH SS 16:232–34 and 258; *Annales Sancti Pauli Virdunensis*, MGH SS 16:500–502. Also see: Constable, "The Second Crusade," 213–79, esp. 224 and 272–73; Wattenbach, *Deutschlands Geschichtsquellen*, pp. 387–94.

[39] "Nam cum per desertum pergerent et escas non invenirent, multi fame perierunt, alii inedia laborantes a paganis aut perempti, aut in captivitatem redacti disperierunt." *Casus Monasterii Petrishusensis, Schwäbische Chroniken Der Stauferzeit* 3 (Sigmaringen, 1978) p. 226. Also see: Constable, "The Second Crusade," 213–79, esp. 224–25, 259–60, 269 and 271; Wattenbach, *Deutschlands Geschichtsquellen*, pp. 279–86.

[40] Michael the Syrian, *Chronicle*, 3:276; Michael's factual detail here is copied in: Bar Hebraeus, *Political History*, p. 274. On Michael also see: Michael the Syrian, *Chronicle*, 1:I–XXXVII. "Universi perierunt fame et siti, transducti in desertum maximum." Helmold of Bosau, *Chonica Slavorum*, p. 117.

[41] "desertum Yconio vicinum intraverunt. Nec satis erat, nichil rerum quibus vesci liberet per tot iam dies repertum fuisse; quin etiam, que solum ad vite solatium hucusque invente fuerant, defecerunt aque." *Annales Herbipolenses*, MGH SS 16:5.

[42] "primo in desertis locis inedia macerati sunt ut plurimi perirent, deinde confecti a paganis." John of Salisbury, *The Historia Pontificalis of John of Salisbury*, ed. and trans. Marjorie Chibnall, (Oxford, 1986), pp. xxxvii and 54; "quibus per loca deserta gratia compendii eos transire oportebat." WT, 16.20, p. 744.

[43] John of Salisbury, *The Historia Pontificalis*, p. 54; Helmold of Bosau, *The Chronicle of the Slavs*, trans. F. Tschan (New York, 1966), p. 174; Helmold of Bosau, *Chronica Slavorum*, p. 117.

of the wider context of their sources in relation to these events and are aware of
Anatolia's geography. Indeed, the references to the lack of water in such sources
again suggests that the chroniclers have in mind a terrain akin to that described in
the Syriac sources, namely a barren desert, when the term *desertum* or *loca deserta*
is used. The image of a barren desert would most certainly correspond to the
description of the landscape the crusaders ultimately reached given in the Pölder
annals. The author states that the crusaders ranged "for fourteen days through a
terrifying wasteland, without paths, happening into a place of dread and vast
emptiness"[44] (the Latin *eremus* is here translated as "wasteland" although it could be
translated as "desert" or "wilderness").[45] Michael Hendy's partial translation of this
text reads that the crusaders initially crossed a "desert" before they entered the
"wilderness." Hendy may be aware of the wider context of his source; he is certainly
au fait with Anatolia's geography, and thus he translates *desertum* as "desert."[46]

Both the context and this terrain are clearly brought out in Arnold of Lübeck's
*Chronica Slavorum*, composed by 1210 and predominately reliant on oral
testimony. Arnold wrote that the army's guide "proceeded into a region which was
uninhabited and very arid. It is said King Conrad halted here with his army and
he was unable to proceed because many of his men were growing weak by hunger
and thirst on account of the great emptiness of the land."[47] Here the Latin *terram
desertam* is translated as "uninhabited." The Pölder annalist provides further details
of the same situation, that is, when the march ceased to continue: "Through these
and other diverse misfortunes many thousands were destroyed, since not only men
but also the beasts of burden were being worn out by the barrenness of the land and
could not survive, because although they might have recovered, they were unable
to find water, and they turned back."[48] William of Tyre provides additional details
of the same circumstances: "While thus, having no knowledge of the region and
concerned by the failure of the provisions, they were wavering – for any kind of
fodder for the pack animals, as well as any kind of food for the people, had entirely
failed ... But the army had located itself in a barren emptiness, far from cultivated
soil."[49] It is clear that Arnold of Lübeck, the Pölder annalist and William of Tyre

---

[44]  Cf. Deut. 32.10.

[45]  "exinde 14 diebus per horribilem eremum, avia secuti, locum horroris et vaste solitudinis
inciderent." *Annales Palidenses*, MGH SS 16:83.

[46]  Hendy, *Studies in the Byzantine Monetary Economy*, p. 40.

[47]  "progressus venit in terram desertam et aridam nimis, ubi dicitur Conradus rex stetisse cum
exercitu suo, quia propter nimiam terre solitudinem multis ibi fame et siti deficientibus procedere non
poterat." Arnold of Lübeck, *Chronica Slavorum*, MGH SS 21:122. Also see: Wattenbach, *Deutschlands
Geschichtsquellen*, pp. 437–41.

[48]  "His et aliis diversis calamitatibus multis milibus extinctis, quoniam amplius subsistere
nequiverunt consumpti a sterilitate terre non solum homines sed et iumenta, quippe quibus refocillandis
nec aqua potuit inveniri, reflexere viam." *Annales Palidenses*, MGH SS 16:83.

[49]  "Dumque sic locorum ignari et pro alimentorum defectu solliciti fluctuarent – defecerat enim
penitus tam quis et iumentis pabulum quam hominibus quodlibet ciborum genus –, Erat autem in
solitudine sterili longe a culto sol constitutus exercitus." WT 16.20, p. 745.

are describing the same terrain, that is, "uninhabited and very arid" and "a barren emptiness" when they write of the place where Conrad had halted before the decision was made by council to retreat.

A number of sources mention the council[50] that witnessed the cessation of the crusaders' advance on Ikonion and our source recital will conclude by reference to a letter written by the king himself from Constantinople, during February 1148, concerning the retreat.[51] Conrad explains in the letter to Abbot Wibald of Corvey and Stavelot that "by the advice of our princes and barons we led the army back to the sea from that uninhabited land in order that it might recover."[52] Again, the most neutral translation has been applied here to the Latin *terra illa deserta* but it should be noted that Dana Munro, perhaps like Hendy aware of the wider context of the source and Anatolia's geography, translated this as "that desert land."[53] Indeed, the image of a desert as in a vast, empty, barren landscape like Anatolia's plateau beyond Dorylaion, would certainly correspond to the descriptions given in the sources of the environment the crusaders had eventually reached and were confronted with in October 1147 before the decision was made and effected to retreat back to Nikaia.

This depiction of a scorched and waterless terrain contrasts sharply with the image of the route through Dorylaion reflected in the aforementioned Greek sources. Even allowing for a certain amount of hyperbole because of the panegyrical nature of the Greek texts, it is clear that what is meant in them as the plain of Dorylaion – namely, the region between the rivers Bathys and Tembros and the course of the Byzantine road – was a perennially verdant and habitable region in the twelfth century. Kinnamos and Choniates certainly knew this and Kugler used them to locate the start of the retreat at Dorylaion. However, it is evident that the Dorylaion as understood by twelfth-century learned Byzantines, was not the same place where the crusaders' advance ceased.[54] It is apparent from our contemporary

---

[50] For example: Odo of Deuil, *De Profectione Ludovici VII in Orientem*, ed and trans. Virginia Berry (New York, 1948) p. 92; WT, 16.20, p. 745; Gerhoh of Reichersberg, *De investigatione*, pp. 375–76; *Annales Herbipolenses*, MGH SS 16:6.

[51] *Epistola Konradis ad Wibaldum, Die Urkunden Konrads III., und seines Sohnes Heinrich*, ed. Fredrich Hausmann, MGH Diplomata 9:354–55. Conrad convalesced in Constantinople in the winter of 1147–48 at the behest of Manuel Komnenos. A number of sources refer to this period. See for example: Odo of Deuil, *De Profectione*, p. 51; Ioannes Cinnamus, *Rerum*, pp. 85–86; John Kinnamos, *Deeds*, pp. 70–71; WT, 16.23 pp. 748–49; Gerhoh of Reichersberg, *De investigatione*, p. 376; *Annales Herbipolenses*, MGH SS 16:7; *Annales Palidenses*, MGH SS 16:83; *Notae Pisanae*, MGH SS 19:266; *Casus Monasterii Petrishusensis*, MGH SS 20:674.

[52] "rogatu principum omnium et baronum, ad mare de terra illa deserta exercitum, ut refocillaretur, reduximus." *Epistola Konradis ad Wibaldus*, MGH Diplomata 9:354.

[53] Dana C. Munro, *Letters of the Crusaders*, Translations and Reprints from the Original Sources of European History 1 (Philadelphia, 1896), pp. 12–14.

[54] A consideration of how many days it would have taken the crusaders to reach Dorylaion supports the inference that the army advanced beyond the plain. On successive evenings from Nikaia, the crusaders are likely to have encamped at Lefke, the grasslands before modern Gülübe and the approximate locations of modern Küplü, Pazaryeri and Bozüyük respectively. The crusaders would have progressed

Latin sources that this was a terrifyingly remote and uninhabited region described as a barren emptiness; Kugler clearly misconstrued Kinnamos' and Choniates' evidence, thus exemplifying the dangers of conferring unwarranted authority to the later Greek sources.

If the descriptions of the terrain the crusaders found themselves in were confined to only one or two texts, or even if they were far removed in time and space from the events they relate, one could reasonably reject them as being the result of an individual's embellished lament of the hardships endured on crusade or the product of expressed grievances snowballing beyond recognition. However, a wide selection of sources has been offered for consideration that are largely contemporaneous with the Second Crusade. Moreover, the texts originate from as far afield as England, Italy and Syria, which negates the likelihood that they originate from a few initial sources, and indeed such a relationship has yet to be discerned amongst the presented texts. Regardless of source partiality and textual inaccuracies, it certainly appears as though the accounts of surviving crusaders were quickly disseminated throughout the crusading world and they all told a similar story: that is, whilst marching in Anatolia, they ultimately advanced into an immense, empty and arid environment reminiscent of the landscape beyond Dorylaion in the month of October.

This is the first occasion that the topographical details contained within these texts have been presented and, as mentioned above, the most neutral translation was applied to the pertinent words and phrases, such as *desertum* and *loca deserta*, so as not to prejudice the evidence. However, it is inescapable that those scholars who have translated a small number of these texts into English have translated such words as "desert." Indeed, following our discussion, it is now reasonable to suggest that a neutral translation such as "wilderness," is actually misleading as it does not accurately convey the landscape the chroniclers apparently had in mind when they used words such as *desertum* and *loca deserta*.

The terrain they envisaged was evidently a desert as in a vast, desolate and barren landscape, which, as elucidated, does not hold with the image of a perennially verdant and habitable Dorylaion and, in actuality, corresponds with the terrain immediately beyond Dorylaion en route to Ikonion. Therefore, if we accept any

---

thus far through verdant land along a mixture of narrow and open, flat and undulating terrain for five days since leaving Nikaia. This is reflected in the average rate of march of 20 kilometres per day, which approximately equates to the average rates of march for most combined forces accompanied by a baggage train throughout recorded history. John Haldon, *Warfare, State and Society in the Byzantine World, 565–1204* (London, 1999), p. 165. It is likely that Conrad struck camp for the River Bathys the morning of day six and reached Dorylaion at the end of day seven. This would equal a total march on days six and seven of approximately 50 kilometres over terrain well suited for the passage of large armies and equates to an absolute average daily rate of march of 22 kilometres per day. Immediately beyond Dorylaion, measured at approximately 151 kilometres from Nikaia, the route enters typical arid plateau country. Jacques Lefort, "Les grandes routes médiévales," in *La Bithynie*, pp. 462–72. Also see map on p. 89.

of this evidence, we should question the traditional notion that Conrad III turned back on the plain of Dorylaion and, indeed, we must now look beyond this location to discover where the crusaders' advance was terminated.

# New Evidence for the Frankish Study of
# Arabic Medical Texts in the Crusader Period

*Emilie Savage-Smith*

University of Oxford

An Arabic medical manuscript now in the Bodleian Library, Oxford, contains hitherto unnoticed Latin annotations that appear to have been added by an unnamed Frankish reader during the crusader period.[1] The manuscript in question is MS Hunt. 202, part of the collection of Robert Huntington that came into the Bodleian in 1693.

The title of the treatise contained in this manuscript is *al-Kutub al-mi'ah fī al-ṣinā'ah al-ṭibbīyah* (The Hundred Books on the Medical Art), and its author was Abū Sahl al-Masīḥī, or more precisely Abū Sahl ʿĪsá ibn Yaḥyá al-Masīḥī, a Christian physician of the late tenth to early eleventh century.[2] He, or his family, apparently originated in Jurjān (Gurgān) on the southeastern coast of the Caspian Sea. He studied in Baghdad, and lived and worked at least part of his life in the Persian province of Khurāsān and then in the province of Khwārazm (south of the Aral Sea) where he was part of the brilliant group of scholars at the court of the Khwārazmshāh Ma'mūn ibn Mā'mūn – scholars that included Ibn Sīnā (Avicenna) and the polymath al-Bīrunī, as well as another Christian physician named Ibn Khammār.

According to medieval biographical sources, Abū Sahl al-Masīḥī died in 1010 [401 H] "at the prime of life," that is, presumably about the age of 40 (see the Appendix for relevant texts). The circumstances of his death were unusual. In the year 1010 a number of scholars at the court in Khwārazm (Ibn Sīnā, Abū Sahl al-Masīḥī, al-Bīrunī, and others) were summoned, rather abruptly, to the court of

---

[1] The annotations in this manuscript were first brought to scholars' attention in a brief notice by the present author, "Between Reader and Text: some medieval Arabic marginalia," in *Écrire dans les marges: une expression de la pensée scientifique (antiquité tardive – renaissance)*, ed. Charles Burnett and Danielle Jacquart (Paris, 2005), pp. 1–20. The present paper is based on a talk presented at the symposium, "Medicine and Disease in the Crusades" held in London in January of 2005 under the auspices of the Wellcome Trust Centre for the History of Medicine at University College London, and organized by Dr. Piers Mitchell. For a description of the paper, ink, and script of Bodleian Library, MS Hunt. 202, see Emilie Savage-Smith, *A New Catalogue of Arabic Manuscripts in the Bodleian Library, Oxford, Volume 1: Arabic Manuscripts on Medicine and Related Topics* (Oxford, forthcoming [2007]).

[2] The treatise was not translated into Latin, and there is no modern translation of it. Recently an edition of the text was published by Floréal Sanagustin, *"Kitāb [sic] al-mi'ah fī l-ṭibb" d'Abū Sahl al-Masīḥī*, 2 vols. (Damascus, 2000); the Bodleian Library manuscript was employed in this edition, but the Latin annotations are not mentioned. For a survey of the treatise, see Ghada Karmi, "A Mediaeval Compendium of Arabic Medicine: Abū Sahl al-Masīḥī's 'Book of the Hundred'," *Journal of the History of Arabic Science* 2 (1978), 270–90.

a rival ruler at Ghazna, in what is now eastern Afghanistan. According to a well-known account given in the twelfth century by Niẓāmī-i ʿArūḍī (see Appendix, section C), rather than go to the court in Ghazna, Abū Sahl al-Masīḥī together with Ibn Sīnā, fled from Khwārazm and travelled west, in the opposite direction from Ghazna. The two of them succeeded in fleeing as far as Māzandarān (a province to the south of the Caspian Sea), at which point they encountered a sudden sandstorm. Abū Sahl al-Masīḥī died in the sandstorm, but Ibn Sīnā continued travelling onward.[3]

There is also persuasive evidence that Abū Sahl was the teacher of Ibn Sīnā for medicine. For our purposes, however, what is particularly pertinent is the fact that this treatise by Abū Sahl al-Masīḥī was much used and recommended by twelfth- and thirteenth-century physicians in Syria and was generally considered to be the best Arabic medical encyclopaedia to be composed by a Christian physician.

To understand the context of this annotated manuscript, it is important to consider the medical education in Syria at the time of the crusader states and the role that Abū Sahl's treatise played in that education. The most important teacher of medicine in Syria in the early thirteenth century was the physician Muhadhdhab al-Dīn ʿAbd al-Raḥīm, known as al-Dakhwār (d. 1230), who said that he had not found any Christian physician, ancient or modern, who was more skilful than Abū Sahl at writing Arabic or more pleasing in turns of phrase (see Appendix, section B, for the text).

Al-Dakhwār worked in the great Nūrī bīmāristān (hospital) built in Damascus in 1154 by Nūr al-Dīn Maḥmūd ibn Zangī. Typical of pre-Ottoman Islamic hospitals, it was entered through a monumental gate; four iwans (vaulted halls with arched openings) were built around a central courtyard having a large rectangular pool. It is evident from inscriptions and book niches, that the largest of the iwans served as a lecture hall. Corner rooms apparently were used as wards for patients, and there were a number of smaller rooms, including one having a large latrine formed of six stalls centred around a pool.[4] The Nūrī hospital became the major centre of medical activity in thirteenth-century Damascus and very probably a centre of medical teaching in the iwan that appears to have been a lecture area.

The reputation of al-Dakhwār attracted many physicians to Damascus, and the list of people who studied with him is long and impressive. These included Ibn Abī Uṣaybiʿah (an oculist as well as important historian of medicine), the botanist Ibn al-Bayṭār and Ibn al-Nafīs (renowned today for his description of the pulmonary

---

[3] On Abū Sahl al-Masīḥī and Ibn Sīnā, see also Floréal Sanagustin, "Le *Canon de la médecine* d'Avicenne, texte de rupture épistémologique?," in *Avicenna and his heritage*, ed. Jules Janssens and Daniel De Smet (Leuven, 2002), pp. 297–311, esp. 304–308.

[4] See Yasser Tabbaa, "The functional aspects of medieval Islamic hospitals," in *Poverty and Charity in Middle Eastern Contexts*, ed. Michael Bonner, Mine Ener, and Amy Singer (Albany, NY, 2003), pp. 95–119, esp. pp. 100–106.

circulation). Al-Dakhwār bequeathed his house in Damascus, in the old goldsmiths' area east of the date-sellers *sūq*, as a charitable trust (*waqf*) for the establishment of a *madrasah* or school in which, following his death, the art of medicine was to be taught. He also bequeathed a number of other properties whose proceeds would serve for the maintenance of the *madrasah*, the salary of the teacher, and the support of students. According to Ibn Abī Uṣaybiʿah, the *madrasah* opened, with considerable ceremony, on 15 January 1231 (8 Rabīʿ I 628) and from other sources we learn that it was still functioning in 1417, when it underwent some repairs.[5] Shortly after this time, according to a sixteenth-century source, there were also in Damascus two other *madrasah*s devoted to medicine, one said to be opposite the Nūrī hospital and the other situated "by the bath of the heavens" ( *ʿinda ḥammām al-falak*). The former was founded by al-Dunaysarī (d. 1283), with some of its teachers expert in *fiqh* (Islamic law) as well as medicine, while the latter was established in 1264 by the physician, poet, and politician Ibn al-Lubūdī (d. 1272).[6]

The point of this digression about medical instruction in Damascus is to provide some context in which to place a Frankish reader of an Arabic medical text. Our sources suggest that Abū Sahl al-Masīḥī's *Hundred Books on the Medical Art* was widely used and recommended in Syria in the twelfth and thirteenth centuries. It is likely that a Syrian Muslim physician at this time, if asked by a Frank, might have recommended a treatise by a Christian writer over other Arabic medical treatises by Muslim writers. Furthermore, the fact that its author was a Christian would have been attractive to a prospective Frankish reader.

With this background, let us now turn to the copy of his treatise that is preserved in MS Hunt. 202. It is a complete copy, comprising 255 folios. In the colophon on folio 256b, the unnamed scribe has stated that the copy was completed in the month of Shaʿbān 592 (= July 1196). The copy appears to be the earliest preserved copy of this treatise, made roughly 180 years after Abū Sahl died. Sometime after its completion in 1196, Latin annotations were added to twenty-seven of its folios. There are fifteen owners' notes, which provide some evidence of the volume's fascinating history.

The earliest dated owner's note occurs on the final page (fol. 256b) and reads: "Transferred by sale to shaykh Shams al-Dīn Abū ʿAbd Allāh Muḥammad al-Samhūrī [that is, from Samhūr near Alexandria], one of the oculists and surgeons in the Islamic lands, from al-shaykh ʿAlāʾ al-Dīn ibn Dawālībī *al-muḥaddith* [transmitter of *ḥadīth*s] al-Ḥanbalī in the middle of the month of Ramaḍān in the

---

[5] Ibn Abī Uṣaybiʿah, *Uyūn al-anbāʾ fī ṭabaqāt al-aṭibbā*, ed. August Müller, 2 vols. (Cairo, 1882–84), 2:244 lines 20–27; ʿAbd al-Qādir al-Nuʿaymī, *al-Dāris fī taʾrīkh al-madāris*, ed. Jaʿfar al-Ḥasanī (Damascus, 1948), 2:127–38.

[6] al-Nuʿaymī, 2:133–38. Compare Ibn Shaddād, *Al-Aʿlāq al-khaṭīrah fī dhikr al-Shām wa-al-Jazīrah*, ed. Sāmī al-Daḥḥān (Damascus, 1956), 266; Gary Leiser, "Medical Education in Islamic Lands from the Seventh to the Fourteenth Century," *Journal of the History of Medicine and Allied Sciences* 38 (1983), 48–75, esp. 57–59. For al-Dunaysarī and al-Lubūdī, see Ibn Abī Uṣaybiʿah 2:185–89 and 267–72.

year 846 [= 13–24 January 1443]."[7] The date is given in *zimāmī* or *rūmī* ("Greek") alphanumeric ciphers, related to Coptic numerals.[8]

In the middle of the folio, beneath the colophon, there is also a faded, possibly defaced, two-line inscription in Hebrew or Judaeo-Arabic. It is virtually illegible, but its presence in this manuscript may provide an additional clue as to the copy's history. The other four owners' notes on this final folio are in Arabic and provide no useful clues as to the manuscript's whereabouts.[9] There are also several Arabic annotations that are not transfers of sale or *ex libris* notes: a recipe said to be useful for the removal of unwanted hair and the prevention of its growth on the chin, armpits, and pubes; a curious unfinished sentence "blood-vessels which are to be bled;" and the subtraction of two sets of numbers, indicating that someone used the end of the volume as a scratch pad for simple arithmetic.

Six Arabic phrases on the folio combine to form a common talismanic formula. At the top of the folio, and again in the middle, there is the Arabic phrase *iḥfaẓ kitābī hādhá* ("Protect this book of mine"). In each of the four corners there is the phrase *yā kabīkaj* ("O Buttercup"). These phrases refer to the magical and protective powers associated with the buttercup (a variety of *Ranunculus*) that was considered especially effective against worms and insects prone to attack old Islamic manuscripts that were mostly made of paper and bound with glues attractive to insects. When the plant itself was not available, then invoking its name was considered equally efficacious. The same pattern of talismanic annotations occurs on the first folio of this volume. Unfortunately these talismanic formulae were not very effective, for the manuscript is riddled with worm holes.

There are yet more owners' notes on the opening folio of the volume (fol. 2a), where there are ten handwritten annotations and one early but illegible square stamp. Above the stamp there is a six-line note that is not readable except for the date 911 [= 1505–6]. Below the stamp is a partially defaced note stating that the volume was sold to one Jamāl al-Dīn Aḥmad al-A[...] *al-mutaṭabbib* [the physician] in the year 960 [= 1552–3]. According to a note written vertically at the bottom of the folio, on the first of Jumādá II 978 [= 13 October 1570] the manuscript was purchased for 105 pieces of gold[10] from [...] Jamāl al-Dīn al-Nuwarnī [?],

---

[7] For illustrations of the final page (fol. 256b) as well as the annotated title page (fol. 2a) and two folios with Latin annotations, see Savage-Smith, "Between Reader and Text" (n. 1 above).

[8] These numerals are not dependent upon place notation and hence can be placed in any order, as here where they are written as 648. For *zimāmī* letter-numerals, see Rosa Comes, "Arabic, *Rūmī*, Coptic, or Merely Greek Alphanumerical Notation? The Case of a Mozarabic 10th-Century Andalusī Manuscript," *Suhayl* 3 (2002–3), 157–85; David A. King, *The Ciphers of the Monks: A Forgotten Number-Notation of the Middle Ages*, Boethius 44 (Stuttgart, 2001); Emilie Savage-Smith, *A Descriptive Catalogue of Oriental Manuscripts at St John's College, Oxford* (Oxford, 2005), p. 47 (entry no. 13).

[9] All are undated. There is a transfer of sale to one Aḥmad ibn ʿAlī al-Simalāwī [?]; another transfer of sale to one ʿAlī ibn Yūnas Ilyās ... [?]; an *ex libris* of a physician *al-faqīr al-ḥājj al-ṭabīb* [name not legible]; and one totally illegible note.

[10] The reading is somewhat uncertain at this point.

possibly the same person as in the previous note. Written diagonally beneath and to the left of the large title of the treatise, there is a five-line note reading: "*Ex libris* al-'abd al-faqīr Muḥammad Fatḥ Allāh, the physician of Dār al-Shifā' al-Nūrī, may God pardon him, in Muḥarram 1034 [= Oct.–Nov. 1624]." The Dār al-Shifā' al-Nūrī is another name for the Nūrī hospital in Damascus that was the centre of medical activity at the time this manuscript was copied and which continued to function as a hospital into the nineteenth century; today it is a museum of medical history.

Thus we know that in 1624 this copy was in Damascus, owned by a physician at the Nūrī hospital, and 70 years after that it came into the collections of the Bodleian Library through the purchase in 1693 of the collection of Robert Huntington. On the basis of the many owners' annotations it seems that this Arabic manuscript remained in the Middle East, apparently in Syria, from the time it was copied in 1196 until it entered the Bodleian Library at the end of the seventeenth century.

The Latin annotations must have been made during the interval between 1196 and its possession in the early fifteenth century by the Ḥanbalī legal scholar who sold it in 1443. A phrase used in the transfer of sale in 1443, however, is quite unusual and possibly significant. It says it was sold to "one of the oculists and surgeons [*aḥad al-kaḥḥālīn wa-al-jarā'iḥīn*] in the Islamic lands [*bil-mamlakah al-islāmīyah*]." Could it be that the Ḥanbalī legal scholar wished to make it clear by using the phrase *bil-mamlakah al-islāmīyah* that the volume was now passing into the hands of an oculist and surgeon in *Islamic* lands and hence leaving the hands of Frankish physicians in one of the crusader states? In any case, this is an unusual phrase, and presumably must have had a particular significance in this context.

Since it is highly unlikely that during this interval it would have been carried to Europe and then back again to the Levant before 1400 or 1440, we can reasonably conclude that the Latin *marginalia* were added in one of the crusader territories. For reasons to be presented below, it is possible that the interval of time can be narrowed even further. First, however, let us look at the annotations themselves.

The treatise by Abū Sahl al-Masīḥī is a general medical encyclopaedia in 100 "books" or chapters, beginning with books on general medical principles and anatomy and physiology, then proceeding to the treatments of diseases presented roughly head to foot, and ending with a book on poisonous bites. Unusually for medical compendia of the day, surgery was not included in Abū Sahl's composition, for his therapeutics relied almost entirely on medicaments. Of the 100 books that constitute the treatise, only thirteen attracted our Frankish reader's attention enough to make annotations. After annotating in Book 14 (On Simple Foodstuffs) some vegetable and fruit names (carrot, onion, leek, endive, and melon), the anonymous reader annotated certain passages in a sequence of six books:

Book 35: On the Disorders of the Psychic Faculties
Book 36: On Disorders of Movements
Book 37: On the Natural Faculties
Book 38: On Retention and Fluxion

Book 39: On Fevers
Book 40: On Swellings/Tumours

Then attention was given to diagnosis by pulse and urine, with annotations being made in two books:

Book 45: On Pulse
Book 46: On Urine

Thereafter there are scattered annotations in four books:

Book 60: On the Treatment of Fevers
Book 66: On the Treatment of Diseases of the Head
Book 76: On the Treatment of Diseases of the Chest
Book 90: On the Disorders of Urine

Most of the marginal notes consist of simply noting the subject matter of a passage, such as *de sompno* "on sleep" in Book 35 (fol. 124a) concerned with disorders of the psychic faculties. Some, however, are more extensive. Book 36, on disorders of movements, opens (fol. 124b) with a discussion of movements which occur involuntarily in the limbs, including twitching, trembling, or spasms (*kuzāz* in Arabic).[11] A statement in the Arabic that quivering movements (*ikhtilāj*) are due to soft air (*rīh*) entering the body, is annotated in the margin as *Nota quod est mollicies*. Below that brief note, the reader has placed a symbol representing the Latin word *Nota*. The symbol is repeated at the bottom of the folio, indicating that the comments at the bottom of the page pertain to the Arabic near the first symbol. These lower marginal annotations read:

> *virtus expulssiva: quando excitatur ad expulssionem alicui superfluitatis ex superfluitatibus ubi dicitur eius operatio naturalis & quando excitatur ad expulssionem l??oris nocivi dicitur eius operatio accidentalis* [?] & *omnia accidentalia*

The Latin annotator is here translating two lines of text (fol. 124a, lines 17–18) but breaks off in the middle of the thought. The Arabic reads in translation: "The expulsive faculty, when it evokes expulsion of some of the superfluities of food, that function is called a 'natural function', and when it evokes expulsion of a harmful mixture, that function is called 'accidental'.[12] And all the accidents (*'arāḍ*)" – but here the Latin annotation stops. The Arabic text, however, continues: "And all the 'accidents' are outside the natural course *except for* those whose cause only, but not its movement, stands outside the natural course – such as shivering, yawning,

---

[11] Also a term for tetanus.
[12] *'araḍan*, contingent.

coughing, belching, spasms, and quivering – and those whose cause *and* movement are outside the natural course when seen from one perspective but which follow the natural course when seen from another perspective." In the latter category Abū Sahl placed trembling and limbs falling asleep.

In this example we have the clear use of the symbol for *Nota* placed in the margin alongside the Arabic text and then repeated at the bottom where the lengthy Latin annotation was placed. Similar symbols for *Nota* appear in the margins of other folios, but in all but one of the other instances there are no Latin annotations. This suggests, perhaps, that someone read through the text and noted where annotations should be placed later, but never returned to complete them. It also suggests the possibility that at least two Latin readers used the volume, one leaving symbols where another was expected to translate or annotate more fully. Symbols for *Nota* occur on ten different folios, and there is considerable variation in the form of the symbols – perhaps again an indication that more than one person was responsible. Further investigation may reveal that the form of these symbols might tell us something about the geographical origins of the annotator(s).

A fistnote (a human hand pointing with the index finger, the cuff of a garment showing at the wrist) is also occasionally placed in a margin to draw attention to certain words or concepts. For example, in this same book on disorders of movements (Book 36) two fistnotes are placed next to each other (fol. 126a) with a Latin note drawing attention to the difference between the Arabic word *ikhtilāj* meaning "twitching," translated as *iactagationem*,[13] and the Arabic *ri'shah* which that Latin commentator renders, accurately, as *tremorem*.

Spasms and tremors of all types seem to have been one of the main preoccupations of the Latin reader. In the book concerned with the natural faculties (Book 37), the Latin annotator is interested in those passages distinguishing spasms (Arabic *al-kuzāz,* rendered in Latin as *acuzez*) from hiccups (Arabic *fuwāq,* Latin *singultum*), and hiccups from vomiting (*al-quyā'*, Latin *vomitum*).[14]

Fevers are the next area of interest to the Latin reader, as judged by the number of annotations in Books 39 and 60. A fistnote draws attention to the opening of the book on fevers (Book 39): "in every body having a malign mixture of superfluities that have not loosened as they ought to do, the bodies quickly develop a fever."[15] Another fistnote later in the chapter is accompanied by a list in Latin of three types of hectic fevers.[16] The chapters on fevers contain most of the marginal symbols for *Nota*, but in all instances no Latin explanation has been added.

---

[13] An unusual form of *iectigatio*, derived from *iactatio–onis* meaning agitated motions, fluttering, or oscillation. On the use of *iectigatio* made by Constantine the African and Arnald of Villanova to translate *ikhtilāj*, see *Translatio libri Galieni De rigore et tremore et iectigatione et spasmo*, ed. Michael R. McVaugh, Arnaldi de Villanova Opera Medica Omnia, 16 (Barcelona, 1981), pp. 22–38.

[14] Fol. 129b.

[15] Fol. 135b.

[16] Fol. 136b, where the Arabic *hummá al-diqq*, "hectic fever" is rendered in Latin as *etice*.

After the sections on fevers and muscular spasms, the books concerned with urine, both diagnostic and therapeutic (Books 46 and 90), have the largest number of Latin annotations. The reader displays an interest in the diagnostic significance of thin or thick urine and also in diabetes (*Cura dyabetis*), incontinence, and the painful discharge of urine.[17] The retention and evacuation of fluids of all sorts seems to be of interest to the Latin reader, with particular attention given to discussions of a state of evacuation involving both vomiting and diarrhoea (Book 37).[18] Later in the same book, the annotator drew attention to passages concerned with *qawlanj* (rendered as *yleos* in Latin), which means not only abdominal pain and colic but also obstruction of the intestines.[19] On the next page, alongside a passage saying that phlegmatic superfluity, when it is throughout the body, is fleshy dropsy, and when it affects only a single part, it is a tumour called *al-tarahhul* ("inflated, swollen"), the Latin annotator has written *Nota de apostemate flegmatico* as well as in Arabic script the word *al-tarahhul*.[20] In Book 38 (On Retention and Fluxion), attention is drawn to the causes of unwanted evacuation, the passing of blood, and diarrhoea and dysentery.[21] Migraine and dizziness get some attention in Book 66, as does pleurisy amongst the diseases of the chest in Book 76. The books on tumours and on pulse have only *Nota* annotations with no accompanying comments or a simple indication of the topic under discussion.

So, to summarize this document, what do we have? A Frankish reader annotating the text of a much admired Arabic medical digest written by a Christian Arab. The Arabic text in the manuscript is unusual in that the text is fully vocalized. In addition, the undotted letters carry diacritic marks (minuscule letters beneath or carons/*hačeks* above) so as to allow no ambiguity in the interpretation of both consonants and vowels. These two characteristics tempt one to speculate that the Arabic text might have been copied in 1196 expressly for the use of someone whose first language was not Arabic.[22]

---

[17] Fols. 158b, 159a, 240b, and 241a.

[18] Fol. 129b, where the term in Arabic for this condition is *al-haydah*, rendered as *colerica* in Latin, from which the modern term cholera is derived although it is an inappropriate translation of the medieval concept.

[19] Fol. 130a.

[20] Fol. 130b, where in the margin the Arabic word *al-tarahhul* appears to be written with the same ink and pen as the Latin note accompanying it.

[21] Fols. 132a, 133a, and 133b.

[22] The editor of the recent edition, Floréal Sanagustin, does not mention these orthographic conventions, though he does notice that the text has some misspellings or mis-dotting of letters (*gharad* for *'arad*, *thiql* for *thufl*, for example). In the instances given by the editor, however, the misspellings are exceptions and the words are written correctly elsewhere. In any case, the errors are no more frequent than what are encountered in other late twelfth-century or thirteenth-century copies of scientific or technical treatises where copyists are unfamiliar with the terminology (see, for example, the illustrated Arabic cosmography copied in the late twelfth or early thirteenth century now in Oxford, Bodleian Library, MS Arab. c. 90, described in a preliminary publication by Jeremy Johns and Emilie Savage-Smith, "*The Book of Curiosities*: A newly discovered series of Islamic maps," *Imago Mundi* 55 (2003), 7–24).

What are the clues as to the European origins of our annotator (or annotators)? An unusual "c" occurs in places (for example, in the word *cepe* on fol. 48a) and is close to that typical of Italian hands of 1250–90. Moreover, the use of a *g* in place of a *c* in certain words such as *De emigranea* instead of *De hemicrania* when discussing migraine (fol. 204a) is a typical Italian convention. The Hebrew or Judaeo-Arabic annotation on the final folio adds further weight to an Italian origin for our Frankish annotator. Others have suggested a non-Parisian French hand of the first quarter of the thirteenth century.[23] Closer analysis may reveal that there was more than one Latin hand. The different forms of the symbol for *Nota* may also suggest more than one Latin reader.

If the Latin *marginalia* were added in one of the crusader territories sometime between 1196 and 1400, as seems likely, then where and when would that have been? When the manuscript was copied, in 1196, the Latin Kingdom of Jerusalem (which included the Syrian coastline) had already fallen to Saladin in the aftermath of the Battle of Ḥaṭṭīn on 4 July 1187. In 1191, however, five years before the manuscript was copied, Saladin had confirmed to Richard I of England that the Franks would again be in possession of the settlements along the coast from Tyre south to Jaffa, including Acre, and that Christian pilgrims would have safe conduct to Jerusalem. Then in 1197, just a year after this manuscript was copied, the Franks recovered other portions of the Syrian coast, from Sidon north to Tripoli, including Beirut. In 1229 the Christians regained control of Jerusalem and Nazareth, only to lose control of Jerusalem again in 1244; and by 1245 most of Palestine was again in Muslim hands. But the Syrian coast remained in Frankish control until 1291, and Acre ('Akkā) was the principal centre of Christian power, with good lines of communication to Damascus. (And it is worth recalling that this manuscript ended up in Damascus.) Then in May 1291 Acre was sacked by the Mamluks, and by 1292 all the remaining Christian outposts in Syria had surrendered.[24]

Therefore, it is likely that the Latin annotations were made sometime between 1196 and 1291, and probably in the city of Acre, which had the best communications with Damascus. Though European trade with Syria and Egypt persisted, and even flourished, through the fourteenth and into the fifteenth century, after 1291 it seems less likely that a Frank would have had access and sufficient time to make the annotations.

---

[23] Various suggestions have been kindly offered by Bruce Barker-Benfield, Charles Burnett, Cristina Dondi, and Martin Kaufmann. It is hoped that a full analysis of all the Latin annotations and corresponding Arabic passages will be published in the near future in collaboration with Charles Burnett.

[24] Joshua Prawer, *Crusader Institutions* (Oxford, 1980); David Abulafia, "The Role of Trade in Muslim–Christian Contact During the Middle Ages," in *The Arab Influence in Medieval Europe: Folia Scholastica Mediterranea*, ed. Dionisius A. Agius and Richard Hitchcock (Reading, 1994), pp. 1–24; Jonathan Riley-Smith, "Government in Latin Syria and the commercial privileges of the foreign merchants," in *Relations between East and West in the Middle Ages*, ed. Derek Baker (Edinburgh, 1973); and David Abulafia, "Crocuses and Crusaders: San Gimignano, Pisa and the Kingdom of Jerusalem," in *Outremer*, pp. 227–43.

The interests of our Latin reader, or readers, were fairly circumscribed: a few foods, migraine, vertigo, digestive and urinary problems, diagnosis of tremors, categorizing fevers. There is no concern with treatment of battle wounds, leprosy, skin lesions, or broken bones. Furthermore, the fact that Abū Sahl al-Masīḥī's treatise did not include surgical techniques meant that those topics could not be annotated by a Frankish reader, though the annotator could, had he wished, have added such material in the marginalia. Nonetheless, given the rarity of comparable material, the presence of Latin *marginalia* in this twelfth-century copy of a tenth-century text is of considerable historical importance. Moreover, Arabic material of any subject matter annotated by Europeans in the crusader states is most unusual.[25] The significance of this manuscript is further enhanced by the fact that the numerous owners' notes in the volume provide additional evidence that the volume remained in Syria until it came into the collections of the Bodleian Library. Furthermore, during the interval between the marginalia being placed in it and its coming to Oxford, the volume was for a time used by a physician in the Nūrī hospital in Damascus, where its author Abū Sahl al-Masīḥī was so admired for having composed an important medical treatise written in excellent Arabic – for a Christian – and also, very possibly, for having instructed Avicenna in the art.

---

[25] In the published literature, only one example has been cited: Istanbul, Topkapı Sarayı, Ahmet III MS 3362, which is an Arabic translation of Aristotle's *Categories* annotated with Latin definitions taken from Boethius' version of the same treatise (see Charles Burnett, "Antioch as a Link between Arabic and Latin Culture in the Twelfth and Thirteenth Centuries", in *Occident et Proche-Orient: Contacts scientifiques au temps des Croisades*, ed. Isabelle Draelants, Anne Tihon, and Baudouin van den Abeele (Louvain-la-Neuve, 1999), pp. 1–78, esp. p. 75 Plate 6). The age and provenance of the manuscript are unknown, but it has been suggested that the Latin hand in the annotations is similar to a hand that annotated a Latin manuscript, now in Milan, copied in the first half of the twelfth century for Stephen the Philosopher working in Antioch (Biblioteca Ambrosiana, Cod. E. 7 sup.); see Burnett, "Antioch as a Link," pp. 67, 71, and 77). If it were true that the Latin annotations in the Istanbul manuscript were added in the twelfth century in Antioch, then it would pre-date the Bodleian manuscript by at least half a century. Until the age and provenance of the Istanbul manuscript can be ascertained, however, its history remains uncertain. I am grateful to Charles Burnett for bringing this material to my attention. A copy made in 1130 (524 H) for the rulers of Saragossa of the treatise on *materia medica* by Ibn Biklārish (fl. 1100), having extensive Latin annotations, has recently come to light and is the subject of current research; there is, however, no apparent association with the crusader states.

## Appendix: Three medieval accounts of Abū Sahl ʿĪsá ibn Yaḥyá al-Masīḥī.

A.  From Ibn al-Qifṭī (d. 1248), *Taʾrīkh al-ḥukamāʾ*, ed. Julius Lippert (Leipzig, 1903), pp. 408–409

Abū Sahl al-Masīḥī *al-mutaṭabbib*. A physician (*ṭabīb*) who was an excellent logician, distinguished, learned in the sciences of the Ancients, well-known in his land. In Khurāsān he was prominently positioned with its ruler, and he was outstanding in his art. He wrote a handbook (*kunnāsh*) known as "The Hundred Chapters" that was well-known. Famous, he died in the prime of life (*fī sinn al-kuhālah*).

B.  From Ibn Abī Uṣaybiʿah (d. 1270), *Uyūn al-anbāʾ fī ṭabaqāt al-aṭibbā*, ed. A. Müller, 2 vols. (Cairo, 1882–84), 1:327–28

Abū Sahl al-Masīḥī – that is, Abū Sahl ʿĪsá ibn Yahyá al-Masīḥī al-Jurjāni. A distinguished physician, outstandingly proficient in the art of medicine, both its theory and its practice, skilful in using the correct Arabic expressions (*faṣīḥ al-ʿibārah*), and a first-rate writer. He had good penmanship in Arabic. I have seen, written in his own hand, his book "On the Revelation of God's Wisdom in the Creation of Mankind" (*Fī iẓhār ḥikmat Allāh taʿālá fī khalq al-insān*), and it was the ultimate of veracity, perfection, correct grammatical expression (*iʿrāb*), and vocalization of Arabic script (*ḍabṭ*). And this book was the best of his books and the most useful, for he had presented in it, with the greatest possible logical arrangement and clarity, a summary of what Galen and others had said about the uses of the parts, augmented with insights of his own displaying brilliant erudition and venerable learning.

For example [lit. therefore], he says in the first of this book of his: No one can understand the superiority of what we have presented over what they [others] have presented except someone who compares, knowledgeably and fairly on his part, our discourse with theirs. For anyone who is not knowledgeable about what we are on about is not soundly equipped to pass judgment on it; and he who is not fair is not able to judge and choose. But those fit for consideration, being fair scholars, apprehending and distinguishing what we have said as opposed to what others have said, will see how we have made sound [that is, improved] what they put down. We polished and completed and smoothed it out, and set it in better order not only for the entire discourse and for every individual section. And we cut out from this branch of knowledge whatever does not belong to it. Then [he will see] how much we added on our own – subtle, admirable additions that were hidden from them because of their [the arguments'] subtleness and their high level. [He will see] how we have arranged the explanations of things from first to last [that is, in a logical order], in contrast to what they did. For our exposition of things by principles and causes provides a true demonstration/proof.

I heard the *shaykh* Muhadhdhab al-Dīn ʿAbd al-Raḥīm ibn ʿAlī [known as al-Dakhwār, the teacher of Ibn Abī Uṣaybiʿah] say: "I have not found any one amongst the Christian physicians, ancient or modern, who is more skilful in using Arabic expressions (*afṣaḥ ʿibārah*) or better in pronunciation (*lafẓ*) or more pleasing in rhetorical/figurative expression (*maʿnan*) than Abū Sahl al-Masīḥī."

And it is said that al-Masīḥī was the teacher of al-Shaykh al-Raʾīs [that is, Avicenna] for the art of medicine, and that afterwards Ibn Sīnā became very distinguished in the art of medicine and expert in it and in the philosophical branches of learning, so that he composed a book dedicated to al-Masīḥī.

ʿUbayd Allāh ibn Jībraʾīl [d. 1058, a member of the influential Bukhtīshūʿ family] said that al-Masīḥī was at Khurāsān and was prominently positioned with its ruler and that he died having reached the age of 40 years.

Amongst the sayings of al-Masīḥī:

> "Sleeping during the day after a meal is preferable to drinking a medicinal remedy."

The books of al-Masīḥī:

> *Kitāb* [*sic*] *al-miʾah fī al-ṭibb* (The hundred books on medicine), which is the best of his books and the most famous. Amīn al-Dawlah ibn al-Tilmīdh [d. 1154 or 1165] wrote glosses on it, and he said that he required that this book be used, for it had the greatest veracity and the least repetition, as well as clarity of writing, and [best] selection of therapies.
>
> *Kitāb Iẓhār ḥikmat Allāh taʿálá fī khalq al-insān* (On the revelation of God's wisdom in the creation of mankind)
>
> *Kitāb fī al-ʿilm al-ṭabīʿī* (Book on natural science)
>
> *Kitāb al-Ṭibb al-kullī* (The book of comprehensive medicine)
>
> *Maqālah fī al-judarī* (Essay on smallpox)
>
> *Ikhtisār Kitāb al-Majisṭī* (Epitome of [Ptolemy's] *Almagest*)
>
> *Kitāb taʿbīr al-ruʾyā* (Book on the interpretation of dreams)
>
> *Kitāb fī al-wabāʾ* (Book on the plague) which he wrote for Khwārazmshāh Abū al-ʿAbbās Maʾmūn ibn Maʾmūn.

C: From Niẓāmī-i ʿArūḍī (12th-century), *Chahār maqālah*, 4th discourse. The translation is that (slightly amended) of Edward G. Browne, *Revised Translation of the Chahár Maqála ('Four discourses') of Niẓámí-i-ʿArúḍí of Samarqand* (London, 1921), pp 78–79 and 85–87.

On the science of medicine the student should procure and read the "Aphorisms" of Hippocrates, ... Then he should take up one of the more detailed treatises, such as the "Sixteen Treatises" of Galen, the "Continens" (*Ḥāwī*) of Muḥammad ibn Zakariyā' al-Rāzī [d. c. 925], or the "Complete Guide to the Art" [by ʿAlī ibn al-ʿAbbās al-Majūsī, fl. 949–982], or the "Hundred Chapters" of Abū Sahl ibn Masīḥī, or the *Qānūn* of Abū ʿAlī ibn Sīnā [Avicenna], or the *Dhakhīra-i Khwārazm-shāhī* [by al-Jurjānī, d. c. 1136]. ...

Abū al-ʿAbbās Maʾmūn Khwārazmshāh [reg. 1009–17 in Gurgānj in the province of Khwārazm] had a minister named Abū al-Ḥusayn Aḥmad ibn Muḥammad al-Suhaylī. He was a man of philosophical disposition, magnanimous nature and scholarly tastes, while Khwārazmshāh likewise was a philosopher and friend of scholars. In consequence of this, many philosophers and men of erudition, such as Abū ʿAli ibn Sīnā, Abū Sahl ibn Masīḥī, Abū al-Khayr ibn al-Khammār, Abū Naṣr ibn ʿArrāq, and Abū Rayḥān al-Bīrūnī, gathered about his court.

Now Abū Naṣr ibn ʿArrāq was the nephew of Khwārazmshāh and in all branches of mathematics he was second only to Ptolemy; and Abū al-Khayr ibn al-Khammār was the third after Hippocrates and Galen in the science of medicine; and Abū Rayḥān [al-Bīrūnī] in astronomy held the position of Abū Maʿshar and Aḥmad ibn ʿAbd al-Jalīl; while Abū ʿAlī [ibn Sīnā] and Abū Sahl Masīḥī were the successors of Aristotle in the science of philosophy, which includes all sciences. And all these were, in this their service, independent of worldly cares, and maintained with one another familiar intercourse and pleasant correspondence.

But Fortune disapproved of this and Heaven disallowed it; their pleasure was spoiled and their happy life was marred. A notable arrived from Sulṭān Maḥmūd Yamīn al-Dawlah [reg. in Ghazna 998–1030] with a letter, whereof the purport was as follows: "I have heard that there are in attendance on Khwārazmshāh several men of learning who are beyond compare, such as so-and-so and so-and-so. Thou must send them to my court, so that they may attain the honour of attendance thereat, while we may profit by their knowledge and skill. So shall we be much beholden to Khwārazmshāh."

Now the bearer of this message was Khwājah Ḥusayn ibn ʿAlī ibn Mikāʾīl ... So Khwārazmshāh assigned to him the best of lodgings and ordered him the most ample entertainment; but, before according him an audience, he summoned the philosophers and laid before them the King's letter, saying: "Maḥmūd hath a strong hand and a large army: he hath annexed Khurāsān and India and covets Iraq, and I cannot refuse to obey his order or execute his mandate. What say you on this matter?"

Abū ʿAlī ibn Sīnā and Abū Sahl [al-Masīḥī] answered: "We will not go." But Abū
Naṣr [ibn ʿArrāq], Abū al-Khayr [ibn al-Khammār], and Abū Rayḥān [al-Bīrūnī]
were eager to go, having heard accounts of the king's munificent gifts and presents.
Then said Khwārazmshāh, "Do you two, who have no wish to go, take your own
way before I give audience to this man." Then he equipped Abū ʿAlī [ibn Sīnā] and
Abū Sahl [al-Masīḥī], and sent with them a guide, and they set off by the way of the
wolves [that is, across the desert?] towards Gurgān/Jurjān.

Next day Khwārazmshāh accorded Ḥusayn ibn ʿAlī ibn Mīkāʾīl an audience, and
heaped on him all sorts of favours. "I have read the letter," said he, "and have
acquainted myself with its contents and the King's command. Abū ʿAlī [ibn Sīnā]
and Abū Sahl [al-Masīḥī] are gone, but Abū Naṣr [ibn ʿArrāq], Abū Rayḥān [al-
Bīrūnī], and Abū al-Khayr [ibn al-Khammār] are making their preparations to
appear at [Maḥmūd's] court." …

… Now when Abū ʿAlī [ibn Sīnā] and Abū Sahl [al-Masīḥī] departed from the
Khwārazmshāh with Abū al-Ḥusayn al-Suhaylī's man, they were so wrought up that
before morning they had travelled 15 farsangs. When it was morning they alighted at
a place where there were wells, and Abū ʿAlī [ibn Sīnā] took up an astrological table
to see under what Ascendant they had started on their journey. When he had
examined it, he turned to Abū Sahl [al-Masīḥī] and said: "Judging by this Ascendant
under which we started, we shall lose our way and experience grievous hardships."
Abū Sahl [al-Masīḥī] replied: "We acquiesce in God's decree. Indeed, I know that I
shall not come safely through this journey, for during these two days the passage of
the degree of my Ascendant falls in Capricorn, which is the [ominous] sector, so that
no hope remains to me. Henceforth, only the intercourse of souls will exist between
us." So they rode on.

Abū ʿAlī [ibn Sīnā] relates that on the fourth day a wind arose and stirred up the
dust, so that the world was darkened. They lost their way, for the wind had
obliterated the tracks. When the wind lulled, their guide was more astray than they
were. And, in the heat of the desert of Khwārazm, Abū Sahl ibn Masīḥī, through lack
of water and thirst, passed away to the World of Eternity, while the guide, along with
Abū ʿAli [ibn Sīnā], after experiencing a thousand hardships, reached … .

# Stephen, the Disciple of Philosophy, and the Exchange of Medical Learning in Antioch[1]

## Charles Burnett

Warburg Institute, London

From the early years of the Common Era, Antioch had held a position of cultural and ecclesiastical prominence. As one of the four seats of the patriarchs in early Christianity, it was always a meeting place for scholars and church dignitaries, and several religious houses and libraries became established in the city. When Antioch capitulated to the First Crusaders in 1098 the population included Greek Orthodox, Arabic Melchite and Jacobite Christians, Muslims and Jews. Arabic was the dominant language, but Christianity was the dominant religion, while the Norman princes attracted immigrants whose language of learning was Latin. This would seem to provide ample opportunities for exchange between Arabic, Latin, Greek and Frankish culture, and in recent years this is precisely what we have found to be the case.[2] One of the pioneers in Latin translations from Arabic in the early twelfth century, Adelard of Bath, spent some time in the principality of Antioch, probably arriving there in the wake of the First Crusaders, and perhaps learning Arabic and picking up locally some of the manuscripts that he later translated. It is significant that of two experiences that he relates concerning his sojourn in the principality, one concerns a lecture on medicine. This is his story of how a certain old man in Tarsus in Cilicia (which formed part of the principality) taught him how the web of the sinews of the human body could be detected by suspending a cadaver in flowing water.[3]

---

[1]  This article summarises and brings up to date the information on Stephen of Antioch published in my earlier articles, "'Abd al-Masih of Winchester," in *Between Demonstration and Imagination: Essays on the History of Science and Philosophy Presented to John D. North*, ed. Lodi Nauta and Arjo Vanderjagt (Leiden, 1999), pp. 59–69; "Antioch as a Link between Arabic and Latin Culture in the Twelfth and Thirteenth Centuries," in *Occident et Proche-Orient: contacts scientifiques au temps des croisades*, ed. I. Draelants, Anne Tihon and Baudouin van den Abeele (Louvain-la-Neuve, 2000), pp. 1–78, and "The Transmission of Arabic Astronomy via Antioch and Pisa in the Second Quarter of the Twelfth Century," in *The Enterprise of Science in Islam: New Perspectives*, ed. Jan P. Hogendijk and Abdelhamid. I. Sabra (Cambridge, MA, 2003), pp. 23–51. An earlier version of this article was presented in January 2005 at the symposium on Medicine and Disease in the Crusades, held at the Wellcome Trust Centre for the History of Medicine, University College, London.

[2]  See the collection of articles by Benjamin Z. Kedar, *The Franks in the Levant, 11th to 14th Centuries* (Aldershot, 1993), Rudolf Hiestand, "Un centre intellectuel en Syrie du Nord? Notes sur la personnalité d'Aimery d'Antioche, Albert de Tarse et Rorgo Fretellus," *Le Moyen Age* 100 (1994), 7–36, and L. Minervini, "Outremer," in *Lo spazio letterario del Medioevo, 2. Il Medioevo volgare*, ed. Piero Boitani, Mario Mancini, Alberto Vàrvaro, 2 vols. (Rome, 2001), 1:611–48.

[3]  Adelard of Bath, Questiones naturales, Q16, in Adelard of Bath, *Conversations with His Nephew: On the Same and the Different, Questions on Natural Science, and On Birds*, ed. Charles Burnett, Italo Ronca, Pedro Mantas España and Baudouin van den Abeele (Cambridge, 1998), p. 122.

A little later in the same century we have more evidence of translating activity taking place within Antioch itself. This is in the person of a certain Stephen, "the disciple of philosophy," whose translations of the various books of the medical compendium, *The Royal Book on Medicine* (*Liber regalis dispositionis*) by 'Ali ibn al-'Abbas al-Majusi (*Haliabbas* in its Latin form), were copied out on specific days within the year 1127 and at Antioch.[4] This translation is not an isolated phenomenon, but can be located within a larger movement of transmission of learning occurring at this time and in this place. Stephen himself gives a clue that his translation of a medical work (significant though it is) is only a prelude to translating more; for, in his preface he writes:

> We have decided to devote the effort of our labour first to these books (of medicine), although the Arabic language has, hidden within it, other things more noble than these: namely, all the secrets of philosophy, to the translating of which, afterwards, if God is kind, we shall devote our skill once it has become practised. We have put these easier subjects first, so that there is a path for us to the more difficult ones, and we provide first what is necessary for bodies so that, when healing has been secured for these by the art of medicine, what belongs to the excellence of the mind, being much more lofty, should follow.[5]

One of these "more lofty" texts is a translation of *On the Configuration of the World* (*Maqala fi hay'at al-'alam*) by Ibn al-Haytham (d. after 1040), which Stephen (now called simply "the Philosopher") entitled *Liber Mamonis*, interspersed with an extensive commentary of his own.[6] In this work Stephen refers to tables that he has translated. These may have some connection with the "Tables of Pisa" that were drawn up in 1149 and were based on lost tables by the astronomer al-Sufi (d. 986), which had presumably been prepared for Baghdad. At least one more astronomical work can be brought into this context, namely a translation of Ptolemy's *Almagest* made by a scholar who called himself *wittoniensis ebdelmessie*, which should mean "the man from Winchester (in Latin) who is the servant of the Messiah (in Arabic)." This translation of the *Almagest*, known from its sole manuscript as the "Dresden *Almagest*," incorporates several references to Euclid's *Elements* that are not in the

---

[4] I shall refer to this text as *The Royal Book*. The title of Stephen's translation in the manuscripts and early printed editions is given in the incipit as "Liber medicine qui dicitur regalis" (+ "dispositio" in the printed editions), and in the explicit as "liber regalis dispositio nominatus in arte medicine completus."

[5] Burnett, "Antioch", p. 31: "His igitur in libris nostri primum consumere laboris proposuimus operam, tametsi alia his preclariora lingua habeat apud se Arabica recondita: omnia scilicet philosophie arcana, quibus deinceps, si divina dederit benignitas, exercitatum dabimus transferendis ingenium."

[6] The identification of Ibn al-Haytham's work was made by Richard Lemay who was preparing an edition of the text at the time of his death in May 2004. It is worth noting that this is the earliest of several translations of this Arabic work, into Latin and into Hebrew, and that its sole Latin manuscript pre-dates any Arabic manuscript of the text by a century. For other Hebrew and Latin translations, see Y. Tzvi Langermann, *Ibn al Haytham's On the Configuration of the World* (New York and London, 1990), pp. 34–41.

original Greek text, and a whole extra section that matches very closely a substantial part of a work by an eleventh-century Baghdadi mathematician, al-Nasawi: the *Sufficient Explanation of the Sector-Figure.*[7] The common features of these texts are:

1   The use of Eastern Arabic authors (Ibn al-Haytham, al-Sufi, and al-Nasawi): it is worth noting that no work of any of these authors was translated by Gerard of Cremona in Toledo later in the same century (or, for that matter, by any other translator in the Iberian peninsula until the mid-thirteenth century), although Gerard was interested in precisely these topics.

2   The use of the same, rather unusual, astronomical terminology in the *Liber Mamonis* and the Dresden *Almagest*.

3   The use of Greek terms and correct transliterations of Greek names in the Arabic texts. The abundance of Greek words and the quality of the transliterations in the Dresden *Almagest* for a long time led scholars to regard the work as a translation from Greek rather than from Arabic. But the *Liber Mamonis* also refers to Ptolemy's *Almagest* by its Greek name – *Syntaxis*, and the *Royal Book* includes a Greek glossary and many Greek terms as translations of Arabic medical vocabulary. This Greek element suggests that Greek scholars and/or manuscripts were available as well as Arabic, a situation that was possible in Antioch, but not so likely in the Iberian peninsula or northern Italy.

4   The use of Latin alphanumerical notation: in other words, using the letters of the Latin alphabet to represent numerals in the same way as the letters of the Greek, Arabic and Hebrew alphabets are used to represent numerals. This experiment in alphanumerical notation is limited almost exclusively to these texts. It spread to Pisa, since it is used in the earliest manuscript of the "Tables of Pisa," and in another self-standing astronomical table in a manuscript that was in Lucca, Pisa's close neighbour, before 1160. One could argue that Stephen of Antioch, who came from Pisa, introduced a convention of Tuscan mathematicians to Antioch, but it is more plausible, I think, that an alphanumerical system was devised in Antioch where the models of Greek and Arabic were so close at hand. This, moreover, has some support from another witness to this notation: namely a manuscript of the *Rhetorica ad Herennium* that was copied in Antioch in 1121 by "Stephen the Treasurer," in which both the individual books and the figures of speech and thought have been numbered with this notation. This alphanumerical notation is also used in the fragment of a translation of Aristotle's *Physics* (the

---

[7]  See Burnett, "The Transmission of Arabic Astronomy," pp. 23–27. The corresponding passages are set side by side in Richard P. Lorch, *Thabit ibn Qurra on the Sector-Figure and Related Texts* (Frankfurt, 2001), pp. 355–57 (general discussion), 362–73 (parallel text) and 374–75. One may add that a "Stephanus Saracenus" appears in the Winton Domesday in 1148, and that the preface to a version of the Pisan tables which refers to the meridian of Winchester in MS British Library, Arundel 377, fols. 56v–63r also gives a starting point of 1149 complete years (see Burnett, "'Abd-al-Masih").

*Physica Vaticana*) which was made by the same scholar as one Latin version of Aristotle's *Metaphysics*.[8] No one has doubted that these translations were made from Greek, but that does not, of course, preclude the possibility that they were made in Antioch, and even by Stephen, who obviously knew some Greek.

5 Both the dates of the completion of the books of the *Royal Book* and of the copying of the *Rhetorica ad Herennium* are in the form of "from the year of the passion of our Lord" (*anno a passione Domini*), an unusual formula, which evidently indicates the starting date of the year (Easter) rather than 33 years after the "year of the nativity."

One must add a further feature which is common to most of these texts. They had virtually no influence: the *Liber Mamonis*, the Dresden *Almagest* and the *Physica Vaticana* each survive incomplete in a single manuscript. The original text of al-Sufi's astronomical tables has disappeared completely, both in the original Arabic and in its Latin translation, although through its adaptation to the meridian of Pisa, which was evidently due to the Jewish polymath Abraham ibn Ezra, it became the model for tables for the meridians of several cities in France and England. The exception to this rule is the *Royal Book* of Stephen of Antioch and Pisa; it is to this work that this paper will now turn.

Who was this Stephen? The manuscripts and early printed editions call him simply "Stephen the disciple of philosophy" (*Stephanus philosophie discipulus*). Later authors who refer to Stephen's version of the *Royal Book* call him "*Stephanon quidam Pisanus*" (*Magister Mathaeus F.*),[9] and "Stephen the nephew of the patriarch of Antioch" (*Stephanus nepos patriarche Antiochene*).[10] If we identify him with the "Stephen the Treasurer" for whom the *Rhetorica ad Herennium* was copied, then we might be able to go further and recognize him as the treasurer of the church of St. Paul, who had been supplied with a house by Bernard, patriarch of Antioch (his uncle?), sometime between 1126 and 1130.[11] Stephen's residence in Antioch seems to be assured. What is less clear is what connection he had with Pisa. There were undoubtedly strong lines of communication between Pisa and Antioch, not least because of the fact that the Pisans had possessed a quarter in Antioch since 1108, and we have seen how the Pisan tables belong to the same context as Stephen's

---

[8] Charles Burnett, "A Note on The Origins of the Physica Vaticana and Metaphysica media," in *Tradition et traduction: les textes philosophiques et scientifiques grecs au moyen âge latin. Hommage à Fernand Bossier*, ed. Rita Beyers et al. (Leuven, 1999), pp. 59–69.

[9] In Erfurt, Wissensch. Bibl., Amplon., O 62, fol. 50r: see Rudolf Creutz, "Die Ehrenrettung Konstantins von Afrika," *Studien und Mitteilungen zur Geschichte des Benediktiner-Ordens und seiner Zweige* 49 (1931), 25–44 (at p. 41).

[10] MS London, British Library, Sloane 2426, fol. 8r. The passage is transcribed and translated in Charles Singer, "A Legend of Salerno: How Constantine the African Brought the Art of Medicine to the Christians," *The Johns Hopkins Hospital Bulletin* 28, no. 311 (1917), 64–69.

[11] This was the proposal of Richard W. Hunt in "Stephen of Antioch," *Medieval and Renaissance Studies* 6 (1950), 172–73.

works. Most relevant for us is the fact that the transmission of al-Majusi's *Royal Book* has links with Pisa even before Stephen comes onto the scene.

The *Royal Book* had first been translated under the title *Pantegni* by Constantine the African, presumably at the Benedictine Abbey of Montecassino, since Constantine became a monk there. The work was dedicated to the famous abbot of the monastery, Desiderius (abbot from 1058 to 1087), and Benedictine monasteries are prominent among the centres possessing the earliest copies.[12] But Constantine did not provide a faithful translation of the whole text, nor, in all likelihood, did he intend to. Rather, he described himself as an "author in the sense of compiler from many books" (*auctor quia ex multorum libris coadunator*) and appears to have used al-Majusi's work as a template for this compilation. For most of the first ten books (the *Theorica*), the *Royal Book* is the main source, but for the second set of ten books (the *Practica*), the *Royal Book* is employed only for the first of them,[13] and the first parts of the second and ninth. For the remaining books, the order of topics of the *Royal Book* is observed, but the material is taken for the most part from elsewhere: from other works translated by Constantine (for example, Ibn al-Jazzar's *Viaticum*, *On Gout* and *On the Degrees of Compound Medicines*, Ishaq al-Isra'ili's *On Fevers*) and works of the Latin tradition.[14] While the actual form of the 20-book *Pantegni*, therefore, corresponds reasonably to Constantine's claim that he was compiling the book from various sources, we cannot be certain that Constantine himself completed the compilation, since the earlier manuscripts of the *Pantegni* only include the first ten books (the *Theorica*) and, at most, Book 1, and the first parts of Books 2 and 9 of the *Practica*, which were those parts which are derived from al-Majusi's work. It is evidently a version of the *Pantegni* similar to this that Stephen came across, and concerning which he records his impassioned reaction:

> Following the injunction of Solomon, for the sake of wisdom I examined thoroughly not only the Latin language, but Arabic as well, so that the more languages I knew, the more clearly I would understand what I had already had an inkling of as a babe in philosophy: what [wisdom] was, how great it was and what it was like.[15] Thus I stumbled upon a certain book which among the Arabs is called "the completion of medicine" and "royal."[16] On investigating whether Latin culture had any portion of this book, I found that it lacked the second and larger part, but that the first part had been disfigured by the cunning fraud

---

[12] See Raphaela Veit, "Quellenkundliches zu Leben und Werk von Constantinus Africanus," *Deutsches Archiv für Erforschung des Mittelalters* 59 (2003), 121–52.

[13] Even this book lacked at least one chapter: see Appendix below.

[14] For an analysis of the sources of individual books see the relevant articles in *Constantine the African and 'Ali ibn al-'Abbas al-Magusi: the Pantegni and Related Texts*, ed. Charles Burnett and Danielle Jacquart (Leiden, 1994), especially Monica Green, "The Re-Creation of Pantegni, Practica, Book VIII," on pp. 121–60; and Raphaela Veit, *Das Buch der Fieber des Isaac Israeli und seine Bedeutung im lateinischen Westen* (Stuttgart, 2004), pp. 268–302.

[15] This implies that he had had a training in the seven liberal arts (= philosophia), and that his experience of Latin literature preceded that of Arabic.

[16] These are reasonably close translations of the alternative names for al-Majusi's book: *al-Kamil fi 'l-tibb* and *al-malaki*, respectively.

of the interpreter. For he had taken out the name of the author and the title, and both made himself the creator (*inventor*) of the book – he who had merely been the interpreter – and had entitled the book with his own name. To do this more easily he missed out many necessary things both in the prologue to the book and in many other places, and, changing the order of much of the subject matter, he put forward some things in a different way, observing this one thing alone: that he added nothing at all of his own. In this he showed himself clearly to us to have been the interpreter rather than the writer. Therefore, he should rather be condemned who, when he translates the book of another author from one language into another, by some overconfidence or impudence has not blushed either to take away from the author what he had laboured over, or to usurp that material for himself. Since this procedure does not please us at all, and this book is very necessary for the life of man, and is outstanding for its learning, we also approach the task of translating this book, but follow another method: ascribing to the author what is his, and to ourselves what belongs to the interpreter, so that what was lacking in Latin is supplied, what was placed in the wrong position is restored to its proper position, and what was put forward wrongly is translated as it is in Arabic.[17]

What can we glean from these passionate statements? First, that, apparently, Stephen came across the Arabic text before Constantine's translation. Second, that the process of completion of the *Pantegni* had hardly begun when Stephen saw it, since, according to him, the second part (the *Practica*) was missing. Moreover, he does not accuse Constantine of adding material from sources other than al-Majusi, which only applies to the completed version. And third, that he saw his task as completing the work, and remedying the deficiencies of Constantine's translation, by means of a detailed comparison with the Arabic text. We can, therefore, see two radically different methods of completing the *Pantegni*, which were probably being used at the same time, but in different places: (1) filling in the gaps in the *Practica* by using pre-existent Latin translations from Arabic and medical works of the Latin tradition; (2) filling in the gaps by going back to an Arabic manuscript of the *Royal Book*. Stephen, in his prologue, appears to be promising to follow the second method. In this he had, as far as we can see, a precursor. For there is a note in two twelfth-century manuscripts, after chapter 43 of *Practica*, Book 9, that "Constantine the African translated this far … ." One of these manuscripts (Montecassino 200 V) states that the book was completed "by a certain Saracen," the other (now Berlin, lat. fol. 74) gives more details: "the rest of book nine of the *Practica* was translated by the doctor John – a Saracen who had recently converted to the Christian faith – and Rusticus of Pisa, son of Bella and a physician by profession, on the expedition to besiege Majorca."[18] The event referred to is the attempt of the Pisans to oust the Arabs from Majorca in a siege which lasted from 1114 to 1115.

---

[17] For the Latin text see Burnett, "Antioch," pp. 26–27.

[18] "Huc [Nunc MS] usque Constantinus Affricanus philosophus ac nobilis medicus translator fidelissimus huius none particule cirurgie practice extitit. Dehinc in expeditione ad obsessionem Maiorice Iohannes quidam Agarenus quondam, qui noviter ad fidem Christiane religionis venerat, cum Rustico Pisano, Belle filius ac professione medicus [these nominatives instead of the expected ablatives

It may be significant that Book 9 receives this treatment, because this is the book on surgery. It circulated without the rest of the *Pantegni* in several manuscripts,[19] and would presumably have been particularly useful on the battlefield. In the Montecassino manuscript the part added by John and Rusticus occurs alone. In the Berlin manuscript, however, both parts of Book 9 are incorporated into a complete *Practica*, the other books of which are in the translation of Stephen. Such a hybrid *Practica* could well be called, as it is by Magister Mathaeus in the thirteenth century, "the Practica Pantegni and Stephanonis."[20] Thus we may hypothesize that the first method of completion is distinctive of the immediate entourage of Constantine and may well have taken place in Montecassino, Salerno and Naples, while the second method is specifically associated with Pisa and Antioch. John the Saracen and Rusticus could have brought an Arabic manuscript of the *Royal Book* to Pisa, and this could have been the manuscript that Stephen saw. However, the situation is not as simple as this. For the earliest manuscript of Stephen's translation (MS Worcester, Cathedral Library, F. 40) omits *Practica* Book 9, and it is possible that the scribe of the Berlin manuscript had such a text (the *Practica* without Book 9) in front of him and added the *Pantegni* Book 9 from elsewhere.

In spite of his claim in his prologue, Stephen did not merely revise and complete Constantine's text by reference to the Arabic. Rather he provided a completely new translation, including, eventually, one of *Practica* Book 9. And he produced this translation in Antioch, as is stated clearly at the end of each of the books. The only indication that he still had a copy of the *Pantegni* with him is a note after the end of the first part of the *Royal Book* (the *Theorica*) where we read: "We found in Latin a chapter which the Arabic truth (*veritas*) does not have, coming after the eighth chapter of the tenth book (of the *Theorica*). Whoever is moved to want to search for this should look at the old translation, since we [emphatic *nos*] are translators only of what was in the Arabic truth."[21] Otherwise it is striking how independent Stephen's

---

are in the manuscript] hanc nonam particulam Practice ad finem usque ad principium decime particule practice in Latinam linguam deo adiuvante transtulerunt:" Berlin, BS-PK, lat. fol. 74, transcribed in Valentin Rose, *Verzeichniss der lateinischen Handschriften der königlichen Bibliothek zu Berlin*, 2.3 (Berlin, 1905), p. 1061.

[19] Book 9 occurs alone in MSS Bethesda, National Library of Medicine, 8, Brussels, Bibliothèque royale, 2419–31 (first part), Erfurt, Wissen. Bibl., Amplon. F. 286 (first part) and Amplon. Q. 179 (incomplete), Montecassino, Biblioteca della Badia, 200 V (second part only), Oxford, Bodleian Library, Laud. Misc. 724 (both parts), and Tortosa, Archivo Capitular, 144 (first part).

[20] See reference in n. 9 above.

[21] "Invenimus autem in Latino capitulum quoddam quod Arabica non habet veritas: post capitulum octavum sermonis decimi qui intueri velle fatigatur a veteri requirat translatione, quoniam nos eorum tantum que in Arabica erant veritate translatores sumus." Haly filius Abbas, Liber totius medicine ... pr. Iacobus Myt (Lyons, 1523), fol. 134v, MS Vat. Lat. 234, fol. 162rb. The printed versions of the Royal Book (Liber regalis dispositionis) insert Constantine's chapter here. Stephen is slightly unfair to Constantine, since Constantine makes it quite clear that he has added this extra chapter, and he has done this because he finds the material on critical days in the Arabic text incomplete and unclear: cf. *Omnia Opera Ysaac* (Lyons, 1515), fol. 54ra: "placuit id subsequens intromitti ut planior daretur introducendis intellectus."

translation is from Constantine's. The usual pattern in medieval translations is for a later translator to take as his basis the earlier translation (as Stephen implies he is doing in the prologue). This is what we find, for example, in Burgundio of Pisa, whose translation of Nemesius' *On the Nature of Man* takes as its starting point Alphanus of Salerno's *Premnon phisicon*, in Gerard of Cremona's translation of ar-Razi's, *Liber ad Almansorem*,[22] and in several of William of Moerbeke's translations. Stephen's translation, however, seems to have been made in complete isolation from any other. This is apparent not only from the fact that it does not repeat any phrases in Constantine's *Pantegni*, but also in that it strikes out on its own in medical terminology. This is a point worth noting, because in general Constantine's terminology rapidly became accepted as the norm. It was followed, for example, by Gerard of Cremona in his medical translations. Stephen's terminology, however, is aberrant (just as the astronomical terminology used in the *Liber Mamonis* and Dresden *Almagest* differs from the usual forms). For example, in listing the ages of man, Stephen gives *grandiorum etas* as the third of the four ages,[23] instead of *senectus / etas perfectionis* found elsewhere. He also uses *porta* for *capitulum* (= chapter),[24] and *beatus* for *fortunatus* (of a planet).[25] Most striking is his list of the eight tastes. Constantine's terms for sharp, harsh, astringent and acrid (*acetosus, stipticus, ponticus, acutus*) are the standard. But Stephen's are quite different (*acerbus, ponticus, gallicus, pungitivus*).[26]

The question remains whether he used different terms deliberately, in order to represent the "Arabic truth" more accurately in his eyes, or whether the differences are on account of his ignorance of the standard terms. In his choice of terms (if he made a choice) he may well have been more influenced by the local vernacular than by earlier medical vocabulary. The use of *grandior* certainly sounds Frankish, as does *castaneus* for "brown" (cf. French *maron*)[27] and *grossus* for "fat" (glossed *crassus*).[28] Moreover, he frequently leaves Arabic terms for *materia medica* (foods and plants) in transcription in the text. In the manuscripts several of these words are glossed in the margin with a Latin equivalent: "*squingibim* (= sakanjabin) *i.e.*

---

[22] See Danielle Jacquart, "Note sur la traduction latine du Kitab al-Mansuri de Rhazes," *Revue d'Histoire des Textes* 24 (Paris, 1994), pp. 359–74, reprinted in eadem, *La science médicale occidentale entre deux renaissances (XIIe s.–XVe s.)* (Aldershot, 1997), article VIII.

[23] *Theorica* I, c. 20, MS Vat. Lat. 234, fol. 13vb.

[24] A literal translation of the Arabic *bab* = door/chapter: *Theorica* I, c. 3: "Decimus sermo .xxviii. portis clauditur ..." (MS Vat. Lat. 234, fol. 6ra).

[25] *Theorica* I, ch. 3, MS Vat. Lat. 234, fol. 5rb.

[26] See Charles Burnett, "Sapores sunt octo: the Medieval Latin Terminology for the Eight Flavours," *Micrologus* 10 (2002), 99–112. Gallicus (for which Stephen also gives as equivalents *asper, durus* and *insuavis*) retains the etymological significance of the equivalent Arabic term *'afis*, which derives from *'afs* = "gall-apple" (*galla* in Latin).

[27] *Theorica* I, c. 10, MS Vat. Lat. 234, fol. 10ra (referring to hair colour).

[28] *Practica* I, c. 8, MS Vat. Lat. 234, fol. 167rb.

*sirupus acetosus*," "*iulab* (= julab)*, i.e. sirupus albus*,"[29] "*benefsegum* (=banafsaj)
*i.e. viole*,"[30] "*candari* (=kundur) *i.e. thuris*" (frankincense).[31] These marginal notes
are almost entirely limited either to giving Latin equivalents, and variant spellings of
the Arabic word (introduced by *id est*), or to indicating a variant reading (introduced
by *in al.*). Such notes could have been added subsequent to the translation of the
*Royal Book*. On the other hand, in that the notes are clearly set off in the margin,
away from the text, they could exemplify Stephen's own claim to distinguish clearly
between the words of the original author and the additions of the translator.[32] As
far as can be ascertained, there are no substantial comments by the translator aside
from the observation concerning the chapter on critical days at the end of the first
part of the *Royal Book*. Stephen's prologue implies that we should expect more,
such as the comments that Gerard supplied to his translation of ar-Razi's *Liber
ad Almansorem*,[33] or even the detailed commentary that Stephen inserted into his
translation of Ibn al-Haytham's *On the Configuration of the World*.

Stephen himself explains why he kept terms in Arabic, in the prologue to the
second part of the *Royal Book*:

> Since we are translating this work from the Arabic language, and almost all the names of
> medicines (*medicamina*) in it appear in the language of the Arabs and we Latins (*Latini*)
> were very unused to them,[34] we present them as they are in Arabic, sometimes, even those
> which are known to us, and in all cases, those that are unknown to us. But we have
> declined them as if they are Latin words.[35]

It may well be, then, that the Arabic words, like *banafsaj* and *kundur*, which have
Latin equivalents in the margin, are those which are known to Stephen. He goes on
to say:

> Had we not used this method, we could not have translated at all, since we have no one
> who knows both languages.[36] I preferred then to seem a little infirm [in my mastery of the

---

[29] *Practica* I, c. 4, MS Vat. Lat. 234, fol. 165ra.

[30] *Practica* I, c. 15, MS Vat. Lat. 234, fol. 174va.

[31] Note that Adelard of Bath, Stephen's predecessor in Antioch, had kept the word *kundur* in transcription in his translation of the text that is associated with his Antioch residence: Thabit ibn Qurra's *De imaginibus* (edition in progress).

[32] See p. 118 above.

[33] These notes are attributed to Gerard in the printed edition *Opera parva Abubetri filii Zacharie filii Arasi* ... (Lyon, 1511).

[34] Or, taking another reading (*Latina*), "we hardly had any common Latin terms for them."

[35] Burnett, "Antioch" (above, n. 1), pp. 35–36: "Set quoniam opus hoc ex Arabica transferimus lingua, omniaque hic fere posita medicaminum nomina Arabum proferuntur lingua, et nos Latini [v.l. Latina] parum habebamus assueta, prout sunt in Arabico ea proferimus etiam que cognita nobis sunt nonnunquam, que incognita ubique, set ad Latine formam declinationis inclinata." For examples of such declined Arabic words see Appendix below, p. 127.

[36] It seems strange that Stephen does not know anyone in Antioch who is competent in both Latin and Arabic.

languages] than not to transmit knowledge, since it is less of a task for someone to ask about a few things than about everything.[37]

At this point he draws an invidious comparison to Constantine's translation which, by contrast, lacks accounts of whole topics. Stephen, by contrast, goes out of his way to provide help for his reader:

> Yet we have not altogether consigned the reader to error and worry. We were able to benefit from something which the Orient provided, and place at the end of the whole work a breviary of all the *materia medica* that is in Dioscorides, presenting on one side the terms in Greek, on the other side, those in Arabic, so that whoever gets this book in his hands, can ask what each thing is if he finds a Greek, or indeed, if he finds an Arab speaker. For the terms that are only in Arabic, I have either presented them with their proper definitions (when I could), or said nothing about them at all. I intend to make an effort, if God gives me the opportunity, to insert the Latin names among the Greek and Arabic ones.[38]

In fact, God did give him the opportunity, because what we find in the manuscripts are not only the columns of Greek terms on the left hand side of the page and their equivalents in Arabic on the right, but a few Latin words written in a central column. In the earliest of these manuscripts (that of Worcester cathedral), the Greek words are written in green, the Arabic in red, and the Latin in black. The presence of both Greek and Arabic in the culture of Antioch made it possible for such a glossary to be compiled for the first time for a Latin reader.[39] Stephen, as we have seen, regards this as a benefit of the Orient, and he repeats this in the explicit to the *Breviarium* where he says: "This is what we have found up to now by our own effort in Syria concerning the interpretations of *materia medica* in Greek and Arabic."[40] A short preface introduces the *Breviarium* in which he says that he took pains to compare books of Dioscorides written in Greek and Arabic and repeats the injunction that

---

[37] Burnett, "Antioch," p. 36: "Nisi etenim sic, nulla esset nobis ad presens transferendi via, cum qui utrasque nosset nullum haberemus linguas. Malui igitur paulo infirmus videri quam scientiam non transferre quoniam minus est pauca quam omnia aliquem interrogare."

[38] Ibid., pp. 37–38: "Nec vero omnino lectorem errori et sollicitudini remisimus, set quod posse nobis fuit et Oriens habebat in totius operis fine omnium que apud Diascoridem sunt medicaminum breviarium subdidimus, hinc eorum Grece, illinc Arabice habens, ut in cuius venerit hoc opus manus, quid queque res sit aut Grecum si invenit aut certe Arabem, sit illi posse consulere. Reliqua vero que Arabica sunt tantum, aut propriis protulimus diffinitionibus, que quidem potuimus, aut omnino siluimus, studium daturi ut si quovis modo nobis posse gratia dederit divina, inter Greca et Arabica nomina inseramus Latina."

[39] "Synonyma" in different languages for names of simple medicines (materia medica) had already been provided in several Arabic medical writings, such as Ibn Biklarish's *Kitab al-Musta'ini* which includes Syriac, Greek, Andalusian and Saragossan Romance, Berber and some Latin equivalents: see Martin Levey, "The Pharmacological Table of Ibn Biklarish," *Journal of the History of Medicine* 26 (1971), 413–21.

[40] Burnett, "Antioch," pp. 39–40: "Hec sunt que in Siria ad presens nostra invenit manus de medicaminum interpretatione Grece et Arabice."

students wishing to identify the *materia medica* should consult Greek and Arabic speakers, which they could find in Sicily and Salerno.[41]

This last statement is revealing. Stephen is imagining that his readers are in Italy, not in the Latin East. The Orient has much to offer, but the schools were in the West. If the works translated in Antioch did not reach these centres of scholarship they were not copied, and this probably explains the very limited diffusion of the texts mentioned at the beginning of this paper. The *Royal Book*, however, had greater success. It was already being used by a doctor called Northungus in Hildesheim by 1140, and at about the same time a copy was being made in the *scriptorium* of Worcester cathedral. Two manuscripts, now in Leipzig and Berlin, and containing the first and second parts of the *Royal Book* respectively, appear to have been written in the same *scriptorium* in the twelfth century, and their distinctive illuminated initials resemble those of manuscripts from the South of France. It is tempting to think that these manuscripts were written in Montpellier, where the school of medicine rivalled that of Salerno. One problem was that the work was so large (especially with the addition of the trilingual glossary), and we find the second part copied on its own a few times (perhaps because doctors were aware that the second part of the *Pantegni* was, for the most part, not a translation of al-Majusi's work). The *Breviarium* provided a major source for the most learned and detailed glossary of medical synonyms of the Middle Ages, that of Simon of Genoa (*Clavis sanitatis*), written at the end of the thirteenth century; the source is acknowledged as "Stephanus in synonymio."[42] The accessibility to Stephen of the works of al-Majusi and Dioscorides in both Greek and Arabic is a testimony to what the Orient could contribute to Western culture in the twelfth century. What needs to be studied now is how the accessibility of such Arabic manuscripts relates to the Arabic culture of the time, and the relationships between Arabic and Frankish doctors in the crusader states.[43]

---

[41] Ibid., pp. 38–39.

[42] Danielle Jacquart, "La coexistence du grec et de l'arabe dans le vocabulaire médical du latin médiévale: l'effort linguistique de Simon de Gênes," in *Transfer de vocabulaire dans les sciences*, ed. Martine Groult (Paris, 1988), pp. 277–90 (see pp. 279 and 280), reprinted in eadem, *La science médicale occidentale entre deux renaissances (XIIe s.–XVe s.)* (Aldershot, 1997), article X; and M. Steinschneider, "Zur Literatur der Synonyma," in Julius L. Pagel, *Leben, Lehre und Leistungen des Heinrich von Mondeville (Hermondaville), 1. Die Chirurgie des Heinrich von Mondeville (Hermondaville)* (Berlin, 1892), pp. 582–95.

[43] A summary of what we know concerning contacts between Frankish and Syriac/Arabic physicians can be found in Piers D. Mitchell, *Medicine in the Crusades, Warfare, Wounds and the Medieval Surgeon* (Cambridge, 2004), pp. 33–40. Two Arabic manuscripts of the Royal Book, copied respectively in 1145 and 1170 (Paris, BNF, ar. 2874 and 2880), were brought to France from Aleppo in 1673, and two more manuscripts from the same source were copied in the eleventh century (Paris, BNF, ar. 2877 and 2878). MS Paris, BNF, ar. 2874, moreover, provides us with the names of two early owners, both described as doctors: 'Abd ar-Rahim ibn Abi Muhammad al-Adib and 'Isa al-Halabi (Jesus of Aleppo!): see Gérard Troupeau, "Les manuscrits du Kamil as-sina'a à la Bibliothèque nationale de Paris," in *Constantine the African* (above, n. 14), pp. 48–56 (at pp. 48–49).

## Appendix: Stephen of Antioch's Translation of the *Royal Book* and Pilgrimage

A curious example of Stephen of Antioch's "supplying what is lacking in Constantine's text" (see p. 118 above) relates to the last chapter (Chapter 31) of the first book of the *Practica* of the *Royal Book*. The Arabic title of this chapter is "About the regimen of travellers on land and sea" (*fī tadbir al-musāfirīn fī'l-barr wa-bahr*).[44] In the *Pantegni* this chapter is lacking, whereas Stephen's version has it, under the title "*De regimine peregrinantium arida aut mare*."[45] We find the following cases among the witnesses that contain the first book of the *Practica Pantegni*:

1 A list of chapter-headings that include what looks like an independent translation of the title of chapter 31 ("*De regimento ambulantium et equitantium et navigantium*"), but the chapter itself is absent: for example, in MSS London, British Library, Sloane 2814, and Paris, BNF, lat. 6887 and lat. 11223.
2 A list of 31 chapter-headings which correspond to the chapters that follow, but do not match the chapter-headings in the Arabic and do not include the chapter on travellers. In these manuscripts Book 1 ends with a chapter on the regimen of weaned children ("*De pueris lac dimittentibus*"): for example, in MSS Oxford, Bodleian Library, Auct. F.5.30 and Rawlinson C.748, and Paris, BNF, lat. 7137.
3 These 31 chapter-headings plus another 45, which combine Books 1 and 2 into one book, and correspond to the chapters that follow: for example, in MSS Bamberg, Staatsbibliothek, med. 6, and London, British Library, Add. 22719.
4 A list of 30 chapter-headings which correspond to the chapters that follow. This is what is found in the majority of the manuscripts and the edition printed by Barthélemi Trot in *Omnia opera Ysaac*, Lyons, 1515.
5 A list of 31 chapter-headings taken from Stephen of Antioch's version, which do not correspond to the chapters that follow, which are in Constantine's version: for example, in MS London, British Library, Sloane 3098.[46]

---

[44] This chapter title appears in the list of contents of *Practica*, Book 1, in the facsimile of MS Istanbul University Library, A. Y. 4713a, Publications of the Institute for the History of Arabic-Islamic Science, ed. Fuat Sezgin (Frankfurt, 1985), p. 3 (without *barr wa*), and in MS British Library, Or. 6591 (1153 A.D.), fol. 114b. The (apparently) remarkably few regimens for travellers written in Greek, Arabic and Latin before the Renaissance are surveyed in Peregrine Horden, "Travel Sickness: Medicine and Mobility in the Mediterranean from Antiquity to the Renaissance," in *Rethinking the Mediterranean*, ed. William V. Harris (Oxford, 2005), pp. 179–99 (at pp. 190–99; al-Majusi is not mentioned). See also Claude Thomasset, "Conseils médicaux pour le voyage en mer au moyen âge," in *L'homme, la santé et la mer* (Paris, 1997), ed. Christophe Buchet, pp. 69–87.

[45] MS Vat. Lat. 2429 gives *preparatione* in place of *regimine*, while the two printed editions give *arida* in the list of contents of *Practica*, Book 1, but *aridam* in the text.

[46] In this manuscript Stephen's headings are usually abbreviated; the chapter-heading on the regimen of travellers is given as "De regimine peregrinantium in terra et in mari." The chapter-headings within the text of Book 1 are those of the *Pantegni*. That Stephen's translation was available to the scribe (or that of

6    Constantine's version of the first 30 chapters of Book 1, with the addition of
     Stephen's version of the 31st chapter: for example, in MS Naples, Biblioteca
     nazionale, VIII.D.39.

In cases 1, 4 and 5, Book 1 ends after the first section (on the care of hair) of chapter
30 in the Arabic text, "on the adornment of the body" ("De corporis ornamento,"
ending with the words *cum oleo violato, adipe anserino et cera*); this chapter, ending
in the same words, can be found in the corresponding places in the other three cases.
We may hypothesize that Constantine translated the list of contents for *Practica*,
Book 1, with all 31 chapters (as in case 1 above). Then for some reason the
translation of the book itself terminated after the first section of chapter 30. In one
early manuscript tradition these chapters were divided into shorter chapters, but
then, perhaps because of an awareness that the original Arabic text included 31
chapters, the first 31 of these shorter chapters were separated from the rest and
regarded as the first book (case 2 above).[47] Then, in later traditions, the *Pantegni*
was compared with Stephen of Antioch's translation and either the list of chapter
headings (case 5), or the missing chapter (case 6), was added from the latter. In
Stephen of Antioch's translation of the *Royal Book* the chapter on the regimen
of travellers regularly occurs and can be found in the printed editions on fols.
93vb–94rb (Bernardino Rizzo, Venice, 1492) and fols. 160ra–161ra (Iacobus Myt,
Lyons, 1523).

    There may be a purely mechanical reason for the omission of the last one and a
half chapters of the first book of the *Practica Pantegni*: for example, that the last
folio of the book was lost at a very early stage in the transmission. But it is more
likely that the choice to stop after the first section of chapter 30 was deliberate.[48]
The remaining sections of the chapter – on cosmetics, on curbing the growth of
breasts and testicles, and on preventing body odour – may have been considered
unnecessary,[49] and even inappropriate, for the monastic audience for which the
*Pantegni* appears to have been initially intended. By the same token, the last chapter
may have been omitted because monks were not expected to travel. Stephen,
however, had no such qualms, and could have expected to have amongst his readers
people who travelled – even pilgrims. For the word that he uses to translate *musafir*

---

his exemplar) is clear from the alternative titles given in the rubric at the beginning of Book 2 (fol. 12ra):
"Incipit particula secunda practice pantegni que vocatur regalis dispositio haly filii abbas ..."

[47]   Hence in MS Paris, BNF, lat. 7137, Book 1 is indicated as ending at the end of the chapter on the
regimen of weaned children (fol. 140v), but the scribe has written at the end of the later chapter on the
adornment of the body: "Here ends Book 1 according to some people" ("Explicit liber 1 secundum
quosdam:" fol. 145v).

[48]   It may be noted that Constantine's chapter 30 closes with substitutions of recipes for getting rid of
unwanted hair, and cracks in the hands and the lips, from Ibn al-Jazzar's *Viaticum*, which became the
main source for filling in the information required by the topics of Books IV–VIII of the Royal Book (see
p. 117 above).

[49]   Cf. the title of the *Theorica Pantegni* in *Constantini ... operum reliqua* (Basel, 1539): "De
communibus medico cognitu necessariis locis."

is *peregrinantes*, which, while being a common enough Latin word for travellers, would have had connotations of pilgrimage, especially in a Frankish context.[50] It would undoubtedly have been a useful guide for the pilgrim, as a glance at the contents will show.[51]

## Chapter 31

Al-Majusi promises to inform the traveller on how he needs to prepare for his journey, and to advise him on how to avoid mishaps. First, he must empty his body (*evacuatio*) by means of blood-letting and laxatives, and should take medicine which will cleanse him of superfluities; for exertion and movement heat the body so that the bad humors liquify and flow from place to place, generating fevers and other illnesses. Then, if he is not used to walking, he must take exercise before he starts off, doing more and more every day until it becomes easy for him. He must also practise staying awake at night, because he might be forced to do this. Likewise, if he is used to taking a bath, he should gradually give this up. He should consider at what time of day it is likely that he will be able to rest from his travelling, and get used to eating at that time of day. In all respects he should prepare himself for doing things that he is normally unaccustomed to doing.

If he is travelling by foot he should firmly bind his lower legs, and put a corset round his waist so that his back is more prepared for movement and firmer. He should have a stick to lean on; it will help him on his journey and relieve distress. He should not starve himself – for lack of food weakens one's strength – but neither should he stuff himself with food, because that will slow him down and dampen his

---

[50]   One may contrast the title of the chapter in the *Pantegni* – "On the regimen of those walking, on horseback or in a ship" – which is hardly as evocative of pilgrimage as is Stephen's title. Another of Constantine's translations was the well-known *Viaticum*, a medical handbook whose Latin title ("provision for a journey") suggests that it was meant for someone who intended to travel. But the full Arabic title of the work of Ibn al-Jazzar of which the *Viaticum* is a translation is "Provisions for the Traveller and Nourishment for the Sedentary," that is, a manual suitable for both the pilgrim and the monk, and Constantine himself, in his preface to the *Viaticum*, makes no mention of its use for travellers, but commends it only for giving in compendious form what is provided at greater length in the *Pantegni*, perhaps drawing on the connotation of via as a "(convenient) way:" cf. the preface printed in *Omnia opera Ysaac*, fol. 144rb, especially the words: "… litteratioribus et provectioribus liber Pantechni a nobis est prepositus … *Viaticum* intitulavi quod (et pr.) pre parvitate sui neque laboriosus neque tediosus est intuenti." ("The book of the Pantegni was offered by us first, to the more learned and advanced students … [but for others I have composed this second book] … I have called it *Viaticum* because, in its brevity it is neither troublesome nor boring for the one who looks into it.") In any case, the *Viaticum* does not include a single mention of the hazards of travel and how to take precautions against them.

[51]   In the following summary I have omitted the ingredients for the foods and medicines mentioned, many of which, as has been remarked above (p. 120), are transliterations of Arabic terms and would require some explanation, and comparison with the terms in Stephen's *Breviarium* and in the marginal glosses in the manuscripts. The summary is based on the text in the Venice printing of 1492, compared with the Arabic text in Istanbul University Library, A. Y. 4713a (as in n. 44 above).

spirits. He should eat food which is small in quantity but rich in nourishment, such as liver, veal, birds, and boiled eggs.

After this preparation he may set out on his journey. But on the first day, he should walk slowly, gradually increasing his pace each day. If the pace causes him discomfort, he should rest, sprinkle himself with water, and have his body rubbed with violet oil, especially his back and feet, to alleviate the dryness caused by movement.

If he is travelling in the summer, he should go by night while the air is cool, and enjoy a rest during the hours of daylight, so that he is not harmed by the heat of the sun. For travelling in the sun's heat brings on terrible diseases like headaches and fevers, especially for those who have a hot and dry complexion and slender bodies, and who are unused to doing things in the heat of the day. But no harm comes to anyone who is used to travelling in the heat, whose complexion is cold and moist, and whose body is fat and fleshy. If one has to travel in the heat of the day one should protect the body with a thick layer of clothes, so that the heat cannot reach the body. The head and face should be covered with a close-fitting felt cap (*pilleus*, for al-Majusi's *'imama*, "turban") or the like, so that one is not breathing in warm air, and harming the air passages. Also, avoid food that makes one thirsty, like fresh or salted fish, milk, matured cheese, cooked beans and anything that is salty, sweet or acrid (*pungitivus*). Rather, take food which cools and moistens (a list of such foods is given) and do not eat too much; for too much food induces thirst. Some prophylactic remedies are prescribed to avoid the onset of thirst on the journey, which include pomegranate juice, and some special pills. If this does not help, keep a sliver of lead or a piece of satin (*adasse*; *atlas*) in one's mouth, and this will allay one's thirst and lessen one's need for water.

If a man suffers from the heat and his body becomes hot, dry and weak, pour over his head cooled rose water, let him also drink water, *julab*, or cold pomegranate juice, and eat fresh fruit cooled with snow, like mulberries, plums, grapes, cucumbers, and the like (other tempting recipes follow). He should inhale the scent of, and be smeared with, sandalwood, rose water and camphor, and should sleep in a place cooled by the north wind, so that his body is strengthened and his natural heat is restored. (A recipe for headache follows.)

If he happens to be travelling in the winter and in cold places, he must travel by day and rest by night, he should cover his body with clothes made out of animal hair, he should put on a fur coat, pelisses and doublets,[52] and cover his head and face with a soft close-fitting felt cap (*pilleus*; *qalansuwa*, "hood").[53] If possible, he should wrap his feet with warm woollen fabric and make sure that they do not get cold,

---

[52] These three words (*pelicium, renones et duplicia*) are equivalent to one word in the Arabic: *farw*, "furs."

[53] The Arabic adds "silk turbans" (*al-'ama'im al-khazz*) which Stephen simply transliterates as *hamahamis gazhinis* (adding the Latin adjectival and ablative plural termination).

especially if he is on horseback; pedestrians have no problem, for the movement keeps their warm.

If his journey takes him through snowy places he should take care of the extremities of his limbs and his face, especially if there is a wind. Before he goes he should eat garlic and onions and foods in which there are hot spices like pepper and ginger. His body and feet should be rubbed with various hot oils which prevent the cold from getting into the body by blocking up its pores, with the result that the heat goes into the depths of the body and its surface is warmed by the oils. He should be especially careful if he is on horseback. He should wrap his joints in soft, close-fitting felt, and put on stockings (*calige*) with trews (*ocree*) on top; he should also cover his hands with gloves made of animal hair.

He should make sure that his eyesight is not impaired by looking at the snow too much; for the snow disperses the vision and weakens it.[54] Thus he should place just under his eyes a black cloth, and his felt cap should be black, and, if possible, his clothes should be violet or green; for these colours gather together his vision, and prevent it from being dispersed.

If at any time the traveller is harmed by cold and his skin becomes rough, he should wear warm clothing and sit for an hour in front of a fire. Then he should enter a bath and stay there for a time, after which he should enter the wash tub (*concha*; *abzan*), and water should be poured over him continuously. He should get dressed and be oiled whilst still in the bath. On leaving the bath he should rest for an hour in a secluded place, then be restored with the juice from meat, with white lead (*espidabago*; *isfidaj*), but in moderation, and have a long sleep under soft, warm covers. If his extremities are harmed by the cold of snow, and one is worried lest they fall off, they should be rubbed with oils, and grey squirrel fur (*grisium varium*; *sinjab*) and soft wool should be placed on and between his fingers; warm woollen coverings should be placed on his feet. Walking is more beneficial than riding a horse. For horse-riders suffer certain ailments, which does not happen to pedestrians, since their motion warms their bodies.

If, when a man travels in cold and snowy places, he thinks the pain has gone, this is dangerous, because he is probably losing his sensation.[55] So he must not neglect to bind his fingers. If they do not become livid or black, but only swell, they must be smeared with hot oils and dipped in hot water in which various warming medicines have been boiled. If his fingers are livid or black he should make several deep cuts in them and place them in hot water until the flowing of blood is cut off spontaneously. A poultice should be made and applied to the fingers by day and night; then they should be washed with wine and covered again until the flesh regrows and the wounds dry out. But if bits of the fingers are falling off, apply a warmed and medicated poultice two or three times a day until whatever is putrid falls off. After this you will use the drying medications by which wounds are cured.

---

[54] Here the author is describing snow blindness.

[55] It is well known that in cases of hypothermia one loses one's sensation.

If the voyage is by sea and the traveller suffers from sea-sickness he should drink syrups made of sour grapes (*heserem*; *hisrim*), pomegranate, mint,[56] apple and tamarind. He should inhale their aroma and refrain from eating. If vomiting gets the better of him, his stomach should be cleansed with warm things before sipping the syrups. He should avoid looking at the sea.

Travellers also tend to suffer from an abundance of lice on their bodies because of the sweat and dust, and their lack of bathing. When this happens put on the traveller's body a poultice whose main ingredient is mercury. He should go to the bath in the morning and have his body rubbed vigorously. His head should be cleaned with effective ingredients and he should wear smooth, clean linen clothes, and thus all the lice will be expelled.

---

[56]  The Arabic omits "mint."

# The Religious Orders of Knighthood in Medieval Scandinavia: Historical and Archaeological Approaches

*Christer Carlsson*

Syddansk Universitet

In 1204, when the crusader army was standing at the gates of Constantinople, Scandinavia was still a remote part of medieval Europe. However, when the news of the fall of Constantinople during the Fourth Crusade reached Scandinavia the *concept of crusading* was nothing new for the population. It is likely that at least some Scandinavians were in the armies that were sent from western Europe to Jerusalem during the First Crusade.[1] Other crusading armies had probably been sent to Finland by the Swedish kings as early as the 1150s,[2] and in 1201, only a few years before the attack on Constantinople, German crusaders started a colonizing project in what is now the Riga area in Latvia.[3] Even the Danish kings were interested in taking part in this Baltic crusading enterprise.[4] These Swedish, Danish and German campaigns quickly expanded the frontiers of Latin Christianity into the Baltic area.

Early on in the German crusading-campaign in the Baltic region the Order of the Sword-brothers played an important role.[5] Religious Orders of Knighthood such as the Sword-brothers were, however, rather new elements in the religious life of early thirteenth-century Scandinavia. Even if the various Orders of Knighthood reached Scandinavia somewhat later than most of the Christian civilization they soon became important religious institutions in Scandinavian societies in the same way as they already were in the rest of western Europe. Even if the Order of the Sword-brothers probably never controlled any land of its own in Scandinavia,[6] other and similar orders certainly did so.

---

[1] Paul Riant, *Expéditions et pèlerinages des Scandinaves en Terre Sainte au temps des Croisades* (Paris, 1865).

[2] Tore Nyberg, "Deutsche, dänische und schwedische Christianisierungsversuche östlich der Ostsee im Geiste des 2. und 3. Kreuzzuges," in *Die Rolle der Ritterorden in der Christianisierung und Kolonisierung des Ostseegebietes, Ordines militares*, ed. Zenon Hubert Nowak, Colloquia Torunensia Historica I (Torun, 1983), pp. 93–114.

[3] Friedrich Benninghoven, "Der Orden der Schwertbrüder: Fratres milicie de Livonia," in *Ostmitteleuropa in Vergangenheit und Gegenwart* 9 (Cologne, 1965).

[4] John Lind, Carsten Selch Jensen, Kurt Villads Jensen and Ane Bysted, *Danske korstog. Krig och mision i Östersjön* (Odense, 2004).

[5] Benninghoven, "Der Orden der Schwertbrüder."

[6] John Lind, "The Order of the Sword-brothers and Finland. Sources and Traditions," in *Vergangenheit und Gegenwart der Ritterorden Die Rezeption der Idee und die Wirklichkeit, Ordines militares*, ed. Zenon Hubert Nowak, Colloquia Torunensia Historica XI (Torun, 2001), pp. 159–63.

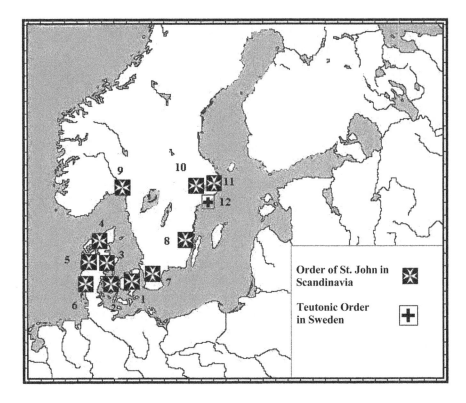

**Fig. 1**    **The major houses of the religious Orders of Knighthood in medieval Scandinavia with their approximate years of foundation**
1: Antvorskov (c. 1165); 2: Odense (c. 1275); 3: Horsens (c. 1350?); 4: Dueholm (c. 1370); 5: Viborg (c. 1280); 6: Ribe (c. 1310?); 7: Lund (c. 1300?); 8: Kronobäck (1479); 9: Varne (c. 1190); 10: Eskilstuna (c. 1180); 11: Stockholm (c. 1332); 12: Årsta (c. 1260?)

The first of these orders to be established in Scandinavia was the Order of St. John known generally as the Hospitallers. This order was probably given its first Scandinavian donation in Antvorskov in Denmark in the 1160s by the Danish king Valdemar the Great (see Fig. 1).[7] They later spread to Sweden in the period 1170–85 when they were given land in the city of Eskilstuna.[8] During the 1190s Varne, the first and only commandery in Norway, was donated to the order.[9]

---

[7] Tore Nyberg, "Zur Rolle der Johanniter in Skandinavien. Erstes Auftreten und Aufbau der Institutionen," in *Die Rolle der Ritterorden in der mitteralterlichen Kultur, Ordines militares*, ed. Zenon Hubert Nowak, Colloquia Torunensia Historica III, (Torun, 1985), pp. 129–44.

[8] Ibid.

[9] Ibid.

The later part of the twelfth century was, however, a time of great political turbulence in the various Scandinavian countries. But, although many of the leading Scandinavian families were fighting against each other in this period, these same families also contributed to the establishment of the Order of St. John in the region. By giving land to the Order it was possible for the leading aristocracy in Scandinavia to acquire a powerful ally in the ongoing conflicts.[10] It is, however, a difficult task to prove that there were specific political intentions behind the first donations to the Hospitallers in Scandinavia.

The political situation in Scandinavia was still unstable when the next Order of Knighthood, the Teutonic Order, reached the region. This group was probably given its first Scandinavian donations in Sweden in the period 1260–1308.[11] In 1308 a *komtur* of the Teutonic Order is mentioned in Årsta,[12] a *komturi* on the Swedish east coast, but it is likely that by then the brothers had already been active in the area for some time.

The only Scandinavian country where the Teutonic Order had land in the Middle Ages was probably Sweden. The reason for this is that perhaps amongst the Scandinavian countries, it was Sweden that had the closest contact with the Baltic Sea. The Baltic region became, after all, the Teutonic Order's main area of interest when the Grand Master moved to Marienburg in 1309.[13] The establishment of the Teutonic Order in Sweden was, as seems to have been the case with the Order of St. John, the result of donations from different noble families with specific political intentions. According to *Erikskrönikan*, a Swedish medieval source of great importance, the Swedish nobleman Karl Ulfsson died in the battle of Durben in 1260 in the service of the Order.[14] Ulfsson belonged to the elite in the country and was related to the powerful jarl Birger, the actual leader of Sweden in these years. Birgitta Eimer has also shown that the noble family Ängel seems to have had much interest in the Order from about the 1260s onwards and according to her it is likely that at least some individuals from this family were members of the brethren.[15]

The early history of the Order of St. John and the Teutonic Order in Scandinavia is, however, filled with problems. Few written sources from the earliest period still survive, since much of the medieval documentation concerning the two groups was destroyed shortly after the Reformation. The history of these two Orders in the region must therefore be studied from both a historical and an archaeological

---

[10] Magnus Wahlberg, *Johanniterordens jord i Sverige. En studie i medeltida jordägande 1231–1520*. Masters thesis, Stockholm University (Stockholm, 1997), pp. 4–5.

[11] Birgitta Eimer, *Gotland unter dem Deutschen Orden und die Komturei Schweden zu Årsta* (Innsbruck, 1966), pp. 53–118.

[12] Johan Gustav Liljegren, *Diplomatarium Suecaneum* (Stockholm, 1829–37), DS 1574–1575.

[13] Marian Arszynski, "Die Deutschordensburgen und der Wehrbau im Ostseeraum," in *Der Deutsche Orden in der Zeit der Kalmarer Union 1397–1521, Ordines militares*, ed. Zenon Hubert Nowak, Colloquia Torunensia Historica X (Torun, 1999), pp. 183–90.

[14] Sven-Bertil Jansson, *Erikskrönikan*, new edition (Stockholm, 2003).

[15] Eimer, *Gotland*, 1966, pp. 53–118.

perspective to help redress this dearth of material. It is, therefore, the aim of this paper to present the archaeological material from the Scandinavian houses of the Orders of Knighthood as it is known today and to point out some areas for further studies.

In all the Scandinavian countries archaeological artefacts from sites that once belonged to the Orders have been preserved in various museums. Although so far mainly used in rather limited and local studies, this archaeological material, if used together with the written sources, offers a far greater potential since archaeological information can sometimes fill the gaps in the written sources, and vice versa. The archaeological material must nonetheless be used with great care. One major methodological problem is that most artefacts from the houses of the Orders of Knighthood are local products that do not differ from those found in other religious houses in the region concerned. Some Scandinavian archaeologists have even claimed that it would be almost impossible to separate archaeological material from the Orders of Knighthood from other archaeological material. This is not always the case, however, since it is actually possible to identify artefacts such as coins from the Teutonic state,[16] seals from the various Orders[17] and building-features with symbols that are specific to the different groups.[18]

During the 1960s the Swedish archaeologist Sune Zachrisson undertook excavations in the medieval building complex that once belonged to the Order of St. John in the central parts of the city of Eskilstuna.[19] Most of the former commandery had actually been destroyed shortly after the Reformation when the sons of king Gustav Vasa erected a new castle on the site, however, it was still possible for Zachrisson to reconstruct the plan of the most central part of the site (see Fig. 2).[20] This part of the complex had been built around a squared yard with the chapel in the north and priory buildings on the southern and eastern sides. There were no traces of the west wing, but it is likely that there was some kind of building on this side as well.

The excavation in the chapel with its thick walls, its many altar-foundations and its numerous graves revealed further information about the commandery. One important discovery was that the chapel seemed to have had at least three different

---

[16] Jörgen Steen Jensen, "Die Münzen des Deutschen Ordens und der Norden," in *Der Deutsche Orden in der Zeit der Kalmarer Union 1397–1521, Ordines militares*, ed. Zenon Hubert Nowak, Colloquia Torunensia Historica X (Torun, 1999), pp. 91–97.

[17] Rune Norberg, "Två medeltida sigillstampar från Eskilstuna," in *Eskilstuna stads museers årsbok 1961* (Eskilstuna, 1961), pp. 23–26.

[18] Nils Lagerholm, "Johanniterordens klosterkyrka i Kronobäck," in *Stranda 1954*, p. 56.

[19] Sune Zachrisson, "Från Vendeltid til Vasatid. Redogörelse för de byggnadsarkeologiska undersökningarna av Eskilstuna kloster och slott 1961–62," in *Eskilstuna stads museers årsbok 1963* (Eskilstuna, 1963).

[20] Ibid., Plansch III.

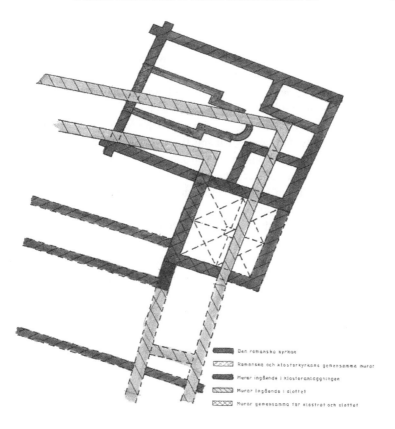

Den romanska kyrkan

Romanska och klosterkyrkans gemensamma murar

Murar ingående i klosteranläggningen

Murar ingående i slottet

Murar gemensamma för klostret och slottet

**Fig. 2     The plan of the commandery in Eskilstuna. Walls from the Romanesque chapel, the commandery of the Order of St. John and the sixteenth-century castle are marked. Based on Zachrisson, 1963**

building phases. From a small Romanesque chapel dating from the twelfth century, it had gradually expanded to a large Gothic commandery church.[21] The second half of the fourteenth century and the fifteenth century seems to have been a period of particularly intensive building activity.[22] Finds from inside the chapel consisted of different bricks from the vaults, items from the graves and fragments of medieval gravestones.[23] Inside as well as outside the chapel a large number of graves were discovered, representing at least four hundred years of burial activity. Some of the skeletons in these graves were of particular interest since it was possible to identify them on account of personal seals that were found in the graves together with the

---

[21]   Ibid., p. 41.

[22]   Ibid., p. 68.

[23]   Ibid., pp. 65–70.

bones. The most famous individual to be identified in this way was a former donor to the commandery named Hemming Hatt Pedersen.[24] Hemming's life has been studied by modern historians and we know today that he died in the commandery in Eskilstuna as a *donati* in about 1475.[25]

Coins and pottery are other examples of artefacts from the excavations in Eskilstuna. Unfortunately these have not yet been subjected to detailed study, but since the excavation was carried out with great care most artefacts can still be tied to different contexts. One way of using these items would be to establish their places of origin and distinguish between local and imported artefacts. This may give an indication of the contact network of the commandery. Another way of using the material would be to identify and date different periods of greater building activity. Enlargements or alterations of the commandery could indicate periods of comparative wealth in the Scandinavian branch of the Order of St. John or in the institution as such. This last point is of particular interest since similar archaeological material is available from the other Scandinavian houses that once belonged to the Order, so this material can therefore be used in a comparative study.

The second commandery in Sweden that belonged to the Order of St. John during the Middle Ages was Kronobäck on the east coast. This commandery was given to the Order in 1479.[26] Excavations in the complex were carried out by the archaeologist Nils Lagerholm in the 1940s (see Fig. 3).[27] They were, however, mainly concentrated on the chapel, the best preserved part of the complex, and no traces from the other buildings were ever identified, although it is likely that the living-quarters were situated to the south of the chapel.[28] Inside the church was a lot of stone rubble from the vaults that had collapsed shortly after the Reformation. Lagerholm removed all this material in order to clear the interior of the chapel. He also identified and dated different building phases in the walls of the chapel and collected a large number of smaller artefacts such as pieces of pottery, coins and liturgical items from the cultural layers inside the church.[29] This material can therefore be used in a similar way to the material from Eskilstuna.

Unfortunately Lagerholm was not as careful during his excavations in Kronobäck as Zachrisson would be in Eskilstuna some twenty years later. This makes it a lot more complicated to work with the archaeological material from Kronobäck since few artefacts can be tied to specific cultural layers. We simply have to trust that Lagerholm's interpretations of the layers inside the chapel are correct

---

[24] Ibid., p. 69.

[25] C. J. Ståhle and Hans Gillingstam, "Otte Torbjörnssons lagbok," in *Naturen och Hembygden*, Skriftserie utgiven av Värmlands nation i Uppsala och Föreningen Naturen och Hembygden V, 1949 p. 85.

[26] Johan Peringskjölds Diplomatarium, 18, letter dated 26 July 1480.

[27] Nils Lagerholm, "Johanniterordens."

[28] Ibid., p. 31.

[29] Ibid., pp. 50–62.

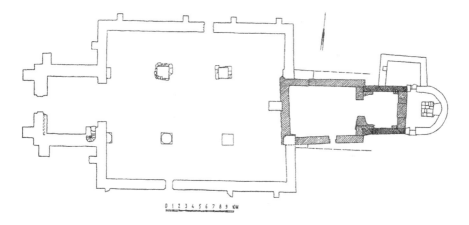

**Fig. 3    Plan showing the chapel of the late-medieval commandery at Kronobäck. Based on Lagerholm 1954**

and that he is right in saying that the building activity in the fifteenth century was especially extensive.[30] Further studies of the standing walls can hopefully confirm this picture.

Prompted by construction work on the former graveyard east of the chapel, further excavations were carried out at Kronobäck in the 1950s.[31] During these investigations some late-medieval skeletons were found, most of which showed signs of recovering from severe war injuries. These individuals must have lived for some weeks after the injuries were inflicted, so it is likely that they had been treated in the commandery for some time before finally dying from infections.[32] If this is the case, the skeletons can hopefully tell us something about the medical skills that existed among the Order of St. John, if studied in more detail by a pathologist.

Excavations have also been carried out in the many Danish commanderies that once belonged to the Order of St. John. From Antvorskov, the headquarters of the Order in the province of Dacia, archaeological investigations between 1887 and 1960 have provided us with much useful information about this large complex.[33] These excavations have now made it possible to reconstruct the commandery and to say something about the functions of the various buildings (see Fig. 4). A more recent excavation was carried out on the site in 1995 by the Danish archaeologist

---

[30] Ibid., pp. 65–66.

[31] *The Kronobäck Infirmary Church*, Länsstyrelsen i Kalmar, 1999 (Kalmar, 1999), p. 4.

[32] Ibid.

[33] Excavations c. 1887–1960 by Magnus Petersén, Terje Schou, H. H. Schou, C. M. Smidt, Poul Nörlund, Mogens Clemmensen and Mogens Brahde. This material is mostly unpublished, but plans, artefacts and documentation from the excavations can be found at the Nationalmuseum in Copenhagen.

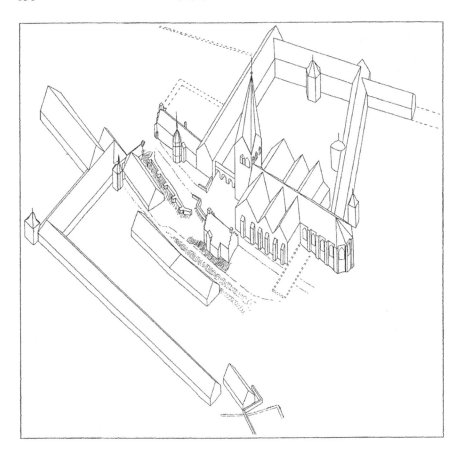

**Fig. 4** The commandery at Antvorskov in the eighteenth century. Reconstruction in
*Danmarks Ruiner*, 1991

Kirstin Eliasen.[34] This excavation is important since it is the only modern
investigation on the site. Eliasen has, for instance, used a modern contextual digging
method where the artefacts have been linked to the various occupation layers right
from the start.

From the former commandery in Ribe there exists also much archaeological
material from two excavations in the 1990s, but this material has so far only been
published in local archaeological reports.[35] In the area of the former commandery in

[34] Kirstin Eliasen, "Arkaeologisk undersögelse ved Antvorskov kloster og slot i juni 1995," in *AMK
1993045 Antvorskov*, in *Sorö Amts Museums Arkaeologiske Afdelnings rapportserie* (Sorö, 1995).

[35] Per Kristian Madsen, "Middelalderkeramik fra Ribe: byarkaeologiske undersögelser 1980–87," in
*Den antikvariske Samlings skriftraekke 2*, ed. Per Kristian Madsen, Jysk Arkaeologisk Selskab 1999

Odense some small-scale excavations were carried out in the 1990s[36] and in Dueholm a number of such investigations have been made since the 1920s.[37] Even the commandery in Viborg has been the subject of some smaller archaeological excavations.[38] Taking all these investigations into account, there now exists enough archaeological material for a larger study of the Scandinavian commanderies. In total, the material has good potential and is now being assessed to determine how it can be used in such a study.

Further information can be obtained by using the various methods that modern archaeology has at its disposal. Demolition-layers and standing walls from reliably dated archaeological contexts, together with detailed studies of the artefacts, can be used to identify periods of more intensive building activity in the various houses. Modern archaeological dating methods, such as dendrochronology, C14 dating and luminescence dating, can be used on both artefacts and standing structures to provide results that can be used in local chronologies for the various sites. All this has so far only been done to a very limited extent.

Årsta, the medieval headquarters of the Teutonic Order on the Swedish mainland, was probably very different from the commanderies that belonged to the Order of St. John. To begin with, Årsta was not situated inside or near a city. Furthermore, the site probably did not have typical convent-buildings, but rather a cluster of different houses. This was at least the situation in the seventeenth century when the complex was documented in a picture by the Swedish architect and artist Erik Dahlberg (see Fig. 5).[39] The site seems to have been a larger farm in the countryside rather than a traditional commandery complex. It is not certain when the Teutonic Order came in possession of the site, but there must have been at least some kind of representation in the farm in 1308 when a *komtur* of the Order is mentioned for the first time.[40]

On account of the economic and administrative problems inside the Teutonic Order that followed its defeat at Tannenberg in 1410, all the Order's land in Sweden

---

(Höjbjerg, 1999); Lis Andersen, "Udgravningen under den gamle bakelitfabrik i Slotsgade," in *By, marsk og geest 11, Kulturhistorisk årbog for Ribe-egnen, 1999* (Forlaget Liljebjerget, 1999), pp. 29–38.

[36] Eskil Arentoft, "Kirkegård. Skt. Hans Kirke, umartikuleret P-plads. Nörregade. Odense. Fyms Amt," in *Odense Bys Museers rapportserie, OBM j. nr. 9395* (Odense, 1997). Dorte Lund Mortensen, "Sankt Hans kirke. Udgravningsberetning KMO 1996/5," in *Odense Bys Museers rapportserie, KMO 1996/5* (Odense, 1996).

[37] Per Bugge Vegger, "Dueholm. Et johanniterkloster på Mors," in *Hikuin 1996* (Forlaget Hikuin, 1996).

[38] Mogens Vedsö, "Undersögelse af stenhus. Sct. Nicolaigade. Viborg by. Nörlyng hrd. Viborg amt," in *Viborgs Stiftsmuseums rapportserie, VSM 410E* (Viborg, 1986). Erik Levin Nielsen, "Viborg Johanniterklosters areal. Viborg by. Nörlyng hrd. Viborg amt," in *Viborgs Stiftsmuseums rapportserie, VSM 833E* (Viborg 1988); Erik Levin Nielsen, "Snitgravninger i forbindelse med vejprojekt. Ibsgade. Viborg Köbstad. Nörlyng hrd. Viborg amt," in *Viborgs Stiftmuseums rapportserie, VSM 581C* (Viborg, 1970).

[39] Original picture in the Royal Library in Stockholm.

[40] Johan Gustav Liljegren, 1829–37, DS 1574–1575.

**Fig. 5    The *komturie* at Årsta. Drawing by Erik Dahlberg from the 1660s. The Royal Library in Stockholm**

was sold in 1467.[41] The building complex itself was finally destroyed in a fire in the 1680s. The site has never been excavated and has therefore a good archaeological potential. An excavation at Årsta, applying modern archaeological standards, can therefore teach us more about the conditions inside the Teutonic Order during the period when it operated as a military organization in the Baltic area. A small-scale excavation on the site is therefore planned to begin in July 2005.[42] When more is known about Årsta it can be compared with similar places in the Baltic region.

While the early history of the Order of St. John and the Teutonic Order in Scandinavia has many problems, the sources from the Later Middle Ages are usually a lot more informative. There exist numerous historical and archaeological sources dating from the fifteenth century and the beginning of the sixteenth, the period shortly before the Reformation, that concern the history of the two Orders. This material is suitable for an international comparative study in which economic, political and religious changes inside the two institutions during the Later Middle

---

[41]  J. H. Schröder and F. J. L. Wulff, *De Ordine Sacro Militari Cruciferorum sive Teutonicorum* (Uppsala, 1845), pp. 11–14.

[42]  Christer Carlsson, 2006. Forthcoming.

Ages can be studied. The economic and religious situation within the Scandinavian branches of the two groups during that period has so far mainly been considered from a local historical perspective.

In a work by the Danish researcher Thomas Hatt Olsen from 1961, founded on information that he found in the archives of the Order of St. John on Malta, the economic situation in the province of Dacia has been studied on the basis of factors such as the ability to pay the *responsions* and other taxes to the priory on Rhodes between the years 1310 and 1522.[43] Hatt Olsen identified several shorter periods of improving, as well as declining, economy in the Scandinavian branch of the Order. One of his most important conclusions was that the Order of St. John often seems to have had extensive economic problems in the province of Dacia until the later part of the fifteenth century.[44]

A similar picture can be seen in a 1997 study by Magnus Wahlberg,[45] in which he identified economic changes in the commandery of Eskilstuna in the Later Middle Ages on the basis of the increasing number of new donations given to the house in this period. Wahlberg also discussed the commandery's increasing ability to pay for new land in the region in these years. Both these factors are seen as indications of an improved economic situation in the commandery from the end of the fourteenth century or the beginning of the fifteenth century.[46] This period of better economic conditions for the Order of St. John in Eskilstuna lasted, according to Wahlberg, until the Reformation finally led to the dissolution, in the 1520s, 1530s and 1540s, of all Catholic institutions in Scandinavia. It is therefore tempting to see the increased building activity from the fifteenth and sixteenth centuries, as indicated by the archaeological material, as a result of the better economic conditions in the province in these years. Unfortunately there does not yet exist any similar study for the Scandinavian branch of the Teutonic Order that left Sweden in 1467.

Another important factor that must be considered when discussing economic changes inside the Orders of Knighthood during the later Middle Ages is that these institutions still were closely associated with the crusading movement. In times of resistance against new crusades and new taxes for these campaigns, criticism was also put forward concerning the Orders of Knighthood. This is a question that Helen Nicholson has dealt with in one of her works on the Orders of Knighthood.[47] During periods when the Military Orders became less popular the number of new donations often went down. This had effects on the economic situations of the different organizations on an international, as well as a more local, level. By adding this economic-historical analysis to the information that we have from the

---

[43] Thomas Hatt Olsen, "Dacia og Rhodos. The Priorate of Dacia of the Order of Saint John of Jerusalem," in *5th Congrès International des Sciences Généalogique et Héraldique* (Stockholm, 1961).

[44] Ibid., pp. 316–30.

[45] Wahlberg, *Johanniterordens jord i Sverige*, pp. 16–34.

[46] Ibid., pp. 30–34.

[47] Helen Nicholson, *Templars, Hospitallers and Teutonic Knights: Images of the Military Orders, 1128–1291* (Leicester, 1993).

archaeological excavations, new perspectives will hopefully open up, perspectives that can serve as a base for further discussions.

In many countries outside Scandinavia there exist numerous archaeological and historical studies about various Orders of Knighthood. The reason for the lack of larger studies in Scandinavia probably has something to do with the complicated source material in combination with different academic traditions. Scandinavia was, after all, not the most important province for these Orders in the Middle Ages. The Scandinavian sites that once belonged to the different institutions cannot, however, be studied as an isolated phenomenon. The international character of these Orders gives us the possibility to make comparisons across the frontiers of modern countries. Further information about the Orders' Scandinavian houses can therefore probably be obtained through studies of their international history.

The key point is this: the full potential of the historical and the archaeological material from the sites that once belonged to the Orders of Knighthood in medieval Scandinavia has not yet been seen. In the SSCLE there exists an established tradition of studies focusing on various Orders of Knighthood. Archaeological studies of the Orders have in recent years been carried out and published by researchers such as Adrian Boas,[48] Ronnie Ellenblum[49] and Denys Pringle,[50] and historical studies have been published by scholars such as Jonathan Riley-Smith,[51] Malcolm Barber[52] and Helen Nicholson,[53] just to mention a few specialists in this particular field. By using these scholars' studies the history of the Orders of Knighthood in medieval Scandinavia can be placed within a more international context and new questions can be raised about the Scandinavian source material. This would not only develop the Scandinavian crusading research but it would also teach us more about the medieval phenomenon of Orders of Knighthood.

---

[48] Adrian Boas, *Jerusalem in the Time of the Crusades: Society, Landscape and Art in the Holy City under Frankish Rule* (London, 2001).

[49] Ronnie Ellenblum, S. Marco, A. Agnon, T. Rockwell and Adrian Boas, "Crusader castle torn apart by earthquake at dawn, 20 May 1202," *Geology* 26 (1988), 303–306.

[50] Denys Pringle, "Templar castles on the road to the Jordan," in *MO, 1*.

[51] Jonathan Riley-Smith, *The History of the Order of St John* (London, 1999).

[52] Malcolm Barber, *The New Knighthood: a History of the Order of the Temple* (Cambridge, 1993).

[53] Nicholson, *Templars, Hospitallers and Teutonic Knights*.

# The Thief's Cross: Crusade and Penance in Alan of Lille's *Sermo de cruce domini*

*Matthew Phillips*

Concordia University, Nebraska

In October 1187, responding to the disastrous defeat of the Christian army at Hattin, Pope Gregory VIII issued the bull, *Audita tremendi*, calling for a new crusade to the Holy Land. Gregory concentrated on the redemptive work of Christ's incarnation and his death on the cross. While God had worked salvation in the Holy Land, now, the pope emphasized that God had brought a severe judgment upon this land because of diabolical dissensions and the malicious sins of all Christians. Gregory's message laid the foundation for the preaching of the Third Crusade with its emphasis on Christ's redemption and the conversion of Christian society. Granting a full indulgence to contrite crusaders, the pope encouraged them to imitate Christ by laying down their lives for their brothers and seeking the recovery of the Holy Land.[1]

Not only had the Christian army been destroyed, but also they had lost their most prized banner, the relic of the True Cross. Since its discovery in 1099 by the victorious crusaders in Jerusalem, the True Cross had played an important role in the religious life and military endeavours of the eastern Franks.[2] The loss of the True Cross to Saladin's forces undermined the faith of western Christians and caused great consternation. Why did God allow the loss of this most holy relic and the destruction of the Christian army? Most apologists argued that the sinful living of the eastern Christians caused God to purge his Holy Land and punish the people. They compared the loss of the True Cross to the Israelites' loss of the Ark of the Covenant. The idea that sin caused defeat had emerged early in crusading thought. Following Bernard of Clairvaux's preaching of the Second Crusade, the pope noted that the Lord had provided Christians a momentous opportunity for spiritual conversion through contrition, penance, and good works. Yet while Bernard, in his explanation of the failure of the Second Crusade, had directly linked military victory with a true, spiritual conversion, Gregory VIII expanded this theme

---

[1] The text of the *Audita tremendi* is in Ansbert, *Historia de expeditione Friderici Imperatoris. Quellen zur Geschichte des Kreuzzuges Kaiser Friedrichs I*, ed. Anton Chroust, MGH, Scriptores rerum Germanicarum nova series 5 (1928), pp. 6–10. See also Penny J. Cole, *Preaching of the Crusades to the Holy Land, 1095–1270* (Cambridge, MA, 1991), pp. 63–65; eadem, "Christian Perceptions of the Battle of Hattin (583/1187)," *Al-Masaq* 6 (1993), 19–21.

[2] On the importance of this relic to the eastern Christians as a battle standard and object of devotion, see Alan V. Murray, " 'Mighty Against the Enemies of Christ': The relic of the True Cross in the Armies of the Kingdom of Jerusalem," in *Crusade Sources*, pp. 217–38; Deborah Gerish, "The True Cross and the Kings of Jerusalem," *The Haskins Society Journal* 8 (1996), 137–55.

by insisting on the reform of western Christendom as a prerequisite for a successful campaign.[3]

This study will examine Alan of Lille's preaching of the Third Crusade, recorded in his *Sermo de cruce domini*, as it relates to the devotion to the cross, the imitation of the crucified Christ and the emerging scholastic teaching on the sacrament of penance.[4] These devotional and theological concepts converged to form a major part of the crusading movement and were the basis for the piety and social reforms that the reform preachers associated with the Parisian schools promoted in western European society in the twelfth and thirteenth centuries.[5] Alan masterfully weaves them together to portray a true crusader as a true penitent. In so doing, he appropriated the monastic teaching concerning the proper response to Christ's call to take up one's cross and applied it the life of the crusader. This paper will focus particularly on Alan's use of the typology of the crosses of the two thieves as a means of delineating between a genuine and false penitent. Using a cross-section of monastic and canonical preachers, it will attempt to demonstrate the ways in which Alan adapted this exegetical tradition to promote a crusader's conversion via the sacrament of penance as symbolized in the penitential cross.

---

[3] On Bernard of Clairvaux, see Cole, *Preaching of the Crusades*, pp. 57–61; on the cross and the Ark see eadem, "Christian Perceptions," 9–39; Elizabeth Siberry, *Criticism of Crusading, 1095–1274* (Oxford, 1985), pp. 69–108. Siberry refers to poets who compared the loss of the True Cross with the loss of the Ark of the Covenant on p. 82. The story of the Israelites' loss of the Ark of the Covenant is in I Sam. 4.11. (All biblical references are made to *Biblia Sacra iuxta vulgatam versionem*, ed. Robert Weber, Stuttgart, 1994.) Two promoters of the Third Crusade referred to the True Cross as the lost Ark: Henry of Albano, *Tractus de peregrinante civitate Dei* 13. PL 204:353D; Peter of Blois, *Passio Reginaldi*, CCCM 194, ed. R. B. C. Huygens (Turnhout, 2002), p. 34. See also Christopher Tyerman, *The Invention of the Crusades* (Toronto, 1998), pp. 26–27; Jessalynn Bird, "Heresy, Crusade and Reform in the Circle of Peter the Chanter, c.1187–c.1240" (unpub. D.Phil. Oxford, 2001), pp. 36–37 and 152.

[4] The text is found in *Alain de Lille: textes inédits*, ed. Marie-Thérèse d'Alverny (Paris, 1965), pp. 279–83. D'Alverny produced this text of the sermon from two manuscripts from the Bibliothèque nationale in Paris, which contain a number of Alan's sermons. Although the manuscripts do not list an author, d'Alverny identified it as Alan's work based on its teaching and style (p. 127). On Alan's preaching on various theological topics, see Jean Longère, *Œuvres oratoires de maitres parisiens au XIIe siècle*, 2 vols. (Paris, 1975), 1:141–51 and 325–33; and on his crusade preaching, see 1:417–18.

[5] On the connection between the devotion to the cross and the origins of the idea of crusading, see Carl Erdmann's *The Origin of the Idea of Crusading*, trans. Marshall W. Baldwin and Walter Goffart (Princeton, 1977), pp. 345–48; Etienne Delaruelle, "Essai sur la formation de l'idée de croisade," *Bulletin de littérature ecclésiastique* 55 (1954), 50–58. On later twelfth- and early thirteenth-century developments, see Cole, *Preaching of the Crusades*, pp. 101–76; Tyerman, *Invention of the Crusades*, pp. 76–83; Christoph T. Maier, "Mass, the Eucharist and the Cross: Innocent III and the Relocation of the Crusade," in *Pope Innocent III and his World*, ed. John C. Moore (Aldershot, 1999), pp. 351–60; see examples of thirteenth-century crusade sermons in Christoph T. Maier, *Crusade Propaganda and Ideology: Model Sermons for the Preaching of the Cross* (Cambridge, 2000). On the group of Parisian scholastics and social reformers, known as the circle of Peter the Chanter, see John Baldwin, *Masters, Princes and Merchants: The Social Views of Peter the Chanter and his Circle*, 2 vols. (Princeton, 1970); and on their activity as crusade preachers, see Jessalynn Bird, "Heresy, Crusade and Reform," on Alan's preaching within this group of reform and crusade preachers see ibid., pp.151–54.

As a theologian and orator, Alan of Lille would have been a well-qualified preacher of the crusades. Born at Lille between 1110 and 1120, Alan studied the liberal arts and Latin literature at Paris in the 1130s and 1140s. He later became a master of arts at Paris and taught at Montpellier in southern France. In the early 1190s he reappeared in Paris as a teacher and entered the Cistercian Order before his death in 1202 or 1203. Known as "Doctor Universalis" by his contemporaries, he produced an extensive and broad range of literature. He wrote works on speculative theology and philosophy, poëtry, a theological dictionary, numerous sermons, a book against heretics, and commentaries on the Christian creeds. Alan likely preached to both Benedictines and Augustinians, while he had contact with Cistercians and participated in anti-heretical preaching in Languedoc. In the last two decades of his long life Alan shifted his attention toward more pastoral concerns, writing a book on preaching and a manual for confessors.[6]

Most likely, Alan of Lille originally preached his *Sermo de cruce domini* on 14 September 1189, the festival for the exaltation of the cross that celebrated the Byzantine Emperor Heraclius' recovery of the relic of the True Cross from the Persian emperor Chosroes in the early seventh century.[7] Although some groups of crusaders had left for the Holy Land before the fall of 1189, the contest between the kings of England and France, the death of Henry II in the previous summer, and infighting among the Angevin nobility, had delayed the departure of Richard I and Philip II. They did not leave until July 1190. In addition, many clerics resented the imposition of the Saladin tithe in 1188 by Henry II and Philip II to pay for the costs of the crusade. Elizabeth Siberry points out that Peter of Blois and other supporters of the crusade opposed the imposition of the Saladin tax on the clergy and gained exemptions for French clergymen. Jean Longère quotes another of Alan's sermons in which he rebukes the clergy for their malice and lack of support for the crusade while commending the repentant laity for taking up the cross. In response both to the royal delay and what he perceived as the lack of clerical enthusiasm for helping fund

---

[6] D'Alverny, *Alain de Lille*, pp. 11–183; Gillian R. Evans, *Alan of Lille* (Cambridge, 1983), pp. 1–19; John M. Trout, "The monastic vocation of Alan of Lille," *Analecta Cisterciensia* 30 (1974), 46–53; P. G. Walsh, "Alan of Lille as a Renaissance Figure," in *Renaissance and Renewal in Christian History*, ed. Derek Baker, Studies in Church History 14 (Oxford, 1977), pp. 119–21. On Alan's recording of an anti-heretical sermon most likely preached by Arnaud Amaury, see Beverly Kienzle, *Cistercians, Heresy and Crusade in Occitania, 1145–1229* (Rochester, NY, 2001), pp. 140–42; and eadem, "*Inimici crucis*: La théologie de la croix et la persécution du catharisme," in *Colloque de Montaillou (25–27 April 2000)*, ed. Emmanuel Le Roy Ladurie (2000), pp. 283–99. Alan's *Summa de arte praedicatoria* is in PL 210:109–98 and the critical edition of his book on penance is *Liber poenitentialis*, ed. Jean Longère, 2 vols., *Analecta Mediaevalia Namurcensia* 17, 18 (Louvain, 1965). (Abbreviated below as *AMN* with volume and page number.)

[7] On this festival in the West see Louis van Tongeren, *Exaltation of the Cross: Toward the Origins of the Feast of the Cross and the Meaning of the Cross in Early Medieval Liturgy* (Leuven, 2000).

the crusade, I believe that Alan composed this sermon for a mixed audience of clergy and laity in northern France.[8]

The scriptural text for Alan's sermon was St. Paul's declaration to the Galatians: "May it be far from me to glory, except in the cross of our Lord Jesus Christ, by which the world is crucified to me and I to the world."[9] Alan contrasts the Christian glorying in the cross with others who boast in riches, honours, pleasures, worldly wisdom, strength and beauty. The cross, he continues, has been made glorious on the breastplates of emperors.[10] Early in the sermon Alan establishes the relationship between the true penitent and Christ by alluding to the biblical account of the two thieves crucified to Christ's left and right. Christ's is a cross of victory in which all should glory. The cross of the thief to Christ's right has mercy, while the cross of the thief to the left is full of misery and madness. One brings about the forgiveness of sins, while the other produces only affliction and pain. The two thieves portray the two responses of Alan's hearers to the vocation of the cross.[11]

After recalling Christ's reconciling work on the cross for humanity, Alan linked the incarnation to the sacramental and liturgical life of the church. Crusaders may bear the sign of the cross on the front of their bodies, but they also carry it in their minds through faith. In baptism and confirmation they received the sign of the cross on their foreheads and hearts as the spiritual fulfilment of the smearing of lamb's blood on the doorframes and overhead post during the Passover.[12] When a deacon

---

[8]   Christopher Tyerman, *England and the Crusades, 1095–1588* (Chicago, 1988), p. 57; d'Alverny, *Alain de Lille*, p. 143; Siberry, *Criticism of Crusading*, pp. 120–24. See also Longère, *Œuvres oratoires*, 1:417, where he quotes Alan's sermon in London, Br. Mus. Add. 19767, f.73v.

[9]   Galatians 6.14. which also inspired the introit for the exaltation of the cross (14 September) and invention of the cross (3 May) that reads: "Nos autem gloriari oportet in cruce Domini Nostri Iesu Christi, in quo est salus, vita et resurrection nostra, per quam salvati et liberati sumus," d'Alverny, *Alain de Lille*, p. 279, n.1.

[10]   Ibid., p. 279. 'Frontes' could be translated 'breastplates' or 'foreheads' here. It is most likely a reference to Constantine's adoption of the cross as his military standard. See Rufinus of Aquileia, *Historia Ecclesiastica*, 9.9, ed. Theodor Mommsen, *Die griechischen christlichen Schriftsteller der ersten drei Jahrhunderte* 9.2 (Berlin, 1909), pp. 827–33. I believe it is a play on words in which he compares the crusader's cross to the marking of the cross on the forehead in baptism or confirmation to which Alan refers shortly. Some crusaders literally branded themselves with the mark of the cross on their foreheads; see Giles Constable, "Jerusalem and the Sign of the Cross," in *Jerusalem: Its Sanctity and Centrality to Judaism, Christianity, and Islam*, ed. Lee I. Levine (New York, 1999), pp. 371–81.

[11]   D'Alverny, *Alain de Lille*, p. 279. On the two thieves, see Luke 23.32–43. Alan is drawing on the tradition prevalent in earlier monastic sermons on the cross of the two thieves portraying the alternate responses to Christ's offer of forgiveness through penance. The earliest use of this typology of the two thieves that I have found is in Augustine, *Sermo* 285.2, PL 38:1293–94. Augustine compared the two thieves' suffering to the martyrs' suffering. His point was that the penitent thief's pious confession of Christ, like a true martyr, made his suffering worthwhile, while the other thief's suffering was of no value, like a Donatist martyr, because he did not rightly believe in Christ.

[12]   Alan's interpretation of Exod. 12.7 is similar to other eleventh- and twelfth-century preachers, cf. Peter Damian, *De inventione sanctae crucis*, 18.5, 13, CCCM 57, ed. Joannes Lucchesi (Turnhout, 1983), pp. 112 and 119; Honorius Augustodunensis, *De inventione sanctae crucis*, PL 172:945; Peter Lombard, *De laudibus sanctae crucis*, PL 171:694; Baldwin of Canterbury, *Sermo de sancta cruce*, 8.30–31, CCCM 99, ed. David N. Bell (Turnhout, 1991), pp. 134–35. Honorius compares the smearing of the

reads the gospels he makes the sign of the cross to sanctify his speech. While believers continue to make the sign of the cross for their protection, they should always remember that the cross marks the entire office of the Mass where the priests present the passion of Christ and the bread is changed into Christ's body.[13]

Following a tradition in monastic exegesis, Alan identified numerous Old Testament prefigurations of the mystery of the salvific cross.[14] Jacob's staff, the staff of Moses that divided the Red Sea and brought water from the stone, the wood on which Moses raised up the bronze serpent, and the pole on which the Hebrew spies carried grapes were all mystical symbols of the cross of Christ. This typological interpretation of Old Testament passages allowed Alan to demonstrate the power of the cross that God displayed throughout history.[15]

Until this point Alan's remarks resemble a typical sermon on the importance of the cross for redemption and the Christian life. Yet after describing the cross as the seal of the Christian religion and banner of the faith, he began to focus on the crusade in general and the loss of the relic of the True Cross in particular. Helena had discovered it, Chosroes had seized it, and Heraclius had liberated it. Now the relic had been lost because of the sins of Christendom. Alan, rhetorically, asked his audience, if there could be any greater sign of Christ's withdrawal from them than the loss of this relic of the Lord's passion.[16]

In response to their iniquity and its consequences, Alan then urged the soldiers of Christ to mark their bodies outwardly with the sign of the cross but, more importantly, mark their hearts with the same holy symbol in penance. They should not follow the example of Simon of Cyrene,[17] taking the cross only because it is

---

lamb's blood to the cross, while the others connect the smearing of the lamb's blood to imitating Christ's passion and rightly carrying the cross in the mind as well as the body. Cf. James of Vitry, *Sermo* 2.11, *Crusade propaganda*, p. 107, where James compares the crusader's cross to the sign of the cross given in baptism.

[13] D'Alverny, *Alain de Lille*, pp. 279–80. In his description of the sign of the cross used at various times during the Mass, Alan follows the twelfth-century instructional manuals on the liturgy. See Honorius Augustodunensis, *Gemma Animae*, 1.23–57, PL 172:551–61; John Beleth, *Summa de ecclesiasticis officiis*, cap. 39 d–g, cap. 46c, CCCM 41A, ed. Heriberto Douteil (Turnhout, 1976), pp. 71–2 and 82.

[14] On this tradition in monastic culture, see Jean Leclercq, *The Love of Learning and the Desire for God*, trans. Catharine Misrahi. 3rd edn. (New York, 1982), pp. 79–84; and Marie-Dominique Chenu, "The Old Testament in Twelfth-Century Theology," in *Nature, Man and Society in the Twelfth Century*, trans. Jerome Taylor and Lester K. Little (Toronto, 1968), pp. 146–61.

[15] D'Alverny, *Alain de Lille*, p. 280. The relevant biblical citations are Genesis 32.10; Exod. 9.23, 10.13, 14.16, 15.25, 17.5–9; Num. 13.24–25, 20.11, 21.8; John 3.14–15. Cf. Alan's *De sancta cruce*. PL 210:223D–224A, Peter Damian's sermons on the cross in CCCM 57, pp. 109–20 and 292–305, and Baldwin, *Sermo de sancta cruce* 8.10, 12, 15–19, 21, 22, CCCM 99, pp. 129–32, 136.

[16] D'Alverny, *Alain de Lille*, pp. 280–81. Helena's discovery of the True Cross is celebrated on 3 May. On the transmission of this story in the Middle Ages, see Stephen Borgenhammar, *How the Holy Cross was Found* (Stockholm, 1991).

[17] On Simon of Cyrene, see Matt. 27.32, Mark 15.21, Luke 23.26. The earliest use of Simon of Cyrene as a negative type of bearing the cross is Gregory the Great, *Homilia* 32.3, CCCM 141, ed. Raymond Etaix (Turnhout, 1999), pp. 280–81.

forced upon them, but patiently bear it as imitators of Christ. Alan implored them to carry the cross like the penitent thief to Christ's right and warned them to avoid the violence of the thief hanging to his left. Having been marked by the cross, they should journey to land of the Crucified and the Holy Sepulchre following Mary Magdalen, Peter, and John. They should seek to recover the True Cross and vindicate Christ's injuries by liberating the land of his inheritance, which is the Virgin's dowry. By affixing a cross to their shoulders and returning with it on their breast, these crusaders will bear the yoke of God, which Christ's love would make delightfully sweet.[18]

The sermon contains many standard features of crusade sermons. Alan called upon the crusaders to avenge the injuries of Christ, liberate the Holy Land and work for the recovery of the True Cross. However, he emphasized that the penitential intent of the crusaders should be in imitation of the penitent thief. He had already contrasted the thieves' crosses with the cross of Christ. Here Alan addressed the soldiers of Christ directly, urging them to carry their crosses like the penitent thief. They must follow the suffering Christ, and not bear their cross like the impenitent thief or Simon of Cyrene.

Alan of Lille drew from an already established tradition of using the typology of the various crosses to explicate the penitential life. The following section of this article will demonstrate the importance of this exegetical tradition for twelfth-century monastic and canonical preachers.[19] Well-known for his devotion to the crucified Christ, Bernard of Clairvaux put forth one of the fullest explanations of the typologies of the various crosses in his *Sententiae*.[20] He identified four crosses, each granting different rewards. The first was Christ's cross of charity, on which Jesus had reconciled God and humanity. Ultimately, Christ desired all believers to be crucified with him on this cross of charity so that they no longer would serve sin, but instead would serve Christ in vigils and fasting with an unfeigned love. This was the cross that the Lord had commanded his disciples to carry.[21]

Identifying the second cross as the one on which the thief to Christ's right had hung, Bernard described this penitent thief as overflowing with penance, humility,

---

[18] D'Alverny, *Alain de Lille*, p. 281; Alan refers to John 20.1–5 and Matt. 11.30.

[19] The two thieves and Simon of Cyrene appear in numerous twelfth-century sermons as examples of true and false bearers of the penitential cross. While I am completing a larger study on those texts, this paper will focus on the most significant preachers in relation to Alan of Lille.

[20] Bernard of Clairvaux, *Sententiae* 3.1, 74, in *S. Bernardi Opera*, vol. 6/2, ed. Jean Leclercq and H. Rochais (Rome, 1972), pp. 59–60, 112–15 and 139 (hereafter abbreviated as SBO). These *Sententiae* give us a better understanding of what Bernard actually may have preached to his own monks; see Jean Leclercq, *Monks and Love in Twelfth-Century France* (Oxford, 1979), pp. 86–87. On Bernard's and other Cistercians' devotion to the crucified Christ, see Sheryl Frances Chen, "Bernard's Prayer before the Crucifix that Embraced Him: Cistercians and the Devotion to the Wounds of Christ," *Cistercian Studies Quarterly* 29 (1994), 23–54; and Giles Constable, "The Ideal of the Imitation of Christ," in *Three Studies in Medieval and Religious Thought* (Cambridge, 1996), pp. 188–90 and 204–205.

[21] Bernard, *Sententiae* 3.1, SBO 6/2, p. 59.

confession, faith, hope and love. He prefigured those who, having recognized their own unrighteousness and God's righteousness, offer their lives on the penitential cross as a sacrifice to God. No one could know Christ, if first he did not hang on the penitent thief's cross and ask the Lord to remember him in his kingdom. Bernard encouraged his audience to stop stealing themselves from God and hang on the cross with heartfelt devotion begging for Christ's mercy.[22]

The impenitent thief to Christ's left, who bore the third cross, suffered similarly to the penitent thief but with an envious, prideful attitude. He represented the wicked that serve God with the same outward works as the truly penitent but do so with a grumbling heart. Simon of Cyrene, the bearer of the fourth cross, signified those who live in outward obedience, but are driven by pride and vainglory. They lack the reward of true obedience, because they will be judged by the intention behind their obedience, not by their outward acts.[23]

The regular canons of St. Victor in Paris used similar typologies in their sermons. A Victorine *Miscellanea*, attributed to Hugh of St. Victor, explained true penance by using the types of the three crosses. The text states that the cross of Christ offered glory, the cross of the thief to the right offered consolation and the cross of the other thief offered confusion. Christ suffered penalty with no guilt, therefore his cross was glorious. Both thieves suffered the penalty on the account of their guilt, but one received remission of sins, while the other was eternally condemned. The thief on the left suffered in vain, because he did not recognize his guilt nor present himself to the judge. The thief to the right humbly recognized his guilt and bore his penalty patiently while begging for mercy.[24]

Baldwin of Forde, the Cistercian abbot who preached the Third Crusade as the archbishop of Canterbury, referred to the thieves beside Christ on the cross in two sermons on the cross. In a sermon in praise of the cross he stated that the cross between the two thieves distinguished their rewards. While the thief to the left mocked Christ and was condemned, the other thief adored him and was saved. This judgment should be an example to all individuals who will stand before Christ.[25] In a sermon on crucifying the old self, Baldwin discussed three crosses of Christ and the two thieves. Christ alone ascended his own cross, thereby justifying others. Sinners carried the other two crosses. While the wicked grumble in their suffering, others penitently confessing their sins hear the Lord assure them of paradise. Baldwin pointed out that malicious sinners bear the cross in vain, because they focus on a worldly prize.[26]

---

[22] Idem, *Sententiae* 3.1, 74, SBO 6/2, pp. 60, 112–13.

[23] Ibid., p. 60.

[24] Attributed to Hugh of St. Victor, *Miscellanea*, PL 177:499C–D. Richard of St. Victor, abbot in the 1160s, applied the typology of the crosses to explain monastic discipline. See Richard of St. Victor, *In medio quadragesimae*, PL 177:1019A–D. On Richard's authorship of these sermons see Jean Longère, *La prédication médiévale* (Paris, 1983), pp. 66–67.

[25] Baldwin, *Sermo de sancta cruce* 8.26, 27, CCCM 99, p. 133.

[26] Idem, *Sermo de crucifixione veteris hominis* 3.1–4, CCCM 99, p. 47.

Other preachers, more closely associated with Alan of Lille's academic circles, also adopted this exegetical tradition. Peter Comestor, the chancellor of Paris from 1168 to 1178, who emphasized the imitation of Christ in his preaching, explained taking up the cross and following Christ in a sermon to monks. After stating that monks should fix themselves to the cross in mind and body, he compared four types of crosses with four ways of living the monastic life. While the truly obedient monks bore the cross of Christ, penitent monks asked God for forgiveness as the penitent thief on the cross had done. A third type of monk bore the impenitent thief's cross, because his superiors forced him to follow the religious life through rebukes and flogging. Finally, some monks carried the cross of hypocrisy with Simon of Cyrene. These monks feigned piety so as to become abbots.[27]

Following Bernard of Clairvaux and the Victorines, in a sermon on the Lord's passion, Maurice of Sully, the bishop of Paris from 1160 to 1196, described the four crosses as types of Christ's love, the thief's penitential confession, the other thief's iniquity, and Simon of Cyrene's hypocrisy.[28] In his *Verbum abbreviatum* Peter the Chanter (d. 1197), Alan's fellow master and reformer, explained the virtue of patience in relation to bearing the cross. Describing the patient sufferers as those who denying themselves take up their cross and follow Christ, he explained the four ways of carrying the cross. Following similar depictions of the crosses of Christ, Simon and the impenitent thief, Peter stated that the penitent thief transformed the penalty of his guilt into meritorious suffering for life. Peter identified the thief as the type of the penitent whom others should imitate by noting the thief's self-accusation, commendation of Christ's righteous cause, and immediate entry into paradise.[29]

Drawing on his contacts with monks, regular canons, and other reform-minded masters, Alan of Lille appropriated this exegetical tradition of distinguishing the four ways of carrying the cross to demonstrate the proper response to the crusading call. In the same manner that a monk or regular canon bore the penitential cross, the penitent knight should affix the cross to his body and heart. Ultimately, the cloistered monk or the crusader could ascend beyond the thief's cross of penance to the cross of Christ, that is, the cross of true love for God and one's neighbour.[30] As we have seen, however, two false ways of taking up the cross led to damnation

---

[27] Peter Comestor, *Ad monachos*, PL 171:897 (falsely attributed to Hildebert of Le Mans). On Peter Comestor's life and preaching of the imitation of Christ, see Longère, *Œuvres oratoires*, 1:20–21 and 103–108.

[28] Vatican City, Biblioteca Apostolica Vaticana, Cod. Reg. Lat. 288, fol. 7ra. On Maurice of Sully's life and preaching, see Longère, *Œuvres oratoires*, 1:14–18.

[29] Peter the Chanter, *Verbum abbreviatum*, cap. 114. PL 205:301D–302C. On Peter's life and career, see Baldwin, *Masters, Princes and Merchants*, 1:3–16.

[30] Jonathan Riley-Smith has shown the appeal to lay down one's life for God and for one's fellow Christian was a central part of crusade propaganda. See Jonathan S. C. Riley-Smith, "Crusading as an Act of Love," *History* 55 (1980), 177–92.

for those in the religious life. Alan warned those who took the crusader's cross to avoid both the symbolic path of Simon of Cyrene, which was hypocrisy, and that of the thief to the left, which was violence and misery that did not result in forgiveness.

To further illustrate his point, Alan then described the proper penitential response to the crusade by using the image of a cross. While many medieval preachers, following Augustine, used similar symbolic interpretations of the cross, Alan's scheme is unique in that he compares the four parts of the cross to the components of the sacrament of penance.[31] The first part, hidden in the ground, signified contrition that was hidden but lies open to God. The second part stretched upward, but attached to the hidden part it symbolized confession that arose from the hidden nature of contrition and was directed toward God. The third part, attached sideways to the second, symbolized satisfaction in which the penitent must persevere to merit forgiveness. The fourth part, the notice that Pilate nailed to the top of the cross, signified the hope of eternal blessedness, because one should participate in the mystery of penance in order to gain the celestial hope. This notice symbolized the human mind, on which this title of Christ should always be inscribed, so that the penitent would always consider the passion and death of Christ. "Without this internal cross," Alan proclaimed, "the external affliction of the cross is frivolous and vain."[32]

In this mystical depiction of the cross Alan illustrated the emerging scholastic theology of penance, which he explained more clearly in his *Summa de arte praedicatoria* and *Liber poenitentialis*. Alan's penitential teaching reflects the theological refinement of the sacrament of penance by twelfth-century Parisian theologians, most notably Peter Lombard. While they did concentrate on the penitent's intent and contrition, nonetheless they affirmed the necessity of confession to a priest and acts of satisfaction to remit the penalty of the sin.[33] Since humans sin in thought, word, and deed, Alan taught that they must make amends through contrition, confession, and satisfaction. Without all these components the penitent, in this case the crusader, could not truly do penance.[34] He defined contrition as the

---

[31] Stephen Langton, Alan's younger contemporary at Paris, presented a similar interpretation; see Longère, *Œuvres oratoires*, 1:156–57. Cf. Alan of Lille, *De sancta cruce*, PL 210:226A. On Augustine see Gerhart B. Ladner, "St. Gregory Nyssa and St. Augustine on the Symbolism of the Cross," in *Late Classical and Mediaeval Studies in honor of Albert Mathias Friend, Jr.*, ed. Kurt Weitzmann (Princeton, 1955), pp. 88–95; and Robert L. Füglister, *Das lebende Kreuz* (Einsiedeln, 1965), pp. 184–215.

[32] "Sine hac cruce interna, exterior crucis afflictio frivola est et nugatoria." d'Alverny, *Alain de Lille*, pp. 281–82. Cf. Siberry, *Criticism of Crusading*, p. 98. This dichotomy of the internal cross and affliction of the external cross mirrors Alan's distinction between interior penance, defined as contrition of the heart, and exterior penance, or satisfaction. See *Liber poenitentialis* 3. 4, *AMN* 18, p. 129.

[33] On this topic see Paul Anciaux, *La théologie du sacrement de pénitence au XIIe siècle* (Louvain, 1949), pp. 84–101; Baldwin, *Masters, Princes and Merchants*, pp. 50–51; Longère, *Œuvres oratoires*, 1:255–71, on Alan especially, 1:265–66.

[34] *Liber poenitentalis* 2.1, *AMN* 18, pp. 45–46; 4.3, *AMN* 18, p. 163; *Summa* 31, PL 210:173C–D.

compunction of the heart that resulted from the remembrance of sins, without which adult baptism and penitential acts would be ineffective. True contrition was the fountain from which confession and satisfaction flow.[35]

In order for contrition to be valid, sinners confessed their sins to a priest, received absolution, and thus escaped future judgment through self-accusation. Alan warned that many obstacles might hinder a penitent from truly confessing sins. These include negligence, the fear of a difficult satisfaction, an evil habit, a delightful sin, the intention of remaining in sin, or the hardening of the heart in malice towards a priest.[36]

Defining satisfaction as the exterior deeds of penance, Alan identified these outward acts as prayers, fasting, vigils, oblations, reading, and alms. The priest should enjoin these remedies to sin as a doctor would give medicine to an ill patient. In order to cure a sin the priest should enjoin its opposite virtue. For example, prayer and fasting could be the medicine for debauchery, or almsgiving for avarice. The virtues of humility, love, patience, cheerfulness of mind, generosity, sobriety, and chastity must be opposed to the vices of pride, envy, anger, sloth, avarice, drunkenness, and debauchery. Perseverance in the penitential life was essential because this struggle against vices by cultivating virtues ended only on the death of the penitent. A true penitent offered as many sacrifices of satisfaction as he or she once offered vices to the devil and the flesh. The sinner should always have the destruction of former sins in mind. An incomplete penance would not suffice. For it was better to suffer the fire of penance in this life than to suffer more in purgatory or, worse, eternally in hell.[37]

By identifying the crusader's cross with the sacrament of penance, Alan followed the message for conversion through penance and pious deeds put forth in *Audita tremendi*. Gregory VIII had granted the indulgence to those who took up the cross with contrition and humility. Alan's identification of the crusader's cross with the sacrament of penance reflects the Parisian reformers' desire to rightly instruct the laity on the nature of penance and its relationship to indulgences. Concerned that indulgences could be understood as a remission of sins without true contrition and confession, they criticized preachers who overstated the remission of sins associated with partial indulgences granted by prelates for such occasions as the building of a church or even a bridge. Ultimately, Parisian masters accepted the use of indulgences, but they did so within the context of their own sacramental theology.

---

[35] *Summa* 30, PL 210:169D–172A; *Liber poenitentalis* 4.4, 10, *AMN* 18, pp.164–65 and 168.

[36] Ibid. 4.5, 8, 10, *AMN* 18, pp. 165–68; *Summa* 31, PL 210:172A–173D.

[37] Ibid., 32, PL 210:173D–175B; *Liber poenitentalis* 2.7, *AMN* 18, pp. 49–51. Alan refers to Gregory the Great, *Homilia* 32.1, CCCM 141, pp. 277–78, concerning the concept of enjoining opposite virtues as medicine for vices. Gregory preaches on "taking up the cross and following Christ" in this homily. On Alan's notion of satisfaction, see Joseph A. Spitzig, *Sacramental Penance in the Twelfth and Thirteenth Centuries* (Washington D.C., 1947), pp. 99–106.

They understood the crusade indulgence as the commutation of all satisfaction enjoined for contritely confessed sins.[38]

Alan's use of the typically monastic examples of the thieves and Simon of Cyrene demonstrates what he believed the papal indulgence offered to potential crusaders. Those who wanted to receive the indulgence in place of the satisfaction necessary to complete the sacrament of penance and avoid further painful penalty in purgatory should contritely confess their sins and take up the cross like the penitent thief. This thief transformed the penalty of his sin into the very way of obtaining paradise by accusing himself before the Lord and begging for mercy. Those crusaders who bore the penitential cross in their heart and persevered in their journey, or died marked by this cross, could expect the same reward.[39] However, Alan forewarned them that those who lacked true contrition, like the impenitent thief, or only took the cross outwardly, like Simon of Cyrene, would still suffer the penalty of sin in purgatory or even worse in hell.

After exhorting his hearers to take up the cross of the penitent thief that he equated to the sacrament of penance, Alan then proclaimed the imitation of the crucified Christ as the crusader's ultimate goal. Drawing upon the image of the crucifix, he presented Christ's passion as a triumph over the Christian's true enemies: the world, the flesh, sin, and the devil.[40] Christ affixed these enemies to the cross with his own body, therefore, counteracting the vices represented by various body parts.[41] Christ turned back the devil's head, pride, through his own humility. He crucified the devil's hand, inordinate desire, by condemning worldly things. Christ also pierced the devil's side, debauchery, and fastened his feet, cunning. Christ crushed the world's head by rejecting glory and pierced its hand

---

[38] On the development of the Parisian reformers' understanding of the crusade indulgence and its effect on crusade preaching in the early thirteenth century, see Bird, "Heresy, Crusade and Reform," pp. 184–236, see especially pp. 196–99, on their conception of the crusade indulgence; eadem, "Innocent III, Peter the Chanter's Circle, and the Crusade Indulgence: Theory, Implementation, and Aftermath," in *Innocenzo III: Urbs et Orbis, Atti del Congresso Internazionale (Rome, 9–15 September 1998)*, ed. Andrea Sommerlechner (Rome, 2003), pp. 501–24. On the changes in indulgence theory and practice in the twelfth century, especially in England, see Nicholas Vincent, "Some Pardoners' Tales: The Earliest English Indulgences," *Transactions of the Royal Historical Society* 12 (2002), 23–58.

[39] Alan referred to the penitent thief as an extraordinary example of a penitent whose contrition and confession sufficed for all satisfaction as evidenced by his immediate entry into paradise with Christ. *Liber poenitentalis* 2.5, *AMN* 18, p. 47. Cf. Peter Lombard, *Sententiarum* 4, dist. 20, PL 192:893.

[40] The anti-Cathar sermon recorded by Alan refers to the crucified Christ. See Kienzle, "Inimici crucis," 291–92, and *Cistercians, Heresy and Crusade*, pp. 141–42. Baldwin of Canterbury drew his audience's attention to the crucifixion by using a cross as a physical prop. An anonymous early thirteenth-century crusade sermon uses the image of the crucified Christ. See *Brevis ordinacio de predicatione crucis, Quinti Belli Sacri Scriptores*, ed. Reinhold Röhricht (Geneva, 1879), pp. 3–26. See Tyerman, *England and the Crusades*, pp. 163–66; Cole, *Preaching the Crusades*, pp. 76–77, 110–12, 117–25; Bird, "Heresy, Crusade and Reform," p. 157.

[41] D'Alverny, *Alain de Lille*, p. 282. On the struggle against these spiritual enemies in medieval religious thought, see Siegfried Wenzel, "The Three Enemies of Man," *Mediaeval Studies* 29 (1967), 47–66.

by condemning pillage. He scorned the appetite of the world's belly and crushed its feet, worldly business. By rejecting sinful impulses and not committing transgression, Christ smashed sin's head and hand. When he scorned sin's pleasure and avoided its increase, Christ crucified its belly and feet. Finally, Christ crucified the tyranny of the flesh or lust. He crushed its head, evil desire, and crucified its hand, the desire for earthly things. He nullified carnal desire, the belly of the flesh, and annulled the increase in evil desire, its feet.[42]

While Christ crucified with himself all these enemies that could keep the crusader from penance and salvation, he endured the passion in his entire body for all his human enemies. His head suffered the imposition of the thorny crown, while his mouth tasted the bitter drink. Christ's ears and eyes heard and beheld the mocking insults. His feet and hands were nailed to the cross while his back was flogged. The soldier's lance ripped open his side and his disciples had deserted him. Alan's graphic depiction of Jesus' passion revealed to his audience what Christ had willingly undergone to overcome their sinful enemies and served as the oratorical bridge to Alan's final rebuke of their sins.[43]

Alan proclaimed that Christ had withdrawn the True Cross, the sign that overcame the devil, because no one in Christendom welcomed him. Prelates cannot welcome Christ, because they received simony as their guest. Since they welcomed pillage, knights denied him hospitality. Christ cannot be found among the deceitful burghers on the account of their usury. Even among the peasants Christ finds no home because robbery dwells among them.[44] According to Alan, only the lonely poor in spirit welcome Christ and they will receive the kingdom of heaven.[45]

This call for the entire society's repentance is analogous to the individual's fulfilment of the sacrament of penance as described by Alan. All Christians should recognize their guilt and confess their sins as the reason for the loss of the True Cross

---

[42] D'Alverny, *Alain de Lille*, p. 282. Alan also compared the crucifixion to a battle between a lord (Christ) and a rebellious vassal (the devil) in a Palm Sunday sermon. Ibid., pp. 246–49. In a sermon addressed to soldiers he explained to them the importance of overcoming the devil, the world, and the flesh through spiritual arms, such as the breastplate of faith, the sword of God's word, the lance of love and the helmet of salvation. *Summa* 40, PL 210:186A–87A. See Eph. 6.11–17; I Thess. 5.8.

[43] D'Alverny, *Alain de Lille*, p. 282. This description reflects the emerging devotion to Christ's passion in the twelfth century.

[44] In "Heresy, Crusade and Reform," Bird demonstrates the link that clerical and monastic reformers established between crusade preaching and attacking the specific sins of various social orders, such as simony, pillage, usury and robbery. Alan seems to be one of earliest preachers to actively promote this idea. On the combination of anti-usury and crusade preaching by Parisian reformers see Jessalynn Bird, "Reform of Crusade? Anti-Usury and Crusade Preaching during the Pontificate of Innocent III," in *Pope Innocent III and his World*, pp. 165–85.

[45] D'Alverny, *Alain de Lille*, pp. 282–83. On Alan's idea of showing hospitality to Christ in one's heart and mind, see *Summa* 37, PL 210:182. Alan's final line is a reference to Matt. 5.3, which was a favourite verse of twelfth-century monastic and clerical reformers who stressed the spiritual poverty of Christ's followers. See Giles Constable, *The Reformation of the Twelfth Century* (Cambridge, 1996), pp. 147–49; Christopher Tyerman, "Who Went on Crusades to the Holy Land?" in *Horns*, pp. 25–26.

and the Holy Land. They should then take up the cross of penance willingly as the proper fruit of repentance. As the priest enjoined satisfaction on an individual in opposition to a particular vice, the pope has now enjoined on all Christendom the crusade as the penitential satisfaction or medicine necessary to counteract the sins that resulted in the loss of the Holy Land and the relic of the True Cross. It was only after the individual and collective fulfilment of this penance that Christ could again be welcomed inwardly or outwardly as symbolized by the relic of the True Cross.

Following the exegetical tradition of equating the penitential cross with the thief to Christ's right, Alan effectively made the penitent thief into a symbol of the truly penitent crusader who bore the cross with patience and thereby gained paradise. After truly adopting the cross of penance, the crusader could glory in the cross of Christ, identified by Alan as the yoke of God made sweet by His love. It was on this cross that Christ overcame all spiritual enemies and embraced suffering for the sins of others. Alternatively, the thief to Christ's left symbolized those who took the cross outwardly but did not repent inwardly of their sins. These impenitent "false" crusaders, who carried the cross of malice, would still be violent, evil men who had not inwardly conquered their spiritual enemies. Simon of Cyrene represented those other "false" crusaders who were driven by pride and ambition instead of inward contrition.

While Alan adopted the typology of these crosses from an interpretive tradition primarily describing the monastic vocation, other factors probably motivated this use of the two thieves as the symbols for the true and false crusaders. As seen above, Alan's indictment of Christian society revolved around sins dealing with money and possessions. Ecclesiastical reformers had traditionally criticized knights for their violent, malicious acts of pillage against other Christians and the Church, while seeking a more positive role for Christian knights.[46] When preaching the First Crusade, Urban II called on those who were once plundering robbers to become soldiers of Christ seeking only an eternal reward.[47] In his *De laude novae militae*, Bernard of Clairvaux had differentiated between the malicious knights, who, driven by selfish ambition, sought earthly possessions and the new soldiers of Christ, who, while destroying the evildoers in defence of the earthly and heavenly Jerusalem, longed for eternal life.[48] Gregory VIII referred to the malice of men as a source of dissension that allowed Saladin to defeat the Christian army at Hattin. Bishop Henry

---

[46] Erdmann, *Origin of the Idea of Crusade*, pp. 201–68; Ian S. Robinson, "Gregory VII and the soldiers of Christ," *History* 58 (1978), 169–92.

[47] FC, 1.3.7, p. 136. See Giles Constable, "The Place of the Crusader in Medieval Society," *Viator* 29 (1998), 379.

[48] Bernard of Clairvaux, *De laude novae militiae* 2, SBO 3 (Rome, 1963), p. 216–19. On Bernard's distinction between worldly, evil knights (malitia) and the new knighthood (militia) of Christ see Aryeh Grabois, "Militia and Malitia: the Bernardine Vision of Chivalry," in *The Second Crusade and the Cistercians*, ed. Michael Gervers (New York, 1992), pp. 49–56.

of Albano appealed to Bernard's distinction between malicious knights and good knights in his promotion of the Third Crusade.[49]

Adopting the tradition of calling worldly knights to repentance, Alan rebuked them for pillaging thievery and assaults on Mother Church.[50] Violence and greed characterized the life of the malicious knight in the same way that the impenitent thief suffered violently, driven only by pride and envy. The crusade offered worldly knights the opportunity to turn from their pillaging ways and bear the cross in true penance as the thief to Christ's right had done. On this cross of penance they could receive the mercy promised to the penitent thief instead of the eternal misery guaranteed by an evil life and death.

Alan instructed not only knights but also the simoniac prelates to carry the cross of penance. By mentioning Simon of Cyrene's way of bearing the cross Alan alluded to clerical hypocrisy. As mentioned above, many clerics promoted the crusade initially, but were unwilling to support it financially on account of their greed. Perhaps Alan's call for clerical financial support encouraged Innocent III's later imposition of the fortieth tax on the clergy in 1199.[51] A similar call to the merchants and peasants regarding their usury and stealing reflected Alan's concern to deal with all social classes and his desire to encourage spiritual and financial support for the crusade imposed on all Christendom as a penance for the malicious iniquity of its members.

Alan of Lille blended the Parisian reformers' teaching on the sacrament of penance with the imitation of the crucified Christ to create a powerful theological and devotional statement on crusading. Adopting the generally monastic teaching on the crosses of the two thieves and Simon of Cyrene, Alan created what became a standard appeal in crusade sermons in the thirteenth century.[52] With the loss of the True Cross God had displayed his displeasure with the avarice of all Christians. Now, according to Alan, the Lord was granting Christians the opportunity to put aside their thievery and be welcomed into paradise after enduring the hardship of the crusade.

---

[49] On Gregory, see n. 1 above. Henry of Albano followed Bernard in his letter to German princes in Ansbert, *Historia de expeditione Friderici*, p. 12. On Henry's crusade preaching, see Cole, *Preaching of the Crusades*, pp. 65–71.

[50] *Summa* 40, PL 210:186.

[51] On clerical greed, see n. 8 above. On Innocent III see Siberry, *Criticism of Crusading*, pp. 126–28. Before Innocent rebuked the French clergy for their lack of financial support, recorded in *Gesta Innocenti*, PL 214:133, he reminded them of Christ's continual suffering because of the loss of the Holy Land and the True Cross.

[52] See Jessalynn Bird, "The Victorines, Peter the Chanter's Circle, and the Crusade: Two Unpublished Crusading Appeals in Paris, Bibliotheque nationale, MS Latin 14470," *Medieval Sermon Studies* 48 (2004), 17, 23; Eudes of Châteauroux, *Sermo* 4.12–13, *Crusade propaganda*, pp. 164–65; Gilbert of Tournai, *Sermo* 3.20, ibid., pp. 208–209; Bonaventure, *Sermo* 1. *Feria III Pentecostes. Opera Omnia Bonaventurae* 13, ed. Adolphe C. Peltier (Paris, 1868), p. 311; Humbert of Romans, *De predicacione sancte crucis*, Vatican City, Biblioteca Apostolica Vaticana, MS Vat. Lat. 3487, fo. 4v. Cf. Bird, "Heresy, Reform and Crusade," p. 199.

# There and Back Again:
# Crusaders in Motion, 1096–1291[*]

*Edward Peters*

University of Pennsylvania

The brief, but happy marriage of St. Elizabeth of Hungary and Landgraf Ludwig IV of Thuringia considerably exercised some of the saint's hagiographers, including Jacobus de Voragine. It also happens to illuminate several important aspects of crusade history: the domestic rupture that leaving on crusade often entailed, rituals of departure, and, dramatically in Ludwig's case, the dangers of the route itself. Ludwig secretly took the cross early in 1227, concealing his decision from his pregnant wife in order not to cause her anxiety. She devotedly accompanied him even beyond the borders of Thuringia when he left, and could only with much effort be persuaded to return home. Finally, her public and demonstrative grief upon receiving the news of his death from fever in Otranto and, later, his remains, suggests the devastating impact on an affectionate marriage that departure and death on crusade might have.[1] Ludwig's death en route is also a reminder that the greatest risks of crusading did not come into play only in the Levant.

Much crusade research and historiography has tended to focus on one of two distinct areas of research: on the one hand, the organization of crusades in western Europe and the circumstances of departure, and on the other the arrival and military activities in the Holy Land (or whatever land crusaders wanted to make holy). The first area – the European impact, or the impact in Europe – includes the papal or royal proclamation through the preaching, recruitment, motivation, specification of privileges, rites for taking the cross, settling disputes, social and financial preparations, arranging protection for family, dependants, and property, and even crusade criticism.

---

[*] An early version of this essay was delivered as part of the Spring Lecture Series on the theme of "Medieval Journeys: Pilgrims, Crusaders, and Explorers," of the Institute for Medieval Studies at the University of New Mexico in Albuquerque in March, 2005. The essay is printed very much as given. I am grateful to Tim Graham for the invitation and hospitality, to the staff of the Annenberg Rare Book and Manuscript Library at the University of Pennsylvania, and to Charles McClelland, Helen Damico, Thomas Madden, and Jay Rubenstein. Jessalynn Lea Bird and James M. Powell graciously read and helpfully commented on an earlier draft of the essay.

[1] *Annales Reinhardsbrunnenses*, ed. Franz X. Wegele, *Thüringische Geschichtsquellen*, Bd. 1 (Jena, 1854), Ad. an. 1227, pp. 198–208. There is a brief English summary, with an illustration of the parting window in the Elizabeth church in Marburg, in Norbert Ohler, *The Medieval Traveller*, trans. Caroline Hillier (Woodbridge, 1989), pp. 136–40. I have not seen the German original, *Reisen im Mittelalter* (Munich, 1986). Louis's uncle and predecessor as Landgraf, Louis III, also died on crusade and became the subject of a rhymed chronicle in Middle High German: *Der Kreuzfahrt des Landgrafen Ludwigs des Frommen von Thüringen*, ed. Hans Naumann, MGH Deutsche Chroniken, Bd. IV, Teil 2 (Munich, 1980).

The other principal focus of research is the activities of crusaders in the Holy Land – settlements, government, family history, communications with western Europe, marriage, relations with the Christian and non-Christian inhabitants, military enterprises, military orders, truces, captivity, ransom, death.

But crusaders in motion – between the European preparations and departure and the arrival in Iberia, Anatolia, Syria, or Egypt, and the return to western Europe – do not often attract the attention of historians – except for occasional spectacular instances like the woman led by a goose on the Popular Crusade in 1096 or the murderous excesses of renegade crusaders on the same crusade, and a few later instances; for example, the riots caused by violent crusaders at Worms in 1147 or the broken transportation contract with the Venetians that ultimately brought the Fourth Crusade to Constantinople in 1203–4.[2]

The death of Ludwig of Thuringia en route to the Holy Land (the same disease that killed Ludwig also struck Frederick II, in whose company Ludwig was travelling) in the midst of elaborate imperial preparations for departure suggests that the actual *passagium* was not only full of its own risks, but that it may also be an illuminating occasion for the history of material civilization, in that it involved the logistical problems of organizing large armed groups and moving them by land or water (usually segments of both on the same journey) across long and dangerous distances. In one respect, of course, this last point may help to explain the exiguous scholarly literature on crusaders in motion; at the moment of departure crusaders seem to dissolve into the larger generic travel categories of military or naval history or general modes and routes of transportation and travel, crusaders differing from other travellers, including other pilgrims, only in their numbers, military equipment, including warhorses, greater need for internal management of men and *matériel*, logistics, and purpose. This becomes more strongly the case when the crusading expeditions consisted of the *passagium particulare* as well as the larger *passagium generale*. But crusaders were not quite ordinary generic travellers. Most travellers in early Europe were from sectors of society that were used to journeying, such as itinerant rulers and their (often quite large) entourages, prelates, nobles, merchants, scholars, couriers, and royal or papal agents. John of Salisbury observed that he crossed the Alps ten times between 1136 and 1154.

But crusaders were usually first-time long-distance travellers, and eventually at some point travellers en masse, and both their purpose and the occasion of their departure for hostile parts was a memorable, if ambivalent experience. And once they were assembled armies, by their very nature they pushed to the limit traditional infrastructures, such as roads, markets, hostels, inns, seaports, local food supplies,

---

[2] An exception for the early period is John France, *Victory in the East: A Military History of the First Crusade* (Cambridge, 1994). Of course, the travel of the armies of the Fourth Crusade is a central theme in its history. Most recently, Jonathan Phillips, *The Fourth Crusade and the Sack of Constantinople* (London, 2004), and John H. Pryor, "The Venetian fleet for the Fourth Crusade and the diversion of the crusade to Constantinople," in *EC, I*, pp. 103–23.

and even the general Christian obligation of charity toward pilgrims. Even the resources and patience of mighty Constantinople could be strained by an influx of crusading armies, no matter how friendly.[3] And until the early thirteenth century virtually all crusades passed through Constantinople. When, in the thirteenth century, the greater use of ships and sea routes took most crusader forces well to the south of Constantinople, the city's importance on crusading routes was considerably reduced.[4]

By the Second Crusade at the latest, leaders of such expeditions had to make increasingly elaborate diplomatic and material preparations well in advance. Odo of Deuil states that Louis VII carefully discussed for both passage and market availability not only with Roger II of Sicily, but with Conrad III and representatives of Geisa II of Hungary, perhaps having been informed of the difficulties in precisely these matters that had troubled the armies of the First Crusade.[5] For kings themselves, of course, regencies had to be established, perhaps for the first time during the Second Crusade, a constitutional novelty, at least for rulers who were not minor children.

The crusading venture of Ludwig IV of Thuringia did not last long, but the experience of another crusader twenty years later offers considerably more information. Here is a crusader, penitent and in motion, in March 1248:

> This same abbot of Cheminon gave me my pilgrim's staff and wallet. I left Joinville immediately after – never to enter my castle again until my return from oversea – on foot, with my legs bare, and in my shirt. Thus attired I went to Blécourt and Saint-Urbain. and to other places where there are holy relics. And all the way to Blécourt and Saint-Urbain I never once let my eyes turn back towards Joinville, for fear my heart might be filled with longing at the thought of my lovely castle and the two children I had left behind.[6]

---

[3] Elizabeth Jeffreys and Michael Jeffreys, "The 'Wild Beast from the West': Immediate Literary Reactions from Byzantium to the Second Crusade," and Angeiki E. Laiou, "Byzantine trade with Christians and Muslims and the Crusades," both in *The Crusades from the Perspective of Byzantium and the Muslim World*, ed. Angeliki E. Laiou and Roy Parvez Mottahedeh (Washington, D.C., 2001), pp. 101–16, and 157–92.

[4] Michael Lower, *The Barons' Crusade: A Call to Arms and Its Consequences* (Philadelphia, 2005), 212, n. 48, citing John H. Pryor, *Geography, Technology, and War: Studies in the Maritime History of the Mediterranean, 649–1571* (Cambridge, 1988).

[5] On crusade memory and the use of earlier crusade experience in later crusade planning, see Jonathan Phillips, "Odo of Deuil's *De Profectione Ludovici VII in Orientem* as a source for the Second Crusade," in *EC, I*, pp. 80–102, and Jay Rubenstein, "Putting History to Use: Three Crusade Chronicles in Context," *Viator* 35 (2004), 131–68. The accounts of earlier crusading ventures were regularly read by later crusaders well into the fourteenth century, some of the more recent accounts (William of Tyre and Jacques de Vitry) replacing older ones.

[6] Joinville, *Vie de Saint Louis*, ed. Jacques Monfrin (Paris, 2002), ch. 122, pp. 218–20. Translation, Jean Sire de Joinville, *The Life of Saint Louis*, in Joinville and Villehardouin, *Chronicles of the Crusades*, trans. Margaret R. B. Shaw (London, 1963), ch. 2, p. 191. On Joinville as crusader, Danielle Quéruel, "Nous de Champaingne …," in *Jean de Joinville: de la Champagne aux royaumes d'outre-mer*, ed. Danielle Quéruel (Langres, 1998), pp. 49–72, and Philippe Ménard, "L'Esprit de la croisade chez Joinville. Étude des mentalités médiévales," in *Les champenois et la croisade*, ed. Yvonne Bellenger and

Six years and 541 editorial sections of the *Vie de Saint Louis* later, Joinville returned to his lovely castle and children via Cyprus, Lampedusa, Panteleria, Hyères, Aix, Beaucaire, and visits to his niece, his uncle and his cousin, after having had a number of dangerous adventures along the way home.[7] And he found, much to his dismay, how much his long absence had cost, not just himself and his king, but the people of his lands in Champagne. Nor did Joinville go on crusade again. He flatly rejected Louis's invitation in 1267, and he stoutly advised the king himself not to go. Once, apparently, had been quite enough. But we are grateful that Joinville went, and that he wrote not a conventional crusade chronicle, but the life of a friend and a saint, which gave his narrative a different perspective on crusading from those of more formal crusade chronicles – the experience of crusading from the inside, as it were.[8] Joinville, distinctive in this as in so many other aspects of his great work, tells us quite a bit about crusaders in motion, and in motion over immense distances which, depending on where one started out, could extend up to three or four thousand kilometers. Occasionally, there is some visual evidence to help.[9]

---

Danielle Quéruel (Paris, 1989), pp. 131–47. There is, alas, no mention on departure or return of Madame de Joinville, a point also made by Margaret Wade Labarge, *Medieval Travellers* (New York, 1983), pp. 96–114, although Labarge's chapter on crusaders as travellers contains a series of picturesque crusade anecdotes rather than a serious analysis of crusaders in motion, a feature characteristic of most popular and even scholarly studies of medieval travel. Arthur P. Newton, ed., *Travel and Travellers of the Middle Ages* (New York, 1926; repr. London and New York, 2004) does not mention crusaders as travellers. There is the brief mention only of Ludwig IV of Thuringia in Ohler, *The Medieval Traveller*. Jean Verdon, *Travel in the Middle Ages*, trans. George Holoch (Notre Dame, 1998), cites Joinville and little else. Albert C. Leighton, *Transport and Communication in Early Medieval Europe AD 500–1100* (Newton Abbot, 1972) adds little more. More recent studies of medieval travel, however, are a considerable scholarly improvement; for example, Rosamund Allen, ed., *Eastward Bound: Travel and travellers, 1050–1550* (Manchester, 2004).

[7]  Monfrin ed., ch. 663, pp. 541–42.

[8]  Accounts like that of Joinville (and of individual pilgrims) seem to be the nearest literary equivalent in the Latin West to the *hodoiporikon* of Byzantine literature: Margaret E. Mullett, "In peril on the sea: travel genres and the unexpected," in *Travel in the Byzantine World: Papers from the Thirty-fourth Spring Symposium of Byzantine Studies, Birmingham, April, 2000*, ed. Ruth Macrides, Society for the Promotion of Byzantine Studies, Publications 10 (Aldershot and Burlington, USA, 2000), pp. 259–84. On the *Hodoeporicon* of Margaret of Beverley, Christoph T. Maier, "The roles of women in the crusade movement: a survey," *Journal of Medieval History* 30 (2004), 61–82, at 64. For the literature on Muslim travel, Shawkat M. Toorawa, "Travel in the medieval Islamic world: the importance of patronage, illustrated by ʿAbd al-Latif al Baghdadi (d. 629/1231) (and other litterateurs)," in *Eastward Bound*, 53–70.

[9]  Pictorial evidence is highly selective. My own very informal inventory of images indicates a considerable emphasis on some aspects of crusading – proclamations, preaching, preparations, and departure, and then arrivals, sieges, and battles, but usually very little of the journey itself. Colin Morris, "Picturing the Crusades: The Uses of Visual Propaganda, c. 1095–1250," in *Crusades Sources*, pp. 195–216. Recent volumes based on museum exhibitions contain somewhat more reliable pictorial information: for example, *Le Crociate: L'Oriente e l'Occidente da Urbano II a San Luigi, 1096–1270*, ed. Monique Rey-Delqué (Milan, 1997), and *Kein Krieg ist heilig. Die Kreuzzüge* ed. Hans-Jürgen Kotzur (Mainz, 2004).

It is worth pointing out four things at the beginning of this essay. The first is that all of our knowledge of travel and communications in early Europe and the Mediterranean must be rethought in the light of the substantial sections on travel and communication in Michael McCormick's great book, *Origins of the European Economy*.[10] The second is that, although geography is not destiny, the geographical and meteorological configuration of Europe, the eastern Atlantic, and the Mediterranean is duplicated nowhere else in the world, and studies of travel in these areas must heed geography and meteorology. The third is that the early eleventh century now appears to be a key turning point in the character of travel, in relation not only to pilgrimage and crusading, but also to commerce and communications as well. The fourth is that the cost of crusading, even more than that of pilgrimage, was immense, although it varied considerably over the twelfth and thirteenth centuries, and it had to be paid in liquid capital, which usually had to be kept in hand and up front.

In the letter of dedication of his work to the future Louis X, Joinville cites four episodes in which Louis IX had placed himself in danger in order to keep his subjects from suffering harm. Three of these four had to do with events on the journey to the Levant and the return, the last a shipwreck on the return to Cyprus in which the king's resolute determination seems to have saved the lives of the 800 passengers on his ship.[11]

Now, Joinville was a remarkably perceptive, well-positioned observer with a fine memory and gift of expression and a willingness to include all sorts of events and impressions if they might illuminate the saintly and often frustrating character of Louis IX. He was also a crusader at a time when – however much one agrees or disagrees with Christopher Tyerman on the subject – the phenomenon of crusade was pretty well defined and clearly understood.[12] And for precisely those reasons he is an ideal – if not my only – informant about crusaders in motion.

Crusaders also appeared to be distinctly different from other kinds of travellers. Although they may have begun their preparations for departure by dressing as

---

[10] Michael McCormick, *Origins of the European Economy: Communications and Commerce AD 300–900* (Cambridge, 2001), and slightly earlier in his "Byzantium on the move: imagining a communications history," in *Travel in the Byzantine World*, ed. Ruth Macrides, pp. 3–29. McCormick's research has been considerably extended by Olivia Remie Constable, *Housing the Stranger in the Mediterranean World: Lodging, Trade, and Travel in Late Antiquity and The Middle Ages* (Cambridge, 2003), an extensive study of the *pandocheion*, *funduq*, and *fondaco*; and Maribel Dietz, *Wandering Monks, Virgins, and Pilgrims: Ascetic Travel in the Mediterranean World, A.D. 300–800* (University Park, PA, 2005). The literature of pilgrimage is now vast. For one distinctive area, Marie-Luise Favreau-Lilie, "The German Empire and Palestine: German pilgrimages to Jerusalem between the 12th and 16th century," *Journal of Medieval History* 21 (1995), 321–41, and generally Aryeh Graboïs, *Le pélerin occidental en Terre Sainte au Moyen Âge* (Paris, 1998).

[11] Monfrin ed., ch. 7–ch. 17. The event was memorable for Joinville – he cites it again at ch. 39–ch. 42.

[12] Christopher Tyerman, *The Invention of the Crusades* (Toronto, 1998). And James M. Powell, *Anatomy of a Crusade, 1213–1221* (Philadelphia, 1986).

pilgrims during their visits to local shrines – consider Joinville's description of his own departure costume – later their distinctive crosses, horses, and weaponry marked them out precisely for what they were.[13] Once sea travel became the primary means of going on crusade, small groups like Joinville's could drift individually to mustering-points like Marseilles – where Louis IX had more difficulties than Joinville, before he departed from the unpropitious Aigues-Mortes – and later Cyprus (or earlier, to Genoa, Bari, or Venice – or, as in the case of the Fourth Crusade, spectacularly, not to Venice), but at some point they, or most of them, had to be brought together. Once combined, such forces had to be set in collective motion as soon as possible. Logistical problems and the limitations of local resources, including local patience, dictated that large military forces could not be left to remain in one place for very long without beginning to unravel; witness the armies of the Fourth Crusade languishing on the island of St. Nicholas in Venice, waiting for fellow-crusaders who never turned up.[14] Evidently, according to Matthew Paris, Louis IX had to leave a significant number of his followers behind at Marseilles. They then went to the pope at Lyons, turned over their traveling supplies to him, were released from their crusade vows and returned home.[15]

Let us follow Joinville as far as he will take us. He was a young man at the time, around twenty-three, and although he had already visited Corbeil, Poitiers, and Paris, his preparations for departure on crusade were necessarily more elaborate. First, he summoned his dependants, including all who held fiefs from him, to celebrate Easter and the birth of his second son, also named Jean. At the end of the celebration, on Friday of Easter Week, Joinville announced that he was taking the cross and going overseas, "not knowing whether I shall return." He invited all present to state and settle their claims against him, making peace, as all pilgrims and crusaders were expected to do. Since his mother was still living and consuming income, Joinville went to Metz to mortgage his lands for 1,000 pounds, that is, to

---

[13] Jonathan Riley-Smith, *The First Crusaders, 1095–1131* (Cambridge, 1997), p. 11. On the fully developed ideas of personal moral reform, rites, and privileges, Powell, *Anatomy*, pp. 15–88.

[14] There is a slender literature on crusade logistics. See Bernard Bachrach, "Logistics in Pre-Crusade Europe," in *Feeding Mars: Logistics in Western Warfare from the Middle Ages to the Present*, ed. John A. Lynn (Boulder, 1993), pp. 57–78; and idem, "The Siege of Antioch: A Study in Military Demography," *War in History* 6 (1999), 127–46. John H. Pryor, "The Venetian fleet for the Fourth Crusade and the diversion of the crusade to Constantinople," *EC, I*, pp. 103–23. The best recent narrative of the Fourth Crusade is that of Jonathan Phillips, *The Fourth Crusade*. There is much on logistics in the earlier period in McCormick, *Origins*, pp. 391–430. And in *Logistics of Warfare in the Age of the Crusades*, ed. John H. Pryor (Aldershot, 2006). Recent books based on museum exhibitions contain somewhat more information: for example, *Le Crociate*, pp. 219–26, and *Kein Krieg ist heilig*, pp. 187–205. The extensive bibliographies of Kelly De Vries are the place to start: *A Cumulative Bibliography of Medieval Military History and Technology* (Leiden, 2002), and *A Cumulative Bibliography of Medieval Military History and Technology: Update 2004* (Leiden, 2005).

[15] Matthew Paris, Giles trans. ad an. 1248 (pp. 269–70). The best study of Louis's preparations, including the logistics, is William Chester Jordan, *Louis IX and the Challenge of Crusade: A Study in Rulership* (Princeton, 1979), esp. pp. 65–104. Cf. Jean Richard, *Saint Louis, Crusader King of France*, trans. and abridged by Simon Lloyd (Cambridge, 1992), pp. 99–112.

obtain his yearly income up front and in cash, the amount he had with him on the day of his departure. Joinville had also arranged to travel with two of his cousins, Jean, Count of Sarrebrück, and the count's brother Gobert d'Aspremont, with whom he hired a ship, although he mentions only the Count of Sarrebrück when he calculates the numbers of knights accompanying him and the count on their voyage.[16] He had sent all of his luggage, including armor and weapons, ahead overland to Auxonne on the Saône.

When he left, Joinville, dressed as a pilgrim, made the local pilgrimages to Blécourt and Saint-Urbain and then proceeded to Fontaine-l'Archevêque, where the abbot of Saint-Urbain gave him and the nine knights with him a number of jewels. At Auxonne, Joinville, his luggage, and his companions boarded riverboats, which moved down the Saône to Lyon, the warhorses being led along the riverbanks beside the boats. From Lyon they sailed down the Rhône to Arles (the horses still walking the bank) and then to Marseilles, where Joinville was sufficiently impressed with the method of loading horses into the ship that he describes the process in some detail, including the careful caulking of the large port in the hull once the horses were loaded.[17] River and sea transport was far easier on baggage trains than overland travel. Odo of Deuil comments sourly on the problem of wagon-trains:

> We say these things to caution subsequent pilgrims; for, since there was a very great number of four-horse carts, if one was damaged, all were delayed to the same extent; but, if they found many roads, all thronged to them at the same time, and the packhorses, in avoiding the obstruction they presented, very frequently ran into more serious hindrances. For this reason the death of horses was a common occurrence, and so were the complaints about the short distance traveled each day.[18]

---

[16] Monfrin ed., ch. 109. Joinville states that both he and his cousin the count each brought nine knights, which, with the two of them added, brought the company up to twenty. He makes no further mention of Gobert d'Aspremont, but there seem also to be other soldiers in the company, as well as a large contingent from the rest of Champagne.

[17] Odo of Deuil reports that Conrad III also walked his army's warhorses along the riverbanks while the main army sailed (Berry ed., 34). On the horse-carrying ships, John H. Pryor, "The Transportation of Horses by Sea during the Era of the Crusades," *The Mariner's Mirror* 68 (1982), 9–27, 103–25; idem, "The Naval Architecture of Crusader Transport Ships," *The Mariner's Mirror* 70 (1984), 171–219, 275–92, 363–86; idem, "The Naval Architecture of Crusader Transport Ships and Horse Transports Revisited," *The Mariner's Mirror* 76 (1990), 255–73. Warhorses wore out quickly when shipped over long distances, and Joinville was well advised: Ralph H. C. Davis, *The Medieval Warhorse: Origin, Development and Redevelopment* (London, 1989). Cf. Bernard S. Bachrach, "On the Origin of William the Conqueror's Horse Transports," and idem, "Some Observations on the Military Administration of the Norman Conquest," both repr. in Bachrach, *Warfare and Military Organization in Pre-Crusade Europe* (Aldershot, 2002), XIII and XIV.

[18] Odo, Berry trans., p. 25. Odo's details about the journey out may offer a corrective to the recent challenge to his authorship by Beate Schuster, "The Strange Pilgrimage of Odo of Deuil," in *Medieval Concepts of the Past: Ritual, Memory, Historiography*, ed. Gerd Althoff, Johannes Fried and Patrick J. Geary (Cambridge, 2002), pp. 253–78. See also Phillips, "Odo of Deuil's *De Profectione Ludovici VII in Orientem* as a source for the Second Crusade." Odo is remarkably informative on a number of details of the expedition omitted by other chroniclers; for example, Louis VII's good fortune to follow the army of

Joinville's party sailed in August, 1248, a sensible season for their route.[19] Like many crusaders and pilgrims, his journey included both land and sea segments.[20]

The ship's captain called for the clergy to perform a paraliturgy of departure, probably not unlike the later "Forms of Prayer to be Used at Sea" at the end of the older versions of the *Book of Common Prayer*, or special public prayers for the safe travel of pilgrims. The whole company chanted the hymn *Veni Creator Spiritus*, the sails were unfurled, and the ship put out to sea.[21]

Their course lay southeast past the west coast of Sicily and then to the passage between Tunis and Malta and east to Lusignan Cyprus, and its reaches clearly involved night sailing. Joinville had never been to sea before, and his reflections on the dangers of the sea on the direct voyage from Marseilles to Cyprus may seem like a few sententious commonplaces about the dangers of seafaring until one realizes that he was probably as apprehensive as he had ever been in his life and the pious moralizations probably conceal some very uncomfortable moments.[22] He tells us of a mountain shaped like a bowl, to which the ship kept returning in the quirky northern Tunisian currents that held them and from which the ship got free only after a series of devotional processions around the deck.[23]

And then to Cyprus, where they found the king and the supplies that his men had been laying in for two years, including vast stacks of wine barrels that from a distance looked like great barns and stacks of grain that looked like large hills. Matthew Paris has some interesting comments on the complexities of supplying Louis's forces on Cyprus – from both Venice and Sicily.[24] Since its conquest by Richard I and his installation of the Lusignan dynasty as its lords (later kings through the grant of the emperor Henry VI), Cyprus had been the key staging

---

Conrad III and therefore have newly built bridges to cross rather than incurring the expense of building his own (Berry ed., 32–33).

[19] There is much useful information about the Mediterranean, its sailing routes and seasons, characteristic ships, and navigation in John H. Pryor, *Geography, Technology, and War: Studies in the Maritime History of the Mediterranean, 649–1571* (Cambridge, 1988). On the differences between warships and cargo vessels, see Richard W. Unger, "Warships and Cargo Ships in Medieval Europe," *Technology and Culture* 22 (1981), 233–52; repr. in Unger, *Ships and Shipping in the North Sea and Atlantic, 1400–1800* (Aldershot, 1997) with same pagination, ch. VIII; idem, *The Ship in the Medieval Economy* (London, 1980), esp. pp. 119–60; idem, ed., *Cogs, Caravels and Galleons: The Sailing Ship 1000–1650* (London, 1994). On Mediterranean sailing seasons, McCormick, *Origins*, pp. 450–68.

[20] Thus, it is often not necessary to distinguish too categorically between land and sea travel on the same expedition: Jonathan Sumption, *Pilgrimage: An Image of Medieval Religion* (London, 1975), pp. 175–92.

[21] On special prayers, McCormick, *Origins*, p. 393 n.2, p. 404 n. 50; idem, "Byzantium on the Move," 10; Margaret E. Mullet, "In peril on the sea"; Sumption, *Pilgrimage*, pp. 175–76.

[22] On the growing use of sea travel, Michel Balard, "Les transports des occidentaux vers les colonies du Levant au Moyen Age," in *Maritime Aspects of Migration*, ed. Klaus Friedland, Quellen und Darstellungen zur hansischen Geschichte, Neue Folge, Bd. 34 (Cologne, 1989), pp. 3–25, as well as other essays in the medieval section of the volume.

[23] On these and other perils, John H. Pryor, "Winds, waves, and rocks: the routes and the perils along them," in *Maritime Aspects of Migration*, pp. 71–85.

[24] Matthew Paris, trans. Giles, ad an. 1249 (pp. 306–307).

area for the eastern Mediterranean.[25] There, Louis had to be persuaded to delay his departure for Egypt to await those of his fellow crusaders who had not yet arrived. As we will see, members of the crusade were still arriving even after Louis had won and lost at Damietta, been captured and ransomed, and gone on to Acre. Joinville's own journey so far looks reasonably efficient and relatively speedy.

But his finances had borne a great strain. Having left with 1,000 *livres tournois*, and paying passage for himself, nine knights, two knights-banneret, and their gear and horses, he found upon reaching Cyprus that he had only 240 *livres tournois* left and, although he does not say so, the prospect of not even this much if the departure for Egypt were delayed on Cyprus much longer. He says nothing of the jewels given by the abbot of Saint-Urbain, but presumably these too had been expended along the way. Such gross underestimation of expenses may seem surprising given the planning that went into the king's crusade. It perhaps highlights the problems of calculating costs in advance and of traveling first-class. But Joinville was stuck. Several of his knights indicated that they would have to leave him if he could not raise more. Fortunately, Louis IX himself took Joinville into his service and gave him 800 pounds to tide him and his knights over.[26] In fact, Joinville's financial difficulties were a microcosm of the king's. Louis IX's expenses on his first crusade cost him five times the annual royal income.

In March, 1249, Louis commanded the fleet to stock itself and leave Cyprus for Damietta:

> King Louis set sail, with all the others in his wake. It was a lovely sight to look at, for it seemed as if all the sea, as far as the eye could reach, was covered with the canvas of the ships' sails. The total number of vessels, both great and small, amounted to about eighteen hundred.[27]

But a sudden storm scattered the fleet, and only seven hundred ships accompanied the king to Damietta, where, according to Joinville, an equally splendid sight awaited them – the glittering army of the sultan.

Faced by a strong hostile force before Damietta, Louis and his reduced forces had no sheltered harbor in which to await the others, and so they had to disembark men and horses, rapidly and chaotically, sometimes from large ships to smaller boats, apparently in great confusion, since Joinville's account can barely be followed at

---

[25] Peter Edbury, *The Kingdom of Cyprus and the Crusades, 1191–1374* (Cambridge, 1991).

[26] Jonathan Riley-Smith, "Early Crusaders to the East and the Costs of Crusading 1095–1130," in *Cross Cultural Convergences in the Crusader period: Essays Presented to Aryeh Graboïs on His Sixty-Fifth Birthday*, ed. Michael Goodich, Sophia Menache, and Sylvia Schein (New York and Bern, 1995), pp. 237–57; Norman Housley, "Costing the crusade; budgeting for crusading activity in the fourteenth century," in *EC, I*, pp. 45–59. Cf. Powell, *Anatomy*, pp. 89–106.

[27] Shaw trans. ch.4, p. 201; Monfrin ed., ch. 146. On the size of earlier fleets, McCormick, *Origins*, pp. 412–13.

this point: "I can assure you that when I landed I had with me neither squire, nor knight, nor servant that I had brought with me from my own lands."[28]

And there is another difference between crusaders and other travellers. Crusaders sometimes had to plunge directly into amphibious combat when they got where they were going, whether or not they and their horses had regained their land legs; for example in Portugal during the Second Crusade and again in 1189, but especially after Egypt had become the landing point of choice.

The mention of Portugal reminds us, of course, of the important role of the North Sea and the eastern Atlantic fleets and shipping routes, from the three-year crusade of Sigurd I of Norway (1107–10) to the siege and capture of Silves in 1189. Several documents, the best known of which is the *De expugnatione Lyxbonensi* by Raol, offer careful detailed accounts of the North Sea–Atlantic route taken by Scandinavian, German, Flemish, Scots, and English crusaders. The *De expugnatione* tells briefly the fascinating story of a composite army, embarked at Dartmouth in May 1147, which, since there seems to have been no obvious leader or leaders, collectively decides that it has to establish its own internal governance and does so by electing a judicial body to make all decisions, comprised of two judges and two fellow-jurors for each one thousand members of the ten thousand-man army, to keep the peace, and manage finances – a collective decision that was probably not unique. The much less well-known and still untranslated *Narratio de itinere navali peregrinorum Hierosolymam tendentium et Silviam capientium, A.D. 1189*, edited by Charles W. David in 1939 from the unique Turin manuscript, offers even further information, perhaps because its author was a landsman on his first long voyage, on such varied topics as weather, St. Elmo's fire, delays caused by wind conditions, the skill of sailors tacking deftly to get through the Straits of Gibraltar in the face of adverse winds, a visit to Santiago, the joining of two different crusading fleets off Lisbon, and a school of dolphins.[29] The slightly later (c. 1200) Danish account, *Historia de profectione Danorum in Hierosolymam*, deals with a North Sea shipwreck and raises the theological question of whether those who die en route to the Holy Land are martyrs; the best-known example was Frederick Barbarossa,

---

[28]  Monfrin ed., ch. 157.

[29]  Charles W. David, ed., *Narratio de itinere navali peregrinorum Hierosolymam tendentium et Silviam capientium, A.D. 1189*, *Proceedings of the American Philosophical Society* 81 (1939), 589–676. Cf. idem, ed. and trans., *De Expugnatione Lyxbonensi: The Conquest of Lisbon* (New York, 1936; repr. with Introduction by Jonathan Phillips, New York, 2000); Matthew Bennett, "Military Aspects of the Conquest of Lisbon, 1147," in *The Second Crusade: Scope and Consequences*, ed. Jonathan Phillips and Martin Hoch (Manchester, 2001), pp. 71–89. On other similar attempts at internal organization, Powell, *Anatomy*, p. 124, and Christopher Tyerman, *England and the Crusades 1095–1588* (Chicago and London, 1988), pp. 60–85. For an account of a later Danish expedition that focuses even more on the difficulties of travel from the North Sea to Jerusalem, see Karen Skovgaard-Petersen, *A Journey to the Promised land: Crusading Theology in the* Historia de profectione Danorum in Hierosolymam *(c 1200)* (Copenhagen, 2001).

drowned in Syria in 1189.[30] There were also several local cults of Ludwig IV of Thuringia. The North Sea and eastern Atlantic, too, are part of the story of crusaders in motion.

Joinville has served me well, but he does not quite tell us everything. And on occasion he may be inadvertently misleading. Remember those late crusaders? We know about them from a trial held at Messina in July, 1250, studied thirty years ago by Benjamin Kedar.[31] The trial took place because a group of crusaders and others had contracted with the owners of the ship *St. Victor*, out of Marseilles, to transport them to King Louis, originally to Damietta. (The thirteenth century saw the increasingly common naming of ships for saints, invoking particular patronal protection.) When they discovered that the king was at Acre and asked to be taken there, the ship's captain refused to transport them farther. They sued, and the court found in their favor.

The *St. Victor* had 453 passengers aboard, and the trial record includes a passenger list, which Kedar thinks is the earliest one discovered. There were 14 knights and group leaders, 90 retainers, 7 clerics, and 342 commoners. The commoners seem to have been divided into coherent subgroups, and their number included women, some wives and others vaguely designated *amicae* and *sociae*, but twenty-two unchaperoned women as well. The nobles and their retainers presumably also had their horses aboard, which indicates that the *St. Victor* may have had the typical thirteenth-century Mediterranean passenger capacity at the period of between 1,000 and 1,500. It would have been a large, round ship, multi-decked and two- or three-masted, lateen-rigged, and often unwieldy and difficult to handle upwind. This reminds us that Joinville and the Count of Sarrebrück almost certainly did not have the sole use of the ship they hired, not if it had the capacity to transport at least twenty horses. In 1248 the demand for ships in France was very great. One French noble contracted a ship from Scotland, another from England, and still another from Norway. Joinville probably saw no reason to record the presence of fellow passengers, but in March 1248 they must certainly have been present, perhaps many of them, like the majority on the *St. Victor*, commoners, since travel costs appear to have dropped considerably during the earlier thirteenth century. By 1250 it is possible that such ships would not have sailed with a full complement of passengers, hence the 453 passengers on the *St. Victor* and perhaps the captain's reluctance to sail considerably farther with a half-full – or half-empty – ship.

---

[30] Skovgaard-Petersen, pp. 56–63. For Barbarossa, p. 65. The Barbarossa legend acquired new life between 1845 and 1874, when Johannes Sepp sought, eventually with Bismarck's support, to recover the emperor's remains which he believed to be buried in the cathedral at Tyre. See Haim Goren, "The Scholar Precedes the Diplomat: German Science in the Service of Political Involvement in Egypt and Palestine until 1870," in *Germany and the Middle East: Past, Present, and Future*, ed. Haim Goren (Jerusalem, 2003), pp. 41–60, at p. 58.

[31] Benjamin Z. Kedar, "The Passenger List of a Crusader Ship, 1250: Towards the History of the Popular Element on the Seventh Crusade," *Studi Medievali*, 3rd series, 13 (1972), 267–79.

A contract around the same time concerning another ship, the *St. Leonard* out of Marseilles, offers the first instance I know of what seems to be ticket-scalping. A certain Master Garnerius purchased from three Marseilles ship-owners two hundred places on the *St. Leonard* at the price of 45 *solidi* of Tours for each place, allowing Garnerius to resell them at a higher cost to actual passengers.

But some passengers, including Joinville, could indeed travel in style. Jacques de Vitry's account of his own journey from Perugia to Genoa and thence to Acre, whose bishop he had been named, recounts a number of disasters that occurred simply in getting to Genoa. He sailed out of Genoa in late October, somewhat late and risky, but, as Jacques observed:

> the men of that city [Genoa] own very seaworthy ships and a great quantity of them, and for this reason they customarily cross the sea in the winter time, because during this season the victuals in the ships do not spoil as easily, nor does the water on the ship putrefy as it does during the summer, nor is it necessary for them to be delayed for a long time at sea on account of a lack of winds and becalmedness of the sea.

Jacques' point about seasonal winds and the supply of drinking water is important. The availability or need of water determined whether or not ships could sail continuously or would have to put into port regularly to renew their supply.[32] On oared galleys, of course, the question of water supply became even more critical.

Thanks to the shrewd Genoese sailing-masters, Jacques de Vitry sailed in considerably greater style, first class, about which he tells us in considerable detail, to take up the pastoral care of distant Acre – a diocese that, less than a century later, would exist only *in partibus infidelium*, and whose sea routes stopped at Cyprus.

Having discussed the generally better-documented sea travel with some land segments, it is now necessary to say somewhat less about land travel. The movement of pilgrims in extremely large, occasionally defensively armed, groups from western Europe to the Holy Land had started by the early eleventh century, although it took much of the century to move such groups – for example, the great German pilgrimage led by Bishop Gunther of Bamberg in 1064 – in any kind of order with reliable sources of supply and hospitality.[33] Recent research has suggested that

---

[32] John Pryor, "'Water, water everywhere, Nor any drop to drink': Water Supplies for the Fleets of the First Crusade," in *Dei gesta per Francos: Etudes sur les croisades dédiés à Jean Richard*, ed. Michel Balard, Benjamin Z. Kedar, and Jonathan Riley-Smith (Aldershot, 2001), pp. 21–28; idem, "Types of ships and their performance capabilities," pp. 52–58. Powell, *Anatomy of a Crusade*, pp. 124–25, 135n.

[33] On the increasing size of pilgrim groups and land and sea travel for pilgrimage, see Sumption, *Pilgrimage*, esp. pp. 114–36, 175–84 and 185–210. For earlier periods, see now McCormick, *Origins*, pp. 123–73, 237–77, and esp. 391–569. Riley-Smith, *The First Crusaders*, pp. 26–27. From the late thirteenth century the size of crusading expeditions varied, especially with the increasing use of garrisons and the new strategic interest in the *passagium particulare*.

extremely large and orderly armies had been mobilized much earlier, such as those of the Carolingian kings and the later Saxon emperors, whose official journey to Rome, the imperial *Römerzug*, also required the managed movement of a very large contingent from Germany into Italy every time a king of the Romans found a pope who would, or could, crown him emperor. Large armies, too, were efficiently assembled and deployed in the eleventh century, most notably that of Duke William of Normandy at Dives-sur-Mer in the autumn of 1066.[34] By the time of the First Crusade, the capacity of western European leaders to mobilize and move large bodies of troops, maintaining both them and discipline on their way, seems reasonably certain. The organization of the Second Crusade was carried out even more carefully, if not always successfully, and it is reflected in the considerable amount of attention paid by Odo of Deuil to the journey from France to Constantinople. And Frederick Barbarossa's careful and detailed organization of the finances and logistics of the imperial armies on the Third Crusade is now, thanks to the work of Rudolf Hiestand, widely acknowledged.[35]

The chief difficulties that land-traveling crusaders encountered seem to have been uncertain roads and bridges: Godfrey of Bouillon apparently had to build his own road from Nicomedia to Nicaea in 1097, as did Frederick Barbarossa elsewhere on the Third Crusade. Other difficulties included arbitrarily opened and closed markets, local suspicion and hostility, nasty turns in the weather, and opposition incited by the aggressive behavior of the crusaders themselves.[36] What is striking even about the four First Crusade armies is how generally efficiently they moved from northern France and the middle Rhineland through Bavaria, Hungary, and into Constantinople. It may well be that the very experience of organized long-distance travel contributed to the military discipline and effectiveness of crusading armies once they reached the Holy Land. Whether on land, river, or sea, large compact assemblies moving through unfamiliar territory were also dangerous epidemiological pools, as witness the frequent devastation of German armies in Italy during the summer months or the fate of Ludwig IV of Thuringia.[37]

One other problem of the land route was that these armies, as had earlier large groups of pilgrims, attracted significant numbers of hangers-on as they moved, something less likely on the sea routes. And the land route via Bavaria, then through

---

[34] Discussion and references in John France, *Victory in the East: A Military History of the First Crusade* (Cambridge, 1994), p. 2, and the essays by Bernard Bachrach (see above, n. 17).

[35] Rudolf Hiestand, "*Precipua tocius christianismi columpna.* Barbarossa und der Kreuzzug," in *Friedrich Barbarossa. Handlungsspielräume und Wirkungsweisen des Stauffischen Kaisers*, ed. Alfred Haverkamp, Vorträge und Forschungen Bd. 40 (Sigmaringen, 1992), pp. 51–108.

[36] On Godfrey's roadbuilding, see Leighton, *Transport and Communication*, p. 58, citing the *Gesta Francorum*, ed. Rosalind Hill (London, 1962), II, 7, p. 14. Roadbuilding remained a necessity for European armies for centuries: Geoffrey Parker, *The Army of Flanders and the Spanish Road, 1567–1659* (2nd ed. Cambridge, 2004), pp. 70–90.

[37] McCormick, "Byzantium on the move," 19–22; Dionysios C. Stathakopoulos, "Travelling with the plague," in *Travel in the Byzantine World*, ed. Macrides, pp. 99–106.

either Hungary (the conversion of which to Christianity late in the tenth century greatly facilitated the land passage) via the *Heerstrasse*, or Dalmatia and the *Via Egnatia*, to Constantinople, remained in use until the armies of Frederick Barbarossa last employed it on the Third Crusade.[38] In spite of their episodic nature, crusades on land and sea benefited from both external developments and considerable attention to specific crusade experience. One measure of the organizational memory of crusade experience is the disastrous ends of the thirteenth-century "spontaneous" expeditions – the Children's Crusade and the two movements of *Pastoureaux*.

Most crusader travel, of course, ran, like Joinville's, in two directions – there and back again. Many early and later crusaders settled in the Holy Land to make new lives in which they and their descendants were no longer crusaders, and some seem to have remained there in order to die and be buried in the holy places. But from the First Crusade onward, departing crusaders contributed to the perennial demographic and military problems of the Latin kingdom of Jerusalem. Although individual crusaders could often receive aid on the journey out from Europe, it would seem that the expenses of returning posed larger problems, not only in terms of cost and reduced financial circumstances, but in the dangers run by the smaller size and diminished resources of returning parties and individuals. Although these seem to have ameliorated during the better organized crusades of the thirteenth and fourteenth centuries, getting home, as even Joinville found, could be far more hazardous than going out.

Returning crusaders were important, however, in other ways. Assuming that they returned alive and without the obloquy attached to crusade preachers and leaders of failed crusades, they were respected and honored locals, and some of their experience and advice seem to have contributed to the building up of both crusade memory and crusade planning. It would be useful to know the extent to which planners and organizers of later crusades consulted those who had gone on earlier ones: for example, meetings such as those called by Philip V of France in the winter of 1319–20 to which veterans of Louis IX's second crusade were invited.[39]

Perhaps the most interesting – or romantic – aspect of travel in connection with crusade planning lies in the accounts of individual diplomats or spies sent out to assess Muslim resources and local conditions in anticipation of a crusade. Adventurous and resourceful individuals like the indefatigable Bertrandon de la

---

[38] On the Balkan and Danube routes, McCormick, *Origins*, pp. 549–62, and Klaus Belke, "Roads and travel in Macedonia and Thrace in the middle and late Byzantine period," in *Travel in the Byzantine World*, ed. Macrides, pp. 73–90; Nenad Fejic, "Les Balkans aux yeux des voyageurs occidentaux au Moyen Age," in *Voyages et voyageurs au Moyen Age, XXVIe Congrès de la S.H.M.E.S. (Limoges-Aubazine, mai 1995)* (Paris, 1996), pp. 281–89.

[39] Norman Housley, *The Later Crusades, 1274–1580: From Lyons to Alcazar* (Oxford, 1992), p. 31.

Broquière are, for anyone interested, the stuff of novels, although this writer is unaware of any literature devoted specifically to their adventures and their results.[40]

By the end of the thirteenth century, the great age of elaborate treatises on the recovery of the Holy Land, travel joined all other aspects of crusading, including extravagant plans for internal European moral, economic, political, and social reform that continued being produced into the sixteenth century.[41] In that process, our subject becomes a rather different subject.[42]

The returning crusader is an image that has been attractive since the first crusaders began to travel back to Europe. The crusader may be a martyred and, in the case of Louis IX, a soon to be sainted king, his body brought back from Tunis to Paris with great ceremony. But the living returned crusader was also an appealing image. Its best known modern representation is probably the burned-out Swedish crusader-knight Antonius Blok, played superbly by Max von Sydow in Ingmar Bergman's film *The Seventh Seal*. But Blok was certainly not the first such image.

The most striking representation is that in the twelfth-century Belval cloister, now at the Musée Historique at Nancy.[43] The statue may be an *ex voto* in gratitude for a safe return, but we cannot really tell. It is, nonetheless, a compelling image. If Joinville ever saw this late twelfth-century image – he did not live all that far from Belval – he would have understood it, if not when he set out in 1248, then certainly when he got home to stay in 1254.

---

[40] Bertrandon de la Broquière, *The Voyage d'Outremer*, ed. and trans. Galen R. Kline (New York, 1988).

[41] Antony Leopold, *How to Recover the Holy Land: The Crusade Proposals of the Late Thirteenth and Early Fourteenth Centuries* (Aldershot, 2000); Sylvia Schein, *Fideles Crucis: The Papacy, the West, and the Recovery of the Holy Land, 1274–1314* (Oxford, 1991).

[42] Just as Constable's research has led her to criticize the "colonialism" thesis of Crusade history (*Housing the Stranger*, p. 357), so a consideration of the circumstances of travel may suggest a similar conclusion.

[43] Nurith Kenaan-Kedar and Benjamin Z. Kedar, "The Significance of a Twelfth-Century Sculptural Group: Le Retour du Croisé," in *Dei gesta per Francos: Etudes sur les croisades dédiés à Jean Richard / Crusade Studies in Honour of Jean Richard* (Aldershot, 2001), pp. 29–44.

# The Crusader Castle of Toron:
# First Results of its Investigation

*Mathias Piana*

University of Augsburg

The castle of Toron in southern Lebanon was of particular importance at the time of the crusades. It is situated about 18 kilometres south-east of Tyre in the mountains of the Jabal 'Āmil range, which geographically belongs to Upper Galilee. It crowns a steep hill – a *tell* – at a height of 725 metres overlooking the village of Tibnīn. After its rebuilding in the eighteenth century, its current appearance is that of a typical Ottoman castle of the region (see Plate 1). Analysis of the pottery found at several spots in stratified deposits suggests an occupation of the site from Late Bronze Age to the end of the Ottoman period. Although occasionally described by some nineteenth-century travellers, it was never explored or surveyed. Investigation of the site started in 2000 and was continued in a second campaign in 2003.[1]

## History

The village of Tibnīn had existed prior to the crusades but there is no evidence for an earlier castle. Many column fragments and large-sized ashlars from the same period, reused in the walls of the castle, indicate a Roman occupation of the site. In 1101 King Baldwin I granted Galilee, with Tiberias as its capital, to the Flemish knight Hugh of Falconberg. Around the end of 1105 or the beginning of 1106 Hugh founded the castle as a fortified base for his raids against Fatimid Tyre.[2] He named it Toron, Old French for a hill. Shortly after Hugh had died on a raid against Damascus,[3] Tibnīn was attacked in 1106/07 by 'Izz al-Mulk, the governor of Tyre, who destroyed its "suburb" (in other words its village) and plundered it.[4] This attack, coming immediately after the erection of the castle, reveals its strategic importance. Together with Hūnīn (Frankish Chastel Neuf) further east, which was built at the same time, Toron blocked the main route from Damascus to Tyre.

---

[1]  Hans H. Curvers and Barbara Stuart, "Qal'at Tibnīn: Archaeology for a Future Conservation Plan," *Archaeology & History in Lebanon* 20 (2004), 9–20; Mathias Piana and Hans H. Curvers, "The Castle of Toron (Qal'at Tibnīn) in South Lebanon: Preliminary Results of the 2000/2003 Campaigns," *Bulletin d'Archéologie et d'Architecture Libanaises* 8 (2004), 333–56.

[2]  WT 11.5, p. 502.

[3]  September 1106: FC 2.36, pp. 509–11.

[4]  Ibn al-Qalānisī, *The Damascus Chronicle of the Crusades*, trans. Hamilton A.R. Gibb (London, 1932), p. 75; Sibṭ Ibn al-Jauzī in *RHC Or* 3:530.

Shortly after Hugh's death a knight named Humphrey was invested with the castle and founded the powerful dynasty named after Toron which held the lordship for nearly the whole period of the Frankish occupation of the site. Shortly before 1118 local forces must have captured Toron since a reconquest by the Franks is recorded that year.[5] The situation changed in 1124 when Tyre fell to the Franks. By the end of the 1120s Toron must have become an independent seigneury indicating the growing influence and power of its owner.[6] In 1180 Humphrey IV ceded the lordship to the king in an exchange agreement.[7] In 1186 Toron was given to Joscelin III of Courtenay, together with Chastel Neuf and Maron.[8] One year later, in July 1187, Saladin sent his nephew Muẓaffar Taqī ad-Dīn 'Umar to besiege the castle. Faced by fierce resistance Saladin had to come himself and after a siege of one week the castle surrendered on 26 July. Saladin then installed an emir of his own,[9] and in 1192 ordered the repair of all the castles of Galilee (Tiberias, Safed and Toron).[10] Five years later a German army, after retaking Beirut, laid siege to the castle from 28 November 1197 to 2 February 1198, but had to abandon it when an Ayyubid force approached.[11] In September 1218, during the siege of Damietta, al-Malik al-Mu'aẓẓam 'Īsā dismantled a number of fortresses in Galilee including Tibnīn and Hūnīn. In 1227, facing the prospect of the arrival of crusaders under Emperor Frederick II, he ordered the total destruction of the castles of Safed and Tibnīn.[12]

In 1229 Frederick regained Toron by treaty. This led to a dispute between the Teutonic Knights, who had bought the possession in 1220 as part of the Seigneurie de Joscelin, and Alice of Armenia, the niece of Humphrey IV of Toron. Alice successfully claimed her hereditary rights before the High Court.[13] In 1241 the possession of Toron by the Christians was newly confirmed in a treaty between Richard of Cornwall and the sultan of Egypt.[14] It was now owned by Philip of Montfort, whose wife, Mary of Poitiers, was the granddaughter of Alice and heiress of Toron. From 1246 Philip also ruled over Tyre and it is likely that he had refortified the castle as an outpost of Tyre, although there is no documentary evidence for this.

---

[5]  15 April 1118: Ibn Khallikan, *Ibn Khallikan's Biographical Dictionary*, trans. William MacGuckin de Slane, 3 (Paris, London, 1868), p. 456; Ibn Taghrībirdī in *RHC Or* 3:487.

[6]  Martin Rheinheimer, *Das Kreuzfahrerfürstentum Galiläa* (Frankfurt/M, 1990), pp. 184–85, 218. This is especially true for Humphrey II (born before 1137, died 1179), who in the mid-twelfth century became royal constable and was one of the wealthiest and most powerful barons of the kingdom.

[7]  WT 22.5, p. 1012; Hans E. Mayer, "Die Seigneurie de Joscelin und der Deutsche Orden," in *Die Geistlichen Ritterorden Europas*, ed. Josef Fleckenstein and Manfred Hellmann, Vorträge und Forschungen 26 (Sigmaringen, 1980), p. 205.

[8]  RRH 653, pp. 173–74.

[9]  'Imād ad-Dīn al-Iṣfahānī, *Conquête de la Syrie et de la Palestine par Saladin (al-Fatḥ al-qussī fī-l-fatḥ al-qudsī)*, trans. Henri Massé, Documents relatifs à l'histoire des croisades 10 (Paris, 1972), pp. 37–39.

[10]  Ibid., p. 398.

[11]  Arnold of Lübeck, *Chronica Slavorum* 5.28–29, MGH SS 21:207–10.

[12]  Abū Shāma in *RHC Or* 5:171.

[13]  "Livre de Jean d'Ibelin", 203, *RHC Lois* 1:112–13, 325–26; Mayer, *Seigneurie*, pp. 204–206.

[14]  Matthew Paris, *Chronica Majora*, ed. Henry R. Luard, RS 57 (London, 1877), 4:141–43.

Latin rule ended in 1266, when Baybars conquered the castles of Hūnīn and Tibnīn, most probably during or immediately after the siege of Safed.[15]

During the Mamluk period the castle was not rebuilt and Tibnīn served only as a local administrative centre. Around 1760 sheikh Nāṣif Naṣṣār, the Shiʿite leader of the region, who was allied with Ḍāhir al-ʿUmar in his struggle against Ottoman authorities, rebuilt the castle.[16] After Nāṣif Naṣṣār's death in 1781, Aḥmed Jazzār Pāshā, the new ruler of Acre and Sidon, conquered all the important fortresses of the region, including Tibnīn, in order to re-establish Ottoman rule.[17] Only after al-Jazzār's death in 1804 did the Shiʿites regain their old possessions, but their castles had meanwhile been destroyed.[18]

In the middle of the nineteenth century, Edward Robinson was the first modern traveller to visit the site. He reported that the houses inside the castle were "broken down and strewn about in shapeless ruin." There was "nothing standing within the enclosure, except the dwelling of the Sheikhs."[19] The first, and up to now most comprehensive, account on the castle is that in the report of the *Survey of Western Palestine*, conducted by Conder and Kitchener in the 1870s.

> The form of the castle was arranged to fit the top of the hill on which it was placed, and is roughly circular, with round and square towers to flank the sides. The lower portions of the masonry of these towers show large Crusading heavy drafted stones, and in some parts the same style without draft. The slopes of the hill were faced with smooth-dressed stones as at Belfort, but not at quite so steep an angle. The interior is principally taken up with ruins. On the west, however, there are some buildings of Dhaher el Omer's time, which still form the Mudîr of the Belâd el Beshârah, and though falling into ruins, show that it was built in good Arabic style. To the south of these there are some Crusading vaults and stables, probably dating from the thirteenth century. On the eastern side there are the foundations of some Crusading walls with drafted stones, six feet thick; they form an irregular rectangular space. A paved road leads along the south-western side, and then bends round to the gate of the castle.[20]

In spite of some substantial restoration work in 1989, the site has never been the focus of scientific research, most likely because of a misleading statement by Paul Deschamps, that practically nothing remained from the crusader period.[21] In fact

---

[15] al-Maqrīzī, *Histoire des Sultans mamlouks de l'Égypte*, trans. Étienne M. Quatremère, I/2 (Paris, 1840), pp. 27–28, 32.

[16] Amnon Cohen, *Palestine in the 18th Century: Patterns of Government and Administration* (Jerusalem, 1973), pp. 84, 101.

[17] Ibid., pp. 101–102.

[18] Ibid., pp. 102–104.

[19] Edward Robinson, *Biblical Researches in Palestine and the Adjacent Regions. A Journal of Travel in the Years 1838 and 1852*, 3 (London, 1856), pp. 57–59.

[20] *The Survey of Western Palestine. Memoirs of the Topography, Orography, Hydrography, and Archaeology, 2: Galilee*, ed. Claude R. Conder and Horatio H. Kitchener (London, 1881), p. 135.

[21] Paul Deschamps, *Les Châteaux des Croisés en Terre Sainte, 2: La Défense du Royaume de Jérusalem. Étude historique, géographique et monumentale*, 1 (Paris, 1939), pp. 117–18.

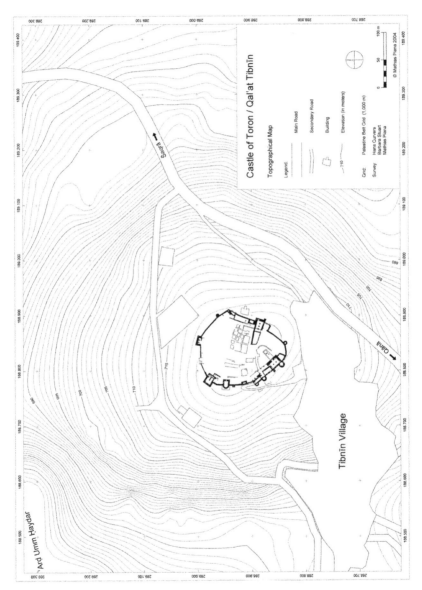

**Fig. 1** Topographical map of the site (houses outside village centre not surveyed/mapped)

although its present appearance is dominated by the Ottoman rebuilding, a more thorough look reveals that a substantial part of the castle's medieval structures has been conserved in its ground walls, allowing one to reconstruct the general layout of the medieval castle.

## Topography

A topographical overview of the site shows that the castle dominates the village south of it. It rises above the tell, covering a platform with an area of about 140 × 170 metres. The enclosure wall follows the contour of the platform, the main entrance to the site being located at the centre of the western side, where a small road leads from the village to the castle gate (see Fig. 1). Apparently this side was the weakest flank of the castle as it was heavily fortified with six strong towers in the Frankish period. At first sight there was no evidence for a moat. The existence of one is recorded, however, and is to be expected as typical of the castle-building at that time. Indeed, older photographs seem to support the hypothesis that the former pond (*birka*), now occupied by the Municipality building, is what remains of it (see Plate 2). According to the *Survey of Western Palestine*, the slopes of the castle hill were covered with a stone revetment.[22] Although the area has been altered, traces of the revetment could be exposed on the northern slope. This stone-revetted glacis must have covered the entire surface of the slopes of the castle hill. It is a distinctive feature of many of the medieval fortifications of the region, having been common long before the crusades.

## The Enclosure Wall

The enclosure wall, together with its adjacent buildings, is the best preserved part of the castle. It encloses an area of 16,700 square metres, with a perimeter of 577 metres. The inner ward of the castle is filled with the ruins and debris of buildings from the late Ottoman period. The workmen of this time generally used the razed walls of the medieval castle for their reconstruction (see Fig. 2). A considerable part of the original structure is therefore preserved, especially at the entrance complex and in the towers. Detailed archaeological investigations were able to trace the outline of the medieval wall together with its adjacent structures. The enclosure is nearly oval in shape and is strengthened with twelve rectangular towers at more or less regular intervals (see Fig. 3). Castles with ring-shaped enclosure walls with interspersed rectangular towers crowning a hill with stone-revetted slopes are a

---

[22]  *Survey*, ed. Conder and Kitchener, p. 135.

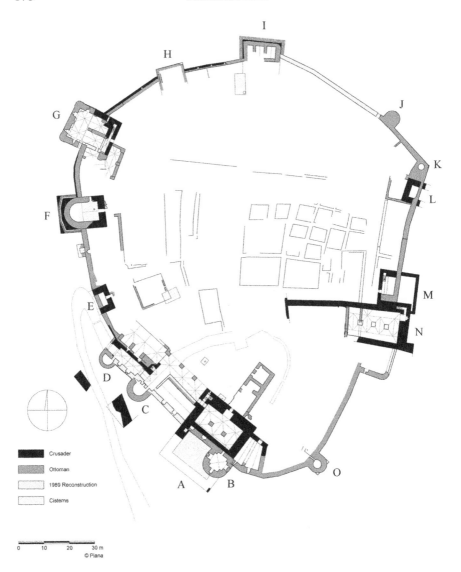

**Fig. 2    Ground plan of the castle displaying general building phases**

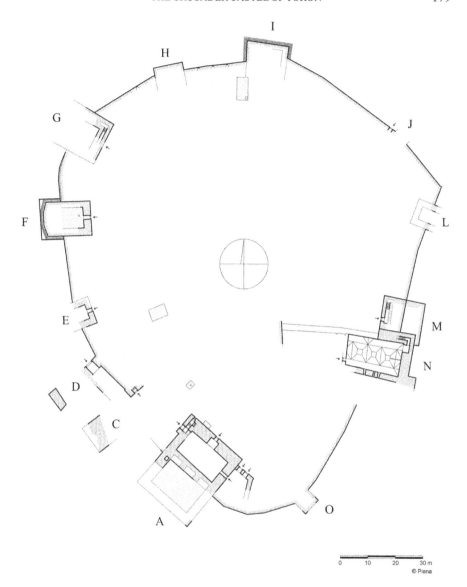

**Fig. 3    Plan of the crusader castle (extant structures hitherto surveyed)**

Northern Syria. The curtain walls between the towers consist of different types of masonry, which do not necessarily belong to different building phases. In the western parts of the enclosure wall, large, crudely hewn boulder-like blocks of stone laid in regular courses are visible on the outer face. The intervals between the blocks are filled with small stone chips in a mortar matrix (see Plate 3). In the three greater towers (A, F and I) an identical masonry is visible (see Plate 10). The curtain walls on the other sides consist of a more regular masonry of medium-sized ashlars with a smooth surface. All these stones are made of the very hard limestone of the region with a colour ranging from off-white to dark brown. Sometimes basalt is used as well.

## The Entrance Complex

The gate building flanking the enclosure wall is a good example of the eighteenth-century architecture of the region. Inside the gate-house a totally different masonry with large smooth-faced ashlars can be detected at the base of the walls on either side. These are clearly part of the original entrance to the medieval castle, as excavations revealed two large hinge sockets, which had been hewn out of the bedrock, at the inner corners of the threshold. The present threshold is part of these structures and must therefore have belonged to the medieval gate. Proceeding further into the entrance hall (11.90 × 4.50 metres) the same masonry can be observed at the north-east wall, while the opposite wall was re-erected in 1989 (see Plate 4). The fine cobblestone pavement covering the floor is certainly medieval. It perfectly matches the outline of the crusader wall to the north-east of it much more closely than it docs thc post-medieval structures of the hall. The pavement is flanked by slightly elevated sections, the borders of which are exactly aligned with the wings of the medieval gate, which may have been sidewalks.

At the opposite side of the hall is located a shallow threshold that belongs to a second crusader-period gate. During the cleaning of this area the remains of a hinge socket were discovered, being part of the north-eastern crusader wall. We assume that this was the true main gate, while the gate flanking the enclosure wall (referred to above) merely served as a barbican. Presumably the inner wall (see Plate 5), which served as the main wall, was stronger and higher than the outer one, thus forming a double line of defence in this section. The space between the walls was probably once open to the sky. This would have made the defence against an enemy that had taken the first gate much more effective. Only a short section of the medieval castle's outer wall in this area has survived. After its excavation it was possible to study the building technique. The foundation of the wall is formed by a mass of rubble bonded by an extremely hard mortar (see Plate 3). The glacis covering the slope must have extended up to this foundation zone. The masonry of the wall, of which two ashlar-like blocks have survived in situ, rested on it.

Leaving the entrance hall via a small corridor, the way leads to a vaulted passage, where it takes a right-angled bend to the left. The floor in this area shows a similar cobble-stone pavement to the gateway, but of poorer quality and less well-preserved. The crusader-period masonry continues around the corner and includes a niche (1.33 × 1.85 metres) in the north-west wall of the passage. Clearing the debris from the floor of this niche, the rear part of which was erected in the Ottoman period, disclosed the beginning of a staircase and two hinge sockets in the bedrock beyond the threshold. This original doorway and staircase were either part of a medieval building or an ascent to the wall-walk of the enclosure wall.

To the south-west of the passage a semicircular Ottoman tower – now in ruins – replaced an earlier crusader tower, the ruins of which lie some distance down the slope. This earlier tower was 10.9 metres wide and must have projected about 10 metres from the enclosure wall. It had a sloping base and was constructed of medium-sized ashlars with some ancient *spolia*. It is not clear whether the present position of its debris is a result of the mining works of 1197/98 or the destruction of the castle by Ayyubids or Mamluks. It is obvious that this massive tower flanked and guarded what we believe to have been the main gate and thus served as a gate-tower. The whole arrangement, consisting of a tower-strengthened main gate defended by a barbican and an entry-passage with a double-bend represents a very elaborate defence system.

## The Crusader Donjon

Opposite the entrance hall is located a nearly rectangular room. In the Ottoman period this served as a stable; it was rebuilt in 1989. The rear wall of this room is of the same typical crusader-period masonry, consisting of the same large crude blocks of stone as in the enclosure wall. A projecting corner is visible there, the quoins of which are formed by well-dressed rusticated ashlars. This wall belongs to a building adjacent to the room identified with the crusader donjon of the castle. Parallel with the front of the room and the passage is a vaulted gallery opening onto the inner ward of the castle. This belongs to the Ottoman period and was also reconstructed in 1989. At its south-eastern end a wall with fine masonry, consisting of large ashlars in the lower courses, and a doorway are visible. These also belong to the crusader donjon (see Plate 6). From this doorway a mural staircase in the northern corner once led to the upper floor of the building. A look at the ground plan of this building reveals very strong walls on three sides. The outer faces of these walls show the rough stone blocks laid in regular courses with quoins formed by rusticated ashlars (see Plate 7).

Inside the building large smooth-dressed ashlars are found at the bottom of the walls, topped by typical Ottoman masonry. The south-west wall is much weaker and coincides with the enclosure wall of the castle. This wall belongs to the Ottoman period and excavations at its base revealed that it rests on a wider foundation wall

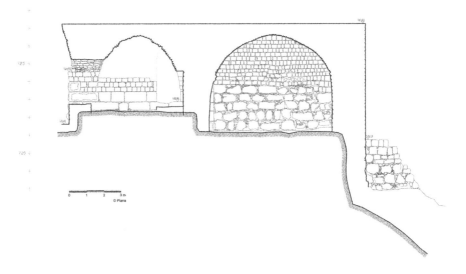

**Fig. 4    Crusader donjon: section/elevation of north-west wall**

linked to the bottom courses of the walls at either side (see Plate 8). A wall stump outside the enclosure wall, but aligned with the north-west wall of this building, indicates the existence of a further part of it stretching down the slope beyond the enclosure wall (see Fig. 4). To determine its extent soundings were made in this area of the slope. The top of a huge mass of rubble bonded by mortar, identified as the foundation of what we consider to have been the south-west wall, was exposed.

From the rising masonry only three ashlars exactly aligned with the outer face of the south-east wall of the building could be found (see Plate 9). These form its south corner and thus enabled its dimensions to be determined. It was 31.03 metres long and 24.43 metres wide. The thickness of the walls varies from 3.01 to 4.34 metres. This building (A) had a main entrance in the middle of the north-east wall, a side entrance with stairs branching off to the upper floor at the northern corner and a postern in the south-east wall. The south-western half of it had projected 14 metres from the enclosure wall (see Fig. 5) and included a basement which once contained a huge cistern. This is indicated by a layer of hydraulic plaster on the interior face of the wall stump and the presence of a water supply shaft.

A comparison with other crusader donjons reveals that Toron's was the largest the crusaders built. It is also the one that resembles most the Western examples, being of a building type that originates from north-western France, where they are known as early as the tenth century. The characteristic features are the rectangular outline, the elevated entrance, the cross-wall, the water-supply installation, the massive walls with mural stairs, and a building technique using irregular stones framed with ashlars at the corners and openings. What we do not know is the internal

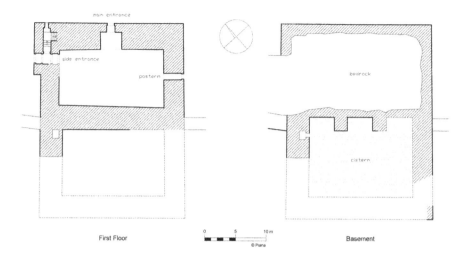

First Floor                                      Basement

**Fig. 5    Ground plan of crusader donjon; the required passage through the cross-wall has not yet been located**

arrangement of the building, or indeed the location of the door-opening in the cross wall.

The level of the ground of the inner ward in front of the donjon's facade is 1.75 metres lower than the threshold of the donjon's main gate, thus forming a depression. It must have served as a moat turning the donjon into a self-defensible unit. The present ramp-like structure leading to the gate is of Ottoman date but may have replaced an earlier construction, most probably one with a wooden bridge leading to the gate.

The position of the donjon was of strategic importance. It is located at the south-west side of the castle, its weakest flank, and directly above the village and the road from Damascus to Tyre. Furthermore this monumental building emphasized the owner's desire to impress. It was a widely visible symbol of the power and wealth of its builder.

## The Wall Towers

The other towers of the medieval castle are also of a rectangular outline, but much smaller in size. A simple example is tower E, which has totally lost its projecting part. A more elaborate type is represented by towers F and I, which are similar. Their projecting parts rest on huge foundations built of large rough boulder-like stone blocks. At tower I, only one course of rusticated ashlars survived of the rising masonry. At tower F, three courses of the same masonry form a sloping polygonal

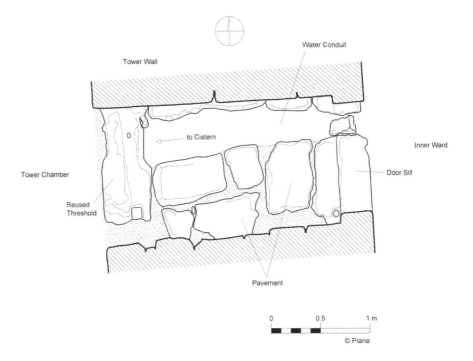

**Fig. 6    Top view/section of doorway in the east wall of tower F: water conduit supplying the cistern in the basement of the tower**

base with two vertical courses of ashlars above it (see Plate 10). It is likely these huge foundations were incorporated in the glacis as their height fits the declination of the slope of the castle hill. Tower F contains a cistern in its basement, the round well-shaft of which was uncovered. The cleaning of the tower's doorway revealed a water conduit under the slabs of its pavement leading to this cistern (see Fig. 6). It must have been part of a pipeline for rainwater drained from the roof of the tower. At the inner rear wall some other interesting features are visible, such as patches of the medieval plaster under the Ottoman whitewash and some traces of coloured painting in the south-east corner.

Tower G, the largest of the castle's Ottoman towers, contains an earlier medieval tower, which was levelled to the line of the enclosure wall most probably after the destruction of its projecting part (see Plate 11). Its basement is preserved and was integrated into the Ottoman tower. Here in the east wall a mural staircase is visible with a landing in the north-east corner, from where stairs lead down to the entrance of the building. It has not yet been cleared of debris. At the east side of the enclosure wall the remains of an earlier tower (M) are visible. Of the projecting part some courses of fine masonry of large rusticated ashlars are preserved (see Plate 12); an opposite wall with remains of a mural staircase leads up from a half-buried entrance, having been part of the same building.

To the south is a large underground hall, its northern wall partly consisting of the tower's south wall (see Fig. 3). To expose its foundations the debris inside was removed and trenches dug alongside the walls. In the western part of this building were found crumbled huge Roman ashlars and strata of a pre-Roman settlement. A doorway is situated at the west wall. This hall in its original design is a crusader-period building, which was re-vaulted in the Ottoman period. After tower M was truncated, its southern part, together with the eastern walls of the hall, were heightened to form an open-backed tower (N). At a later date, most probably in the thirteenth century, the transverse walls of tower N were extended to form a long building projecting into the inner ward. The terminating wall there is older and does not exactly match the side walls of the building. Furthermore its inner face is rusticated with the bosses of the ashlars pointing to the interior of the building. This wall occupies the highest point of the platform forming the inner ward of the castle. We believe that it may have been part of an early tower, probably the nucleus of the first castle built by Hugh of Falconberg. The investigation of this structure is therefore an important item on the agenda for future research.

## Chronology

The establishment of a complete chronology of the medieval building phases was not yet possible. However, the layout of the castle undoubtedly points to a date of construction in the first half of the twelfth century. It is comparable to contemporary examples such as Saône (Ṣahyūn; Qal'at Ṣalāḥ ad-Dīn) and Giblet (Jbail), especially with regard to the construction and design of the towers.[23] The main construction phase must have finished as late as the end of the 1120s when, after the conquest of Tyre, the crusaders' reign was consolidated. The castle does not seem to have suffered much from the Saladin's campaign of 1187. The destruction of most of the towers has to be attributed to the long-lasting siege of 1197/98, when skilled miners were engaged to break the castle walls.[24] At some points there is evidence of repairs, for example at the north wall of tower G. There the levelling of a crusader tower can be observed. In order to close the breach left by the tower's destruction a new field-side wall was erected, most probably during the Ayyubid period. From architectural evidence there is no indication of an extensive rebuilding in the thirteenth century, either by the crusaders or by the Mamluks. The castle must have lain in ruins for about five hundred years before it was rebuilt in the Ottoman period.

---

[23] See further: Denys Pringle, "Crusader Castles. The First Generation," *Fortress* 1 (1989), 14–25; Ronnie Ellenblum, "Three Generations of Frankish Castle Building in the Latin Kingdom of Jerusalem," in *Autour*, pp. 517–51.

[24] Arnold of Lübeck, *Chronica Slavorum* 5.28–29, MGH SS 21:207.

Plate 1    View of the castle from the south-west, the village of Tibnīn in the foreground

Plate 2    Aerial view of Tibnīn (about 1930), in the foreground the former *birkat* and supposed location of the moat (Deschamps 1939, Album Pl. XXXII A)

**Plate 3**    **Curtain wall D–C: remains of the crusader wall showing two blocks of the rising masonry above the foundation, topped by an Ottoman relieving arch**

**Plate 4    Entrance hall looking north-west**

Plate 5    North-east wall of entrance hall, southern section: crusader masonry below
           black line, to the left *in situ*, to the right partly rearranged; above black line,
           Ottoman masonry (mid-eighteenth century)

Plate 6    The north corner of tower A (background), the crusader donjon, showing the
           remains of its former side entrance with original threshold

Plate 7    North-east facade of the crusader donjon with characteristic masonry made
           up of huge stone blocks in regular courses with bossed quoins; the remains of
           the main entrance are visible in the central section; the upper courses were
           reconstructed in 1989

Plate 8    Ottoman hall inside extant part of A, looking north-west: bottom courses
           show blocks of the donjon's north-west wall, partly topped by Ottoman
           masonry; in the foreground are foundation stones of the donjon's cross-wall
           exposed during excavation

**Plate 9    South corner of donjon during excavation**

**Plate 10    Tower F, western face: preserved talus with three courses of bossed ashlars above substructure made up of huge stone blocks**

Plate 11    Ottoman tower G, northern flank: seam left of the arrows indicating the
            extent of levelled medieval tower; below white line is original crusader
            masonry of wall and tower; above the white line, Ayyubid reconstruction,
            topped by Ottoman rebuilding

Plate 12    Towers M/N, eastern elevation: in the foreground, preserved courses of
            bossed masonry of crusader tower M; behind it the well-preserved facade of
            tower N, to the left a turret walled up in 1989

# Thanks to a Neighbour's Bad Reputation: Reconstructing an Area of Thirteenth-Century Acre[*]

*Pnina Arad*

The Hebrew University of Jerusalem

A new reading of two charters promulgated in Acre in 1198 and 1235, in conjunction with a fourteenth-century plan of the city, allows for the reconstruction of a small area in the northern part of Acre, in close proximity to the Hospitaller compound.

The charter of 1198, issued by King Aimery in Acre,[1] contains three distinct grants to a private individual, William de Petra: the Prison Tower (*Turris Carceris*), a "house" and the income from "another house." The charter specifies the location of several structures adjacent to the two houses (see Fig. 1).[2] Both houses border on the gate of *Boveria Templi* to the west, and on the Prison Tower to the east; the southern side of the "house" is adjacent to a structure with an oven, named after its owner, *furnus Malivicini*, that is, "the oven of the bad neighbour." (*Malus vicinus* appears to have been a nickname that later became a surname.) The fact that the same structures, both from east and west, stood adjacent to both houses, indicates that the "other house" stood to the north of the "house." The charter explicitly mentions that the "other house" stood in the area between the city wall and the external fortifications (*barbacana*). It concludes with a prohibition against transferring the residential property to communes, secular churches and religious orders. This prohibition appears in the early thirteenth-century *Livre au Roi* with respect to *borgesies* (burgage tenures) and fiefs.[3]

The *furnus Malivicini* is also mentioned in the later charter and thereby connects both documents. This charter, issued in 1235, deals with the exchange of houses between the Hospitaller Order and a private individual, Nicholas Antelinus.[4] Figure 2 shows the arrangement of the structures vis-à-vis each other, as mentioned in the

---

[*] I am grateful to Benjamin Z. Kedar and David Jacoby for their helpful remarks.

[1] Sebastiano Pauli, *Codice diplomatico del sacro militare ordine gerosolimitano oggi di Malta*, 2 vols. (Lucca, 1733–37), 1:287, no. 8; RRH, no. 746.

[2] The figures are not to scale; they only reflect the layout of the structures as mentioned in the charters.

[3] With respect to *borgesies*, see *Le Livre au Roi*, ed. Myriam Greilsammer (Paris, 1995), chap. 43, p. 265: "nules borgesies, si come est maisons ou terres ou vignes ou jardins qui soyent as devises dou roy, ce est en sa terre, ni en la terre de ces homes, ne peut estre doné a yglise ne a relegion, par dreit." With respect to fiefs, see ibid., chap. 45, p. 271: "Et si juge la raison c'on ne det soufrir a acheter nul fié a nule religion, ni a yglise, ni as gens de coumune." On the nature and status of *borgesies*, see Joshua Prawer, *Crusader Institutions* (Oxford, 1980), pp. 250–52.

[4] *Cart. Hosp.* no. 2126; RRH, no. 1063 (in his summary, Röhricht mistakenly wrote *portum civitatis* instead of *portam civitatis*).

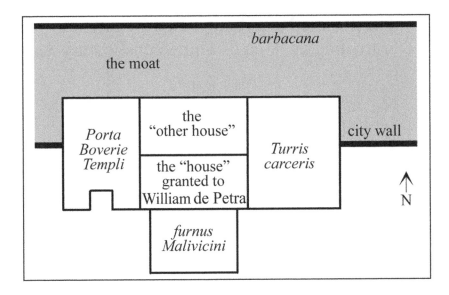

**Fig. 1**    **Proposed reconstruction of the layout of the structures mentioned in the 1198 charter**

charter. The house exchanged with Nicholas borders the moat on its northern side; to the west it borders on a house of the Templars and other houses paying royal tax; to the east it borders on a public road (*via publica et regia*) leading through the *Porta Nova* and the tower situated above it in such manner that the walls of the house and the tower touch each other; to the south it borders on the oven of the bad neighbour (*furno quod dicitur de Malvesin*).[5]

Both charters undoubtedly deal with the same house. Both mention a house bordering the oven of *Malivicinus* or *Malvesin* on its south and the moat on its north.[6] In addition, both charters connect the house to a single family. In the charter of 1198 the house is granted to William de Petra and his heirs, while the charter of 1235 indicates that the house which is exchanged with Nicholas Antelinus belonged to Ysabella de Petra prior to its acquisition by the Hospitaller Order. Additional proof

---

[5] The directions indicated in contemporary charters dealing with landed property are always full (north, south, east and west), whereas halfway directions such as south-west are never registered; see David Jacoby, "Three Notes on Crusader Acre," *Zeitschrift des Deutschen Palästina-Vereins* 109 (1993), 89–90. Because of this practice, the house of Margaret, apparently located at the south-east corner of the house of Nicholas, is mentioned twice: from the west ("the corner of Margaret's house") and from the south.

[6] Since the charter of 1235 mentions only one house in the area between the oven and the moat, it seems that the "house" was enlarged so as to include the area of the "other house." The charter specifies that the house, on its northern flank, *protenditur in longum super fossatum civitatis* – that means, it protruded above the moat of the city, at the same place where the "other house" had stood.

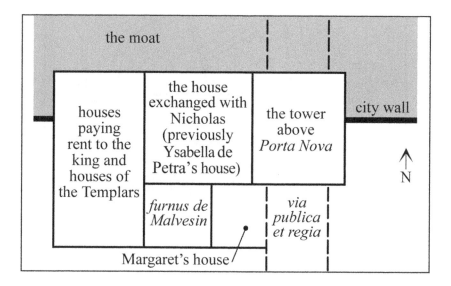

**Fig. 2**     **Proposed reconstruction of the layout of the structures mentioned in the 1235 charter**

that we are dealing here with the same family appears on the reverse of the later charter: a thirteenth-century entry mentions William and Ysabella de Petra as a married couple and as previous owners of the house.[7] A comparison between the two charters indicates that between 1198 and 1235 the husband died and his widow sold the property to the Hospitaller Order. It transpires that at some time between 1198 and 1235 the prohibition to transfer the property, a burgage tenure, to an ecclesiastical institution had been lifted either by a king, an officer replacing an absentee king, or else by the *Cour des Bourgeois*, after the Commune of Acre, established in 1231, took over the city's government.[8] Although compiled in Cyprus in the mid-fourteenth century, the *Abrégé du Livre des Assises de la Cour des Bourgeois* hints at the procedure applied in the kingdom of Jerusalem. It states that members of secular churches, religious orders and foreign communes are barred from obtaining property on behalf of the communities to which they belong, unless by special permission of the territory's lord, who is vested with authority like the chief lord or king.[9] Indeed, the charter of 1235 states that the exchange between

---

[7] "privilegium recuperatum de heredibus Nicholai Ancelini de possessione quadam domine Ysabellis de Petra et ejus mariti Guillelmi." *Cart Hosp*, no. 2126, *in fine*.

[8] On the Commune of Acre, see Jonathan S. C. Riley-Smith, *The Feudal Nobility and the Kingdom of Jerusalem, 1174–1277* (London, 1973), pp. 177–84; Prawer, *Crusader Institutions*, pp. 57–66.

[9] "Abrégé du Livre des Assises de la Cour des Bourgeois," chap. 32, in *RHC Lois* 2:263: "se ce ne fusse par congé dou seignor, qui a le poier de tout coumander et à faire à son gré et à sa olenté, come chief seignor."

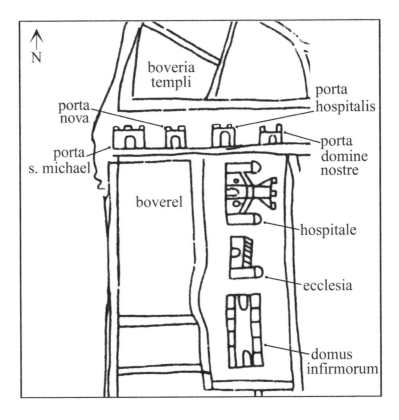

**Fig. 3    The north-western part of Acre, based on Paolino Veneto's plan**

the Hospitaller Order and Nicholas Antelinus was certified *in presencia curie et juratorum Acconensium*. As regards the earlier purchase from Ysabella de Petra, it could have been possible only if authorized by the king or as an exchange confirmed by the Commune of Acre after 1231.

The city plan of Acre by Paolino Veneto, dating from the 1320s, mentions a gate called *Porta Nova*, situated in the twelfth-century inner city wall (see Fig. 3). The plan also notes an area designated as *Boveria Templi* in the Montmusard suburb, directly north of the *Porta Nova* and the city moat. The proximity of the gate to the *Boveria Templi* on Paolino's plan concurs with the data from both charters.[10]

---

[10] In his reconstruction of Montmusard, Jacoby was the first to link the charters of 1198 and 1235 on account of the oven mentioned in both of them. However, he doubted the accuracy of the gate's name – *porta Boverie Templi* – in the 1198 charter, contending that, on the Paolino Veneto plan, the location of *Boveria Templi* north of the moat is erroneous. See David Jacoby, "Montmusard, Suburb of Crusader Acre: The First Stage of its Development," in *Outremer*, p. 208 n. 20. Now he accepts the accuracy of plan and charter: see David Jacoby, "L'apogeo di Acri nel medioevo, Secc. XII–XIII," in: *Le città del*

A comparison between the two charters throws light on the urban development in this part of the city during the first decades of the thirteenth century. Both charters deal, within a time gap of 37 years, with two gates located at opposite sides of the same house. The *porta Boverie Templi*, which in 1198 led northwards to the *Boveria Templi* in Montmusard, was probably demolished later, and some houses built in its stead. By 1235 a new gate stood at the other side of the house, as confirmed by its name – *Porta Nova*. This gate apparently pierced the lower part of what had been the Prison Tower in 1198. We can assume that the *via publica et regia*, which is mentioned in 1235 as running through the *Porta Nova*, and which connected the city with the new suburb, was also constructed during these 37 years. It may be identified with the north–south street which, on Paolino's plan, runs west of the Hospitaller compound.

The 1235 charter reveals the urban reality developing near the *Porta Nova*. The gate and the tower above it are property of the Hospitaller Order, which also possesses the right to passage at the gate and the public road. On the Paolino plan two gates stand in close proximity to the Hospitaller compound in the inner city wall: the *Porta Domine Nostre*, located in the north-eastern corner of the compound, and the *Porta Hospitalis* in the north-western one.[11] The *Porta Nova* is located to the west of these two gates. The charter of 1235 suggests that by that time the Hospitallers had extended their compound westward up to the *Porta Nova*.[12]

As for the tower above the *Porta Nova*, the charter does not indicate whether it continued to function as a prison in 1235. We do know that somewhere within the Hospitaller compound was a prison, but its location remains unknown.[13] Since it appears now that the tower above *Porta Nova* used to be a prison in 1198 and became a property of the Hospital Order in 1235, it is possible that the Order continued to use it as a prison.

The area around the supposed location of *Porta Nova* has yet to be excavated, but we are now able to reconstruct some of its main features. This reconstruction is made possible owing to two charters, one plan, and a neighbour's bad reputation.

---

*Mediterraneo all'apogeo dello sviluppo medievale: Aspetti economici e sociali* (Pistoia, 2003), p. 501 and "Aspects of Everyday Life in Frankish Acre," *Crusades* 4 (2005), 77, 80–81.

[11] According to Jacoby the *Porta Nova* was located in the north-west corner of the compound, and the *Porta Hospitalis* in the north-east one, whereas the *Porta Domine Nostre* was detached from the compound and stood to its east. In contrast Riley-Smith reconstructs the gates of the Hospital according to Paolino Veneto's plan. See David Jacoby, "Crusader Acre in the Thirteenth Century: Urban Layout and Topography," *Studi Medievali* 3.20 (1979), 41 n. 212 and plan; and Jonathan Riley-Smith, "Guy of Lusignan, the Hospitallers and the Gates of Acre," in *Dei Gesta per Francos: Études sur les croisades dédiées à Jean Richard*, ed. Michel Balard, Benjamin Z. Kedar and Jonathan Riley-Smith (Aldershot, 2001), pp. 112–13.

[12] See Jonathan Riley-Smith, "Further Thoughts on the Layout of the Hospital in Acre," in *Chemins d'outre-mer. Études sur la Méditerranée médiévale offertes à Michel Balard*, 2 vols, ed. Damien Coulon, Catherine Otten-Froux, Paule Pagès and Dominique Valérian (Paris, 2004), 2:755.

[13] Ibid, p. 757.

# REVIEWS

Alfred Andrea, *Encyclopedia of the Crusades*. Westport, CT: Greenwood Press, 2003. Pp. xxiii, 356. ISBN 0 313 31659 7.

Corliss K. Slack, *Historical Dictionary of the Crusades* (Historical Dictionaries of War, Revolution, and Civil Unrest, 25). Lanham, MD: Scarecrow Press, 2003. Pp. xxiv, 273. ISBN 0 8108 4855 4.

Despite their similarity of purpose, these volumes differ from one another in both content and format. The reason for the difference lies in the approaches taken by the two authors, which was probably dictated in part by the publishers. The Andrea volume is intended to stand alone, while that of Slack is part of a series. The difference in format makes it difficult to compare the length of these books, but Andrea clearly has devoted more space to long articles, while Slack has more short articles. I counted 235 articles in Andrea and 270 in Slack, which is quite significant given the greater length of Andrea's work. It is explained in part by the fact that he devotes long articles to individual crusades, while Slack has much shorter articles. Still, Andrea has a three-page article on Jews and the crusades in which he treats persecution of Jews in each period; Slack has an article on Emicho of Flonheim, one on Jews, Judaism, and another, one of the longer in the book, on the Spanish Inquisition. These points illustrate the differences in approach taken by the two authors. While there is considerable overlap, there are numerous cases in which each is distinctive.

Andrea's volume provides a more interpretative approach. As we might expect, his treatment of the Fourth Crusade is extensive. He follows Queller/Madden in their view that the Venetians were not involved in a conspiracy to divert the crusade. He also follows their work in pointing to the problems faced by the crusaders in meeting the terms to which they agreed to secure a Venetian fleet for transport to their destination, which was Alexandria in Egypt. His account of the attack on Zara points out that the Franks never actually fulfilled the terms of their absolution by the papal legate. One of the most difficult questions was the decision by the crusaders to support the claim of the young Alexius IV against the reigning emperor, his uncle, Alexius III. Andrea's treatment of the diversion of the crusade takes the approach that each stage was influenced by the circumstances at the time, thus supporting the general line of the Queller thesis. While there is strong evidence to support this view, we need to recognize that the crusade leaders were themselves rather more willing to deceive the pope and to engage in conspiracies to secure their objectives than that line of argument suggests. But, given the controversial nature of the Fourth Crusade, it is important to stress that this article is both accurate and well written. Treatment of the other crusades also reveals considerable attention to organization and an effort to provide the clarity needed for student use.

Andrea gives the same care to shorter articles. His treatment of Eleanor of Aquitaine provides a valuable caution to the more extreme portrayals of this queen on crusade. One point that might have been made is the fact that Eleanor was accustomed to exercise her rule in Aquitaine. Her active role in Antioch may have caused resentment among some of the crusader barons. His article on Pope Eugenius III rightly emphasizes the importance of the letter, *Quantum praedecessores*. It clearly signals a further development in the idea of crusade. Anyone who attempts a brief description of Francis of Assisi faces a complex body of myth and legend. Andrea's article is certainly a strong effort in the right direction, but it is important to note that Francis first preached to the crusaders in their camp near Damietta before crossing over to the Muslim camp. Evidence suggests that he gave the same message to both sides, namely, conversion as an alternative to war. While this message was not received well by either side, nor was it rejected. Given al-Kamil's desire for a truce that would free him to advance his ambitions in Syria, it is likely that Francis's message was read by him as a possible opening of negotiations. But these remarks should not detract from Andrea's work, a very considerable achievement for one scholar that reveals both a breadth and depth of knowledge of the crusades.

The approach taken by Corliss Slack is closer to that found in many reference works, which place a major emphasis on factual narrative rather than interpretation. She provides an introduction on the history of the crusades, in which she gives greater scope to her own views. Her volume also has a useful chronology covering the period from 1009 to 1312. But the major value of her work lies in the articles dealing with Muslim topics. They total fifty compared to thirty-one in Andrea, many of them being very brief, such as that on Baha al-Din ibn Shaddad, the biographer of Saladin, which runs to only four lines. Her article on Muslims provides a good brief introduction to Islam in a manner accessible to students. I would suggest, however, that her contrast of Muslim tolerance to Christian intolerance, though a commonplace in the literature, does not reflect the full reality of minority life under Muslim rule. I believe it springs in part from a misunderstanding of the evolution of the place of *dhimmi* in various Muslim societies. Unfortunately, there is no article on *dhimmi* in either volume. Slack also has a useful article on sufism, a movement within Islam that stressed mysticism. She treats both the Muwahhids and the Murabits (Almoravids) of north-west Africa as well as the Spanish reconquista, topics that are also treated by Andrea. Slack has a number of individual articles on eastern churches, such as the Nestorians and the Jacobites.

Her brief article on the First Crusade makes no mention of the Council of Piacenza and the presence there of Byzantine envoys. Her treatment of the Children's is too short and contains little substantive information. She devotes considerable space to the Inquisition and the Spanish Inquisition, neither of which is given a separate article by Andrea. Her account of the Inquisition seems to me to be a bit hard to follow and her opening statement joining the Spanish Inquisition to the Papal or Roman is misleading. This problem persists in her article on the

Spanish Inquisition. Admittedly, these are difficult topics about which considerable controversy still swirls.

In the article on the Latin Patriarchs, we should note that Soffredus, cardinal priest of Santa Prassede, was never actually Patriarch. He was elected and refused the office. The article on John of Brienne states that Francis of Assisi "attempted to preach the gospel to the sultan in Cairo." The article on Francis repeats this point. Actually, Francis visited the Sultan's camp south of Damietta, most likely during a truce. He had earlier preached to the crusaders. There are all kinds of speculations in the secondary literature, but we have a basic account in James of Vitry, which is fairly consistent with Thomas of Celano. The article on Cyprus makes no mention of the Emperor Frederick II. It is interesting to note the considerable space allotted to the various regencies during the reign of Baldwin IV of Jerusalem, but Baldwin himself is treated very briefly. Hamilton's judgment would suggest need for a longer treatment. Still there is much of value in this volume. Used with a certain caution, it provides a useful supplement to Andrea. It is especially helpful for its detailed bibliography. Both of these authors should be commended for undertaking the difficult task of selecting topics and deciding how to organize their subjects.

JAMES M. POWELL
SYRACUSE UNIVERSITY (EMERITUS)

Michael Angold, *The Fourth Crusade. Event and Context* (The Medieval World). Harlow: Pearson-Longman, 2003. Pp. xxii, 281. ISBN 0 582 35610 5 (paperback).

Marco Meschini, *1204 L'incompiuta. La IV crociata e le conquiste di Costantinopoli.* Milan: Ancora, 2004. Pp. 256. ISBN 88 514 0183 7.

Jonathan Phillips, *The Fourth Crusade and the Sack of Constantinople.* London: Jonathan Cape, 2004. Pp. xxvi, 374. ISBN 0 224 06986 1.

Whether by coincidence or design, a number of books dealing with some aspect of the Fourth Crusade were published in or around the eight-hundredth anniversary of the conquest of Constantinople in 1204. The first two under review here are distinct in that they are directed at a popular audience. Although a vast body of scholarship exists on this complex and controversial crusade, sadly very little of that work has made it to a general readership. These two books go a long way to rectifying that problem. It is refreshing indeed to see professional historians taking up the challenge of writing popular history.

Jonathan Phillips brings to his volume a wide expertise in the history of the crusades. But he brings much more. Through evocative and stirring prose, Phillips breathes life not only into the Fourth Crusade but the medieval world in which it took place. No detail is too small or insignificant for Phillips not to make use of in order to give depth to his narrative. Every activity, every building, every item provides a potential opportunity for Phillips to teach. He knows that his readership may be just as unfamiliar with the Middle Ages as they are with the Fourth Crusade, so he takes his time, pointing out important components of medieval life as he guides them in the footsteps of the crusaders. Occasionally one almost gets the impression that the crusade itself is simply a vehicle for Phillips to educate his reader about the Middle Ages. To that end, he cleverly engages them with references to their own world. Comparing a medieval roundship to an Airbus A320 might seem a stretch, but it works perfectly here. All of this makes Phillips' rendering of the Fourth Crusade strikingly rich and colorful.

The story that Phillips tells will already be familiar to crusade historians. He traces the expedition from its inception until the fall of Constantinople in 1204. He then devotes one chapter to the Latin Empire while a final summing up appears in an afterword. Phillips avoids old historiographical fights between "Accident Theorists" and "Treason Theorists," instead crafting his narrative according to the best current scholarship. Footnotes are largely kept to occasional references to primary sources, although full references to the scholarly literature that informs this book are available in a separate bibliography. Leaving aside the dark intrigue and malevolent secret plans that adorned earlier popular histories, Phillips demonstrates that the events of the Fourth Crusade are fascinating enough without the embellishment. His crusaders, both Frankish and Venetian, are men driven by a desire to complete their spiritual vows yet beset by all-too-earthly problems that incrementally lead them astray.

Like Phillips, Marco Meschini seeks to bring the story of the Fourth Crusade to a popular audience. Unlike Phillips, however, Meschini also has something to say about the various controversies and debates that have characterized its historiography. He, therefore, divides his book into two sections. In, "The Facts," Meschini provides a solid yet concise narrative of the course of the crusade. Like Phillips, Meschini has no scheming villains dotting his landscape, but neither does he have the rich asides that so beautifully add depth to Phillips's prose. In lieu of that, Meschini includes several textboxes that describe such things as a crusade vow, siege machinery, and vessels in the crusade fleet. There are a number of color plates, including excellent reproductions of the floor mosaics from San Giovanni Evangelista in Ravenna that depict various real and imagined episodes of the crusade. However, the color maps of Constantinople, which are rendered from a bird's eye perspective, are a bit cartoonish. Not only are several buildings misplaced but most of the great city appears to have been a forest.

The second section of Meschini's book is "The Interpretations." It is here that he describes some recent scholarship and offers some of his own solutions to problems. For example, in a section called "Numbers," he contends that despite the fact that only one-third of the crusaders rendezvoused at Venice they nevertheless used all of the vessels that had been assembled. Yet, if this is true, how can one square the statements made by Geoffrey of Villehardouin and Robert of Clari that the Venetians had prepared all that they had promised with the need to transport more than 20,000 additional troops if the army had arrived as expected? Indeed, Meschini would increase those numbers even further, since he includes prostitutes and the poor among those travelling with the crusade. Yet we know that the papal legate, Peter Capuano, relieved the poor of their vows and sent them home before the crusade began. As for prostitutes, were they not available locally?

Meschini joins a growing number of scholars eschewing the usual lamentations that seem to set the sack of Constantinople apart from every other conquest in history. He notes that it was done according to the standards of the time and compellingly argues that later references to massacres are simply not credible. It is certainly true that enormous booty was obtained in the sack, but Meschini points out that the destroyed or pilfered treasures so often described were themselves pilfered from other cities at the order of Constantine or his successors. Among the most memorable scenes during the sack is that of the French prostitute singing and dancing at the throne of the patriarch in Hagia Sophia. Meschini argues that this was an isolated incident magnified by Nicetas Choniates and Constantine Stilbes as a symbol of the Frankish defilement of the Byzantine Empire. He is certainly correct that this became a potent symbol, yet was it also a factual event? One might, for example, wonder how Choniates, who was hiding at a Venetian friend's house at the time, was so well informed about events in Hagia Sophia. Meschini generally presents his conclusions in a tentative way, which is proper given the evidence he has at hand. Nevertheless, many of his suggestions are provocative and could well lead others to fruitful avenues of new research.

Unlike the books by Phillips and Meschini, Michael Angold's work is not at all meant for a popular audience. Indeed, it assumes at the outset that the reader is well familiar with the intricacies of the crusade and its aftermath. Angold's purpose, as his title suggests, is to place the Fourth Crusade within a larger context, examining the political, social, and cultural environments of Byzantium and the West before and after 1204. In so doing, Angold casts new light on the course of the crusade, bringing several factors into sharper relief. He begins with an overview of the principal sources for the crusade, describing and critiquing each in turn. It is clear from the outset that, unlike many earlier Byzantinists who have treated this subject, Angold does not privilege his Greek sources. Quite the contrary, he provides an excellent analysis of their limitations as well as those of Western writers. He then traces a brief history of Byzantium's relations with the Latin West and describes the Byzantine factional landscape into which the Fourth Crusade sailed. Angold provides the best treatment yet of the Byzantine perspective on the events leading up to the conquest of their capital.

In a short chapter, Angold addresses the events of the crusade itself. Yet even here he declines to provide a full narrative. Instead, this chapter provides an opportunity for a chronological discussion of various key points in the expedition. Angold then moves on to the most valuable portion of this book, a fascinating analysis of the consequences of the fall of Constantinople. Like Meschini, Angold discounts much of the hyperbole concerning the sack of the city, noting that it derives principally from the pens of Nicetas Choniates and Innocent III, both of whom had reasons to exaggerate. More importantly, Angold makes the case that our understanding of 1204 is heavily colored by the subsequent failure of the Latin Empire. He examines not only the weaknesses of the short-lived state, but the longer lasting effects of the coming of the Latin church, a new Latin aristocracy, and the Venetians and other Italians. He also describes the intricate matrix of competing aims in the Greek world as would-be emperors, military adventurers, and pious churchmen found themselves faced with a new and unprecedented landscape in the wake of Latin occupation. In the last section, Angold addresses the myth of Byzantium that he sees fashioned in response to the cataclysm of 1204. Although the event led to a renewal culminating in the restoration of 1261, it also shifted the Byzantine gaze to restoring a grandeur of a pre-conquest past rather than adapting to a changing present.

It is not possible in a short review to do justice to all of the insights that Angold provides for the student of the Fourth Crusade in this excellent book. Almost every page brims with a banquet of food for further thought. Still, one could posit a few criticisms. Angold may be the first Byzantine historian to write a history of the Fourth Crusade in which Doge Enrico Dandolo is not portrayed as a scheming devil. His treatment of twelfth-century Venice is, on the whole, admirable. Nevertheless, Angold is occasionally unable to shake the shopworn stereotype of Venetians as a nation of cynical merchants and zealous patriots. In contrast to "the crusade leadership conscious of its moral responsibilities" the "Venetians thought in terms of the honour of their patria and of commercial interests" (p. 258). The fact that the Venetians, unlike other Italians, sought a papal dispensation to trade with Muslims is not evidence of their piety but simply part of a "new image that the Venetians were fashioning of their city as the loyal daughter of the Apostolic See" (p. 76). One might also quarrel with his assertion that for Byzantines 1204 "was a more traumatic event than the final fall in 1453" (p. 126), particularly in light of the elation and mirth evidenced by the Greek provincials upon hearing of the crusader conquest. Yet, these are matters for future discussion and research. They take nothing away from this truly remarkable work that advances our understanding of the Fourth Crusade as well as its causes and effects.

The Fourth Crusade has always been an event both fascinating and complex. Thanks to these new books the complexity of the expedition may act no longer as a stumbling block, but a gateway to the medieval world of the crusaders.

THOMAS F. MADDEN
SAINT LOUIS UNIVERSITY

*The Book of Deeds of James I of Aragon. A Translation of the Medieval Catalan* Llibre des Fets, trans. and with notes by Damian Smith and Helena Buffery (Crusade Texts in Translation 10). Aldershot: Ashgate, 2003. Pp. xii, 405. ISBN 0 7546 0359 8.

The "Llibre dels fets" is indeed an extraordinary source. Written in the thirteenth century on behalf of King James I of Aragon, it counts among the few auto-biographical texts composed by a monarch of the Middle Ages. With a mixture of propaganda, education, and legitimisation, King James, who is rightfully known as the Conqueror, passed on to his successors his personal vision of royal power and the purpose of monarchy. By narrating the successes of his military campaigns, King James strove to demonstrate that his deeds (*fets*) were in fact guided by God. This intent causes considerable problems for historians, for James had no interest in detracting from his image by including references to defeats or failures. In order to obtain a reliable picture of his reign, one must compare James's narrative with further sources, in particular documentary evidence. In spite of these limitations, the "Llibre dels fets" is far more than a literary gem. It offers an invaluable insight into a medieval monarch's frame of mind and draws a vivid, albeit highly subjective picture of fifty crucial years in the history of a Mediterranean kingdom.

The last complete English translation of this important work dates from 1883, and in the past decades new editions and further studies have considerably enhanced our knowledge of the text's historical background and philological status. It was thus high time for an up-to-date and reliable new translation. Helena Buffery has accomplished the difficult task of rendering medieval Catalan into modern English very well. One could argue if "usages" is the correct equivalent for the term "usatges" (pp. 368–69), which may well have designated the well-known Catalan law code. One could also criticise the inconsistent use of "Moor" and "Muslim" throughout the notes. But these are very few minor points in a task well done. A particularly welcome element is the excellent historical commentary compiled by Damian Smith. He not only presents pertinent remarks to the places, individuals and occurrences mentioned in the text, but also points out where James took a one-sided view of affairs or where the king chose to omit essential information.

Thanks to Smith's annotations, those readers not well acquainted with Iberian history will be able to understand to what extent James reduced the chronicle of his reign to the story of his military successes and failures. The military aspect dominates throughout, while much of what later historians consider to be particularly remarkable in James's reign plays a secondary role, such as his administrative, economic and cultural innovations. Even the young king's difficult early years are described as a sort of playing-ground, a learning phase for later successful campaigns. These were to come with the conquest of Majorca and the lengthy expeditions against the kingdom of Valencia, which succumbed to the Christians after many years of fighting. Though militarily successful, the reconquest of Murcia in the 1260s could not compare to these achievements, because James could not maintain his acquisition, and noble uprisings further darkened the last years of his reign. All this is told from the highly subjective viewpoint of the ruler himself, and the reader can sense the monarch's rage, disappointment, satisfaction and pride according to situation.

It may come as a surprise to find the translation of the "Llibre dels fets" in the series Crusade Texts in Translation. This work in fact presents the inside view of a crusading society, in which the struggle with Muslim foes often had more in common with border warfare than with holy war. In this sense, it resembles William of Tyre's famous chronicle. At first sight, honour and dynastic self-consciousness were the key motives behind James's actions. Consequently, crusaders from beyond the Pyrenees are, at best, mentioned in passing (p. 170), and throughout the text the pope is noticeably absent. This only changes towards the end of the book where first-hand information is offered about crusade diplomacy during the Council of Lyon in 1274. It is mostly through Damian Smith's expert footnotes that the reader learns about the crusading background which the text itself often does not mention (unfortunately this valuable information was not included in the index).

But if one reads the text attentively, the "Llibre dels fets" offers more to crusade historians than meets the eye. For example, this text can be read as an excellent military manual on warfare in the thirteenth century: it describes an enormously wide range of violent and peaceful ways of vanquishing one's foes – from open battles to raids, from tactics of devastation to siege warfare, from bribery to diplomacy. The author proudly unfolds how he gradually became an expert in all these fields, thereby presenting first-hand information on the procedures of medieval warfare. Furthermore, James effectively organised a military expedition to the Near East in 1269, which failed largely due to adverse weather. The king not only gives a vivid description of the preparations for this expedition and its fate, but also goes to great pains to explain its failure by giving a compelling account of his vain attempts to master the seas (pp. 335–44). In this chapter, one can observe that the author subtly hints at certain crusading traditions. Thus he terms the expedition a *passatge* (*passagium*) or *ida* (*iter*) instead of using the more customary term *viatge*, and James claims to have used the First Crusade's catchword *Deus vult* in a speech to his troops intended to persuade the men (p. 335).

While these references, mostly lost in translation, illustrate the unique prestige of the Eastern Crusade, other passages clearly show that James also perceived religious warfare on the Iberian front as something special – or, at any rate, the king wanted it to be remembered in this way in his memoirs. In his eyes, wars against Muslims were clearly a service to God, as he repeatedly claims. The fact that some rebellious Aragonese nobles interpreted the wars in purely economic terms only serves to prove the king's point (pp. 164, 223). It is surely no coincidence that the campaign against Majorca is depicted as a penance for Peter II's failings in the Albigensian wars (p. 71), that James terms the campaigns against Muslims as "good works" (*bones obres*) or that the battle-cry of both Catalans and Aragonese is "Saint Mary" when fighting the Muslims opposing "Aragon" in other conflicts (pp. 107, 193).

If the king's memoirs are to be trusted, he appealed to the crusading spirit of his warriors during all three major Iberian campaigns of his reign in both speeches and prayers, describing those killed in battle as martyrs and comparing Iberian expeditions to the crusades in Palestine (pp. 81, 86, 92, 188, 290). James also reports on the positive effect that visions and warrior saints are supposed to have had on the outcome of certain campaigns (pp. 107, 290). Thus, though more a "mirror of princes" than a crusader chronicle, the "Llibre dels fets" is indeed an excellent source for the history of the crusades. This finely annotated translation will undoubtedly make a wide circle of students and historians aware of it.

Nikolas Jaspert
Ruhr-Universität Bochum

*The Catalan Rule of the Templars: A Critical Edition and English Translation from Barcelona, Archivo de la Corona de Aragón, Cartas Reales, MS 3344*, ed. and trans. Judi Upton-Ward (Studies in the History of Medieval Religion, 19). Woodbridge: The Boydell Press, 2003. Pp. xxviii, 113. ISBN 0 85115 910 9.

Historians of the military orders have long been aware that Curzon's edition of the French rule of the Templars (1886) and Schnürer's edition of the order's "primitive" Latin rule (1903) do not constitute a complete corpus of the Templars' normative texts. As early as 1889, Delaville Le Roulx described another manuscript which is today known as Barcelona, Archivo de la Corona de Aragón, Cartas Reales, MS 3344. Shortly thereafter, d'Albon included a transcription of this text in his collection of Templar materials (Paris, Bibliothèque nationale, nouvelles acquisitions latines, 1–71, here 68). Judi Upton-Ward's new book, *The Catalan Rule of the Templars*, is the first complete scholarly edition and the first English translation of the Barcelona manuscript. For this alone she deserves our gratitude.

The book opens with a short preface and two useful maps of the Templar commanderies in the Corona de Aragón and of the Holy Land. From the introduction we learn that the Barcelona manuscript was written in the late thirteenth century (the last datable incident mentioned is the surrender of the Templar castle Gaston which occurred in 1268), that its language, apart from a short Latin passage dealing with the reception of chaplain brothers, is "Catalan, with influences from Provençal/Occitan, Old French and Aragonese/Castilian" (p. xviii) and that – while much of the text is related to that of the French rule – there are some clauses that are completely unique. The manuscript can be divided into four parts: the holding of ordinary chapters (§§ 1–45), penances (§§ 46–120), further details on penances (§§ 121–202), and reception into the order (§§ 203–206); it is incomplete in that it stops in mid-sentence. Very helpful are the brief description of the Templars' hierarchy, penance system, and provincial structure in the introduction, its concordance of the clauses of the Barcelona manuscript with related clauses in Curzon's 1886 edition of the French rule and Delaville Le Roulx's 1889 description of the Barcelona manuscript, as well as its brief summary of the contents of the Barcelona manuscript's individual clauses. This reader would have appreciated an explanation of how the manuscript became a part of the *Cartas Reales* (a result of royal confiscations during the trial of the Templars?), but this is a minor omission. To the description of the penance system (as related in the Barcelona manuscript) one might add that, while § 120 does not further explain what happened when brothers were sent to the chaplain brother to receive their sentences (p. xvii), other clauses seem to suggest that maybe only those brothers who were not well (§§ 23, 32) and chaplain brothers who had sinned (§ 48) were sent to a chaplain brother to receive their sentences from him in private.

According to Upton-Ward, "the greatest interest of the Barcelona manuscript lies in the historical examples of infringements of the Rule which are not found in the French" (p. xiii). There are, for example, new cases here that seem to indicate that alcoholism may have been a much more serious problem in the order than historians have acknowledged so far (§§ 34, 192); delinquent brothers were offered to either forgo wine altogether or join another (that is, stricter) order. Secondly, considering medieval standards of dental hygiene, it comes as no surprise that there were cases of halitosis even in the military orders, but the Barcelona manuscript's stipulations with regard to cases of bad breath amongst the Templars (§ 41) are nonetheless unique and of value for the study of medieval 'Alltagsgeschichte.' Thirdly, it is of interest that the questions a candidate for reception into the order was asked (for example with regard to his marital status, vows, debts, health, and so on), while fairly similar in the French and the Catalan texts (§ 62), appear in a different order here: the Barcelona manuscript's first concern was to ensure that no one would be admitted by way of simony (which ranks only fifth in the French text). Was simony a major issue in the Templar province of Catalonia and Aragón? Then there is the fascinating case of a brother in Catalonia who was a forger of papal indulgences (§ 174). Finally, the Barcelona manuscript shows that the standard bearer (§ 203: "ganfanoner") seems to have played a more important role in the reception of brothers into the order than has been recognized so far.

The critical apparatus of the edition takes into account variations from d'Albon's transcription, Delaville Le Roulx's readings, and – in cases where the wording is related to that of the French rule – Curzon's edition. To those familiar with Upton-Ward's English translation of the French rule (1992), it will come as no surprise that the prose of her translation of the Barcelona manuscript is marvelous. One exception may be the last sentence of § 5 which contains the awkward phrase "if any brother wishes to remind him of him anything" (*sic*) which is undoubtedly an editorial oversight. With regard to the lacuna in § 70 (a clause reiterating that Templars were to avoid women), I would like to submit that it makes more sense that the Templars were not to have their hands and feet washed by women, rather than the other way around, because there is an analogous stipulation in the rule of the Hospitallers (§ 4: "let no women wash their heads or their feet"). Finally, the explanation of the term "baylia" (in the context of § 39 on Templars in Muslim captivity) as a "Templar province comprising of a group of commanderies managed from a center in regions too small to warrant the creation of grand commanderies, but too distant to manage within the provincial structure" (p. 21, note 20) may be too narrow. I would argue that "baylia" should be translated in more general terms as a "function", an "office", an "assignment", or an "area of responsibility". To sum up: apart from minor issues, Judi Upton-Ward's *Catalan Rule of the Templars* is an extremely valuable addition to the corpus of edited and translated Templar sources.

JOCHEN BURGTORF
CALIFORNIA STATE UNIVERSITY, FULLERTON

*The Crusades. A Reader*, ed. Sarah Jane Allen and Emilie Amt (Readings in Medieval Civilizations and Cultures, 8). Peterborough, Ontario: Broadview Press, 2003. Pp. xix, 430. ISBN 1 551111 537 9 (paperback).

This is the most comprehensive collection of crusader sources in translation published so far and is, therefore, to be welcomed wholeheartedly. It comprises 104 documents from almost all areas of crusading and its historical contexts stretching from the fourth to the sixteenth centuries. This wide scope not only reflects a sympathetic take on the many different ways in which the crusading movement was shaped by, and in turn permeated, medieval culture generally. It also concords with the didactic design of the book which is principally meant as an aid in teaching undergraduate students. The collection starts with a number of texts (docs. 1–11) about early Christian pilgrimage and just war, Muslim tradition and expansion in the early Middle Ages, the beginnings of the Reconquista and the Gregorian Reform. These represent some of the major historical context in which the origins of the crusade movement were couched. The vast majority of texts concerns the crusades between the late eleventh and the early fourteenth centuries (docs. 12–81, 84–97), concentrating on the Holy Land crusades and the so-called crusader states in the eastern Mediterranean. There are two texts about the Albigensian Crusade (docs. 59–60) and two whole sections on the Baltic Crusade (docs. 64–73) and the conflicts between Muslims and Christians on the Iberian Peninsula (docs. 74–83). The final seven texts (docs. 98–104) concern snippets of crusading and related topics of the late fourteenth to the early sixteenth centuries. The omission of further documents relating to the rich history of the later crusades is regrettable, but probably reflects the chronological boundaries which still dominate the teaching of the crusades at most universities. This is no great loss, however, since Norman Housley's *Documents on the Later Crusades, 1274–1580* (1996) fills the gap, providing an excellent tool for teaching the crusades of the fourteenth to sixteenth centuries.

Allen and Amt have included a refreshing variety of texts alongside the more commonly known chronicles. Some are central to the business of crusading, such as reports about preaching the cross, indulgences, liturgical texts or financial accounts of crusaders. Other documents explore the wider context of crusading – for example, texts about the military orders, conversion, law codes or accounts of Arab learning. The editors have also included a fair share of Byzantine and Muslim texts which provide perspectives not available in the Western sources. There is a short but valuable index of topics (pp. 427–30) which helps in tracing common themes treated by these documents.

Most translations are reprinted from previous publications but Allen and Amt also provide their own reliable translations where none were available. Unfortunately reference to the editions of the original texts is only given in the latter cases making it a cumbersome task to check translations if and when needed. In some cases it is also not obvious why a particular passage was selected and how this passage relates to the overall document. For example, Innocent III's letter to the archbishop and clergy of Magdeburg (doc. 56) could well have been printed in its entirety without taking up too much space.

Each document is prefaced by a short heading giving information about author, historical setting and, if necessary, the text from which a passage is taken. Whilst being useful, these introductions are often too short and selective. Anyone using these texts in teaching will have to add further information. At the end of each document there are a number of didactic questions meant to help students interpret the sources. I wonder how useful and necessary these really are. They seem pedantic in that they represent a very personal take on the reading of these sources by the editors and many teachers might not find them very useful for their own purposes. Some references to secondary materials relating to the subject matter of the documents would have been more useful.

All in all, however, this is an extremely useful collection of texts in translation, which will be welcomed by anyone teaching the crusades at undergraduate level.

CHRISTOPH T. MAIER<br>UNIVERSITÄT ZÜRICH

*The Deeds of Pope Innocent III by an Anonymous Author*, trans. with an introduction and notes by James M. Powell. Washington D.C.: The Catholic University of America Press, 2004. Pp. xlv, 286. ISBN 0 8132 1362 2.

This is the first complete translation of the *Gesta Innocentii III* into any modern language, and through it James M. Powell has made a unique source of insight into the first ten years of the pontificate of Innocent III (1198–1216) more readily accessible to students and scholars. The *Gesta* was composed in the years from about 1204 to 1209 by an anonymous author who was clearly close to the pope and at some point a member of the papal curia. Powell suggests that he was the canonist and later cardinal Peter of Benevento, who compiled a collection of Innocent's decretals in 1209. Whoever he was, he included a large number of letters to and from the pope, some of which are not found in the papal registers and most of which have never been translated into English before.

The *Gesta* provides an insight into the papacy's view of European politics as well as its activities and policies at a decisive point of development of the papal office. Naturally, it is the affairs of Rome, the Patrimony, and the Kingdom of Sicily that are in focus, but the author clearly wanted to present Pope Innocent's commitment to the reform of the whole church. Thus we learn of the pope's decisions in cases of translations of bishops "from the whole world" and of his concerns for the rights of the church even as far away as Norway. The author appears to be very well informed of the marital case of the French king Phillip Augustus and Danish princess Ingeborg, which is treated at some length (pp. 64–71), followed by the case of the union of the king of Leon and his niece, the daughter of the king of Portugal. Both cases are presented to show the determination of Pope Innocent to make the kings of Europe follow the canonical enforcements.

Of principal interest to the readers of our journal is the lengthy treatment of the Fourth Crusade and Innocent's dealings with the Greeks, Franks, and Venetians in this intricate business (pp. 131–228). This section is composed mainly of Innocent's letters of admonition and instruction to the crusaders, and the intermediate commentaries by the author make no secret of the fact that they were selected and arranged in order to clear the pope of complicity in the siege of Zara and the sack of Constantinople. The pope is presented as angered and frustrated by these events, but also as confronted by a series of impossible situations and hard choices in his efforts to direct the crusaders towards the Holy Land and to establish unity of the Roman and Greek churches

The translation is very readable and the text has been furnished with helpful explanatory notes. On top of it, Powell has written a highly informative and stimulating introduction to the *Gesta* and to the pontificate of Innocent III. The only thing missing in the eyes of this reviewer is an index of the letters cited in the *Gesta*, which would have made this edition even more useful to the students of Innocent III, the development of the papacy, and the Fourth Crusade.

ANE L. BYSTED
UNIVERSITY OF SOUTHERN DENMARK

Bernhard Demel, *Der Deutsche Orden im Spiegel seiner Besitzungen in Europa* (Europäische Hochschulschriften, Reihe III, Geschichte und ihre Hilfswissenschaften, 961). Frankfurt am Main: Peter Lang, 2004. Pp. 742. ISBN 3 631 51017 9.

To many colleagues Bernhard Demel is known as the archivist of the Teutonic Order in Vienna and also the author of many publications, books and important articles on the history of this religious military order. A first volume of his collected essays was published in 1999 in the same series: *Der Deutsche Orden einst und jetzt: Aufsätze zu seiner mehr als 800jährigen Geschichte.*

The present volume includes seven substantial, sometimes expanded and revised papers, most of them lectures from the years 1999 to 2002. Only the first paper touches upon the medieval period at least initially: "Die Deutschordensballei Sachsen vom 13.–19. Jahrhundert – ein Überblick" (pp. 7–189) gives a short sketch of about 15 houses and commanderies, among them Dommitzsch, Langeln, Lucklum, Bergen near Magdeburg, Weddingen. Most pages are devoted to activities of the provincial commanders during the sixteenth to eighteenth centuries. By that time the region was predominantly Protestant. Therefore, both the medieval origins and the later fate of the Teutonic Order's possessions have so far been somewhat neglected. This article is a first and important step forward. "Die Rekuperationsbemühungen des Deutschen Ordens um Livland von 1558/62 bis zum Ende des 18. Jahrhunderts" (pp. 190–258) shows the futile discussions at the imperial diet and the Order's futile appeals to the emperor that were made until the final partition of Poland in 1795. "Bausteine zur Deutschordensgeschichte vom 15. bis zum 20. Jahrhundert" (pp. 259–378) reviews recent literature on the stormy times from the Reformation to the Nazi régime. "Der Deutsche Orden in Schlesien und Mähren in den Jahren 1742–1918" (pp. 379–472), first published in 1997, pursues the acquisitions of the Teutonic Order that were possible after the Habsburg victory over the Bohemian rebellion in 1620, especially Freudenthal, Troppau (where the Teutonic Order held properties in medieval times), Eulenberg and Busau. "Zur Geschichte des Piaristen- und späteren Staatsrealgymnasiums in Freudenthal (1730–1945)" (pp. 472–537) describes the Master's attempts to engage a teaching order to secure Catholic education for the subjects in the Teutonic Order's dominions in Silesia and Moravia. "Hoch- und Deutschmeister Leopold Wilhelm von Österreich (1641–1662)" (pp. 538–603) outlines the career of this archduke, who was also active as military commander during the Thirty Years War, as governor of the Spanish Netherlands and as bishop of Breslau. "Die Reichstagsgesandten des Deutschen Ordens von 1495 bis Ende 1805" (pp. 604–56) furnishes prosopographical data about the lawyers and diplomats employed by the order, mostly from papers of the seventeenth and eighteenth centuries. The index of persons and places (pp. 666–725) was compiled by Friedrich Vogel.

The printing is somewhat careless, as no difference is made between various types of dashes and I is frequently used for 1, I45 for 154, and so on. The sentences are sometimes complicated and crowded with learned asides. The strength of Bernhard Demel lies in his great expertise and knowledge about the archives and their sources. In sum, the book may be consulted with profit for many fascinating details and for a long series of general topics concerning the Teutonic Order from the fifteenth to twentieth centuries, for example the Reformation, the Thirty Years' War, the Enlightenment, the Napoleonic Wars or the revolutions of 1848/49 and 1918.

KARL BORCHARDT
UNIVERSITÄT WÜRZBURG

Christine Dernbecher, *"Deus et virum suum diligens."* *Zur Rolle und Bedeutung der Frau im Umfeld der Kreuzzüge* (SOFIE. Saarländische Schriftenreihe zur Frauenforschung, 16). St. Ingbert: Röhrig Universitätsverlag, 2003. Pp. 197. ISBN 3 86110 342 7.

Sabine Geldsetzer, *Frauen auf Kreuzzügen 1096–1291*. Darmstadt: Wissenschaftliche Buchgesellschaft, 2003. Pp. 304. ISBN 3 534 13736 1.

The study of the role of women in the context of the crusades has finally taken off. These two monographs in German, each based on the author's Ph.D. thesis, were written independently and published only a few months apart. Whether this reflects the missing network among German crusade historians or a deliberate attempt at studying the same topic from two separate personal vantage points remains a moot point. Both books in essence treat the topic within the same traditional limits of time and scope in studying the involvement of women in the crusading campaigns to the Holy Land between 1095 and 1291. But here the similarities end.

Dernbecher's book is by far the weaker. It is under-researched, shows very little critical appraisal of the sources and betrays a general lack of analytical vigour. The study is divided into three main sections: (i) a general introduction; (ii) a section on women on the home front; and (iii) a section on women participants in the crusade campaigns, which is by far the longest and thus the central element of the book. Within these sections the author treats a number of subthemes which describe women's roles on the home front, their functions and standing within crusade armies, and particular female concerns such as childbearing and rape on crusade. For each theme Dernbecher draws on a variety of primary and secondary materials, but her selection of sources is in no way comprehensive nor does she adopt a critical stance towards the scholarship she cites. What is more, there is (surprisingly for a German Ph.D.) very little evidence of serious "Quellenkritik." Too often isolated passages from the sources are taken literally and at face value without questioning the authors' intentions or the compositional strategies governing the texts. As a result Dernbecher's narrative seems flat, stringing apparent fact onto apparent fact while reiterating the sources rather than interpreting them. By the same token she does not, for the most part, manage to embed her argument within the context of the relevant scholarship. The fact that a surprisingly large proportion of her references to secondary materials concerns encyclopaedia entries may go some way towards explaining this.

When Dernbecher presents her own interpretations, they more often than not seem far from the sources she discusses. A good example is her reading of two passages by Fulcher of Chartres and Guibert of Nogent according to whom some of the first crusaders scratched crosses into the skin of their foreheads. Without really arguing her point, Dernbecher interprets these crosses as a reaction of women crusaders whom crusade preachers had allegedly barred from taking the crusade vow and who as a result declared themselves crusaders by unofficially signing themselves with the cross in an act of self-mutilation (p. 54). This reading is not based on any evidence and entirely goes against what Fulcher and Guibert themselves wrote. Not only did they make it clear that these crosses were discovered on the dead bodies of both men and women, but nothing in their texts suggests that this had anything to do with who was and who was not allowed to go on crusade.

Dernbecher's somewhat haphazard procedure is well illustrated by her chapter on the financial contributions to crusading by women on the home front (pp. 46–52). In essence the chapter is a discussion of a short passage about a number of Genoese women who took the cross, which James of Vitry reported in one of his letters. As James Powell, who first studied this passage, showed, the connections between this text and the question to what extent women contributed towards vow redemption payments is by no means straightforward. Dernbecher does not, however, seem to be interested in laying open the difficulties of interpreting this particular source or indeed other sources. Nor does she discuss any of the other relevant sources about women's involvement in either paying crusade vow redemptions or providing crusade finance, thus disregarding the materials presented by J. Riley-Smith, E. Siberry, C. Tyerman, J. Bird, C. Maier and others, and ignoring the scholarly debates surrounding crusade taxation and vow redemption payments.

Geldsetzer's book is of an altogether different calibre. Her study is based on about 175 carefully researched prosopographical portraits of women known to have been involved in the crusade campaigns to the Holy Land. These portraits are listed in a number of appendices at the end of the book (pp. 181–215) which group women participants into different categories according to the type of their involvement in the crusading campaigns. Drawing on the evidence presented in these prosopographical portraits, Geldsetzer tackles five principal questions in her five chapters: (i) Which women can be counted as participating in crusades?; (ii) What did the relevant authorities think about women on crusade?; (iii) Why did women go on crusade?; (iv) How did women on crusade live?; (v) What did women do on crusade?

In the first chapter Geldsetzer grapples with the question of defining a woman crusader. The problem is twofold. On the one hand it is a question of terminology as reflected in the sources and on the other a matter of perception, in other words, which women were perceived as crusaders. Given the fact that up until the early thirteenth century there was no uniform term for describing a crusader and that medieval authors were often not concerned about clearly describing a participant's status, it is in many cases ultimately impossible to decide whether a women mentioned in the context of crusading was technically someone who had taken a crusade vow or not. Geldsetzer is well aware of these problems, but nevertheless ends up putting the women she encountered in the crusading sources into more or less narrowly defined and not always very clear categories: she distinguishes between *crucesignatae*, potential participants (*crucesignatae*), participants strictly speaking, potential participants (non-*crucesignatae*), travellers to the East during crusade campaigns, women accompanying crusade armies, travellers to the East outside crusade campaigns, alleged crusade pilgrims. Despite Geldsetzer's careful attempts to justify these divisions on the basis of the textual evidence, this is a dangerous game because in many cases her decisions are based on arguments *e silentio*. The sources, for example, never describe women among the train, washerwomen, cooks or prostitutes as *crucesignatae*. But this is also true of many knights and noblemen mentioned as participants of crusade armies who were undoubtedly crusaders. Geldsetzer's rigid categories, which, for example, put prostitutes into a group of women "accompanying" (rather than being part of) crusade armies, run the danger of pasting over the unclear terminology of the sources and unnecessarily narrowing the interpretative scope that terminology opens up. A case in point is Margaret of Beverly, a crusading pilgrim of the 1180s, whom Geldsetzer categorises as a traveller to the East during a crusade campaign (p. 203). The sources do not call her a *crucesignata* nor did she travel with a crusading army. But she took part in military action in the Holy Land and was described as "having taken the cross and following Christ", which was a standard way of describing crusading status (see C. T. Maier, "The roles of women in the crusading movement: a survey," *Journal of Medieval History* 30 (2004), p. 65). On a different note, one might ask if the prostitute of a brothel in Caesarea, who got involved with a crusader in 1251/52 and is listed by Geldsetzer under women accompanying crusade armies (pp. 207/8), should at all be part of her list of women on crusade. Local prostitutes were presumably visited by crusaders all over the place. Geldsetzer's effort of categorising women on crusade is indicative of her sincere and laborious attempt at coming to grips with the unsystematic terminology of the sources. But her categories are at times too rigid and show a tendency to obscure as much as elucidate the problems inherent in the interpretation of those sources.

Having said this, Geldsetzer's study of women participants in the crusades to the Holy Land is a meticulous and competent analysis of the available sources set against the background of previous scholarship. Geldsetzer considers the various ways in which women contributed to the crusade effort and explores the different experiences of women on crusade. She rightly insists upon the fact that women's tasks and experiences differed greatly and were for the most part predicated on social origin. All in all, Geldsetzer succeeds well in presenting the first comprehensive and reliable overview of women on crusade, couching her findings within the current state of crusade scholarship.

Both Geldsetzer's and Dernbecher's studies, however, suffer from a number of limitations which are connected with their overall approach. It is regrettable that both authors limited themselves to the crusades to the Holy Land in the twelfth and thirteenth centuries (even though for no clear reason Dernbecher includes the Albigensian Crusade). Figures such as Catherine of Siena or Bridget of Sweden show that not only did the involvement of women in the later crusades continue, they also lend women crusaders a voice of their own which is not available for the earlier centuries. Both studies also avoid serious discussion of the religious

motivation behind women's participation in the crusade, which means that they miss
out on a large proportion of the story that they are telling. Given the wealth of recent
scholarship which emphasises the religious side of crusading, this is not entirely
understandable. In addition, neither author made the attempt to approach their topic
from the point of view of modern gender history. This is surprising since gender
history (in particular in the German-speaking world) has recently opened up a
number of interesting approaches on warfare and gender in the modern era which
could have been successfully adapted to a medieval context.

CHRISTOPH T. MAIER
UNIVERSITÄT ZÜRICH

Cristina Dondi, *The Liturgy of the Canons Regular of the Holy Sepulchre of
Jerusalem. A Study and a Catalogue of the Manuscript Sources* (Bibliotheca
Victorina, 16). Turnhout: Brepols, 2004. Pp. 343. ISBN 2 503 51422 7.

While the institutional life of the Latin Church in the crusader states can be
reconstructed to a considerable degree through surviving narrative, legislative and
diplomatic sources, very little is known about the liturgical usages of the church of
the Holy Sepulchre under crusader rule. The tools for a study of the liturgy of the
Holy Sepulchre lie to hand, however, in the form of the eighteen surviving liturgical
manuscripts from the crusader states. That it has taken so long for a full liturgical
study to appear is testimony to the technical complexity of the material and
the methodological difficulties presented by the project. Indeed, much of this
impressive book consists of a presentation of the technical demands of the research
through a full reconstruction of the content of the manuscripts themselves. Cristina
Dondi begins with an introduction to the historiography of the liturgy of the Holy
Sepulchre and to the comparative method employed in the book, which uses more
than a hundred other manuscripts. In Part I, on the liturgy of the canons, she
proceeds to a discussion of the possible Western origins of the liturgy that developed
at the Holy Sepulchre in the twelfth century; there follow discussions of the
manuscripts themselves, originating from Jerusalem in the twelfth century, and
from Acre, Caesarea, Tyre and Antioch in the thirteenth century. Manuscripts
from Cyprus are dealt with in a separate chapter. The specific elements used for
comparative study – the chant repertories of the office books – are then treated in
a chapter devoted to liturgical analysis. Part II comprises a detailed catalogue
of the eighteen manuscripts: sacramentaries, missals, ordinaries, breviaries and
psalters. The calendars of these manuscripts are presented in an easily readable
appendix.

　　Because of the highly technical nature of much of the information in the book, the
chapters dealing with the historical development of the liturgy will probably be
consulted more often by most readers than the liturgical analysis and catalogue.
Dondi argues that the liturgy that eventually emerged in twelfth-century Jerusalem,

and was adopted not only by cathedral chapters in the patriarchate of Jerusalem but also by the Templars and Hospitallers and in the thirteenth century by the Carmelites, was a composite of different elements derived from a number of Western liturgical traditions. Understanding the process through which this happened entails studying the foundation of the Latin church in Jerusalem in the years immediately following 1099. Dondi demonstrates that the influence of early twelfth-century Rheims reformed usage must have arrived with Arnulf of Choques, who as archdeacon of Jerusalem became the driving force behind the adoption of the Augustinian rule by the canons of the Holy Sepulchre. Specific links can be established to the customs of Rheims through appeals directed to Manasses, archbishop of Rheims (the notorious simoniac of Guibert of Nogent's Monodiae, but here rehabilitated as a reformer), and to Lyons through the presence of Archbishop Hugh as papal legate in Jerusalem in 1101–3. Although comparative study of elements such as the chants or calendars can indicate the likeliest sources for the Holy Sepulchre usages, it is another thing to show how those usages made their way to the East. Thus, for example, the All Saints responsaries in the Holy Sepulchre office derive ultimately from the usage at Evreux, and are also found in York and Sées; but how did these usages in particular come to be adopted in Jerusalem? Dondi's reconstruction of this process is based on a prosopographical study of influential individuals in the early history of the chapter of the Holy Sepulchre. Arnulf can be assumed to have contributed usages of Evreux and Bayeux from books given to him by the bishops of those places, both of whom had been present at Clermont in 1095 and who accompanied Duke Robert of Normandy's army as far as Palermo. The Sées usages can be traced through the Augustinian house of St. Victor to Paris. Ansellus, a canon of Notre-Dame in Paris, and cantor of the Holy Sepulchre from 1112 to 1138, is assumed to have brought liturgical books with him from Paris that then contributed to the chant repertory at the Holy Sepulchre. Similarly, Chartrian elements can probably be traced to the installation of Fulcher as a canon of the Holy Sepulchre in 1114. The Chartres connection is also evident in office books from Antioch, where Bohemond's followers included the vidame of Chartres.

These conclusions, while necessarily speculative, are probably as far as it is possible to go in explaining how the liturgy developed. Beyond their value for liturgical studies, however, they also shed light on the institutional history of the Church in Jerusalem itself. The argument that the liturgical life of crusader Jerusalem was formed from the varied experiences brought by individuals from their home communities echoes the famous reflection of Fulcher of Chartres on the creation of a hybrid society from different Western elements. In the thirteenth century, however, the usage of the Holy Sepulchre was influencing the Church throughout the crusader states, including Cyprus. Although some local variations appear in the calendars of Cypriot manuscripts, such as the inclusion of the "Cypriot" saints Hilarion and Epiphanius, it is also apparent that Holy Sepulchre usages were adopted in Cyprus even before the removal of the Holy Sepulchre chapter to the island. This fits nicely with the dependence of the Cypriot Church on that of Jerusalem established in Odo of Châteauroux's Statutes of 1253–4, and suggests that institutional links between the kingdoms existed despite the separation of the crowns for most of the thirteenth century. Cristina Dondi's book, despite its sharp focus on liturgy, has a great deal to offer to crusader historians more generally, and will be a valuable source of reference for those interested in the construction of institutions in the crusader states.

ANDREW JOTISCHKY
LANCASTER UNIVERSITY

*The Fall of Acre 1291. Excidii Aconis Gestorum Collectio. Magister Thadeus Civis Neapolitanus: Ystoria de Desolatione et Concvlcatione Civitatis Acconensis et Totivs Terre Sancte*, ed. Robert B. C. Huygens, with contributions by Alan Forey and David C. Nicolle (Corpus Christianorum Continuatio Medievalis, 202). Turnhout: Brepols, 2004. Pp. 225. ISBN 2 503 05029 8 (hardback), 2 503 03000 9 (series). Includes *Instrumenta Lexicologica Latina: Excidium Acconis, curante Centre Tradition Literarum Occidentalium* (Corpus Christianorum Instrumenta Lexicologica Latina, 162 [CM 202] Series A Formae). Turnhout: Brepols, 2004. Pp. 50 including 4 micofiches. ISBN 2 503 65022 8 (paperback), 2 503 63000 6 (series).

This book contains new editions of two accounts of the fall of Acre to the Mamluk sultan al-Ashraf Ṣalāḥ al-Dīn Khalīl after a 44-day siege on 18 May 1291, the Templar castle falling ten days later. Both texts have been known and used by historians from R. Röhricht onwards, but the previous editions left much to be desired. An edition of the *Excidium Aconis* was published by Dom Martène in 1724 on the basis of three fourteenth-century manuscripts, two in Paris and one in Liège, though he appears to have relied mostly on the latter. For this edition, Huygens also makes use of another, in Madrid, also fourteenth century, as well as two Old French translations, one of them tacked on to a manuscript of the Rothelin continuation of William of Tyre. The *Ystoria de Desolatione et Conculcatione Civitatis Acconensis* by Magister Thadeus was first published by Riant, in 1873 – an unsatisfactory edition based on manuscripts in Turin and London which had been transcribed for him. These like the other four that Huygens uses in this edition date to the fourteenth and fifteenth centuries and are associated with texts of the *Historia Orientalis* of James of Vitry. While the author of the *Excidium* is quite unknown, Thadeus is described as citizen of Naples in all six manuscripts. A colophon added by another hand in some manuscripts also states that he wrote it in Messina in December 1291 (pp. 10–11, 164), a date that is consistent with the *terminus post quem* of August 1291 provided by his mention of the fall of 'Atlit and Tartus, though the Mamluk naval raid on Cyprus *instante mense Maii* would have to be placed in May 1291, rather than 1292 (p. 139), to conform with this dating. Both writers indeed appear to have composed their texts in the West within months of the event itself; and while both drew on eye-witness accounts, Thadeus writes with the advantage of having visited the East at some time in his past.

Both texts are of considerable historical value, adding as they do significant details to the principal Western account of the fall of Acre by the Templar of Tyre (*Cronaca*, ed. L. Minervini [Liguori: Naples 2000], pp. 206–26), on which Marino Sanudo's account was also largely based (*Liber Secretorum Fidelium Crucis*, ed. J. Bongars [Hanau, 1601], pp. 230–31). The *Excidium* falls into two parts. The first describes the events before the siege: the breaking of the truce by newcomers from the West raiding nearby Muslim villages, the subsequent diplomatic exchanges with Sultan Qalawūn, the failure of negotiations, the exhortation of the patriarch, the sending for help from the West, the arrival of King Henry II of Cyprus with 300 men, and the preparations for defending the town walls. The latter were divided into four wards, each patrolled by two groups of defenders operating alternate eight-hour watches. The first two were commanded by the constable of the kingdom, John of Grailly, and the commander of the English troops, Otto of Grandson; the second, by King Henry and the master of the Teutonic Knights; the third, by the grand master of the Hospital and the rector of the *milicia Spate*; and the fourth, by the grand master of the Templars and the prior of the *milicia Sancti Spiritus*. Alan Forey's suggestion (p. 62) that the *milicia Spate* was the same as the Spanish confraternity of St. James seems to be confirmed by a document of 1254, by which the confraternity's two priors were received into the Hospital of St. John and their brethren were required to swear allegiance to the grand master once a year (*Cart Hosp*, no. 2666). The *milicia Sancti Spiritus* was an Italian confraternity, established in Acre on the eve of the Fifth Crusade at Whitsun 1216, whose statutes were confirmed in 1218 by Giles, cardinal bishop of Tusculum and papal legate, and in 1220 by James of Vitry, bishop of Acre, who was himself a *confrater* (Alexander IV, *Registres*, ed. C. Bourel de la Roncière [Paris, 1902–59], I, pp. 103–105, no. 346); although it evidently had a military function, it may well have been associated with the hospital that the hospital of the Holy Spirit in Bologna had established in the Pisan quarter of Acre sometime before 1187 (G. Müller, *Documenti sulle relazioni delle città toscane coll'oriente* [Florence, 1879], pp. 94–95, no. 63; Gregory IX, *Registres*, ed. L. Auvray [Paris, 1896–1955], I, p. 124, no. 209).

The second part of the *Excidium* concentrates on the siege itself. The sultan sets out for Acre but dies on the way, leaving his son, al-Ashraf Khalīl, to conduct the siege. Contrary to other sources, the *Excidium* has King Henry departing for Cyprus, on 15 May, before the first breach in the walls had been made. The author was probably not very familiar with Acre's topography, for he says that the breach was made near St. Antony's gate. This was situated on the inner wall of the Montmusard suburb, just at the point where it met the ditch in front of the north wall of the "old city" of the twelfth century. From the Templar of Tyre and other sources, however, we know that the breach occurred at the exposed north-eastern corner of the old city, some 750 metres further east, where the Mamluks undermined the "new tower" of King Henry II on the outer wall and proceeded to attack the *Turris Maledicta* on the inner wall. From there, one group broke into the German quarter of the old city, while another pressed westwards between the inner and outer walls towards St. Antony's gate and the particularly vulnerable spot in the re-entrant angle where the inner wall of Montmusard crossed the old city ditch. The description in the *Excidium* of fighting by Hospitallers and Templars around St. Antony's gate suggests that its author's informants may have been fighting in the Hospitallers' sector of Montmusard, away from the crucial breach in the inner wall at the *Turris Maledicta*. He also seems unaware of what happened to those left besieged in the Templar castle, as though his informants had already left the city before it fell. They may perhaps have been among the ten Templars, including Theobald Gaudin, who escaped with the order's treasury and relics to Cyprus, or the seven Hospitallers, who likewise escaped with their wounded master, John of Villiers.

While the *Excidium* ends with a lament and exhortation to the church to avenge the disaster, Thadeus, who had visited the Holy Land and writes with evident feeling about it, composed his treatise as a heartfelt complaint against those Christians who had allowed such a thing to happen. His account is not strictly chronological, but consists of short sections, usefully headed by inserted rubrics, which illustrate different aspects of the disaster. For this both authors blame the military orders, the people of Acre and western leaders, though both praise the patriarch, Nicolas of Hanapes, the grand master of the Templars, William of Beaujeu, and the grand master and marshal of the Hospitallers, John of Villiers and Matthew of Clermont respectively. The Teutonic Knights are praised by Thadeus; and, while Henry II of Cyprus is criticized by the *Excidium* for abandoning the city, Thadeus excuses him in part on account of his youth, disability and inexperience of war. The constable, John of Grailly, and commander of the English troops, Otto of Grandson, both get a bad press; and Thadeus also inveighs heavily against the foreign merchants for continuing to trade with the enemy.

As Huygens remarks (p. 16), it is a pity that neither text gives us much information about the layout of the city itself, though Thadeus mentions the house of the Teutonic Order, "in which a tower stood out, lofty and strong, near the beach and seashore" (*in qua turris circa littus maris atque crepidinem sublimis prominebat et fortis*: p. 120; cf. pp. 8–9). He also gives an impressionistic description of the now-vanished Templar castle, which, taken together with the Templar of Tyre's account (*Cronaca*, ed. Minervini, pp. 220–22, 224–26), indicates that it would have consisted of a massive construction of vaults, galleries and paved fighting platforms, probably not unlike the order's other castles of 'Atlit (Pilgrims' Castle) and Tartus, whose remains may still be seen today.

Huygens' clear and authoritative edition of the texts is preceded by a valuable introduction, in which he discusses the authors and their texts, the manuscripts and the establishment of the texts, and the characteristics of the Latin and its orthography. A particularly useful addition for both historians and archaeologists is a glossary of the terms for medieval arms, armour and siege weaponry used in the *Excidium*, compiled by D. Nicolle. The edition is accompanied by a separate fascicule in Corpus Christianorum's Instrumenta Lexicologica Latina series containing lists of word forms.

Huygens declares on p. 6 that this edition marks his farewell to crusader studies – one hopes not!

DENYS PRINGLE
CARDIFF UNIVERSITY

*France and the Holy Land: Frankish Culture at the End of the Crusades*, ed. Daniel H. Weiss and Lisa Mahony (Parallax: Revisions of Culture and Society). Baltimore: The Johns Hopkins University Press, 2004. Pp. xx, 375. ISBN 0 8018 7823 3.

The papers published in this volume were, with one exception, originally presented at a conference held at the Johns Hopkins University in March 2000 on the theme of "Frankish Culture at the End of the Crusades: France and the Holy Land." As the editors appear to regard the crusades as having ended in 1291 (despite the surprise that this may cause to some members of the SSCLE), the focus of the book is on the transmission of social, political and artistic relations between France and the Holy Land in the thirteenth century.

The thirteen essays are grouped into five parts. The first part focuses on "Art and Poetry in Crusader Paris." In his paper, "The Old Testament Image and the Rise of Crusader Culture in France," Daniel Weiss discusses the illustrations in the Morgan Picture Bible and argues that the contemporary issues highlighted in them point to the development in Paris in the later thirteenth century of a specifically "crusader community," keenly interested in the affairs of the Holy Land. Without necessarily dissenting from his thesis, one may ask, however, whether it is helpful to refer to such crusade-inspired art and the cultural milieu in which it developed as "crusader," an adjective that is more normally used in relation to people who actually went on crusade, or in a looser sense to the society and culture (including the art and archaeology) of westerners settled in the East. The difficulties that can arise when the term is stretched to include the residents of the French capital are illustrated in the other paper in this part, in which Stephen Nichols shows how the theme of courtly love in contemporary "crusader" poetry was used as a vehicle for anti-crusade polemics. Would not such lyrics be better described as "crusade-inspired," "crusade-related," or simply "crusade" poetry?

Part II deals with the Frankish presence in the Levant and opens with a survey by Jonathan Riley-Smith of the military and political involvement with Acre of the French kings Louis IX, Philip III and Philip IV between 1254 and 1291. Gustav Kühnel examines the interest that westerners, settled in both East and West, had in the Byzantine emperor Heraclius (or as Kühnel calls him, "Heracles"), whose retrieval of the relic of the Holy Cross from the Persians in 631 made him an ideal model for crusading monarchs to emulate. Robert Ousterhout points out that, although the introduction of rib-vaulting in crusader buildings in the Holy Land was doubtless a local response to French Gothic, the fact that the ribs are only very rarely integral with the vault suggests that the builders were locals who continued to build using their own traditional construction techniques.

Part III, focusing on Acre as a cultural centre, begins with a wide-ranging review of society, culture and the arts in the city in the twelfth and thirteenth centuries by David Jacoby. His paper challenges the normal eurocentric view of the city and argues that art historians' preoccupations with luxury items and patrons have tended to obscure the multicultural nature of its inhabitants and of its artistic and artisanal output. Jacoby also questions whether some of the manuscripts attributed to Acre may not in fact have been produced in Cyprus. Jaroslav Folda (who for reasons which are obscure calls Acre by its post-medieval French name, *St. Jean d'Acre*) looks at some aspects of the art produced in the medieval city between 1191 and 1244. He concludes that in the years before the arrival of St. Louis not only were more art objects produced there than was previously thought to be the case, but also that a significant German influence may be detected in them.

In Part IV, on the uses of secular history, Bianca Kühnel shows how the manuscripts of the *Histoire universelle* and *Histoire d'Outremer*, produced in Acre during the final decades of the crusader kingdom, attempted to bolster the legitimacy and position of the monarchy in a period of uncertainty. Anne Derbes and Mark Sandona suggest that the sympathetic depiction of Amazons and other historical and biblical women in Acre-produced manuscripts of the *Histoire universelle* reflects the involvement of women both in the crusades and also quite possibly in the commissioning of manuscripts. Rebecca Corrie, on the other hand, argues that the Chantilly *Histoire ancienne* was most likely produced in Naples for a member of the court of Charles I.

The fifth part deals with cultural exchange. Anthony Cutler discusses Muslim influences on crusader art. Scott Redford examines the recurring motif of the *sāqī*, or seated cup-bearer, found on Port Saint-Symeon ware, a type of *sgraffiato* pottery first identified by Sir Arthur Lane on the basis of finds made in the 1930s at al-Mina, the port of Antioch. Redford shows that this ware, which is decorated with both figural and non-figural motifs in a manner related to but distinct from contemporary products from Muslim-controlled areas, was produced at a number of different centres in the region of Antioch and Armenian Cilicia, and that the quantities exported around the eastern Mediterranean suggest that it is unlikely to have been regarded as a luxury item. In the final paper, Annemarie Weyl Carr, somewhat extends the date-range of the book's title by examining a group of icons made under Lusignan patronage between 1350 and 1430 in imitation of the icon of St. Mary in the monastery of Kykkos, in Cyprus.

Frankish culture in the final decades of the Latin kingdom is a neglected subject on which this volume sheds new light. One of its particularly welcome features is the interdisciplinarity of its contributions. It will be quarried for its information and ideas for many years to come.

DENYS PRINGLE
CARDIFF UNIVERSITY

Cristian Guzzo, *Templari in Sicilia. Le storia e le sue fonti tra Federico II e Roberto d'Angiò* (Insigna et arma, 2) Genoa: Name edizioni, 2003. Pp. 122. ISBN 88 87298 58 0

Benefiting from an introduction by Malcolm Barber, this book covers the history of the Templars in the kingdom of Sicily – or rather on the mainland part of it – from the minority of Frederick II to their suppression. It concentrates on their economic activities. The approach is a narrative one and Cristian Guzzo provides a useful guide to the source material, particularly that revealed by one of the great late twentieth-century enterprises, the reconstruction of the Angevin archives. He makes the point that relations with Frederick never recovered from his crusade and he draws attention to the way the order was favoured by Charles II. He is particularly interesting on the importance of the Templar house at Barletta.

But while the evidence revealed is interesting there is very little detailed analysis. It may not be possible to explain just how the number of French brothers in the south Italian houses grew exponentially under the Angevins, but attention should have been paid to another issue of wider significance, the institutional measures the order had to take to cope with the fact that the grand commandery was split between two warring kingdoms after 1282, at a time when it had a grand master, William of Beaujeu, who was committed to French interests: his brother was to die on the Aragonese crusade. The order seems, for a time at least, to have treated the island of Sicily sometimes as a *baiulia*, sometimes as an independent grand commandery. Of even greater importance is the issue of the relationship between Charles I of Anjou and William of Beaujeu, who was provincial grand commander and then grand master and has traditionally been seen as an agent of the Angevin government in Palestine. From the moment he returned to Acre in September 1275 William certainly pursued a course of action that favoured Charles's claims to the throne of Jerusalem. Documents from the Angevin archives illustrate how close he was to Charles's vicar-generals and their assistants after the Angevin takeover in 1277. As late as February 1283 he was still regarded in Naples as acting almost as co-ruler with one of them.

The Sicilian Vespers of 1282, the capture of Charles's heir, Charles of Salerno, by the Aragonese in 1284, the deaths of Hugh of Cyprus-Jerusalem in 1284 and Charles of Anjou in 1285, and, perhaps most significant of all, the death of Philip III of France later in the same year led the French government to rethink its approach to the kingdom of Jerusalem. Until then it had supported the claims of Charles, who seems to have taken over from the French crown the responsibility for financing a mercenary force established in Acre by Louis IX in 1254. It is clear, however, that as soon as Philip IV came to throne he or his advisers decided to jettison the Angevin cause in Palestine and to provide support for the Lusignan claimant, Henry of Cyprus-Jerusalem, whose rule, they seem to have considered, was the only hope for the Latin settlement. On 27 June 1286 Henry of Cyprus informed the French knights in Acre, who were still reinforcing Angevin rule, that he had knowledge that they were acting against the wishes of the king of France. Philip seems to have resumed paying directly for the French soldiers. John of Grailly, who arrived in Acre in 1287 as the new "capitaneus soldatorum regis Franciae," had been one of a delegation from Acre to the papal curia, then at Lyons, which in 1274 had tried to block any discussion of Maria of Antioch's claim to the throne of Jerusalem, and therefore of Charles of Anjou's purchase of it, arguing that the curia had no jurisdiction, because the only competent court was the high court of Jerusalem. His appointment must, therefore, have been one which was acceptable to Henry of Cyprus.

William of Beaujeu had joined the masters of the Hospitallers and Teutonic Knights in persuading the French soldiers to surrender the citadel of Acre in 1286 and his name appears on the safe-conduct offered to them by Henry. So the Templars had switched their support to Henry and it is clear that William of Beaujeu only acted as Charles's agent until he was given instructions to the contrary by the French government. He was related to the Capetians by marriage – it was probably because of this that he had served as provincial commander in the kingdom of Sicily – but the prime loyalties of his family were to the crown of France itself. Three brothers had been on the Tunis crusade with King Louis IX and one, who had held the marshalcy of France, had died there. The eldest, Humbert, had been constable of France and, as has already been noted, died on the Aragonese crusade of 1285. As the master of the Hospital had written to the count of Flanders in 1273, William had been elected "por la reverence dou seignor roy de France et por le vostre."

It was reported that Robert of Artois, the regent of Naples, was so enraged by the support given to Henry by the Templars and Hospitallers that he confiscated their properties in Apulia. Cristian Guzzo unfortunately does not describe the consequences of this affair. His book is a useful step in the right direction but much more work still needs to be done.

JONATHAN RILEY-SMITH
EMMANUEL COLLEGE, CAMBRIDGE

Jonathan Harris, *Byzantium and the Crusades* (Crusader Worlds). London and New York: Hambledon and London, 2003. Pp. xvii, 259 pp. ISBN 1 85285 298 4.

Ralph-Johannes Lilie, *Byzanz und die Kreuzzüge*. Stuttgart: Kohlhammer, 2004. Pp. 280. ISBN 3 17 017033 3 (paperback).

One can only welcome the publication of two engaging Byzantine perspectives on the crusades, both pitched at a general readership. Jonathan Harris's contribution to Hambledon's "Crusader Worlds" series is a successful synthesis that will appeal to a wide anglophone audience, and will satisfy the needs of most undergraduates. His well-written survey of the first four crusades and their aftermath offers the view from Constantinople, incorporating important work by Jonathan Shepard, Paul Magdalino and Michael Angold, up to but not including Angold's recent study of 1204. Harris also makes use of Lilie's important research on Byzantium and the crusader states, the forerunner to, and foundation for, the second work under review. Both offer a political narrative, Lilie's a little longer, and therefore fuller. The story is familiar, but bears retelling. Ultimately, while Harris offers the more provocative work, Lilie's is more successful and authoritative.

Harris advances a particular vision of Byzantine foreign policy, which he perceives behind the clashes he surveys, and to which he returns whenever possible in the course of his narrative. His argument is coherent and well-documented, and thus will convince his intended audience, although academic historians may find it a little too neat, and at times naive. Byzantine foreign policy, Harris maintains, was driven by two imperatives: first, to defend the *oikoumene*, which may be understood as either the empire proper, or all lands subject to the will of the emperor, and in particular to preserve its capital, Constantinople; second, to enforce recognition of the Byzantine ruler as emperor of the Romans, the ultimate ruler in Christendom. The first point is unimpeachable, and the second at first glance a perfectly reasonable reading of the evidence. However, if one asks why the Byzantines wished at all costs to enforce recognition of their ruler, one might find oneself short of a decent explanation that did not replicate the first. That is, recognition for the emperor reinforced a system, in Ostrogorsky's understanding a hierarchical world view, that ensured the integrity of the empire. In practical terms, a cowed, submissive barbarian was most unlikely to attack the empire, and less still its capital. Thus we are left with one imperative: to defend the empire, by effecting submission of others to its ruler, by defeating them in battle or by all manner of diplomatic means. What administration, one might ask, does not pursue, as its primary foreign policy objective, the defence of the "homeland"? And which is beyond, when pushed for explanation or justification, cloaking the uglier aspects of that policy in rhetoric, which may involve reference to a special covenant or duty? By reducing every initiative to the two imperatives, Harris diminishes the flexibility of Byzantine policy. He sees himself cutting through political and economic ephemera to the ideological underpinnings, whereas others may consider his reductionism as floating above the essential minutiae, so carefully excavated in secondary literature, to expose the rhetorical veneer the Byzantine bureaucrats wished to foist on us, and those with whom they negotiated.

Lilie revels in the minutiae, and his observations frequently clarify situations over which Harris has, of necessity in such a compact work, glossed. More detail is offered on key episodes and themes, such as the calling of the First Crusade and the role of Alexius I (if any), the testimony of Anna Comnena, and the centrality of Antioch to Byzantine and Frankish policy. Harris believes it is not immediately clear why Alexius courted the pope in 1094–5, although the unsettled situation in the Muslim world is surely the answer. Scepticism regarding Anna's reliability as a witness to the First Crusade, given that she was writing at the time of the Second Crusade, is too swiftly dismissed. Lilie draws attention to parallels with Cinnamus' account of the latter, and might have also looked at the contemporary orations of "Manganeius" Prodromus. Attributing Byzantine interest in Antioch primarily to "ideology," which term is never adequately defined by Harris, does little justice to the city's strategic situation, and ignores the local population, which, as Lilie notes, was never able to come to terms with Latin rulership. There was more at stake here than the right to appoint the patriarch, although that was extremely important.

Harris is stronger on the last years of the twelfth century, when he is able to offer clever observations from a close reading of Choniates, with most of which Lilie agrees. Neither is convincing when dealing with – or more accurately dispensing with – the Byzantine notion of "holy war." Harris falls back on the canon of St. Basil of Caesarea, that nobody who has spilt blood in battle may receive communion for three years. This ruling was indeed used at a synod in the 960s, but there is no indication that it was observed before that, nor indeed afterwards, until it was excavated by twelfth-century canonists confronted with maturing Latin articulations of "crusade". There is, to the contrary, strong evidence not just that some Byzantines understood Latin sentiments, but for long periods shared them, for example in the seventh and tenth centuries. Lilie notes this, but believes these periods to be anomalous. He cites the Life of St. Antony the Younger as evidence that Byzantines fought wars for pragmatic reasons, against both Christians and infidels. But one can certainly detect a lost tradition, in unique religious services and martyria, works of art and literature, that flirted with the idea of offering spiritual rewards for fighting the infidel and dying at his hands. The eventual orthodox rejection of such ideas was surely a consequence of the confrontation with Western ideas, which the Byzantines understood only too well.

PAUL STEPHENSON
UNIVERSITY OF WISCONSIN
AND DUMBARTON OAKS

*The History of the Holy War. Ambroise's Estoire de la Guerre Sainte.* 2 vols: *I. Text*, ed. Marianne Ailes and Malcolm Barber; *II. Translation*, trans. Marianne Ailes with notes by Marianne Ailes and Malcolm Barber. Woodbridge: The Boydell Press, 2003.Vol. 1: Pp. xv, 211. Vol. 2: Pp. xvi, 214. ISBN 1 84383 001 9.

The historical value of the rhymed narrative of the Third Crusade by Ambroise has long been recognized, and the appearance of this new edition with a prose translation into English and extensive notes is much to be welcomed. Ambroise himself was evidently a participant in the crusade, and internal evidence suggests a date of composition in the period between King Richard's release from captivity in 1194 and his death in 1199. Ambroise tells the story of Richard's expedition from 1187 until his departure from the East in 1192 with an extended flashback to recount the defeat at Hattin and the other events which led to the crusade being called. The work seems not to have been widely known in the Middle Ages – just one manuscript survives together with a single leaf from another – although around 1220 the author of the *Itinerarium Peregrinorum et Gesta Regis Ricardi* drew on it extensively. Ambroise was unashamedly partisan in his support for Richard and in his criticism of his opponents, most notably King Philip Augustus and Conrad of Montferrat, but made no attempt to conceal the disappointment shared by many crusaders that Richard attempted no direct assault on Jerusalem. The poem was written in French, and Ambroise shows considerable ability in his use of language and his employment of various literary devices to hold the reader's attention.

Marianne Ailes's translation is much to be commended. Many of us familiar with the older verse translation of M. J. Hubert and J. LaMonte found their relentless doggerel hard to cope with for more than a few pages at a time. It was also, as the present editors point out, not as precise as we might expect. What of course cannot be rendered into English is the author's wordplay, but the accuracy and readability of the translation is a great help and will be welcomed by all of us who in the future will be urging our students to use it. Even so, I have a few minor quibbles: I am not convinced that "l'amulaine" (line 5,142; translation p. 103) should be translated "caliph"; "gent" (e.g. lines 6,733, 6,735; translation p. 123) would be better rendered as "people" than "race" – certainly it does not seem to carry any connotations of ethnicity; and "guaste" (line 12,030; translation p. 190) in this context at least means "abandoned" and not "in ruins".

The introduction and notes in volume 2 are also extremely useful. At page 190 it might have been pointed out that "the sepulchre of the body where God became flesh" – a phrase that I am sure will baffle most of my students – relates to the tomb of the Virgin Mary at the abbey of St. Mary of the Valley of Jehosaphat. There are, however, a few points that I would take issue with in the introduction: the misprint at page 3 of "1186" for "1187" is particularly unfortunate; the Christians did not always carry the relics of the Cross into battle (p. 3); Belvoir, Montréal, Kerak and Safad all remained in Christian control for over a year after the battle of Hattin (p. 3); the ancient tell on which Guy established his camp for the siege of Acre was, if

Professor Kedar's understanding of the location of the walls of Acre is correct, considerably nearer the city than is supposed, and the Templar fortress in Acre was at the south-western extremity of the city and not on "the northern promontory" (p. 7); and the Latin continuation of William of Tyre, at least in the form in which it has been transmitted to posterity, is considerably later than the 1190s (p. 14). The archbishop of Caesarea who became patriarch of Jerusalem and died in 1202 was named Monachus and not Aimery (p. 17); he was not "the only senior eastern cleric" to survive from before Hattin to the early years of the thirteenth century – he shared that distinction with Archbishop Joscius of Tyre – and, more importantly, he was not the author of the narrative of the siege of Acre that many, following Paul Riant its nineteenth-century editor, have attributed to him.

It is helpful to have the Old French text and the translation in separate volumes, and the editors are to be congratulated on a very considerable achievement that will be of service for many years to come.

PETER W. EDBURY
CARDIFF UNIVERSITY

Andrew Jotischky, *The Carmelites and Antiquity. Mendicants and their Pasts in the Middle Ages*. Oxford: Oxford University Press, 2002. Pp. xii, 370. ISBN 0 19 820634 8.

Until John XXIII revised the Roman Breviary in 1961 the fourth lesson appointed for Mattins on the feast of Our Lady of Mount Carmel was as follows: "When, on the feast of Pentecost, the Apostles, being divinely inspired, spoke in many languages [...] many men (so it is said) who followed in the footsteps of Elijah and Elisha and who had been prepared for the coming of Christ by the preaching of John the Baptist [...] immediately accepted the faith of the Gospel and began to hold the Blessed Virgin in veneration with a special degree of affection [...] And they built the first chapel in honour of the most pure Virgin [...] on Mount Carmel." Andrew Jotischky, in this learned and sensitive study, examines why the Carmelites adopted this legendary account of their origins, and the ways in which they developed it. This inquiry is set in the context of general Western attitudes towards the past in the late-medieval centuries. As Jotischky has shown in his earlier study, *The Perfection of Solitude: Hermits and Monks in the Crusader States*, the Latin hermits of Mount Carmel had evolved in the late twelfth century, having been strongly influenced by Orthodox communities, and were given a rule by St. Albert of Jerusalem (d. 1214). After 1241 the Order began to establish foundations in Western Europe, and in 1247 Pope Innocent IV modified their Rule in his bull *Quae honorem conditoris*, which effectively transformed them from a contemplative into a mendicant order. Consequently the Carmelites faced a double problem: first, how they should explain their role in the Church to people in the West who were not familiar with them; second, how they should evade the ban of the Second Council of Lyons (1274) that no order founded after 1215 should remain in existence. For although the Rule of St. Albert dated from before 1215, the new rule of 1247 had radically changed the character of the order.

The brethren began by capitalizing on their connection with Mount Carmel. The prologue to the Carmelite constitutions of 1281 stated that the order was the successor "in manner of living" of the hermits of Carmel in Elijah's day. In 1287 the brethren abandoned their traditional parti-coloured habits for white ones, claiming that in this way they were fulfilling the dream of Elijah's father, that his son would be greeted by men dressed in white. This apocryphal story was already well known in the West through the work of Peter Comestor. From these simple beginnings the story grew in complexity. Its full late-medieval form is exemplified in the writings of John Bale, an English Carmelite professed in 1506, whose voluminous works, still largely in manuscript, have been drawn on by Jotischky. In this later version of their history the Carmelites identified themselves with the *viri religiosi* (in the 1611 Bible "devout men") of Acts 2:5, who heard the apostolic preaching at Pentecost and became Christians. The gaps in the order's history between Elijah and Christ and Christ and St. Albert of Jerusalem were filled by claiming some well-known figures as members. These included the prophet Obadiah, St. John the Baptist, St. Basil the Great (probably an acknowledgement by the order of its Orthodox roots) and St. Cyril of Alexandria, whose devotion to Our Lady warranted him a favoured place in Carmelite historiography. The prophet Agabus, mentioned in Acts 11:28, was reckoned among the first generation of Christian Carmelites, and was said as a young man to have been in love with the Virgin and to have become a hermit of Carmel when she rejected his suit. The order's Marian devotion was a constant theme in its historiography: the brethren had shared in the prophetic vision that salvation would come through a Virgin (Isaiah 7:14), while those present at the first Christian Pentecost had had the privilege of meeting with and talking to Mary.

In making these claims the Carmelites were asserting that theirs was the original form of Christian monasticism, and that all the other orders merely approximated to it. Their account of Church history did not go unchallenged and the Dominicans were particularly incisive critics. Such scepticism was more widely shared. Jotischky begins his study by describing how at Milan in 1499, when the prior of the Carmelites claimed precedence over representatives of other orders in a procession, the duke's jester intervened: " 'The father [prior] speaks truly, for at the time of the apostles there were no other friars beside these. It is of them that St. Paul wrote [...] [when he spoke of being] "in peril among false brethren" (II Cor. 11: 26). They are some of these false brethren.' And at this clever joke [...] everyone started to laugh." It would have been easy for Jotischky to invite his readers to join them, but that is not the route which his investigation has taken. Instead, he examines the influence on Carmelite thinking of Joachimism, which saw the Old Testament as an exact prophecy of Christian history; and he also makes clear that Carmelite historiography differed from that of their contemporaries only in degree. Their fellow mendicants, the Dominicans and Franciscans, for example, while not claiming apostolic foundation, did claim that their orders were embodying apostolic practices; while some secular scholars approached family history in much the same way as the Carmelites, annexing unrelated historical figures to their genealogies as evidence of ancient lineage. It was possible to use such devices because historical time was perceived as static rather than dynamic: it was therefore possible to conceive that "the sons of the prophets" in ancient Israel had lived like the Carmelites, though lacking a full knowledge of the Christian dispensation.

The Carmelites are the one major religious order in the Middle Ages which has been comparatively neglected by historians, partly because members of the order were for a long time deterred by their own version of events from examining their own historical tradition using new historical methods so little congruent with it. In this sympathetic study, Jotischky has helped us to understand how and why the Carmelites evolved this myth of their origins, and in so doing has also shed much welcome light on late-medieval attitudes to antiquity.

BERNARD HAMILTON
UNIVERSITY OF NOTTINGHAM

*Der Kreuzzug Friedrich Barbarossas 1187–1190: Bericht eines Augenzeugen*, trans. and with an introduction and notes by Arnold Bühler (Fremde Kulturen in alten Berichten, 13). Sigmaringen: Thorbecke, 2002. Pp. 191. ISBN 3 7995 0612 8.

Angesichts abnehmender Lateinkenntnisse hat eine Übersetzung heute eine größere Bedeutung als noch vor fünfzig Jahren. Sie wendet sich mehr denn je nicht allein an ein fachfremdes Publikum, sondern wird auch von Spezialisten für eine erste Annäherung an den Text sowie als Hilfsmittel in der Lehre eingesetzt. Übersetzer stehen daher vor der schwierigen Aufgabe, den Text so zu übertragen, dass er historisch interessierte Laien anspricht, ohne sich zu weit vom lateinischen Original zu entfernen. Sprachlich gesehen ist das Arnold Bühler zweifelsohne gelungen. Seine Übertragung ins Deutsche ist ebenso korrekt wie lebendig und bleibt selbst an schwierigen Passagen verständlich. Kritisierbar ist jedoch seine Entscheidung, anders als seine Vorlage, die Ausgabe des lateinischen Texts durch Anton Chroust, nur die den dritten Kreuzzug betreffenden Teile der Überlieferung zu berücksichtigen. In der einzigen vollständigen mittelalterlichen Handschrift geht der Bericht vom Kreuzzug Friedrichs I. in eine chronikalisch gestaltete Darstellung über, die der Geschichte Heinrichs VI. zwischen 1190–1197 gewidmet ist. Sie würdigt ausführlich Herzog Leopold V. von Österreich und seine Rolle im Kreuzzug. Dieser Anhang setzt sich zwar inhaltlich und stilistisch vom Hauptteil ab, enthält aber Verbindungen zur Einleitung und zum Abschluss des Kreuzzugsberichts. Ihre sprachliche Gestalt und ihr Horizont setzen sie ebenfalls vom eigentlichen Textkern ab. Innerhalb des Hauptteils lassen sich weitere Einschübe identifizieren. Die einen Zugaben zu berücksichtigen und die andere wegzulassen, ist angesichts der Schwierigkeit einer sicheren Zuordnung schwer zu rechtfertigen. Hinzu kommt, dass sich in der Literatur und Geschichtswissenschaft der letzten Jahre eine Rückkehr zum handschriftlichen Originalbefund abzeichnet. Sie hat zur Folge, dass Varianten, Fortsetzungen und Bearbeitungen nicht mehr als Entstellungen, sondern als kreative Verarbeitungen der Vorlage betrachtet werden. Die Überlieferung um ihren Schluss zu amputieren, entzieht solchen Fragestellungen die Grundlage. Nicht zuletzt entspricht die Präsentation eines Augenzeugenberichts durch einen Bearbeiter in der mittelalterlichen Kreuzzugsgeschichtsschreibung einer eingeführten, geradezu klassischen Form der Vermittlung. Daher stellt sich die Frage, ob es sich bei der Mehrschichtigkeit nicht um einen literarischen Gestus handelt. Aus einer vielschichtigen Überlieferung, die bewusst als solche konzipiert sein könnte, nach modernen Vorstellungen den originalen Kern herausschneiden zu wollen, scheint daher verwegen.

Neben der Vermittlung des Texts stellt sich einem Übersetzer eine zweite Aufgabe. Er muss den Inhalt des übersetzten Berichts so situieren und vorstellen, dass sich Laien orientieren und Leser vom Fach nicht langweilen. Was die Kreuzzugsgeschichte betrifft, entledigt sich Arnold Bühler dieser Aufgabe mit Bravour. Er vermittelt ein kurzes, konzises Bild von der Geschichte des Kreuzzugs, in dem die wesentlichen Forschungsperspektiven zu einem ausgewogenen Gesamtbild vereinigt werden (S. 10–15). Auch die Vorgeschichte und Organisation des dritten Kreuzzugs werden ansprechend und zugleich so eingehend dargestellt, dass sich Laien und Fachleute informieren können (S. 15–23). Die daran anschließende Darstellung des dritten Kreuzzugs ordnet die parteiliche Perspektive des Berichts in eine distanzierte Interpretation ein. Sie wirbt bei den Lesern um Verständnis für die vorgebrachten Deutungen, leitet sie aber zugleich an, sich von ihnen zu distanzieren. Bühler erklärt die zum Ausdruck kommende Feindschaft gegenüber den Griechen mit der Undurchschaubarkeit der politischen Situation im byzantinischen Reich (S. 23–26). Da die griechischen Versprechungen nicht eingehalten werden können und sich das Heer Angriffen ausgesetzt sieht, werden ihm zufolge die bereits bestehenden antigriechischen Vorurteile der Kreuzfahrer bestätigt. Die Plünderung Griechenlands durch das Kreuzfahrerheer erscheint damit subjektiv gerechtfertigt. Ähnlich unverständig wie gegenüber der Situation in Griechenland erweist sich der mittelalterliche Verfasser und mit ihm das deutsche Heer sowie der Kaiser für die Machtkämpfe im Reich der Seldschuken (S. 29–32). Die Angriffe münden hier in einem Racheakt, der Einnahme von Konya, die die Kreuzfahrer nicht unerheblich bereichert. Die eingeschlagene Route hat jedoch später erhebliche Verluste zur Folge und verlangt den Kreuzfahrern das Letzte ihrer Kräfte ab. Der unvermutete Tod des Kaisers besiegelt vor diesem Hintergrund den sich bereits abzeichnenden Misserfolg des Kreuzzugs (S. 32–37). Bühlers Darstellung der Ereignisse ist zweifellos für moderne Leser ansprechend, weil sie von der Wahrnehmung der Teilnehmer ausgeht. Die vermittelte Augenzeugenperspektive als Zugang zum historischen Geschehen zu benutzen, unterschätzt jedoch die intentionale Komponente des Berichts. Trotz der Distanzierung entgeht dem modernen Leser so, dass das geschilderte Verhalten des Heers auch in mittelalterlicher Perspektive moralisch gesehen problematisch ist. Der später hinzugefügte Textbeginn unterstreicht das, denn das Verhalten der Kreuzfahrer sticht deutlich von den päpstlichen Vorstellungen ab, die dort zugänglich gemacht werden. Die im Bericht vermittelte und von Bühler übernommene Vorstellung, die Kreuzfahrer seien schutzlos permanenten Angriffen ausgesetzt gewesen und hätten sich getäuscht gefühlt, hat daher auch eine rechtfertigende Funktion.

Angesichts des sich mit den Kreuzfahrern und dem mittelalterlichen Verfasser identifizierenden Ansatzes der Präsentation, der bis in die Fussnoten hinein wirkt, ist es wenig erstaunlich, dass die Charakterisierung des Texts im Vergleich zur ereignisgeschichtlichen Einführung erstaunlich kurz ausfällt. Im Einklang mit der älteren Forschung erhebt Bühler den Verfasser zum Augenzeugen, der das Geschehen "dicht" und "detailreich" schildert und "eindringliche, psychologisch, genaue Stimmungsbilder" von der "Kreuzzugsfront" liefert. Wer jedoch Ovid und Otto von Freising zitiert, Bibelzitate aus dem Ärmel schüttelt, die Indiktionszählung beherrscht und über rechtliche Kenntnisse verfügt, ist in den freien Künsten, und d.h. auch in der Rhetorik, bewandert. Die einseitige Darstellung des Geschehens hat daher einen ideologischen und polemischen Charakter. Die ältere Forschung hat das noch anerkannt. Die Nähe des Erzählers zum Kaiser und der von ihm formulierte Alleinvertretungsanspruch des westlichen Kaisers haben Chroust dazu bewegt, von einer "offiziösen" Darstellung zu sprechen, die das Geschehen im Reich bekannt machen sollte. Die damit greifbar gemachte politische und ideologische Tendenz kommt in der Präsentation Bühlers eindeutig zu kurz. Obwohl die Einladung zu einer identifizierenden Lektüre ansprechend ist, leistet sie also einem naiven Textverständnis Vorschub. Er liefert moderne Leser der Rhetorik des mittelalterlichen Texts aus.

BEATE SCHUSTER
UNIVERSITÄT BASEL

John H. Lind, Carsten Selch Jensen, Kurt Villads Jensen and Ane Bysted, *Danske korstog. Krig og mission i Østersøen*. Copenhagen: Høst & Søn, 2004. Pp. 404. ISBN 87 14 29712 4.

At last the European crusading movement and its Danish elements have found their way into modern Danish historiography of the Middle Ages. This book will stand as a work of reference for years to come and as such should find a very broad and wide audience. It signals a change in the historiography of Danish medieval history. With this book the authors argue for the necessity of a focus on the crusades as both a feature of a specific historical period and at the same time a defining characteristic of that same period. Following this line of thought, the authors argue the need to break away from a narrow but very traditional, nationalist focus of Danish medieval research. In this the book is very consistent: the borders of present-day Denmark do not in any way limit the lively account of medieval Denmark's experiences with Christian expansion and the crusades. The authors are to be admired for their successful handling of the complicated course of events. This is not an easy task considering that, throughout the book, the authors also consistently reflect on the other political and religious players around the Baltic Sea. This is all very well done.

The layout of the book includes numerous boxes of "facts." This may seem a slightly surprising choice in a book of this kind, but in fact it works very well. The "facts boxes" deliver short and lucid lexical information, while the main text of the book presents a clever mixture of sober account, in-depth source studies and careful analysis. It is all presented in ordinary, no-nonsense language, satisfying both lay and learned. The illustrations in the book also deserve mentioning as there are many, dispersed generously throughout the book and accompanied by informative captions. One critical remark about this, however: the book includes a number of illustrations by the artist Niels Willum Andreasen which are surely meant to depict themes and historical events in a realistic manner. This reviewer does not doubt the illustrator's profound knowledge of medieval clothing, weaponry and the like. But, considering that the book wishes to take crusades seriously and to recognize, for better or worse, the enormous civilizing role played by the Christian Church in the European Middle Ages, why is it that almost every cleric represented is depicted as a most ugly and hysterical creature (for example, the preacher on pp. 98–99)? This reinforces a traditional affront against the medieval Christian Church, an often-uttered prejudice in much unconsciously Protestant historiography and a line of thought the book itself actually wishes to expose.

However, in no way must this slight criticism stand in the way of the many titbits in this book which coming generations of historians and those generally interested in history will enjoy alike. An example of this is the authors' analysis of the martyred Duke Knud Lavard of Slesvig (ca. 1096–1131), a popular figure well-known in Denmark. He has often been represented as a true crusader, among other things, because of his position as knes (king?) of the Obadrites, a Wend tribe on the south coast of the Baltic Sea. However, his exact role in the Northern German region has often seemed somewhat dubious at the same time. When his rival Magnus, heir to the Danish throne, killed Knud Lavard, the murder thrust Denmark into a civil war which only ended in 1157 with the sole rulership of Valdemar I. Knud Lavard was canonized in 1170, thus furnishing the Valdemarian royal line with a touch of divinity. The authors, however, convincingly modify this seemingly successful story. Knud's popularity is mainly the result of his apparently very deliberate portayal as a crusader saint by his immediate decendants. The authors prove that at the time the most important crusading activities actually originated with the Danish King Niels (d. 1134), and that Knud Lavard appears as a proper crusader only after his death in connection with crusading activities linked to his saint's day and his role as patron saint for the so-called St. Knud guilds all over Denmark. This reinterpretation was only possible thanks to the careful reading and thorough analysis of the relevant sources.

The scholarly exactitude in the authors' handling of the sources is a prominent and valuable feature of this book. Furthermore, their capability in handling sources other than those traditionally used in Danish historiography also makes this book extraordinary. Especially impressive are the parts involving the Danes' Orthodox Russian co-players. Through meticulous studies of the Russian chronicles, the authors succeed in exposing a number of intricate and decisive rifts between the Russian princes with their differing views of the Latin church at a time when they were threatened by the Mongols. The chapters on the Russians in the Baltic crusades make impressive reading and are a much-needed corrective to traditional accounts mostly biased towards the Western powers and the Latin church. Equally deserving of praise are the chapters on Prussians, Lithuanians, the Teutonic Order, the Latin church and many other participants in this complicated fight for pagans' souls and lands.

It is hard to find insufficiencies or inadequacies in this book, but I shall try anyhow. Were the book longer than its not inconsiderable 404 pages, some chapters on the conquered Balts and Wends would have been appropriate. As it is, we hear next to nothing of the fate of the pagan tribes following their submission to Christianity. They were, of course, illiterate cultures, and all written sources about them are Christian, but there are some important questions that deserved recognition. For example: in which way did the conversion of the Baltic result in fundamental changes for these societies besides the one of confession? Which new ties of exploitation were the conquered pagans subjected to? What did the administrative and religious structures in the Baltic look like after conquest and conversion? Moreover, in a specific Danish context: Who exactly were the Danish vassals in Estonia and what caused the Danish king to reorganize his system of vassalage after the Treaty of Stensby 1238? Were the authors to continue their fruitful cooperation in another book, I am sure they would provide us with clever and thoughtful answers to questions such as these.

TORBEN K. NIELSEN
AALBORG UNIVERSITY

Thomas F. Madden, *Enrico Dandolo and the Rise of Venice*. Baltimore: The Johns Hopkins University Press, 2003. Pp. xix, 298. ISBN 0 8018 7317 7.

Was Enrico Dandolo, the leader of the Venetians in the Fourth Crusade, blind? Thomas Madden does not content himself with a brief answer. Instead, he provides a complete discussion of the doge's blindness and its ramifications, disposing of false explanations, and tracing Enrico's signature until it no longer appears, showing that he signed no document during his dogeship, thus confirming his blindness. This devotion to research is characteristic of this well-written and interesting study of the Dandolo family and their role in the development of Venetian power in the Mediterranean.

This is not another study of the Fourth Crusade. Madden places Enrico Dandolo into the broader context of the rise of his family and their increasingly important role in twelfth-century Venice. At the beginning of this century, Venice was already the most important Western sea power in the Adriatic and the eastern Mediterranean. Its ties to the Byzantine Empire as well as its support for the First Crusade put it at the center of efforts to defend the gains made by the crusaders, especially against the Fatimid navy. Madden shows us the Dandolos in a rather minor role in the fleet commanded by Doge Domenico Michiel. They were members of a solidly middle-class family, mostly involved in professional business. The real founder of the family's rise to prominence was Domenico Dandolo, who had supported Pietro Polani as doge and was rewarded with a judgeship in the doge's court. Doge Pietro Polani chose his son, Enrico, the uncle of the later doge, to be Patriarch of Grado. Patriarch Enrico was at the center of efforts to introduce major reforms into the Venetian church. As a result, he came into conflict with Giovanni Polani, bishop of Castello, under whose jurisdiction the church of Venice fell. Madden views this dispute more as a jurisdictional dispute than as a difference over reform. Certainly this was an important dimension; but we ought not to rule out the fact that Venice was seeking greater prestige on the ecclesiastical front. As Madden demonstrates, Patriarch Enrico Dandolo worked tirelessly to place his church at the center of Venice. One of the most important aspects of the reform program was a concern over the rights attached to churches and monasteries. The good bishop or abbot was valued for his husbanding of the resources under his charge. Enrico was tireless in this regard. If this aspect of his effort did not bring him into conflict with Doge Pietro, his opposition to the ducal alliance with Byzantium on religious grounds did. What needs a bit more emphasis here, I believe, is that the patriarch acted in close alliance with the papacy, a point made by Madden but perhaps not strongly enough. There can be no doubt, however, that the victory of the patriarch benefited his family. Does it mark a turning point in their fortunes? Perhaps not, but a defeat would have spelled disaster, as it almost did. As it was, the recovery of the Dandolo from their exile, which had been due to the conflict between the doge and the patriarch, benefited from the victory of Patriarch Enrico. A major beneficiary was Vitale Dandolo, Enrico's younger brother and the father of the future doge. He rose quickly in wealth, power, and prestige in the 1160s. Madden describes the important role he played in the conflicts between Venice and Frederick Barbarossa and between them and the Byzantines. This is an important phase in the advancement of his son and his election as doge.

Enrico Dandolo owed much to his father and uncle. He was scion of a family that had participated in the First Crusade and had been leaders in the reform of the Venetian church. Madden stresses this background in contrast to the view of historians who portray Enrico and the Venetians as more interested in material than spiritual matters. At the same time, he argues for a distinctive Venetian separation of religious and secular affairs. While I agree that such a distinction existed, I don't see it as uniquely Venetian. In my view, it was quite common to Western political thought and practice. One reason that historians have made such a hash of the papal–imperial conflicts of the period is that they have insisted on seeing them in purely ideological terms rather than recognizing that ideology was subordinated to a profound concern over rights on both sides. In fact, if we reread the documents of the time, we see ample evidence that both sides recognized that there was a profound separation between spiritual and temporal; they just could not agree on how it should be expressed on the ground. Madden has touched on this nerve point again and again, and properly so, for it is central to understanding this period and, in this context, the Fourth Crusade. One cannot read the documents of the period without realizing that there are two very different worlds represented. These worlds do not really communicate very well with one another, even though they share much in common. Neither Enrico Dandolo, the crusaders, nor the pope believed that the diversion of the crusade was a rejection of faith; for them it was a difference in interests and goals that drove a wedge between them.

Madden's study of Enrico Dandolo moves the discussion much further along. His important contribution rests on the depth of his research concerning the Dandolos in the Venetian archives. He has not merely produced a classic of family history but has also raised issues that historians of Venice and of the crusades must now come to grips with. This volume provides a new context for examining some very important questions.

JAMES M. POWELL
SYRACUSE UNIVERSITY (EMERITUS)

*The Medieval Crusade*, ed. Susan J. Ridyard (Sewanee Medieval Studies, 14). Woodbridge: The Boydell Press, 2004. Pp. x, 177. ISBN 1 84383 087 6.

In his introduction to this volume of ten essays, Jonathan Phillips speaks of "a consensus amongst most academics" (p. 1) about the nature of crusading. A consensus there may have been at the conference, but there is still considerable resistance to the "pluralist" view of crusading. The contributions are of very high quality, though it is rather odd that two contributors have each provided two essays, together occupying over a third of the volume. Robert Chazan's "Latin and Hebrew Crusade Chronicles: Some Shared Themes" analyses Jewish accounts of the First Crusade and suggests that common themes united such works as the *Gesta Francorum* and the Jewish writers in that both perceived "the centrality of human will, commitment and action in the drama of the First Crusade." Is this anything more than the notion that God works through humankind, which is the common heritage of the two religions? His second essay, "Crusading in Christian–Jewish Polemics," explores the idea that Christian attempts to convert the Jews were an alternative form of that aggressiveness which had produced the crusading. This represents another contribution by this distinguished historian to our knowledge of Judaeo–Christian relations in the era of the crusades. The other "double contributor" is Jonathan Riley-Smith, the first of whose essays asks the very radical question, "Were the Templars Guilty?" In a very scholarly analysis, Riley-Smith handles the difficult evidence carefully and his conclusions are appropriately tentative. The secrecy of the order over its reception rites is very curious, as he says; however, he may underestimate the tendency of all inquisitors to shape the responses of their victims. Nonetheless, Riley-Smith has opened the door to enquiry. It may be that rituals like that confessed to by John of Stoke, who claimed that he was forced to deny Christ, may well have had their origins in obedience ordeals, testing the faith and obedience of the new postulants. Such possibilities are substantially reinforced by Riley-Smith's "The Structures of the Orders of the Temple and the Hospital in c.1291," which draws a picture of a Templar Order in organizational chaos, incapable of renewing itself and adapting to new circumstances. The comparison with the Hospitallers, who had restructured their Order, is telling. In this context the existence of dubious practices becomes understandable and the case made in the earlier essay more convincing. These are important studies which will contribute to the agenda for research on the orders.

Two articles explore a theme somewhat neglected in recent years, the impact of apocalypticism on the crusades. Jay Rubenstein, in his "How, or how much, to reevaluate Peter the Hermit," draws attention to the apocalyptic passages in Guibert of Nogent's account of Pope Urban II's speech. He suggests that Guibert, who confessed that he could not precisely report what Urban said, emphasizes them to explain (though in rationalized and non-imminent terms) the apocalyptic preaching which moved people in northern France where he lived and where Peter preached. However, the account of Peter's preaching does not make it sound at all apocalyptic and Guibert does not mention Albert of Aachen's story that Peter claimed to have received a divine commission to inspire an expedition. In fact it is possible that Guibert does not give an account of Peter preaching the crusade. Rather, he reports that he did and that he later led an army, but describes what seems to be a preaching expedition of an entirely different kind. In many ways it is comparable to Baudri of Dol's account of the early preaching of Robert of Arbrissel. And while there is much that is miraculous, there is not much apocalyptic about Albert of Aachen's account. However, this makes Urban's apocalyptic passages even more mysterious, but perhaps the pope (or Guibert) was trying to emphasize the significance of the movement by viewing it as a step (albeit a remote one) on the way to the "Last Days." Alfred J. Andrea in his "Innocent III, the Fourth Crusade, and the Coming Apocalypse," shows that the great pope drew on the ideas of Joachim of Fiore in his reaction to the fall of Constantinople in 1204, which he saw as the gathering of the faithful which might portend the "Last Days." Remarkably, Innocent persisted in this view despite the difficulties which quickly set in. Thomas Madden, "Venice, the Papacy and the Crusade before 1204" charts the much more prosaic business of the worsening of relations between Innocent and the Venetians in the period immediately before 1204. Perhaps the most original essay in the volume is that of Christopher MacEvitt. Studies of the crusader settlements have concentrated on the Latin Kingdom of Jerusalem, although Thomas Asbridge's work on Antioch has changed the focus somewhat. However, this essay, "Christian Authority in the Latin East: Edessa in Crusader History," analyses Matthew of Edessa's prejudices and concludes that sometimes, though not invariably, local and Latin Christians cooperated. This fits rather well with the archaeological evidence for the Latin Kingdom examined by R. Ellenblum (*Frankish Rural Settlement in the Latin Kingdom of Jerusalem* [1998]). William E. Rogers' "The C-Revisions and the Crusades in Piers Plowman" analyses references to the crusades in one version of that famous poem and suggests the author ascribed the failures of the movement to the fault of the priesthood. As it is likely that he was patronized by the famous crusading family of the Despensers, this would appear to have been a remarkably brave stance. In the last essay, Kelly Devries considers the reasons for "The Failure of Philip the Good to fulfil his Crusade promise of 1454." This failure has been attributed to the death of Pope Nicholas V, which deprived Philip of an urgent taskmaster, and that of Bishop Rudolf of Utrecht which plunged him into a local war. Devries points out that Nicholas's successor, Calixtus III, was equally enthusiastic for the crusade while the issue of the Utrecht election had been settled by 1456, the delayed time (from 1455) of Philip's departure. Devries concludes that Philip was deeply concerned by the intentions of the king of France in his absence. Overall this is a stimulating collection of essays and a volume which is essential for any serious student of the crusades.

JOHN FRANCE
UNIVERSITY OF SWANSEA

Jörg Oberste, *Der Kreuzzug gegen die Albigenser. Ketzerei und Machtpolitik im Mittelalter*. Darmstadt: Primus Verlag, 2003. Pp. 222. ISBN 3 89678 464 1.

Despite its title this is not strictly speaking a book about the Albigensian Crusades. The author himself actually distances himself from the term crusade by putting it into inverted commas on the title page and throughout the introduction, thus following well-trodden paths of traditional German crusade history which treats all crusades outside the Holy Land as aberrations or at least unwarranted copies of the real thing. Oberste is not really interested in the discussions about the definition and institutional character of the crusades and does not pick up the leads of Anglo-American crusade historians who have for some time tried to integrate the history of the Cathar wars into the wider context of the medieval crusade movement. Books with "crusade", or German "Kreuzzug", in the title sell and it is presumably because of this that Oberste's monograph sports the label of crusade history.

In scope and subject matter the book compares to Malcolm Barber's recent *The Cathars* (reviewed in *Crusades 1* [2002]). It begins by discussing the origins of Catharism in Languedoc in the twelfth century and follows through the various stages of the fight against the heretics by the Church and the secular authorities up to the establishment of the inquisition and the fall of the last Cathar stronghold of Montségur in 1244. But while Barber's book is written for students and budding researchers, providing an introduction into the multi-layered scope and research issues of the history of Catharism complete with full bibliographical information, it is not quite clear whom Oberste's book is aimed at. It is minimally footnoted, has a bibliography of less than two pages and is written in an affirmative style sometimes bordering on the colloquial which does not lend itself to scholarly debate. Nevertheless, the scholarship behind Oberste's story is sound and reliable, and the book could be profitably read by undergraduates seeking first information about Catharism or by (the dying breed of) educated laymen interested in traditional academic narrative.

Oberste's history of Catharism is mainly political history. He devotes five pages only to discussing Cathar religion, the rest is – as predicted by the book's subtitle – a history of diplomacy, wars and the changing political alliances which marked the rise and fall of the Albigensian heresy. As such, it is a story that is more linear and less rich than that painted by Barber. At times in Oberste's narrative the overarching lines of conflict between the papacy, the great nobility and the monarchs involved in the Cathar wars tend to overshadow the very intricate and ever changing patterns of power on the ground. Just as the majority of Cathars were never part of a fixed political alliance, so the representatives of the Catholic church in Languedoc showed different degrees of allegiance and obedience to papal policies. The strengths of Oberste's story are its narrow delineations and clear contours, its weakness perhaps a certain lack of attention to the details and intricacies of a conflict which is ultimately difficult to grasp in its complexity and its many layers of human experience and suffering.

Christoph T. Maier
Universität Zürich

*L'Ordine Teutonico nel Mediterraneo, Atti del Convegno internazionale di studio Torre Alemanna (Cerignola) – Mesagne – Lecce 16–18 ottobre 2003*, ed. Hubert Houben (Acta Theutonica, 1). Galatina: Mario Congedo Editore, 2004. Pp. xi, 321. ISBN 8 8808 6544 7.

The Teutonic Order cannot be regarded as a genuinely or predominantly "international" corporation if compared to Templars or Hospitallers. Nevertheless, the Teutonic Order held important possessions and pursued great aims outside Germany and the Baltic regions. Its activities around the Mediterranean from the Holy Land through Cilicia, Cyprus, Greece and Italy to Spain reflect early thirteenth-century imperial politics, mainly of the Staufen dynasty and Emperor Frederick II. Moreover, as a religious military order the Teutonic Knights were strongly involved in crusades against the infidel not only in the Baltic but also the Levant, where the *domus Teutonica sancte Marie in Jerusalem* had originated and continued to have its spiritual focus. The present volume reveals a truly international interest in the history of this corporation by thirteen scholars from different countries. The papers are published as the first volume of the new series Acta Theutonica published by the Centro di Studi sulla Storia dell'Ordine Teutonico nel Mediterraneo at Torre Alemanna (Cerignola), Capitanata. Hubert Houben ("Nuovi orientamenti nelle ricerche sull'Ordine Teutonico," pp. 3–16) sums up old controversies between German and Polish historiography on the Teutonic Order and outlines new approaches initiated by the Ordines Militares conferences at Torun, started in 1981 and organised by Karol Górski and Zenon Hubert Nowak, the Internationale Kommission zur Erforschung des Deutschen Ordens founded at Vienna in 1985 and, as might be added, by Udo Arnold who, on top of his publications organised an important exhibition at Nuremberg in 1990. Giancarlo Andenna ("Città padane e carità verso i poveri e i pellegrini tra XII e XV secolo," pp. 17–32) notes the absence of the religious military orders in late-medieval communal statutes concerning public charity. Benedetto Vetere ("L'ideologia degli Ordini religioso-militari [Templari e Cavalieri Teutonici]," pp. 33–52) portrays the twelfth-century fighting monks as standing in a tradition of the church militant of the eleventh-century Gregorian reform and the spiritual strife presented in the military overtones of the Benedictine rule. The following nine contributions provide an excellent, up-to-date survey of the Teutonic Order in the Mediterranean. Marie-Luise Favreau-Lilie ("L'Ordine Teutonico in Terrasanta [1198–1291]," pp. 55–72) stresses its active role at Montfort and Acre in the thirteenth-century defence of the Holy Land before, under and after Grand Master Hermann von Salza (d. 1239), the great but unsuccessful mediator between Frederick II and the papacy. Andreas Kiesewetter ("L'Ordine Teutonico in Grecia e in Armenia," pp. 73–107) identifies possessions especially in Cilicia, Constantinople and above all Achaia where the Teutonic Knights apparently participated in the initial Latin conquest of 1205. This article is based on a vast range of sometimes remote sources and publications, and represents a great advance on previous studies. Nikolas Jaspert ("L'Ordine Teutonico nella penisola iberica: limiti e possibilità di una provincia periferica," pp. 109–32) gives an expanded version of his paper in España y el Sacro Imperio (ed. Klaus Herbers et al., 2002), investigating the history of the domus La Mota in Léon, founded by Beatrix von Staufen, wife of King Ferdinand III, estates in Aragón (Calatayud, Monzón) and Andalusia (Sevilla, Carmona, Córdoba, Jaén) up to the sixteenth century. Kristjan Toomaspoeg ("L'Ordine Teutonico in Puglia e in Sicilia," pp. 133–60) describes the foundation of the commanderies at Brindisi (probably with a castrum at Mesagne), Bari, Barletta, Siponto, Corneto, Ginosa, then at Messina, Palermo, Margana, Polizzi, Agrigento and Noto. He also explains how they survived the fall of the Staufen dynasty and the retreat of the order's headquarters to Marienburg in 1309. This is a welcome summary of his thesis on the Teutonic Order in Sicily 1197–1492 (Collection de l'École française de Rome 321, 2003) and of numerous other articles. Pietro Dalena ("Gli insediamenti dell'Ordine Teutonico e la rete viaria nell'Italia meridionale," pp. 161–74) looks at houses near pilgrim routes to Monte Gargano or to Apulian ports. Raffaele Licinio ("Teutonici e masserie nella Capitanata dei secoli XIII–XV," pp. 175–95), despite the scarcity of the source material, detects some differences between the agricultural organisation of Templar and royal estates. Barbara Bombi ("L'Ordine Teutonico nell'Italia centrale. La casa romana dell'Ordine e l'ufficio del procuratore generale," pp. 197–216) reviews the order's well-known presence in Rome and in places such as Viterbo, Montefiascone and Orvieto. Rome was especially important for the order's procurators at the papal curia. Piotr Cierzniakowski ("L'Ordine Teutonico nell'Italia settentrionale," pp. 217–35) treats commercial privileges at Venice and elsewhere in the region and the German students in the order's *domus* at Padua. His article refers to many unpublished sources from Padua and Treviso. Thomas Krämer ("Der Deutsche Orden in Frankreich – Ein Beitrag zur Ordensgeschichte im Königreich Frankreich und im Midi," pp. 237–76) offers a masterly survey of the donations made from the Fifth Crusade onwards and the order's fortunes both in the north, at Beauvoir (near Troyes) and Orbec (between Nevers and Auxerre), and the south, at Arles and Montpellier, about which so far almost nothing had been known. A summary of the symposium by Cosimo Damiano Fonseca concludes the volume ("L'Ordine Teutonico nel Mediterraneo. Una pista di lettura," pp. 277–89). Kristjan Toomaspoeg compiled the three indexes of persons, places and authors (pp. 293–321). The volume includes numerous maps, which are extremely helpful. Generally speaking, it provides an up-to-date review of the state of research concerning the Mediterranean activities of the Teutonic Order. Moreover, many contributions mark a considerable step forward in our knowledge about the Teutonic Order in the Mediterranean. Thus the book offers more than an instrument of research for the years to come. Indeed many articles will in themselves be noted as milestones of research.

KARL BORCHARDT
UNIVERSITÄT WÜRZBURG

Carmen von Samson-Himmelstjerna, *Deutsche Pilger des Mittelalters im Spiegel ihrer Berichte und der mittelhochdeutschen erzählenden Dichtung* (Berliner Historische Studien, 37). Berlin: Duncker & Humblot, 2004. Pp. 328. ISBN 3 428 11556 2.

Literary texts are not always purely fictional and historical reports are not always based on pure fact. Comparing the two genres can therefore be helpful for understanding phenomena such as medieval pilgrimage. The first part of this thesis reviews seven historical accounts about journeys to the Holy Land: Johannes von Würzburg's *Descriptio Terrae Sanctae* and his contemporary Theodericus's *Libellus de locis sanctis* describe visits to Jerusalem and its environs in the 1160s and early 1170s respectively. Burchard von Straßburg's *Itinerarium* informed Frederick Barbarossa about Saladin's dominions in 1175. Arnold von Lübeck wrote

the chapter *De peregrinatione Heinrici ducis* in his *Chronica Slavorum* about the
visit to Jerusalem by Duke Henry the Lion in 1172 probably under Henry's son, the
Emperor Otto IV, in about 1210. Wilbrand von Oldenburg's *Itinerarium* described
his experiences as Otto IV's envoy to the Levant in 1212. The *Descriptio Terrae
Sanctae* was compiled by an otherwise unknown Philippus in the decade before
1291. The Dominican Wilhelm von Boldensele's (originally Otto von Neuhaus's)
*Hodoeporicon ad Terram Sanctam* was addressed to Cardinal Elié de Talleyrand-
Périgord in the 1330s. The second part of Samson-Himmelstjerna's thesis discusses
pilgrims and pilgrimages in nineteen German literary texts. This starts with five epic
tales usually dated to the twelfth century: *König Rother*, Lord of Bari in Apulia,
who wins the daughter of the Greek Emperor Constantine; *Herzog Ernst*, a Swabian
duke in conflict with his stepfather Emperor Conrad II; *Salmân und Môrolf*, the king
of Jerusalem, who is in search of his eloped heathen wife, and his brother; *St.
Oswald*, the king of England, who wins the daughter of the heathen lord Aron as his
wife; *Orendel*, a king of Trier, who marries the queen of Jerusalem and wins Christ's
seamless shirt for Trier; and the two poems *Graf Rudolf* and *Dukus Horant*, written
down in the later Middle Ages, the latter one in Hebrew. Three major classical
works of c. 1180–c. 1210 follow: Hartmann von Aue's *Gregorius*, Wolfram von
Eschenbach's *Parzival*, and Gottfried von Straßburg's *Tristan*. Furthermore,
pilgrims appear as marginal figures in five thirteenth- and early-fourteenth-century
texts: Rudolf von Ems's *Barlaam und Josaphat* and *Der guote Gêrhart*; Konrad
Fleck's *Flore und Blanscheflur* and *Kudrun*; and Johann von Würzburg's *Wilhelm
von Österreich*. They also feature as main figures in four works datable between
1250 and 1300: Ulrich von Lichtenstein's *Frauendienst* (the tale of a knight from
Styria who wonders about going on pilgrimage or crusade in the service of his lady);
Konrad von Würzburg's *Das Herzmaere*, in which a lady counsels her lover to go on
pilgrimage whilst the husband contemplates doing the same in order to have his wife
always in his company; *Mai und Beaflor*, a love story about the king of Greece and
the daughter of the emperor of Rome; and Ulrich von Etzenbach's *Wilhelm von
Wenden*, in which a heathen prince is baptized in Jerusalem, fights for the Holy
Sepulchre and is finally rewarded by reunion with his family.

 The two parts of the thesis are only loosely connected. The author mainly
restricts herself to a translation or rehearsal of the contents or the plot. For each text
the historical background and the literary tradition is conveniently summarized on
the basis of existing studies. This makes the book valuable as a work of reference
despite the fact that it sometimes lacks precision (p. 120 Groningen not Gröningen;
p. 121 Donauwörth not Donauwerth; p. 151 rubber instead of mastic on Chios).
Not unexpectedly, pilgrims used to tell news, and people disguised themselves as
pilgrims to further their more or less honest plans. It is not surprising that the seven
historical accounts do not reveal a growing familiarity with, and understanding
for, foreign cultures. The choice of these seven texts from Germany is perhaps too
small to justify the author's disillusioned statement that the Middle Ages did not
show any progress towards enlightenment. Nor is it surprising that literary texts

often present the pilgrims in nostalgic ways: as wise counsellors although people of dubious moral standards went on pilgrimages, as pious individuals although masses thronged to holy places, and as travellers to the Holy Land although the crusades to that region had come to an end. Also, the choice of these nineteen German texts is perhaps too small to justify the author's optimistic conclusion that there was progress towards individuality in the Middle Ages. Taken together, these two remarks about medieval progress appear to be somewhat contradictory. So although the book offers an interpretation of twenty-six texts on pilgrims and pilgrimages, it makes only a modest contribution to the debate on medieval experiences with strangers and foreigners.

KARL BORCHARDT
UNIVERSITÄT WÜRZBURG

Iris Shagrir, *Naming Patterns in the Latin Kingdom of Jerusalem* (Prosopographica et Genealogica, 12). Oxford: Unit for Prosopographical Research, 2003. Pp. xiii, 112. ISBN 1 900934 11 1.

Over the past century scholars of the crusades have treated at length all of the standard subdivisions of the topic – government, economy, artistic/intellectual, the military, and so on – but one subject almost completely neglected has been that of the crusaders' personal names. Iris Shagrir has now filled this gap with her short, compact monograph on the naming customs of those who settled in the Latin kingdom during the twelfth and thirteenth centuries. Her objective is to find out how these transplanted European Christians named their children: that is, which names they favored as opposed to which they used only occasionally or rarely. And to see how their preferences evolved over this two-century period. Did they duplicate, resemble, or differ in any significant way from customs in the West, and, if so, how and why? She took her names from published charters, much the most abundant source of such information, nearly 2,500 in all. These yielded 6,200 personal names for the period under examination. Since multiple appearances by the same person would have falsified the data (by leading the researcher to believe she was dealing with three different Roberts whereas in fact it was only one person of that name) Shagrir has sought first to identify individuals before measuring name frequencies. This reduced her group to about 3,300 people. These she grouped in four different social categories: ecclesiastics, nobles, burgesses, and members of military orders. She has divided the two hundred years into six segments of thirty years each, thus enabling her to compare the relative popularity or rarity of individual names over successive generations. The numbers of individuals encountered in any given 30-year period varied from as low as 600 to as high as 1,800. As was to be expected, very few women figured in the charters, hence this study deals almost exclusively with masculine names. With the aid of the computer she has carried out a sophisticated analysis of her data which includes measuring "concentration" (increasing popularity of a few preferred names), and "condensation" (the reduction of the number of different names borne by a given population sample).

Having introduced her book with 1: Names Studies: an Overview, and 2: Data and Method, in her third chapter Shagrir presents the results of her study by listing the most popular male names (John, Peter, William, Hugh, Gerard) as well as those of secondary rank, and describing their changes in popularity throughout the period. In her fourth chapter she compares her findings with those of studies of personal naming in several parts of western Europe during her period, most recently by French, Italian, and Spanish collaborators in the Genèse médiévale de l'anthroponymie moderne. On the whole she concludes that the main trends in crusader-states naming paralleled those in the West: a steady decline in the use of Germanic names accompanied by an increase in names of Latin origin, particularly saints' names. The crusaders differed slightly, however, in giving greater ascendancy to certain saints' name – John, James, Nicholas, and Thomas – which hint at what the author calls an "Italian, or rather eastern Mediterranean accent" (p. 72). This may "raise the possibility of a shared influence of Eastern Christendom in the Mediterranean realm [... and] may have produced an exposure to a more particular naming fashion which stressed central and highly revered figures in Oriental Christian hagiology, often with a Palestinian connection" (p. 77). Other slight differences: the total stock of different names in use did not decline as markedly in the crusader states as it did in western Europe in the thirteenth century, nor was there as much homonymy (different people bearing the same name), nor did the number of rarely used names drop drastically over time. In her conclusion (chapter 5) the author suggests some factors which may have colored the naming practices of the settled crusaders – exposure to the habits of the indigenous Syrian-Palestinian Christian population through simple proximity in settlement as well as intermarriage, and finally their sense of mission as leaders of a religious movement.

Considering the crusades as not only a series of military invasions but also a sustained emigration movement which saw many western Europeans settle permanently in the eastern Mediterranean, can only lead the historian to wonder about its long-term effects on those who never returned home. Without wishing to exaggerate the importance of the evidence, and Iris Shagrir does not do this, her study of the personal naming habits of the European settlers in the Latin kingdom of Jerusalem provides new material for answering this question. In certain respects the transplanted Europeans were influenced by local naming customs, but their overall reliance on ancestral names shows that in at least one regard they remained closely linked with their earlier homelands.

The following traits stood out as I read this book: the author's mastery of the methods involved in name studies, the clarity of her presentation of her results, her reluctance to draw sweeping conclusions in the face of equivocal data (see a good example of this on p. 93), and above all her understanding that the significance of her findings could only be brought out clearly through comparison with naming practices in western Europe. I find this an admirable book.

GEORGE BEECH
WESTERN MICHIGAN UNIVERSITY

*"De Sion exibit lex et verbum domini de Hierusalem." Essays on Medieval Law, Liturgy, and Literature in Honour of Amnon Linder*, ed. Yitzhak Hen (Cultural Encounters in Late Antiquity and the Middle Ages). Turnhout: Brepols, 2001. Pp. vii, 214. ISBN 2 503 51091 4.

Potential readers of this Festschrift will be pleased by the absence of glossy reproductions, fuzzy reproductions of manuscript pages, pretentious appendixes, otiose maps with irritatingly minimalist print, and pompous prefaces of laudation. Instead, what is presented here are thirteen papers which are unadorned, original, lucid, and edited to a standard that is rare these days. The Preface, written by Yitzhak Hen, one of Amnon Linder's students, is concise, and its sparing expression conveys the unmistakable respect and gratitude of the contributors.

Hen has arranged the papers chronologically, stating modestly, that whatever unity the papers may have stems from the fact that they reflect Linder's own interests, as evidenced in his record of publications, which are listed (pp. 211–14). Thus, Bat-Sheva Albert, "Le judaïsme et les juifs dans l'hagiographie et la liturgie visigothique," Aviad M. Kleinberg, "Depriving Parents of the Consolation of Children: Two Legal *Consilia* on the Baptism of Jewish Children," and Esther Cohen, "Who Desecrated the Host?" examine causes and expressions of Jewish–Christian conflict in Europe. Ora Limor, "Reading Sacred Space: Egeria, Paula, and the Christian Holy Land," Benjamin Z. Kedar, "Convergences of Oriental Christian, Muslim, and Frankish Worshippers: The Case of Saydnaya," Sylvia Schein, "*Servise de Marriage* [*sic*?] and Law Enforcement in the Latin Kingdom of Jerusalem," Yvonne Friedman, "Did Laws of War Exist in the Crusader Kingdom of Jerusalem?," and David Jacoby, "Pilgrimage in Crusader Acre: The *Pardouns dAcre*," discuss social and religious issues arising from the Western Christian experience of the East, and problems stemming from their settlement there during the period of the crusades. Finally, there are five highly engaging papers treating purely Western concerns: Yitzhak Hen, "Educating the Clergy: Canon Law and Liturgy in a Carolingian Handbook from the Time of Charles the Bald," Phyllis B. Roberts, "Sermons, Preachers, and the Law," Michael Goodich, "Liturgy and the Foundation of Cults in the Thirteenth and Fourteenth Centuries," Joseph Ziegler, "Text and Context: On the Rise of Physiognomic Thought in the Later Middle Ages," and Michael Toch, "The Peasant Community and its Laws: Medieval Bavaria."

For those who believe that the experience of mediaeval people was diverse, and that academic efforts to impose a continuity or a construct of socio-religious conformity are largely delusory, these papers will have particular appeal. Inventiveness, novelty, and the passion to develop new ways of understanding their world and the people in it inspired mediaeval people, and impelled them to actions and modes of thought that were adventuresome, odd and not infrequently bizarre. What, they asked, did Christ really look like? How could one tell? What congruency existed between the external appearance of Christ, indeed of any person, and his moral and spiritual nature? These questions, and their answers, according to Joseph Ziegler, were shaped by the incorporation of Eastern physiognomic thought, in the thirteenth century, into Western exegetical, pastoral, and theological thought and writings.

What was sacred space? How did early Christians think about it? How did they translate their experiences of sacred space into text? And, what critical problems do these texts present to modern readers? In a study of the pilgrimages of Egeria and Paula to the Holy Land, Ora Limor stresses their different modes of perceiving holy sites and of textualising their experience of them. The differences, which are striking, derive, Limor shows, from assumptions which had less to do with the sites themselves than with the two women's respective cultural contexts. This is a study of considerable interest, and has the merit, in my view, of personalising Egeria and redeeming her text from its dull patina of biblical literalism.

The degree to which historians must learn to contextualise if they are to understand pilgrimage and pilgrims is underscored further by David Jacoby's fascinating study of the thirteenth-century Acre pilgrimage. Acre was never considered part of the Holy Land, and yet, on the evidence of the *Pardouns dAcre*, a list of indulgences attached to forty locations in Acre, it is evident that between 1258 and 1264, scarcely more than a generation before its fall, a new pilgrimage itinerary was instituted. By this time, Jerusalem and other major holy sites had been lost. Acre was to fill the gap by providing a valid surrogate pilgrimage for the thousands of Western pilgrims who continued to arrive. Drawing upon external evidence, including contemporary maps of Acre, Jacoby contextualizes this novelty brilliantly. What we see, as the result of his meticulous scholarship, is the birth, as it were, of a pilgrimage.

Critical persistence and seriousness of purpose characterize this Festschrift. It is, however, in those papers treating aspects of Jewish suffering in Christian society where these features are evinced most poignantly. Aviad Kleinberg, analysing *consilia* of two late-mediaeval Christian jurists, explores socio-juridical implications of forced baptism of Jewish children. Kleinberg is dispassionate in his analysis, but his narrative makes all too evident the potentially devastating consequences of this for the children and for Jewish family life. Kleinberg does readers a service by providing a Latin edition and English translation of the *consilia*. Forced baptism, persecution of converted Jews for rejecting trinitarian doctrine, and anti-Jewish secular and ecclesiastical legislation comprise what Bat-Sheva Albert terms "le triste tableau des relations judéo-chrétiennes" (p. 41). This is a fascinating, forcefully argued study. Albert, who knows her manuscript sources well, demonstrates that Catholic liturgists in Visigothic Spain laced some of the saints' *Passiones* and the liturgical texts of their festivals with anti-Jewish polemic. The faithful listened as the priests read of the sufferings of the very popular Saint Eulalia, and their faith and devotional fervour were deepened. At the same time, they heard how a Jewish protagonist, "*l'adversarius fidei*" (p. 24), who featured in some of the versions of Eulalia's *Passio*, recognized, miraculously, the innate truth of Christianity and converted from his Jewish infidelity to Christ.

If converted Jews were suspect, unconverted Jews were the menacing "Other", a convenient scapegoat adduced to rationalize aberrant Christian behaviour. This is evident in Esther Cohen's riveting examination of an act of desecration of the consecrated host. The story-line is straightforward. In 1493 a Catholic priest burst in upon a mass being celebrated at Notre-Dame in Paris. The priest allegedly blasphemed against Catholic eucharistic truth, and attacked the host and chalice. Scandal followed, and the priest was tortured. He repented and was executed at the pig-market. Now, as Cohen states, the evidence is conflicting and woefully incomplete; the full story will never be known. What matters, however, is that the contemporary records attributed the priest's act of desecration not to his own aberration of mind or will, but to Jewish influences experienced at Avignon. He was, the record declares, "*prestre judaizant*" (p. 205).

PENNY J. COLE
TRINITY COLLEGE, UNIVERSITY OF TORONTO

William L. Urban, *The Livonian Crusade*, 2nd edn., revised and enlarged. Chicago: Lithuanian Research and Studies Center, 2004. Pp. xvi, 549. ISBN 0 929700 45 7.

More than twenty years after the first edition of his *Livonian Crusade* the American scholar William Urban has released a revised and enlarged version, which presents itself as a typical print-on-demand book with self-made setting and glued spine. The author has incorporated many new publications that reflect the state of research on different topics. In some cases, however, he has not taken due account of the literature. The Teutonic Order's Table of Honor, for example, was usually set up before (not after) a campaign, and it was not really modelled on King Arthur's Round Table, as Urban states (p. 141). The knights at the table were ranked according to their chivalric achievements elsewhere. Werner Paravicini's study on the *Preußenreisen des europäischen Adels*, which is otherwise quoted by the author, has made this clear.

In twenty-one chapters Urban unfolds the history of the Teutonic Knights in Livonia (roughly the modern Latvia) and Estonia, covering the period from the late thirteenth century to the downfall of the Order's rule over Livonia in 1562. This is an epic scope indeed. The book picks up the thread of *The Baltic Crusade* (2nd edition, 1994), which dealt with the beginnings of the Livonian conquest. Without question *The Livonian Crusade* is the most detailed account on late-medieval Livonia that is available in English, it offers considerable help in unpicking a difficult and at times confusing subject. Urban, who has worked on the Baltic region for many years, sets out by portraying that area on "the eve of the thirteenth century" (the table of contents displays a slightly different chapter heading). The military and political conflicts and relations between the Teutonic Order in Livonia, the bishops and burghers, the native Balts and neighbouring peoples and powers such as Lithuania and Rus form the main content of the book. In addition, the internal development of the Teutonic Order in Livonia is considered.

With his concept of narrative history Urban aims at scholars and a wider public alike. He relies on published sources and literature written mainly in English, German and Polish. The chapters are arranged chronologically. Urban narrates his story vividly and judges with verve. As in all his books, he has a tendency to draw analogies between his medieval subject and modern times as well as to make more general statements about life and man, revealing the teacher in him rather than the researcher (see, for example, p. 39 n. 11). General readers may enjoy this style; scholars, however, will have to check details before quoting the book too confidently.

Urban assures the reader that the wars of the Teutonic Order in Livonia were "a genuine crusade." This would be well worth a discussion which he evades by stating that medieval Europeans by and large "never doubted the legitimacy of this crusade" (p. i). Because contemporaries were "better placed than we to judge this matter," this statement counts as sufficient proof for Urban. Accordingly, he considers it best "to let the facts speak for themselves" (p. v). But what do the "facts" tell us? It is, after all, the historian who arranges them and gives them his voice.

This becomes clear, for example, from the use of the term "crusader". Crusaders are, in the terminology of the book, almost all persons who fought in Livonia. But the term is also applied to the brothers of the Teutonic Order as well as to visiting knights. Thus, Urban applies a wide meaning of the term "crusader" that corresponds to his loose concept of the term "crusade". As the latter appears in the title of his book, it might have deserved greater consideration, especially as the author himself addresses the modern preconceptions of such terms (p. 535).

There are numerous computer-generated maps of lamentable quality: most are too small and of confusing style, legends are missing in numerous cases and the labelling is inconsistent. Several photographs of buildings and coins have been included in the new edition, but unfortunately the quality of reproduction is poor and renders some of the pictures fairly useless.

Urban uses a puzzling system of short titles, quoting by title in one case, by author in the next. The alphabetical ordering of the short titles is confusing: for example, the short title "*A History of Latvia*" cannot be found under "History" nor under "Latvia", but under "B" for "Bilmanis, Alfred." Urban quotes "Mastnak, *Crusading Peace*" in the footnotes (p. 5 n. 9), but in the list of short titles this book can be found only under "C" for *Crusading Peace*, rather than under "M" for "Mastnak", and "Friedrich, *Der deutsche Ritterorden und die Kurie*" (p. 78 n. 11) reappears in the list under "D" (not "F") as "*Der Deutscheritterorden* [!] *und die Kurie*" (p. viii). Elsewhere, "Voigt, IV" (p. 28 n. 47) means "Johannes Voigt, *Geschichte Preussens*, vol. 4," but this remains obscure, nor is there an explanation for "*Rom und Byzanz, I*" (p. 49 n. 33; apparently: *Rom und Byzanz im Norden: Mission und Glaubenswechsel im Ostseeraum während des 8.–14. Jahrhunderts*, vol. 1, ed. Michael Müller-Wille. Mainz, 1997). Moreover, Stephen Rowell's study "*Lithuania ascending*" sometimes turns into "*The Ascent of Lithuania*" (p. 48 n. 31; p. 84 n. 28), while Bernhart Jähnig becomes Bernard Jähnig (p. 29 n. 49). A collection of articles by Erich Maschke (*Domus hospitalis Theutonicorum*) is said to contain "Bohm, Die Besetzung der livländischen Bistümer," which cannot be found in that volume (p. 7 n. 13), but probably refers to Fritz Schonebohm, *Die Besetzung der livländischen Bistümer bis zum Anfang des 14. Jahrhunderts*, Riga, 1909. A most bewildering hyperlink (apparently the complete URL of a search query) was pasted into a footnote on page 494 (n. 22). A bibliography is missing. Readers who are "addicted to footnotes" (p. iv) are served ill by this book.

In sum, *The Livonian Crusade* is a book that demands respect for the scope of the subject and the author's supreme knowledge of medieval Livonia. It surely is a mine of information and a cornerstone for future studies. One can only regret that it often lacks analytical clarity and was produced without the appropriate care.

AXEL EHLERS
HANNOVER, GERMANY

# SOCIETY FOR THE
# STUDY OF THE CRUSADES
# AND THE LATIN EAST

## BULLETIN No. 26, 2006

**Editorial**

It is a pleasure for the SSCLE to announce that its new treasurer is **Prof. James Ryan, Apt. 26M, 100 W. 94th St., New York NY 10025-7013, U.S.A.; email: james.d.ryan@ verizon.net**. Many members will have noticed already that he tries hard and with great success to establish the individual accounts and to answer queries concerning fees or subscriptions. We apologize for any confusions, troubles or delays during the past few years. And we want to thank all our members for their great patience und their loyalty to the SSCLE.

Our journal entitled *Crusades*, now 5 (2006), allows the Society to publish articles and texts; encourages research in neglected subfields; invites a number of authors to deal with a specific problem within a comparative framework; initiates and reports on joint programmes; and offers reviews of books and articles. Editors: Benjamin Z. Kedar and Jonathan Riley-Smith; associate editor: Jonathan Phillips; reviews editor: Christoph Maier; archaeology editor: Denys R. Pringle.

Colleagues may submit papers for consideration to either of the editors, Professor Benjamin Z. Kedar and Professor Jonathan S. C. Riley-Smith. A copy of the style sheet is to be found in the back of this volume.

The journal includes a section of book reviews. In order to facilitate the reviews editor's work, could members please ask their publishers to send copies to: **Dr Christoph T. Maier, Reviews editor, *Crusades*, Sommergasse 20, CH-4056 Basel, Switzerland**. Please note that *Crusades* reviews books concerned with any aspect(s) of the history of the crusades and the crusade movement, the military orders and the Latin settlements in the Eastern Mediterranean, but not books which fall outside this range.

The cost of the journal to individual members is £20, $30 or €33; the cost to institutions and non-members is £65, $95 or €105. Cheques should be made payable to SSCLE.

Members may opt to receive the Bulletin alone at the current membership price (single £11, $15 or €17; student £6, $9 or €10; joint £15, $23 or €25). Those members who do not subscibe to the journal will receive the Bulletin from the Bulletin editor.

The Bulletin editor would like to remind you that, in order to avoid delays, he needs to have information for the Bulletin each year at an early date, usually in January or February: **stadtarchiv@rothenburg.de**. Postal address: **Prof. Karl Borchardt, c/o Stadtarchiv, Milchmarkt 2, D-91541 Rothenburg, Germany**.

Dr Zsolt Hunyadi has been appointed to run our official website: **http://www.sscle.org**. There you can find news about the SSCLE and its publications as well as links to related sites. It is planned to show the members' publications recorded in our Bulletins from 1980 onwards and some additional bibliography related to the crusades, the Latin East and the military orders.

Karl Borchardt

**Message from the President**

Dear Member,

After some three years of turbulence, our Society is getting back to good health, thanks to the fine efforts of our new treasurer, James Ryan, who has brought our accounts up to date and has tried successfully to find new members. Our journal *Crusades* draws many proposals of papers; the next issue will include some of those presented at our conference in Istanbul. Of the others, Thomas Madden is editing a selection of the main papers concerned with the Fourth Crusade, for a book to be published by Ashgate. So, next year, our publications will be completely up to date.

Currently, we have to prepare the next conference, in commemoration of the Albigensian Crusade. It will be held in France, not without some problems. The hospitality offered by the Centre d'Études cathares does not seem to be forthcoming: for financial reasons the Director of the Centre was dismissed last year, and all our academic colleagues have left. I am currently working to find another solution with the help of a university in Southern France, for a conference in August 2008. You will receive the information as soon as possible.

Best wishes to all and good work on the crusades.

Michel Balard

# Contents

**List of abbreviations**

CISH Sydney: 20th International Congress of Historical Sciences, Sydney, University of New South Wales, Australia, 3–9 July 2005.

CLE-Seminar: The Crusades and the Latin East Seminar, Institute of Historical Research and Emmanuel College, Cambridge or London.

CyprusSoCu: Cyprus: Society and Culture 1191–1374, ed. Angel Nikolaou-Konnari and Chris Schabel, The Medieval Mediterranean 58 (Leiden – Boston: Brill, 2005), xvi+403pp. + 32 illustrations.

DOM: Dictionnaire des ordres militaires au Moyen Âge, ed. Nicole Bériou and Philippe Josserand (Paris: Fayard, 2007).

EI: The Encyclopedia of Islam (Leiden: Brill).

EncycCru: Encyclopedia of the Crusades, ed. Alan V. Murray (ABC-Clio, 2006).

HES: International colloquium on the History of Egypt and Syria in the Fatimid, Ayyubid and Mamluk Eras, Katholieke Universiteit Leuven.

IMC: International Medieval Congress, Kalamazoo or Leeds.

IMMO: International Mobility in the Military Orders (Twelfth to Fifteenth Centuries): Travelling on Christ's Business, ed. Jochen Burgtorf and Helen Nicholson, Religion and Culture in the Middle Ages (Cardiff: University of Wales Press and Tuscaloosa: University of Alabama Press, 2006), xxii + 218pp.

MO3: The Military Orders, vol. 3: Their History and Heritage, ed. William G. Zajac (Aldershot: Ashgate, NYP).

MO4: The Military Orders on Land and by Sea, The Fourth International Conference of the London Centre for the Study of the Crusades, the Military Religious Orders and the Latin East, Clerkenwell, London, 8–11 September 2005, ed. Judi Upton-Ward (Aldershot: Ashgate, NYP).

OM13: Selbstbild und Selbstverständnis der geistlichen Ritterorden [Self-Image and Self-Perception of the Military Orders], ed. Roman Czaja and Jürgen Sarnowsky, Universitas Nicolai Copernici, Ordines militares, Colloquia Torunensia Historica XIII (Toruń: Wydawnictwo Universytetu Mikolaja Kopernika, 2005), 285pp.

OM 2005: Die Ritterorden als Träger von Herrschaft: Territorien, Grundbesitz und Kirchen, 13th congress Ordines militares, Universitas Nicolai Copernici, Toruń, 23–25 September 2005.

Runciman–Conference: Terceras Jornadas Internacionales: Medio siglo de estudios sobre las Cruzadas y las Órdenes Militares, 1951–2001, A Tribute to Sir Steven Runciman, Universidad de Zaragoza y Ayuntamiento de Teruel, Teruel (Aragon), 19–25 July 2001, ed. Luis García-Guijarro Ramos (Madrid: Castelló d'Impressió SL).

Saladin und die Kreuzfahrer, Ausstellungskatalog, ed. Alfried Wieczorek, Mamoun Fansa and Harald Meller, Publikationen der Reiss-Engelhorn-Museen 17, Schriftenreihe des Landesmuseums für Natur und Mensch Oldenburg 37 (Mainz: Zabern, 2005), xxiii+517pp.; Konfrontation der Kulturen? Saladin und die Kreuzfahrer, Begleitband, ed. Heinz Gaube, Bernd Schneidmüller and Stefan Weinfurter, Publikationen der Reiss-Engelhorn-Museen 14, Schriftenreihe des Landesmuseums für Natur und Mensch Oldenburg 34 (ibid.), 207pp.

Urbs capta: La quatrième croisade et ses conséquences, The Fourth Crusade and its Consequences, ed. Angeliki E. Laiou, Réalités byzantines 10 (Paris: Lethielleux, 2005), 371pp.

**1. Recent publications**

ALLARD, Jean-Marie, Templar Mobility in the Diocese of Limoges According to the Order's Trial Records, in: IMMO 130–141.

ALVIRA CABRER, Martín, Dimensiones religiosas y liturgia de la batalla plenomedieval: Las Navas de Tolosa, 16 de julio de 1212, in: XX Siglos 19 (1994), 33–46; Las Cruzadas y la España Medieval, in: Historia 16 229 (1995), 82–90; La muerte del enemigo: cifras e ideología (El modelo de Las Navas de Tolosa), in: Hispania LV/190 (1995), 403–424; El *venerable* Arnaldo Amalarico (h. 1196–1225): idea y realidad de un cisterciense entre dos Cruzadas, in: Hispania Sacra 48 (1996), 569–591; La concepción de la batalla como *duelo* y la propaganda de cruzada en Occidente a principios del siglo XIII: el *desafío* de *Miramamolín* a la Cristiandad antes de la batalla de Las Navas de Tolosa (16 de julio de 1212), in: Heresis 26/27 (1996), 57–76; Guerra e ideología en la España Plenomedieval: La conquista de Mallorca según la *Crònica* de Bernat Desclot, in: En la España Medieval 19 (1996), 37–50; La imagen del *Miramamolín* al-Nâsir (1199–1213) en las fuentes cristianas del siglo XIII, in: Anuario de Estudios Medievales 26/2 (1996), 1003–1028; De Alarcos a las Navas de Tolosa: idea y realidad de los orígenes de la batalla de 1212, in: Actas de 'Alarcos 1195' Congreso Internacional Conmemorativo del VIII Centenario de la Batalla de Alarcos (Cuenca, 1996), 249–264; El *Desafío del Miramamolín* antes de la batalla de Las Navas de Tolosa (1212): Fuentes, datación y posibles orígenes, in: Al-Qântara 18/2 (1997), 463–490; Peregrinaciones medievales hacia Jerusalén, Roma y otras metas, in: XX Siglos 41 (1999), 83–100; Le *vénérable* Arnaud Amaury: image et réalité d'un cistercien entre deux croisades, in: Heresis 32 (2000), 3–35; La Cruzada Albigense y la intervención de la Corona de Aragón en Occitania: El recuerdo de las crónicas hispánicas del siglo XIII, in: Hispania 60/3–206 (2000), 947–976; El papel de maestres y caballeros en la batalla de Las Navas de Tolosa (1212) según las Historias Modernas de las Órdenes Militares, in: Las Órdenes Militares en la Península Ibérica, vol. 1: Edad Media, ed. R. Izquiero Benito and F. Ruiz Gómez (Cuenca, 2000), 537–554; with Emilio Mitre Fernández, Ideología y Guerra en los Reinos de la España Medieval, in: Conquistar y Defender: Los recursos militares en la Edad Media Hispánica, Jornadas de Historia Militar de la España Medieval (Madrid, 23–24 y 30–31 de Octubre; 6–7 y 13–14 de Noviembre de 2000), Revista de Historia Miltar (Madrid, 2001), 291–334; Alphonse, par la grâce de Dieu, Roi de Castille et de Tolède, Seigneur de Gascogne: Quelques remarques à propos des relations entre Castillans et Aquitans au début du XIIIᵉ siècle, in: Aquitaine et Espagne (VIIIᵉ–XIIIᵉ siècle), ed. with Pascal Buresi (Poitiers, 2001), 219–232; El Jueves de Muret: 12 de Septiembre de 1213 (Barcelona, 2002); Los reinos hispánicos y los movimientos heréticos en la plenitud medieval (repertorio bibiliográfico de 'Herejía y cultura antiherética en la España Medieval' de Emilio Mitre Fernández), in: Iglesia y Religiosidad en España: Historia y Archivos, Actas de las V Jornadas de Castilla-La Mancha sobre investigación en archivos, Archivo Histórico Provincial de Guadalajara, Guadalajara, 8–11 mayo 2001), 2 vols. (Guadalajara, 2002), 1: 507–551; with Jaafar Ben Elhaj Soulami, Una misma exclamación del sultán Salâh al-Dîn y del Miramamolín an-Nâsir en las batallas de Hittîn/Hattîn (583 H./1187 JC.) y al-'Iqâb/Las Navas de Tolosa (609 H./1212 JC.), in: Anaquel de Estudios Árabes 13 (2002), 9–20; *Ut stulticie Hispanorum et hominum terre hujus, qui sompnia curant et auguria, plenius contrairem*: Sobre superstición y herejía durante la Cruzada contra los Albigenses, in: Heresis 36/37 (2002), 253–257; Guerra e ideología en la España medieval: cultura y actitudes históricas ante el giro de principios del siglos XIII – Batallas de Las Navas de Tolosa (1212) y Muret (1213), CD-Rom (Madrid: Servicio de Publicationes de la University Complutense de Madrid, 2003); with Emilio Mitre Fernández, Movimientos heréticos y conflictos populares en el Pleno Medievo, in: Historia del Cristianismo, vol. 2: El mundo medieval (Madrid: Trotta, Univ. de Granada, 2004), 385–437; La Couronne d'Aragon, entre hérétiques et croisés: la croisade albigeoise (1209–1211) selon le *Chronicon Rotense*, in: Heresis 38 (2003), 71–87; Le Jeudi de Muret: Aspects idéologiques et mentaux de la bataille de 1213, in: La Croisade albigeoise, Colloque de Carcassonne, Centre d'Études Cathares, Carcassonne – octobre 2002 (Balma: CEC, 2004), 197–207; with Martin Aurell, Francisco García Fitz, Laurent Macé, Flocel Sabaté and Esteban Sarasa, *Muret, Muret, Muret "Morne Plaine!"*: Réflexions sur "El Jueves de Muret" de Martín Alvira Cabrer, in: Heresis 41 (2004), 13–54; Introduction, in: Les grandes batailles méridionales, 1209–1271, ed. Laurent Albaret and Nicolas Gouzy (Toulouse: Privat, 2005), 15–24; Le triomphe de la Croix: La bataille de Las Navas de Tolosa (16 juillet 1212), in: ibid. 61–71; Le jugement de Dieu punit le roi d'Aragon: La bataille de Muret (12 septembre 1213), in: ibid. 73–82; Los cátaros, "herejes" o *Buenos Hombres*?, in: Clio 40 (February 2005), 20–27.

AMITAI, Reuven, ed. with Michal Biran, Mongols, Turks and Others: Eurasian Nomads and the Sedentary World (Leiden: Brill, 2005), xx + 550pp.; The Resolution of the Mongol-Mamluk War, in: ibid. 359–390; Ilkhanids, in: Encyclopaedia Iranica 12 (2004), 645–654; The Conquest of Arsūf by Baybars: Political and Military Aspects, in: Mamluk Studies Review 9 (2005), 61–83 [Hebrew version to appear in a volume on Arsuf/Appolonia, ed. Israel Roll and Michael Winter]; Some Remarks on the Inscription of Baybars at Maqam Nabi Musa, in: Mamluks and Ottomans: Studies in Honour of Michael Winter, eds. David J. Wasserstein and Ami Ayalon (London – New York: Routledge, 2005), 45–53.

ANDREA, Alfred J., Christendom and the *Umma*, in: Crusades: The Illustrated History (London: Duncan Baird, 2004), 10–31; Innocent III, the Fourth Crusade, and the Coming Apocalypse, in: Medieval Crusade (Woodbridge: Boydell & Brewer, 2004), 97–106; Innocent III and the Byzantine Rite, 1198–1216, in: Urbs capta 111–122.

ARNOLD, Udo, Die Sicht des Deutschen Ordens im 16.–18. Jahrhundert auf seine Anfänge, in: OM13, 253–265.

ATTA, Zubaida, Jews in the Middle Ages in the Middle East (Cairo, 2004).

BALARD, Michel, L'eau et son utilisation à Gênes à la fin du Moyen Âge, in: Famille, violence et christianisation au Moyen Âge, Mélanges offerts à Michel Rouche, ed. Martin Aurell and Thomas Deswarte (Paris, 2005), 119–131; ed. with Élisabeth Malamut and Jean-Michel Spiesser, Byzance et le monde extérieur: contacts, relations, échanges, Actes du 21ᵉ congrès international des études byzantines, Paris août 2001, Byzantina Sorbonensia 21 (Paris: Publ. de la Sorbonne, 2005); Bilan de la Quatrième Croisade, in: 1204, la quatrième croisade, de Blois à ... Constantinople, éclats d'empires, catalogue d'exposition, Musée-Château de Blois et Bibliothèque nationale de France, Musée du cabinet des Médailles, octobre 2005–janvier 2006, red. Inès Villela-Petit, Revue française d'Héraldique et de Sigillographie 73/75 (2003/5), 79–85; L'historiographie des croisades en France au XXᵉ siècle, publ. Université Soongsil Corée du Sud (en coréen).

BALLETTO, Laura, I Genovesi e la caduta di Costantinopoli: riflessi negli atti notarili, in: Νέᾳ Ρώῃ, Rivista di ricerche bizantinistiche, Studi di amici e colleghi in onore di Vera von Falkenhausen (2004, published 2005), 1: 67–312; Il Mar Nero nei notai genovesi: panoramica generale, stato degli studi, progretti di pubblicazione, in: The Black Sea Region in the Middle Ages, VI, ed. Sergei Pavlovich Karpov, Center of Byzantine and Black Sea Region Studies, Historical Faculty Moscow State University (St. Petersburg: Aletheia, 2005), 22–42; Uomini dell'Alessandrino nel Vicino Oriente sulla fine del medioevo, in: Alle origini di Alessandria. Dal Gonfalone del Comune nella Lega Lombarda all'Aquila imperiale degli

Staufen (Alessandria, 2005), 153–167; Les Génois à Phocée et à Chio du XIII$^e$ au XIV$^e$ siècle, in: Byzance et le monde extérieur: contacts, relations, échanges, ed. Michel Balard, Élisabeth Malamut and Jean-Michel Spiesser, Actes du 21$^e$ congrès international des études byzantines, Paris août 2001, Byzantina Sorbonensia 21 (Paris: Publ. de la Sorbonne, 2005), 45–57; L'impresa del genovese Filippo Doria contro Tripoli di Barberia nel 1355, in: Intemelion, Cultura e territorio, Quaderno di studi dell'Accademia di cultura intemelia 11 (2005), 79–117.

BARBER, Malcolm, with Keith Bate, ed. and transl., The Templars, Manchester Medieval Sources (Manchester: Manchester UP, 2002), 350pp.; with Marianne Ailes, ed. and trans., The History of the Holy War: Ambroise's Estoire de la Guerre Sainte, 2 vols. (Woodbridge: Boydell & Brewer, 2003), 211pp. + 214pp.; The Career of Philip of Nablus in the Kingdom of Jerusalem, in: The Experience of Crusading, vol. 2, ed. Peter Edbury and Jonathan Phillips (Cambridge: Cambridge UP, 2003), 60–75; The Templar Preceptory of Douzens (Aude) in the Twelfth Century, in: The World of Eleanor of Aquitaine: Literature and Society in Southern France between the Eleventh and the Thirteenth Centuries, ed. Marcus Bull and Catherine Léglu (Woodbridge: Boydell & Brewer, 2004), 37–55; The Impact of the Fourth Crusade in the West: The Distribution of Relics after 2004, in: Urbs capta 325–334.

BEECH, George T., A Little Known Armenian Historian of the Crusading Period: Gregory the Priest (1136–62), in: Truth as Gift: Studies in Medieval Cistercian History in honor of John R. Sommerfeldt, ed. Marsha Dutton, Daniel M. La Corte and Paul Lockey (Kalamazoo, 2004), 119–143.

BELLOMO, Elena, Mobility of Templar Brothers and Dignitaries: The Case of North-Western Italy, in: IMMO 102–113.

BEREND, Nora, Frontiers, in: The Crusades, ed. Helen Nicholson, Palgrave Advances (London: Palgrave Macmillan, 2005), 148–171.

BIRD, Jessalynn, Crusade and Conversion after the Fourth Lateran Council: James of Vitry's and Oliver of Paderborn's Missions to the Muslims Reconsidered, in: Essays in Medieval Studies, Proceedings of the Illinois Medieval Association 21 (2004), 23–47.

BISAHA, Nancy, Creating East and West: Renaissance Humanists and the Ottoman Turks (University of Pennsylvania Press, 2004); Pope Pius II and the Crusade, in: Crusading in the Fifteenth Century: Message and Impact, ed. Norman Housley (Palgrave, 2004).

BOAS, Adrian, Latrun, in: Crusades 4 (2005), 159–160.

BOMBI, Barbara, Innocent III and the 'praedicatio' to Heathens in Livonia (1198–1204), in: Medieval History Writing and Crusading Ideology, ed. Kurt Villads Jensen and Tuomas M.S. Lehtonen, Studia Fennica Historica 9 (Tampere, 2005), 232–241.

BONNEAUD, Pierre, Catalan Hospitallers in Rhodes in the First Half of the Fifteenth Century, in: IMMO 155–166.

BORCHARDT, Karl, Leitbilder und Ziele von Ordensreformen bei deutschen Johannitern während des 14. Jahrhunderts, in: OM13, 69–80.

BOWLUS, Charles R., Lechfeld (955), in: The Seventy Great Battles in History, ed. Jeremy Black (London: Thames & Hudson, 2005), 51–54; Gondolatok Boba Imre Morávia tortenetéröl vallott kapecsán, transl. István Petrovics Kijevtöl Kalocsáig emlékkönyv Boba Imre Tisztelletére (Budapest: Historia Ecclesiastica Hungarica Alapitvány, 2005).

BRONSTEIN, Judith, The Mobilization of Hospitaller Manpower from Europe to the Holy Land in the Thirteenth Century, in: IMMO 25–33; The Hospitallers and the Holy Land: Financing the Latin East, 1187–1274 (London: Boydell & Brewer, 2005), 200pp.; Cambios estructurales y economicos en la orden de San Juan de Jerusalén en la mitad del siglo XIII, in: As Ordens Militares e as Ordens de Cavalaria na Construção do Mundo Ocidental, Actas do IV Encontro sobre Ordens Militares, ed. Luís Adão da Fonseca and Fernanda Olival (Palmela: Edições Colibri, 2005), 227–235.

BRUNDAGE, James A., The Chronicle of Henry of Livonia [reprint of 1961 book with new introduction] (New York: Columbia UP, 2003); The Profession and Practice of Medieval Canon Law, Variorum (Aldershot: Ashgate, 2004), xii + 336pp.

BURGTORF, Jochen, ed. with Helen Nicholson, IMMO; The Templars' and Hospitallers' High Dignitaries: Aspects of International Mobility, in: ibid. 11–24; Das Selbstverständnis der Templer und Johanniter im Spiegel von Briefen und Urkunden (12. und 13. Jahrhundert), in: OM13, 23–45.

BURNS, Robert I., 100,000 Crossbow Bolts for the Crusader King of Aragon, in: Journal of Medieval Military History 2 (2004), 159–164.

CARR, Annemarie Weyl, Art, in: CyprusSoCu 285–328; Cyprus and the Devotional Arts of Byzantium in the Era of the Crusades (Aldershot: Ashgate, 2005), xiv + 378pp.; Cypriot Funerary Icons: Questions of Convergence in a Complex Land, in: Medieval Paradigms, Essays in Honor of Jeremy DuQuesnay Adams, 2 vols., ed. Stephanie Hayes (Boston: Palgrave Macmillan, 2005), 1: 153–174; Thoughts on Mary East and West, in: Images of the Mother of God: Perceptions of the Theotokos in Byzantium, ed. Maria Vassilaki (London: Ashgate, 2005), 277–291.

CARRAZ, Damien, L'Ordre du Temple dans la basse vallée du Rhône (1124–1312): Ordres militaires, croisades et sociétés méridionales, Collection d'histoire et d'archéologie médiévales 17 (Lyon: Presses University, 2005), 662pp.

CATLOS, Brian A., The Ebro Valley and Valencia: Mudéjar Experiences Related, Distinct, in: Revista d'Historia Medieval, Dossier 12 (2002), 293–305; Contexto social y "conveniencia" en la Corona de Aragón: Propuesta para un modelo de interacción entre grupos etno-religiosos minoritarios y mayoritarios, in: Revista d'Historia Medieval (Valencia) 12 (2002), 220–235; Intereses comunes: la çaualquenia musulmana de Huesca y el poder real a finales del siglo XIII, in: XVIII Congreso de la historia de la Corona de Aragón, Actas, vol. 2 (Barcelona: University de Barcelona, 2003), 65–70.

CHRISTIE, Niall G. F., Crusade Literature, in: The Encyclopedia of Women and Islamic Cultures, ed. Suad Joseph et al. (Leiden: Brill, 2003), 1: 16–21; with Deborah Gerish, Parallel Preachings: Urban II and al-Sulami, in: Al-Masāq 15 (2003), 139–148; Just a Bunch of Dirty Stories? Women in the "Memoirs" of Usamah ibn Munqidh, in: Eastward Bound: Travel and Travellers, 1050–1550, ed. Rosamund Allen (Manchester: Manchester UP, 2004), 71–87; Reconstructing Life in Mediaeval Alexandria from an 8th/14th Century Waqf Document, in: Mamluk Studies Review 8 (2004), 163–190.

CLAVERIE, Pierre-Vincent, Les débuts de l'ordre du Temple en Orient, in: Le Moyen Âge 111 (2005), 545–594; Les "mauvais chrétiens" dans l'Orient des croisades, in: Egypt and Syria in the Fatimid, Ayyubid and Mamluk Eras 4, ed. Urbain Vermeulen (Louvain: Peeters, 2005), 143–163; L'ambassade au Caire de Philippe Mainebeuf (1291), in: ibid. 383–396; with Emmanuel and Jean-Pierre Grélois, Apud Ciprum Nicossiam: notes sur les relations cyprio-auvergnates au XIIIᵉ siècle, in: Epeterida 31 (2005), 199–231.

CIPOLLONE, Giulio, La cultura della convivenza per un avvenire di pace tra cristiani e musulmani, in: Rivista di studi politici internazionali 282 (2004), 213–229; L'Europa è la sua eredità e il suo progetto: il contributo del Cristianesimo alla costruzione dell'Europa, in: ibid. 286 (2005), 233–264.

COBB, Paul M., Usāma ibn Munqidh's Book of the Staff: Autobiographical and Historical Excerpts, in: Al-Masāq 17 (2005), 109–122; Usama ibn Munqidh: Warrior-Poet of the Age of the Crusades (Oxford: Oneworld, 2006), 136pp.; Usāma ibn Munqidh's Kernels of Refinement (Lubāb al-ādāb): Autobiographical and Historical Excerpts, in: Al-Masāq 8 (2006), 67–78.

CORRIE, Rebecca W., with George Contis and Robert Allison, Byzantium to Russia: Popular Icons for Personal Devotion, exhibition catalogue (Bates College, 2003), 13pp.; The Kahn and Mellon Madonnas and their Place in the History of the Virgin and Child Enthroned in Italy and the East, in: Images of the Mother of God: Perceptions of the Theotokos in Byzantium, ed. Maria Vassilaki (Aldershot and Burlington, 2005), 293–303; Angevin Ambitions: The Conradin Bible Atelier and a Neapolitan Localization for Chantilly's Histoire Ancienne et jusqu'a Cesar, in: France and the Holy Land: Frankish Culture at the End of the Crusades, ed. Daniel H. Weiss and Lisa Mahoney (Baltimore – London, 2004), 230–249; 14 entries, in: Byzantium: Faith and Power (1261–1557), ed. Helen C. Evans (New York: Metropolitan Museum of Art, 2004), 465–470, 473–483.

COUREAS, Nicholas S., Cyprus and Euboea in the Mid-Fourteenth Century, in: Symmeikta 16 (Athens, 2003/04), 87–100; I mercanti genovesi e le loro attività a Nicosia dall'marzo all'ottobre 1297, in: Alle origini di Alessandria (Alessandria, 2005), 189–201; Economy, in: CyprusSoCu 103–156; The Genesis and Development of Cyprus' Modern Latin Community after 1571 [expanded English version], in: Journal of Mediterranean History (Malta, 2005); transl., George Boustoronios, A Narrative of the Chronicle of Cyprus, 1456–1489, Cyprus Research Centre and Greece and Cyprus Research Centre (Nicosia and Albany, NY, 2005), 250pp.

CRAWFORD, Paul F., Imagination and the Templars: The Development of the Order-State in the Early Fourteenth Century, in: Annual Review of the Cyprus Research Centre 30 (2004), 113–121.

CUNHA, Maria Cristina, Internal Mobility in the Order of Avis (Twelfth to Fourteenth Centuries), in: IMMO 190–201.

CZAJA, Roman, Das Selbstverständnis der geistlichen Ritterorden im Mittelalter: Bilanz und Forschungsperspektive, in: OM13, 7–21.

DEMEL, Bernhard, Unbekannte Aspekte der Geschichte des Deutschen Ordens (Köln – Weimar – Wien: Böhlau, 2006), 160pp.

DEMIRKENT, Isin, Son Donem Bizans Imparatorlugu Tarihi Bibliyografyasi (1261–1453) [The Bibliography of the Last Period of Byzantium], Istanbul Universitesi Rektorlugu Yayinlari 4440 (Istanbul, 2003); Râvendân (A Castle of the Crusader Era), in: Tarih Dergisi 40 (2004), 141–157; Maarretünnu'mân, in: DIA – Türkiye Diyanet Vakfi İslâm Ansiklopedisi 27 (Ankara, 2003), 274–276; Menbic, in: ibid. 29 (Ankara, 2005), 123–124; Mevdûd b. Altuntegin, in: ibid. 427–429; Misis, in: ibid. 30 (İstanbul, 2005), 178–181; Niketas Khoniates'in Historia'si (1195–1206): İstanbul 'un Haçlılar Tarafindan Zaptı ve Yağmalanması [Historia of Niketas Khoniates (1195–1206): Conquest and Plunderage of Istanbul by the Crusaders] (İstanbul: Dünya Yayınları, 2004); Bizans Tarihi Yazıları [Papers on Byzantine History] (İstanbul: Dünya Yayınları, 2005); Haçlı Seferleri Döneminde Doğu-Akdeniz'de Deniz Hâkimiyeti [Marine Domination in the Eastern Mediterranean During the Crusader Era], in: Tarih Boyunca Dünyada ve Türkler'de Denizcilik Semineri, 17–18 Mayıs 2004 (İstanbul: Dünya Yayınları, 2005), 49–70.

DEMURGER, Alain, Between Barcelona and Cyprus: The Travels of Berenguer of Cardona, Templar Master of Aragon and Catalonia (1300–1), in: IMMO 65–74.

Dɪ Vɪᴛᴛᴏʀɪᴏ, Antonio, L'Ordine dei Cavalieri di S. Giovanni: la struttura economica, in: Gli archivi per la storia del Sovrano Militare Ordine di Malta, Atti del III Convegno Internazionale di Studi Melitensi, Taranto 18–21 ottobre 2001 (Taranto: Centro Studi Melitensi).

Dᴏᴅᴅ, Erica Cruikshank, Christian Arab Sources for the Madonna Allattante in Italy, in: Arte Medievale 2/2 (2003), 33–39; Medieval Painting in the Lebanon (Wiesbaden: Reichert, 2004).

Eᴅʙᴜʀʏ, Peter W., Franks, in: CyprusSoCu 63–101.

Eᴅɢɪɴɢᴛᴏɴ, Susan B., Medicine and Surgery in the *Livre des Assises de la Cour des Bourgeois de Jerusalem*, in: Al-Masāq 18 (2005), 87–97; Administrative Regulations for the Hospital of St John in Jerusalem dating from the 1180s, in: Crusades 4 (2005), 21–37.

Eʜʟᴇʀs, Axel, John Malkaw of Prussia: A Case of Individual Mobility in the Teutonic Order, c.1400, in: IMMO 75–84.

ᴠᴀɴ Eɪᴄᴋᴇʟs, Klaus, Secure Base and Constraints of Mobility: The Rheno-Flemish Bailiwick of the Teutonic Knights between Regional Bonds and Service to the Grand Master in the Later Middle Ages, in: IMMO 167–172.

Eᴋᴅᴀʜʟ, Sven, Crusades and Colonization in the Baltic, in: The Crusades, ed. Helen Nicholson, Palgrave Advances (Basingstoke – New York: Palgrave Macmillan, 2005), 172–203.

Fɪsᴄʜᴇʀ, Mary, The Books of the Maccabees and the Teutonic Order, in: Crusades 4 (2005), 59–71.

Fᴏʟᴅᴀ, Jaroslav, Crusader Art in the Holy Land from the Third Crusade to the Fall of Acre, 1187–1291 (Cambridge and New York: Cambridge UP, 2005), lxxvi+714pp, 11 colour plates, 415 b+w illustrations, CD with 501 b+w illustrations; The Figural Arts in Crusader Syria and Palestine, 1187–1291: Some New Realities, at: Dumbarton Oaks Papers 58 (2004 [2005]), 315–331.

Fᴏʀᴇʏ, Alan, Templar Knights and Sergeants in the *Corona de Aragón* at the Turn of the Thirteenth and Fourteenth Centuries, in: As Ordens Militares e as Ordens de Cavalaria na Construção do Mundo Ocidental, Actas do IV Encontro sobre Ordens Militares, ed. Luís Adão da Fonseca and Fernanda Olival (Palmela: Edições Colibri 2005), 631–642; How the Aragonese Templars Viewed Themselves in the Late Thirteenth and Early Fourteenth Centuries, in: OM13, 59–68; Introduction, in: IMMO 1–7; with Jochen Burgtorf and Helen Nicholson, Conclusion, in: ibid. 202–206.

Fʀɪᴇᴅᴍᴀɴ, Yvonne, Violence towards Captives in the Latin Kingdom of Jerusalem, in: Historia 11 (2003), 1–22 [Hebrew]; Miracles, Meaning and Narrative in the Latin East, in: Signs, Wonders, Miracles: Representations of Divine Power in the Life of the Church, ed. Kate Cooper and Jeremy Gregory, Studies in Church History 41 (2005), 123–134; A Room of Her Own: Sylvia Schein's Contribution to Medieval History, in: Sylvia Schein, Gateway to the Heavenly City (Aldershot: Ashgate, 2005), vii–ix.

Gᴀʙʀɪᴇʟᴇ, Matthew, 'Asleep on the Wheel?' Apocalypticism, Messianism and Charlemagne's Passivity in the Oxford *Chanson de Roland*, in: Nottingham Medieval Studies 43 (2003), 46–72.

Gʀᴀʙᴏɪs, Aryeh, Das Vermächtnis und die Legende Karls des Großen in hebräischen Schriften des Mittelalters, in: Ex Oriente: Isaak und der weiße Elefant, vol. 3: Aachen, Der Westen: 800 und Heute (Aachen, 2003), 122–139; The First Crusade and the Jews, in: The Crusades, Other Experiences, Alternate Perspectives, Proceedings of the 32rd Annual

CEMERS Conference, ed. Khalil I. Semaan (Binghamton/NY, 2003), 13–26; La description de l'Egypte au XIV<sup>e</sup> siècle par les pèlerins et les voyageurs occidentaux, in: Le Moyen Âge 109 (2003), 529–543.

GRIVAUD, Gilles, Literature, in: CyprusSoCu 219–284.

VON GUTTNER SPORZYNSKI, Darius, Protestant Nobility in Poland: Index of Families, in: Materialy do biografii, genealogii i heraldyki polskiej [Sources on Biography, Genealogy and Heraldry in Poland], vol. 10, ed. Stefan K. Kuczyński (Warszawa: DiG, 2005), 55–75; The Order of Saint John [English summary], in: Zakon Maltański w Polsce [The Order of Malta in Poland], ed. Jerzy Baranowski, Marcin Libicki, Andrzej Rottermund, Maria Starnawska (Warszawa: DiG, 2000), 281–288.

HAMILTON, Bernard, The Impact of the Crusades on Western Geographical Knowledge, in: Eastward Bound: Travel and Travellers 1050–1550, ed. Rosamund Allen (Manchester: Manchester UP, 2004), 15–34; The Albigensian Crusade and the Latin Empire of Constantinople, in: Urbs capta 335–343.

HARRIS, Jonathan, ed., Byzantine History, Palgrave Advances (Basingstoke: Palgrave/ Macmillan, 2005), xiii+252pp.

HECKMANN, Dieter, Vom *eraftigen* zum *erwirdigen*: Die Selbstdarstellung des Deutschen Ordens im Spiegel der Anreden und Titulaturen (13.–16. Jahrhundert), in: OM13, 219–225.

HOLMES, Catherine, Basil II and the Governance of Empire, 976–1025 (Oxford, 2005).

HOUSLEY, Norman, Perceptions of Crusading in the Mid-Fourteenth Century: the Evidence of Three Texts, in: Viator 36 (2005), 415–433.

HOUBEN, Hubert, Eine Quelle zum Selbstverständnis des Deutschen Ordens im 14. Jahrhundert: der Codex Vat. Ottobon. lat. 528, in: OM13, 139–153.

HUNT, Lucy-Anne, Art in the Wadi al-Natrun: An Assessment of the Earliest Wallpaintings in the Church of Abu Makas, Dayr Abu Makas, in: Coptica 3 (2004), 69–103; Orientalische Christen: Kunst und Kultur zur Zeit der Kreuzfahrer, in: Saladin und die Kreuzfahrer, Ausstellungskatalog 191–203; For the Salvation of a Woman's Soul: An Icon of St. Michael Described within a Medieval Coptic Context, in: Icon and Word: The Power of Images in Byzantium, ed. Antony Eastmond and Liz James (Aldershot – Burlington/VT: Ashgate, 2003), 205–232.

HUNYADI, Zsolt, Hospitaller Officials of Foreign Origin in the Hungarian-Slavonian Priory (Thirteenth and Fourteenth Centuries), in: IMMO 142–154; (Self)Representation: Hospitaller Seals in the Hungarian-Slavonian Priory up to c.1400, in: OM13, 199–212.

HUYGENS, Robert B. C., Excidium Aconis – Magister Thadeus, Corpus Christianorum Continuatio Medievalis 202 (Turnhout, 2004), 225pp., 4 illustrations; Inventio Patriarcharum, in: Crusades 4 (2005), 131–155.

JACKSON, Peter, The Mongols and the West, 1221–1410, Longman's Medieval World series (Harlow: Pearson, 2005), xxxiv+414pp.; The Mongols and the Faith of the Conquered, in: Mongols, Turks and Others: Eurasian Nomads and the Sedentary World, ed. Reuven Amitai and Michal Biran (Leiden: Brill, 2005), 245–290.

JACOBY, David, The Demographic Evolution of Euboea under Latin Rule, 1205–1470, in: The Greek Islands and the Sea, Proceedings of the First International Colloquium held at the Hellenic Institute, Royal Holloway, University of London, 21–22 September 2001, ed. Julian Chrysostomides, Charalambos Dendrinos and Jonathan Harris (Camberley/Surrey: Porphyrogenitus, 2004), 131–179; Silk Economics and Cross-Cultural Artistic Interaction: Byzantium, the Muslim World and the Christian West, in: Dumbarton Oaks Papers 58 (2004),

197–240; Les Latins dans les villes de Romanie jusqu'en 1261: le versant méditerranéen des Balkans, in: Byzance et le monde extérieur: contacts, relations, échanges, eds. Michel Balard, Élisabeth Malamut and Jean-Michel Spiesser, Actes du 21ᵉ congrès international des études byzantines, Paris août 2001, Byzantina Sorbonensia 21 (Paris: Publ. de la Sorbonne, 2005), 13–26; Bishop Gunther of Bamberg, Byzantium and Christian Pilgrimage to the Holy Land in the Eleventh Century, in: Zwischen Polis, Provinz und Peripherie: Beiträge zur byzantinischen Geschichte und Kultur, ed. Lars M. Hoffmann and Anuscha Monchizadeh, Mainzer Veröffentlichungen zur Byzantinistik 7 (Wiesbaden: Harassowitz, 2005), 267–285; The Economy of Latin Constantinople, 1204–1261, in: Urbs capta 195–214; Aspects of Everyday Life in Frankish Acre, in: Crusades 4 (2005), 73–105.

JANKRIFT, Kay Peter, International Mobility in the Order of St Lazarus (Twelfth to Early Fourteenth Centuries), in: IMMO 59–64.

JASPERT, Nikolas, Zwei unbekannte Hilfsersuchen des Patriarchen Eraclius vor dem Fall Jerusalems (1187), in: Deutsches Archiv 60 (2005), 483–516; Kleinere Ritterorden Palästinas – und der Kanonikerorden vom Heiligen Grab, in: Ritterorden im Mittelalter, ed. Feliciano Novoa Portela and Carlos de Ayala Martínes (Darmstadt, 2005), 77–100; Von Karl dem Großen bis Kaiser Wilhelm: Die Erinnerung an vermeintliche und tatsächliche Kreuzzüge in Mittelalter und Moderne, in: Saladin und die Kreuzfahrer, Begleitband, 136–160; Jerusalem und sein Königshaus, in: Saladin und die Kreuzfahrer, Ausstellungskatalog 61–82; Jerusalem und die Kreuzfahrerherrschaften im Leben und Denken des Maimonides, in: The Trias of Maimonides: Jewish, Arabic and Ancient Culture of Knowledge / Die Trias des Maimonides: Jüdische, arabische und antike Wissenskultur, ed. Georges Tamer, Studia Judaica 30 (Berlin, 2005), 41–64.

JENSEN, Kurt Villads, Politikens bog om korstogene [Politiken's Book about the Crusades], Copenhagen, 2005, 249pp.; Crusading at the Fringe of the Ocean: Denmark and Portugal in the Twelfth Century, in: Medieval History Writing and Crusading Ideology, ed. Tuomas M. S. Lehtonen and Kurt Villads Jensen with Janne Malkki and Katja Ritari, Studia Fennica Historica 9 (Helsinki: Finnish Literary Society, 2005), 195–204; Introduction, in: ibid. 16–33; Det Danske Imperium – storhed og fald [Rise and Fall of the Danish Empire], with Michael Bregnsbo (Copenhagen: Aschehougs, 2004), 256pp.; Danske korstog: Mission og omvendelse i Østersøområdet [Danish Crusades: Mission and Conversion in the Baltic Sea Area], with Ane Bysted, Carsten Selch Jensen and John Lind (Copenhagen: Høst og Søns, 2004), 404pp.; Imitatio Christi i den grad: Korstogene som en spirituel rejse [Imitatio Christi indeed: The Crusades as a Spiritual Journey], in: Undervejs mod Gud: Rummet og rejsen i middelalderlig religiøsitet [Towards God: Space and Travel in Medieval Religiosity], ed. Mette Birkedal Bruun and Britt Istorf (Copenhagen: Museum Tusculanum UP, 2004), 46–65; Danske korstog før og under korstogstiden [Danish Crusades before and during the Crusading Period], in: Ett Annat 1100-tal: Individ, kollektiv och kulturella mönster i medeltidens Danmark [Another Twelfth Century: Individual, Collectivism, and Cultural Pattern in Medieval Denmark], ed. Peter Carelli, Lars Hermanson and Hanne Sanders (Stockholm: Makadam, 2004), 246–283.

JUBB, Margaret A., The Crusaders' Perceptions of Their Opponents, in: The Crusades, ed. Helen Nicholson, Palgrave Advances (Basingstoke: Palgrave / Macmillan, 2005), 225–244, bibliography 295–296.

KEDAR, Benjamin Z., The Crusader Motif in the Israeli Political Discourse, in: Alpayyim 26 (2004), 9–40 [Hebrew]; Dimensioni comparative del pellegrinaggio medievale, in: Fra Roma e Gerusalemme nel Medioevo: Paesaggi umani ed ambientali del pellegrinaggio meridionale, Atti del Congresso Internazionale di Studi, Salerno – Cava de' Tirreni – Ravello,

26–29 ottobre 2000, ed. Massimo Oldoni, 3 vols. (Salerno, 2005), 1: 255–277; with Daniella Talmon-Heller, Did Muslim Survivors of the 1099 Massacre of Jerusalem Settle in Damascus? The True Origins of the al-Salihiyya Suburb, in: Al-Masāq 17 (2005), 165–169; The Voyages of Giuàn-Ovadiah in Syria and Iraq and the Enigma of his Conversion, in: Giovanni-Ovadiah da Oppido, proselito, viaggiatore e musicista dell'età normanna, Atti del convegno internazionale, Oppido Lucano 28–30 marzo 2004, ed. Antonio Da Rosa and Mauro Perani (Florence, 2005), 133–147; Holy Men in a Holy Land: Christian, Muslim and Jewish Religiosity in the Near East at the Time of the Crusades, Hayes Robinson Lecture series 9, Royal Holloway, University of London (London, 2005), 24pp.

KOSTICK, Conor, William of Tyre, Livy, and the Vocabulary of Class, in: Journal of the History of Ideas 65 (2004), 353–368; Women and the First Crusade, in: Studies on Medieval and Early Modern Women, ed. Christine Meek and Catherine Lawless, vol. 3 (Dublin: Courts Press, 2005), 57–68.

KREEM, Juhan, Einige Bemerkungen über die Siegel der Gebietiger des Deutschen Ordens in Livland, in: OM13, 213–218.

KRÜGER, Jürgen, Outremer: Architektur im Heiligen Land als Kolonialarchitektur?, in: Saladin und die Kreuzfahrer, Begleitband 57–89.

KWIATKOWSKI, Krzysztof, Die Selbstdarstellung des Deutschen Ordens in der *Chronik* Wigands von Marburg, in: OM13, 127–138.

KWIATKOWSKI, Stefan, Auf der Suche nach den moralischen Grundlagen des Deutschen Ordens in Preußen, in: OM13, 155–179.

LICENCE, Tom, The Templars and the Hospitallers, Christ and the Saints, in: Crusades 4 (2005), 39–57.

LOUD, Graham A., Monastic Chronicles in the Twelfth Century Abruzzi, in: Anglo-Norman Studies 27 (2005), 101–131; Monastic Miracles in Southern Italy, c. 1040–1140, in: Studies in Church History 41 (2005), 109–122; Some Reflections on the Failure of the Second Crusade, in: Crusades 4 (2005), 1–14.

LUTTRELL, Anthony, Ermengol de Aspa, *Provisor* of the Hospital: 1188, in: Crusades 4 (2005), 15–19; Las Órdenes Militares de San Juan de Jerusalén y del Temple, in: Las Órdenes Militares en la Europa Medieval, ed. Feliciano Novoa Portela and Carlos de Ayala Martínez (Barcelona, 2005), 45–76 = Der Johanniter- und der Templerorden, in: Ritterorden im Mittelalter, ed. iidem (Stuttgart, 2006), 45–76.

MADDEN, Thomas F., Crusades: The Illustrated History (Ann Arbor: University of Michigan Press, 2004; paperback edition, 2005); The Fourth Crusade: A Tragic Misfire, in: ibid. 100–116; The New Concise History of the Crusades (Lanham: Rowman & Littlefield, 2005), 304pp.; translated as Le crociate: una storia nuova, transl. D. Ballarini (Torino: Lindau, 2005); Cruzadas: La verdadera historia, transl. Garciela Lehmann and Alicia Lorefice (Buenos Aires: Lumen, 2005); Korean transl. (Seoul: Rubybox Publishing, 2005).

MÄRTL, Claudia, Donatellos Judith – Ein Denkmal der Türkenkriegspropaganda des 15. Jahrhunderts?, in: Osmanische Expansion und europäischer Humanismus, Akten des interdisziplinären Symposions vom 29. und 30. Mai 2003 im Stadtmuseum Wiener Neustadt, ed. Franz Fuchs, Pirckheimer Jahrbuch 20 (2005), 53–95.

MAYER, Hans Eberhard, Die porta nova de Belcayra im Jerusalem der Kreuzfahrer, in: Zeitschrift des Deutschen Palästina-Vereins 119 (2003), 183–190; Geschichte der Kreuzzüge, 10th edition (Stuttgart, 2005), 406pp. [updated]; Drei oberrheinische Kreuzfahrer des 13. Jahrhunderts: Berthold von Nimburg (Vater und Sohn) und Werner von Egisheim, in: Zeitschrift für die Geschichte des Oberrheins 153 = Neue Folge 114 (2005), 43–60.

MARCOMBE, David, Lepers, Land and Loyalty: The Order of St Lazarus of Jerusalem in England and the Holy Land, c.1150–1300, in: IMMO 173–189.

MENACHE, Sophia, A Clash of Expectations: Self Image versus the Image of the Knights Templar in Medieval Narrative Sources, in: OM13, 47–58.

MESCHINI, Marco, Note sull'assegnazione della viscontea Trencavel a Simone di Montfort nel 1209, in: Mélanges de l'École française de Rome – Moyen Âge 116/2 (2004), 635–655; "Pourquoi Béziers?" La chute de Béziers (22 juillet 1209), in: Les grandes batailles méridionales (1209–1271), ed. Laurent Albaret and Nicolas Gouzy (Toulouse, 2005), 25–38.

MINERVINI, Laura, Gli orientalismi nel francese d'Oltremare, in: Sprachkontakte in der Romania: Zum 75. Geburtstag von Gustav Ineichen, ed. Volker Noll and Sylvia Thiele (Tübingen: Niermeyer, 2004), 123–133; Les Gestes des Chiprois et la tradition historiographique de l'Orient Latin, in: Le Moyen Âge 110 (2004), 315–325; Filippo da Novara, Lingue, regno di Gerusalemme, Teodore d'Antiochia, in: Enciclopedia Fridericiana (Roma: Istituto dell'Enciclopedia Italiana, 2005), !: 637–638, 2: 186–187, 818–821.

MITÁČEK, Jiří, Čeští johanité 1367–1397 – správci a diplomaté [Czech Hospitallers – Administrators and Diplomats, in: Časopis národního muzea – řada historická 174 (2005), 113–135; Převorství Havla z Lemberka (1337–1366) [The Priory of Havel of Lemberk (1337–1366)], in: Acta Musei Moraviae 90 (2005), 197–218; Starobrněnští Johanité a jižní Morava za vlády Lucemburků (1310–1419) [The Hospitallers of Old Brno and southern Moravia during the Luxemburg reign (1310–1419)], in: Brno v minulosti a dnes 18 (2005), 43–55.

MÖHRING, Hannes, König der Könige: Der Bamberger Reiter in neuer Interpretation (Königstein: Langewiesche, 2004); al-Mahdī, al-Mansūr and faras al-nawba, in: Words, Texts and Concepts Cruising the Mediterranean Sea, ed. Rüdiger Arnzen and Jörn Thielmann (Leuven: Peeters, 2004), 603–617; Saladin: Der Sultan und seine Zeit, 1138–1193 (München: Beck, 2005); Saladin, der edle Heide – Mythisierung und Realität, in: Saladin und die Kreuzfahrer, Begleitband 160–175; Muslimische Reaktionen: Zangi, Nuraddin und Saladin, in: Saladin und die Kreuzfahrer, Ausstellungskatalog 83–99; Sultan Saladin und Kaiser Friedrich Barbarossa, in: ibid. 151–155; Saladin und die Frage der religiösen Toleranz, in: ibid. 157–161; "Hedwigsbecher", in: ibid. 441–442.

MURRAY, Alan, Prosopography, in: The Crusades, ed. Helen Nicholson, Palgrave Advances (Basingstoke: Palgrave Macmillan, 2005), 109–129.

NICHOLSON, Helen, ed., The Crusades, Palgrave Advances (Basingstoke: Palgrave Macmillan); ed. with Jochen Burgtorf, IMMO; International Mobility versus the Needs of the Realm: The Templars and Hospitallers in the British Isles in the Thirteenth and Fourteenth Centuries, in: ibid. 87–101; Saints Venerated in the Military Orders, in: OM13, 91–113.

NICOLAOU-KONNARI, Angel, ed. with Chris Schabel, CyprusSoCu; Greeks, in: ibid., 13–62; Onomastics in the Manuscripts of the Chronicle of Leontios Makhairas, in: Anadromika kai Prodromika: Approaches to Texts in Early Modern Greek, Papers from the Conference Neograeca Medii Aevi V, Exeter College, University of Oxford, September 2000, ed. Elizabeth and Michael Jeffreys (Oxford, 2005), 327–371 [Greek].

NICOLLE, David, with Viacheslav Shpakovsky, Russkaya Armiya 1250–1500 (Moscow, 2004); Crusader Castles in the Holy Land 1192–1302, Osprey Fortress 32 (Oxford, 2005); Carolingian Cavalryman AD 768–987, Osprey Warrior 96 (Oxford, 2005); Acre 1291, Osprey Campaign 154 (Oxford, 2005); The Third Crusade 1191, Osprey Campaign 161 (Oxford, 2005).

NIELEN, Marie-Adélaïde, Nouvelles preuves de l'histoire des vicomtes de Tripoli: tentative de reconstruction de la généalogie de la famille Visconte, in: Epeterida 30 (Nicosia, 2004), 23–38; Les réseaux familiaux dans les seigneuries de Gréce franque au XIIIᵉ siècle, in: 1204: La Quatrième croisade: éclats d'empire, Catalogue de l'exposition, ed. Inès Villela-Petit (Paris: Léopard d'Or, 2005), 87–96; Georges Chastellain, Philippe de Commynes, Jean Froissard, Guibert de Nogent, Guillaume de Nangis, Guillaume le Breton, Suger, Geoffroy de Villehardouin, Orderic Vital, in: Dictionnaire des Historiens, ed. Christian Amalvi (Paris: Boutique de l'Histoire, 2004).

NOBLE, Peter, Robert de Clari, La conquête de Constantinople, British Rencesvals Publications 3 (Edinburgh, 2006), 149pp.

O'MALLEY, Gregory, The Knights Hospitaller of the English Langue, 1460–1565 (Oxford: Oxford UP, 2005); Collective Image and Individual Insufficiency among the Hospitallers of the English Langue in the Fifteenth and Sixteenth Centuries, in: OM13, 81–89.

OMRAN, Mahmoud Said, Europe in the Middle Ages (Beirut/Lebanon, 2006), 472pp. [Arabic]; Historical Research Methodology and Medieval Sourcebook (Alexandria/Egypt, 2006), 344pp. [Arabic].

OTTEN, Catherine, Les Occidentaux dans les villes de province de l'empire byzantin: le cas de Chypre, in: Byzance et le monde extérieur, contacts, relations, échanges, ed. Michel Balard, Élisabeth Malamut and Jean-Michel Spiesser, Actes du 21ᵉ congrès international des études byzantines, Paris août 2001, Byzantina Sorbonensia 21 (Paris: Publ. de la Sorbonne, 2005), 27–44.

PARTNER, Peter D., Corsari e crociati: volti e avventure nel Mediterraneo (Torino: Einaudi, 2003), 229pp.

PAVIOT, Jacques, Le rêve d'un Empire latin d'Orient après 1261, in: 1204, la quatrième croisade, de Blois à ... Constantinople, éclats d'empires, catalogue d'exposition, Musée-Château de Blois et Bibliothèque nationale de France, Musée du cabinet des Médailles, octobre 2005 – Janvier 2006, red. Inès Villela-Petit, Revue française d'héraldique et de sigillographie 73/75 (2003/05), 161–167.

PHILLIPS, Jonathan, La quarta cruzada y el saco de Constantinopla (Madrid: Critica, 2005).

PIANA, Mathias, Konfrontation der Kulturen? Saladin und die Kreuzfahrer, Kolloquium am 4./5. November 2004 in den Reiss-Engelhorn-Museen Mannheim, Tagungsbericht, in: Kunstchronik 58 (2005), 277–281; Die Kreuzfahrerstadt Tortosa, in: Saladin und die Kreuzfahrer, Ausstellungskatalog 248–251; Kreuzfahrerarchitektur im Orient, Die Kreuz-fahrerstadt Tortosa (Tartus), Kathedrale von Tortosa (Tartus), Türstürze des Eingangsportals des Grabeskirche, Fragment eines Knotensäulenbündels, in: ibid. 395–397, 399–400.

POSPIESZNY, Kazimierz, Die Architektur des Deutschordenshauses in Preußen als Ausdruck- und Herstellungsmittel der Ordensmission und Herrscherpolitik, in: OM13, 227–241.

PURKIS, William J., Stigmata on the First Crusade, in: Signs, Wonders, Miracles: Representations of Divine Power in the Life of the Church, ed. Kate Cooper and Jeremy Gregory, Studies in Church History 41 (Woodbridge: Boydell & Brewer, 2005), 99–108.

RANDO, Daniela, Antitürkendiskurs und antijüdische Stereotypen: Formen der Propaganda im 15. Jahrhundert am Beispiel Trient, in: Osmanische Expansion und europäischer Humanismus, Akten des interdisziplinären Symposions vom 29. und 30. Mai 2003 im Stadtmuseum Wiener Neustadt, ed. Franz Fuchs, Pirckheimer Jahrbuch 20 (2005), 31–52.

RICHARD, Jean, National Feeling and the Legacy of the Crusades, in: The Crusades, ed. Helen Nicholson, Palgrave Advances (Basingstoke, 2005), 204–222; La quatrième croisade en son contexte, in: 1204, la quatrième croisade, de Blois à ... Constantinople, éclats d'empires, catalogue d'exposition, Musée-Château de Blois et Bibliothèque nationale de France, Musée du cabinet des Médailles, octobre 2005 – janvier 2006, red. Inès Villela-Petit, Revue française d'heraldique et sigillographie 73/75 (2003/05), 21–25; Au-delà de la Perse et de l'Arménie: l'Orient latin et la devouverte de l'Asie ultérieure, Quelques textes inégalement connus aux origines de l'alliance entre Francs et Mongols 1145–1262, Miroir du Moyen Âge (Turnhout: Brepols, 2005), 218pp.

RUBENSTEIN, Jay, Putting History to Use: Three Crusade Chronicles in Context, in: Viator 35 (2004), 131–168; What is the Gesta Francorum and Who was Peter Tudebode?, in: Revue Mabillon 16 (2005), 179–207.

RYAN, James D., The Choir Stalls of Toledo and the Crusade to Capture Granada, in: Bible de bois du Moyen Âge: Bible et liturgie dans les stalles médiévales, ed. Frédéric Billet (Paris: Édition L'Harmattan, 2003), 193–209; Missionary Saints of the High Middle Ages: Martyrdom, Popular Veneration and Canonization, in: Catholic Historical Review 90/1 (January 2004), 1–28.

SARNOWSKY, Jürgen, Hospitaller Brothers in Fifteenth-Century Rhodes, in: IMMO 48–58; Ritterorden als Landesherren: Münzen und Siegel als Selbstzeugnisse, in: OM13, 181–197.

SAVVIDES, Alexios, Latinokratia-Frankokratia after A.D. 1204 – Identical Terms? A Bibliographical Essay on the Early Centuries of Western Domination in Greek Lands, in: Byzantiaka 23 (Thessalonike, 2003 [2004]), 185–209 [Greek]; Seven Important Late Medieval Muslim Historiographical Sources (14th–15th Centuries) Regarding the Relations of the Oriental World with Byzantine Pontos of the Grand Komnenoi, in: Archeion Pontou 50 (Athens, 2003/04), 139–149 [Greek]; Essays on Ottoman History, 2nd edition (Athens: Papazesses, 2004), 301pp. [Greek]; The Foundation of the Mongol Empire, A.D. 1206–1294 (Athens: Iolcos, 2004), 146pp. [Greek]; Notes on the Ionian Islands and Islam in the Byzantine and Post-Byzantine Periods (Arab and Ottoman Raids), in: Journal of Oriental and African Studies 12 (Athens, 2004), 63–76; George Maniakes, Conquests and Undermining in 11th-Century Byzantium, A.D. 1030–1043 (Athens: Periplous, 2004), 94pp. [Greek]; Kos as an Early Basc and Starting Point of Nikephoros Melissenos' Sedition in 1080/81, in: Studies in Memory of Charis Kantzia (Athens: Greek Ministry of Culture, 2004), 397–404 [Greek]; Byzantine Diplomacy (with a bibliographical appendix on Byzantine diplomacy and diplomatics), in: Byzantinos Domos 14 (Thessalonike, 2004/05), 13–26 [Greek]; The Empire of Nicaea in a Diplomatic Tangel, A.D. 1213/14–1236/38, in: Byzantiaka 24 (2004 [2005]), 211–224 [Greek]; The Grand Komnenoi of Trebizond and the Pontos: An Historical Survey of the Byzantine Empire of Anatolia Hellenism (Athens: Epitrope Pontiakon Meleton, 2005), 282pp. [Greek]; Some Major Seljuk, Persian and Ottoman Sources regarding Byzantine-Seljuk Relations, in: Les Seldjoukides d'Anatolie, ed. G. Leiser, Mésogeios 25/26 (2005), 9–25; The Utopia of Expecting a Complete One-Volume Byzantine History Manual, in: Byzantion 75 (2005), 523–539.

SCHABEL, Christopher, ed. with Angel Nicolaou-Konnari, CyprusSoCu; Religion, in: ibid. 157–218; The Status of the Greek Clergy in Early Frankish Cyprus, in: "Sweet Land ...", Cyprus through the Ages: Lectures on the History and Culture of Cyprus (Camberley/Surrey: Porphyrogenita, 2005); The Myth of Queen Alice and the Subjugation of the Greek Church of Cyprus, in: Acts du Colloque "Identités croisées en un milieu méditerranéen: le cas de Chypre", ed. Sabine Fourrier and Gilles Grivaud (Rouen, 2005).

SCHMITT, Oliver Jens, Skanderbeg als neuer Alexander: Antikenrezeption im spätmittelalterlichen Albanien, in: Osmanische Expansion und europäischer Humanismus,

Akten des interdisziplinären Symposions vom 29. und 30. Mai 2003 im Stadtmuseum Wiener Neustadt, ed. Franz Fuchs, Pirckheimer Jahrbuch 20 (2005), 123–144.

SCHMITT, Reinhard, with Stefan Tebruck, Jenseits von Jerusalem: Spuren der Kreuzfahrer zwischen Harz und Elbe, Begleitheft zur Sonderausstellung "Saladin und die Kreuzfahrer" im Landesmuseum für Vorgeschichte in Halle (Halle/Saale, 2005), 228pp.

SHAGRIR, Iris, Personal Names in the Latin Kingdom of Jerusalem (Oxford, 2003); The Naming Patterns of the Inhabitants of Frankish Acre, in: Crusades 4 (2005), 107–116.

SHARON, Moshe, Vassal and Faal: The Evidence of the Farkhah Inscription from 608/1210, in: Crusades 4 (2005), 117–130.

SHEPARD, Jonathan, How St James the Persian's Head was Brought to Cormery: A Relic Collector around the Time of the First Crusade, in: Zwischen Polis, Provinz und Peripherie: Beiträge zur byzantinischen Geschichte und Kultur, ed. Lars M. Hoffmann and Anuscha Monchizadeh, Mainzer Veröffentlichungen zur Byzantinistik 7 (Wiesbaden: Harassowitz, 2005), 287–335.

SVOBODA, Miroslav, Postavení a správa patronátních kostelů johanitského řádu v předhusitských Čechách [Position and Administration of Hospitaller Churches in Pre-Hussite Bohemia], in: Časopis národního muzea – řada historická 174 (2005), 1–21.

STAHL, Alan M., Venetian Commerce in the Later Middle Ages: Feast or Famine, in: Medieval Cultures in Contact, ed. Richard F. Gyug (New York, 2003), 139–159.

STARNAWSKA, Maria, Das Bild der Kreuzherrn-Hospitaliterorden (der Chorherren des Heiligen Grabes, der Kreuzherren mit dem roten Stern, der Chorherren des Heiligen Geistes) auf polnischem Gebiet in der Frühen Neuzeit, in: OM13, 243–252.

STEFANIDOU, Alexandra, The Medieval Rhodes based on the Manuscript and Illustrations of Johannes Hedenborg (1854) (Thessalonike: Stamules, 2004), 128pp.

STERN, Eliezer, The Church of St John in Acre, in: Crusades 4 (2005), 157.

TESSERA, Miriam Rita, Dalla liturgia del Santo Sepolcro alla biblioteca di Sidone: note sulla produzione libraria latina di Oltremare nel XII–XIII secolo, in: Aevum 79 (2005), 407–415.

URBAN, William, Žalgiris ir kas po jo (Vilnius, 2004) [Lithuanian transl. of Tannenberg and After]; Kryžiaus karas Žemaitijoje (Vilnius, 2005) [Lithuanian transl. of The Samogitian Crusade]; A Teuton Lovagok (Budapest, 2005) [Hungarian transl. of The Teutonic Knights]; Krzyżacy (Warsaw, 2005) [Polish transl. of The Teutonic Knights].

VANN, Theresa M., The Exchange of Information and Money between the Hospitallers of Rhodes and their European Priories in the Fourteenth and Fifteenth Centuries, in: IMMO 34–47.

VOGEL, Christian, The Mobility of Templars from Provence, in: IMMO 114–129.

WEBER, Benjamin, La croisade impossible: étude sur les relations entre Sixte IV et Mathias Corvin (1471–1484), in: Byzance et ses périphéries: hommages à Alain Duceiller, ed. Bernard Doumerc and Chistophe Picard (Toulouse, 2004), 309–321.

WENTA, Jarosław, Der Deutschordenspriester Peter von Dusburg und sein Bemühen um die geistige Bildung der Laienbrüder, in: OM13, 115–125.

## 2. Recently completed theses

CLAVERIE, Pierre-Vincent, L'ordre du Temple en Terre sainte et à Chypre au XIII$^e$ siècle, PhD University Paris I – Sorbonne, 2004, supervised by Michel Balard.

DEMOSTHENOUS, Anthoulles, The Fantasy-Community of Byzantine Cyprus through the Writings of Neophytos the Recluse (1134–c.1214): Social Critique and Class-Differentiation of a Byzantine Saint, PhD, Aegean University, Rhodes-Greece, 2005 [Greek], supervised by Alexios Savvides.

FERGUSSON, Jack, Crusades as Anti-Heresy Strategy: The Cathar and Hussite Crusades, MA, History Dept., University of Canterbury, Christchurch, New Zealand, 2004.

FONNESBERG SCHMIDT, Iben, The Popes and the Baltic Crusades, 1147–1254, PhD, Cambridge, 2003.

GABRIELE, Matthew, *Imperator Christianorum*: Charlemagne and the East, 814 – ca. 1100, PhD, History, Berkeley, 2005.

GAT, Shimon, The City of Ramla in the Middle Ages, PhD, Bar-Ilan University, 2004, supervised by Yvonne Friedman and Joseph Drory.

GUTER, Yael, Aspects of Christian Pilgrimage to the Holy Land: The Pilgrim's Experience, PhD, Bar-Ilan University, 2005, supervised by Yvonne Friedman.

KOSTICK, Conor, The Language of *ordo* in Crusading Histories, 1096–1184, Trinity College, Dublin, 2005.

MITÁČEK, Jiří, Česká provincie řádu sv. Jana Jeruzalémského za vlády Lucemburků (1310–1419), University of Brno, 2005.

MPAIRAKTARES, Gregorios, The Greek Verses of Jelal al-Din Rumi and those of his Son, Sultan Veled, PhD, Aegean University, Rhodes-Greece, 2006, supervised by Alexios Savvides.

PHILLIPS, Simon D., The Role of the Prior of St John in Late Medieval England, c.1300–1540, PhD, University of Southampton, April 2005, supervised by Michael Hicks and Thomas Beaumont James.

PURKIS, William J., Crusade and Pilgrimage Spirituality, c.1095 – c.1187, PhD, Emmanuel College, Cambridge, supervised by Jonathan Riley-Smith.

SCHENK, Jochen, Family Involvement in the Order of the Temple in Burgundy, Champagne and Languedoc, c.1120–c.1307, PhD, Emmanuel College, Cambridge, supervised by Jonathan Riley-Smith.

SNYDER, Matt, God Willed It Too: Preparations of the Fourth Crusade by Those Who Participated in It, BA, Reed College, 2004.

STILES, Paula R., Christian and Non-Christian Templar Associates in the 12th and 13th Century Crown of Aragon, PhD, Dept. of Mediaeval History, University of St Andrews, November 2004.

### 3. Papers read by members of the Society and others

AMITAI, Reuven, Did Chinggis Khan have a Jewish teacher? An examination of a 14th-century Arabic text, at: Orientalisches Seminar der Rheinischen Friedrich-Wilhelms-Universität Bonn, 23 November 2004; Mongol provincial administration: Syria in 1260 as a case-study, at: Sonderforschungsbereich "Differenz und Integration", Martin-Luther-Universität Halle-Wittenberg, 26 November 2004; also at: Annual Meeting of the American Oriental Society, Philadelphia, 18 March 2005; The Islamization of the Mongols and theories of conversion, at: Institut für Islamwissenschaft der Freien Universität zu Berlin, 30 November 2004; also at: Baer Forum of the Israel Oriental Society, Tel Aviv University, 7 January 2005; From a nameless officer class to identified officers: the Mamluks in Palestine as seen from the epigraphic evidence, at: In honour of the appearance of volume 3 of the

"Corpus Inscriptionum Arabicarum Palaestinae" by Moshe Sharon, Institute of Asian and African Studies, The Hebrew University of Jerusalem, 29 December 2004; Between Europe and the Middle East: crusades then and now, at: The Middle East and the Eastern Mediterranean in the Aftermath of the War in Iraq, Yeditepe University, Istanbul, 8 April 2005; Buddhism in Iran under the Mongols, at: Fourth Annual Conference of Asian Studies in Israel, Jerusalem, 30 May 2005; Towards a pre-history of the Islamization of the Turks: a re-reading of Ibn FaĀlān's *Riḥla*, at: Islam in Central Asia, Institute for Advanced Studies, Nehemia Levtzion Center for Islamic Studies, The Hebrew University of Jerusalem, 16 June 2005; The Mongols in the Muslim world: confrontation, tolerance, conversion, at: Dschingis Khan und seine Erben: Das Weltreich der Mongolen, Kunst- und Ausstellungshalle der Bundesrepublik Deutschland, Bonn, 19 June 2005; The Mongol army of the Ilkhanate: long-term nomadic continuity in the midst of a sedentary society, at: Nomads versus Standing Armies in the Iranian World, 1000–1800, Institut für Iranistik, Österreichische Akademie der Wissenschaften, Wien, 5–6 December 2005; The ongoing refinement of Mamluk siege warfare: the conquest of Hisn al-Akrad (Crac des Chevaliers) in 1270, at: Castles and Towns of the Crusader Period in the Eastern Mediterranean, Braubach, Germany, 27–29 January 2006.

ANDREA, Alfred J., What remains to be said about relic thievery and the fourth crusade?, at: IMC Kalamazoo, 6–9 May 2004; The crusades in the context of world history, at: CLE-Seminar London, 21 February 2005; God wills it! The crusade in medieval and modern perspective, at: The Norbert Kuntz Lecture, Saint Michael's College, Winooski/VT, U.S.A., 23 March 2005; Just war, crusade and jihad in medieval perspective, at: Northern Kentucky University, 5 April 2005, and at: The University of Louisville, 7 April 2005; Teaching the crusades, at: A Teacher Institute Sponsored by Primary Source, Boston, 27 July 2005.

BALARD, Michel, The Black Sea in the international trade of the 14th and 15th centuries, at: Crimea at the Crossroads: Byzantine, Russian and Western influences across the Black Sea in the medieval and early modern periods, London, February 2005; Crociate e Giovanniti, at: Alle origini dell'Europa: l'Ordine dei cavalieri giovanniti, Lagopesole, June 2005; Le regard de l'Europe médiévale sur l'Orient, at: CISH Sydney; Il Mediterraneo crocevia di culture, at: Festival della Scienza, L'Acquario de Gênes, October 2005.

BALLETTO, Laura, Genova ed il Mediterraneo Orientale nel tardo medioevo, at: The Nautical Cities of Italy and the Eastern Mediterranean, Athens, 24 Mai 2005.

BARTOS, Sebastian, Bishops and dukes: negotiations of power in Little Poland, at: IMC Kalamazoo, 5–8 May 2005.

BELLOMO, Elena, Images of the Templar Order in the Middle Ages, at: Center for Medieval and Renaissance Studies, State University of New York, Binghamton, 17 April 2005.

BIRD, Jessalynn, Prophecy and the rhetoric of holy war: creating, maintaining, and justifying the identity and goals of the fifth crusade (1217–1221), at: Berkeley/CA, February 2005; Law and the crusaders: papal judges delegate and the negotiation, enforcement, and ramifications of crusaders' privileges in the early 13th century, at: Midwest Medieval History Conference, October 2005.

BISHOP, Adam, Violence in crusader law in the 12th century, at: Crusades: Medieval Worlds in Conflict, Saint Louis University, 18 February 2006.

BOMBI, Barbara, Celestine III and the conversion of the heathen on the Baltic Sea, at: IMC Leeds, 12–15 July 2004; Innocenzo III e la relazione sulle condizioni del Medio Oriente coevo, at: Fedi a contronto: Ebrei, Cristiani e Musulmani fra X e XIII secolo, Montaione, 22–24 September 2004; "Fishing for souls in the Baltic": mission to northern Europe in the early 13th century, at: CISH Sydney; International network of proctors: the Teutonic Knights, at: 2nd British-Scandinavian Colloquium of Church Historians, Lund, 8–10 September 2005; The Teutonic Order and its archives, at: Medieval Church and Culture, Harris Manchester College, Oxford, 31 January 2006; Le Crociate: nuove prospettive di ricerca, at: Seminario Internazionale di Studi, Rome, 16–17 March 2006.

BONNEAUD, Pierre, Un catalan en Rodas: Antoni de Fluvià, maestre del Hospital, 1421–1439, at: 7th Annual Congress of the Mediterranean Studies Association, Barcelona, 26–29 May 2004.

BOWLUS, Charles R., The Hungarians as mercenaries, at: conference on mercenaries, University of Wales, Swansea, 8–10 July 2005; The conversion of Bulgaria in a larger Eurasian context, at: conference on Slavic languages, Sofia, Bulgaria, 28–30 September 2005; Richard and the Bulgar Khan: an important essay on an ignored subject, at: conference in memoriam for Richard Sullivan, 10 December 2005, East Lansing/MI, U.S.A.; Zwischen Byzanz und dem Abendland: Mitteleuropa 600–1000, at: Historisches Seminar, Heidelberg, 17 January 2006.

BURGTORF, Jochen, The Templar Matthew Sauvage and Baybars: enemies and blood-brothers in the thirteenth-century Latin East, at: IMC Kalamazoo, 5–8 May 2005; Die Herrschaft der Johanniter in Margat im Heiligen Land, at: OM 2005.

BURNS, Robert I., Footprints of the conqueror: the registers of James I of Aragon, at: 34th Annual Convention, Society for Spanish and Portuguese Historical Studies, UCLA, 1–4 April 2004; Dogs of war in 13th-century crusader garrisons, IMC Kalamazoo, 6–9 May 2004; Perfil de una sociedad de frontera: el reino de Valencia de Jaime I, at: XVIII congreso de historia de la Corona de Aragon, Valencia, 9–14 September 2004.

CARLSSON, Christer, A new chronolgy for the Scandinavian branches of the military orders, at MO4; A research-excavation at the Teutonic comturi in Årsta: first results, at: OM2005.

CATLOS, Brian A., Perceived utility among individuals and organizations: *conveniencia* in medieval Iberia, at: Interrogating Iberian Frontiers: Cross-Disciplinary Approaches in Mudéjar History, Religion, Art and Literature, Cornell University, 13 November 2004; Towards a general theory of ethno-religious interaction: the case of medieval Iberia, at: UCLA California Medieval History Seminar, Huntingdon Library, Los Angeles, 26 February 2005; Marriage, foreign policy and the confessional frontier in medieval Iberia, at: IMC Kalamazoo, 5–8 May 2005; Impuestos e identidad: comunidades fiscales y confessionales en la Corona de Aragón, at: X Simposio Internacional de Mudejarismo, Teruel, Spain, 15 September 2005.

CHRISSIS, Nikolaos, Crusading in Romania: the aftermath of the 4th crusade in Byzantine-Western relations in the 13th century, at: Late Antique and Byzantine Studies Theses Workshop, Institute of Classical Studies.

CHRISTIE, Niall G. F., Conflict in the eastern Mediterranean: Byzantium and Islam, 635–717, at: Pharos: The Canadian Hellenic Cultural Society, Vancouver, February 2003; Preaching the divine plan: the *Kitab al-Jihad* of 'Ali ibn Tahir al-Sulami (d. 1106), at: 33rd medieval workshop "Noble Ideals and Bloody Realities: Warfare in the Middle Ages, 378–1492", University of British Columbia, Vancouver, October 2003; From distant barbarians to invading infidels: the "Franks" through Muslim eyes, 900–1169, at: Lanagara College / Vancouver Public Library lecture series, Vancouver, March 2004; The *Kitab al-Jihad* of 'Ali ibn Tahir al-Sulami: a progress report, at: 214th annual meeting of the American Oriental Society, San Diego, March 2004; Motivating listeners in the *Kitab al-Jihad* of 'Ali ibn Tahir al-Sulami (d. 1106), at: Crusading and Against Whom?, Middlebury College,

Middlebury/U.S.A., October 2005; The nature of Islam, at: The Newman Association, Vancouver, November 2005.

CIPOLLONE, Giulio, A historical overview of tolerance and respect between Christianity and Islam: theory and practice at the time of the crusades and jihad (XI–XIII centuries), at: CISH Sydney.

CLAVERIE, Pierre-Vincent, La marine du Temple dans l'Orient des croisades, at: 130ᵉ Congrès national des sociétés historiques et scientifiques "Voyage et voyageurs," La Rochelle, 21 April 2005; Une source méconnue sur la bataille de La Mansurah: la chanson de Guillaume Longue-Epée, at: HES, Leuven, May 2005; The relations between Cyprus and Auvergne at the time of the crusades, at: University of Cyprus, Nicosia, 19 September 2005.

COBB, Paul M., La vie religieuse des Banu Munqidh, 1080–1180: une famille musulmane entre les croisés et les sultans, at: Le Bilâd al-Shâm face aux mondes extérieurs (XIᵉ–XIVᵉ s.), Institut français du Proche-Orient, Damascus, 8 February 2005; On getting crusaded: Muslims and medieval holy war, at: Middle East Center, University of Pennsylvania, Philadelphia, 1 March 2006.

CORRIE, Rebecca W., Constantinople, Siena, and the Polesden Lacey triptych: an Angevin commission for a crusader empress, at: 28th Annual Byzantine Studies Conference, Ohio State University, Columbus/Ohio, 4–6 October 2002; Sicilian ambitions renewed: Byzantine painting and Aragones kingship, at: IMC Kalamazoo, 6–9 May 2004; The Polesden Lacey triptych and the presence of Greek painters in late medieval Italy, at: Symposium in honor of Ernst Kitzinger, Dumbarton Oakes, Washington/DC, 5 March 2005.

COSGRAVE, Walker Reid, Crucesignatus: a refinement or one more term among many?, at: Crusades: Medieval Worlds in Conflict, Saint Louis University, 15–18 February 2006.

COUREAS, Nicholas S., Commerce between Mamluk Egypt and Hospitaller Rhodes in the mid-fourteenth century: the case of Sidi Galip Ripolli, at: 14th HES, May 2005; Mamluks in the Cypriot chronicle of George Boustronios and their place within a wider context, at: 3rd Medieval Chronicles International Conference, University of Reading, July 2005; The migration of Syrians and Cypriots to Hospitaller Rhodes in the 14th and 15th centuries, at: MO4.

CRAWFORD, Paul F., *Quid pro quo? Gerard of St. Victor and the Templars, at: MO4.

DEMIRKENT, Isin, Birinci, İkinci, Üçüncü Haçlı Seferlerinin Anadolu'dan geçişi hakkında [In relation with the transition of the first, second and third crusades through Anatolia], at: Boğaziçi Üniversitesi Tarih ve Kültür Vakfi, İstanbul Üniversitesi Tarih Bölümü, İtsanbul, 18 May 2005; Kudüs Haçli Krallığında Devlet İdaresi [Statecraft in the Crusader Kingdom of Jerusalem], at: Tarih Boyunca Saray, Hayatı ve Teşkilâtı Semineri, İstanbul, 23 May 2005; Fetih Öncesinde Bizans 'ın Durumu [The Status of Byzantium in the Pre-Conquest Era], at: Yeniden Müdafaa-i Hukuk Hareketi Derneği, İstanbul, 29 May 2005.

DODD, Erica Cruikshank, The Syrian style in Mar Musa al-Habashi, at: Netherlands Institute for the Near East, Leiden University, Damascus, May 2004; Evidence for a Syrian style in the medieval Mediterranean, at: Index of Christian Art and International Society of Medieval Art Historians, Princeton University, October 2004; Sources from Outremer in the Development of Western medieval art, at: Interactions: Artistic Interchange between the Eastern and the Western Worlds in the Medieval Period, Princeton Index of Christian Art, April 2005.

DOUROU-ELIOPOULOU, Maria, Allusions of the fourth crusade in Latin sources of the 13th and 14th centuries, at: The Fourth Crusade, Andros, 27–30 May 2004; Western institutions in the principality of Achaea, at: The Peloponnese after the Fourth Crusade (1204), Mystras, 1–3 October 2004; The Albanians in Romania according to Latin Sources of the 13th and

14th centuries, at: 9th International Congress of South-East European Studies, Tirana, 30 August–3 September 2004; Latin presence in Romania and its process of Hellenisation, at: SSCLE-Sydney; Latin colonialism in the eastern Mediterranean during the crusades, at: CISH Sydney; The Latins in Peloponnese after the fourth crusade: the example of the barony of Patras, at: 7th International Congress of Peloponnesian Studies, Pyrgos, 12–19 September 2005; Latin settlement in Romania after the fourth crusade, at: 4th Congress of the Greek Heraldic and Genealogical Society, Athens, 4–6 November 2005.

EDBURY, Peter W., The crusades and their critics, Nicosia, January 2005; John of Ibelin, Philip of Novara and the French William of Tyre: exploring French vernacular texts from the crusader kingdom of Jerusalem, at: Swansea University, March 2005, Bristol University, October 2005.

EKDAHL, Sven, The Teutonic Order's mercenaries during the "Great War" with Poland-Lithuania (1409–11), at: conference on mercenaries, University of Wales, Swansea, 7–10 July 2005; Heliga Birgitta, slaget vid Tannenberg och grundandet av klostret Triumphus Mariae i Lublin, at: University of Lund, together with the Polish-Scandinavian Research Institute, Copenhagen, 16–17 September 2005; The turning-point in the battle of Tanneberg (Grunwald/Žalgiris) in 1410, at: Lithuanian Academy of Sciences, Vilnius, 4 October 2005 [inauguration lecture]; The siege machines of the military orders during the Baltic crusades, at: 10th Conference on Medieval Arms and Armour, Łódź, 3–4 November 2005.

FOLDA, Jaroslav, Crusader art and the East: Eurasian contacts, at: Interactions, Symposium at the Index of Christian Art, Princeton University, 8–9 April 2005.

FOREY, Alan, *Milites ad terminum* in the military orders during the 12th and 13th centuries, at: MO4; A Templar lordship in northern Valencia in the late 13th and early 14th centuries, at: OM2005.

FRIEDMAN, Yvonne, Peace processes between Muslims and Christians in the Middle East during the crusader period, at: IMC Kalamazoo, 6–9 May 2004; Gestures of conciliation, at: Institute of Historical Research, London, 21 May 2005; Peacemaking processes between Muslims and Christians in the Latin kingdom of Jerusalem, at: CISH Sydney.

GABRIELE, Matthew, The *Descriptio qualiter Karolus Magnus* and the origins of the first crusade, at: Midwest Medieval Conference, Knoxville, 8 October 2004; Charlemagne and Jerusalem: the afterlife of Einhard's *Vita Karoli* and the *Annales regni Francorum* to 1100, at: IMC Kalamazoo, 5–8 May 2005; The legend of Charlemagne and the survival of Christendom, at: University of California, Berkeley, 20 January 2006; Some early evidence of Charlemagne's legendary dominion over the East, at: Medieval Academy of America, Boston, 30 March 2006.

VON GUTTNER SPORZYNSKI, Darius, Relic or relevant: the Knights of Saint John, at: 15th Biennial Conference of the Australasian Association of the European History, Melbourne, 11–15 July 2005; Polish historiography on the Crusades, at: MO4; The crusades: beyond a definition, at: Polish Czech Medievalists Forum, Gniezno, 26–29 September 2005.

HARRIS, Jonathan, Constantinople as city state, 1369–1453, at: Unities and Disunities in the Late Medieval Eastern Mediterranean World, University College, Oxford, March 2005.

HOLMES, Catherine, Shared world: a question of evidence?, at: Unities and Disunities in the Late Medieval Eastern Mediterranean World, University College, Oxford, March 2005.

HOLT, Andrew P., The lure of the Orient: sexual propaganda during the crusades, at: IMC Kalamazoo, 6–9 May 2004; "The snare of the devil": women, sin, and crusades propaganda, at: Bette Soldwedel Gender Research Center, Jacksonville/FL, 12 April 2005; Virtue and vice: contrasting portrayals of Muslim and Christian women in crusades propaganda, at:

Southwestern Medieval Association, 31st Annual Meeting, Daytona Beach/FL, September/ October 2005; "Sinful Women" and the defeat of the crusaders, at: Southern Historical Association: European History Section, Annual Conference, Atlanta/GA, November 2005; The saints at war: sin and saints in crusade propaganda during the siege of Antioch, at: New College Conference on Medieval and Renaissance Studies, Sarasota/FL, March 2006.

IRWIN, Robert, The crusades and the arrest of the advance of Islamic civilization, at: Jerusalem, November 2004; Jerusalem in late medieval Islamic spirituality and culture, at: The Eastern Mediterranean in the Late Middle Ages, Oxford, March 2005.

JENSEN, Kurt Villads, European and Scandinavian crusades in the middle of the twelfth century – similarities and differences in the mental world of Bishop Henry, at: Kristinusko Soumessa Kaukainen menneisyys ja nykyinen yhteiskunta, organized by Suomen kirkkohistoriallisen seuran, Helsinki, 19 January 2005; Crusading elites in North and South around 1100 and around 1200, at: Les élites nordiques et l'Europe occidentale (XII$^e$–XV$^e$ siècle), organized by Toumas M. S. Lehtonen and Élisabeth Mornet, Société de littérature finlandaise, Institut finlandais de Paris and Université Paris I – Laboratoire de médiévistique occidentale de Paris, Paris, 9 June 2005; War and peace in the High Middle Ages – Ideological obligations of Christian rulers, at the workshop: Religion and State Formation: Medieval Europe in Comparative Perspective, Central European University, 7 March 2006.

JUBB, Margaret A., The relationship between text and image in manuscripts of the *Estoires d'Outremer et de la naiccsance Salehadin* and the Ernoul-Bernard *abrégé*, at: Medieval Chronicles Conference, University of Reading, 15–19 July 2005.

KEDAR, Benjamin Z., Rashi's map of the land of Canaan, ca. 1100, and its cartographic background, at: Cartography in Antiquity and the Middle Ages, University of British Columbia, Vancouver, 28–29 October 2005; Un santo venuto da Gerusalemme: Ranieri da Pisa, at: I santi venuti dal mare, Bari – Brindisi, 14–17 December 2005.

KOSTICK, Conor, *Iuvenes* on the first crusade, at: IMC Leeds, July 2005; Re-interpreting the youth: *iuvenes* in Robert the Monk and Albert of Aachen, at: Borderlines VIII, Dublin, 2005.

LOUD, Graham A., Tipologie della disciplina monastica nell'Italia meridionale tra XI e XII secolo, at: Centro Europeo di Studi Normanni, Ariano Irpino, Italy, October 2005.

MADDEN, Thomas F., The crusades and the modern world, at: 2004 Phi Beta Kappa Keynote Address, Saint Louis University, 22 April 2004; Medieval and modern perspectives on the crusader conquest of Constantinople in 1204, at: 2005 Distinguished Lecture, Institute for Medieval Studies, University of New Mexico, 30 March 2005; The fourth crusade and historical memory, at: IMC Kalamazoo, 5–8 May 2005.

MENACHE, Sophia, The reputation of Don Alonso de Aragon, at: SSCLE-Conference Istanbul, 25–30 August 2004; Chronicles, narratives, and historiography: the interrelationship of text and context, at: The Medieval Chronicle, Reading, 2005; Fighting for the monarchy or against the infidel? The military career of Don Alonso de Aragon, at: OM 2005.

MESCHINI, Marco, Rileggere la quarta crociata, at: Fedi a confronto: ebrei, cristiani e musulmani fra X e XIII secolo, Centro Internazionale di studi La Gerusalemme di San Vivaldo, 22–24 September 2004; 1204: né caso, né complotto, at: IV crociata: rapporti tra Oriente e Occidente, Istituto di studi ecumenici San Bernardino, Venezia, 4 November 2004; "Pro negotio crucesignatorum": Innocenzo III e il sostegno della guerra santa, at: Cruce de miradas sobre la guerra santa: guerra, religion e ideologia en el espacio mediterraneo latino (siglos XI–XIII), Casa de Velazques – FRAMESPA, Toulouse – CRHIA, Nantes – SIREM, CNRS, Madrid, 11–13 April 2005.

MITCHELL, Piers, Archaeological evidence for disease and medicine in the crusades, at: Medicine and Disease in the Crusades, University College London, January 2005; A comparison of child health in a medieval farming village and castle in the crusader kingdom of Jerusalem, at: Paleopathology Association, Milwaukee, April 2005; Healing pilgrimages to Christian religious shrines in the eastern Mediterranean at the time of the crusades, at: American Assosciation for the History of Medicine, Alabama, April 2005; A comparison of health at a village and castle in the kingdom of Jerusalem during the twelfth century, at: MO4.

NICOLAOU-KONNARI, Angel, Genoa: external politics and internal strife, at: National Hellenic Research Foundation, Athens, 24 May 2005; Lingusitic Construction of Group Awareness in Lusignan Cyprus (13th–15th centuries): the example of literary languages and ethnic names, at: Ethnicity and Prejudice in Pre-Modern Europe, organized by S. Barber and Andrew Jotischky, Lancaster University, Dept. of History, 14–15 September 2005.

NICOLLE, David, Warfare in the medieval Islamic World, at: Dept. of Archaeology, Damascus University, June 2005.

NIELEN, Marie-Adélaïde, Guillaume de Tibérida, un itinéraire en Orient, at: Seminar of Christophe Picard, 13 January 2006.

O'MALLEY, Gregory, The English Hospitallers and Mediterranean trade, at: MO4.

OMRAN, Mahmoud Said, New intellectual dimensions of historical research methodology, at: 1st Annual Conference on Literary Criticism, Crisis in the Methodology of Studies, The Humanities, Faculty of Arts, University of Alexandria/Egypt, 22–27 November 2005.

PHILLIPS, Christopher Matthew, Crucified with Christ: the imitation of the crucified Christ and crusading spirituality, at: Crusades: Medieval Worlds in Conflict, Saint Louis University, February 2006.

PHILLIPS, Simon D., The prior of St John in late medieval England, at: History Research Seminar, University of Winchester, February 2003.

PIANA, Mathias, Zur Wasserversorgung von Kreuzfahrerburgen, at: Internationales Frontinus-Symposium Wasserversorgung auf Burgen des Mittelalters, Blankenheim/ Germany, 6–9 October 2005.

POWELL, James M., St. Francis of Assisi's way of peace, at: IMC Kalamazoo, 6–9 May 2004; Following sources: a seminar, at: University of Tennessee, Marco Center, October 2004.

PURKIS, William J., Disciplining Iberian arms-bearers: first thoughts on the development of crusading in Spain, at: 44th Conference of the Ecclesiastical History Society, Lancaster University, 21 July 2005; Pilgrimage, religious poverty and the military orders, at: MO4; Jerusalem, Compostela, and the early development of crusading in Iberia, at: CLE-Seminar, London, 21 November 2005.

ROCHE, Jason T., Byzantine literary representations of the 12th century "barbarian" crusader, at: Outsider Conference, Stirling University, March 2004; Anatolia and the second crusade: who clashed with Louis VII?, at: IMC Leeds, July 2004; Conrad III and the second crusade: retreat from Dorylaion?, at: SSCLE-Conference, Boğaziçi Üniversitesi, Istanbul, August 2004; Conrad III and the Greek sources for the second crusade: errors, omissions and flawed assumptions, at: IMC Leeds, July 2005; Conrad III and the second crusade: Dorylaion reconsidered, at: CLE-Seminar, London, December 2005.

RYAN, James D., Missionaries, crusaders and martyrs in early 13th century Spain, at: IMC Kalamazoo, 6–9 May 2004.

RYAN, Laurent, Kings need not apply? Innocent III, Richard the Lionheart and preliminary preparations for the fourth crusade, at: Midwest Medieval History Conference, University of

Tennessee, Knoxville, October 2004; "Appeased by the prayer of my mother, I shall be merciful to the Franks": the Virgin and Marian devotion in the chroniclers of the first crusade, at: Medieval Association of the Pacific, San Francisco State University, San Francisco, March 2005.

SCHABEL, Christopher, Peter of Candia and the reaction to Duns Scotus on Divine Foreknowledge, at: International Workshop on Peter of Candia, the Last Greek Pope, Alexander V, University of Cyprus, Nicosia, 23–24 April 2005; with William Duba and Eftychia Zachariadou, The historical context of the Cistercian convent of St Theodore in Nicosia, at: Cyprus-American Archaeological Research Institute, Nicosia, 18 May 2005; Antelmus the Nasty (1205–41): new information on the first archbishop of Patras, at: SSCLE-Symposium "From the West to the Holy Land in the Age of the Crusades," University of Sydney Centre for Medieval Studies, Sydney, 1 July 2005; Greeks, Latins, and the quarrel over the Eucharist in Frankish Cyprus, at: CISH Sydney, 4 July 2005.

SCHENK, Jochen, Family networks in the Temple, at: CLE-Seminar, 20 March 2006.

STAHL, Alan M., The Sterling abroad, at: Haskins Society Conference, Washington/DC, November 2005; Michael of Rhodes: a medieval mariner in service to Venice, at: The World of Michael of Rhodes, Debner Institute for the History of Science and Technology at MIT, December 2005.

STILES, Paula R., New wine in old bottles: oral tradition and the written rule in the Iberian Temple, at: IMC Leeds, July 2005.

STRUCKMEYER, Myra, The hospital of Saint John, the bedroom of caritas, at: MO4.

VAN WINTER, Johanna Maria, Crusades and sugar, at: MO4.

## 4. Forthcoming publications

ALVIRA CABRER, Martín, Pedro el Católico, Rey de Aragón y Conde de Barcelona (1196–1213): Documentos, Testimonios y Memoria Histórica [including transcription of PhD thesis 1932 of M. Á. Ibarra y Oroz], 2–3 vols. (Zarazoza, 2006); Rebeldes y herejes vencidos en las fuentes cronísticas hispanas (siglos XI–XIII), in: El cuerpo derrotado: cómo trataban musulmanes y cristianos a los enemigos vencidos, Península Ibérica, ss. VIII–XIII, Instituto de Filología, CSIC Madrid 30 June – 1 July 2005, ed. M. Fierro and F. García Fitz (2006); Dal *Sepulcro* y los sarracenos meridionales a los herejes occidentales: apuntes sobre tres "guerras santas" en las fuentes del sur de Francia (siglos XI–XIII), in: Cruce de miradas sobre la guerra santa: Guerra, religión e ideología en el espacio mediterráneo latino, siglos XI–XIII, Casa de Velázquez 11–13 april de 2005, ed. D. Baloup and Philippe Josserand (2006); Les itinéraires du roi Pierre II d'Aragon (septembre 1212 – septembre 1213), in: Montaillou, mémoire pyrénéenne: II Colloque International historique et archéologique de Montaillou 4–6 août 2004 (Cahors: L'Hydre, 2006); with Damian J. Smith, Política antiherética en la Corona de Aragón: una carta inédita de Inocencio III a la reina Sancha (1203), in: Acta Mediaevalia (Barcelona, 2006); Sobre la denominación *Albigenses* en las fuentes hispanas del siglo XIII, in: Religión, Etnia y Nación: II Congreso de Historia de la Iglesia en España y el Mundo Hispánico, CSIC Madrid 18–20 October 2001 (2006).

AMITAI, Reuven, Did the Mongols in the Middle East Remain Nomadic Pastoralists?, in: Conditions of Pastoral Mobility, ed. Günther Schlee and Anatoly Khazanov; Mongol Provincial Administration: Syria in 1260 as a Case-Study, in: Festschrift in honour of Benjamin Z. Kedar, ed. Iris Shagrir, Ronnie Ellenblum and Jonathan Riley-Smith; The Mamluk State and its Relations to Jerusalem, in: The History of Jerusalem: The Mamluk Period, ed. Joseph Drory and Yvonne Friedman (Jerusalem: Yad Itzhaq Ben-Zvi); A Mongol

Governor of al-Karak in Jordan?: A Re-Examination of an Old Document in Mongolian and Arabic, in: Zentralasiatische Studien.; Ayn Jālūt, in: EI.

EL-AZHARI, Taef, The Muslim Perspective of the Fourth Crusade, in: Crusades 5 (2006); The Career of Balak the Artukid, in: Annals of Japan Association of Middle East Studies (2006).

BALARD, Michel, Latins in the Near East, 11th–15th Centuries [book].

BALLETTO, Laura, Il mondo del commercio nel *Codex Comanicus*: alcune riflessioni, in: Atti del Colloquio Internationale *Il Codice Cumanico e il suo mondo* (Venezia); Da Pera a Genova dopo la conquista di Costantinopoli (1453), in: Miscellanea in onore di Carme Battle (Barcelona); Greci a Genova dopo la conquista turca di Costantinopoli, in: Geschehenes und Geschriebenes. Studien zu Ehren von Günther S. Heinrich und Klaus-Peter Matschke, ed. S. Kolditz and R. C. Müller (Leipzig, 2005); Battista di Felizzano e Domencio di Novara fra Genova ed il Vicino Oriente a metà del Quattrocento, in: Societdad y memoria en la Edad Media. Estudios en homenaje de Nilda Guglielmi (Buenos Aires, 2005).

BARBER, Malcolm, The Trial of the Templars, 2nd edition (Cambridge UP, 2006).

BELLOMO, Elena, The Order of the Temple in North-west Italy (1142–middle 14th Century), Medieval Mediterranean (Brill) [book]; The Templar Order in North-western Italy: A General Picture (1142–1312), in: MO3; L'Ordine del Tempio in Italia nord-occidentale (1142–1308): problemi, riflessioni e nuovi indirizzi di ricerca, in: I Templari in Italia, ed. C. Guzzo, introduction by Malcolm Barber, Quaderni di Sacra Militia 3 (Genova: Name Editori).

BEREND, Nora, The Expansion of Latin Christendom, in: The Short Oxford History of Europe (2006).

BIRD, Jessalynn, Paris Masters and the Justification of the Albigensian Crusade, in: Crusades 5 (2006).

BOMBI, Barbara, ed. with G. Andenna, Oliviero di Colonia, La quinta Crociata (Milano, 2006); Novella plantatio fidei: Missione e crociata nel nord Europa tra XII e XIII secolo (Roma: Istituto storico italiano per il medio evo, 2006); The *Dialogus miraculorum* of Caesarius of Heisterbach as a Source for the Livonian Crusade, in: Power and Authority, ed. Brenda Bolton and C. M. Meek (Turnhout: Brepols, 2007).

BONNEAUD, Pierre, Catalan Hospitallers in Rhodes in the First Half of the Fifteenth Century, in: IMMO; Los Hospitalarios catalanes en la primera mitad del siglo XV, in: Actes de les Primeres Jornades de Genealogia I Heràldica dels Països Catalans (Barcelona, 2006).

BOWLUS, Charles R., Mobility, Politics, and Society in Medieval Germany, in: German Literature of the High Middle Ages, ed. Will Hasty, Camden History of German Literature (February 2006); The Battle of Lechfeld and Its Aftermath, August 955: The End of the Age of Migrations in the Latin West (Aldershot: Ashgate, May 2006).

CHRISTIE, Niall G. F., ed. with Maya Yazigi, Noble Ideals and Bloody Realities: Warfare in the Middle Ages (Leiden: Brill, 2006); Religious Campaign or War of Conquest? Muslim Views of the Motives of the First Crusade, in: ibid.; Abbasids, Arabic Sources, caliph al-Hakim, 'Imad al-Din Al-Isfahani, 'Ali ibn Tahir Al-Sulami, caliphate, Homs, Ibn al-Qalanisi, Ibn Shaddad, Ibn Wasil, Kamal al-Din, Nur al-Din, Shi'ites, Sibt ibn al-Jawzi, Sunni Islam, Zangi, for EncycCru; Crusades, in: Medieval Islamic Civilization: An Encyclopedia, ed. Josef Meri (New York: Routledge, 2006).

CLAVERIE, Pierre-Vincent, La perception des musulmans dans l'œuvre d'Héthoum de Korykos, in: HES (Louvain, 2006); Notes sur la mort de saint Louis et les finalités de sa croisade, in: ibid.; Un *illustris amicus Venetorum* du début du XIII^e siècle: l'évêque Nivelon de Quierzy et son temps, in: Atti del Convegno internazionale di studi su Quarta Crociata: la partecipatione europea, le reazioni, la risonanza, 5–6 maggio 2004, ed. G. Ortalli (Venice: IVSLA, 2006); Les remembrements épiscopaux dans la Syrie franque, in: L'espace du diocèse à l'époque médiévale, ed. F. Mazel (Rennes: Presses University, 2006); L'image de l'Islam dans les traductions vernaculaires de Guillaume de Tyr, in: Festschrift Prof. Dr. Urbain Vermeulen: Traditions and Changes in the Realms of Islam, ed. A. van Tongerloo (Louvain: Peeters, 2006).

COBB, Paul M., Infidel Dogs: Hunting Crusaders with Usama ibn Munqidh, in: Crusades (2007?); Islam and the Crusades: Usama ibn Munqidh and Ibn Jubayr (Harmondsworth: Penguin, 2008?).

CORRIE, Rebecca W., The Virgin Mary in Art, in: Women and Gender in Medieval Art, ed. Margaret Schaus (Routledge, autumn 2006); 3 entries on crusader icons for an exhibition, Getty Museum (fall 2006).

COUREAS, Nicholas S., Controlled Contacts: The Papacy, the Latin Church of Cyprus and Mamluk Egypt, in: Egypt and Syria in the Fatimid, Ayyubid and Mamluk Eras 4, Proceedings of the 9th, 10th and 11th HES, ed. Urbain Vermeulen (Leuven: Peeters, 2004); The Role of Cyprus in provisioning the Latin Churches of the Holy Land in the 13th and early 14th centuries, in: ibid.; Commercial Relations between Cyprus and Mamluk Egypt and Syria with special reference to Famagusta and Nicosia in the 15th and 16th centuries, in: 12th HES; The Copts in Cyprus during the 15th and 16th centuries, in: 13th HES; A Political History of Nicosia, in: A History of Nicosia, ed. D. Michaelides (Nicosia, 2005); An Ecclesiastical History of Nicosia, in: ibid.; The Development of Nicosia as the Judicial Centre of Lusignan Cyprus, in: Cyprus Research Centre Annual Review 31 (Nicosia, 2005); Apple of Concord: The Great Powers and Cyprus from 400 AD onwards, in: Kypriakai Spoudai 68 (2003/04 [Nicosia, 2005]); articles on Sinai, Cyprus, Catherine Cornaro, Nicosia, Limassol, Paphos and Kerynia for EncycCru; Punishments and Imprecations in the Cypriot Monastic Rules and how they compare with those in other Orthodox Monastic Rules [in Greek], in: Epeteris tes Kypriakes Hetaireias Historikon Spoudon (Nicosia, 2006).

CRAWFORD, Paul F., The Trial of the Templars and the University of Paris, in: MO3; articles for EncycCru and for the New Westminster Dictionary of Church History, ed. Christopher Ocker (Westminster: Knox, 2006).

CUSHING, Dana, An Anonymous German Crusader's Voyage to the Reconquista: De Itinere Navali, Dallas Medieval Texts in Translation (University of Dallas, 2007).

DANSETTE, Béatrice, with É. Deluz, edition and French transl. of the Peregrinatio in Terram Sanctam of Bernhard von Breidenbach (1486).

DODD, Erica Cruikshank, Byzantine Silver Stamps, in: Cahiers archéologiques 92/1; Jerusalem: Fons et Origo, in: Princeton Index of Christian Art.

DONDI, Cristina, Gerusalemme e gli ordini militari: liturgia e santo, in: Amadeus, special issue ed. Giacomo Baroffio (December 2005); Liturgical Policies of the Hospitallers between the Invention of Printing and the Council of Trent: the Evidence of the Early Printed Breviaries and Missals, in: MO3; Liturgy, in: DOM.

DOSTOURIAN, Ara, Armenia and the Crusades: The Chronicle of Matthew of Edessa, transl. and commentary, 2nd edition, paperback.

EDBURY, Peter W., Ramla: The Crusader Town and Lordship (1099–1268), for a collection of studies on Ramla, ed. Denys Pringle; British Historiography on the Crusades and Military Orders: from Barker and Smail to Contemporary Historians, in: Runciman–Conference; Crusader Sources from the Near East, in: Byzantium and the Crusades: the non-Greek

Sources (1025–1204), ed. M. Whitby; The Suppression of the Templars in Cyprus, 1307–1312, in: St John Historical Society Proceedings; The French Translation of William of Tyre's *Historia*: the Manuscript Tradition, in: Crusades 6 (2007); The Old French William of Tyre and the Origins of the Templars, for a festschrift.

EDGINGTON, Susan B., Pagans and "Others" in the *Chanson de Jerusalem*, in: Languages of Love and Hate (Brepols); A Female Physician on the Fourth Crusade? Laurette de Saint-Valery, in a festschrift; Albert of Aachen, Historia Ierosolimitana, edition and transl., Oxford Medieval Texts (2006); The Crusaders Write Home: the Experience of the First Crusade as Described in Participants' Letters, in: Segundas Jornadas Internacionales sobre la Primera Cruzada, ed. Luis García-Guijarro Ramos (Zaragoza); Crusader Chronicles: Revisions and Additions to the Nineteenth-Century Texts, in: Runciman–Conference; entries on Albert of Aachen, Chanson d'Antioche, De Expugnatione Lyxbonensi, Excidium Acconis, Fulcher of Chartres, Holy Sepulchre, Hospital of St John (Jerusalem), Christian Martyrdom, Medicine, Motivation, Peter Tudebode, Raymond of Aguilers, Teutonic Source, Thadeus of Naples, Walter the Chancellor, Western Sources, for EncycCru; La Chanson d'Antioche, transl. and commentary with Carol Sweetenham (Aldershot: Ashgate, 2007).

EHLERS, Axel, Die Ablaßpraxis des Deutschen Ordens im Mittelalter, Quellen und Studien zur Geschichte des Deutschen Ordens (Marburg: Elwert, 2006) [book]; entries on Indulgence, Anno de Sangershausen, Paul de Rusdorf, Albrecht de Brandenbourg, for DOM.

EKDAHL, Sven, The Battle of Tannenberg-Grunwald-Žalgiris (1410) as Reflected in Monuments of the Twentieth Century, at: MO3; Christianisierung – Siedlung – Litauerreise: Die Christianisierung Litauens als Dilemma des Deutschen Ordens, in: Christianisierung Litauens im mitteleuropäischen Kontext, ed. Romualdas Budrys and Vydas Dolinskas (Vilnius: Lithuanian Art Museum, 2006); The Teutonic Order's Mercenaries during the "Great War" with Poland-Lithuania (1409–11), in: Mercenaries and Paid Men: The Mercenary Identity in the Middle Ages, ed. John France (Leiden: Brill, 2006); Heliga Birgitta, slaget vid Tannenberg och grundandet av klostret Triumphus Mariae i Lublin, in: Östersjönationernas relationer och ömsesidiga kulturpåverkan, med fokus på Skandinavien och Polen, ed. Barbara Törnqwist-Plewa and Eugeniusz S. Kruszewski (Lund, 2006); The Siege Machines of the Military Orders during the Baltic Crusades, in: The Invaders and their Weapons in Antiquity and the Middle Ages, ed. Witold Świętosławski, Fasciculi Archaeologiae Historicae 16 (Łódź: Institute of Archaeology and Ethnology of the Polish Academy of Sciences, Lodz Branch, 2006); Verträge des Deutschen Ordens mit Söldnerführern aus den ersten Jahrzehnten nach Grunwald, in: Quaestiones Medii Aevi Novae vol. 11: Militaria, ed. Jan Szymczak (2006); entries for EncycCru.

FOLDA, Jaroslav, East Meets West: The Art and Architecture of the Crusader States, in: Companion to Medieval Art, ed. Conrad Rudolph (Oxford: Blackwells, 2006).

FOREY, Alan, Desertions and Transfers from Military Orders (12th to early 14th Centuries), in: Traditio 60 (2005).

GABRIELE, Matthew, Against the Enemies of Christ: The Role of Count Emicho in the Anti-Jewish Violence of the First Crusade, in: Christian Attitudes toward the Jews in the Middle Ages: A Casebook, ed. Michael Frassetto (New York: Routledge, 2006).

GRABOIS, Aryeh, Acre as Seen by French-Writing Pilgrims in the Thirteenth Century, in: Crusader Acre (Jerusalem) [Hebrew]; Image and Reality of the Holy Land in the Descriptions of the Fourteenth-Century Pilgrims, in: Proceedings of the Pilgrimage Conference, Cork, Ireland; Les pèlerinages du XIᵉ siècle dans la chronographie occidentale contemporaine, in: Revue d'Histoire Ecclesiastique.

HARRIS, Jonathan, Collusion with the Infidel as a Pretext for Military Action against Byzantium, in: Clash of Cultures: the Languages of Love and Hate, ed. Sarah Lambert and Liz James (Turnhout: Brepols, 2006/07); Introduction, in: Chronology of the Byzantine Empire, ed. Timothy Venning (Basingstoke: Palgrave/Macmillan, 2006); Greek sources, Manuel II, John V, Bessarion, Paul II, Innocent VIII, for EncycCru; Constantinople: The Queen of Cities (Hambledon/London, 2007).

HOCH, Martin, Hattin, battle (1187), for EncycCru.

HOLMES, Catherine, Constantinople in the reign of Basil II, in: Byzantine Style, Religion and Civilisation: In Honour of Sir Steven Runciman, ed. E. Jeffreys (Oxford); Treaties between Byzantium and the Islamic World, in: War and Peace in Antiquity and the Medieval World, ed. P. de Souza (Cambridge).

HOLT, Andrew P., Crusades Scholarship from the Enlightenment to the Present, and Medieval Historical Studies, in: Handbook of Medieval Studies: Concepts, Methods, and Trends in Medieval Studies, ed. Albrecht Classen (Berlin: de Gruyter).

HOUSLEY, Norman, Indulgences for crusading, 1417–1517, in: Promissory Notes on the Treasury of Merits: Indulgences in the Late Middle Ages, ed. R. N. Swanson (Leiden: Brill, 2006).

HUNT, Lucy-Anne, Christian Art in the 13th Century: Cultural Convergence between Jerusalem, Greater Syria and Egypt, at: Ayyubid Jerusalem: The Holy City in Context, 1187–1250, ed. S. Auld and L. Hillenbrand (London, 2006); The Art of Outremer and Cyprus, Melisende Psalter, for EncycCru; Byzantium – Venice – Manchester: Study of some Little-Known Sculpture, in: Byzantine Style, Religion and Civilisation: In Honour of Sir Steven Runciman, ed. E. M. Jeffreys (Cambridge: UP, 2006); Oriental Orthodox Iconographic and Architectural Traditions, in: The Blackwell Companion to Eastern Christianity, ed. K. Parry (Oxford: Blackwell's, 2006); Artistic Interchange in Old Cairo in the 13th – early 14th Centuries: The Role of Painted and Carved Icons, in: Artistic Exchange between the Eastern and the Western Worlds in the Medieval Period, ed. C. Honishare, Proceedings of the Index of Christian Art Conference, Princeton University, 8–9 April 2005; The Bible in Arabic, in: The Bible in Arabic, Proceedings of the 5th Wordbrokke-Megara Conference, Birmingham, 14–17 September 2005 (Leiden: Brill, 2006).

HUYGENS, Robert B. C., Editorisch Verfehltes zum Hospital von Jerusalem, in: Deutsches Archiv (2005).

IRWIN, Robert, For Lust of Knowing: The Orientalists and their Enemies (London: Allen Lane, January 2006); An Introduction to a Re-Issue of Hamilton Gibb's The Life of Saladin (Saqi Books, winter 2005); Petrarch and "that rabid dog Averroes," in: Re-Orienting the Renaissance: Cultural Encounters with the East, ed. Gerald Maclean (Palgrave, autumn 2005).

JACKSON, Peter, Hulegu, Ilkhans, Mongke, Mongols, for EncycCru.

JASPERT, Nikolas, Forgotten Brethren – Historiography on the Non-Military Orders and Congregations of the Crusader States (in print); Carlomagno y Santiago en la memoria histórica catalana (in print); Alfons I of Aragon, Alfons IV of Aragon, Aragón, Arnau de Torroja, James I of Aragon, Montegaudio, Ramon Berenguer IV, Reconquista, Tortosa, True Cross, for EncycCru.

JUBB, Margaret A., Saladin in the Continuation of the *Chanson de Jérusalem*, in: British Branch of the Société Rencesvals (2005/06).

KEDAR, Benjamin Z., Some Reflections on Maps, Crusading and Logistics, in: Proceedings for the conference "The Logistics of Crusading," Sydney 2002, ed. John Pryor (Ashgate,

February 2006); I due *Montes Gaudii* di Gerusalemme, in: Proceedings of the conference "La Puglia tra Gerusalemme e Santiago di Compostella", Bari 2002, ed. Maria Stella Calò Mariani [in press]; The Fourth Crusade's Second Front, in: Urbs capta; Ramla: The Evidence of World War I Aerial Photographs, in a volume on the history and archaeology of Ramla, ed. Denys Pringle; with Reuven Amitai, Franks in the Eastern Mediterranean, 1047, in a volume of Marco Tangheroni; ed. with Nicolas Faucherre, an issue of the "Bulletin Monumental" on "Saint Louis en Terre Sainte" (2006); The Size of Frankish Jaffa, in: ibid.

LOUD, Graham A., History Writing in the Twelfth-Century Kingdom of Sicily, in: Chronicling History in Medieval Italy, ed. S. Dale, A. Williams Lewin and D. Osheim (Penn State Press, 2006); Amalfi, Arnold of Lubeck, Conrad III, Frederick Barbarossa, Gregory VIII, Otto of Freising, The Pilgrimage of Henry the Lion, Roger I of Sicily, Roger II of Sicily, Sicily and the Crusades, for: EncycCru.

MADDEN, Thomas F., Food and the Fourth Crusade: A New Approach to the "Diversion Question", in: Logistics of Warfare in the Age of the Crusades, ed. John Pryor (Ashgate, 2006); Boniface of Montferrat, Enrico Dandolo, Fourth Crusade, Domenico Michiel, Venetian Crusade of 1112, Venice and the Crusades, Treaty of Venice, Zara, for EncycCru.

MARVIN, Laurence W., The Massacre at Beziers, July 22, 1209: A revisionist View, in: Dissent and Persecution: R. I. Moore and Heresy in the Middle Ages (Brill, 2006).

MESCHINI, Marco, Validità, novità e carattere della decretale «Vergentis in senium» di Innocenzo III (25 marzo 1199), in: Bulletin of Medieval Canon Law 25 (2002/03 [2006]); Innocenz III. und der Kreuzzug als "Mittel" im Kampf gegen die Häresie, in: Deutsches Archiv für Erforschung des Mittelalters (2006); Innocenzo III e il «negotium pacis et fidei» in Linguadoca (1198–1215) (Roma, 2006).

MITCHELL, Piers, Child Health in the Crusader Period Inhabitants of Tel Jezreel, Israel, in: Levant; with Y. Nagar and Ronnie Ellenblum, Weapon Injuries in the 12th Century Crusader Garrison of Vadum Iacob Castle, Galilee, in: International Journal of Osteoarchaeology; with J. Huntley and E. Sterns, Bioarchaeological Analysis of the 13th Century Latrines of the Crusader Hospital of St. John at Acre, Israel, in: MO3; entries on Disease, War Injuries, for EncycCru; The Infirmaries of the Order of the Temple in the Medieval Kingdom of Jerusalem, in: The Medieval Hospital and Medical Practice: Bridging the Evidence, ed. B. Bowers (Ashgate); The Torture of Military Captives during the Crusades to the Medieval Middle East, in: Noble Ideals and Bloody Realities: Warfare in the Middle Ages, 378–1492, ed. N. Christie and M. Yazigi (Brill); Challenges in the Study of Health and Disease in the Crusades, in: Diachronic Patterns in the Biology and Health Status of Human Populations of the Eastern Mediterranean, ed. M. Faerman (Oxford: Archaeopress); Trauma in the Crusader Period City of Caesarea, a Major Port in the Medieval Eastern Mediterranean, in: International Journal of Osteoarchaeology; Medicine, in: Oxford Dictionary of the Middle Ages, ed. R. E. Bjork (Oxford UP).

MURRAY, Alan, Money and Logistics in the Armies of the First Crusade: Coinage, Bullion, Service and Supply, 1096–99, in: Logistcs of Warfare in the Age of the Crusades, ed. John Pryor (Ashgate, 2006); Kingship, Identity and Name-Giving in the Family of Baldwin of Bourcq (2007); Barschaft und Beute: Komposition und Entstehung des "Barbarossa-Schatzes" im Umfeld des Dritten Kreuzzugs, in: Vom Umgang mit Schätzen, ed. Elisabeth Vavra and Thomas Kühtreiber.

NICOLAOU-KONNARI, Angel, Giorgio de Nores, Della legittima successione al Regno di Cipro, ed. with introduction, comments, and appendices, Cyprus Research Centre (Nicosia, 2006).

NICOLLE, David, The Military Artefacts, in: Final Report on the Late Mamluk Finds Uncovered during the Franco-Syrian Excavations in the Citadel of Damascus (IFPO Beirut); with Viacheslav Shpakovsky, Armies of Ivan the Terrible: Russian Troops 1505–1700 (Osprey, 2006); A Medieval Islamic Arms Cache (Cairo University); Byzantine, Western European, Islamic and Central Asian Influence in the Field of Arms and Armour from the 7th to 14th Century AD (Cambridge University); Crusader Castles in Cyprus, Greece, the Aegean & Black Seas, 1191–1522 AD (Osprey Fortress 2006/07); Islamic art, Arms and Armour before 1500, in: Dictionary of Art; Ayn Jalut, al-Mansura 1221, al-Mansura 1250, Muslim Armies, Arms and Armour, Lake Peipus 1242, Siege Warfare, Warfare in Greece, Warfare in Iberia, Saladin and the Art of War, for EncycCru; The Normans, Osprey World of the Warriors, reprint.

O'MALLEY, Gregory, The English Knights Hospitaller and the Reformation, in: Ritterorden und Reformation, ed. Johannes A. Mol, Helen Nicholson and Jürgen Sarnowsky (2006).

OTTEN, Catherine, Les actes du notaire génois Antonio Foglietta passés à Famagouste (milieu XVᵉ siècle), Cyprus Research Centre.

PARTNER, Peter D., Pope Alexander VI.

PAVIOT, Jacques, ed., Projets de croisade, fin XIIIᵉ s.–début XIVᵉ s., Documents relatifs à l'historie des croisades (Paris: Académie des Inscriptions et Belles-Lettres, 2006); ed. with Philippe Contamine, Philippe de Mézières, Epître lamentable et consolatoire sur le croisade de Nicopolis (Paris: Société de l'histoire de France, 2006).

PIANA, Mathias, with Hans Curvers, The Castle of Toron (Qal'at Tibnīn) in South Lebanon: Preliminary Results of the 2002/2003 Campaigns, in: Bulletin d'Archéologie et d'Architecture Libanaises 8 (2004); Burgen und Städte der Kreuzzugszeit im östlichen Mittelmeerraum (Petersberg: Imhof, 2006); The Crusader Castle of Toron: First Results of its Investigation, in: Crusades 5 (2006).

POWELL, James M., St. Francis of Assisi's Way of Peace (University of Minnesota).

PURKIS, William J., Elite and Popular Perceptions of *imitatio Christi* in Twelfth-Century Crusade Spirituality, in: Elite and Popular Religion, ed. K. Cooper and J. Gregory, Studies in Church History 42 (Woodbridge: Boydell & Brewer, 2006).

ROCHE, Jason T., Niketas Choniates as a Source for the Second Crusade in Anatolia, in a festschrift for Prof. Isin Demirkent (Ankara, 2006).

SAVVIDES, Alexios, Notes on Byzantine-Norman Relations in the Period prior to the Norman Invasions (till A.D. 1081), in: The Ancient World, Festschrift for John Fossey (Montreal, 2005); The Empire of Trebizond and the Importance of the Study of its History: The Sources and the Diachronic Development of Research, in: Archeion Pontou 52 (Athens, 2006); Queen Tamara – Thamar of Georgia (Iberia): A Medieval Semiramis of the Caucasus, in: Historika Themata (Athens, 2006); with Nikolaos Nikoloudes, The Late Medieval World, 11th–15th Centuries (Athens: Herodotos, 2006) [Greek]; entries for EncycCru and Encyclopaedic Prosopographical Lexicon of Byzantine History and Civilization, vols. 5–6 (Athens: Metron-Iolcos, 2006) [Greek].

SCHABEL, Christopher, with Nicholas Coureas and Gilles Grivaud, The Capital of the Sweet Land of Cyprus: Frankish and Venetian Nicosia, in: A History of Nicosia, ed. Demetrios Michaelides (Nicosia, 2006); with Gilles Grivaud, Nicosie, in: Camille Enlart, L'art gothique et la renaissance en Chypre, ed. Alain Erlande-Brandenberg (Paris: Académie des Inscriptions, 2006); Attitudes toward the Greeks and the History of the Filioque Dispute in 14th-Century Oxford, in: Acts of the Andros Conference on the Fourth Crusade, ed. E. Chrysos et al. (Paderborn: Schöningh, 2006).

SEEBERG-SIDSELRUD, Kaare, The roll of arms of the Catholic hierarchy of the Nordic countries post-Reformation (University Press of Southern Denmark).

SHEPARD, Jonathan, ed., The Cambridge History of the Byzantine Empire (Cambridge, 2006/07), with contributions relating to the crusades by M. Angold, P. Magdalino, P. Stephenson, David Jacoby, Michel Balard, Angeliki Laiou and others.

STEFANIDOU, Alexandra, The Cannons of the Medieval City of Rhodes based on the Manuscript and Illustrations of J. Hedenborg, in: Proceedings of the 6th International Conference on Greek Research, Flinders University, Adelaide/Australia, June 23–26 2005 (2006); Byzantium: Children's Books and the Illustrators from the Past and Today, in: Proceedings of the Pedagogical Society of Greece (2006); The Island of Chalki based on the Texts and Iconography of Travellers, in: Neohellenica 1 (2006).

STILES, Paula R., Arming the Enemy: Non-Christians' Roles in the Military Culture of the Crown of Aragon during the Reconquista, in: Noble Ideals and Bloody Realities (Leiden: Brill, 2006).

UPTON-WARD, Judi M., ed., MO4.

URBAN, William, The Samogitian Crusade, 2nd edition, much enlarged and revised (Chicago: Lithuanian Research and Studies Center, 2005).

WEBER, Benjamin, Encore sur la lettre de Pie II à Mehmed II: conversion, croisade et oeucuménisme à la fin du Moyen Âge, in: Crusades (2007/8?).

## 5. Work in progress

ALVIRA CABRER, Martín, with Laurent Macé, Los Sellos de Pedro el Católico, Rey de Aragón y Conde de Barcelona (1196–1213) [book]; with Laurent Macé and Damian J. Smith, La Grande Couronne d'Aragon du roi Pierre II (1213): une évidence documentaire, in: Annales di Midi (Toulouse) [article]; with Laurent Macé and Florent Laborie, L'itinéraire du roi Pierre II d'Aragon en 1204 [article].

AMITAI, Reuven, The Military History of the Mamluk Sultanate.

ANDREA, Alfred J., Jihad and Crusade, Key Themes in World History series (Pearson Prentice Hall Publishers).

BALARD, Michel, Spices in the Middle Ages [book].

BARBER, Malcolm, The Crusader States in the 12th Century (Yale UP) [book].

BELLOMO, Elena, The Order of Montjoie in North-west Italy; The Letter of Jobert, Master of the Hospital, to the Citizens of Savona; Crusade and Diplomacy in the Early Fourteenth Century Mediterranean: The Savonese Franciscan Filippo Brusserio; see also Bulletin 23, 2003.

BIRD, Jessalynn, The "History of the West" (Historia Occidentalis) of Jacques de Vitry (Liverpool UP) transl. with critical introduction and notes; Women and the Crusades (London Books); with Edward Peters and James Powell, Christian Society and the Crusades, 1198–1274 (University of Pennsylvania Press) a sourcebook; manuscript tradition and influence of Jacques de Vitry's Historia Orientalis.

BISAHA, Nancy, An intellectual biography of Pope Pius II, with special attention to his views on the Turks and crusading.

BONNEAUD, Pierre, Els Hospitallers catalans a la fí de la Edat Mitjana, 1396–1472 (2007) [book].

BOWLUS, Charles R., Mitteleuropa: The Making of Europe between Byzantium and the Latin West ca. 800–1025, in: Paradigms and Methods in Late Ancient and Early Medieval Studies:

A Reconsideration, ed. Celia Chazelle and Felice Lifshitz (under consideration by Palgrave Macmillan).

BURNS, Robert I., Diplomatarium regni Valentiae, vol. 4 (Princeton UP) [finished, going into publication].

CARR, Annemarie Weyl, with Andreas Nicolaides, Asinou [book]; Pursuing the Life of an Icon: The Virgin of Kykkos.

CHRISTIE, Niall G. F., with Deborah Gerish, The Sermons of Urban II and the *Kitab al-Jihad* of 'Ali ibn Tahir al-Sulami, edition, transl., and study [book].

CIPOLLONE, Giulio, Retrospettiva culturale della tolleranza nella documentazione tra Papato e Islam nel Medioevo (on behalf of the Gregoriana Pontifical University, Rome, and al-Azhar, Cairo).

CLAVERIE, Pierre-Vincent, The Oriental Policy of Pope Honorius III (1216–1227) [book].

CORRIE, Rebecca W., Conradin Bible; Arezzo Manuscripts as Art on Political Frontiers; Images of Virgin and Child between Tuscany and the East [books]; Siena and Byzantine Imagery, for: College Art Association; Arezzo and Byzantine and Crusader Sources, for: IMC Kalamazoo, May 2006; Polesden Lacey Triptych and Sterbini Diptych, for Byzantine congress, London 2006.

COBB, Paul M., Lords of Shayzar: A Medieval Muslim Family in the Age of the Crusades, ca. 1050–1250.

COUREAS, Nicholas S., The Latin Chruch in Cyprus 1313–1378; The Life of Peter Thomas by Philippe de Mézières, transl. into English, Cyprus Research Centre [books].

CRAWFORD, Paul S., articles on crusade-related topics for ABC-Clio's World History Encyclopedia, ed. Alfred Andrea; see also previous Bulletins.

DEMIRKENT, Isin, Niketas Khoniates'in Historia'si (1180–1195) [The History of Niketas Khoniates (1180–1195)]; Antakya Haçlı Devleti Tarihi [The History of the Principality of Antioch].

DODD, Erica Cruikshank, The Double-Naved Church in the Lebanon; Inscriptions in the Mosque of the Wazir Khan, Lahore; Byzantine Silver Stamps, revised edition, including 75 vessels with stamps discovered since the publication of 1962.

DOUROU-ELIOPOULOU, Maria, see Bulletin 22 (2002); with Nikoletta Giantsi, The Institutions, the Social Welfare and the Economy in the Mediterranean in the Age of the Crusades (12th–15th Centuries) [research programme]; From Western Europe to the Eastern Mediterranean during the crusades: Latin Settlement in Romania [book].

EDBURY, Peter W., A critical edition of Philip de Novara, *Livre de forme de plait*; further work on the Old French William of Tyre; The Third Crusade [book]; with E. Walker, transl. of the *Chronique d'Amadi*; Celestine III and the Crusades [article].

EDGINGTON, Susan B., *Regimen sanitatis* of Guido da Vigevano, edition and commentary.

EHLERS, Axel, The use of vow redemptions by the military orders.

FOLDA, Jaroslav, Crusader Art [an introductory book for the general reader].

FOREY, Alan, The Papacy and the Spanish Reconquest; Marriage and Sexual Relations between Western Christians and Outsiders in the Crusading Period; Western Converts to Islam in the Crusading Period.

FRIEDMAN, Yvonne, Interludes of Peace: Peace Processes between Muslims and Franks in the Latin East.

GABRIELE, Matthew, The Legend of Charlemagne and the Origins of the First Crusade.

VON GUTTNER SPORZYNSKI, Darius, Transmission of the idea of crusade to Poland and the subsequent Polish experience of crusading 11th and 12th centuries; Polish understanding and response to the crusading call; Cardinal Hubald's Charter of 1146 for the Canons Regular in Trzemeszno; Henry, Duke of Sandomierz; Piast Dynasty.

HAMILTON, Bernard, The Crusades and the Wider World (London Books).

HOUSLEY, Norman, Experiencing the Crusades (Yale UP, December 2007) [book].

IRWIN, Robert, Circassian Mamluk History; History of Orientalism.

JACKSON, Peter, The Seventh Crusade, 1244–1254: Sources and Documents, Crusade Texts in Translation series (Ashgate, 2007).

JORDAN, William Chester, Comparative study of the relations between Westminster Abbey and the English crown and Saint-Denis and the French crown in the 13th century.

JUBB, Margaret A., Text and Image in Manuscripts of Crusader Texts, principally the *Eracles* and the Crusade Epics.

KEDAR, Benjamin Z., A cultural history of the kingdom of Jerusalem [book]; Hebron, 1119 [article]; The Battle of Arsuf, 1191 [article].

KRÜGER, Jürgen, Architectural history of the hospital of the Order of the Hospitallers in Jerusalem.

LOUD, Graham A., The Latin Church in Norman Italy (Cambridge UP, September 2006).

MADDEN, Thomas F., Memory and the crusader conquest of Constantinople in 1204.

MAIER, Christoph T., see Bulletin 25 (2005).

MENACHE, Sophia, Jacques de Molay, the Last Master of the Temple: A Reconsideration.

MESCHINI, Marco, La prima crociata contro gli albigesi (1207–1215) [book].

MITCHELL, Piers, Palaeopathological study of crusader period health at Blanchegarde Castle (Tel Safi) in Israel; Palaeopathological study of a crusader period cess pool in Acre.

MURRAY, Alan, Prostitution in the First Crusade [article]; The Crusade of Frederick Barbarossa.

NICOLLE, David, Warfare in the Crusader World (Hambledon); Atlas of Ottoman History (Thalamus); Armament, Equipment, Archers, Banniere, Escadon, Pietons, for EncycCru; Archery, for EI³; with M. Alvira Cabrer, Las Navas de Tolosa 1212, Osprey Campaign; The Hospitallers, Osprey World of Warriors; Horse-Armour from Roman to Medieval Times in the Middle East and Europe [article]; research for the Royal Jordanian Institute for Furusiyya; contributions to the Encyclopedia of the History of the Philosophy of War and Strategy; Dating and Provenance of a Recently "Rediscovered" Cache of 13th–14th Century Mamluk Military Equipment and Horse-Harness in Damascus.

NIELEN, Marie-Adélaïde, participation à un projet de programme archéologique à Tyr (Liban), présenté par l'UMR 5189, HISOMA, Maison de l'Orient et de la Méditerranée, Lyon, France.

NOBLE, Peter, Baldwin of Flanders and Henry of Hainault as Military Commanders; translations of Villehardouin and Henri de Valenciennes.

O'MALLEY, Gregory, Officials and Servants of the Order of St John in Britain and Ireland.

OTTEN, Catherine, History of Famagusta under the Lusignan.

PHILLIPS, Simon D., Fighting for the Faith? The Military Role of the Hospitaller Prior in Late Medieval England [article]; with Richard Brown of QAA Gloucester, Secularisation in Pre-Reformation England: The Bishopric of Winchester and the Hospitallers [article]; Prior and Sire: The Knights Hospitaller Prior in Late Medieval England, 1272–1540 [book].

RICHARD, Jean, with Christopher Schabel, Bullaire de Chypre, lettres pontificales 1316–1378; entries for DOM.

ROCHE, Jason T., Turkish tactics employed against the second crusade [article].

RUBENSTEIN, Jay, History and Holy War: The Legacy of the First Crusade in 12th Century Europe.

RYAN, James D., Two related reform orders of secular canons in the 15th century, one in Italy and one in Portugal, The Secular Canons of St. John the Evangelist, playing a part in Portuguese involvement in the Congo and in Asia, an expansion seen as part of the larger effort to outflank the Turks and recover the Holy Land.

SAVVIDES, Alexios, Georgios Kedrenos, The Undervalued Byzantine Chronicler: A Bibliographical Note [Greek]; A Note on the 13th-Century Byzantine Chronicler Theodore Skoutariotes and the Synopsis Chronike [Greek].

SCHABEL, Christopher, St Theodore Abbey, Nicosia: A Cistercian Monastery of Women; Martyrs and Heretics, Intolerance of Intolerance: The Azymo Dispute and the Execution of 13 Greek Monks in Cyprus in 1231; with Jean Richard, Bullarium Cyprium: Papal Letters Involving Cyprus 1196–1378, Texts and Studies in the History of Cyprus, 3 vols. (Nicosia: Cyprus Research Centre, 2007/08); with William Duba, Bullarium Hellenicum I: Pope Honorius III's Letters Involving Frankish Greece (Leiden: Brill).

SEEBERG-SIDSELRUD, Kaare, The Sonnenburg collection of coats-of-arms of members of the Order of St. John – Ballei Brandenburg, spanning the period c.1600–1920, with the hope of publishing the complete collection of 1140 paintings.

SHAGRIR, Iris, The Breviary of the Holy Sepulchre, ms. of Santo Sepolcro di Barletta.

STAHL, Alan M., with Pamela O. Long and David McGea, The Book of Michael of Rhodes, edition and transl. with studies of a 15th century Venetian maritime manuscript (MIT Press, 2007).

STEFANIDOU, Alexandra, The Coats-of-Arms of the Medieval City of Rhodes based on the Manuscript and Illustrations of Johannes Hedenborg, 1854.

TESSERA, Miriam Rita, with Marco Petoletti, Monachus of Caesarea's The Expugnata Accone liber tetrastichus, critical edition, Italian transl. and commentary [book]; The Papacy and the Latin Kingdom of Jerusalem in the 12th Century [book]; Amalric I's Dream and the True Cross sent to Clairvaux Abbey [article].

TOKO, Hirofumi, Byzantium, in: A Companion to the History of the Mediterranean World.

URBAN, William, Medieval Mercenaries; Three Chapters on Crusades in the Baltic.

## 6. Theses in progress

BISHOP, Adam, PhD, Centre for Medieval Studies, University of Toronto.

CARLSSON, Christer, The Religious Orders of Knighthood in Medieval Scandinavia 1291–1536, PhD, University of Southern Denmark, Odense.

CARRIER, Marc, L'image des Byzantins et les systèmes de représentation selon les chroniqueurs occidentaux des croisades 1096–1261, PhD, University Paris I Sorbonne.

CHRISSIS, Nikolaos, Crusading in Romania: A Study of Byzantine-Western Relations and Attitudes, 1204–c.1282, PhD, Royal Holloway, University of London, supervised by Jonathan Harris.

DANSETTE, Béatrice, Les pèlerins occidentaux en Terre Sainte, XIII$^e$ – XVI$^e$ siècle, Habilitation, supervised by Michel Balard.

VON GUTTNER SPORZNSKI, Darius, Crusading in Poland: Its Idea, Reception and Experience, 1102–1298, PhD, University of Melbourne.

IKONOMOPOULOS, Konstantinos, The Influence of the Orthodox Patriarchate of Jerusalem on the Launching of the First Crusade, MPhil, PhD, University of London, supervised by Jonathan Harris.

KARTSEVA, Tatiana, Latin East in a Dialogue of Medieval Civilizations, PhD in Culturology, Russian State Humanitarian University, Moscow.

MAIOR, Balazs, The Medieval Settlement Pattern of the Syrian Littoral, 11th to 13th Centuries, PhD, Cardiff University, supervised by Denys Pringle.

MILLIMAN, Paul Richard, Disputing Identity, Territoriality, and Sovereignty: Constructing Historical Memory in Medieval Poland and the Teutonic Ordensstaat, PhD, Cornell University

O'SULLIVAN, Rhiain, The Principality of Antioch, 1136–1192, PhD, Queen Mary, University of London.

PELEG, Peter S., Emperor Frederick II and the Military Orders, PhD, Haifa University, supervised by Sophia Menache.

PERRA, Photeine, The Venetian-Ottoman Antagonism for the Conquest of the Helladic Area (1463–1503): The First Two Venetian-Ottoman Wars and the Southeastern Mediterranean World, PhD, Aegean University, Rhodes-Greece, supervised by Alexios Savvides.

PETRO, Theodore D., Returning Crusaders in the 12th Century, PhD, University of Cincinnati.

PHILLIPS, Christopher Matthew, "O magnum crucis misterium": Devotion to the Cross, Crusading and the Imitation of the Crucified Christ in the High Middle Ages, c.1050–c.1215, PhD, Saint Louis University, supervised by Thomas Madden.

PORRO, Clive, The Order of Christ in 14th Century Portugal, PhD, Queen Mary, University of London, supervised by Thomas Asbridge.

ROCHE, Jason T., Conrad III and the Second Crusade: Anatolia Reconsidered, PhD, University of St Andrews.

RYAN, Vincent, The Virgin and the Cross: The Crusaders, Marian Devotion, and the Expansion of the Cult of the Virgin in the Medieval West, PhD, Saint Louis University.

STRUCKMEYER, Myra, Female Hospitallers in the High Middle Ages, PhD, University of North Carolina at Chapel Hill.

WAGNER, Thomas, Krankheiten und Krankenversorgung zur Zeit der Kreuzzüge: Epidemien, Verwundetenpflege, historische Krankheitsbilder, PhD, University Würzburg.

WEBER, Benjamin, Lutter contre les Turcs: les formes nouvelles de la croisade pontificale au XV<sup>ème</sup> siècle, PhD, University de Toulouse le Mirail.

NN, The Chronicles of al-Kamil by Ibn al-Athir: A Comparative Study on the Crusades, 1097–1230, PhD, Faculty of Education and Arts, Buraida, Saudi Arabia, supervised by Taef el-Azhari.

## 7. Fieldwork planned or undertaken recently

CARLSSON, Christer, research-excavation at the Teutonic Order commandery of Årsta, Sweden.

DODD, Erica Cruikshank, spent the summer of 2005 in Syria and Lebanon, covering medieval paintings, including those that have been discovered since the publication of Medieval Painting in the Lebanon in 2004.

MENACHE, Sophia, relations between medieval monarchs and the military orders, especially royal attempts to interfere in the elections of masters, comparative research of developments in the Iberian Peninsula as against England and France, prior and after the suppression of the Temple.

MITCHELL, Piers, has been to Syria, Egypt and Israel to research pilgrimage centres regarded as sources of healing by pilgrims in the crusader period, and he has done research at Bar-Ilan University, Israel, to study crusader period human skeletal remains excavated from Blanchegarde Castle (Tel Safi).

PIANA, Mathias, 4th campaign of survey and excavation on the castle of Toron/Qal'at Tibnīn, April/May 2006.

ROSEN-AYALON, Myriam, excavations at Khirbat al-Minya.

## 8. News of interest to members

### a) Conferences and seminars

2005 January 25: Piers Mitchell organised the conference "Medicine and Disease in the Crusades" at University College, London. The meeting was funded by a grant from The Wellcome Trust. Guest speakers from Britain, France, Germany, Israel and the USA discussed the evidence for ill health and medical treatment in the military expeditions and resulting Frankish states established in the East. Papers were presented by medical historians, crusades historians and palaeopathologists. Over fifty people attended, and all appreciated the multidisciplinary approaches employed to investigate the topic.

2006 January 27–29: Castles and Towns of the Crusader Period in the Eastern Mediterranean / Burgen und Städte der Kreuzzugszeit im Vorderen Orient, an international symposium at Castle Marksburg near Braubach/Germany. Contact: mathias.piana@phil.uni-augsburg.de Programme: www.deutsche-burgen.org/crusader.pdf

2006 February 15–18: An international symposium "Crusades: Medieval Worlds in Conflict" held at Saint Louis University by Thomas F. Madden. Plenary lectures included Jonathan Riley-Smith (Cambridge), Carole Hillenbrand (Edinburgh), and Jaroslav Folda (North Carolina). Lectures were delivered during the late afternoon and evening of 15–17 February. A full day of sessions of 20-minute papers was presented on 18 February. For more information see http://crusades.slu.edu

2006 June 22–25: The World History Association annual conference in Long Beach, California. For further information, consult the WHA's website www.thewha.org or e-mail the conference organizer Alfred J. Andrea at aandrea@uvm.edu

2007 May 3–6 and July 9–12, IMC Kalamazoo and Leeds: As 2007 will be the 700th anniversary year of the arrest of the Templars, Helen Nicholson, Paul Crawford and Jochen Burgtorf will organise sessions on the trial of the Templars. Themes may include (but are not limited to) the religious, political and social context of the trial, the papacy, royalty, biography of individual participants, regional aspects, procedural aspects, the aftermath of the trial, the historiography of the trial, both contemporary and later, and fictional writing about the trial. While the language of both conferences as well as of the intended publication will be English, it will be possible to submit papers in French, German, Spanish, Italian, Portuguese, or Dutch.

## b) Other news

Since the autumn of 2004, Reuven Amitai has been director of the newly founded Nehemia Levtzion Center for Islamic Studies at the Hebrew University. In the summer of 2006 he will be in Ulaan Baatar, Mongolia, for the conference of the International Assosciation of Mongolian Studies.

Andrew P. Holt is the editor, originator and author of www.crusades-encyclopedia.com, a work in progress offering references to over 800 subjects concerning the crusading movement. A secondary purpose is to offer trustworthy external links to hundreds of articles, sources, and other material concerning the crusading movement. The project is anticipated to be completed sometime in 2007.

Ideata e curata da Marco Meschini, la versione italiana dell'opera di Jean Richard, La grande storia delle crociate, è stata pubblicata nella Collana dedicata al Medioevo del quotidiano Il Giornale, 50 volumi, 1 uscita settimanale a partire dalla fine di agosto del 2005, e ha venduto oltre 500.000 copie.

The MA in Crusader Studies run by the History Departments of Royal Holloway, University of London and Queen Mary, University of London has a new website giving details of the course and associated talks, seminars and events, www.crusaderstudies.org

Burgen und Basare / Castles and Bazaars, an exhibition prepared by the International Castle Research Society, Aachen/Germany, shown from 5 November 2005 through 26 February 2006 at the Archaeological Museum in Frankfurt/Main (Germany). Main objects are two large-scale models of the Crac des Chevaliers and of a section of the Bazaar of Aleppo. The exhibition was shown from 3 April through 4 September 2006 at the Museum of the National Geographic Society in Washington/DC.

Paul Crawford reports that the Syrian Antiquities Department is preparing a full survey of Margat (Marqb) Castle, with publication of the plans to follow.

Alexios Savvides reports that in 2006 an English edition of the Encyclopaedic Prosopographical Lexicon of Byzantine History and Civilization, of which he is editor since 1996 (Athens: Metron-Iolcos, so far 4 vols., 1996–2002 [Greek], will commence by Brepols, Tournhout, with Prof. Benjamin Hendricks of Johannesburg University, South Africa, and Assistant Prof. Alicia Simpson, Koc University, Istanbul, as coeditors. Vols. 1–2 of the English edition, expected in 2006 and 2007, will cover entries from A to E, including several personages directly or indirectly connected with the crusades, especially the first four crusades. New entries from letter F onwards will be allocated in 2006 for vol. 3 (F, G, H, I and J) of the English edition, expected in 2008. SSCLE members interested in contributing should contact the editors, Alexios Savvides (savvides@rhodes.aegean.gr), Benjamin Hendricks (thekla@telkomsa.net) or Alicia Simpson (asimpson@ku.edu.tr).

There is now a listserv for the scholarly discussion of the crusades, the military orders and the Latin East. For information, please contact the administrator, Myra Struckmeyer, at: struckme@email.unc.edu

## 9. Members' queries

Dana Cushing is interested in making Arabic texts available in English, in any crusade-era contact with/from Ethiopia, in any Nevada-based members of the SSCLE, and would like to establish an e-library of out-of-print articles and books free of copyright but helpful for crusade studies.

## 10. Officers of the Society

President: Professor Michel Balard. Honorary Vice-Presidents: Professor Jean Richard, Professor Jonathan Riley-Smith, Professor Benjamin Z. Kedar, Secretary: Professor Sophia Menache. Assistant Secretary: Professor Luis García-Guijarro Ramos. Editor of the Bulletin: Professor Karl Borchardt. Treasurer: Professor James D. Ryan. Website: Dr Zsolt Hunyadi.

Committee of the Society: Professor Antonio Carile (Bologna), Professor Robert Huygens (Leiden), Professor Hans Eberhard Mayer (Kiel).

## 11. Income and expenditure for the SSCLE from 17 September 2002 to 30 September 2005

There has been no proper treasurer's report since 17 September 2002 (published in Bulletin No. 23), submitted at that time by Helen Nicholson as she turned over the records of the treasury to her successor. The undersigned was asked to assume the duties of treasurer during the summer of 2005, and completed the steps necessary to have access to and control over the society's bank accounts on 20 November. Dr. Nicholson forwarded some treasury records (for which the current treasurer is very grateful) but no records have been supplied by either of those who assumed the duties of treasurer between Dr. Nicholson's resignation and the undersigned's appointment. As a consequence no proper account of the income or expenditures can be made for the above-mentioned period. In lieu thereof, this report recapitulates the balances brought forward on 17 September 2002, and states the balances in the bank accounts on 30 September 2005, at a time when there were unpaid bills and before any new deposits for 2005–6 (cheques, bank transfers, or standing order transfers) were made. The cash in hand on 30 September 2005 will become the new baseline for future reports, and the next report, in Bulletin No. 27, will detail receipts and expenditures for 1 October 2005 through 30 September 2006.

BALANCES CARRIED FORWARD, 17 SEPTEMBER 2002

| U.S. Accounts ($) | U.K. Accounts (£) | Euro Accounts (€) |
| --- | --- | --- |
| $9,485.06 | £6,583.77 | €243.30 |

BALANCES ON HAND, 30 SEPTEMBER 2005

| U.S. Accounts ($) | U.K. Accounts (£) | Euro Accounts (€) |
| --- | --- | --- |
| $12,588.89 | £(1,493.57) | €1,270.98 |

The balances shown for 30 September 2005 represent a reduction in Society assets equalling approximately £5,618 (or $9,831 or €8,427). Once the undersigned achieved control over the bank accounts, funds were transferred to erase the negative balance in the sterling accounts, and monies received in subscriptions for 2005 and 2006 have allowed the Society to pay several significant bills, including (*inter alia*) sums owed for publication of *Crusades* Vol. 4, for postage and bank fees, and for dues to the International Committee of Historical Sciences. At present the Society for the Study of the Crusades and the Latin East is in a sound fiscal position. Nevertheless, costs are increasing faster than income, and it may be necessary to institute a slight increase in subscription costs for the journal *Crusades* in the near future if the society is to engage in activities customary in past years and remain solvent in years to come.

Respectfully submitted,
James D. Ryan, Treasurer

## 12. List of members and their addresses

Shawn D. ABBOTT, 924 Greenbriar Road, Muncie IN 47304-3260, U.S.A.; sdbabbott@hotmail.com

Prof. Baudouin van den ABEELE, Rue C. Wolles 3, B-1030 Bruxelles, BELGIUM; vandenabeele@mage.ucl.ac.be

Dr Anna Sapir ABULAFIA, Lucy Cavendish College, Cambridge CB3 0BU, ENGLAND, U.K.

Dr David S. H. ABULAFIA, Gonville and Caius College, Cambridge CB2 1TA, ENGLAND, U.K.

Gabriella AIRALDI, Dipartimento di Scienze dell'antichità e del medioevo (DISAM), Università di Genova, Via Lomellini 8, I-16124 Genova, ITALY; tel.: 0039-010-2465897 and 2099602, fax: 0039-010-2465810

Brian ALLISON LEWIS, c/o Sabic, P.O. Box 5101, Riyadh 11422, SAUDI ARABIA

Dr Martín Alvira Cabrer, C/Marañosa, 2, 4° Izquierda, E-28053 Madrid, ESPAÑA; martinalvira@yahoo.es

Prof. Reuven AMITAI-PREISS, Dept. of Islamic and Middle Eastern Studies, Hebrew University, Jerusalem 91905, ISRAEL; r_amitai@mscc.huji.ac.il

Dr Monique AMOUROUX, 2, Avenue de Montchalette, Cassy, F-33138 Lanton, FRANCE

Prof. Alfred J. ANDREA, 161 Austin Drive #3, Burlington VT 05401, U.S.A.; aandrea@uvm.edu

Pnina ARAD, P.O.B. 8609, Jerusalem 91086, ISRAEL; parad@netvision.net.il

Dr Benjamin ARBEL, School of History, Tel-Aviv University, Tel-Aviv 69978, ISRAEL; arbel@ccsg.tau.ac.il

Dr Marco AROSIO, Università del Sacro Cuore, Milano, ITALY; marco_arosio@tin.it

Dr Thomas S. ASBRIDGE, Dept. of History, Queen Mary and Westfield College, University of London, Mile End Road, London E1 4NS, ENGLAND, U.K.; t_asbridge@qmul.ac.uk

Prof. Zubaida ATTA, 15 Sphix 5Q    Sphinx Tower Apt. 85, Cairo, EGYPT

Dr Hussein M. ATTIYA, 20 Ahmed Sidik Street, Sidi Gaber El-Shiek, Alexandria, EGYPT

Prof. Taef K. EL-AZHARI, Faculty of Education and Arts – Shabaka, Safraa – Burida P.O. Box 1300 – SAUDI ARABIA; taef@tedata.net.eg

Dr Mohammed AZIZ, P.O. Box 135513, Beirut, LEBANON

Dr Bernard S. BACHRACH, University of Minnesota, Dept. of History, 633 Social Sciences Building, Minneapolis MN 55455, U.S.A.

Dr Dan BAHAT, P.O. Box 738, Mevasseret Zion 90805, ISRAEL; danbahat@yahoo.com

Prof. Michel BALARD, 4, rue des Remparts, F-94370 Sucy-en-Brie, FRANCE, Michel.Balard@univ-paris1.fr

Laura BALLETTO, Via Orsini 40/B, I-16146 Genova, ITALY; Laura.Balletto@lettere.unige.it

Paul Walden BAMFORD, 2204 West Lake of the Isles Parkway, Minneapolis MN 55405-2426, U.S.A.

Prof. Malcolm BARBER, Dept. of History, University of Reading, P.O. Box 218, Whiteknights, Reading RG6 6AA, ENGLAND, U.K.; m.c.barber@reading.ac.uk

Dr Michael BARDOT, Dept. Behavioral and Social Sciences, Lincoln University, 820 Chestnut Street, Room 310 Founders Hall, Jefferson City MO 65102, U.S.A.; Bardotm@lincolnu.edu

Prof. John W. Barker, Dept. of History, University of Wisconsin, 3211 Humanities Building, Madison WI 53706, U.S.A.; jwbarker@wisc.edu

Sebastian Bartos, 6762 4th Avenue, Brooklyn NY 11220, U.S.A.; sebartos@hotmail.com

The Rev. Fr. Robert L. Becerra, Senior Associate Pastor, St Luke Catholic Church, 2892 South Congress Avenue, Palm Springs FL 33461-2170, U.S.A.; SinaiPantocrator@aol.com

Dr Bruce Beebe, 1490 Mars Lakewood OH 44107, U.S.A.; lgbeebe@aol.com

Prof. George Beech, Dept. of History, Western Michigan University, Kalamazoo MI 49008, U.S.A.; beech@wmich.edu

Elena Bellomo, via dei Rospigliosi 1, I-20151 Milano, ITALY; elena.bellomo@libero.it

Jacob Ben-Cnaan, 52 Katz Street, Petakh-Tikva 49374, ISRAEL; ponar@zahav.net.il

Matthew Bennett, 58 Mitchell Avenue, Hartley Wintney, Hampshire RG27 8HG, ENGLAND, U.K.; mattbennett@waitrose.com

Dr Nora Berend, St Catharine's College, Cambridge CB2 1RL, ENGLAND, U.K.; nb213@cam.ac.uk

Jessalynn Bird, 1514 Cortland Drive, Naperville IL 60565, U.S.A.; jessalynn.bird@iname.com

Prof. Nancy Bisaha, Dept. of History, Vassar College, Maildrop 711, 124 Raymond Avenue, Poughkeepsie NY 12604, U.S.A.; nabisaha@vassar.edu

Adam Bishop, 57 Charles Street West, Apt. 1702, Toronto, Ontario MS5 2X1, CANADA; adam.bishop@utoronto.ca

Prof. John R. E. Bliese, Communication Studies Dept., Texas Tech University, Lubbock TX 79409, U.S.A.

Dr Adrian J. Boas, Institute of Archaeology, Hebrew University of Jerusalem, Jerusalem 91905, ISRAEL; adrianjboas@yahoo.com

Prof. Mark S. Bocija, Columbus State Community College, 550 E. Spring Street, Columbus OH 43216-1609, U.S.A.; mbocija@cscc.edu

Louis Boisset, Université Saint-Joseph de Beyrouth, BP 166 778, Achrafieh, Beirut, LEBANON

Brenda M. Bolton, 8 Watling Street, St Albans AL1 2PT, ENGLAND, U.K.; brenda@bolton.vianw.co.uk

Barbara Bombi, Corpus Christi College, Merton Street, Oxford OX1 4JF, ENGLAND, U.K.; barbara.bombi@history.ox.ac.uk

Pierre Bonneaud, Carretera de Sant Vicenç 47, E-08394 Sant Vicenç de Montalt (Barcelona), ESPAÑA; pierrebonneaud@yahoo.es

Prof. Karl Borchardt, Wiesenstraße 18, D-91541 Rothenburg ob der Tauber, GERMANY; stadtarchiv@rothenburg.de

Prof. Charles R. Bowlus, History Dept., University of Arkansas, 8081 Mabelvale, Little Rock AR 72209-1099, U.S.A.; Haymannstraße 2A, D-85764 Oberschleißheim, GERMANY; crbowlus@ualr.edu and carolus22000@yahoo.com

Prof. Charles M. Brand, 508 West Montgomery Avenue, Haverford PA 19041-1409, U.S.A.; cmbrand4@earthlink.net

Dr Michael Brett, School of Oriental and African Studies, University of London, Malet Street, London WC1E 7HP, ENGLAND, U.K.

Robert BRODIE, 61 St Saviours Wharf, 8 Shad Thames, London SE1 2YP, ENGLAND, U.K.; robert@dbrodie.demon.co.uk

Judith BRONSTEIN, Ilanot 29/2, Haifa 34324, ISRAEL; judith_bronstein@hotmail.com

Prof. Elizabeth A. R. BROWN, 160 West 86th Street PH4, New York NY 10024, U.S.A.; rsbrown160@aol.com

Prof. James A. BRUNDAGE, 1102 Sunset Drive, Lawrence KS 66044-4548, U.S.A.; jabrun@ku.edu

Dr Marcus G. BULL, Dept. of Historical Studies, University of Bristol, 13–15 Woodland Road, Clifton, Bristol BS8 1TB, ENGLAND, U.K.; m.g.bull@bris.ac.uk

SSG Almyr L. BUMP, 7070 Austrian Pine Way #1, Portage MI 49204, U.S.A.

Dr Jochen BURGTORF, California State University, Dept. of History, Fullerton CA 92834-6846, U.S.A.; jburgtorf@fullerton.edu

Olivier BURLOTTE, Appartment 79, Smolensky Boulvard 6–8, Moscow 119 034, RUSSIA, oburlotte@yahoo.com

Charles BURNETT, Warburg Institute, Woburn Square, London WC1H 0AB, ENGLAND, U.K.; ch-burne@sas.ac.uk

The Rev. Prof. Robert I. BURNS, History Dept., UCLA, Los Angeles CA 90095, U.S.A.; fax: (310) 338-3002

Dr Peter BURRIDGE, Harmer Mill, Millington, York YO4 2TX, ENGLAND, U.K.

Ane Lise BYSTED, Dept. of History, University of Southern Denmark, Campusvej 55, DK-5230 Odense M, DENMARK; bysted@hist.sdu.dk

Dr J. P. CANNING, History Dept. University College of North Wales, Bangor, Gwynedd, WALES, U.K.

Franco CARDINI, P.O. Box 2358, I-50123 Firenze Ferrovia, ITALY

Christer CARLSSON, Litsbyvägen 66, S-18746 Täby, SWEDEN; cc_arch75@hotmail.com

Alan Brady CARR, 2522 20th Street, Lubbock TX 79410, U.S.A.

Dr Annemarie Weyl CARR, Division of Art History, Southern Methodist University, P.O. Box 750356, Dallas TX 75275-0356, U.S.A.; during the calendar year 2006: 608 Apple Road, Newark DE 19711, U.S.A.; acarr@mail.smu.edu

Marc CARRIER, 500 Alexandre-Dumas, Granby, Quebec J2J 1B2, CANADA; marctcarrier@yahoo.ca

Jennifer CASTEN, 875 Western Avenue, Apt. 3, Brattleboro VT 05301, U.S.A.; nulla@macol.net

Prof. Brian A. CATLOS, Dept. of History, University of California Santa Cruz, Stevenson Academic Center, 1156 High Street, Santa Cruz CA 95064, U.S.A.; bcatlos@ucsc.edu

Prof. Fred A. CAZEL Jr., 309 Gurleyville Road, Storrs Mansfield CT 06268-1439, U.S.A.

Dr Simonetta CERRINI[-ALLOISIO], Via Antonio Gramsci 109/32, I-15076 Ovada (Alessandria), ITALY; alloisiocerrini@inwind.it

Anton CHARLTON, 16 Muswell Hill, Muswell Hill, London NJ0 3TA, ENGLAND, U.K.

Dr Martin CHASIN, 1125 Church Hill Road, Fairfield CT 06432-1371, U.S.A.; mchasin@worldnet.att.net

Nikolaos CHRISSIS, C522 Canterbury Hall, 12–18 Cartwright Gardens, London WC1H 9EE, ENGLAND, U.K.; nchrissis@yahoo.uk

Dr Katherine CHRISTENSEN, CPO 1756 Berea College, Berea KY 40404, U.S.A.; katherine_christensen@berea.edu

Dr Niall G. F. CHRISTIE, Dept. of Classical, Near Eastern and Religious Studies, The University of British Columbia, BUCH C260-1866 Main Hall, Vancouver, B.C. V6T 1Z1, CANADA; niall.christie@yahoo.com

Ioanna CHRISTOFORAKI, Aristotelous 26, Chalandri, Athens 15234, GREECE; joanna.christoforaki@archeology.oxford.ac.uk

Dr Julian CHRYSOSTOMIDES, Dept. of History, Egham Hill, Egham, Surrey, ENGLAND, U.K.; j.chrysostomides@rhul.ac.uk

Padre Giulio CIPOLLONE, B.S.S.T., Padri Trinitari, Piazza S. Maria alle Fornaci 30, I-00165 Roma, ITALY; cipolloneunigre6009@fastwebnet.it

Dr G. H. M. CLAASSENS, Departement Literatuurwetenschap, Katholieke Universiteit Leuven, Blijde Inkomststraat 21, Postbus 33, B-3000 Leuven, BELGIUM

Dr Pierre-Vincent CLAVERIE, 9, rue du Bois-Rondel, F-35700 Rennes, FRANCE; pvclaverie@minitel.net

Paul M. COBB, Dept. of History, University of Notre Dame, Notre Dame IN 46556, U.S.A.; pcobb@nd.edu

Dr Penny J. COLE, Trinity College, 6 Hoskin Avenue, Toronto, Ontario M5S 1HB, CANADA; pjcole@trinity.utoronto.ca

Prof. Eleanor A. CONGDON, Dept. of History, Youngstown State University, 1 University Plaza, Youngstown OH 44420, U.S.A.; eacongdon@ysu.edu

Prof. Giles CONSTABLE, 506 Quaker Road, Princeton NJ 08540, U.S.A.

Prof. Olivia Remie CONSTABLE, Dept. of History, University of Notre Dame, Notre Dame IN 46556-0368, U.S.A.; constable1@nd.edu

Prof. Robert F. COOK, French Language and General Linguistics Dept., University of Virginia, 302 Cabell Hall, Charlottesville VA 22903, U.S.A.

Prof. Rebecca W. CORRIE, Phillips Professor of Art, Bates College, Lewiston ME 04240, U.S.A.; rcorrie@bates.edu

Walker Reid COSGRAVE, History Dept., Saint Louis University, 3800 Lindell Boulevard, Saint Louis MO 63108, U.S.A.; cosgrawr@slu.edu

Prof. Ricardo Luiz Silveira da COSTA, Rua Joao Nunes Coelho 264 apto. 203, Ed. Tom Jobim – Bairro Mata da Praia – Vitória – Espíritó Santo (ES), CEP 29.065-490, BRAZIL; riccosta@npd.ufes.br or ricardo@ricardocosta.com

Dr Nicholas S. COUREAS, P.O. Box 26619, Lykarittos, CY-1640 Nicosia, CYPRUS; ncoureas@moec.gov.cy

The Rev. H. E. J. COWDREY, 19 Church Lane, Old Marston, Oxford OX3 0NZ, ENGLAND, U.K.; fax (0)1865 279090

Prof. Paul F. CRAWFORD, History Dept., Alma College, 614 West Superior Street, Alma MI 48801, U.S.A.; crawford@alma.edu

Prof. Larry S. CRIST, 6609 Rolling Fork Drive, Nashville TN 37205, U.S.A.

B. Thomas CURTIS, 36 Brockswood Lane, Welwyn Garden City, Herts. AL8 /BG, ENGLAND, U.K.; btcurtis@btinternet.com

Dana CUSHING, 1030 San Jacinto Drive, Apt. 2034, Irving TX 75063, U.S.A.; dana@paternostery.com

Charles DALLI, Dept. of History, Faculty of Arts, University of Malta, Msida MSD06, MALTA; cdalli@arts.um.edu.mt

Philip Louis DANIEL, Archivist, Equestrian Order of the Holy Sepuchre of Jerusalem, 37 Somerset Road, Meadvale, Redhill, Surrey RH1 6LT, ENGLAND, U.K.; fax: 01737-240722

Dr Béatrice DANSETTE, 175, Boulevard Malesherbes, F-75017 Paris, FRANCE

Nicole DAWE, 21 New Road, Okehampton, Devon EX20 1JE, ENGLAND, U.K.; ndawe@hotmail.com

Julian DEAHL, c/o E. J. Brill, P.O. Box 9000, NL-2300 PA Leiden, THE NETHERLANDS; deahl@brill.nl

Prof. Bernhard DEMEL O.T., Leiter des Deutschordenszentralarchivs, Singerstraße 7, A-1010 Wien, AUSTRIA; tel. 513 70 14

John A. DEMPSEY, 218 Edgehill Road, Milton MA 02186-5310, U.S.A.; milton1@bu.edu

Prof. Alain DEMURGER, 5, rue de l'Abricotier, F-95000 Cergy, FRANCE; ademurger@wanadoo.fr

Prof. George T. DENNIS, Loyola Marymount University, P.O. Box 45041, Los Angeles CA 90045-0041, U.S.A.; nauarchos@aol.com

Americo DE SANTIS, 88 East Main Street, Box Number 141, Mendham NJ 07945, U.S.A.; ricodesantis@hotmail.com

Dr M. Gary DICKSON, History, School of History and Classics, University of Edinburgh, Wm. Robertson Building, 50 George Square, Edinburgh EH8 9JY, SCOTLAND, U.K.; GaryDickson77404@aol.com

Prof. Richard DIVALL, 301 Arcadia, 228 The Avenue, Parkville, Victoria 3052, AUSTRALIA; naestro@spin.net.au

Dr Erica Cruikshank DODD, 4208 Wakefield Place, Victoria, B.C. V8N 6E5, CANADA

César DOMÍNGUEZ, Universidad de Santiago de Compostela, Facultad de Filologia, Avda. Castealo s/n, E-15704 Santiago (La Coruna), ESPAÑA

Cristina DONDI, 128 Berkeley Court, Glentworth Street, London NW1 5NE, ENGLAND, U.K.; cfd@bodley.ox.ac.uk

Ara DOSTOURIAN, Box 420, Harmony RI 02829, U.S.A.

Maria DOUROU-ELIOPOULOU, Kephallenias 24, Althea 36km.Sounion Ave., 19400 Attiki, GREECE; meliop@cc.uoa.gr

Dr Jean DUNBABIN, St Anne's College, Oxford OX2 6HS, ENGLAND, U.K.

Mark DUPUY, 119 South Sixth Avenue, Apartment A, Clarion PA 16214, U.S.A.; mdupuy@clarion.edu

John DURANT, 32 Maple Street, P.O. Box 373, West Newbury MA 01985, U.S.A.

Dr Valerie EADS, 308 West 97th Street, New York NY 10025, U.S.A.

Prof. Richard EALES, School of History, University of Kent, Canterbury CT2 7NX, ENGLAND, U.K.; rgel@ukc.ac.uk

Ana ECHEVARRÍA ARSUAGA, Facultad de Geografía e Historia, Departimento de Historia Medieval, C/ Senda del Rey, E-28040 Madrid, ESPAÑA; anaevjosem@wanadoo.es

Prof. Peter W. EDBURY, School of History and Archaeology, Cardiff University, P.O. Box 909, Cardiff CF10 3XU, WALES, U.K.; edbury@cf.ac.uk

Dr Susan B. EDGINGTON, 3 West Street, Huntingdon, Cambs PE29 1WT, ENGLAND, U.K.; s.b.edgington@btinternet.com

Axel EHLERS, Gehägestraße 20 N, D-30655 Hannover, GERMANY; aehlers1@gwdg.de

Prof. Sven EKDAHL, Sponholzstraße 38, D-12159 Berlin, GERMANY; Sven.Ekdahl@t-online.de

Dr Ronnie ELLENBLUM, 13 Reuven Street, Jerusalem 93510, ISRAEL; msronni@pluto.mscc.huji.ac.il

Prof. Kasper ELM, Koserstraße 20, D-14195 Berlin, GERMANY

Prof. Steven A. EPSTEIN, Dept. of History, 204 Hellems, Campus Box 234, University of Colorado, Boulder CO 80309-0234, U.S.A.; steven.epstein@colorado.edu

Dr Helen C. EVANS, The Medieval Dept., The Metropolitan Museum of Art, 1000 Fifth Avenue, New York NY 10028, U.S.A.; helenevans@metmuseum.org

Michael EVANS, Flat 6, Marston Ferry Court, Oxford OX2 7XH, ENGLAND, U.K.; m_r_evans@hotmail.com

Prof. Theodore EVERGATES, 146 West Main Street, Westminster MD 21157, U.S.A.

John C. FARQUHARSON, 19 Long Croft Lane, Cheadle Hulme, Cheadle Cheshire SK8 6SE, ENGLAND, U.K.; johnfarquharson@easicom.com

Prof. Marie-Luise FAVREAU-LILIE, Kaiser-Friedrich-Straße 106, D-10585 Berlin, GERMANY; mlfavre@mail.zedat.fu-berlin.de

Jack FERGUSSON, 17 Bethel Crescent, Christchurch 5, NEW ZEALAND; jb.fergusson@xtra.co.nz

P. J. FLAHERTY, 9 Oak Street, Braintree MA 02184, U.S.A.

Prof. Richard A. FLETCHER, Low Pasture House, Nunnington, York YO62 5XQ, ENGLAND, U.K.; richardfletcher@ukonline.co.uk

Prof. Jean FLORI, Docteur d'État des Lettres et Sciences Humaines, Directeur de Recherche au Centre d'Études Supérieures de Civilisation Médiévale de Poitiers, 69 rue Saint Cornély, F-56340 Carnac, FRANCE; flori.jean@wanadoo.fr

Prof. Jaroslav FOLDA, Dept. of Art, University of North Carolina, Chapel Hill NC 27599-3405, U.S.A.; jfolda@email.unc.edu

Dr Michelle FOLTZ, M.D., PMB 33, P.O. Box 1226, Columbus MT 59019, U.S.A.; mfoltz@imt.net

Dr Iben FONNESBERG SCHMIDT, Dept. of History, Aalborg University, Fibgerstraede 5, DK-9220 Aalborg, DENMARK; imfs@ihis.aau.dk

Dr Alan FOREY, The Bell House, Church Lane, Kirtlington, Oxon. OX5 3HJ, ENGLAND, U.K.

Edith FORMAN, 38 Burnham Hill, Westport CT 06880, U.S.A.

Barbara FRALE, via A. Gramsci 17, I-01028 Orte (VT), ITALY; barbara-frale@libero.it

Dr John FRANCE, History Dept., University of Wales, Swansea SA2 7PP, WALES, U.K.; j.france@swansea.ac.uk

Dr Peter FRANKOPAN, Worcester College, Oxford OX1 2HB, ENGLAND, U.K.; peter.frankopan@worcester.ox.ac.uk

Dr Yvonne FRIEDMAN, Dept. of History, Bar-Ilan University, Ramat-Gan 55900, ISRAEL; yfried@mail.biu.ac.il

Stuart FROST, 44 Ratumore Road, Charlton, London SE7 7QW, ENGLAND, U.K.; stuartfrost@fsmail.net

R. FROUMIN, P.O. Box 9713, Hadera 38001, ISRAEL; robin_fr@zahav.net.il

Michael and Neathery FULLER, 13530 Clayton Road, St Louis MO 63141, U.S.A.

Matthew GABRIELE, Dept. of Interdisciplinary Studies, Virginia Tech, 342 Lane Hall, Blacksburg VA 24061, U.S.A.; gabriele@berkeley.edu

Prof. Luis GARCÍA-GUIJARRO RAMOS, Professor titular de Historia Medieval, Facultad de Huesca, Plaza de la Universidad 3, E-22002 Huesca, ESPAÑA; luguijar@posta.unizar.es

Dr Christopher K. GARDNER, Postdoctoral Fellow in History, George Mason University, MS: 3G1, Fairfax VA 22030, U.S.A.; cgardner@jhu.edu

Dr Giles E. M. GASPER, History Dept., University of Durham, 43 North Bailey, Durham DH1 3EX, ENGLAND, U.K.; g.e.m.gasper@durham.ac.uk

F. Gregory GAUSE Jr., 207 Bayard Avenue, Rehoboth Beach DE 19971, U.S.A.; prgause@aol.com

Sabine GELDSETZER, M.A., Westheide 6, D-44892 Bochum, GERMANY; sabine.geldsetzer@ruhr-uni-bochum.de

Prof. Maria GEORGOPOULOU, Dept. of the History of Art, Yale University, P.O. Box 208272, New Haven CT 06520-8272, U.S.A.; maria.georgopoulou@yale.edu

Deborah GERISH, Dept. of Social Sciences Box 32, Emporia State University, 1200 Commercial, Emporia KS 66801, U.S.A.; dgerish@netscape.net

Dr Ruthy GERTWAGEN, 30 Ranas Street, P.O. Box 117, Qiryat Motzkin 26317, ISRAEL; ruger@macam.ac.il

Prof. John B. GILLINGHAM, 49 Old Shoreham Road, Brighton, Sussex BN1 5DQ, ENGLAND, U.K.; john@jgillingham.wanadoo.co.uk

Prof. Anne GILMOUR-BRYSON, 1935 Westview Drive, North Vancouver, B.C. V7M 3B1, CANADA; annegb@telus.net

J. L. GILS, Gouden Leeuw 820, NL-1103 KS Amsterdam, THE NETHERLANDS

Prof. Dorothy F. GLASS, 11 Riverside Drive, Apartment 6-OW, New York NY 10023, U.S.A.; dglass1@att.net

Prof. Aryeh GRABOIS, History Dept., University of Haifa, Mount Carmel, Haifa 31905, ISRAEL; arag@research.haifa.ac.il

Michael GRAYER, 192 York Road, Shrewsburg Shropshire SY1 3QH, England, U.K.

Gilles GRIVAUD, 8 rue de Général de Miribel, F-69007 Lyon, FRANCE

The Rev. Joseph J. GROSS, Trinitarian History Studies, P.O. Box 42056, Baltimore MD 21284, U.S.A.; jjgross@trinitarianhistory.org

Prof. Klaus GUTH, Greiffenbergstraße 35, D-96052 Bamberg, GERMANY; klaus.guth@ggeo.uni-bamberg.de

Darius von GUTTNER SPORZYNSKI, 8 Waters Road, Shepparton, Victoria 3630, AUSTRALIA; gutties@bigpond.net.au

Dr Mark E. HALL, 6826 Walso Avenue, El Cerrito CA 94530, U.S.A.; markhall@aol.com

Adina HAMILTON, 469 Albert Street, Brunswick, West Victoria 3055, AUSTRALIA or History Dept., University of Melbourne, Parkville, Victoria 3052, AUSTRALIA

Prof. Bernard HAMILTON, 7 Lenton Avenue, The Park, Nottingham NG7 1DX, ENGLAND, U.K.

Peter HARITATOS Jr., 1500 North George Street, Rome NY 13440, U.S.A.

Jonathan HARRIS, Dept. of History, Royal Holloway, University of London, Egham, Surrey TW20 0EX, ENGLAND, U.K.; jonathan.harris@rhul.ac.uk

Kathryn D. Harris, 6 Gallows Hill, Saffron Walden, Essex CB11 4DA, ENGLAND, U.K.

Dr Alan Harvey, Dept. of Historical and Critical Studies, University of Northumbria, Newcastle-upon-Tyne NE1 8ST, ENGLAND, U.K.; alan.harvey@unn.ac.uk

David Hay, 164 McCaul Street Apt. 1, Toronto, Ontario M5T 1WA, CANADA

Dr Bodo Hechelhammer, Erzbergerstraße 8, D-64823 Groß-Umstadt/Heubach, GERMANY; bodo.hechelhammer@t-online.de or Institut für Geschichte, Residenzschloß, D-64283 Darmstadt, GERMANY; bh@polihist.pg.tu-darmstadt.de

Prof. Thérèse de Hemptinne, Universiteit Gent, Faculteit van de Letteren, Vakgroep Middeleeuwse Geschiedenis, Blandijnberg 2, B-9000 Gent, BELGIUM

Michael Heslop, 2, Boulevard J.-Dalcroze, CH-1204 Geneva, SWITZERLAND; michaelheslop@atlworld.com

Dr Paul Hetherington, 15 Luttrell Avenue, London SW15 6PD, ENGLAND, U.K.; phetherington@ukonline.co.uk

Dr Avital Heyman, 12 Hertzel Street, Ness-Ziona 74084, ISRAEL; avital-h@internet-zahav.net

Prof. Rudolf Hiestand, Brehmstraße 76, D-40239 Düsseldorf, GERMANY

Charles A. Hilken, P.O. Box 4825, St Mary's College, Moraga CA 94575, U.S.A.; chilken@stmarys-ca.edu

James Hill, 2/4 Cassam Place, Valley Heights, New South Wales 2777, AUSTRALIA

Dr George Hintlian, Armenian Patriarchate, P.O. Box, Jerusalem 14001, ISRAEL

Dr Martin Hoch, Konrad-Adenauer-Stiftung, Rathausallee 12, D-53757 Sankt Augustin, GERMANY; Lobebaer@web.de

Laura Hollengreen; laurah@u.arizona.edu

Dr Catherine Holmes, University College, Oxford OX1 4BH, ENGLAND, U.K.; catherine.holmes@univ.ox.ac.uk

Andrew P. Holt, 747 Superior Street, Jacksonville FL 32254, U.S.A.; a-holt@comcast.net

Prof. Hubert Houben, Via Marugi 38, I-73100 Lecce, ITALY; houben@sesia.unile.it

Prof. Norman J. Housley, School of Historical Studies, The University of Leicester, Leicester LE1 7RH, ENGLAND, U.K.; hou@le.ac.uk

Prof. Lucy-Anne Hunt, Dept. of History of Art and Design, Righton Building, Cavendish Street, Manchester M15 6BK, ENGLAND, U.K.; l.a.hunt@mmu.ac.uk

Zsolt Hunyadi, 27 Szekeres u., H-6725 Szeged, HUNGARY; hunyadiz@hist.u-szeged.hu

Prof. Robert B. C. Huygens, Witte Singel 28, NL-2311 BH Leiden, THE NETHERLANDS

Sheldon Ibbotson, P.O. Box 258, Rimbey, Alberta T0C 2JO, CANADA; bronwen@telusplanet.net

Robert Irwin, 39 Harleyford Road, London SE11 5AX, ENGLAND, U.K.; robert@robertirwin.demon.co.uk

John E. Isles, 10575 Darrel Drive, Hanover MI 49241, U.S.A.; jisles@voyager.net

Prof. Peter Jackson, History Dept., University of Keele, Keele, Staffs. ST5 5BG, ENGLAND, U.K.; hia08@keele.ac.uk

Martin Jacobowitz, The Towers of Windsor Park, 3005 Chapel Avenue – 11P, Cherry Hill NJ 08002, U.S.A.

Prof. David Jacoby, Dept. of History, The Hebrew University, Jerusalem 91905, ISRAEL; jacobgab@mscc.huji.ac.il

Dr Kay Peter JANKRIFT, Institut für Geschichte der Medizin der Robert Bosch Stiftung, Straußweg 17, D-70184 Stuttgart, GERMANY.

Prof. Nikolas JASPERT, Ruhr-University Bochum, Historisches Institut – Lehrstuhl Mittelalter II, Universitätsstraße 150 (GA 4/31), D-44801 Bochum, GERMANY; nikolas.jaspert@ruhr-uni-bochum.de

Prof. Carsten Selch JENSEN, Dept. of Church History, University of Copenhagen, Købmagergade 46, POB 2164, DK-1150 Copenhagen K, DENMARK; csj@teol.ku.dk

Janus Møller JENSEN, Institute of History and Civilization, University of Southern Denmark, DK-5230 Odense M, DENMARK; jamj@hist.sdu.dk

Prof. Kurt Villads JENSEN, Dept. of History, Odense University, Campusvej 55, DK-5230 Odense M, DENMARK; kvj@hist.sdu.dk

Prof. William Chester JORDAN, Dept. of History, Princeton University, Princeton NJ 08544, U.S.A.; wchester@princeton.edu

Philippe JOSSERAND, Dépt. histoire, chemin la Censive du Tertre, BP 81227, F-44312 Nantes Cedex 3, FRANCE; philippe.josserand@humana.univ-nantes.fr

Dr Andrew JOTISCHKY, Dept. of History, University of Lancaster, Bailrigg, Lancaster LA1 4YG, ENGLAND, U.K.; a.jotischky@lancaster.ac.uk

Dr Margaret A. JUBB, Dept. of French, Taylor Building, University of Aberdeen, Old Aberdeen, AB24 3UB, SCOTLAND, U.K.; m.jubb@abdn.ac.uk

Dr Fotini KARASSAVA-TSILINGIRI, Chrysostomou Smyrnis 14, N. Smyrni, Athens 17121, GREECE

Tatiana Kartseva, 73–50 Vavilova Street, Moscow 117335, RUSSIA; tvkartseva@hotmail.com

Prof. Benjamin Z. KEDAR, Dept. of History, The Hebrew University, Jerusalem 91905, ISRAEL; fax (home): 972-8-970-0802, bzkedar@h2.hum.huji.ac.il

Alexander KEMPTON, Skøyenveien 30, N-0375 Oslo, NORWAY; alexansk@student.hf.uio.no

Prof. Nurith KENAAN-KEDAR, Dept. of Art History, Tel-Aviv University, Tel-Aviv 69978, ISRAEL; kenaank@post.tau.ac.il

Dr Hugh KENNEDY, Medieval History Dept., University of St Andrews, St Andrews, Fife KY16 9AL, SCOTLAND, U.K.

Dr Andreas KIESEWETTER, Via La Sila 16/8, I-00135 Roma, ITALY; leonidas@ilink.it

Sharon KINOSHITA, Associate Professor of Literature, University of California Santa Cruz, Santa Cruz CA 95064, U.S.A.

Dr Klaus-Peter KIRSTEIN, Lerchenstraße 60, D-45134 Essen, GERMANY; kirstein-musemeyer@t-online.de

Dr Michael A. KOEHLER, Hertogenlaan 14, B-1970 Wezembeek-Oppem, BELGIUM

Prof. Athina KOLIA-DERMITZAKI, Plateia Kalliga 3, Athens 11253, GREECE; akolia@arch.uoa.gr

Wolf KONRAD, 6240 Phillips Road, Mundaring, West Australia 6073, AUSTRALIA; wolf17@telstra.easymail.com.au

Dr Conor KOSTICK, Dept. of Medieval History, Trinity College, Dublin 2, IRELAND; kostick@tcd.ie

Prof. Barbara M. KREUTZ, 1411 Orchard Way, Rosemont PA 19010, U.S.A.

Prof. Jürgen KRÜGER, Steinbügelstraße 22, D-76228 Karlsruhe, GERMANY; krueger-kunstgeschichte@t-online.de

Hans-Ulrich KÜHN, Silcherstraße 9/1, D-71254 Ditzingen-Schöckingen, GERMANY; hans-ulrich.kuehn@web.de

Sarah LAMBERT, 35 Cromer Road, London SW17 9JN, ENGLAND, U.K.; slambert@gold.ac.uk

The Rev. William LANE, Charterhouse, Godalming Surrey GU7 2DF, ENGLAND, U.K.; wjl@peperharow.freeserve.co.uk

Dr Robert A. LAURES, 1434 West Maplewood Court, Milwaukee WI 53221-4348, U.S.A.; dr001@voyager.net

Stephen LAY, c/o Dept. of History, Monash University, Melbourne, AUSTRALIA

Eric LEGG, PSC 98 Box 36, Apo AE 09830, U.S.A.; ericlegg@hotmail.com

Robert D. LEONARD Jr., 1065 Spruce Street, Winnetka IL 60093, U.S.A.; rlwinnetka@aol.com

Dr Antony LEOPOLD, 62 Grafton Road, Acton, London W3 6PD, ENGLAND, U.K.

Richard A. LESON, 2720 St Paul Street #2FF, Baltimore MD 21218, U.S.A.; ral2@jhunix.hef.jhu.edu

Dr Yaacov LEV, P.O. Box 167, Holon 58101, ISRAEL; yglev@actcom.net.il

Dr Christopher G. LIBERTINI, 27 Lombard Lane, Sudbury MA 01776, U.S.A.; clibertini@aol.com

Dr Giuseppe LIGATO, Viale San Gimignano 18, I-20146 Milano, ITALY; giuseppeligato@virgilio.it

Prof. Ralph-Johannes LILIE, Kaiser-Friedrich-Straße 106, D-10585 Berlin, GERMANY; mlfavre@zedat.fu.berlin.de

Dr Ora LIMOR, The Open University, 16 Klausner Steet, Tel Aviv 61392, ISRAEL; orali@openu.ac.il

Prof. John LIND, Dept. of History, University of Odense, Campusvej 55, DK-5230 Odense M, DENMARK; john_lind@hist.ou.dk

Dr Simon D. LLOYD, Dept. of History, University of Newcastle-upon-Tyne, Newcastle Upon Tyne NE1 7RU, ENGLAND, U.K.; s.d.lloyd@ncl.ac.uk

Prof. Peter W. LOCK, 9 Straylands Grove, Stockton Lane, York YO31 1EB, ENGLAND, U.K.; p.lock@venysj.ac.uk

Scott LONEY, 4153 Wendell Road, West Bloomfield MI 48323, U.S.A.; scottloney@ameritech.net

Prof. Graham A. LOUD, School of History, University of Leeds, Leeds LS2 9JT, ENGLAND, U.K.; g.a.loud@leeds.ac.uk

Prof. Michael LOWER, Dept. of History, University of Minnesota, 614 Social Sciences Building, 267 19th Avenue South, Minneapolis MN 55455, U.S.A.; mlower@umn.edu

Zoyd R. LUCE, 2441 Creekside Court, Hayward CA 94542, U.S.A.; zluce1@earthlink.net

Dr Svetlana LUCHITSKAYA, Institute of General History, Leninski pr. 89-346, Moscow 119313, RUSSIA; svetlana@mega.ru

Andrew John LUFF, Flat 3, The Hermitage, St Dunstans Road, Lower Feltham, Middlesex TW13 4HR, ENGLAND, U.K.; andrew@luffa.freeserve.co.uk

Dr Anthony LUTTRELL, 20 Richmond Place, Bath BA1 5PZ, ENGLAND, U.K.

Christopher MacEvitt, Dumbarton Oaks, 1703 32nd Street NW, Washington DC 20007, U.S.A.

Merav Mack, 48 Regent Street, Cambridge CB3 1FD, ENGLAND, U.K.; merav@cambridgeresearch.co.uk

Dr Alan D. MacQuarrie, 173 Queen Victoria Drive, Glasgow G14 7BP, SCOTLAND, U.K.

Thomas F. Madden, Dept. of History, Saint Louis University, 3800 Lindell Boulevard, P.O. Box 56907, St Louis MO 63108, U.S.A.; maddentf@slu.edu

Ben Mahoney, 19 Bond Street, Mount Waverly, Victoria 3149, AUSTRALIA; BMahoney@abl.com.au

Dr Christoph T. Maier, Sommergasse 20, CH-4056 Basel, SWITZERLAND; ctmaier@hist.unizh.ch

Chryssa Maltezou, Istituto Ellenico di Studi Bizantini e Postbizantini di Venezia, Castello 3412, I-30122 Venezia, ITALY; hellenic.inst.@gold.ghnet.it

Prof. Lucy Der Manuelian, 10 Garfield Road, Belmont MA 02178-3309, U.S.A.; lucy.manuelian@tufts.edu

Prof. Michael Markowski, Dept. of History, Westminster College, 1840 South 1300 East, Salt Lake City UT 84105, U.S.A.

Dr Christopher J. Marshall, 8 Courtyard Way, Cottenham, Cambridge CB4 8SF, ENGLAND, U.K.

Dr Carlos de Ayala Martinez, Historia Medieval, Ciudad Universitaria de Cantoblanco, Ctra. De Colmenar, E-28049 Madrid, ESPAÑA

Prof. Laurence W. Marvin, History Dept., Evans School of Humanities and Social Sciences, Berry College, Mount Berry GA 30149-5010, U.S.A.; lmarvin@berry.edu

Kathleen Maxwell, 4016 26th Street, San Francisco CA 94131, U.S.A.; kmaxwell@scu.edu

Prof. Hans Eberhard Mayer, Historisches Seminar der Universität Kiel, D-24098 Kiel, GERMANY

Robert Maynard, The Old Dairy, 95 Church Road, Bishopsworth Bristol BS13 8JU, ENGLAND, U.K.; maynard966@btinternet.com

Andreas Mazarakis, Rizou 3, Athens 10434, GREECE; amazarakis@tee.gr

Prof. Rasa Mazeika, 48A Arcadian Circle, Toronto, Ontario M8W 4W2, CANADA

Brian C. Mazur, 718 W. Webster, Royal Oak MI 48073, U.S.A.; bcmazur1066@yahoo.com

Arthur H. S. Megaw, 27 Perrins' Walk, London NW3 6TH, ENGLAND, U.K.

Prof. Sophia Menache, Dept. of History, University of Haifa, Haifa 31905, ISRAEL; menache@research.haifa.ac.il

Marco Meschini, Via Fé 15, I-21100 Varese, ITALY; marco.meschini@libero.it; marco.meschini@unicatt.it

Margaret Meserve, Assistant Professor of History, University of Notre Dame, 219 O'Shaughnessy Hall, Notre Dame IN 46556, U.S.A.; margaret.h.meserve.1@nd.edu

Prof. D. Michael Metcalf, Ashmolean Museum, Oxford OX1 2PH, ENGLAND, U.K.

Françoise Micheau, 8bis, rue du Buisson Saint-Louis, F-75011 Paris, FRANCE; fmicheau@univ-paris1.fr

Paul Richard Milliman, 618 W Willow St #3, Chicago IL 60614, U.S.A.; prm7@cornell.edu

Dr Jonathan P. PHILLIPS, Dept. of History, Royal Holloway University of London, Egham, Surrey TW20 0EX, ENGLAND, U.K.; j.p.phillips@rhul.ac.uk

Dr Simon D. PHILLIPS, 21 Perikleous Street, Apt. 101, Strovolos, CY-2020 Nicosia, CYPRUS; simonas@rocketmail.com

Dr Mathias PIANA, Benzstraße 9, D-86420 Diedorf, GERMANY; mathias.piana@phil.uni-augsburg.de

Brenda POCHNA, 17 Berryhill, Eltham Park, London SE9 1QP, ENGLAND, U.K.

Clive PORRO, 36 Castle Road, Whitstable, Kent CT5 2DY, ENGLAND, U.K.; clive.porro@btinternet.com

Dr John PORTEOUS, 52 Elgin Crescent, London W11, ENGLAND, U.K.

Prof. James M. POWELL, 5100 Highbridge Street, Apartment 18D, Fayetteville NY 13066, U.S.A.; mpowell@dreamscape.com

Jon POWELL, 711 SE 11th #43, Portland OR 97214, U.S.A.; jonp@pdx.edu

Dr Karen PRATT, French Dept., King's College London, Strand, London WC2R 2LS, ENGLAND, U.K.

Jennifer Ann PRICE, Dept. of History, University of Washington, P.O. Box 353560, Seattle WA 98195-3560, U.S.A.; japrice@u.washington.edu

Prof. R. Denys PRINGLE, School of History and Archaeology, Cardiff University, P.O. Box 909, Cardiff CF10 3XU, WALES, U.K.; pringlerd@cardiff.ac.uk

Dragan PROKIC, M.A., Rubensallee 47, D-55127 Mainz, GERMANY; dp.symbulos@t-online.de

Prof. John H. PRYOR, Centre Medieval Studies, University of Sydney, John Wolley Building A20, Sydney, New South Wales 2006, AUSTRALIA; john.pryor@arts.usyd.edu.au

William J. PURKIS, 46 Fennec Close, Cherry Hinton, Cambridge CB1 9GG, ENGLAND, U.K.; william_purkis@hotmail.com

Ian D. QUELCH, 27 Barn Meadow Lane, Great Bookham, Surrey KT23 3EZ, ENGLAND, U.K.; Ian.Quelch@ntlworld.com

Yevgeniy / Eugene RASSKAZOV, Worth Avenue Station, P.O. Box 3497, Palm Beach FL 33480-3497, U.S.A.; medievaleurope@apexmail.com

Susan REYNOLDS, 19 Ridgemount Gardens, London WC1E 7AR, ENGLAND, U.K.; smreynolds@btinternet.com

Prof. Geoffrey W. RICE, History Dept., University of Canterbury, Private Bag 4800, Christchurch, NEW ZEALAND; g.rice@hist.canterbury.ac.nz

Prof. Jean RICHARD, 12, rue Pelletier de Chambure, F-21000 Dijon, FRANCE

Maurice RILEY Esq., P.O. Box 15819, Adliya, BAHRAIN, Arabian Gulf; mriley@batelco.com.bh

Prof. Jonathan S. C. RILEY-SMITH, The Downs, Croxton, St Neots, Cambridgeshire PE19 4SX, ENGLAND, U.K.; jsr22@cam.ac.uk or jonathan.rileysmith@btinternet.com

Rebecca RIST, 50 Roseford Road, Cambridge CB4 2HD, ENGLAND, U.K.; raw2@corn.ac.uk

The Rev. Leonard Stanley RIVETT, 47 Ryecroft Avenue, Woodthorpe, York YO24 2SD, ENGLAND, U.K.

Prof. Louise Buenger ROBBERT, 709 South Skinker Boulevard Apartment 701, St Louis MO 63105, U.S.A.; lrobbert@mindspring.com

Jason T. ROCHE, Seaview, Kings Highway, Largoward, Fife KY9 1HX, SCOTLAND, U.K.; jtr@st-andrews.ac.uk

José Manuel RODRÍGUEZ-GARCÍA, C/ San Ernesto 4.5° C, E-28002 Madrid, ESPAÑA; anaevjosem@wanadoo.es

Prof. Israel ROLL, Dept. of Classics, Tel-Aviv University, Ramat Aviv, Tel-Aviv 69978, ISRAEL; rolli@post.tau.ac.il

Dean Richard B. ROSE, 119 Grandview Place, San Antonio TX 78209, U.S.A.

Prof. Myriam ROSEN-AYALON, Institute of Asian and African Studies, The Hebrew University, Jerusalem 91905, ISRAEL

Dvora ROSHAL, P.O. Box 3558, Beer-Sheva 84135, ISRAEL; devorahr@afikim.co.il

Linda Ross, Dept. of History, Royal Holloway University of London, Egham, Surrey TW20 0EX, ENGLAND, U.K.; linde@lross22.freeserve.co.uk

Prof. John ROSSER, Dept. of History, Boston College, Chestnut Hill MA 02467, U.S.A.; rosserj@bc.edu

Jay RUBENSTEIN, Dept. of History, UNM, ABQ NM 87131, U.S.A.; jrubens@unm.edu

James RUEL, Ground Floor Flat, 63 Redland Road, Redland, Bristol B56 6AQ, England, U.K.; james-ruel@hotmail.com

Prof. Frederick H. RUSSELL, Dept. of History, Conklin Hall, Rutgers University, Newark NJ 07102, U.S.A.; frussell@andromeda.rutgers.edu

Prof. James D. RYAN, 100 West 94th Street, Apartment 26M, New York NY 10025, U.S.A.; james.d.ryan@verizon.net

Vincent RYAN, Dept. of History, Saint Louis University, 3800 Lindell Boulevard, St. Louis MO 63108, U.S.A.; ryanv+@slu.edu

Dr Andrew J. SARGENT, 33 Coborn Street, Bow, London E3 2AB, ENGLAND, U.K.; andrewsargent@newham.gov.uk

Prof. Jürgen SARNOWSKY, Historisches Seminar, Universität Hamburg, Von-Melle-Park 6, D-20146 Hamburg, GERMANY; juergen.sarnowsky@uni-hamburg.de

Christopher SAUNDERS OBE, Watery Hey, Spring Vale Road, Hayfield, High Peak SK22 2LD, ENGLAND, U.K.

Prof. Alexios G. C. SAVVIDES, Aegean University, Dept. of Mediterranean Studies, Rhodes, GREECE; or: 7 Tralleon Street, Nea Smyrne, Athens 17121, GREECE; savvides@rhodes.aegean.gr

Christopher SCHABEL, Dept. of History and Archaeology, University of Cyprus, P.O. Box 20537, CY-1678 Nicosia, CYPRUS; schabel@ucy.ac.cy

Dr Jochen SCHENK, Emmanuel College, Cambridge CB2 3AP, ENGLAND, U.K.; or Spardorferstraße 7, D-91054 Erlangen, GERMANY; jg.schenk@gmail.com

Prof. Paul Gerhard SCHMIDT, Seminar für lateinische Philologie des Mittelalters, Albert-Ludwigs-Universität Freiburg, Werderring 8, D-79085 Freiburg i. Br., GERMANY

Dr Beate SCHUSTER, 19, rue Vauban, F-67000 Strasbourg, FRANCE; beaschu@compuserve.com

Prof. Rainer C. SCHWINGES, Historisches Institut der Universität Bern, Unitobler – Länggass-Straße 49, CH-3000 Bern 9, SWITZERLAND

Kaare SEEBERG SIDSELRUD, Solbergliveien 87 B, NO-0683 Oslo, NORWAY; kaasid@online.no or heraldikk@gmail.com

Per Seesko, Heden 18, 2., lejl. 10, DK-5000 Odense C, DENMARK; seesko83@yahoo.com

Iris Shagrir, Dept. of History, The Open University, P.O. Box 808, Raanana 43107, ISRAEL; irissh@openu.ac.il

Prof. Maya Shatzmiller, Dept. of History, The University of Western Ontario, London, Ontario N6A 5C2, CANADA

Karl W. Shea, GPO Box 1526, Hobart, Tasmania 7001, AUSTRALIA; sangrail@bigpond.com

Dr Jonathan Shepard, 14 Hartley Court, Woodstock Road, Oxford OX2 7PF, ENGLAND, U.K.; nshepard@easynet.co.uk

Dr Elizabeth J. Siberry, 28 The Mall, Surbiton, Surrey KT6 4E9, ENGLAND, U.K.

Alicia Simpson, 8 Karaiskaki Street, Athens GR-18345, GREECE

Raitis Simsons, A/k 209, Riga LV 1082, LATVIA; raitiss@btv.lv

Dr Gordon Andreas Singer, P.O. Box 235, Greenbelt MD 20768-0235, U.S.A.; andysinger@att.net

Dr Corliss K. Slack, Dept. of History #1103, Whitworth College, Spokane WA 99251, U.S.A.; cslack@whitworth.edu

Rima E. Smine, 25541 Altamont Road, Los Altos Hills CA 94022, U.S.A.

Sheila R. Smith, 111 Coleshill Road Chapelend, Nuneaton Warwickshire CV10 0PG, ENGLAND, U.K.

Matt Snyder, 57 Egham Hill, Egham, Surrey TW20 0ER, ENGLAND, U.K.; calidus@gmail.com

Simon Sonnak, P.O. Box 1206, Windsor, Victoria 3181, AUSTRALIA; heliade@bigpond.com.au

Arnold Spaer, 4 Alharizi Street, Jerusalem 91272, ISRAEL; hui@spaersitton.co.il

Brent Spencer, 3 9701 89 Street, Fort Saskatchewan, Alberta T8L 1J3, CANADA; ktcrusader@yahoo.com

Dr Alan M. Stahl, Curator of Numismatics, Firestone Library, Princeton University, Princeton NJ 08544; amstahl@optonline.net or astahl@princeton.edu

Prof. Harvey Stahl, Dept. of the History of Art, University of California, Berkeley CA 94720, U.S.A.; hstahl@socrates.berkeley.edu

Dr Alexandra Stefanidou, 35 Amerikis Street, Rhodos 85100, GREECE; aleste@otenet.gr or stefanidou@rhodes.aegean.gr

Eliezer and J. Edna Stern, Israel Antiquities Authority, P.O. Box 1094, Acre 24110, ISRAEL; fax: 04-9911682 or 9918074

Alan D. Stevens, Campbell College, Dept. of History, Belmont Road, Belfast BT4 2ND, NORTHERN IRELAND, U.K.; alan.d.stevens@ntlworld.com

Paula R. Stiles, 552 Barstow Road, Shelburne VT 05482, U.S.A.; thesnowleopard@hotmail.com

Myra Struckmeyer, 29 Flemington Road, Chapel Hill NC 27517, U.S.A.; struckme@email.unc.edu

Shaul Tamiri, Hachail-Halmoni #8, Rishon le Zion 75255, ISRAEL

Olivier Terlinden, Avenue des Ramiers 8, B-1950 Kraaïnem, BELGIUM; olivierterlinden@yahoo.com

Miriam Rita Tessera, via Moncalvo 16, I-20146 Milano, ITALY; monachus_it@yahoo.it

Kenneth J. THOMSON, Edessa, 8 Salterfell Road, Scale Hall, Lancaster LA1 2PX, ENGLAND, U.K.; kenneth@thomsonk91.fsnet.co.uk

Prof. Peter THORAU, Historisches Institut, University des Saarlandes, Postfach 15 11 50, D-66041 Saarbrücken, GERMANY

Prof. Hirofumi TOKO, 605-3 Kogasaka, Machida, Tokyo 194-0014, JAPAN; ttokou@toyonet.toyo.ac.jp

Prof. John Victor TOLAN, Département d'Histoire, Université de Nantes, B.P. 81227, F-44312 Nantes, FRANCE, or: 2, rue de la Chevalerie, F-44300 Nantes, FRANCE; john.tolan@humana.univ-nantes.fr

Prof. François-Olivier TOUATI, Le Navril, F-49250 La Ménitré, FRANCE; francoistouati@aol.com

Catherine B. TURNER, Flat 3, 1055 Christchurch Road, Boscombe East, Bournemouth BH7 6BE, ENGLAND, U.K.

Dr Judith M. UPTON-WARD, Flat 6, Haywood Court, Reading RG1 3QF, ENGLAND, U.K.; juptonward@btopenworld.com

Prof. William L. URBAN, Dept. of History, Monmouth College, 700 East Broadway, Monmouth IL 61462, U.S.A.; urban@monm.edu

Theresa M. VANN, Hill Monastic Manuscript Library, St John's University, Collegeville MN 56321, U.S.A.; www.hmml.org

Dr Marie-Louise von WARTBURG MAIER, Paphosprojekt der Universität Zürich, Rämistraße 71, CH-8006 Zürich, SWITZERLAND; paphos@hist.unizh.ch

Benjamin WEBER, 24, rue du Tour, F-31000 Toulouse, FRANCE; benyi_tigrou@hotmail.com or benjamin-weber@laposte.net

Dr Daniel WEISS, History of Art Dept., Johns Hopkins University, 3400 North Charles Street, Baltimore MD 21218, U.S.A.; dweiss@jho.edu

Brett E. WHALEN, 119 Quillen Court, Stanford CA 94305, U.S.A.

Dr Mark WHITTOW, St Peter's College, Oxford OX1 2DL, ENGLAND, U.K.

Timothy WILKES, A. H. Baldwin & Sons Ltd., 11 Adelphi Terrace, London WC2N 6BJ, ENGLAND, U.K.; timwilkes@baldwin.sh

The Rev. Dr John D. WILKINSON, 7 Tenniel Close, London W2 3LE, ENGLAND, U.K.

Dr Ann WILLIAMS, 40 Greenwich South Street, London SE10 8UN, ENGLAND, U.K.; ann.williams@talk21.com

Prof. Steven James WILLIAMS, Dept. of History, New Mexico Highlands University, P.O. Box 9000, Las Vegas NM 87701, U.S.A.; stevenjameswilliams@yahoo.com

Gayle A. WILSON, P.O. Box 712, Diamond Springs CA 95619, U.S.A.; gayle@inforum.net

Peter van WINDEKENS, Kleine Ganzendries 38, B-3212 Pellenberg, BELGIUM

Prof. Johanna Maria van WINTER, Brigittenstraat 20, NL-3512 KM Utrecht, THE NETHERLANDS; j.m.vanwinter@let.uu.nl

Prof. Kenneth B. WOLF, Dept. of History, Pomona College, Pearsons Hall, 551 North College Avenue, Claremont CA 91711-6337, U.S.A.

Dr Noah WOLFSON, 13 Avuqa Street, Tel-Aviv 69086, ISRAEL; noah@meteo-tech.co.il

Peter WOODHEAD, Tarry Cottage, Church Lane, Daglingworth near Cirencester, Gloucestershire GL7 7AG, ENGLAND, U.K.

Dr John WREGLESWORTH, Fountain Cottage, 98 West Town Road, Backwell, North Somerset BS48 3BE, ENGLAND, U.K.; john@wreg.freeserve.co.uk

Prof. Shunji YATSUZUKA, 10–22 Matsumoto 2 chome, Otsu-shi, Shiga 520, JAPAN

William G. ZAJAC, 9 Station Terrace, Pen-y-rheal, Caerphilly CF83 2RH, WALES, U.K.

Prof. Ossama Zaki ZEID, 189 Abd al-Salam Aref Tharwat, Alexandria, EGYPT; ossama_zeid@hotmail.com

Joseph ZELNIK, 25 Wingate Street, Raanana 43587, ISRAEL

Prof. Monique ZERNER, Villa Stella, Chemin des Pins, F-06000 Nice, FRANCE; zernerm@unice.fr

## Institutions subscribing to the SSCLE

Brepols Publishers, Steenweg op Tielen 68, B-2300 Turnhout, BELGIUM

Bibliothécaire Guy Cobolet, Le Bibliothécaire, École Française d'Athènes, 6, Didotou 10680 Athènes, GREECE

Centre de Recherches d'histoire et civilisation de Byzance et du Proche-Orient Chétien, Université de Paris 1, 17, rue de la Sorbonne, 75231 Paris Cedex, FRANCE

Centre for Byzantine, Ottoman and Modern Greek Studies, University of Birmingham, Edgbaston, Birmingham B15 2TT, ENGLAND, U.K.

Couvent des Dominicains, École Biblique et Archéologique Français, 6 Nablus Road, Jerusalem 91190, ISRAEL

Deutsches Historisches Institut in Rom, Via Aurelia Antica 391, I-00165 Rome, ITALY

Deutschordenszentralarchiv (DOZA), Singerstraße 7, A-1010 Wien, AUSTRIA

Dumbarton Oaks Research Library, 1703 32nd Street North West, Washington D.C. 20007, U.S.A.

Europäisches Burgeninstitut, Schlossstraße 5, D-56338 Braubach, GERMANY; ebi@deutsche-burgen.org

Germanisches Nationalmuseum, Bibliothek, Kornmarkt 1, D-90402 Nürnberg, GERMANY

History Department, Campbell College, Belfast BT4 2ND, NORTHERN IRELAND, U.K.

The Jewish National and University Library, P.O. Box 34165, Jerusalem 91341, ISRAEL

The Library, The Priory of Scotland of the Most Venerable Order of St John, 21 St John Street, Edinburgh EH8 8DG, SCOTLAND, U.K.

The Stephen Chan Library, Institute of Fine Arts, New York University, 1 East 78th Street, New York NY 10021, U.S.A.

Metropolitan Museum of Art, Thomas J. Watson Library, Serials Dept., 5th Avenue at 82nd Street, New York NY 10028, U.S.A.

Museum and Library of the Order of St John, St John's Gate, Clerkenwell, London EC1M 4DA, ENGLAND, U.K.

Order of the Christian Knights of the Rose, Brent R. Spencer, Grand Master, P.O. Box 3423, Fort Saskatchewan, Alberta T8L 2T4, CANADA

Order of the Temple of Jerusalem and the Industrial Temple, Grand Priory of Knights Templar in England and Wales, Treasurer, 14 Goldthorne Avenue, Sheldon, Birmingham B26 3JY, ENGLAND, U.K.

Serials Department, 11717 Young Research Library, University of California, Box 951575, Los Angeles CA 90095-1575, U.S.A.

Sourasky Library, Tel-Aviv University, Periodical Dept., P.O. Box 39038, Tel-Aviv, ISRAEL

Teutonic Order Bailiwick of Utrecht, Dr John J. Quarles van Ufford, Secretary of the Bailiwick, Springweg 25, NL-3511 VJ Utrecht, THE NETHERLANDS

Türk Tarih Kurumu [Turkish Historical Society], Kizilay Sokak No. 1, Sihhiye 06100 Ankara, TURKEY

The Warburg Institute, University of London, Woburn Square, London WC1H 0AB, ENGLAND, U.K. [John PERKINS, Deputy Librarian, jperkins@a1.sas.ac.uk]

Eberhard-Karls-Universität Tübingen, Orientalisches Seminar, Münzgasse 30, D-72072 Tübingen, GERMANY

University of California Los Angeles Serials Dept. / YRL, 11717 Young Research Library, Box 951575, Los Angeles CA 90095-1575, U.S.A.

University of London Library, Periodicals Section, Senate House, Malet Street, London WC1E 7HU, ENGLAND, U.K.

University of North Carolina, Davis Library CB 3938, Periodicals and Serials Dept., Chapel Hill NC 27514-8890, U.S.A.

Universitätsbibliothek Tübingen, Wilhelmstraße 32, Postfach 26 20, D-72016 Tübingen, GERMANY

University of Reading, Graduate Centre for Medieval Studies, Whiteknights, P.O. Box 218, Reading, Berks. RG6 6AA, ENGLAND, U.K.

University of Washington, Libraries, Serials Division, P.O. Box 352900, Seattle WA 98195, U.S.A.

University of Western Ontario Library, Acquisitions Dept., Room M1, D. B. Weldon Library, London, Ontario N6A 3K7, CANADA

W. F. Albright Institute of Archaeological Research, 26 Salah ed-Din Street, P.O. Box 19096, Jerusalem 91190, ISRAEL

# Guidelines for the Submission of Papers

The editors ask contributors to adhere to the following guidelines. Failure to do so will result in the article being returned to the author for amendment, or may result in its having to be excluded from the volume.

**1. Submissions.** Submissions should be made on 3.5 inch, high-density IBM compatible disks and in two typescripts, double-spaced with wide margins. Please send these to one of the editors. Remember to include your name and address on your paper.

**2. Length.** Normally, the maximum length of articles should not exceed 6,000 words, not including notes. The editors reserve the right to edit papers that exceed these limits.

**3. Notes.** Normally, notes should be REFERENCE ONLY and placed at the end of the paper. Number continuously.

**4. Style sheet.** Please use the most recent *Speculum* style sheet (currently *Speculum* 75 (2000), 547–52). This sets out the format to be used for notes. Failure to follow the *Speculum* format will result in accepted articles being returned to the author for amendment. In the main body of the paper you may adhere to either British or American spelling, but it must be consistent throughout the article.

**5. Language.** Papers will be published in English, French, German, Italian and Spanish.

**6. Abbreviations.** Please use the abbreviation list on pp. ix–xi of this journal.

**7. Diagrams and Maps** should be referred to as figures and photographs as plates. Please keep illustrations to the essential minimum, since it will be possible to include only a limited number. All illustrations must be supplied by the contributor in camera-ready copy, and free from all copyright restrictions.

**8. Italics.** Words to be printed as italics should be italicised if possible. Failing this they should be underlined.

**9. Capitals.** Please take every care to ensure consistency in your use of capitals and lower case letters. Use initial capitals to distinguish the general from the specific (for example, "the count of Flanders" but "Count Philip of Flanders").

*Editors*

Professor Benjamin Z. Kedar
Department of History
The Hebrew University
Jerusalem 91905, Israel

Professor Jonathan S. C. Riley-Smith
Emmanuel College
Cambridge CB2 3AP
U.K.

## SOCIETY FOR THE STUDY OF THE CRUSADES AND THE LATIN EAST
### MEMBERSHIP INFORMATION

The primary function of the Society for the Study of the Crusades and the Latin East is to enable members to learn about current work being done in the field of crusading history, and to contact members who share research interests through the information in the Society's Bulletin. There are currently 420 members of the SSCLE from 30 countries. The Society also organizes a major international conference every four years, as well as sections on crusading history at other conferences where appropriate.

The committee of the SSCLE consists of:
Prof. Michel Balard, *President*
Prof. Jean Richard, Prof. Jonathan Riley-Smith and Prof. Benjamin Z. Kedar, *Honorary Vice-presidents*
Prof. Sophia Menache and Luis Garcìa-Guijarro Ramos, *Secretary and Assistant Secretary*
Prof. James D. Ryan, *Treasurer*
Prof. Karl Borchardt, *Bulletin Editor*
Dr Zsolt Hunyadi, *Website*.

Current subscription fees are as follows:
- Membership and Bulletin of the Society: Single £11, $15 or €17;
- Student £6, $9 or €10;
- Joint membership £15, $23 or €25;
- Membership and the journal *Crusades*, including the Bulletin: £20, $30 or €33.

#0022 - 210917 - C0 - 234/156/17 [19] - CB - 9780754656562